Origins

CANADIAN HISTORY TO CONFEDERATION

SEVENTH EDITION

Origins

CANADIAN HISTORY TO CONFEDERATION

SEVENTH EDITION

R. DOUGLAS FRANCIS
University of Calgary

RICHARD JONES

DONALD B. SMITH
University of Calgary

ROBERT WARDHAUGH
University of Western Ontario

NELSON EDUCATION

NELSON EDUCATION

Origins, Seventh Edition

by R. Douglas Francis, Richard Jones, Donald B. Smith, and Robert Wardhaugh

Vice President, Editorial Higher Education: Anne Williams

Executive Editor: Laura Macleod

Senior Marketing Manager: Amanda Henry

Developmental Editor: Jacquelyn Busby

Photo Researcher/Permissions Coordinator: Lynn McLeod

Senior Content Production Manager: Imoinda Romain

Production Service: MPS Limited, a Macmillan Company

Copy Editor: Rodney Rawlings

Proofreader: Barbara Storey

Indexer: Richard Shrout

Production Coordinator: Ferial Suleman

Design Director: Ken Phipps

Managing Designer: Franca Amore

Interior Design: Dianna Little

Cover Design: Martyn Schmoll

Cover Image: *The Lower City of Quebec, from the Parapet of the Upper City*, 1833, by James Pattison Cockburn (1779–1847), National Gallery of Canada (no. 41828.6)

Compositor: MPS Limited, a Macmillan Company

Printer: R.R. Donnelley

Printed and bound in the United States of America
1 2 3 4 15 14 13 12

For more information contact Nelson Education Ltd., 1120 Birchmount Road, Toronto, Ontario, M1K 5G4. Or you can visit our Internet site at http://www.nelson.com

Library and Archives Canada Cataloguing in Publication

Origins: Canadian history to Confederation/R. Douglas Francis . . . [et al.].—7th ed.

Includes bibliographical references and index.
ISBN-13: 978-0-17-650250-8

1. Canada—History—To 1763 (New France)—Textbooks.
2. Canada—History—1763–1867—Textbooks. I. Francis, R. D. (R. Douglas), 1944–

FC161.F73 2012 971 C2011-908267-5

ISBN-13: 978-0-17-650250-8
ISBN-10: 0-17-650250-5

Part opener photo credits Page 22: D.G.G. Kerr, ed., *A Historical Atlas of Canada* (Toronto: Thomas Nelson & Sons, 1961); Page 162: Thomas Davies, *A View of the Château Richer, Cape Torment, and Lower End of the Isle of Orleans near Quebec, 1787.* Watercolour on laid paper, 35.4 × 52.7 cm. National Gallery of Canada, Ottawa. Photo © NGC; Page 278: Library and Archives Canada, Acc. No. 1934-402/C-012632; Page 388: Library and Archives Canada/C-041605; Page 474: ART GALLERY OF ONTARIO. Gift from The Canadian Club Classic Fund, purchased with assistance from the Government of Canada through the Cultural Property Export and Import Act, 1989. © 2011 AGO.

We wish to dedicate this seventh edition to our students over the years who have taught us so much.

Brief Contents

Contents

PART TWO   Colonial Societies in British North America, 1760 to 1815

CHAPTER 8   The Conquest of Quebec, 1760–1774 164

CHAPTER 9   Quebec Society in the Late Eighteenth Century 186

PART FOUR Colonies and Hinterlands, 1815 to 1867

List of Maps

The Nature of History

"History" refers to both the events of the past and the study of them. Students of history realize, however, that these events are "filtered" by historians and then "presented" as history. As a result, our knowledge of the past is subjective, open to interpretation, and in a continuous process of revision. What the historian tells us about past events is not objective or definitive; no conclusive or final study of any event in the past is possible. As a result, our understanding of history is always being revised and history is always being rewritten. This textbook—a project in its seventh edition and going back a quarter century—is part of that process.

The revising of history occurs for good reasons. New evidence emerges through the discovery of new sources and documents. The borders and boundaries of the "discipline" of history are being challenged by scholars in other disciplines—archaeology, anthropology, native studies, demography, sociology, geography, political science, women's studies, to name a few. Besides the discovery of new sources and the emergence of new fields, new theoretical approaches also push our understanding of history in new directions. Theories of Marxism, feminism, postcolonialism, poststructuralism, and postmodernism question the nature of history, the role of the historian, and even the ability to write history. In addition, the writing and reading of history is a much an exercise in understanding the present as it is in understanding the past. Historians and students of history are products of their own time. History will be rewritten by and for each new generation. Most importantly, new perspectives result from historians asking new questions. Historical revisionism (and indeed, a fuller understanding of the past) relies on the art of questioning.

The writing of history is about making choices, and those choices have certainly changed in Canada over time. When historians were preoccupied with the study of political, economic, and military figures and events, their perspectives and priorities framed an understanding of the past. They dictated the topics deemed worthy of study, the sources consulted to provide the evidence, the questions asked of those sources, and ultimately, the interpretations and even the answers. When a new generation of historians, beginning in the 1970s, began to question, challenge, and even reject these choices, the discipline of history was literally turned upside down. Reflecting the social changes of the time, these "social historians" claimed that we needed to reorient our perspectives, we needed to approach the past "from the bottom up." They wanted to learn about the lives of "ordinary people" and "ordinary events" and not simply the "great men" and their wars, elections, and economies. If history was indeed a study of our "entire" past, should we not be studying everyone?

The emergence of social history revolutionized the history of Canada and the result was a much deeper and richer understanding of the past. These challenges were not accepted easily and the resulting changes were not embraced without friction. The "history wars" in Canada led to often bitter debate. To an extent, these wars continue. But the "new history" must face the same scrutiny as the "old history." The pendulum swung too much toward social history, unfortunately often at the exclusion and even disdain of political history. In time, the social historians became part of the establishment they had fought to depose and those studying the "traditional" topics were marginalized. But the process of revisionism continues apace. Again, this textbook is part of that process.

The Nature of this Textbook

Origins and *Destinies,* our companion volumes of Canadian history, cover the study of Canada's past from the beginnings to the present. First and foremost, the texts seek to tell the story of Canada in a narrative framework. In some ways, this is a traditional structure and approach that continues to "privilege" the grand design of nation-building, wars, political development, and economic cycles. But we believe that a narrative approach remains the best way to tell a good story. While we are influenced by new theoretical approaches, and while social history often dominates the narrative, it is essential that readers are presented with a clear, engaging, educational, and entertaining story. And while the texts are framed around the nation, they seek to question the process and the results at every turn. The texts also attempt to reflect and incorporate the current trends in historical writing. We include the most recent and up-to-date research by Canadian historians and expose students to the most innovative approaches presently being employed.

While the history of the nation of Canada obviously frames these texts, we do not seek to promote nationalism. Canada's past offers much to celebrate, but it also offers much to mourn. Our objective is to question how we came to be who we are. These two volumes highlight the historical development and contribution of the Aboriginal peoples, the French and the English colonists, women, and the waves of immigrants and minority groups, realizing that together they make up Canada's past. As well, we focus on the history of each of the country's regions. Finally, up-to-date annotated bibliographies appear at the end of each chapter to identify the major historical writings on the events covered.

The format for *Origins* and *Destinies* is chronological, to help students understand how events developed through time. The texts are further divided into thematic sections, each introduced by a brief overview of themes highlighted in the chapters within the section. Each chapter treats a major topic or period, and begins with a "Time Line" listing the key events discussed. Headings and subheadings throughout the chapters assist in organizing the material. As well, a section entitled "Related Readings" identifies useful articles, primary sources, and visual documents in the companion resource, *Visions: The Canadian History Modules Project.*

Regarding content, *Origins,* the first volume, tells the story of pre-Confederation Canada. It begins with the earliest history of North America and the Indigenous peoples prior to contact. It then tells the story of the coming of the Norse, the Portuguese, the Spanish, the Basques, and particularly the French and the British, who eventually established permanent European settlements. From the imperial wars to industrialization, the chapter examines the regional personalities formed in Atlantic Canada, the St. Lawrence River valley, the Great Lakes region, the Red River area, and the Pacific coast.

Destinies, the second volume, takes Canada's story from Confederation in 1867 to the present day. Unlike the United States, Canada did not experience a uniform wave of expansion westward from the Atlantic seaboard. In many cases, the European communities in Canada began as pockets of settlement, independent of one another, founded at different times, and with people of various European backgrounds. In *Destinies,* we show how Canada came to take the transcontinental form it did, and how the various groups within its boundaries came together. We focus on various regional, ethnic, and social tensions and unifying forces.

Origins and *Destinies* feature two types of boxed inserts, entitled "Where Historians Disagree" and "Where Social Scientists Disagree." These debate boxes provide a "historiographical" feature to the texts by highlighting some of the most contentious debates in Canadian history and some of the fields where the most innovative work is being done. They remind students that the writing of Canadian history is interpretive and revisionary.

But although social history shifts the spotlight away from individuals and toward social groups, the role of the individual remains important. Accordingly we include a boxed feature entitled "Historical Portraits" that highlight the lives of well-known, or not-so-well-known, persons whose lives and experiences reflect important issues and trends.

Finally, to demonstrate the contribution of selected communities to Canada's history, boxed "Community Portraits" also appear.

We hope *Origins* and *Destinies* will provide students of Canadian history with a knowledge of Canada's past, a desire to explore that past in greater depth in more specialized courses in Canadian history, and an appreciation of the multilayered, vibrant, and exciting nature of the writing of Canadian history within the discipline of history as a whole.

Acknowledgments

In preparing each of the seven editions of *Origins* and *Destinies,* we have benefited enormously from the advice and suggestions of many Canadian historians who have read chapters and often the entire manuscript, and provided us with useful criticism within their respective research areas. In particular, we wish to thank the following: William Acheson, Gratien Allaire, Douglas Baldwin, Jean Barman, Matthew J. Bellamy, John Belshaw, Theodore Binnema, David Bright, Penny Bryden, Phillip Buckner, Anne Buffam, Robert Burkinshaw, Kristin Burnett, Robert A. Campbell, Sarah Carter, Joseph Cherwinski, Lisa-Anne Chilton, Colin Coates, Gail Cuthbert-Brandt, Jean Daigle, George A. Davison, A.A. den Otter, Olive Dickason, Mark Dickerson, Marcel Dirk, Robert Englebert, John English, A. Ernest Epp, Robin Fisher, Rae Fleming, Gerald Friesen, Donald Fyson, Michael Granger, Roger Hall, John David Hamilton, James Helmer, James Hiller, Raymond Huel, Bonnie Huskins, Robert Irwin, Helen Towser Jones, Jeffrey Keshen, Douglas Leighton, Ernest LeVos, Maureen Lux, Alan MacEachern, Ingeborg Marshall, Marcel Martel, Lynn Marks, Bea Medicine, James Miller, Dale Miquelon, William Morrison, Suzanne Morton, James Muir, Ken Munro, the late Howard Palmer, Martin Pâquet, Gillian Poulter, Margaret Prang, Colin Read, Keith Regular, Daniel Richter, Patricia Roome, R.H. Roy, Eric Sager, Daniel Samson, Phyllis Senese, Thomas Socknat, Angela Sottosanti, Donald Swainson, M. Brook Taylor, John Herd Thompson, Elizabeth Vibert, Jill Wade, Keith Walden, William Westfall, William Wicken, and John Zucchi.

At Nelson, we benefited enormously from a dedicated and enthusiastic editorial team. In particular, we wish to thank Laura Macleod, Executive Editor; Jacquelyn Busby, Developmental Editor; Imoinda Romain, Senior Content Production Manager; and Rodney Rawlings, Copy Editor. It was our pleasure to work with each of them. We also wish to thank our partners Barbara Grant, Lilianne Plamondon, and Nancy Townshend for their support throughout this project.

We would also like to thank the following Ph.D. candidates who helped with the "Where Historians Disagree" boxes: Jeremy Marks, Daniel Heidt, Carly Simpson, Craig Greenham, Michael Del Vecchio, Michelle Hutchinson-Grondin, and Tim Compeau. Special thanks go to Jonathan Scotland, who also helped with the bibliographies, photos, maps, and captions, and Adrian Ciani for his editing work. We wish to dedicate this seventh edition to our students over the years, who have taught us so much.

Chapter One

THE FIRST PEOPLE

TIME LINE

70 000–14 000 years ago	Land bridge (Beringia) forms between North America and Siberia People likely contact Pacific Coast by sea
c. 15 000 years ago	Glaciers begin to melt and retreat
c. 12 000 years ago	Human settlement known to exist in southernmost portion of Americas (Chile)
10 000 years ago	Settlements established throughout large sections of what is now Canada
5000 years ago	Glacial ice recedes to present northern position Climate stabilizes
3500–2000 years ago	Maya, Aztec, and Inca civilizations develop in Mexico, Central America, and Peru
A.D. 1–50	Mound Builders' culture flourishes in Ohio
c. 500	First Nations societies based on agriculture (corn) in present-day southern Ontario
c. 700–1000	Mississippian culture arises in Mississippi Valley
c. 1500	Eleven linguistic First Nations groups reside within what is now Canada; more than 50 languages spoken
c. 1730	Plains people acquire horse

When, where, and how were the Americas first settled? The First Nations are the descendants of the original inhabitants of the Americas, but archaeological evidence indicates that human beings came relatively late to these continents, during the last Pleistocene geological age (the Wisconsin stage). This evidence indicates that the Americas were settled through numerous mass migrations of early humans, likely coming across a land bridge that then spanned the Bering Strait, allowing passage from what is now Siberia to Alaska. Archaeologists disagree, however, on when these migrations first began.

According to the Bering Strait theory, the migrations moved southward all the way to the southern tip of South America, and then back northward. There is general consensus that the original inhabitants of North America lived on this continent at least 12 000 years before the Europeans' arrival. But other theories exist as well. Evidence continues to mount that people may well have travelled to the Pacific coasts of North America by sea over the course of thousands of years. The First Nations often reject the theories of the newcomers and instead have their own creation stories that place the peoples here since time immemorial. Eldon Yellowhorn, an archaeologist and a member of the Piikani First Nation in southern Alberta, welcomes the insights the scientific approach contributes: "A scientific perspective of antiquity may challenge traditional interpretations, but it also opens exciting possibilities for imagining the past."[1]

Origins of the First Peoples of North America

Archaeologists believe the first direct ancestors of modern-day human beings appeared about 2 million years ago in Africa. Physical evidence of hominid bones, dating back 60 000 years, has been found in Africa, Asia, and Europe, but not in the Americas. Bones have not preserved well in the soils of the Americas; dating has instead been performed on artefacts. On the basis of these findings, it is assumed that the Eastern Hemisphere was populated by *homo sapiens* who then made their way to the Western Hemisphere. Physical and genetic data link Aboriginal peoples in the Americas to Asian populations, adding weight to the theory that peoples migrated to the Americas.

The most well-accepted archaeological theory posits that the early inhabitants of North America crossed from Siberia during the last Ice Age, when sea levels dropped and the continental shelf was exposed.[2] This land bridge, known as Beringia, existed from 70 000 to 14 000 years ago. At its largest, the expanse of open grassland and tundra was more than 2000 kilometres wide. For thousands of years, Beringia served as a highway for animals and humans passing between Asia and the Americas. But if the Americas were peopled via the Bering Strait, why are the oldest societies in the Americas in the south rather than the north? Archaeologists argue that after crossing Beringia, humans travelled south in pursuit of game and warmer climes. It is also believed that they went southward along the Pacific Coast by sea. Whether by foot or boat, or a combination of the two, humans gradually advanced throughout North, Central, and South America, eventually crossing more than 15 000 kilometres from Alaska to Patagonia, at the tip of South America. When the glaciers retreated, people migrated northward. In this way, North America was populated last, with the high Arctic settled only 4000 years ago.

Some archaeologists believe human migration to the Americas occurred, not via the Bering Strait, but via the sea. While many argue that such migration either to the west or east coasts was unlikely due to unfavourable ocean current and wind patterns, others claim that even the most primitive boats were capable of crossing both the Atlantic and the Pacific, and such crossings would have inevitably occurred over the course of tens of thousands of years. Evidence of coastal settlements has not been found, but rising sea levels would mean they are now underwater. Theories of migration will continue to be revised as more evidence emerges, providing an excellent example of history as a constant process of revision.

Canada between approximately 80 000 and 20 000 years ago. At this time, almost all Canada was buried beneath a kilometre or more of glacial ice. A large ice-free area known as the Bering Land Bridge connected Siberia and Alaska. Animals and human hunters moved between the Old World and the New across this arctic landscape. It has also been suggested that peoples who had adapted to a maritime way of life in the southern fringes of Beringia might have later travelled southward along ice-free pockets of land that opened up along the Pacific coast from what is now Alaska to Washington State.

Source: © Canadian Museum of Civilization, illustrator Gilles Archambault, 1989, image no. S98-10739.

Canada about 12 000 years ago. Rapidly retreating glaciers were fringed by large lakes of glacial meltwater. The ancient beaches of some of these lakes reveal the remains of camps occupied by First Nations peoples who moved north to occupy the land now known as Canada.

Source: © Canadian Museum of Civilization, illustrator Gilles Archambault, 1989, image no. S98-10741.

While most archaeologists support the Bering Strait theory, they disagree on when the migrations occurred. The dates of arrival are being pushed back. Originally, it was believed that the migrations occurred some 30 000 years ago. This time frame is now believed to have been at least 40 000 and possibly even 50 000 years ago. Sites such as Monte Verde in south-central Chile show evidence of human occupation more than 12 500 years ago.

Archaeologists generally accept as evidence only artefacts found in sealed deposits with organic matter that can be radiocarbon-dated. In addition, they require evidence of distinctively styled artefacts. One example of such evidence is the "fluted point," a stone projectile head with one or more flutes, or hollowed-out channels that allowed for attachment of the point to a wooden or bone shaft.

Four Canadian sites—Debert, Nova Scotia; Vermilion Lakes, Banff National Park; Charlie Lake Cave, north of Fort St. John, British Columbia; and Wally's Beach (St. Mary's Reservoir) in southwestern Alberta—confirm the presence of humans in Canada at least 10 000 years ago.

About 10 000 years ago, a drastic change in climate occurred in the northern hemisphere. The great ice sheets—more than 3 kilometres thick—that once covered 97 percent of Canada began to melt. The runoff raised the sea level, causing the Beringian land bridge to disappear and the Bering Strait to form. The absence of ice sheets in formerly glaciated territories meant that wind and rainfall patterns shifted. Forests replaced grasslands and deserts developed. Some animals became extinct, especially large grazing animals such as mammoths (giant elephants), American camels, and a very large race of bison that foraged on the grasslands. These changes allowed people to migrate northward.

"Civilizations" of the Americas

Maya, Aztecs, and Incas

About 5000 years ago, the ice receded to approximately its present northern position and the climate became similar to what it is today. The Bering Strait attained its present width of approximately 80 kilometres, and land animals could no longer cross between Siberia and Alaska. People still made the journey, but no longer from Asia's inland centres. They were sea-mammal hunters and fishers who traded across the strait.

From 3500 to 2000 years ago, the population of the Americas underwent significant changes and developments. The peak of technological and social complexity was achieved in present-day Mexico, Central America, and the Andes of Peru, where permanent communities had the highest population densities on the two continents. In central and southern Mexico, a series of classical "civilizations" developed. The dominant one, the Aztec, emerged around 800 years ago. Agriculture (corn, beans, and squash) and rich sea resources formed the basis of these civilizations. Their technological levels were impressive, with advancements in science, medicine, architecture, astronomy, and mathematics that might easily rival and often surpass those of the Eastern Hemisphere.

These civilizations developed without the aid of Europe's domesticated animals—horses, oxen, and donkeys. They had discovered the wheel, but because they lacked animals other than the dog and, in the Andes, the llama for transport, they had little use for it. They also lacked sufficient supplies of useable copper and tin to allow for the replacement of stone tools. The Peruvians made a few tools from metal that had washed down in the streams, but in Mexico and Central America only stone tools were used. When the Europeans reached the Americas, they assumed that these "stone-age" civilizations were primitive and inferior.

Despite the absence of the wheel and metal tools, the peoples of the Americas were well advanced in arts and sciences. The Maya in Central America, whose civilization flourished between 1700 and 1100 years ago, developed a sophisticated system of mathematics, applying the concept of zero 500 years before the Hindus. The Maya, with their sophisticated knowledge of astronomy, outlined a 365-day annual calendar and plotted the cycle of the planet Venus. They calculated eclipses and recorded their calculations in a writing system that was both pictographic and phonetic.

In the Andes, the Incas, between 800 and 500 years ago, developed irrigation systems, built bridges and roads, erected stone walls using enormous rocks cut to fit so tightly that a knife blade could not be pushed between two blocks, and did metalwork of the highest quality in gold and silver. Farmers developed more than 100 species of plants, including two of the world's four basic food crops: corn (maize) and potatoes (the other two are wheat and rice). Other North American plants included tomatoes, peanuts, cacao, tobacco, gourds, squash, avocados, beans, and chilli peppers.

Canada today.

Source: © Canadian Museum of Civilization, illustrator Gilles Archambault, 1989, image no. S98-10742.

Canadian artist Franklin Arbuckle (1909–2001) drew this sketch of the hunt of a mammoth, used as an illustration in Selwyn Dewdney and Franklin Arbuckle, They Shared to Survive: The Native Peoples of Canada *(Toronto: Macmillan, 1975), p. 6.*

Source: © Franklin Arbuckle

The Mound Builders

About 2000 years ago, immediately south of the Great Lakes, farming and more permanent settlements replaced gathering and hunting in the Ohio and later the Mississippi valleys. The "Mound Builders" of the Ohio River valley (the Hopewell culture) constructed gigantic sculptured earthworks—some nearly 25 metres high—in geometric designs, sometimes in the shape of humans, birds, or serpents.

Archaeologists have located thousands of mounds used as burial sites and have excavated several earthen-walled enclosures, including one fortification with a circumference of more than 5 kilometres, enclosing the equivalent of fifty modern city blocks. Once a settled civilization was established, the Ohio peoples developed an extensive trading network. Archaeologists have found, among the artefacts in the burial mounds, large ceremonial blades chipped from obsidian (a volcanic glass) from deposits in what is now Yellowstone National Park in Wyoming; embossed breastplates, ornaments, and weapons made from copper nuggets from the Great Lakes; decorative objects cut from mica sheets from the southern Appalachians; and ornaments made from shells and shark and alligator teeth from the Gulf of Mexico. When Europeans arrived, they mistakenly assumed the "Indians" did not understand economics and only traded for necessities among their neighbours.

The Mound Builders' culture evolved slowly, reaching its peak roughly 2000 years ago. The Ohio mounds may have influenced the building of the Serpent burial mounds on a point overlooking Rice Lake, near present-day Peterborough, Ontario. From approximately 1900 to 1700 years ago, the local people built the earthworks 400 metres long, 15 metres across, and rising half a metre to a metre above the surface. Excavation has revealed numerous burials, with objects from afar—copper from western Lake Superior, silver from deposits in northern Ontario, and conch shells from the Gulf of Mexico. These findings confirm the extensive nature of the trading networks.

About 1500 years ago, the Ohio Mound Builders' culture declined, perhaps because of attacks by other nations or severe changes in climate that undermined agriculture. It was replaced by a similar, agriculture-based culture farther west, around present-day St. Louis. This culture extended over most of the Mississippi watershed, from Wisconsin to Louisiana and from Oklahoma to Tennessee. The influence of the trading centre of Cahokia extended throughout most of North America. In its day, it was the greatest settlement north of Mexico. From about 1300 to 800 years ago, this Mississippian culture influenced the Aboriginal nations to the east. Indeed, its example led the Iroquoian-speaking peoples of the lower Great Lakes and the St. Lawrence Valley to adopt agricultural techniques similar to those of the Mound Builders and the Mississippians.

A Cahoika mound located in Illinois.
Source: © Michael S. Lewis/CORBIS

Population Growth

Agriculture and a settled lifestyle supported larger populations than hunting and gathering. The cultivation of as little as 1 percent of the land could significantly increase the food supply. Estimates of the Aboriginal population of the Americas in the mid-fifteenth century indicate numbers as high as 100 million people, or approximately one-sixth of the human race at that time. The population north of Mexico may have reached 10 million before European contact. These numbers would have astounded the European explorers, who assumed they were contacting small, tribal populations.

The Iroquoians, in what is now southern Ontario and southwestern Quebec, for instance, domesticated high-yield cereals and tubers, which allowed them to feed a large population. Approximately half a million people (the most widely accepted estimate) lived within the boundaries of present-day Canada. Roughly half lived along the Pacific coast, with its abundant and more available resources, and in present-day southern Ontario and Quebec, where the Iroquoians practised farming. Aboriginal populations also reached such numbers because they lived in a relatively disease-free zone not touched by epidemics from other regions of the world.

European Diseases

The Europeans reduced the Aboriginal populations dramatically by exposing them to diseases new to the Americas. The population lacked defences against such contagious diseases as smallpox and measles. Because these foreign diseases often spread in advance of European contact through the extensive trade networks spanning the continent, many First Nations were devastated before ever meeting Europeans directly. As a result, when the Europeans arrived, they often assumed the "Indian" populations were small and the land largely empty.

According to Alfred Crosby, "the initial appearance of these diseases is as certain to have set off deadly epidemics as dropping lighted matches into tinder is certain to cause fires."[3] Aboriginal healers had never before encountered these epidemic diseases. They could not combat them, nor could the Europeans, until the twentieth century—long after the Aboriginal population had been repeatedly devastated. After European contact, death rates in some areas of the Americas reached as high as 95 percent. By the early twentieth century, the entire First Nations population in Canada and the United States had been reduced to less than 1 million, or one-tenth of the estimated population at the time of contact. Olive P. Dickason notes that in the seventeenth century, "the lands that appeared 'vacant' to the new arrivals were either hunting areas or else had been recently depopulated because of introduced epidemics."[4]

Classifying the First Nations

Languages

The First Nations population has been classified according to three distinct categories: linguistic, national, and cultural. None is completely satisfactory. A linguistic division in Canada reveals eleven Indigenous language units. One is Eskimo-Aleut, the language spoken by the Inuit; the other ten are First Nations linguistic groups. Seven of them (Salishan, Tsimshian, Haidan, Wakashan, Tlingit, Kutenaian, and Athapaskan) are found in the most densely populated and therefore most linguistically complex region of the Pacific Coast, in present-day British Columbia. The Siouan speakers are found on the Prairies and in the foothills of the Rockies. The Iroquoian speakers live in the woodlands of eastern Canada. The Algonquian (or Algonkian) linguistic family, geographically the largest group, extends from the Atlantic coast to the Rockies. The Athapaskan language group can be found throughout the Yukon, the Northwest Territories, Nunavut, and the northern sections of the four western provinces. As nearly as can be determined, the First Nations spoke about fifty different languages.

This linguistic classification links together widely disparate groups that had little in common. While the language base might have been the same, the dialects were often very different. The language of one group might differ as much from that of another as English from

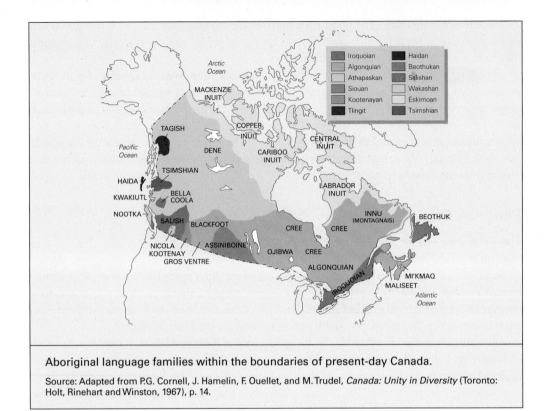

Aboriginal language families within the boundaries of present-day Canada.

Source: Adapted from P.G. Cornell, J. Hamelin, F. Ouellet, and M. Trudel, *Canada: Unity in Diversity* (Toronto: Holt, Rinehart and Winston, 1967), p. 14.

German or Portuguese from Romanian. Within the same linguistic family, the groups were often very different from each other. The Mi'kmaq of the Maritimes and the Blackfoot of the Prairies, for instance, although separated by 4000 kilometres, were joined together in the Algonquian linguistic family. Conversely, the Haidas of the Queen Charlotte Islands culturally resembled their mainland neighbours, the Tsimshians, but their languages were unrelated.

Nations

To classify Canada's original inhabitants by national and political categories also poses problems. The term "tribe" was formerly used, but it was derisive and failed to recognize the Aboriginal peoples as "nations" on equal terms with the Europeans. When the French first came in contact with the Iroquoians, they referred to them as "nations." Nations—groups of people bound by a common culture and language and acting as a unit in relations with their neighbours—certainly existed. But between some nations, the ties were not strong. More remote groups often diverged considerably in dialect, and in some cases had so thoroughly assimilated the customs of other peoples around them that they had lost all sense of political unity with their nation.

Still, these were the classifications most often used by the Europeans to identify "Indians." At times the newcomers identified them with labels used by their enemies. For example, some argue that the term "Sioux" originates from an Odawa term that means "snake"; it was a derisive term. Such names are gradually being replaced by those used by the First Nations' people themselves.

The Beothuk, Mi'kmaq, Maliseet, and Abenaki were the First Nations of the Maritimes. The Confederacies of the Iroquois and Wendat (Huron) dominated the eastern woodlands. The Odawa, Algonquin, Ojibwa, and Cree lived in the vast territory of the Shield. The Plains groups consisted of the Ojibwa, Cree, Dakota, Assiniboine, and the Blackfoot Confederacy. Numerous

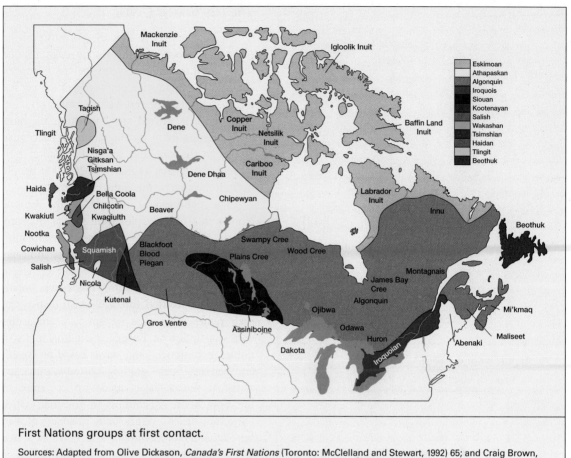

First Nations groups at first contact.

Sources: Adapted from Olive Dickason, *Canada's First Nations* (Toronto: McClelland and Stewart, 1992) 65; and Craig Brown, *The Illustrated History of Canada*, (Montreal/Kingston: McGill-Queen's University Press, 2007), p. 7.

tribes dwelt on the Pacific Coast, including the Haida, Tsimshian, Bella Coola, Chilcotin, Nisga'a, Nootka, Tlingit, Squamish, Salish, Gitskan, Cowichan, and the Sto:lo. In the northern regions dwelt the Inuit and the Dene.

Cultures

Another classification of Aboriginal North Americans is by cultural area. This classification revolves around geography, and it is useful because it recognizes how the environment—climate and resources—influenced the development of societies and technologies. According to this classification, Indigenous societies in Canada consisted of six culture areas: Northwest Coast, Plateau, Plains, Subarctic, Arctic, and Northeast. The cultural areas tend to coincide with ecological zones.

As the bands settled in various territories of what is now Canada, they based their lifestyles around the available resources. Whether they became settled, semi-settled, or nomadic depended on the geography. They constantly adapted to new environmental conditions, especially climate change. The peoples of northern North America were not isolated, but part of a hemisphere-wide civilization. They articulated their own spiritual beliefs and philosophies; they developed trade networks that extended across the continent; they developed their own concepts of war and diplomacy. Over time, Indigenous societies dynamically changed. As archaeologist Robert McGhee observes: "Native North American cultures were not fixed in ancient traditions, any more than were those of Old World peoples, and were remarkably flexible to change in response to new ideas or circumstances."[5]

The Northwest Coast

Archaeologists believe that the ancestors of the Aboriginal peoples of the Pacific coast resided there for thousands of years before European contact. The linguistic complexity of the coastal region, with its nineteen distinct languages, suggests that it is an "old area," and thus the most likely starting point for migrations of successive groups to the east and south. Population estimates indicate that as many as 200 000 people lived in the area by the eighteenth century.

The culture and lifestyle of the various Northwest Coast peoples were similar in many aspects. Evidence exists of wide-scale adaptation to a similar environment. Evidence also indicates that about 2500 to 1500 years ago, hierarchical societies emerged, with ruling classes who maintained their position through lavish displays of their riches. This class system had similarities with that found in Europe, including ranks of nobles, commoners, and slaves based on wealth and heredity. Social grading existed within each class. At times, slaves made up one-third of the population. According to historian Olive Dickason, slaves "were usually prisoners of war, but sometimes individuals who had lost status because of debt; one could also be born into slavery, one of the few regions in North America where this happened. In any event, slaves had no rights of any kind and could be put to death at the will of their masters."[6]

Some of the northern groups had clan divisions which recognized descent through the female line. In general, social divisions often interlocked and overlapped. A person's life became part of a kinship web of reciprocal obligations and privileges, the aim being to reinforce the community. Beginning about 1500 years ago, Northwest Coast peoples took on increased cultural complexity. Artistic traditions became further elaborated. Warfare became common, with competition over important trade routes. Wars were also fought in order to gain slaves and canoes.

On the eve of European contact in the mid-eighteenth century, the coastal inhabitants relied on the sea and the abundant fish for their livelihood: herring, smelt, oolichan (candle-fish), halibut, and several species of cod. Salmon, which they speared, netted, and trapped in large quantities, then sun-dried or smoked, became their basic, year-round staple. In addition, they hunted sea mammals, such as whales, seals, sea lions, porpoises, and sea otters. The abundant food supply made the Pacific coast region the most densely populated area in Canada.

The Northwest Coast peoples used the giant cedars and firs of the coastal rain forest to build houses and to make dugout canoes and woodwork, such as carved boxes, bowls, dishes, and ladles. They lived year round in villages located in sheltered island coves or on channels near the mouths of rivers. Each village was self-contained, but on occasion, particularly in times of war, several settlements joined together. Their communal activities included the *potlatch*, a large ceremonial feast, which they used to mourn the dead, to celebrate the investiture of new chiefs, or to mark the completion of a new house. The potlatch became the best known of the Pacific coast rituals. Originally it was used for subsistence functions to facilitate food exchanges between

Aboriginal culture areas.

Source: Based on *Handbook of North American Indians, vol. 4, History of Indian-White Relations* (Washington: Smithsonian Institution, 1988).

Gitsaex village.

Source: R. Cole Harris, ed., *Historical Atlas of Canada vol. 1, From the Beginning to 1800* (Toronto: University of Toronto Press, 1987), plate 13. Reprinted by permission of the University of Toronto Press Incorporated.

those who had surpluses and those who had shortages. But these elaborate giveaway feasts were also used to show and gain wealth and social status.

The Plateau

The Plateau culture area, the smallest of the six regions, takes in the high plateau zone between the Coast Range and the Rocky Mountains in the south-central interior of British Columbia. It extends southward through western Montana, Idaho, and eastern Washington and Oregon. The Canadian portion of the Plateau area is a region noted for its hot, dry summers and cold winters and includes the Kootenai (Ktunaxa) in the east, the Interior Salish in the west (Shuswap and Lillooet), and the Athapaskan-speaking groups to the north. These nations depended on salmon, and thus their populations were concentrated downriver, where the fish were most abundant. Their Northwest Coast neighbours influenced them greatly.

Canadian artist Franklin Arbuckle (1909–2001) drew this sketch of Pacific coast whale hunters, used as an illustration in Selwyn Dewdney and Franklin Arbuckle, They Shared to Survive: The Native Peoples of Canada (Toronto: Macmillan, 1975), p. 133.

Source: © Franklin Arbuckle

Over 8000 years ago the Plateau people adopted more settled ways, living in village sites. The western Plateau became a strategic trading area and the population, due to the major salmon runs, much denser than in the eastern Plateau. The villages along the Fraser River appear to have reached their largest size about 2000 to 1000 years ago. In the eastern Plateau, after the arrival of the horse more than 250 years ago, the resident Kootenay (Ktunaxa) had more contact with the Plains people. In dress, customs, and religion, the most easterly Plateau people came to resemble those on the Great Plains.

The Plains

East of the Plateau region lies the Plains (or Great Plains) culture area, the broad central region of North America west of the Mississippi and Red River valleys, and east of the Rockies. The open grasslands, with tall grass in the east and short grass in the west, extend on a north–south axis from northern Alberta and Saskatchewan and western Manitoba to Texas. The region has a continental climate—hot, dry summers and cold winters. The harshness of the climate dictated the lifestyles of the people, who were nomadic by necessity. They moved according to the seasons and the availability of food. The Plains groups also came to learn that their region was subject to cycles of severe drought.

Throughout the buffalo era, the northwestern Plains attracted Aboriginal communities from all directions in pursuit of the vast herds. In the eighteenth century, First Nations belonging to three linguistic groups lived on the Canadian Plains: the Algonquian, the Athapaskan, and the Siouan. As the Plains became a crossroads for many First Nations, a sign language developed to allow people to communicate. These groups specialized in the communal hunt of the buffalo, or bison, an animal central to their way of life. They ate its flesh and used the hide to make teepee covers, clothing, and robes. From the thick hide of the buffalo's neck they made shields, from the horns they fashioned spoons and drinking cups, and from the sinew they created thread and bow string. On the treeless Great Plains, dried buffalo dung provided fuel.

The Plains peoples hunted the buffalo on foot in nomadic bands of roughly 50 to 100 people. Finding the herds required knowledge of their migratory habits. Large herds existed in abundance, but one could go for days or weeks without seeing a single animal. Hunting also required considerable skill in approaching the animals, because neither the lance nor the bow was effective against them at long range. Buffalo could run at speeds of over 50 kilometres per hour, making it impossible for hunters on foot to run them down.

Over the centuries, the Plains peoples developed effective subsistence strategies. The "drive" became the best way of harvesting the herds. The Plains peoples lured the buffalo into corrals or pounds of poles and brush in small valleys, where they could ambush them. Where the land was uneven, as in the foothills to the west, the ambush frequently took the form of a "jump," where the hunters stampeded the animals over a cliff or steep cutbank.

One such location is Head-Smashed-In Buffalo Jump in the Oldman River valley, 130 kilometres south of Calgary in southwestern Alberta. Used for at least 6000 and possibly 9000 years, it is one of the oldest, largest, and best preserved of all the buffalo jumps in North America. Evidence remains of several of the drive paths, marked by rock piles about a metre in diameter and a third of

A Blackfoot couple with horse-drawn travois.

Source: Edward S. Curtis/Glenbow Archives, Calgary, Canada/ NA-1700-156.

a metre high, stretching back, in one case, as far as 8 kilometres from the cliff.

The arrival of the horse on the northern prairie in the early eighteenth century provides perhaps the most dramatic example of the ability of Plains peoples to adapt to new situations and to take advantage of new opportunities. It also demonstrates an example of the Europeans influencing First Nations without making direct contact. The horse originally existed in the Americas, but then it disappeared, until it was reintroduced by the Spaniards into Mexico in the sixteenth century. Escaped or freed horses reproduced and spread across the continent. The horse quickly replaced the dog as the chief transporter of goods. The Plains peoples adopted the dog *travois* (two trailing poles on which was attached a platform or net for holding a load) for use with the horse. Their horse-drawn travois carried a load of 150 kilograms, in contrast to 35 kilograms for a dog travois. As well, a horse

One of the most dramatic of the representations at the Agawa Pictograph Site is that of Mishipeshu, the great water lynx, from the Agawa pictograph site in Lake Superior Provincial Park, Ontario.

Source: Courtesy of Lake Superior Provincial Park.

could travel 20 kilometres a day, twice as far as a dog. With the horse, the nomadic Plains peoples could take more than just the basic necessities as they moved from one hunting camp to another and to keep extra suits of clothing, additional buffalo robes for winter, and more dried provisions. The horse transformed the buffalo hunt. Mounted hunters could now surround a buffalo herd, without having to drive it into an enclosure or over a cliff. They could pursue the animals, taking them down at close range with spear or bow.

The Subarctic

To the north lies the sparsely populated Subarctic culture area. A low-lying region covered with coniferous trees, it extends across the Canadian Shield, from the Labrador coast to the mouth of the Yukon River, covering over a quarter of present-day Canada. Its northern boundary is below the tree line. The winters are long and harsh, but the forests provide shelter for its human inhabitants. Not surprisingly, the peoples lived a nomadic existence, migrating according to the seasons in pursuit of game.

Members of two linguistic families lived in the Subarctic: in the west, the Athapaskan-speaking groups, or "Dene" (pronounced "de-ne" or "de-nay" and meaning "the people"); and in the east, the Subarctic Algonquians. Because small groups of hunters left few traces, this area of vast northern forests remains one of the least known of the archaeological areas in Canada. The acidic soils of the Subarctic have reduced the hunters' remains to a few stone tools.

Because of the thin distribution of game animals over vast areas of the boreal forest, the Subarctic human population was among the lowest in the world. In the summer the peoples lived in communal encampments of several hunting bands (about 100 individuals) situated at good fishing sites. In the autumn they divided into individual hunting bands of approximately 25 people, closely related either by family ties or by marriage, to hunt for food. A senior male directed the group and, in consultation with the other men, decided where and when they would hunt and camp. Many Dene and Algonquians relied on caribou and moose, whose importance to them was comparable to that of the buffalo to the Plains peoples.

The Arctic

Immediately north of the Subarctic, above the tree line, lies the Arctic culture area. Today, this area includes much of Alaska, all of the Canadian North above the tree line, and Greenland. The region has one of the world's harshest climates. For about eight months of the year it remains snow-covered and its seas frozen.

Today, the various Inuit groups speak related languages, suggesting that they are all derived from a single ancestral tongue. The languages are also similar to those of the Chukchi, Koryak, and Itel'men peoples of northeastern Siberia. Racially as well, the Inuit resemble First Nations, which suggests that the Inuit originated in Asia.

About 4000 years ago, humans developed skills and technologies to hunt and fish to enable them to survive winters on the treeless tundra of Arctic Canada. They constructed dog sleds, snow houses, and soapstone lamps. They killed sea mammals with harpoons attached to retrieving lines, and used barbed stone spears to fish and hunt birds. They also used the bow and arrow. Although fewer species of animals exist in this region, they are relatively larger. In certain areas, migration and the availability of food led to dense seasonal concentrations of many mammals, such as caribou, walrus, and seals.

Copper Inuit archers in the early twentieth century.

Source: © Canadian Museum of Civilization, photo G. H. Wilkins, 51165.

About a thousand years ago, an Alaskan people, the Thule—direct ancestors of the modern Inuit—entered the central Arctic. Four hundred years later, a sparse Thule population occupied most of Arctic Canada north of the tree line. In the relatively mild weather conditions at the time of their arrival, they were able to adapt their rich maritime hunting culture to the Canadian Arctic. They introduced many new items of technology for sea-mammal hunting. After perfecting the techniques of hunting on the open seas, they could even take on the bowhead whale. The colder climate of the sixteenth century onward made this life untenable and they developed the well-known classic Inuit culture. Modern Canadian and Greenlandic Inuit are descended from the Thule.

The Northeast

The Northeast (or Eastern Woodlands) culture area extended roughly from the Atlantic to the Great Lakes, and north to the Subarctic. The Northeast Aboriginal peoples hunted a variety of large game, particularly deer, as well as smaller game. They also fished and gathered edible wild plants and roots. Dramatic changes followed when hunters in southern Ontario adopted the bow and arrow from the Ohio region, about 1500 years ago. Climate and soil conditions south of the Canadian Shield allowed some nations to grow corn, beans, and squash, thereby allowing for a settled lifestyle. Two linguistic families lived in the Northeast: the Algonquians, a migratory people primarily dependent on hunting and fishing; and the Iroquoians, a semi-nomadic and agricultural people. The Algonquians occupied the northern part of the region, while the Iroquoians inhabited much of present-day southern Ontario and neighbouring New York state.

The Algonquian-speaking peoples were widespread on the eve of European contact. The Mi'kmaq (Micmac) lived in the Maritimes, and the closely related Maliseet (Malecite), in what is now western New Brunswick. North of the St. Lawrence and east of the St. Maurice River dwelt the Innu (Montagnais). The Algonquins (Algonkins), the group that gave its name to the Algonquian linguistic family, lived in the Ottawa Valley. (Note that the tribe's name ends in "quin" and that of the linguistic family in "quian.") Still farther west lived the Nipissings on Lake Nipissing, the Odawas (Ottawa) on Manitoulin Island in Lake Huron, and the Anishinabe (Ojibwas, Chippewas) around Lake Superior. The Beothuk, now extinct, lived in Newfoundland; they might have been Algonquian speakers, but the evidence is inconclusive.

Ojibwa (Anishinabeg) birchbark canoe, photographed about 1895, probably in northern Minnesota.

Source: Smithsonian Institution, National Anthropological Archives.

Although many Algonquian groups grew crops, those north of the Great Lakes chiefly hunted and fished. During the winter they broke up into small, independent family groups to hunt deer, elk, bear, beaver, and other animals. In the early spring, families came together at maple groves to gather and boil the tree sap. In the summer, by lakes and at river mouths, the women undertook agricultural work, while the men fished. During the fall they gathered wild rice, and, farther south, harvested corn.

Several winter hunting groups joined together for summer fishing. Each fishing band had its own name, territory, and leader. The leader, however, had relatively little power or authority.[7] The men of these male-centred hunting groups usually married women from neighbouring bands, maintaining friendly ties. Adjacent bands, having a common language and customs, constituted a local community. Their unity was more cultural than political, since the band was the only clearly defined political unit. They traded extensively with their neighbours.

Initially, the Northeast peoples were hunters and gatherers, but gradually many in the area south of the Canadian Shield became farmers. Crops that originated in Mexico and Central America played an important role in the development of Iroquoian culture. About 1500 years ago, corn spread northward via the Ohio and Illinois areas to southern Ontario. It adapted to the shorter growing season and the more rigorous climate. Tobacco probably entered eastern Canada 2500 years ago and beans about 1000 years ago. Beans, high in protein, partially freed the Iroquoians from having to supplement their corn diet with animal protein. This new food supply contributed to rapid population growth.

At first, small-scale gardening supplemented hunting and fishing, but later the opposite was true. By the time of European contact, the Iroquoian farming nations of the lower Great Lakes depended on their crops for up to four-fifths of their food. Every 10 to 15 years, they moved their village sites as the soil and firewood became depleted. Iroquoian women assumed the tasks of planting, cultivating, and harvesting the crops, freeing the men to clear the land for farming and to hunt, fish, trade, and wage war.

Canadian artist Franklin Arbuckle (1909–2001) drew this sketch of Iroquoian men building a village with pallisade, used as an illustration in Selwyn Dewdney and Franklin Arbuckle, They Shared to Survive: The Native Peoples of Canada *(Toronto: Macmillan, 1975), p. 65.*

Source: © Franklin Arbuckle

Women and Power in Iroquoian Society

Generalizations are often made about Aboriginal society, but it is important to note the remarkable diversity that differentiated the various First Nations. One generalization is that Aboriginal society was much less patriarchal than European society. These matriarchal assumptions usually derive from the Iroquois. The extent and nature of women's authority in Iroquois society has long fascinated historians. Much of the discussion centres on information provided by the Jesuits in their annual reports, or *Relations*, published from the early seventeenth century to the 1670s, and Jesuit writings in the early eighteenth century.

Ethnologists a century ago noted that the Iroquois organized their societies on different lines than did the patrilineal western Europeans. The American ethnologist Lucien Carr, for instance, believed Iroquois women controlled their societies. In 1884, he wrote that the Iroquois woman, "by virtue of her functions as wife and mother, exercised an influence but little short of despotic, not only in the wigwam but also around the council fire."[1] Another American ethnologist, J.N.B. Hewitt, himself of Iroquois background (Tuscarora), agreed. In 1933, he noted that the Iroquois woman "indeed possessed and exercised all civil and political power and authority. The country, the land, the fields with their harvests and fruits belonged to her . . . her plans and wishes molded the policy and inspired the decisions of council."[2]

Scholars in the mid-twentieth century returned to this topic, re-examining the same material but arriving at different conclusions. Anthropologist Cara E. Richards, for instance, argued that Iroquois women enjoyed little real power in the seventeenth century.[3] It was only in the eighteenth and nineteenth centuries, when population losses and other post-contact pressures necessitated a change to the early-seventeenth-century power structure, that women's power and influence prevailed.

In her book *Chain Her by One Foot: The Subjugation of Women in Seventeenth-Century New France*, Canadian sociologist Karen Anderson took a middle position, arguing that before Huron contact with the French, equality existed between males and females. The Jesuit fathers, however, upset this balance by imposing Christianity and European standards on male–female relations. By 1650, Anderson notes, "Women, especially, had been profoundly changed, accepting the domination of their husbands and fathers." Elsewhere she emphasizes, "What is astonishing is how quickly women's status was changed once Christianity was established."[4]

Controversy also centred on the sources Anderson and others used: the *Jesuit Relations*. As anthropologist Judith K. Brown points out, "the *Relations* cover an extended period of time and are anecdotal rather than descriptive. They are the work of many authors, whose prime purpose was to describe not the customs they found, but their own missionary activities."[5]

In the 1970s, the Iroquoianist William N. Fenton and French-language specialist Elizabeth L. Moore made available an English translation of the early-eighteenth-century ethnological classic *Moeurs des sauvages amériquains, comparées aux moeurs des premiers temps* (1724) by Joseph-François Lafitau. While Lafitau's remarks on male–female relations apply to only one Iroquois community near Montreal, at a specific period of time during the 1710s, it is invaluable.

The Jesuit missionary lived for nearly six years (1712–17) with the Christianized Iroquois converts at Sault St. Louis (later known as Caughnawaga or Kahnawake). He based his study on his own observations, information from another Jesuit who had worked in New France for over half a century, and on the *Jesuit Relations*. Lafitau summarized the status of Iroquois women: "Nothing is more real . . . than the women's superiority. It is they who really maintain the tribe, the nobility of blood, the genealogical tree, the order of generations and conservation of the families. In them resides all the real authority: the lands, fields and all their harvest belong to them; they are the soul of the councils, the arbiters of peace and war; they hold the taxes and the public treasure; it is to them that the slaves are entrusted; they arrange the marriages; the children are under their authority; and the order of succession is founded on their blood."[6]

Anthropologist Elisabeth Tooker added a fresh, new geographical dimension to this topic in her 1984 essay "Women in Iroquois Society." She emphasized the importance of the two different domains of Iroquois societies: the clearing, which is the domain of females, and the forest, which is that of males. "As the women did all the agricultural work of planting, tending, and harvesting of crops, the whole clearing (village and fields) also was regarded as the domain of women. The land beyond the clearing, the forest, was the domain of men."[7]

1.   Lucien Carr, "On the Social and Political Position of Woman among the Huron–Iroquois Tribes," *16th and 17th Annual Reports of the Trustees of the Peabody Museum*, 3(3–4) (1884): 211, reprinted in William Guy Spittal, ed., *Iroquois Women: An Anthology* (Ohsweken, ON: Iroqrafts, 1990), p. 13.

2.   J.N.B. Hewitt, "Status of Women in Iroquois Polity Before 1784," *Annual Report of the Board of Regents of the Smithsonian Institution for the Year Ending June 30, 1932*, p. 487, reprinted in Spittal, ed., *Iroquois Women*, p. 67.

3.   Cara E. Richards, "Matriarchy or Mistake: The Role of Iroquois Women Through Time," in V.F. Kay, ed., *Cultural Stability and Cultural Change*, proceedings of the 1957 Annual Spring Meeting of the American Ethnological Society, reprinted in Spittal, ed., *Iroquois Women*, pp. 149–59. (The quote appears on p. 153.)

4.   Karen Anderson, *Chain Her by One Foot: The Subjugation of Women in Seventeenth-Century New France* (London/New York: Routledge, 1991), pp. 52, 162.

5.   Judith K. Brown, "Economic Organization and the Position of Women Among the Iroquois," *Ethnohistory* 17(3–4) (1970): 165, n. 5, reprinted in Spittal, ed., *Iroquois Women*, p. 196.

6.   Joseph-François Lafitau, trans., *Customs of the American Indians Compared with the Customs of Primitive Times*, 2 vols. (Toronto: Champlain Society, 1974, 1977), vol. 1, p. 69.

7.   Elisabeth Tooker, "Women in Iroquois Society," in *Extending the Rafters: Interdisciplinary Approaches to Iroquoian Studies* (Albany: State University of New York Press, 1984), pp. 109–23, reprinted in Wendy Mitchinson et al., eds., *Canadian Women: A Reader* (Toronto: Harcourt Brace, 1996), p. 28.

With the development of agriculture and more settled societies, large confederacies formed. Two Iroquoian confederacies existed in the Great Lakes area at the time of European contact. The Wendat (Huron) were located on the north shores of Lake Ontario before migrating to Georgian Bay. The Huron Confederacy was an alliance of four nations: Attignawantans (People of the Bear), Attigneenongnahacs (People of the Cord), Arendarhonons (People of the Rock), and Tahontaenrats (People of the Deer). The Huron were the economic power of the region. Their villages were surrounded by wooden pallisades for defensive purposes, and the pallisades were surrounded by

Caroline Parker, Seneca, around 1850, wearing beaded clothing.

Source: Courtesy of The Autry National Center, Southwest Museum, Los Angeles. Photo # N.24963.

corn fields. Because they were permanently settled, the Huron became the traders of the region, situated as they were at a crossroads in a trading network that crisscrossed North America.

The League of Hodenosaunee (People of the Longhouse) was located south of Lake Ontario and Lake Erie. The Five Nations Iroquois (note that "Iroquois" is the name of the linguistic and national group) Confederacy consisted of (from east to west) Mohawk, Oneida, Onondaga, Cayuga, and Seneca. It became the Six Nations in 1722 when the Tuscaroras joined. These nations were more distinct from each other than those of the Wendat. While they controlled a larger territory, their population was smaller (16 000 as against 30 000). The Iroquois were the military power of the region. While they farmed, they were semi-nomadic. Their location allowed them to control the trade routes extending from the coast to the interior. Each member nation of the Iroquois Confederacy had its own council, which met in the group's largest village. The national councils sent representatives to the League, or Confederacy Council. The Great League of Peace was formed on the eve of contact in the fifteenth century. It was governed by a council of fifty chiefs representing the nations. The aim was to maintain peace within the Confederacy and to coordinate relations with other groups.

The Iroquoian peoples lived in stockaded villages of up to 1500 inhabitants. From ten to thirty families belonging to the same clan lived together in "longhouses," some the size of half a football field in length, and consisting of a framework of saplings, often arched in a barrel shape, covered with sheets of bark. The Iroquoians divided the longhouses into apartments, occupied by closely related families. A corridor ran down the middle of the house, and families on each side shared fireplaces. The villages were moved every ten to fifty years or so, when the soil became exhausted and the local resources depleted.

The core of any household consisted of a number of females descended from a common ancestor. When a man married, he moved to his wife's home, where authority was invested in an elderly woman. In Iroquoian society, the older women had social and political power. The matrons of the appropriate families elected the chiefs, who were men; these women could also vote out of office any chief. By the mid-1530s, another group of Iroquoians—neither Huron nor Iroquois—occupied the St. Lawrence River valley: the St. Lawrence Iroquoians.

SUMMARY

At the time of European contact, First Nations groups lived in six very different culture areas that parallel Canada's major geographical areas: the West coast, the interior of British Columbia, the prairies, the Canadian Shield, the eastern woodlands, and the Arctic. Linguistic diversity also existed, with more than fifty different languages being spoken in the six culture areas. On the eve of European contact, the Aboriginal peoples had been living throughout North America for thousands of years. Their societies were culturally, politically, religiously, and economically complex.

But the First Nations were also very distinct. It is dangerous to make generalizations about these groups. In each culture area, nature and the availability of natural resources dictated the lifestyle of the particular groups. Indigenous societies were accustomed to adjusting to change and new opportunities. First Nations communities traded across linguistic and cultural boundaries, and indeed, their trade networks were remarkably extensive and complex. These exchanges sealed economic, political, and military relationships.

NOTES

1. Eldon Yellowhorn, in Alan D. McMillan and Eldon Yellowhorn, *First Peoples in Canada* (Vancouver: Douglas & McIntyre, 2004), p. x.

2. Alice Kehoe discusses this subject in her book *North American Indians: A Comprehensive Account*, 2nd ed. (Englewood Cliffs, NJ: Prentice-Hall, 1992), pp. 2–3; in the 3rd ed. (Upper Saddle Creek, New Jersey: Pearson/Prentice-Hall, 2006), pp. 1–2; and also in her *America Before the European Invasions* (London: Pearson Education, 2002), pp. 9, 20.

3. Alfred W. Crosby, "Virgin Soil Epidemics as a Factor in the Aboriginal Depopulation in America," *William and Mary Quarterly*, 3rd series, 33 (1976): 290.

4. Olive P. Dickason, *Canada's First Nations: A History of the Founding Peoples from Earliest Times* (Toronto: McClelland & Stewart, 1992), p. 43.

5. Robert McGhee, "Canada YIK: The First Millennium," *The Beaver* (December 1999/January 2000): 10.

6. Dickason, *Canada's First Nations*, p. 67.

7. Bruce G. Trigger, *The Indians and the Heroic Age of New France* (Ottawa: Canadian Historical Association, 1977), p. 6.

RELATED READINGS

See Chapter 1, "First Nations in Their Own Words: The Early History of Canada to 1500," pp. 4–48 in Bryden et al., *Visions: The Canadian History Modules Project* (Toronto: Nelson Education, Ltd., 2011). Robert McGhee's "Canada Y1K: The First Millennium," pp. 15–20, and "Report of the Royal Commission on Aboriginal Peoples," pp. 21–48, are especially useful.

BIBLIOGRAPHY

Three overviews of pre-contact Aboriginal society by anthropologists include Alice B. Kehoe, *North American Indians: A Comprehensive Account*, 3rd ed. (Upper Saddle Creek, NJ: Pearson/Prentice-Hall, 2006); R. Bruce Morrison and C. Roderick Wilson, eds., *Native Peoples: The Canadian Experience*, 3rd ed. (Don Mills, ON: Oxford University Press, 2004); and Alan D. McMillan and Eldon Yellowhorn,

First Peoples in Canada (Vancouver: Douglas & McIntyre, 2004). A good survey of the area that would become Canada is Olive P. Dickason, *Canada's First Nations: A History of the Founding Peoples from Earliest Times*, 3rd ed. (Don Mills, ON: Oxford University Press, 2002); and her shorter work *A Concise History of Canada's First Nations* (Don Mills, ON: Oxford University Press, 2006). Other useful overviews include Arthur J. Ray, *I Have Lived Here Since the World Began: An Illustrated History of Canada's Native People* (Toronto: Key Porter Books, 1996; rev. ed. 2005); and Bruce G. Trigger ansd Wilcomb E. Washburn, eds., *The Cambridge History of the Native Peoples of the Americas*, vol. 1, *North America* (Port Chester, NY: Cambridge University Press, 1996); Bruce Trigger, *Natives and Newcomers: Canada's 'Heroic Age' Reconsidered* (Montreal/Kingston: McGill-Queen's University Press, 1985), and James Axtel, *The Invasion Within: The Context of Cultures in Colonial North America* (New York: Oxford University Press, 1985).

Alice Kehoe provides an account of the development of human cultures in North America in *America Before the European Invasions* (London: Pearson Education Limited, 2002). A popular account of the archaeological record is Robert McGhee's *Ancient Canada* (Ottawa: Canadian Museum of Civilization/Libre Expression, 1989). For a review of the human occupation of what is now Ontario just after the glaciers retreated, see Peter L. Storck, *Journey to the Ice Age: Discovering an Ancient World* (Vancouver: UBC Press, 2004). For a comprehensive study of the Huron (Wendat) Nation, see Bruce Trigger, *The Children of Aateaentsic: A History of the Huron People to 1600*, 2 vols. (Montreal/Kingston: McGill-Queen's University Press, 1976). A speculative work is Elaine Dewar's *Bones: Discovering the First Americans* (Toronto: Random House, 2001). For a study of cultural contact in eastern North America, see Denys Delage, *Bitter Feast: Amerindians and Europeans in Northeast North America, 1600–1664* (Vancouver: University of British Columbia Press, 1993), and, A.G. Bailey, *The Conflict of European and Eastern Algonkian Cultures, 1504–1700* (Toronto: University of Toronto Press, 1969). For a study of the Iroquois, see Francis Jennings, *The Ambiguous Iroquois Empire* (New York: Norton, 1984), and Daniel K. Richter, *The Ordeal of the Longhouse: The Peoples of the Iroquois League in the Era of European Colonization* (Chapel Hill: University of North Carolina Press, 1992). Richter's *Facing East from Indian Country: A Native History of Early America* (Cambridge/London: Harvard University Press, 2001) is another important work that offers an alternative way of viewing this period of history. Richard White gives a comprehensive account of contact relations in the Great Lakes region in *The Middle Ground: Indians, Empire and Republics in the Great Lakes Region, 1615–1815* (New York: Cambridge University Press, 1991).

Henry F. Dobyns, *Native American Historical Demography: A Critical Bibliography* (Bloomington: Indiana University Press, 1976), provides demographic information. For details on the impact of disease, consult Alfred W. Crosby, "Virgin Soil Epidemics as a Factor in the Aboriginal Depopulation in America," *William and Mary Quarterly*, 3rd series, 33 (1976): 289–99, and his *Ecological Imperialism: The Biological Expansion of Europe, 900–1900* (Cambridge: Cambridge University Press, 1986). In *Numbers from Nowhere: The American Indian Contact Population Debate* (Norman: University of Oklahoma Press, 1998), David Helge challenges Dobyns's estimates on the magnitude of the demographic decline.

Short reviews of Aboriginal culture areas appear in Morrison and Wilson, *Native Peoples*; Kehoe, *North American Indians*; and McMillan and Yellowhorn, *First Peoples in Canada*. There are useful essays in Paul Robert Magocsi, ed., *Canada's Aboriginal Peoples: A Short Introduction* (Toronto: University of Toronto Press, 2002). Six volumes in the series *Handbook of North American Indians* (Washington: Smithsonian Institution) are important: vol. 1, David Dumas, ed., *Arctic* (1985); vol. 6, June Helm, ed., *Subarctic* (1981); vol. 7, Wayne Suttles, ed., *Northwest Coast* (1990); vol. 12, Deward E. Walker, ed., *Plateau* (1998); vol. 13, Raymond J. Demaillie, ed., *Plains* (2001); and vol. 15, Bruce G. Trigger, ed., *Northeast* (1978). A useful study of Aboriginal languages is Michael K. Foster's "Native People, Languages" in *The Canadian Encyclopedia*, 2nd ed., vol. 3 (Edmonton: Hurtig, 1988), pp. 1453–56.

The early maps in R. Cole Harris, ed., *Historical Atlas of Canada*, vol. 1, *From the Beginning to 1800* (Toronto: University of Toronto Press, 1987), are based on recent archaeological discoveries. This atlas contains a wealth of new information about the first inhabitants of present-day Canada. The most up-to-date summary of our current understanding is Dickason's *Canada's First Nations*.

A survey of developments in Ontario appears in Edward S. Rogers and Donald B. Smith, eds., *Aboriginal Ontario: Historical Perspectives on the First Nations* (Toronto: Dundurn Press, 1994); and in Peter A. Baskerville's chapter, "Change and Exchange: 9000 B.C.E.–1500 C.E.," in his *Ontario: Image, Identity, and Power* (Don Mills, ON: Oxford University Press, 2002), pp. 1–11. One of the best overviews on First Nations groups embracing change is Theodore Binnema's *Common and Contested Ground: A Human and Environmental History of the Northwestern Plains* (Norman: University of Oklahoma Press, 2001). For bibliographical information, consult Shepard Krech III, *Native Canadian Anthropology and History: A Select Bibliography*, rev. ed. (Winnipeg: Rupert's Land Research Centre, University of Winnipeg, 1994). John S. Lutz's *Makuk: A New History of Aboriginal–White Relations* (Vancouver: UBC Press, 2008), incorporates oral history and examines the topic from contact through the 1970s.

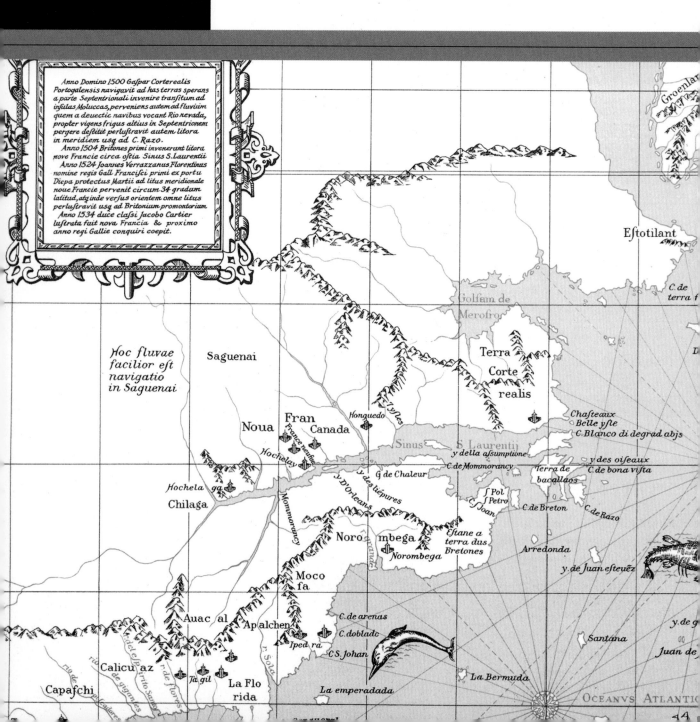

Part 1
EARLY EUROPEAN SETTLEMENT TO 1760

*Anno Domino 1500 Gaspar Corterealis
Portogalensis navigavit ad has terras sperans
a parte Septentrionali invenire transitum ad
insulas Moluccas, perveniens autem ad fluvium
quem a deuectis navibus vocant Rio nevada,
propter vigens frigus altius in Septentrionem
pergere destitit perlustravit autem litora
in meridiem usq ad C. Razo.*
*Anno 1504 Britones primi invenerunt litora
nove Francie circa ostia Sinus S. Laurentii*
*Anno 1524 Joannes Verrazzanus Florentinus
nomine regis Gall Francisci primi ex portu
Diepa protectus Martii ad litus meridionale
noue Francie pervenit circum 34 gradum
latitud, atq inde versus orientem omne litus
perlustravit usq ad Britonium promontorium.*
*Anno 1534 duce classi Jacobo Cartier
lustrata fuit nova Francia & proximo
anno regi Gallie conquiri coepit.*

Groenla

Estotilant

C. de
terra f

Golfam de
Merofro

Terra
Corte
realis

*Hoc fluvae
facilior est
navigatio
in Saguenai*

Saguenai

Chasteaux
Belle yste
C. Blanco di degrad abjs

Noua
Fran
Canada

Honguedo

y. des
Sinus S Laurentii
y della assumptione

y des oiseaux
C. de bona vista

Hochelay

C. de Mommorancy

Terra de
bacallaos

y des lièpures

G de Chaleur

Pol
Petro
C. Joan

Hochela ga

y. D'Orleans

Chilaga

Mommorancy

C. de Breton

C. de Razo

Noro mbega

Estane a
terra dus
Bretones

Arredonda

Norombega

y. de Juan esteuèz

Moco
fa

Auac al

Apalchen

C. de arenas

C. doblado

Iped ra

C.S. Johan

Santana

y. de g

Juan de

Calicu az

Ja gil

La Flo
rida

La Bermuda

Capafchi

La emperadada

OCEANVS ATLANTI

4

INTRODUCTION

When Western Europeans crossed the North Atlantic Ocean during their "Age of Discovery" in the fifteenth and sixteenth centuries, they entered what they considered a new world. They assumed they were "discovering" for the first time a continent that was open and empty, and theirs to claim, conquer, colonize, and exploit. They considered the Aboriginal peoples uncivilized. These assumptions, recorded in writing, became the foundation for the histories of the Western Hemisphere for centuries. Thus, the "voices" of the First Nations were muted.

But the First Nations were ancient civilizations with their own understandings of trade and economics, and they recognized what the newcomers represented in terms of new, revolutionary trade goods. As a result, many First Nations aggressively pursued trading relationships with the Europeans.

The Europeans, likewise, recognized the bounty of the New World. The Spanish and the Portuguese led the "Age of Discovery," and by the late fifteenth century had established bases in South and Central America. The French and the English, slower to centralize their power and to send expeditions across the Atlantic, were forced to explore farther north. While the English began settling along the eastern seaboard of North America, the French went even farther north.

The objective of all the Europeans was a route to the riches of the Orient through what was assumed to be a relatively small land mass. But wealth was discovered right on the continent. The Spanish found gold and silver. To the north it was fish and then furs that brought the Europeans back annually, eventually leading the French to establish permanent settlements in what they called New France. The colony was large geographically; but in comparison with New England to the south, founded at about the same time, the population remained small—only 65 000 people at the time of the Conquest in 1760, almost 150 years after Champlain founded Quebec in 1608.

The nature of the fish and fur trade created a different colony in what would become Canada. Neither resource required settlement of vast stretches of land. The small population became a constant problem, but the likelihood of conflict with the First Nations was lessened as a result. In addition, the fur trade benefited from, indeed relied on, participation of the First Nations. A mutually beneficial relationship developed early. In addition, the French colony depended on its "Indian" allies for defence.

The existence of New France was never guaranteed, and its survival was often in doubt. Wars with the Iroquois and their allies, the British, posed a constant threat. But the colony developed over the next century and a half. The Crown attempted to create a "little France" in North America, but the colony's institutions were inevitably shaped by their North American character. By the mid-eighteenth century, the contours of the "Canadien" and Acadian identities were evident. The British conquest in 1760 ended the French regime in North America, but not the French character of the St. Lawrence Valley or the Maritimes.

Chapter Two

THE ARRIVAL OF THE EUROPEANS

TIME LINE

985	Eric the Red establishes Norse settlements in Greenland
1492	Christopher Columbus reaches North America
1497	Giovanni Caboto (John Cabot) lands in Newfoundland
1524	Giovanni da Verrazzano explores Atlantic coast between Florida and the Gulf of St. Lawrence
1534–35	Jacques Cartier enters the Gulf of St. Lawrence and makes contact with Laurentian Iroquois
1536	Cartier visits Hochelaga (Montreal) and Stadacona (Quebec City)
1540s	Basque whalers operate stations on south coast of Labrador
1542	Cartier–Roberval expedition establishes French settlement but it is abandoned
1576	Martin Frobisher makes first attempt to find Northwest Passage
1583	Humphrey Gilbert claims Newfoundland for England

The massive boat emerging from the edge of the world likely amazed the Aboriginal hunters along the Labrador and Newfoundland coast. Upon the sea monster's back arose a tall, leafless tree from which hung a gigantic white blanket. Around the tree stood ugly beings covered with hair of numerous colours and skin the colour of a fish's underbelly. They looked sickly, and smelled as if they had not bathed for a long time. But they were armed with formidable weapons that seemed almost unbreakable. And they were clad in seemingly impenetrable armour and shields.

The year was 1000 and the newcomers were the Norse. This early contact would not be long-lasting, however. After perhaps a decade of settlement, the Norse were gone. And so too was knowledge of their voyages, other than vague references in the Norsemen's ballads. After an interval of nearly five centuries, other Europeans (Spanish, Portuguese, English, and French) came to the Americas thinking they were the first to "discover" this new world.

The absence of written source materials makes the narrative of the Europeans' arrival uncertain. And without benefit of a written language, the First Nations' perspective is completely absent. Indeed, it was the lack of surviving source material that allowed knowledge of the Norse excursions to slip into obscurity. Accounts of the Europeans' return five centuries later did survive, but the explorers' journals are not abundant. According to Morris Bishop, a biographer of Samuel de Champlain, the founder of Quebec in 1608, "In reading history one must always be impressed by the fact that our knowledge is only a collection of scraps and fragments that we put together into a pleasing design, and often the discovery of one new fragment would cause us to alter utterly the whole design."[1]

Up to only a few decades ago, the history of North America was taught without knowledge of the Norse arrival. Christopher Columbus had "discovered" America in 1492, and Canadian history started in 1497 with the discoveries of John Cabot or 1534 with the arrival of Jacques Cartier. Even now, the story of the Europeans' arrival in northeastern North America remains subject to amendment, as does all history.

The Norse Expeditions

Irish monks, the guardians of lost knowledge from classical antiquity, were probably the first European navigators both interested in voyaging westward and capable of reaching North America. They travelled in *curraghs,* wood-framed boats covered with sewn ox hides, powered by oars and a square sail. In the early Middle Ages, tales circulated about the celebrated Irish saint Brendan, said to have found new lands by sailing west in the sixth century; however, no medieval claim that he reached lands to the west has ever been substantiated.

But it was likely those the Irish monks feared most—the Norse—who first crossed the Atlantic. From the ninth to the twelfth centuries, Scandinavia led the European sea powers with a commercial empire extending from Russia in the east to Sicily in the south and Normandy in the west. But even farther west, the Norse occupied small coastal areas on the southwestern coast of Greenland, as part of their voyages from the European mainland. Eric the Red (Eirikr Thorvaldsson) founded the Norse settlements in Greenland in A.D. 985. Exiled from his native Norway as punishment for committing murder, he escaped to Iceland, only to become involved in a feud there. Banished for more killings, he fled farther west to a vast uninhabited subcontinent. On its southwestern coast, he found that the land had green, reasonably level pastures and impressive fiords and headlands, all of which reminded him of his native Norway. Finding it rich in game animals, with a sea full of fish and large mammals such as seals and walrus, he believed that the land could support many Icelanders. Eric named the country "Greenland." On returning to Iceland, Eric encouraged others to migrate with him. Accompanied by fifteen shiploads of Icelanders, the Norse adventurer founded two settlements, where they raised cows, horses, sheep, pigs, and goats. Excavations of the remains of Eric's own farm have revealed a surprisingly large and comfortable establishment, built with thick walls of stone and turf.

Viking ship, or knarr, *a reconstruction by Louis S. Glanzman.*

Source: National Geographic Society Image Collection.

In 986, Bjarni Herjölfsson, owner of a ship that traded between Norway and Iceland, went to join Eric in Greenland. En route, he and his crew met with stormy weather, which drove them off course for several days. When the thick mists cleared they sighted a flat land covered with woods. As this country did not fit the description he had of Greenland, Bjarni sailed north. Bjarni thus became the first known European to sight eastern North America (probably Labrador), although he never landed there.

Eric's second son, Leifr (or Leif) Eiriksson, grew up hearing tales about Bjarni's discovery. In 1001, he assembled a crew of 35 and set out to explore the lands southwest of Greenland. He sailed past Baffin Island, which he called "Helluland" (Flat Stone Land). Farther south, he landed in a forested area—probably the coast of central Labrador—that he called "Markland" (Wood Land). Continuing on, he reached an attractive location with a moderate climate, which he named "Vinland" (Wineland) for its plentiful "wineberries" (probably wild red currants, gooseberries, or mountain cranberries). A year later Leif and his crew loaded a cargo of timber and "wineberries" and set sail for Greenland. They did not encounter any other humans during their stay.

Conflict Between the Norse and the First Peoples

Leif's brother, Thorvaldr, led the next voyage to Vinland. With his crew of thirty he reached the Vinland houses and settled there for the winter, catching fish to supplement provisions brought from Greenland. During the second summer, Thorvaldr and his crew apparently followed the coast northward, where they encountered nine *skraelings* (barbarians), as the Norse called them, sleeping under three "skin boats" on shore (because of this reference in the Vinland Sagas, some experts believe these *skraelings* were not First Nations, but Inuit using kayaks). The Norse murdered eight of the nine. The individual who escaped later returned with others in a fleet of skin boats. In the skirmish that ensued, Thorvaldr was killed. The crew returned to Vinland and then to Greenland. Similar skirmishes occurred on subsequent expeditions, preventing the establishment of a permanent colony.

The Historical Value of the Norse Sagas

We know of the journeys of Eric the Red, Bjarni Herjölfsson, Leif Eiriksson, and the later Viking explorers from sagas, or adventure stories, passed orally from generation to generation for about 300 years before being written down. As expert storytellers told these sagas to spellbound audiences, they no doubt embellished them considerably, but the accounts still have value. The Norse journeys were largely forgotten for centuries.

In 1960, Helge Ingstad and his archaeologist wife, Anne Stine Ingstad, used the sagas to locate the first known site of European settlement in North America, L'Anse aux Meadows, on the northeastern tip of the Great Northern Peninsula of Newfoundland. Here, they unearthed the remains of eight sod-walled structures (the largest is 25 metres long) similar to those constructed by the Norse in Iceland and Greenland. Excavation led to the discovery of Norse artefacts, including a bronze cloak pin used to fasten a cloak on the right shoulder in order to leave arms free to wield a sword, and a soapstone disk that served as the weight on a spindle used in spinning yarn from wool. Radiocarbon-dating of Norse artefacts found at the site indicated occupancy in the vicinity of A.D. 1000—the date of the Vinland expeditions. The absence of a *midden* (refuse heap) containing bones and other debris, together with the fact that none of the buildings had been rebuilt or had major repairs, hints at a short occupancy. L'Anse aux Meadows remains the only authenticated Viking site in northeastern North America.

The Norse in Greenland

For nearly 500 years, the Norse occupied Greenland. Their economy was based on raising stock, hunting, and fishing. They travelled to the west for timber and to the north to trade with the Inuit along the Greenland coast and Baffin and Ellesmere Islands. Norse specimens, including ship rivets, chain-mail pieces, two items of woven woollen cloth, barrel-bottom fragments, and many copper and iron artefacts, have been excavated on the east coast of Ellesmere Island.

Reconstruction of the turf houses originally built by the Norse at L'Anse aux Meadows.

Source: Robin Bodnaruk

The Greenland settlements prospered in the twelfth century, when an estimated 2000 to 4000 people, or perhaps as many as 6000, lived there. Then, in the thirteenth century, Greenland's climate became colder, which threatened agriculture. Furthermore, the settlements' prosperity, precariously built on the walrus-ivory trade, declined when the Portuguese imported African elephant ivory. As well, the Black Death of 1349 struck Norway and Iceland. The epidemic of bubonic plague killed one-third of the population—a loss that cost the Norse their command of the seas. Thereafter, the annual ship that brought vital supplies from Norway no longer appeared. By 1450, the Greenlandic settlements disappeared.

The Portuguese and the Spanish

The Portuguese replaced the Scandinavians as the leading European sea power by the fifteenth century. Following the chaos of the Black Death, Portugal was able to centralize its power and begin to focus its energies externally. It went in search of trade routes and sources of wealth to increase its power. The Portuguese also developed the fast, efficient *caravels* (long, narrow ships with two masts).

By 1420 the Portuguese reached Madeira, and by 1427 the Azores. Their voyages across the Atlantic then ceased because they had reached latitudes at which strong westerly winds made sailing dangerous. Instead, they focused on discovering a sea route around Africa to India to gain access to valuable spices and other "exotic" trade goods. In 1487, Bartolomeu Dias rounded the Cape of Good Hope and reached India. In addition to locating a passage to India, the Portuguese also found a new source of wealth—African slaves.

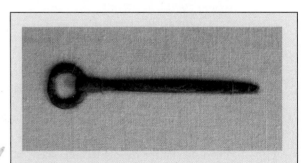

A bronze ringed pin found at L'Anse aux Meadows.

Source: © Parks Canada

European Interest in Expansion

The Age of Discovery was primarily motivated by economics and politics. The capture in 1453 of Constantinople by the Ottoman Turks, the key city in Europe's trade with the Orient, caused a desperate search to find a new route to "the Indies" (as China, Japan, Indonesia, and India were then collectively called) for spices to preserve their meat. The emerging kingdoms of Western Europe realized that these expeditions could result in riches to fill their coffers and place them in an advantageous position in the balance of power with their neighbours.

But there were other motives. The New World provided thousands of souls to be saved. The race was on to convert the "heathens" to Christianity. In addition, curiosity, adventure, and the search for a new and better world (particularly after the ravages of the Black Death) spurred the Portuguese—and later the Spanish, French, English, and Dutch—to expand beyond Europe.

The Europeans become the great explorers at the end of the fifteenth century, even though the Chinese and the Arabs both had extensive maritime experience, and in many ways were the more learned civilizations. The Arabs living on the western and northwestern shores of the Indian Ocean, for example, were more advanced than their European contemporaries in the seafaring sciences (astronomy, geography, mathematics, and navigation). Long before the Portuguese travelled along the west coast of Africa, Arabs had explored the east coast of that continent to the island of Madagascar. But the Arabs felt no need to go farther, since their territories included the rich variety of tropical plants and animals, as well as minerals, sought by Europe.

Similarly, well over a thousand years before European exploration, the Chinese had evolved a strong maritime tradition. The Chinese had introduced the compass to Europe and developed elaborate navigational charts showing detailed compass bearings. In the early fifteenth century, the Chinese built the world's largest navy, using it to sail as far as the Islamic world and Africa. But by the mid-1430s, they withdrew under orders from the emperor to suppress seafaring. An austere isolationism was imposed. Just at the time when Europeans were embarking on their great explorations, China turned inward.

The Voyage of Columbus, 1492

The Europeans had no idea what lay beyond the western seas. Even though Christian theologians claimed the Earth was flat, most educated Europeans knew it was spherical. Two thousand years previously, Aristotle had claimed it was possible to sail westward from Spain to "the Indies." When the Italian mariner Christopher Columbus proposed his expedition to the Spanish King and Queen, Ferdinand I of Aragon and Isabella I of Castile, he argued that there was a direct sailing route to India across the Atlantic. If it were found, recently united Spain could undercut the Portuguese, who were taking the long route around Africa. Columbus promised to find this route.

At the age of 41, Columbus already had extensive seafaring experience. Under the Portuguese flag he had sailed from the Arctic Circle to the equator, and from the eastern Mediterranean west to the outer Azores in the mid-Atlantic. Although, in the end, he found he had underestimated the circumference of the globe, his knowledge of the winds for sailing was impeccable.

In 1492, he sailed south to the Canary Islands, avoiding the strong westerly winds of the North Atlantic, and then west, reaching the Caribbean (the Bahamas). Convinced that he had reached islands near mainland Asia, he named the inhabitants he came across (the Lucayan, Taíno, or Arawak) "Indians." Over the course of Columbus's four expeditions, the motive shifted from the search for the passage to India and exploration to the establishment of colonies for settlement.

The voyages led to fierce rivalry between Spain and Portugal. In 1493, Ferdinand and Isabella approached Pope Alexander VI and asked for exclusive rights over the territories they had "discovered." The Spanish-born Pope drew a line of division through the mid-Atlantic, from the North to the South Pole. By the Treaty of Tordesillas in 1494, Spain and Portugal agreed to move the Pope's line of division one hundred leagues farther west. All land west of the line belonged to Spain and that to the east to Portugal. (This division brought Newfoundland and much of Brazil into Portugal's sphere.) This treaty, however, left no room for the emerging kingdoms of France and England.

The English Cross the North Atlantic

When news of Columbus's first two Atlantic voyages to "Asia" reached England, King Henry VII sponsored his own expedition. In 1496, he chose John Cabot (Giovanni Caboto), an experienced Italian mariner, to lead it. He instructed Cabot to "seek out, discover, and finde, whatsoever isles . . . and provinces of the heathen and infidelles," and to claim them for England. The merchants of the English port of Bristol, anxious to secure direct access to the spices of the east, sponsored the expedition.

Cabot set sail in late May 1497. He journeyed north of the Portuguese and Spanish claims. Unlike the Norse, the Italian navigator had the benefit of compass, quadrant, and traverse table. On June 24 he reached land, probably the eastern coast of Newfoundland. Here, he planted the flags of England and his native Venice and claimed the territory for Henry VII. He realized that the seas swarmed with fish. When baskets were dropped off the sides of the ships, weighted with stones, they were hauled up full of cod. Cabot's expedition had located the great continental shelf of Newfoundland, the shallow areas called banks, and the favourite breeding places of the cod. Cabot also entered the Gulf of St. Lawrence, believing it to be a direct route to China and India.

In 1997, the 500th anniversary of Cabot's voyage, a reconstructed Matthew *faced the same perils as did Cabot's ship.*

Source: Reprinted with permission from *The Telegram*.

Encouraged by this information, Henry VII sponsored a second voyage. In May 1498, Cabot sailed again from Bristol with five ships. Shortly out of port, one vessel turned back in distress to Ireland, but the other four were lost. Cabot's disappearance, followed shortly afterwards by the death of Henry VII, caused English interest in the search for a Northwest Passage to lapse. Nevertheless, John Cabot's first voyage announced England's interest in the Americas. The voyage also brought to Western Europe's attention the Grand Banks fishery. Bristol fishers had possibly been fishing the Grand Banks since the 1480s, but now their secret was out.

The Portuguese in the North Atlantic

When Portugal claimed Brazil in 1500, the kingdom focused on discovering a sea route around Africa to its new colony. Even though they had the African route to the Orient, the Portuguese also participated in the search for the Northwest Passage by sponsoring three North Atlantic expeditions. In 1500, João Fernandes, a *lavrador* (small farmer), reached Greenland. When he first sighted the huge land mass, Fernandes humorously called it "Tierra del Lavrador" (Land of the Farmer). A century later, when mapmakers learned of the old Norse name "Greenland," they revived it and applied the name Labrador to the southwest. In the same year, Gaspar Corte-Real sailed to Newfoundland. The Azorean sea captain kidnapped 57 First Nations people and sent them back to Europe with his brother Miguel; their fate there remains unknown. The fate of Gaspar Corte-Real and his crew is also unknown. Like Cabot and his four ships, he was lost with all hands, as was Miguel when he came back to search for his brother.

Despite the dangers of navigating the uncharted North Atlantic, the Portuguese annually fished the Grand Banks and the coastal waters of Newfoundland. Several place names, now corrupted in English or French versions, testify to their travels: Cape Race (from *raso*, shaved), at the southeastern corner of Newfoundland; Fermeuse Harbour (from *fremoso*, beautiful), about halfway from the cape to St. John's harbour; and Cape Spear (from the Portuguese *de espera*, hope), just south of St. John's harbour.

Since the Corte-Real expeditions did not produce any riches, the Portuguese lost interest in North Atlantic exploration for two decades. But around 1520, João Alvares Fagundes made a voyage along the south coast of Newfoundland and into the Gulf of St. Lawrence. Upon his return, he obtained colonists from Portugal and the Azores and established a colony, probably on the eastern coast of Cape Breton Island. After a year or so, difficulties arose with the local First Nations, and the settlement—the first European settlement since the Norse—died out. After the failure of this settlement, the Portuguese lost interest, apart from the cod fisheries in the North Atlantic.

The French Cross the North Atlantic

Of all the European powers in the early sixteenth century, France was perhaps the best situated to dominate northeastern North America. It had twice the population of Portugal and Spain together, and six times that of England. It also had more ocean-facing territory, at least as many seaports as England, and far greater wealth. Yet, due to its involvement in European conflicts, France did not become involved in North Atlantic exploration until 1524.

France was interested in the passage to India. Two possible entry points existed: between Florida and Newfoundland (the most promising) and between Labrador and Greenland. The French selected Giovanni da Verrazzano, an Italian navigator, as commander of their expedition. He searched the North American coast from the Carolinas to Gaspé. At one point, just north of what is now North Carolina, beyond a narrow strip of coastline, he claimed to have seen an immense, ocean-like body of water. But it was a mirage. The illusion, however, was enduring. For years afterward, cartographers put the Pacific Ocean just north of Florida, almost reaching the Atlantic. Gradually, as more became known, they put it farther west. Still, as late as the mid-eighteenth century, one European map showed a sea covering much of present-day western Canada connected to the Pacific.

Despite Verrazzano's failure to find the passage to Asia, France gained a better understanding of the eastern North American coastline. But discoveries were abandoned due to war against the Hapsburgs (the rulers of Austria, the Low Countries, and Spain).

The Voyages of Jacques Cartier

Jacques Cartier, a mariner from the wealthy port of Saint-Malo in Brittany, northwestern France, succeeded Verrazzano. Fishers from Saint-Malo and other northern French ports were already sailing to the Grand Banks for the plentiful cod. Cartier probably gained his first maritime experience on these runs. In April 1534, he left Saint-Malo with two ships and 61 men in search of a passage to China and India. The expedition reached the Strait of Belle Isle between Labrador and Newfoundland a month later. Unimpressed with the area, Cartier called it "the land God gave to Cain," after the biblical wasteland.

Cartier entered the Gulf of St. Lawrence and landed at present-day Prince Edward Island. Next, he sailed north to Chaleur Bay, which divides Quebec from New Brunswick, and met Mi'kmaq traders. Cartier's journal contains the first reference since the Vinland Sagas to a trading exchange between Aboriginal peoples and Europeans—initiated by the Mi'kmaq. According to Cartier, they "set up a great clamour and made frequent signs to us to come on shore, holding up to us some furs on sticks." The Mi'kmaq's enthusiasm for trade indicates that they had likely participated in previous exchanges and that word had been passed on through the generations by oral history.

As the French moved north to Gaspé they encountered Iroquoians who had come from the interior to fish. Unaccustomed to trading with Europeans, they brought no furs with them. The French gave the Iroquoians "knives, glass beads, combs, and other trinkets of small value" to win their friendship as well as information about the area. Then the French kidnapped two sons of the chief, Donnacona, and took them back to France to learn French, so that they could serve as guides on the next voyage.

It was standard practice among early Europeans in the Americas to capture inhabitants and take them back to Europe as proof of having reached the new lands or to serve as slaves. Columbus, for example, shipped 550 Aboriginals to Europe. Often, the captives perished on the voyage or died in Europe, unable to fight off illnesses that did not exist in the Americas and to which they had not immunity. In this instance, however, Donnacona's sons, Taignoagny and Domagaya, defied the odds and survived. They assisted Cartier in his next expedition.

Cartier in the St. Lawrence Valley, 1535–36

In 1535, Cartier returned with three ships and sailed up the St. Lawrence to the Iroquois village of Stadacona (present-day Quebec), the home of his guides, Taignoagny and Domagaya. Cartier recorded a word they used to refer to their home: "They call a town, *Canada*."[2] En route, the French sea captain gave the name "St. Lawrence" to a cove at which the French stopped, after the Christian martyr whose feast day it was (August 10). The entire gulf and the great river later were given the same name.

The Iroquoians at Stadacona saw the French as valuable trading partners. Access to the French trade goods provided the Laurentian Iroquois an essential economic advantage over their neighbours. Thus, when Cartier told Chief Donnacona he intended to travel inland to continue the search for the passage to Asia, the chief strongly objected. The Stadaconans wanted to monopolize the trade with the French and to barter the interior groups' furs for the precious European iron tools.

Regardless, Cartier pushed on and travelled inland in early October. By his own estimate, more than 1000 people greeted him at Hochelaga, a palisaded Iroquois town of fifty longhouses, much more impressive than Stadacona. That afternoon, Cartier climbed the large hill he called

Mont Royal (which eventually became "Montréal"). From the summit he had a magnificent view of the well-cultivated cornfields and longhouses below, but he also sighted rapids to the west, which no boat larger than a canoe could pass. Believing China lay beyond, he called them the Lachine Rapids. The French stayed just one day, then returned downriver. It being too late in the year to depart safely for France, Cartier and his men wintered at Stadacona.

The winter of 1535–6 was difficult for Cartier's crew. Tension prevailed at Stadacona. By travelling upriver without Donnacona's permission, Cartier had angered the Laurentian Iroquois. But the climate posed the greatest danger. The winter, much longer and colder than in France, proved a nightmare. By January and February, ice—nearly 4 metres thick—locked the ships in. On land, the snow lay more than a metre deep. To add to the sailors' problems, scurvy—a disease caused by insufficient ascorbic acid (vitamin C) in the diet—broke out. Twenty-five men (one-quarter of Cartier's crew) died before the French learned the Aboriginal cure: a brew with a high vitamin C content made by boiling bark and leaves of the *annedda* (white cedar).

Despite the help of the Iroquois, Cartier's relationship with Donnacona and his people deteriorated. The French were intent on obtaining information about the lands to the west, particularly the "kingdom of the Saguenay" alluded to by Taignoagny and Domagaya—which they believed to be, like Mexico, rich in gold and silver. (The stories of the Saguenay probably referred to copper deposits around Lake Superior.) This elusive destination provided Cartier with the dual objectives of his expedition—the Northwest passage and a source of wealth. If he failed to attain these objectives, he risked losing financial support for future expeditions. The French kidnapped Donnacona, his two sons, and three of the chief's principal supporters. Cartier left in the spring of 1536, promising to return his hostages the following year, but the captives never saw "Canada" again.

Cartier entered Saint-Malo in July 1536, after an absence of 14 months. Although he had discovered neither great wealth nor the Northwest Passage, he had proved Newfoundland was an island, charted much of the Gulf of St. Lawrence, and recorded in his journal the existence of a great river flowing from deep in the interior—the St. Lawrence. His geographical exploration remained unsurpassed by any other French explorer until Champlain, in the early 1600s.

The Cartier–Roberval Expedition, 1541–42

War between France and Spain delayed Cartier's third voyage until 1541. This time, the French navigator left with a mandate to found a colony and locate the famed "kingdom of the Saguenay" and the Northwest Passage. The expedition split into two groups. Cartier led the first group to Cap Rouge, about 15 kilometres upstream from Stadacona. Here, he unloaded cattle and supplies and planted crops, making it quite clear that he and the 150 French colonists intended to stay. Very little information has survived regarding the settlement that winter, but according to one report, at least 35 settlers died in attacks by the First Nations.

By spring, Cartier wanted to leave. With a cargo of iron pyrites and quartz that he thought were gold and diamonds, he sailed for France. A French proverb still used in Brittany and Normandy owes its origin to this episode: "*Faux comme un diamant du Canada*" (fake as a Canadian diamond).

Jean-François de La Rocque de Roberval arrived at Cap Rouge with the second part of the expedition, just after Cartier's hasty departure. He had with him some 200 settlers, and they too experienced a terrible winter at the site of Cartier's rebuilt settlement. Fifty died from scurvy. Apparently Cartier had neglected to communicate to Roberval the Aboriginal remedy. The next summer Roberval also returned to France. An inscription on a French map of 1550 explains the reasons for the colony's failure: "It was impossible to trade with the people of that country because of their austerity, the intemperate climate of said country, and the slight profit."

Not only did the failure of the Cartier–Roberval settlement dampen enthusiasm for further expeditions, but also war in Europe prevented the French return for the next half-century.

France, still at war with Spain, was torn in the 1560s by religious conflict. For thirty years Catholics battled Protestants, and not until the Edict of Nantes in 1598 did hostilities end. The Edict acknowledged Catholicism as the official religion of France, while allowing the Huguenots (as the Protestants were called) the right to worship and to enjoy political privileges, including the holding of public office.

During the French Wars of Religion (1562–1598), France made no excursions in search of wealth or the Northwest Passage, nor did they again attempt colonization. Although French fishers, whalers, and traders continued to sail to the northeastern coasts, the harsh climate, hostile relations with the Indigenous peoples, and failure to find gold combined to give the French a poor image of Canada, particularly relative to the wealth gained by Portugal and Spain in their New World exploits. In the late 1550s, France directed its colonization efforts toward Brazil and, in the early 1560s, toward the southeastern coasts of North America.

Fishing and Trading off the East Coast of North America

Despite setbacks further inland, European fishers maintained a constant presence in Newfoundland. Between March and October of each year, large fishing fleets—Portuguese, Basque, French, and English—gathered on the Grand Banks. They supplied the markets of Western Europe and the Mediterranean with cod, the "beef of the sea." The Newfoundland fishery was big business by the mid-sixteenth century. With an estimated 10 000 people visiting annually, it provided a livelihood for twice as many fishers as did the fisheries of the Gulf of Mexico and the Caribbean combined, where the Spanish fleets sailed.

The success of the Newfoundland cod fishery initially depended on the harvesting of salt left by the evaporation of seawater. This salt was better than the mineral variety for curing fish, because it was more uniform in quality. France, Spain, and Portugal produced an abundance of "solar salt," but England, not so blessed with sunshine, did not. This hurt England in the age of the "green fishery," the term sailors used to describe a method of salting fish immediately upon catching them, then transporting them back to Europe for drying. To compensate for their lack of solar salt, the English developed "dry fishing"—drying their lightly salted fish before returning home. The sun-cured codfish lasted indefinitely if kept dry and could be reconstituted by soaking in water.

English fishing expeditions to Newfoundland were an annual event. From December to February the English cleaned, overhauled, and fitted their ships. Then in March they left from the bustling ports in southwestern England—Plymouth, Poole, Dartmouth—with sufficient provisions and stores for eight months. Estimates of the number of English ships involved in Newfoundland expeditions around the year 1600 vary from 250 to 400, and the number of men from 6000 to 10 000. These expeditions made good England's claims to the Avalon Peninsula on Newfoundland's east coast, the location of the best English fishing and processing sites.

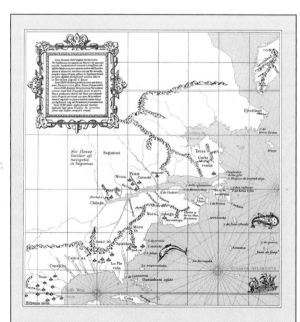

Part of Mercator's map of 1569, showing what was then known of eastern North America.

Source: D.G.G. Kerr, ed. *A Historical Atlas of Canada* (Toronto: Thomas Nelson & Sons, 1961), p. 11.

An artist's depiction of the French fishing and drying cod.

Source: Library and Archives Canada/C-003686

The English practised inshore fishing methods they had first used off the coast of Iceland. They fished from open boats or from barrels suspended over the ship's side. Before the fishing began, they searched for the most convenient "room"—a tract of land on the waterfront of a cove or harbour adjacent to their fishery. There they constructed the sheds, drying racks ("flakes"), wharves ("stages"), and other facilities where they landed their boats and processed their catch. A large fishing room was called a "plantation," and its owner, if he lived permanently on it, a "planter." Most of the ships carried a crew of 20, of whom a dozen fished while the rest cured the fish on shore. The fishing day was arduous. Up before dawn, the men fished until late afternoon. Then, at dusk, the first boat reached the staging to unload. The men worked 18 to 20 hours daily to take advantage of the run of fish. Curing involved splitting, lightly salting, and drying the cod, producing an excellent "stock" fish that did not spoil during the long voyages to the Caribbean.

England profited greatly from the decline of Spain's naval strength after the defeat of the Spanish Armada in 1588. No longer was Spain the power it had been in the mid-sixteenth century. England, in the seventeenth century, gained a market for its dried cod in southern Europe, including Spain. The English sold the firmest and whitest cod in the Mediterranean. They classified slightly damaged fish as second-grade and shipped it to overseas buyers. They packed the poorest-grade fish in casks and sold it to slave owners in the West Indies.

The Basque Whaling Stations

From their homeland in the border region of France and Spain, Basque whalers joined the cod fishers in the early sixteenth century and carried out whaling in the Strait of Belle Isle. Europe's first commercial whalers came prepared to set up a long-distance fishery. The south coast of Labrador became the first region of northeastern North America to undergo extensive exploitation by Europeans. Whaling stations flourished there for half a century. Sixteenth-century Europeans treasured whale oil as a fuel for lamps, an all-purpose lubricant, an additive to drugs, and a major ingredient of scores of products, such as soap and pitch. At its peak, the fishery employed about 2000 men, who remained in Newfoundland–Labrador waters from June until January every season. At the Basque shore stations, Inuit and First Nations groups obtained European materials annually from fixed locations in southern Labrador, and perhaps on the Gaspé coast also. Marc Lescarbot, the early French chronicler, noted that the Aboriginal people trading along the Gaspé shore during the first decade of the seventeenth century came to speak a trade language that was "half Basque." This Basque–Algonquian language became a "contact" language, used in trade with Europeans. Other trade languages later developed elsewhere, such as Chinook on the Pacific coast.

English Activity in the North Atlantic and Arctic

England sponsored a number of expeditions north of Newfoundland in the late sixteenth and early seventeenth centuries. In 1576, only a few months before Sir Francis Drake left to plunder

Spanish shipping in the Pacific Ocean, Martin Frobisher, 37 years old and a mariner of great repute, sailed northerly in search of a Northwest Passage to India and China. Off southern Baffin Island, Frobisher encountered Inuit, who came to trade meat and furs for metal objects and clothing. The Inuit's behaviour indicated that they were no strangers to Europeans, their ships, or their trade goods. Evidently, they had already encountered vessels of the Newfoundland fishing fleet and had probably traded for iron. Frobisher discovered this the hard way when he was struck by an iron-tipped arrow during a skirmish with the Inuit.

COMMUNITY PORTRAIT

The Basque Whaling Community of Red Bay, Labrador, 1550–1600

In the mid-1970s, Selma Barkham, a researcher employed by the Public Archives, discovered a forgotten chapter of Canadian history. Although it had long been known that Basque whalers had hunted off the Labrador coast, the extent of their operations, and the location of their whaling stations, was not known. While examining wills, lawsuits, mortgages, and insurance policies in Basque archives in Spain, Barkham came across a wealth of information on the whale fishery in the Strait of Belle Isle, separating Labrador from the northern tip of Newfoundland. The strait was ideal for whale hunting, as it acted as a funnel through which migrating whales passed in large numbers.

Barkham made a preliminary investigation of the southern Labrador coast with James Tuck, an archaeologist from Memorial University of Newfoundland, and several other scientists in the summer of 1977. All down the coastline they found evidence that the Basques had been in the region. At several locations they found red patches on the beaches, the remains of the imported red roof tile used by the Basque whalers for their buildings.

Tuck returned in the summer of 1978 to excavate the most promising site, on Saddle Island in Red Bay, one of the finest harbours in the Strait of Belle Isle. On

the harbour side of the island, he found fragments of old stone walls stained with a black material, later identified as burnt whale oil. The archaeologist had discovered the remains of the ovens where whale blubber was tried (boiled down) into oil. During future visits to Saddle Island, Tuck and his team located additional evidence of Basque activity. They found the remains of houses and of the workshops where the coopers (barrel-makers) constructed the barrels to ship whale oil.

In 1978, Robert Grenier, head of marine archaeology for Parks Canada, began underwater investigations that complemented Barkham's archival research and Tuck's archaeological work on Saddle Island. He discovered the well-preserved remains of a sunken Basque ship only 30 metres offshore of the Saddle Island station. It had gone down in a squall with a load of nearly 1000 barrels of whale oil. Subsequent investigations in the icy waters led to the location of the ship's compass, anchor, rudder, and loaded swivel gun. In 1979, the Historic Sites and Monuments Board of Canada designated the forgotten Basque whaling station of Red Bay a place of national historic interest.

Red Bay appears to have been the favourite whaling station of the Basque whalers. Normally, about ten galleons

An artist's reconstruction of Basque galleons riding at anchor in Red Bay, Labrador.

Source: "Discovery in Labrador: A 16th-Century Basque Whaling Port and Its Sunken Fleet," *National Geographic,* 168(1) (July 1985): 42–43. Painting by Richard Schlecht.

arrived in Red Bay every summer in the late sixteenth century. Depending on a ship's tonnage, crews ranged from 50 to 120 men. During the whaling season, the men harpooned whales from small open whaleboats and towed them back to the galleon left moored in the harbour. After they had removed large strips or slabs of blubber, they hauled it ashore. At the whaling station they rendered it into oil in huge ovens, or *tryworks,* containing several ovens, sheltered by roofs of red tile brought to Red Bay for that purpose.

The graves located at Red Bay reveal that the tradespeople were sturdy and relatively young. Basque males of all ages, some as young as 11, participated. The captains hired crews in the late winter and early spring. The Basque crews earned shares in the season's catch rather than fixed salaries. Crew members were able to climb the shipboard hierarchy and, with special training, to become harpooners or pilots. The ships brought large

amounts of cider, wine, and ship's biscuit. At Red Bay the men enjoyed a diet based largely on cod and salmon, with an occasional piece of caribou or a wild duck.

Between mid-June and early July the whaling ships left for Labrador. An average Atlantic crossing in the sixteenth century took a month. Basque whalers commonly stayed in Labrador well into the winter, returning to Spain by the end of January, by which time the Strait of Belle Isle had normally frozen over. Their residency in Labrador in winter required solid buildings; hence, the Basques imported large amounts of Iberian tile for the construction of their buildings.

The whaling effort at stations such as Red Bay proved so effective that it led to a massive depletion in northwestern Atlantic whale stocks. Another factor that helped to put an end to the Basque Labrador whale fishery by the end of the sixteenth century was the ill-fated Spanish Armada of 1588. The failed Spanish naval invasion of Britain claimed many Basque ships and lives. One written source indicates that another contributing factor was Inuit resistance to the Basque presence on the southern Labrador coast. The Basque whaling community at Red Bay vanished shortly after the beginning of the seventeenth century.

FURTHER READING

Selma Barkham, "The Basques: Filling a Gap in Our History between Jacques Cartier and Champlain," *Canadian Geographical Journal*, 96(1) (February/March 1978): 8–19.

James A. Tuck and Robert Grenier, *Red Bay, Labrador: World Whaling Capital, A.D. 1550–1600* (St. John's, NL: Atlantic Archaeology Ltd., 1989).

Frobisher failed to find a passage to the Orient, either on this first journey or on two subsequent voyages in 1577 and 1578. Ten years later, John Davis followed up on Frobisher's work in three successive summers (1585–87), but without success. The necessary maritime technology for penetration of the Arctic Archipelago did not exist in the late sixteenth century.

European Trade with the First Nations

The Eurocentric nature of our history reveals how the newcomers first perceived the First Nations and Inuit. There is little information, however, to reconstruct how the Aboriginal groups viewed the Europeans. The information that does exist attests to the value the Aboriginal peoples placed on European material goods. This, of course, is a Eurocentric generalization and it is important not to exaggerate the importance of the technological factor. The Aboriginals were not simply "awed" by the European trade goods and local conditions usually determined their effectiveness. Generally, however, the First Nations were impressed by the range of goods and their abundance. They likely were also impressed by those who could make such valuable goods. The Hurons of the Great Lakes called the French "Agnonha," or Iron People.

The Inuit and First Nations were likely not so impressed by the Europeans themselves, whose technology was remarkable and who could sail across the great water on massive boats, but who lacked even the most rudimentary survival techniques. The Europeans had difficulty withstanding the winters and died of a sickness easily cured by boiling tree bark. Nor were they a physically impressive people, covered in hair like animals but not knowing enough to bathe themselves—which animals at least did.

On the other hand, while the Europeans viewed the Aboriginals as barbaric and Stone-Age peoples, they were impressed by their ability to survive in such a climate. The early explorers commented on the physical prowess of the First Nations. Even when it came to technology, at times Aboriginal goods were superior. First Nations people held onto their superbly crafted bark canoes, snowshoes, toboggans, and bark-covered wigwams, because they were superior to what the Europeans could offer.

The Europeans assumed that the Aboriginal groups were not civilized enough to understand

Ojibwa women mending a birchbark canoe, North-West Angle of Lake of the Woods, October 1872. The Indigenous canoe made travel possible throughout the Eastern Woodlands and beyond.

Source: Library and Archives Canada/PA-074670.

trade and economics. They viewed them as hunter-gatherer peoples who used stone tools and wore animal skins. They perceived a simplistic people who were willing to trade many valuable furs for mere trinkets. But what if the trade is viewed from an Aboriginal perspective? The First Nations perceived the newcomers as willing to trade remarkably valuable metal tools and weapons for mere clothing. The furs were abundant and easy to obtain. In addition, the Europeans apparently wanted used clothing. The most valuable beaver pelts were those already worn, because the coarse guard-hair had already fallen off. The most important "trinkets" provided by the newcomers, including knives, axes, and pots, were of immense value. Steel blades did not break like stone or obsidian blades; copper pots did not crack and break like clay pots. The newcomers' steel axes lightened the labour of gathering firewood. Steel awls and needles made sewing and the working of hides and leather much easier.

The goods offered by the Europeans were so valuable that their availability affected not only the lifestyles of the Aboriginal groups but also their relations with each other. The Inuit and First Nations aggressively pursued trade. They were willing to fight to maintain their position in the trade and to prevent other groups from taking the coveted position. A direct trading relationship with the Europeans put the Aboriginal group in the role of middleman to then trade with other groups. European trade goods entered the extensive Aboriginal trading networks, and interior groups obtained them long before they ever saw a European. Archaeology has confirmed, for example, the presence, by the early sixteenth century, of European trade goods among the Seneca south of Lake Ontario, an Iroquoian nation located hundreds of kilometres from the Atlantic. This also means, however, that the impact was being felt long before direct contact occurred, for better and worse.

Yet, if the Aboriginal peoples of North America and the Europeans initially regarded each other with awe, the amazement quickly passed. Missionary reports from the early seventeenth century reveal that First Nations soon noted the slowness of the French in mastering Aboriginal languages and learning to use canoes, snowshoes, and other commonplaces. The more they learned about European customs and religion, the stranger and more bizarre these things appeared. Likewise, the Europeans' view of the First Nations as the "noble savage," an innocent people akin to Adam and Eve in the Garden of Eden before the Fall, was soon replaced by more negative perceptions.

A HISTORICAL PORTRAIT

Martin Frobisher

Martin Frobisher was one of the most famous mariners of Elizabethan England. In the late sixteenth century, his name was as well known as those of Francis Drake and John Hawkins. Brave and impetuous, a man of action, he became the first English pioneer of northern Canadian exploration. His first Arctic voyage of 1576 marked the beginning of a more than two-century-long quest to find the Northwest Passage, the route to Asia through Arctic waters. Historian Leslie Neatby has written that, as his original achievements were all in Canadian waters, "he may justly be recognized as the first Anglo-Canadian."[1]

As a boy Frobisher does not appear to have received much schooling. On documents his name appears in several versions, including "Furbiser," "Frobiser," "Furbisher," and even "Flourbyssher." In 1553, at the age of 14, young Martin left on his first sea voyage. Frobisher survived the trip to West Africa, although three-quarters of the expedition did not. Other African voyages followed, as well as privateering ventures seizing enemy vessels on the high seas.

For years the veteran sea rover dreamt of leading a search for the North-west Passage. Finally, in 1576, a group of London merchants financially backed his proposed expedition. Of the three ves-sels that left England, only Frobisher's made it to the huge bay on Baffin Island that now bears his name. He travelled up the bay for 200 kilometres, which he took to be a strait with the Americas on one side and Asia on the other. Before returning to England, he took back samples of ore that he believed con-tained gold. Several London assayers pronounced the ore valueless, but one stated it contained gold. That single upbeat report sufficed to send Frobisher back the next year to search for more ore. He returned with 200 tonnes and a gold rush began.

Frobisher's third voyage in 1578 involved fifteen ships, the largest naval fleet ever used in Arctic exploration. In spite of a hazardous journey, all but two vessels reached Frobisher Bay. The sailors spent the following weeks gathering and loading ore. On Kodlunarn Island, one of the mining sites at the southeastern tip of Baffin Island, they built a house of stone and lime. Expecting to return, they wanted to test the durability of the structure over the winter. Believing they had struck pay dirt, the expedition then returned with 1350 tonnes of ore.

But all attempts to smelt precious metal out of the rock failed. Frobisher's "gold" turned out to be only pyrite, cre-ating a huge scandal and financial ruin for Frobisher's backers. The veteran sea cap-tain's reputation fell, and only rebounded

Encounter with Eskimos, a watercolour by John White, an English artist who travelled with Martin Frobisher on his second expedition to Baffin Island in 1577.

Source: ©The Trustees of the British Museum.

when he took a leading role in repelling the Spanish Armada in 1588. Frobisher died six years later while storming an enemy fort in France.

During all of his voyages Frobisher was in contact with the Inuit. Nearly three centuries later, in the early 1860s, the American Charles Francis Hall found the ruins of the expedition's house on Kodlunarn Island. He also discovered that the Inuit, with whom Frobisher had had hostile relations (he kidnapped several of them and took them back to England, where they died from disease), had an accurate oral record of his voyages three centuries earlier. Their stories, which had been passed from generation to gen-eration, confirmed many details in the written record.

1. Leslie H. Neatby, "Martin Frobisher," *Arctic*, 36(3) (September 1983): 374.

SUMMARY

The original inhabitants of present-day Atlantic and Arctic Canada witnessed the arrival of the first Europeans—the Norse—around A.D. 1000, and that of the English, Portuguese, French, Spanish, and Basques five centuries later. The early European navigators crossed the North Atlantic at great personal risk. John Cabot, the Corte-Real brothers, and Sir Humphrey Gilbert (who claimed Newfoundland for England in 1583) lost their lives during their explorations: "North America became a graveyard for European ships and sailors."[3] Yet the Europeans persisted. Some came in search of a profitable Northwest Passage to China and the Indies. Others—the vast majority—were lured by the promise of economic gain in the ruthless exploitation of the cod and whale fisheries, and later in the fur trade. As late as 1600, however, no permanent European settlement existed in northern North America.

NOTES

1. Morris Bishop, *Champlain: The Life of Fortitude* (Toronto: McClelland & Stewart, 1963 [1948]), p. 26.

2. H.P. Biggar, ed., *The Voyages of Jacques Cartier* (Ottawa: King's Printer, 1924), p. 245. For an important discussion of other possible origins of the word "Canada," see Olive P. Dickason, "Appendix 1: Origin of the Name 'Canada,'" in *The Myth of the Savage and the Beginnings of French Colonialism in the Americas* (Edmonton: University of Alberta Press, 1984), pp. 279–80.

3. Samuel Eliot Morison, *The European Discovery of America: The Northern Voyages*, A.D. *500–1600* (New York: Oxford University Press, 1971), p. xi.

RELATED READINGS

Module 2, "Contact Zones from the Sixteenth to Eighteenth Century" in *Visions: The Canadian History Modules Project Pre-Confederation* discusses how Aboriginal peoples responded to and perceived European settlers and colonists (pp. 52–96). See especially the secondary source articles, which include Neil Salisbury, "The Indians' Old World: Native Americans and the Coming of Europeans"; Ramsay Cook, "Donnacona Discovers Europe: Rereading Jacques Cartier's Voyages"; Cornelius J. Jaenen, "The *Other* in Early Canada."

BIBLIOGRAPHY

Summaries of the early European explorers' accounts include Samuel Eliot Morison, *The European Discovery of America: The Northern Voyages*, A.D. *500–1600* (New York: Oxford University Press, 1971); Daniel J. Boorstin, *The Discoverers: A History of Man's Search to Know His World and Himself* (New York: Random House, 1983); and Robert McGhee, *Canada Rediscovered* (Ottawa: Canadian Museum of Civilization/Libre Expression, 1991). Primary texts are available in David Quinn, ed., *New American World: A Documentary History of North America to 1615*, 5 vols. (New York: Arno Press, 1979). Economic aspects are briefly reviewed by Michael Bliss in *Northern Enterprise: Five Centuries of Canadian Business* (Toronto: McClelland & Stewart, 1987). *Dictionary of Canadian Biography*, vol. 1, *1000–1700* (Toronto: University of Toronto Press, 1966), contains biographical portraits and is available online: www.biographi.ca.

Ralph T. Pastore provides a bibliographical guide to the secondary literature in his essay "Beginnings to 1600," in M. Brook Taylor, ed., *Canadian History: A Reader's Guide*, vol. 1, *Beginnings to Confederation* (Toronto: University of Toronto Press, 1994), pp. 3–32.

For a look at Aboriginal response and adaptation to European settlement and colonialism, see Keith Thor Carlson, *The Power of Place, the Problem of Time: Aboriginal Identity and Historical Consciousness in the Cauldron of Colonialism* (Toronto: University of Toronto Press, 2010).

Helge and Anne Stine Ingstad tell the story of the discovery of L'Anse aux Meadows in *The Viking Discovery of America: The Excavation of a Norse Settlement in L'Anse aux Meadows, Newfoundland* (St. John's, NL: Breakwater, 2000). Joel Berglund reviews the end of the Norse Greenlandic communities in "The Decline of the Norse Settlements in Greenland," *Arctic Anthropology*, 23(1–2) (1986): 109–35. For an overview of Viking landings in North America, see Eugene Linden, "The Vikings: A Memorable Visit to America," *Smithsonian*, 35(9) (2004): 92–5, 97–9.

Peter E. Pope reviews the various theories of where Cabot landed in *The Many Landfalls of John Cabot* (Toronto: University of Toronto Press, 1997). Another study is Peter Firstbrook's *The Voyage of the Matthew: John Cabot and the Discovery of North America* (Toronto: McClelland & Stewart, 1997). For two accounts of early Prince Edward Island, see David Keenlyside, "New Finds from the Island's Offshore. *Island Magazine*, 59 (2006): 10–12; Earle Lockerby, "Two Early Descriptions of Prince Edward Island," *Island Magazine*, 60 (2006): 28–32.

Bruce G. Trigger, *The Children of Aataentsic: A History of the Huron People to 1660*, vol. 1 (Montreal/Kingston: McGill-Queen's University Press, 1976), provides background information on the St. Lawrence Iroquoians' reactions to Cartier and Roberval. See also Trigger's *Natives and Newcomers: Canada's "Heroic Age" Reconsidered* (Montreal/Kingston: McGill-Queen's University Press, 1985). For an understanding of the Cartier–Roberval expeditions, consult Olive P. Dickason, *The Myth of the Savage and the Beginnings of French Colonialism in the Americas* (Edmonton: University of Alberta Press, 1984). Ramsay Cook has edited H.P. Biggar's translation of Cartier's journeys; see Jacques Cartier, *The Voyages of Jacques Cartier* (Toronto: University of Toronto Press, 1993). Cornelius Jaenen reviews the cultural interaction between the French and the Aboriginal peoples in *Friend and Foe* (Toronto: McClelland & Stewart, 1976). Ralph Pastore reviews "The Sixteenth Century: Aboriginal Peoples and European Contact" in Phillip A. Buckner and John G. Reid, eds., *The Atlantic Region to Confederation: A History* (Toronto: University of Toronto Press, 1994), pp. 22–39. Leslie C. Green and Olive P. Dickason examine the ideology that motivated the European occupation of the Americas in *The Law of Nations and the New World* (Edmonton: University of Alberta Press, 1989).

On Basque activity in northeastern North America, see Selma Barkham, "A Note on the Strait of Belle-Isle During the Period of Basque Contact with Indians and Inuit," *Etudes/Inuit/Studies*, 4 (1980): 51–58; "The Basque Whaling Establishments in Labrador, 1536–1632: A Summary," *Arctic*, 37 (1984): 515–19; Nicolas Landry, "Les Basques dans le golfe du Saint-Laurent se racontent," *Acadiensis*, 37(2) (2008): 117–29. An illustrated series of articles (including contributions by James A. Tuck and Robert Grenier) entitled "Discovery in Labrador: A 16th-Century Basque Whaling Port and Its Sunken Fleet" appeared in *National Geographic*, 168(1) (July 1985): 40–71. Jean-Pierre Proulx reviews the Basque arrival in *Basque Whaling in Labrador in the 16th Century* (Ottawa: National Historic Sites, Parks Services, 1993). For an introduction to the Gaspe region's prehistory, see Christian Gates St-Pierre, "Les collections archéologiques préhistoriques de la Gaspésie au Musée McCord," *Archéologiques*, 20 (2007): 55–70.

Laurier Turgeon examines First Nation and French contact in "French Fishers, Fur Traders, and Amerindians during the Sixteenth Century: History and Archaeology," *William and Mary Quarterly*, 3rd series, 55(4) (October 1998): 585–610. The ecological consequences of the European arrival in the waters off northeastern North America are described by Farley Mowat in his popular study *Sea of Slaughter* (Toronto: McClelland & Stewart, 1984). A delightful book is Mark Kurlansky's *Cod: A Biography of the Fish That Changed the World* (London: Penguin Books, 1998).

The impact of the Europeans on the First Nations' relationship to nature is reviewed by Calvin Martin in *Keepers of the Game: Indian–Animal Relationships and the Fur Trade* (Berkeley: University of California Press, 1978). This controversial study should be supplemented by Shepard Krech III, ed., *Indians, Animals and the Fur Trade: A Critique of* Keepers of the Game (Athens: University of Georgia Press, 1981).

A survey of the Frobisher and Davis expeditions in Arctic waters appears in L.H. Neatby, *In Quest of the North West Passage* (Toronto: Longmans, 1958). Robert McGhee's *The Arctic Voyages of Martin Frobisher* (Montreal/Kingston: McGill-Queen's University Press, 2001) provides a readable introduction to the story of early British Arctic exploration. Susan Rowley has written an article on the Inuit oral accounts of the Frobisher expeditions: "Frobisher Miksanut: Inuit Accounts of the Frobisher Voyages," in William W. Fitzhugh and Jacqueline S. Olin, eds., *Archeology of the Frobisher Voyages* (Washington: Smithsonian Institution Press, 1993).

For maps of early European exploration, see R. Cole Harris, ed., *Historical Atlas of Canada*, vol. 1, *From the Beginning to 1800* (Toronto: University of Toronto Press, 1987); Derek Hayes, *Historical Atlas of Canada: Canada's History Illustrated with Original Maps* (Vancouver: Douglas and McIntyre, 2002); Raymonde Litalien et al., *Mapping a Continent: Historical Atlas of North America, 1492–1814* (Montreal/Kingston: McGill-Queen's University Press, 2007). For an excellent geographical survey of pre-Confederation Canada, see R. Cole Harris, *The Reluctant Land: Society, Space, and Environment in Canada Before Confederation* (Vancouver: UBC Press, 2008).

Chapter Three

THE BEGINNINGS OF NEW FRANCE

TIME LINE

1603	Samuel de Champlain travels to northeastern North America
1605	Port-Royal established by Champlain and Pierre Du Gua de Monts
1608	Trading post at Quebec (Stadacona) established
1609	French under Champlain clash with Five Nation Iroquois
1627	The Company of One Hundred Associates established
1629	English "privateers" seize and hold Quebec for three years
1632	The Jesuits obtain monopoly over mission work in New France
1634	Settlement of Trois-Rivières founded
1635	Champlain dies
1639	Marie de l'Incarnation and two Ursuline sisters arrive at Quebec
1642	Montreal founded
1645	The Habitants' Company established

The Spanish discovered wealth in the New World in the form of Aztec and Inca gold and silver. For the English, it came in the form of the tobacco plantations. For the French, it was furs. While the Europeans continued to fish cod off the Grand Banks, the lure of the fur trade led the French to establish a permanent colony along the St. Lawrence. In the late sixteenth century, no fabric then available rivalled the warmth, wearability, and beauty of furs. In Europe, they were worn to display rank and wealth. The beaver had become almost extinct in northern Europe. When they were shown to be abundant in North America, merchants eagerly sought them through trade with the First Nations. When the beaver robes worn by the "Indians" were worn or slept in, the long guard hairs of the pelts loosened and fell out, leaving only the soft underfur, which hat makers could then process into a smooth felt unmatched by any woven cloth. By the end of the sixteenth century, hundreds of French traders sailed to Tadoussac, at the mouth of the Saguenay River in Quebec, to bargain for pelts.

Jacques Cartier's three voyages established a French claim to the Gulf of St. Lawrence, but recognition of that claim would come only through successful occupation. In the early 1580s, the fur trade led to France's return and to its permanent occupation of the St. Lawrence Valley. In the Gulf and along the Atlantic coastline, the fur trade began as a by-product of the fishing industry. By returning each year to the same locality, the French established mutually beneficial trading relationships with the local First Nations. In the 1580s, French merchants sent out ships commissioned solely to trade for furs. The French Crown decided to bring the trade under the control of fur-trading companies. For a private fur-trading company to obtain a monopoly, it had to fulfill two promises: to promote settlement and to send Roman Catholic missionaries to Christianize the Aboriginal peoples. As a result, merchant, settler, and priest were brought under the joint enterprise of the Crown to create the colony of New France.

The Rise of the Fur Trade

The First Nations generally welcomed the trade in furs. Those groups strategically located gained advantages through access to the French trade goods and weapons. This factor had an impact on relations among the Aboriginal nations, as neighbouring and rival groups worked aggressively in competition for the trade. In this way, the French entered into a foreign and dangerous world of First Nations politics and economics. The French inevitably got caught up in these rivalries and had to take sides. Their trade goods quickly moved through the complex trade networks, affecting groups far into the interior.

The fur trade often ushered in rapid change for the First Nations. It did not take long for the effects to be felt. The metal implements certainly made life easier, but by the early 1600s the Algonquians on the Atlantic coast were already losing some of their self-sufficiency and becoming reliant to an extent on the Europeans for their goods. The fur trade transformed the coastal groups from hunters and fishers into trappers. Prior to European contact, the Mi'kmaq spent more than half the year living on the coast, since the sea supplied as much as 90 percent of their diet. Now, they spent long periods every year hunting inland for fur-bearing animals. This change in their traditional activities affected their winter diet. They no longer accumulated their usual summer food stores and instead now relied partly on the dried foods they received in trade.

Tadoussac, at the mouth of the Saguenay River, became the principal French trading centre on the northern Gulf of St. Lawrence. Established in 1559, pre-existing Aboriginal trading networks led from this location all the way north to Hudson Bay and west to the Great Lakes. In the mid-1580s, as many as twenty vessels at a time called at Tadoussac in the summer, while approximately 1000 Aboriginals arrived each year to trade. The French fur trade was set up in one fixed location, and the First Nations, mainly the Algonkian groups such as the Odawa, Algonquin, and Montagnais, brought furs to the site. The furs were then loaded onto ships and sent to France for processing.

Trade reached such a volume by the 1590s that the French Crown established a monopoly to control it. The trade was profitable and made for good business, but it did not result in settlement. The fur trade could be run with a relatively small number of men working the trade post at Tadoussac. The Crown wished to establish a colony to secure its claims in the new world, and to compete with the English and Spanish colonies to the south. Only a substantial colony would allow the enterprise to possess a spiritual dimension. Only a colony would allow Catholic missionaries from France a foothold to begin winning the souls of the "heathens." The Crown hoped a monopoly would provide a stable structure to the trade. In return for the elimination of competition, the new company would establish a colony. But colonization schemes were expensive and the harsh climate did not help. All early attempts failed. The French colonists suffered a disastrous year at Tadoussac in 1600–1601, when only five of the sixteen settlers survived the winter. An outpost established in 1598 on Sable Island (about 200 kilometres off the coast of Nova Scotia, close to the fishing grounds) also failed.

In 1603, François Gravé Du Pont, an experienced captain who had already made fishing voyages up the St. Lawrence, became the representative of the French monopoly. Samuel de Champlain, a young mariner in his twenties, was in the crew. The two men remained partners for nearly thirty years and together helped establish the first permanent French settlement in the Americas.

Samuel de Champlain

Champlain was born around 1580 and likely came from Brouage, on the Bay of Biscay in western France—one of the principal sources of salt for the fishing fleet. At an early age he went to sea and became a ship's captain and an authority on navigation. The earliest references to Champlain document his service in the royal army. As a soldier in his mid-teens, he was toughened by service in a Renaissance European army whose soldiers' actions could be summarized by five phrases: to steal possessions, to carry off cattle, to burn homes, to kill men, and to rape women.[1] After his army service, Champlain undertook a voyage to the West Indies that kept him away from France for two and a half years. He returned to France in 1601, and two years later was invited to sail with Gravé to North America.

Much had changed in the St. Lawrence Valley since the journeys of Cartier and Roberval in the 1530s and 1540s. Champlain saw large numbers of Montagnais and Algonquins, both Algonquian-speaking groups, at Tadoussac and small groups at several encampments along the St. Lawrence. But the St. Lawrence Iroquois of Donnacona, who lived in the large and impressive settlements of Stadacona and Hochelaga, had vanished without a trace.

With no knowledge of what befell the St. Lawrence Iroquois, historians could only speculate on their fate. Harold Innis believed competition for the coveted position of middleman with the French caused the eastern Algonquian nations to drive them from the location. These Algonquian groups obtained iron weapons from the coastal trade even before the St. Lawrence Iroquoians, which gave them a technological advantage in warfare.

In the 1970s, historian Bruce Trigger speculated that the landlocked New York Iroquois had wanted European trade goods, but found them difficult to obtain from either the St. Lawrence Iroquois or the Algonquians. Consequently, the Iroquois had moved north and dispersed their neighbours, the St. Lawrence Iroquois, some of whom may have moved west to join the Wendat on Georgian Bay on Lake Huron. Archaeologists, Trigger states, have established that European goods reached all the New York Iroquois groups by 1600. These, he surmises, must have been largely obtained as booty from the St. Lawrence Iroquois.

Both explanations are plausible. But there is another possibility: European diseases, inadvertently introduced by Cartier, Roberval, and the French settlers, may have wiped out these people. Regardless, the St. Lawrence Iroquois were likely victims of contact with the French. There was no sign of the First Nations people Cartier described in his journals.

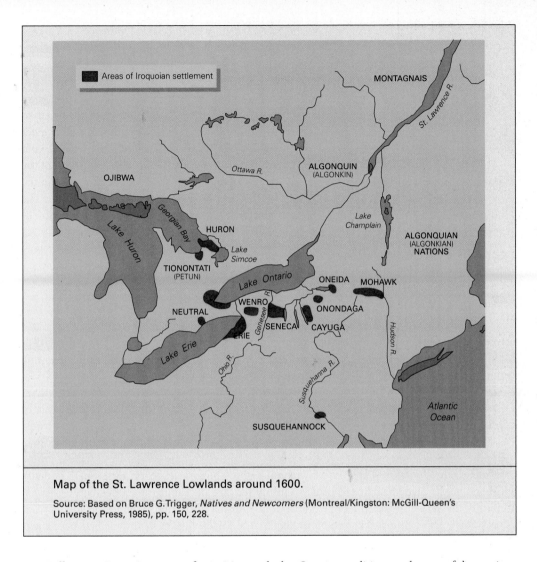

Map of the St. Lawrence Lowlands around 1600.

Source: Based on Bruce G. Trigger, *Natives and Newcomers* (Montreal/Kingston: McGill-Queen's University Press, 1985), pp. 150, 228.

Following Cartier's route as far as Montreal, the Gravé expedition made a careful examination of the St. Lawrence Valley during the summer of 1603. They heard much about the *pays d'en haut* (upper country), north and west of the St. Lawrence Valley, from the Algonquians, who had a good working knowledge of the lower Great Lakes, since their trading network reached far inland. The French learned for the first time of a nation called the "good Iroquois" (the Wendat) who lived by a great lake to the northwest (Lake Huron). The Algonquians were enemies of the Five Nation Iroquois. The French also heard about other massive lakes (Ontario and Erie) and remarkable waterfalls (Niagara Falls).

The French in Acadia

From 1604 to 1607 Pierre Du Gua de Monts, the man in charge of the fur-trade monopoly, accompanied by Gravé and Champlain, searched for the best place to establish a colony. The St. Lawrence provided inland access to the furs, but a coastal colony provided its own strategic advantages. To escape competition from traders who refused to respect the monopoly of the St. Lawrence fur trade, the French sailed south to the Maritime region, an area that had a climate milder than that of the St. Lawrence region and was potentially rich in minerals. They also searched for a more southerly location for the colony, in hopes a finding a route to Asia.

An early line drawing of Champlain's Port-Royal settlement.

Source: Courtesy Northern Blue Publishing.

Armed with vice-regal powers and a ten-year fur-trading monopoly, de Monts led his colonists to the south coast of what is now Nova Scotia. They sailed up the Bay of Fundy and entered the Annapolis Basin, which Champlain named Port-Royal. The party crossed to the New Brunswick shore, passed a large river (which they named the Saint John River), and wintered on a small island near the mouth of the St. Croix River, now on the American side of the border between Maine and New Brunswick. The miserable French experience with the harsh climate continued. Roughly half of the expedition's 79 men died of scurvy before spring, and many more were close to death.

The French at Port-Royal

After a summer exploring the coastline, the French stayed the next winter on the mainland at Port-Royal. This colony became the first European agricultural settlement in what is now Canada. The French continued to explore the coastline the following summer and then wintered again at Port-Royal.

In 1606–07, the French (with the aid of the Mi'kmaq) had their first successful winter. Despite the improved situation, de Monts decided to abandon Port-Royal. After three years of considerable expenditures, unsuccessfully searching for mineral resources and the Northwest Passage, de Monts realized the area's limitations. He could not enforce his fur-trade monopoly along the winding and indented Maritime coast—a rival needed only a ship, a crew, and a supply of trade goods to challenge it. Annually, about eighty ships poached on de Monts's domain. Furthermore, he made insufficient profit to justify the cost of maintaining a post at Port-Royal. Ironically, the very year that the French abandoned Acadia (the name given to the area of what is now Maine, New Brunswick, and Nova Scotia), the English established their first permanent settlement to the south at Jamestown in Virginia. While de Mont lost the monopoly on the fur trade in 1607, within several years the small colony of Port Royal was re-established as an agricultural settlement under Jean de Poutrincourt. Jesuits arrived and established a French religious mission, but by 1613 the English colonists from Virginia attacked and burned the French colony.

The Founding of Quebec

In 1608 Champlain and Gravé returned to the St. Lawrence Valley, to find a location where they could control access to the interior and prevent competition from other traders. At the point where the St. Lawrence narrowed and in the shadow of a towering cliff, Champlain constructed a *habitation*, a collection of wooden buildings built in the

Champlain's Port-Royal settlement has been rebuilt at the original site.

Source: © Stephen Saks Photography/Alamy.

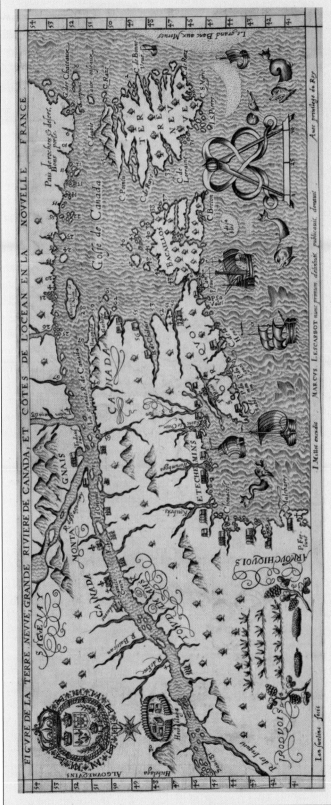

This map by Marc Lescarbot shows "*Kebec*" and "*La grande R. de Canada.*" Figure de la Terre Neuve, Grand rivière de Canada et côtes de l'ocean en la Nouvelle France (Paris: 1609).

Source: Library and Archives Canada/NMC 97952.

ABITATION.DE QVEBECQ

The habitation at Quebec, from Champlain's Voyages, 1613. The walls have loopholes, and a moat and drawbridge surround the wooden buildings. Today, Notre-Dame-des-Victoires, one of the oldest churches in Canada, located at the Place Royale in Quebec's Lower Town, raises its spire almost on the site of Champlain's habitation.

Source: Rare Book Collection/Library and Archives Canada/8759.

form of a quadrangle and surrounded by a stockade and moats. He called it *Québec*—after the Algonquian word *Kebec* for "strait" or "narrow passage." It was also the site of the former St. Lawrence Iroquois village of Stadacona. Champlain's *habitation* became the heart of the first permanent and continuous French settlement in Canada.

Habitation Quebec largely replaced Tadoussac as the centre of the fur trade. Gravé departed with a load of furs in mid-September. Once again, the French were badly prepared for a severe Canadian winter. Twenty of the 28 Frenchmen died, two-thirds from scurvy and the other third from dysentery. Champlain himself was stricken with scurvy but survived.

The Montagnais (Innu) around Tadoussac and Quebec welcomed the French arrival—especially since they saw them as potential allies who possessed muskets. The French had entered a war zone, and the Montagnais could certainly use help against Iroquois raiders from the south. It is important to note that the muskets, while impressive, had limited use in warfare among the First Nations of the eastern woodlands. The wooded terrain meant that subterfuge was an essential aspect of combat. The European musket in the early seventeenth century was a clumsy, complex, and unreliable weapon. It required extensive training and took over twenty steps just to load and fire. If the powder got wet, or even too damp, the musket would not discharge. Even if properly loaded and fired, the weapon had a short range (approximately 46 metres) and was highly inaccurate. To make matters worse, the lighted, smoke-producing wick revealed the shooter's location. Of more value were the iron goods offered at the trading post at Quebec, which the Montagnais could obtain at advantageous rates. As historian Arthur J. Ray notes, "The Montagnais obtained their furs from their partners in the interior at much lower prices than they charged the Europeans for them."[2]

The French and Aboriginals held contradictory concepts of land ownership, but because the newcomers were not yet threatening to take large tracts of land, the issue was not contentious. Like other Europeans, the French did not recognize the First Nations' rights to the land. They officially claimed the St. Lawrence Valley for France on the basis of Jacques Cartier's "discoveries." And, as a Christian nation, the newcomers assumed they had the right to occupy the lands of "heathens." Within a few decades, France began to provide land to colonists. In 1627, for instance, the Crown granted all of North America not then occupied by a Christian prince to the newly created Company of One Hundred Associates.

But making broad claims was one thing; occupying the land was another. As long as the fur trade remained the major industry and the colony struggled to attract settlers, there would be no struggle over land between the French and First Nations.

It is just as important to understand Aboriginal concepts of land ownership. Cartier may have claimed the area for Francis I when he erected a cross at Stadacona, but the Laurentian Iroquois did not accept the claim. Donnacona objected, and according to Cartier, "the chief, dressed in an old black bearskin, arrived in a canoe with three of his sons and his brother; but they did not come so close to the ships as they had usually done. And pointing to the cross he made us a long harangue, making the sign of the cross with two of his fingers, and then he pointed to the land all about, as if he wished to say that all this region belonged to him, and that we ought not to have set up this cross without his permission." The First Nations regarded the land as theirs. Each Montagnais group around Tadoussac and Quebec, for example, occupied a specific territory. The boundaries were well known, and usually well defined by recognizable geographical features. The groups jealously guarded their territories and often went to war over transgressions.

Early French–Aboriginal Relations

The French negotiated an alliance with the Algonquians (the Montagnais around Quebec and the Algonquins further to the west in the Ottawa Valley). The Montagnais asked Champlain to join their war parties against their enemies—the Five

Indian Preparing Birch Bark Map for Professor Hind, *by William G.R. Hind, 1861–62.*

Source: J. Ross Robertson Collection/Toronto Reference Library/T31956.

Nation Iroquois to the south. To secure the alliance and keep the furs coming, the French complied. In 1609, Champlain and two other Frenchmen joined about sixty Montagnais and Wendats (whom the French called Hurons). The war party travelled south from the St. Lawrence and into a region near what is now called Lake Champlain. They came upon an Iroquois (Mohawk) war party numbering 200. The two sides greeted each other and prepared for battle with a night of songs and ceremony. The following morning, the French muskets proved their psychological value: the Mohawks fled in panic. Next summer, the French and their Aboriginal allies defeated another Mohawk war party near the mouth of the Richelieu River.

The alliance proved invaluable to the French. The Algonquians taught them how to adapt to winter and supplied them with geographical information about the interior. The French learned the value of birchbark canoes, and when the waterways froze, of toboggans and snowshoes. As well, they relied on the Aboriginals for food supplies. As late as 1643, Quebec depended almost entirely on Aboriginal hunters for its supply of fresh meat. The French also gathered wild berries, particularly blueberries, and learned from the Indigenous peoples how to make maple sugar. Most importantly, the Algonquians became the first French middlemen in supplying furs. But Champlain soon learned of a potentially more valuable middleman partner in furs—the Hurons.

The French colonial experience was set against what was occurring in the other colonial ventures throughout the Western Hemisphere, and lessons were often taken from these contexts. In Brazil in the mid-sixteenth century, for example, the French began the practice of sending young men to live with various Aboriginal groups to learn their languages and ways. To gain allies, advance trade, and ultimately to convert the "heathens" to Christianity, it proved useful to gain an understanding of the particular group's culture. Champlain wanted to establish the same practice in New France. He arranged for *coureurs de bois* ("runners of the woods") to live with the Algonquians and Hurons.

In 1610, Champlain arranged such an exchange with the Hurons. He sent Étienne Brûlé, a young Frenchman, to live with them. In return, Champlain took Savignon, brother of a Huron headman and roughly the same age as Brûlé, into his custody.

From Brûlé and Savignon the French learned about the Huron Confederacy, an alliance of several nations with a population of up to 30 000 on Lake Huron. Not only was the Huron Confederacy large and powerful and able to challenge the Iroquois Confederacy, it was also the

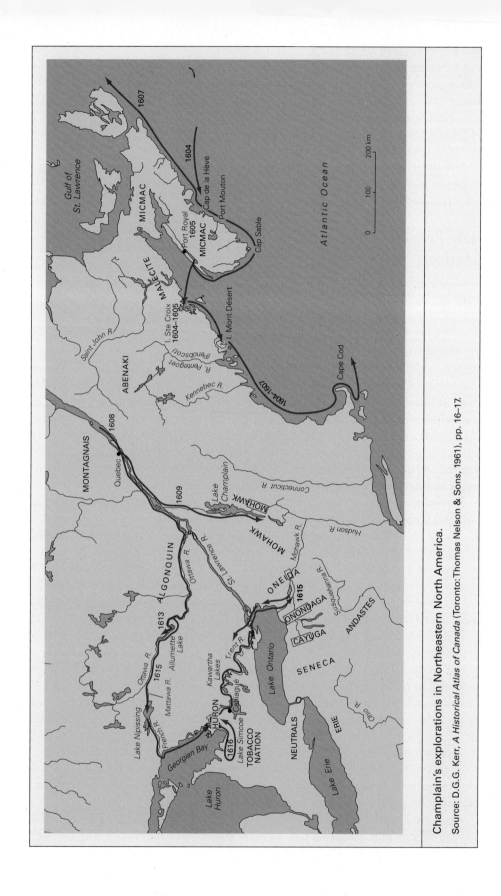

Champlain's explorations in Northeastern North America.

Source: D.G.G. Kerr, *A Historical Atlas of Canada* (Toronto:Thomas Nelson & Sons, 1961), pp. 16–17.

economic power in the region. The Huron trading area extended as far west as Lake Superior and as far north as James Bay. Huron was the trading language of the entire Upper Great Lakes. Champlain had found his ideal middleman for the fur trade. In 1611 Champlain even took Savignon on a trip to France.

Champlain made his last journey into the interior in the summer of 1615, for the purpose of strengthening the Franco–Huron alliance. While in Huronia, Champlain formed alliances with individual Wendat leaders, affirming French support in their wars—provided that the Hurons continued to trade with the French. By joining a large war party against the Iroquois (Oneida), he convinced the Hurons of his support. Attempts by the Algonquins to keep the French from forming such a close relationship with the Hurons failed. While the Hurons had to pay compensation to the Algonquins for the use of the Ottawa River, they took their own furs to New France. By the 1620s, the Hurons supplied from one-half to two-thirds of the furs obtained by the French. The scale of the fur trade increased. Over the next three decades, the annual flotilla travelling from Huronia to Quebec consisted of about 60 canoes and 200 men. Approximately 12 000 to 15 000 pelts were traded each year from Huronia. But the alliance between the Hurons and the French ensured that both groups were now involved in a long and costly war with the Five Nation Iroquois, who were the military power of the region and soon to be allies of the English.

The French Crown and the Fur Trade

The colony of New France grew slowly. During the winter of 1620–21, for example, no more than 60 persons lived at Quebec. The reality was that the fur trade could be run with relatively few people. All that was required was a handful of men to run the trade outpost, and a port facility for ships to transport the furs and supplies back and forth to France. While the size of the colony was not of concern to the fur traders, who focused on accruing profits, it did concern the French Crown, who was monitoring the colonies of its rivals. New France was pathetically small when compared with the English colony of Virginia, with its tobacco-based economy and 2000 inhabitants by 1627 (twenty times the French colony's population). Even the newly established Dutch colony of New Netherlands in the Hudson River valley had 200 settlers by 1625.

A HISTORICAL PORTRAIT

Jean Nicollet

Very little is known about Jean Nicollet, apparently one of the most colourful characters of early New France. None of his own accounts survive and there are just a few references to him in the *Jesuit Relations*—their annual reports back to France—and in church and legal records. The priests seemed to hold him in high regard. As Father Barthélemy Vimont wrote in 1643, "His disposition and his excellent memory led one to expect worthwhile things of him."

Nicollet's father was the King's postal courier between the French port of Cherbourg on the English Channel and Paris. At the age of about 20, in either 1618 or 1619, Jean came to the infant colony of New France, then just the tiny trading post of Quebec. Samuel de Champlain, badly in need of interpreters and representatives to consolidate his Aboriginal alliances, immediately dispatched him to Allumette Island, a strategic Algonquin community on the Ottawa River. He was the first European to live with the important Algonquin trading chief Tessouat and his followers, where he learned both Algonquin, the language of the Algonquian-speaking First Nation in the Ottawa Valley, and Huron, the trading language of the Upper Great Lakes. According to Father Vimont: "He tarried with them two years, alone of the French, and always joined the Barbarians in their excursions and journeys."

Impressed by his wilderness skills and his ability to promote the fur trade, Champlain next sent Nicollet among the Nipissings, a group who lived north of the Algonquins by the lake that bears their name, between the Ottawa River and Lake Huron. Nicollet got close to these people, who were important intermediaries with the First Nations south of James Bay. He lived "eight or nine years with the Algonquin Nipissiriniens, where he passed for one of that nation, taking part in the very frequent councils of those tribes, having his own separate cabin and household, and fishing and trading for himself."

The Jesuits found his behaviour preferable to that of other Frenchmen in the interior, such as the coureur de bois Étienne Brûlé, disliked by the priests for what they regarded as his loose moral conduct. Father Vimont, at least, overlooked the fact that while among the Nipissing, Nicollet took an Aboriginal wife, outside of Christian marriage, and had at least one daughter by her, whom he brought with him to the colony in 1633. At this point, according to Father LeJeune, Nicollet asked to stay in the settlement, "to assure his salvation." He became an interpreter and fur-trade clerk at Trois-Rivières.

In 1637 Nicollet married Marguerite, the Canadian-born daughter of Guillaume Couillard and Guillemette Hébert. At the time of their marriage, the average age of women in New France was 22, and the legal age 12. Marguerite was only 11 years old. Nevertheless, on account of their esteem for Nicollet, the Jesuits allowed the ceremony to proceed. The couple had a son and a daughter. The children would have few memories of their father, however. Unable to swim, Nicollet drowned after his boat was overturned by a strong gust of wind near Quebec in late 1642.

Jean Nicollet is best remembered for a voyage in 1634 to the Winnebagos, a Siouan-speaking group in Wisconsin. A statue of him, the first European to reach Lake Michigan, commemorates his arrival at Green Bay, Wisconsin, and a national forest in Wisconsin bears his name. In reality, however, the voyage never occurred. It appears that Nicollet did make a western voyage in the mid-1630s, but it was to the north shore of Lake Superior, not to Lake Michigan. The error was due to a misreading of a passage in the *Relations* by mid-nineteenth-century American historian John Gilmary Shea. Other scholars over the next century simply repeated the error and ignored the original reference, until Canadian historians Marcel Trudel[1] and Jacques Gagnon[2] corrected it.

---

1. Marcel Trudel, "Jean Nicollet dans le lac Supérieur et non dans le lac Michigan," *Revue d'histoire de l'Amérique française* 34 (2) (September 1980): 183–96.

2. Jacques Gagnon, "Jean Nicollet au lac Michigan: Histoire d'une erreur historique," *Revue d'histoire de l'Amérique française* 50 (1) (Summer 1996): 95–101.

From the perspective of the French Crown, the colony of New France was failing. In 1627, the Crown took action. Cardinal Richelieu, Louis XIII's most influential minister, made the decision to end New France's dependency on furs. If the colony was to rival those of England and Spain, it had to be based on more industries than the fur trade. In particular, it had to possess an agricultural base in order to demonstrate its level of civilization and attract settlers.

Richelieu's efforts coincided with his larger vision of a united France under the Crown and the Catholic Church. If France was to become the leading power in Europe, it needed impressive and wealthy colonies in the new world. From his appointment in 1624 to his death in 1642, the Cardinal worked to extend French overseas commerce and authority through mercantile trade. Mercantilism, the dominant economic philosophy of Europe, held that colonies existed for the mother country's benefit. Colonies supplied goods required by the mother country while also providing markets for goods produced at the imperial centre. Direct trade by foreigners with the colonies was forbidden.

Company of One Hundred Associates

Cardinal Richelieu sponsored a new company called the Compagnie des Cent-Associés (Company of One Hundred Associates), which obtained

The demonstration of the Jeunesse catholiques (Catholic Youth) at the foot of the statue of Champlain, Quebec City, during the Quebec Tercentenary celebrations, late July 1908.

Source: *Illustrated London News*, August 8, 1908, page 197.

working capital from 100 investors to develop and exploit New France's resources and to encourage Catholic missionary activity. Despite the promises of the Edict of Nantes in 1598, Protestants were barred from participation and were officially excluded from the colony. The company became the seigneur of all the lands France claimed in North America. It had a monopoly on all commerce, including the fur trade, and the right to cede land to settlers in seigneurial tenure. In return for its trade monopoly, the company promised to bring out 4000 settlers, all French and Catholic, within fifteen years and to promote missions to the First Nations.

Unfortunately for New France, the project began at the worst possible time. War had just broken out between France and England. In 1627 the Kirke brothers, English privateers, seized Tadoussac and captured, off the shores of the Gaspé, French ships bringing 400 settlers to New France. In 1629, the English attacked Quebec itself. Cut off from France and their provisions long exhausted, Champlain and his starving garrison surrendered in July 1629. Champlain, the ailing Gravé, and the garrison left Quebec.

Still New France's greatest champion and lobbyist, Champlain urged the French ambassador in England to begin negotiations for the return of Quebec. For three years, the St. Lawrence remained closed to the French, which meant heavy losses for the One Hundred Associates. King Charles I of England, who had married Louis XIII's sister, refused to return the captured territories until his French brother-in-law had paid his sister's full dowry. In 1632, Louis XIII settled his debts and the English left the St. Lawrence. Champlain returned to New France and undertook one last initiative: he founded a fur-trading post above Quebec in 1634 at Trois-Rivières.

With Champlain's death on Christmas Day, 1635, the leadership of the fur-trading colony passed into the hands of the religious orders, particularly the Jesuits.

The French Religious Orders

For nearly a century, France experienced civil strife between Catholics and Protestants (Huguenots). In reaction to an increasingly corrupt and seemingly unredeemable papacy, church reformers, led by Martin Luther—a German priest who broke with Rome in 1517—began the Reformation. The followers of Luther and other reformers, such as the Frenchman John Calvin in Geneva, came to be known as "Protestants," individuals who no longer recognized the spiritual and moral authority of the Pope, and instead recognized the authority of biblical scripture and the right of individuals to have a direct relationship with their god. By the mid-sixteenth century a number of Protestant churches had arisen in many parts of northern Europe (most of Germany, Switzerland, Holland, Scandinavia, Scotland, and England) and a substantial Huguenot minority lived in France.

In response to the Protestant Reformation, the Roman Catholic Church began to reform from within. Southern Europeans, including the Catholic majority in France, launched a Counter-Reformation, which sought to root out the corruption in the Catholic Church and then win back those lost to Protestant "heresies." The Jesuits, the papacy's most dedicated missionaries, led the struggle. Other groups, such as the Ursulines, a female

The Arrival of the Ursulines at Quebec, August 1639, *painted by Frank Craig (1874–1918).*

Source: Library and Archives Canada, Acc. No. 1996-23-4/C-001549.

teaching order, followed. Contact between France and North America occurred during this era of religious turmoil in Europe. The First Nations were caught up in the evangelizing zeal that gripped Catholics and Protestants. The various religious orders, including the Jesuits and the Ursulines, were dispatched to the far reaches of the French Empire to bring the "heathens" to God.

Fur-trading entrepreneurs, such as Champlain, could not ignore the directives of the Church or Crown. Champlain realized that even the fur trade would be shaped by the religious zeal in Europe and the desire for an agricultural colony. He urged the neighbouring Algonquians to convert to Christianity and give up their nomadic ways and settle on farms. Champlain also encouraged relationships between the French men and Aboriginal women. He believed children from such unions would ultimately produce an even stronger race in North America.

The first French missionary order to begin work in New France was the Récollets, a branch of the Franciscan Friars. Three Récollet priests and a lay brother arrived at Quebec in 1615. That same year, Father Joseph Le Caron was accepted among the Attignawantans, the first missionary to Huronia. In 1620 the Récollets opened a monastery close to Quebec. They initially hoped that their seminary would train an Indigenous clergy for the colony, but they found the Aboriginals had no desire to assimilate into French society. The seminary soon closed for lack of students and funds.

The Jesuit and Ursuline Orders

The Récollets lacked a financial base and soon found themselves in difficulty. In an attempt to solve their problems, they sought to collaborate with the Society of Jesus (commonly known as the Jesuits), a wealthy and powerful order founded by the soldier-priest Ignatius Loyola a century earlier. From 1625 to 1629, the Jesuits assisted the Récollets in establishing missions in New France.

This highly disciplined order, renowned for its ability to attract able candidates often of high rank, was also known for its willingness to take on the most dangerous missions—even to martyr themselves for the cause.

While the Récollets believed the First Nations should be assimilated to European ways before converting, the Jesuits disagreed. They focused on taking their religion to the various groups, even if it meant journeying far into the interior. They were prepared to learn Aboriginal languages, culture, and even spirituality, in order to aid in conversion. Thanks to their *Relations*, or annual reports back to France, a great deal is known about Jesuit activities in New France.

The Récollets did not survive the English occupation of Quebec. In 1632, Cardinal Richelieu gave the Jesuits a monopoly over the Canadian mission field. Their work began in earnest. But despite their different approaches, the Jesuits experienced similar problems to the Récollets'. The Algonquins and Hurons had no reason or desire to convert to Christianity. When the missionaries attempted to focus on Aboriginal children, the parents refused to let their young go off to live in the seminaries. The priests usually had to give presents to the parents in order to gain students. Many ran away; others got ill and died of sickness, which only heightened resistance among parents. In addition, the French custom of physically punishing children was abhorrent.

A Jesuit preaching to the Algonquians of the Great Lakes. By C.W. Jefferys (1869–1951).

Source: Library and Archives Canada/C-005855.

The First Nations found the French religion foreign and often bizarre. While they could appreciate many of the morality tales told by the "black robes," the emphasis on a man named Jesus who was apparently killed in a distant land so they could achieve salvation made little sense. Even more strange were the efforts of the Jesuits to starve themselves of many of the most basic instincts and pleasures, such as sex. But the Aboriginal groups had little choice but to accept and tolerate the Catholic missionaries among their people. Champlain made it clear that no missionaries meant no trade.

The Ursuline nuns arrived in Quebec in 1639. The Jesuits invited them to Christianize and to "civilize" young Aboriginal girls. But the Ursulines also failed. In 1668 Marie de l'Incarnation, founder of the Ursuline order in New France, wrote: "We have observed that of a hundred that have passed through our hands we have scarcely civilized one. We find docility and intelligence in these girls but, when we are least expecting it, they clamber over our wall and go off to run with their kinsmen in the woods, finding more to please them there than in all the amenities of our French house." The Ursulines proved relatively more successful in their hospital work. A number of First Nations people agreed to leave their aged and infirm at what they called the "house of death" (the mortality rate being so high) rather than to abandon them to die while travelling to their hunting territories.

The Jesuits and the Algonquians

Both the Récollets and the Jesuits encouraged the Algonquians to abandon their nomadic ways, which the priests regarded as contrary to the laws of the church and incompatible with Christian life. The lure of the woods was a constant obstacle for the missionaries. It prevented them

A nineteenth-century lithograph depicting the Jesuits in New France.
Source: Jules Benoît Livernois/Library and Archives Canada/C-04462.

from monitoring and ministering to the Aboriginals. It also kept them tied to their traditional cultures and seemed to undermine the process of assimilation and conversion, which went hand-in-hand. The Catholic missionaries urged the Algonquians to live in the French manner, in settled agricultural communities, or *réductions*, adjacent to French settlements in the St. Lawrence Valley. These became, in effect, the first reserves in Canada. To accomplish their goal, the Jesuits hired workmen to help the Montagnais clear farmland and build a small village between the St. Lawrence and the cliff of Cap aux Diamants (where Jacques Cartier's men had mined for diamonds a century earlier), about 6 kilometres west of Quebec. The Jesuits called the 3500 hectare *réduction* St. Joseph de Sillery, after a former minister and ambassador of the king, who donated his fortune to establish a model Aboriginal settlement.

By 1641 the Sillery reserve contained some 30 families—about 150 baptized First Nations people. Some Algonquians from Trois-Rivières joined them in clearing land and planting crops. The village became divided into a Christian faction and a somewhat larger non-Christian faction. The Jesuits' limited financial support and the constant threat of Iroquois attacks, however, checked the development of the community. Throughout the 1640s, the village men frequently left for long periods on war parties, at which time those left behind abandoned the village for the safety of Quebec. Disease also struck, leading to the death of a number of the converts. An Iroquois raid in 1655 and a fire in 1656 that destroyed the mission residence, the church, and most of the small houses ended the experiment. It never recovered. By 1663, French farmers occupied most of the Sillery land.

The Jesuits were responsible for much of the education in New France. In 1635, they established a college for First Nations boys at Quebec. It became the first institution of higher learning north of Mexico, established a year before Harvard University in Massachusetts. Four years later, in 1639, the Jesuits encouraged the Ursulines and the Hospital nuns of Dieppe to begin a school for girls and a hospital at Quebec. They were also in contact with the Société de Notre-Dame, an association of priests and laypeople founded in 1639 in Paris.

The Jesuits and Indentured Workers in New France

The church, in effect, became the second industry of the colony. The Jesuits, the Ursulines, and the Hospital nuns came in number to work with the Aboriginal peoples and in turn brought out engagés, or indentured workers, on three-year contracts, to help them. These newcomers created a market for agricultural produce in the colony. Upon being discharged, many left to return to France rather than stay on in a land that had little to offer in terms of security or comforts, with its formidable winters, heavy forests to clear, and shortage of marriageable women. But some engagés stayed and began to farm.

The Founding of Montreal

The Société de Notre-Dame planned a mission settlement remote and independent from the main settlement at Quebec. Members believed that once

Statue of Chomedey de Maisonneuve and Notre-Dame Church, Place d'Armes, Montreal.

Source: © Carl & Ann Purcell/CORBIS.

a church, school, and hospital were built, the First Nations would come and settle, and be converted to Christianity. The organizers chose the former site of Hochelaga, on the island of Montreal, at the crossroads of the Ottawa and the St. Lawrence rivers, a location that could be easily reached by the Algonquian-speaking peoples.

Paul de Chomedey de Maisonneuve, a 33-year-old career soldier, led the first settlers to establish what they hoped would become a model Christian community. The citizens at Quebec did their best to discourage Maisonneuve and his band of 40 colonists from continuing up the St. Lawrence, then beset by Iroquois attacks. Maisonneuve replied that even if every tree on the island were changed into an Iroquois, his honour would oblige him to establish the new religious colony. In mid-May 1642 they founded Ville-Marie, the future Montreal.

The first settlers farmed on the grassy areas where the villages of the Laurentian Iroquoians once stood. The only sizable influx of new settlers, 100 in all, arrived in 1653. Despite an initial burst of enthusiasm, the outpost grew slowly, and underpopulation remained a problem until the late 1660s. Two factors prevented the colony's expansion: the Société's quick loss of enthusiasm for its missionary enterprise, and repeated raids by the Iroquois, who resented the founding of a French village in their northern hunting grounds. In 1663 the Sulpicians, another French religious order, took over the direction of the settlement and became the seigneurs of the island of Montreal.

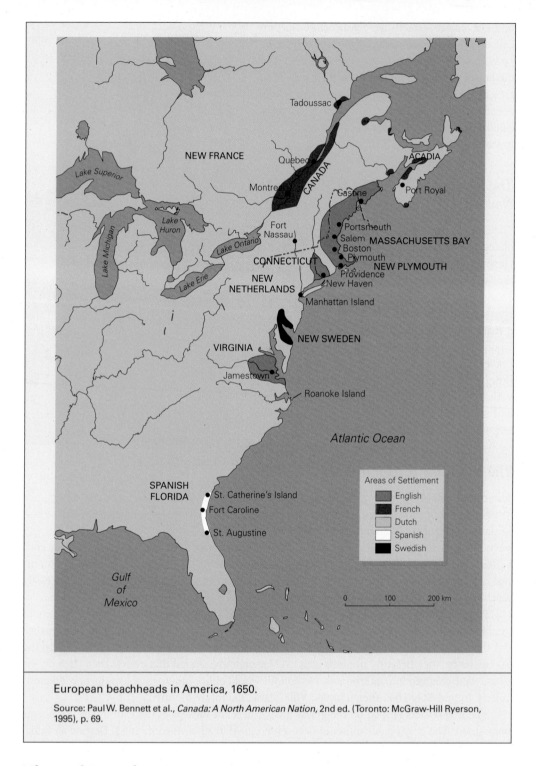

European beachheads in America, 1650.

Source: Paul W. Bennett et al., *Canada: A North American Nation*, 2nd ed. (Toronto: McGraw-Hill Ryerson, 1995), p. 69.

The Habitants' Company

The Company of One Hundred Associates never overcame the effects of the English occupation of Quebec between 1629 and 1632. By the early 1640s, the Company teetered on the verge of bankruptcy, heavily in debt and unable to supply the funds needed to maintain and defend the colony. The leading settlers in 1645—a group of about 15 merchants—took matters into their own hands and formed the *Compagnie des habitants* (Habitants' Company). While reserving its rights of ownership over all of New France, the Company of One Hundred Associates ceded the fur monopoly to the new enterprise. Henceforth, the Habitants' Company had to pay the costs of administering the colony, including payments to the governor and the military officers for the maintenance of forts and garrisons, the upkeep of the clergy, and the responsibility of bringing 20 male and female settlers to the colony each year.

New France in the Mid-1640s

In 1645—a decade after Champlain's death—the French colony in the valley of the St. Lawrence contained only 600 residents and a few hundred engagés. Despite attempts to grow the settlement through farming, the colony remained a fur trade outpost that was smaller than an Iroquoian village. New France tried to lure colonists from France with land, economic mobility, and the avoidance of royal taxes, but immigration was expensive and rarely did people leave unless they were pushed out or the opportunities were too great to pass up. The English used their colonies as dumping grounds for the undesirables—from religious dissenters to convicted prisoners. The French, however, wished to avoid the religious turmoil that was dividing France. As a result, the Huguenots were not allowed to settle. Catholic settlers were loath to leave France for a strange land, characterized by a harsh and hostile climate, dominated by the fur trade, and threatened constantly by annihilation though "Indian" attacks. Even the journey to get to the new land was perilous. Colonists faced the dangers of crossing the North Atlantic, a journey that took anywhere from three weeks to more than three months. On these voyages, if headwinds continued too long, food supplies could run out, and then scurvy would take its toll. If fewer than 10 percent of the ship's company died during a crossing, the captain considered the voyage a success.

The peasants and artisans who arrived safely then had to face the challenge of clearing the virgin forest. A man could clear one hectare a year at best. Much of this difficult work had to be performed in the summer months, when the blackflies and mosquitoes made life intolerable. Most harrowing, however, were the Iroquois raids, which resumed in earnest in the 1640s. All men—and many women—capable of bearing arms had to be ready at all times to fight for their lives.

Hundreds of emigrants did leave France for the Americas in the 1630s and 1640s. But rather than New France, most settled in the French Antilles, in the Caribbean, and in the islands of Martinique and Guadeloupe in particular. Unlike the northern fur trade, tobacco and cotton farming required a great deal of unskilled labour. Within a decade, the European population of the French Antilles was estimated at 7000.

SUMMARY

The fur trade *was* New France. The colony depended on the Algonquians and Hurons who hunted, trapped, and prepared the beaver pelts, and then transported them hundreds of kilometres to Quebec. Within a generation, France had advanced 1000 kilometres into the interior, establishing a firm trading alliance with the Hurons. But in early 1649 it was doubtful whether New France, with a resident population of barely 1000, could survive in the face of determined Iroquois attacks. The entire enterprise teetered on the edge of collapse.

NOTES

1. E. Pocquet, *Histoire de Bretagne*, vol. 5, p. 310, cited in Morris Bishop, *Champlain: The Life of Fortitude* (Toronto: McClelland & Stewart, 1963 [1948]), p. 8.

2. Arthur J. Ray, *I Have Lived Here Since the World Began: An Illustrated History of Canada's Native People* (Toronto: Key Porter Books, 1996), p. 56.

RELATED READINGS

Module 3 in *Visions: The Canadian History Modules Project: Pre-Confederation* textbook offers a selection of documents and secondary source readings on early Quebec. Alan Greer's article "The Feudal Burden" and Colin Coates' "Seigneurial Landscapes" are accompanied by eight primary source documents covering the early settlement period in New France. See pages 99–142.

BIBLIOGRAPHY

Marcel Trudel provides an overview of the period in *The Beginnings of New France, 1524–1663* (Toronto: McClelland & Stewart, 1973). A shorter summary appears in W.J. Eccles, *The Canada Frontier, 1534–1760* (Toronto: Holt, Rinehart and Winston, 1969). His later work, *France in America*, rev. ed. (Markham, ON: Fitzhenry & Whiteside, 1990 [1972]), also contains information on the early French colonies in the Caribbean as well as New France and Acadia. See also John Bosher's study *Business and Religion in the Age of New France, 1600–1700* (Toronto: Canadian Scholars' Press, 1994); Hubert Charbonneau et al., *The First French Canadians: Pioneers in the St. Lawrence Valley* (Newark/London/Toronto: University of Delaware Press and Associated University Presses, 1993); Leslie Choquette, *Frenchmen into Peasants: Modernity and Tradition in the Peopling of French Canada* (Cambridge: Harvard University Press, 1997); Louise Dechene, *Habitants and Merchants in Seventeenth-Century Montreal.* (Montreal/Kingston: McGill-Queen's University Press, 1992); Dale Miquelone, *The First Canada: to 1791* (Toronto: McGraw-Hill Ryerson, 1994); and Peter Moogk, *La Nouvelle France: The Making of French Canada—A Cultural History* (East Lansing: Michigan State University Press, 2002).

Bibliographical guides include Jacques Rouillard, ed., *Guide d'histoire du Québec du régime français à nos jours: Bibliographie commentée* (Montreal: Éditions du Méridien, 1991); and Thomas Wien, "Canada and the *Pays d'en haut*, 1600–1760," in M. Brook Taylor, ed., *Canadian History: A Reader's Guide*, vol. 1, *Beginnings to Confederation* (Toronto: University of Toronto Press, 1994), pp. 33–75.

Contemporary maps and illustrations appear in André Vachon, in collaboration with Victorin Chabot and André Desrosiers, *Dreams of Empire: Canada Before 1700* (Ottawa: Public Archives of Canada, 1982); and Derek Hayes, *Historical Atlas of Canada: Canada's History Illustrated with Original Maps* (Vancouver: Douglas and McIntyre, 2002). See also R. Cole Harris, *The Seigneurial System in Early Canada: A Geographical Study* (Madison: University of Wisconsin Press, 1966).

For First Nations affairs, Bruce G. Trigger's *The Children of Aataentsic: A History of the Huron People to 1660*, 2 vols. (Montreal/Kingston: McGill-Queen's University Press, 1976), and his *Natives and Newcomers: Canada's "Heroic Age" Reconsidered* (Montreal/Kingston: McGill-Queen's University

Press, 1985), are important. Denys Delâge's *Bitter Feast: Amerindians and Europeans in Northeastern North America, 1600–64*, trans. Jane Brierley (Vancouver: University of British Columbia Press, 1993), also provides an overview. An older study, A.G. Bailey's *The Conflict of European and Eastern Algonkian Cultures, 1504–1700* (Toronto: University of Toronto Press, 1969 [1937]), is still important. Arthur J. Ray, *Indians in the Fur Trade* (Toronto: University of Toronto Press, 1974), and Carolyn Gilman, *Where Two Worlds Meet: The Great Lakes Fur Trade* (St. Paul: Minnesota Historical Society, 1982) cover the economic aspects of early Aboriginal–European contact. An overview of early French–First Nation relations is the chapter "The Native People and the Beginnings of New France" in John A. Dickinson and Brian Young's *A Short History of Quebec*, 3rd ed. (Montreal/Kingston: McGill-Queen's University Press, 2003), pp. 3–27. J.B. Jamieson reviews the disappearance of the St. Lawrence Iroquoians in "Trade and Warfare," *Man in the Northeast* 39 (1990): 79–86. Another treatment is James F. Pendergast, "The Confusing Identities Attributed to Stadacona and Hochelaga," *Journal of Canadian Studies* 3(4) (Winter 1998): 149–67.

Two examinations of the early French missionaries' policies toward First Nations women are Eleanor Leacock, "Montagnais Women and the Jesuit Program for Colonization," in Mona Etienne and Eleanor Leacock, eds., *Women and Colonization. Anthropological Perspectives* (Brooklyn, NY: J.F. Bergin Publishers, 1980): 25–42, and Carol Devens, *Countering Colonization: Native American Women and Great Lakes Missions, 1630–1900* (Berkeley: University of California Press, 1992). For a discussion of missionary impressions and interactions with the landscape, see Lynn Berry, "Le ciel et la terre nous ont parlé: Comment les missionnaires du Canada français de l'époque coloniale interprétèrent le tremblement de terre de 1663," *Revue d'histoire de l'Amérique française* 60(1–2) (2006): 11–36. For a look at textual images of the landscape, territory, and bodies of water in New France, see Stephanie Chaffray, "Corps, territoire et paysage à travers les images et les textes viatiques en Nouvelle-France (1701–1756)," *Revue d'histoire de l'Amérique française* 59(1–2) (2005): 7–52.

Biographies of Champlain include: Morris Bishop, *Champlain: The Life of Fortitude* (Toronto: McClelland & Stewart, 1963 [1948]), and Samuel Eliot Morison, *Samuel de Champlain: Father of New France* (Boston: Little, Brown, 1972). See also Raymonde Litalien and Denis Vaugois' illustrated *Champlain: The Birth of French America* (Montreal/Kingston: McGill-Queen's University Press, 2004), David Hackett Fischer's Pulitzer Prize–winning *Champlain's Dream* (Mississauga, ON: Random House, 2008), and Francoise Niellon, "Québec au temps de Champlain," *Archéologiques* special issue 2 (2008): 1–17. For an understanding of Champlain's Aboriginal policy, one should, however, supplement these studies with Trigger's *Children of Aataentsic* and his *Natives and Newcomers*. For a more general look at the first voyages to New France, see Marie Renier, "Le récit au service du vécu ou de l'imaginaire?: Premier voyageurs en Nouvelle-France," *Ethnologies* 29(1–2) (2007): 239–66. Andrew D. Nicholls' *A Fleeting Empire: Early Stuart Britain and the Merchant Adventurers to Canada* (Montréal/Kingston: McGill-Queen's University Press, 2010) examines Franco–British rivalries and the importance of privateering in North America.

Sources on the Algonquians in the St. Lawrence Valley include Alain Beaulieu, *Convertir les fils de Caïn: Jésuites et Amérindiens nomades en Nouvelle-France, 1632–1642* (Quebec: Nuit blanche, 1990); Marc Jetten, *Enclaves amérindiennes: Les "réductions" du Canada 1637–1701* (Sillery, QC: Septentrion, 1994); John A. Dickinson, "Native Sovereignty and French Justice in Early Canada," in Jim Phillips, Tina Loo, and Susan Lewthwaite, eds., *Essays in the History of Canadian Law*, vol. 5, *Crime and Criminal Justice* (Toronto: University of Toronto Press, 1994), pp. 17–40; James P. Ronda, "The Sillery Experiment: A Jesuit–Indian Village in New France, 1637–1663," *American Indian Culture and Research Journal* 3(1) (1979): 1–18; and Cornelius J. Jaenen, *Friend and Foe: Aspects of French–Amerindian Cultural Contact in the Sixteenth and Seventeenth Centuries* (Toronto: McClelland & Stewart, 1976). François-Marc Gagnon examines early French racial attitudes in *Ces hommes dits sauvages: L'Histoire fascinante d'un préjugé qui remonte aux premiers découvreurs du Canada* (Montreal: Libre Expression, 1984). Olive P. Dickason's *The Myth of the Savage and the Beginnings of French Colonialism in the Americas* (Edmonton: University of Alberta Press, 1984); John Webster Grant's *Moon of Wintertime: Missionaries and the Indians of Canada in Encounter since 1534* (Toronto: University of Toronto Press,

1984); and James Axtell's *The Invasion Within: The Contest of Cultures in Colonial North America* (New York: Oxford University Press, 1985), are very useful for their review of early missionary activities in New France. For a review of European opinions about the land rights of Aboriginal peoples in the Americas, see Leslie C. Green and Olive P. Dickason, *The Law of Nations and the New World* (Edmonton: University of Alberta Press, 1989). Biographical articles appear in *Dictionary of Canadian Biography*, vol. 1; see in particular the entries on Jacques Noël, p. 520; François Gravé Du Pont, pp. 345–46; Pierre Du Gua de Monts, pp. 291–95; Étienne Brûlé, pp. 130–33; Marie Guyart (Marie de l'Incarnation), pp. 351–59; and Paul de Chomedey de Maisonneuve, pp. 212–22. The volumes of *Dictionary of Canadian Biography* are available online: www.bibliographi.ca.

For the early history of the settlement of Quebec, see John Hare, Marc Lafrance, and David Thiery Ruddel, *Histoire de la Ville de Québec, 1608–1871* (Montreal: Boréal Express, 1987). Hubert Charbonneau et al., *The First French Canadians: Pioneers in the St. Lawrence* Valley, trans. Paola Colozzo (Newark: University of Delaware Press, 1993), discusses the first French settlers in the St. Lawrence Valley. For the early history of Montreal, consult Robert Prévost, *Montréal: A History*, trans. Elizabeth Mueller and Robert Chodos (Toronto: McClelland & Stewart, 1993); and the beautifully illustrated *Pour le Christ et le roi: La vie au temps des premiers Montréalais, sous la direction d'Yves Landry* (Montreal: Libre Expression/Art Global, 1992). For a consideration of how New France became a political unit within British North America, see Douglas Hunter, "Was New France Born in England?," *Beaver* 86(6) (2006–2007): 39–44.

Maps of early Acadia and New France are contained in R. Cole Harris, ed., *Historical Atlas of Canada*, vol. 1, *From the Beginning to 1800* (Toronto: University of Toronto Press, 1987). Jacob Ernest Cooke et al., eds., *The Encyclopedia of the North American Colonies*, 3 vols. (New York: Scribner's, 1993), contains many useful articles on New France. See also R. Cole Harris, *The Reluctant Land: Society, Space, and Environment in Canada Before Confederation* (Vancouver: UBC Press, 2008).

Chapter Four

THE IROQUOIS, THE HURONS, AND THE FRENCH

TIME LINE

1475–1525	League of the Iroquois (Five Nations) established
1609	First clash occurs between French and Iroquois
1615	First Roman Catholic missionaries reach Hurons
mid-1630s	Epidemics sweep through Huronia
1649	Huronia falls to the Iroquois
1653	French coureurs de bois replace Hurons as middlemen in fur trade
1660	Dollard's last stand at Long Sault
1667	Truce between French and Iroquois
1687	Conflict between French and Iroquois resumes
1701	"Great Peace" of Montreal ends French–Iroquois war

From Champlain's first encounter with the Mohawks in 1609 to the "Great Peace" of Montreal in 1701, the Five Nations Iroquois were the major concern of the settlers in New France. Sometime between 1475 and 1525, the confederacy of Mohawk, Oneida, Onondaga, Cayuga, and Seneca formed. The Iroquois called it the League of Ho-dé-no-sau-nee (People of the Longhouse). Over the course of the sixteenth century, they consolidated their position across what is now upstate New York. Although less populous than their enemy—the Wendat (Hurons)—the League controlled more territory. The organization handled relations with other Aboriginal groups. By the seventeenth century, it coordinated affairs with the European newcomers. The geographic location of the League provided an advantage after contact, because the Iroquois controlled the major routes from the coast to the interior.

The French viewed the Five Nations as an alliance bent on war and the Iroquois as the military power of the region. The Iroquois seemed to be enemies of almost every other First Nation. The French first learned of the existence of the Five Nations from the Algonquians. The name the Montagnais attached to them indicated the extent of their animosity—"Hirokoa" or "the killer people." The word originated in the Algonquian–Basque trade language that developed in the late sixteenth century. From the Algonquians, Basque fishers first learned of the Hirokoa, the Algonquians' formidable enemies who lived in the distant interior. When the French heard the word, they revised the spelling to fit their own language, and the word "Iroquois" was born. It was not the name the Five Nations applied to themselves. Like so many names applied to Aboriginal groups, it was their enemies' designation. The name "Mohawk" was itself derived from a New England Algonquian word meaning "eater of human flesh." The labels indicate the fierce reputation of the Iroquois as feared warriors.

The Formation of the Iroquois League

The French view of the Iroquois was shaped by their conflict with the League and their alliances with the Algonquians and Hurons. The Iroquois called their confederacy the "Great League of Peace," because one of its main purposes was to prevent hostilities among the Iroquois and to coordinate its energies externally. Its symbol was the White Tree of Peace, above which hovered an eagle, a bird of wisdom, observation, and preparation. According to Iroquois legend, the League of Five Nations was founded by the nations from east to west: the Mohawks, the Oneidas, the Onondagas, the Cayugas, and the Senecas. After the Tuscaroras from the Carolinas joined the confederacy in the early eighteenth century, the Five became the Six Nations.

The founders conceived their League as the nucleus of a larger union. Historians now generally agree that it was established by the late fifteenth century. According to Iroquois elders, the League's origins go back to a story of how the hero Dekanahwideh brought the Great Peace to the five nations. Dekanahwideh was born among the Wendat but it was prophesied that he would save the Iroquois. He travelled to the country of the Onondaga in a canoe of white stone. Dekanahwideh sought out the home of a notorious murderer and cannibal, and finding the cabin empty, he climbed onto the bark roof and waited, peering down through the smoke hole. When the murderer returned, he cut up and placed his latest victim's body in a cooking pot. But while bending over the kettle, he saw Dekanahwideh's calm, strong, and wise face reflected from the water's surface. The image of the peacemaker's face was in stark contrast to his own and it forced the cannibal to ponder what had become his own brutal existence. In revulsion, the cannibal emptied the kettle and resolved to change his life. Dekanahwideh entered the cabin and delivered his message of peace and power. The man "took hold of the message" and offered himself as a disciple. Dekanahwideh gave him the name Hiawatha, which meant "he who combs," for he would comb the twists out of people's perverted minds. The first obstacle to peace was the tyrant Atotarho, head chief of the Onondagas, whose body was deformed and whose hair consisted of live snakes.

Iroquois trail, taken a century ago in the territory of the Seneca, near Conesus Lake, New York.

Source: National Anthropological Archives/Smithsonian Institution/947A.

The lawgiver and his new spokesperson visited the five warring nations and persuaded each to come under the Tree of Peace and to form the union of the Ho-dé-no-sau-nee. Dekanahwideh then planted the Tree of Peace, a great white pine with healthy white roots that extended to the four corners of the earth, allowing all nations of good will to follow those roots to their source and to take shelter with the others under the great tree. On top of the tree, he placed the Eagle That Sees Afar, a symbol of military preparedness. Then he put antlers on the heads of the 50 chiefs representing the Five Nations and gave them the Words of the Law.

A new political structure was thus created to maintain peace among the Iroquois. Carrying gifts of deerskin and wampum, ambassadors travelled to settle disputes among the member nations. War parties used the forest paths to attack outsiders who encroached on Five Nations lands. In the eyes of the Iroquois, the Hurons' refusal to come under the Tree of Peace proved their hostile intent.

The Arrival of the Missionaries in Huronia

At the time of French contact in the seventeenth century, the Hurons and the Iroquois were already at war. Warfare among the eastern woodland groups differed from European conflicts. Rather than fighting for conquest or economic gain, the Aboriginals of the area fought what are called "mourning wars" as a means of coping with grief and depopulation. Often begun at the behest of women, war was a means of avenging the loss of loved ones and to capture enemies to replace those lost. A desire for war honours and prestige also served as justifications for hostility. Participation in a war party, if successful, raised a warrior's standing in his clan and village. Honour, strength, and courage were essential traits to uphold in battle. It was common for captives to be ritually tortured so as to test their warrior spirit. This ritual was reciprocal in the sense that it allowed the victor to wreak vengeance upon his enemy while allowing the captive to demonstrate his strength and courage by suffering but not crying out. Regardless of the motivation, war was fought through raiding in small groups rather than in large pitched battles.

As with most aspects of Aboriginal culture, the Europeans judged the differing modes of warfare according to their own standards, and not surprisingly failed to understand them. The Europeans found the Aboriginal use of subterfuge as cowardly, the motivation of vengeance as emotional, and the use of torture as barbaric. But even though "Indian" warfare continued to dominate the eastern woodlands for over two centuries after contact, the arrival of the Europeans transformed the process. Economic motives joined those of prestige and the blood feud as causes of conflict.

Both the Iroquois and the Hurons needed a steady supply of furs to buy European trade goods. By the 1620s, the Hurons had become the principal economic partner of the French, exchanging furs for corn and European goods with the neighbouring Algonquians, who, in turn, traded as far north as James Bay and along the shores of Lakes Michigan and Superior. As elsewhere on the continent, the fur trade and the goods that it brought enriched Huron culture. The Hurons began to decorate their pottery with more elaborate patterns and to use iron knives to make more intricate bone carvings. By choosing the Hurons, however, the French became enemies of the Iroquois.

The Jesuits and the Hurons

After establishing an alliance with the Hurons, the French obtained permission to send Roman Catholic priests to Huronia. Champlain dispatched Récollet missionaries in 1615 and Jesuit fathers in 1627. As a condition for renewing the Franco–Huron alliance after the English ended their occupation of Quebec in 1632, the French insisted that the Hurons allow Jesuits to live in Huronia. Reluctantly, the Hurons agreed, in order to maintain the now essential trade. In 1634, Jean de Brébeuf and two companions reopened the Huron mission. Dressed in black gowns, wearing broad-brimmed black hats, and with iron chains and black beads hanging from their belts, the "Black Robes" went from village to village to spread the Christian gospel and to seek converts. The Hurons met them with apprehension and a growing fear, particularly after the outbreak of European diseases. The Jesuits soon became associated with the diseases.

The Jesuit order put great effort into building up its mission. It used French lay workers (*donnés*), whose contracts assured them of lifetime support but no wages. The Jesuits mastered the Huron language and then communicated their ideas to the would-be converts. They also used non-verbal methods: pictures of holy subjects or images of the sufferings of lost souls; religious statues; coloured beads as prizes for successful memorization; ceremonies, chants, and processions on holy days and on such occasions as baptisms, marriages, and funerals. They decorated the churches with crosses, bells, and candles, creating a colourful visual display. While the Hurons had difficulty accepting the teachings of the "Black Robes," they understood the importance of pomp, ceremony, and ritual.

Cultural Differences

In this initial period the Jesuits made some progress, but the gulf between the two societies when it came to matters of spirituality remained vast. For the Hurons, the meaning of life was to maintain harmony with nature. They did not consider humans superior to other entities in the natural world, but rather equal partners. Their sacred stories explained their perception of the universe: the relationship between humanity and the earth, between people and animals, between the sun and the moon, between sickness and health. Christianity differed from the Hurons' religion in viewing the world as provisional and preparatory to the afterlife.

To gain an audience among the Hurons, the Jesuits emphasized the similarities between the Hurons' faith and their own. They pointed out that both believed in a supernatural power that influenced their lives, one that the Hurons located in the sun or sky and the Jesuits in heaven. Both Huron shamans (*arendiwane*) and Roman Catholic priests encouraged personal contact with the supernatural. At puberty, every young Huron man was expected, through fasting and a vision quest, to find his own guardian spirit. The Jesuits also encouraged spiritual quests and valued fasts and vigils. The common reliance on prayer revealed a shared conviction that divine power controlled warfare, caused rain or drought, and gave health or disease. Finally, both Jesuits and Hurons accepted the idea of an afterlife; for the Hurons it was a pleasant place where life continued essentially as on earth, and for Christians it was heaven.

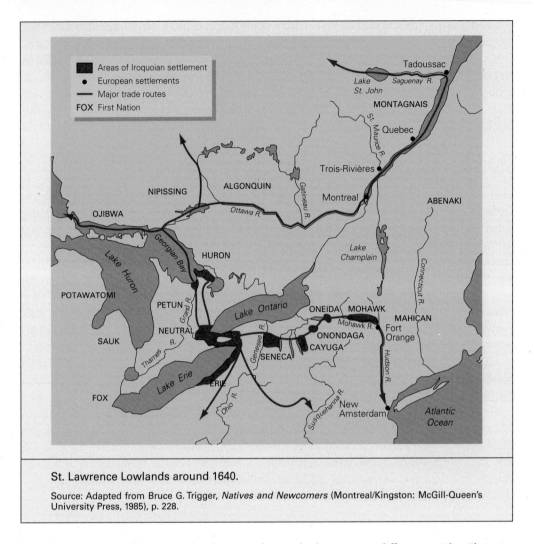

St. Lawrence Lowlands around 1640.

Source: Adapted from Bruce G. Trigger, *Natives and Newcomers* (Montreal/Kingston: McGill-Queen's University Press, 1985), p. 228.

These common elements aside, the two religions had enormous differences. The Christian understanding that only one deity ruled the universe conflicted with the Huron belief in many supernatural beings. Furthermore, the Hurons had nothing remotely close to the Jesuits' concepts of the Trinity and the Incarnation. Marriage was another controversial issue. The Jesuits found the Hurons' sexual behaviour aberrant. Among the Hurons, divorce was easy and frequent, in contrast with the Jesuits' ideal of the indissolubility of marriage. Since Huron children by custom belonged to the mother, divorce did not endanger family stability. The Hurons failed to see lifetime marriage as superior to their own custom. Moreover, they could not understand the Jesuits' practice of celibacy and sexual self-denial.

The two cultures also disagreed on issues of human sinfulness and the need for salvation. Although the Hurons distinguished between good and evil, they had no concept similar to the missionaries' idea of universal guilt, of a fundamental inadequacy in human nature. Like most Aboriginal North Americans, the Hurons believed that almost all people would experience the same pleasant afterlife, regardless of how they had lived on earth. For the Jesuits, there was both a heaven and a hell. The only way to escape hell was through Christianity. This concept of a place of torment proved very difficult to convey to the Hurons.

The Jesuits tried to convince the Hurons of the worthiness of biblical standards. They insisted that the Hurons curtail easy divorce, marry for life, and end their undue reliance on dreams. To the Hurons, the missionaries threatened to subvert the very customs and beliefs essential to successful hunting, good health, and survival. As Aenons, a Huron chief, complained to Father Brébeuf, "When you speak to us of obeying and acknowledging as our master him whom you say has made Heaven and earth, I imagine you are talking of overthrowing the country."

Epidemics Decimate Huronia

The French brought with them more than European trade goods and their Christian message. Unknowingly, they brought European diseases that devastated the Hurons and their neighbours. It was one thing to tolerate and even accommodate the "Black Robes" out of the necessity of maintaining trade; it was quite another to allow them to bring strange diseases that threatened to annihilate the population. By 1639 smallpox raged throughout Huronia, killing more than half the population and reducing their numbers to 10 000. Since old people and children died in the largest numbers, the Hurons lost much of their traditional religious lore, which tended to be the preserve of the elderly, and suffered a shortage of warriors in the next decade with the deaths of so many children.

By the late 1630s, the Hurons concluded that the Jesuits were sorcerers who brought disease. The Hurons recognized three major sources of illness: natural causes, unfulfilled desires of a person's soul (alleviated by a form of dream fulfillment), and witchcraft. Not surprisingly, the Hurons blamed the new diseases on their visitors, since the Jesuits alone seemed immune. The Jesuits' celibacy also suggested that the "white shamans" nurtured supernatural power for the purposes of witchcraft. Furthermore, they seemed to cause death by their rituals: after they touched sick babies with drops of water, many died.

As the epidemics spread, the Hurons' suspicion and fear of the Black Robes increased. They denied the Jesuits entry into their longhouses and villages. The Hurons harassed and threatened the Jesuits. On at least two occasions, in 1637 and 1640, Huron councils discussed killing the missionaries or at least forcing "the sorcerers" to return to Quebec. Yet they pursued neither course of action. Many of the leading chiefs realized that the Hurons depended on the French for European trade goods. Already weakened, the Hurons would be destroyed by the Iroquois if they lost their French ally.

Huron Converts

During the epidemics of the mid-1630s, the missionaries under Jean de Brébeuf's direction worked in selected Huron villages. Jérôme Lalemant, the new superior of the Huron mission, changed this policy in 1638. He constructed a permanent mission headquarters of stone and timber buildings. Sainte-Marie, begun in 1639, included residences, chapels, workshops, and a hospital within its fortified walls. Nearby, the Jesuits cleared fields and planted crops.

Inspired by accounts of the Jesuits' mission in Paraguay, Lalemant hoped that the Huron Christian converts would settle at Sainte-Marie and adopt French customs. When they refused to leave their villages and abandon their clans, he established permanent Jesuit residences in the major Huron towns. The priests visited other villages on assigned circuits.

Model of a Huron-Ouendat (Wendat) village, based on historical and archaeological information in Midland, Ontario.

Source: Courtesy Huronia Museum.

Huron Christians praying. From Bressani's map of New France, Novae Franciae Accurata Delineatio (1657).

Source: Library and Archives Canada/C-71502.

Some Huron traders realized the benefits of conversion, and by the 1640s the Jesuits were able to boast of increasing numbers. French traders and government officials accorded Aboriginal Christians far greater honour, and gave them additional presents at Quebec and Trois-Rivières. Another incentive to convert came from the French policy of selling guns only to Aboriginals who were baptized. In 1648, when only 15 percent of the Huron population had been baptized, half of those in the Huron trading fleet were already Christians or were receiving instruction. By 1646, the Christian Huron community numbered 500 and was growing.

The development of a Christian faction divided the Huron. Jesuit priests forbade Huron converts to participate in Aboriginal feasts and celebrations. To avoid involvement in Huron rituals, Christian warriors often refused to fight alongside traditionalists. Conversion on occasion also resulted in divorce and in the Christian warriors' expulsion from their wives' or mothers' longhouses.

The Final Conflict Between the Hurons and the Iroquois

The Huron were weakened by disease and internal division at the worst possible time. Their war with the Iroquois was reaching its climax. When the French first established Quebec in 1608, the Iroquois were at a disadvantage. They had no access to a European trade partner. When the Dutch arrived on the Hudson River, the Mahicans blocked Iroquois access. By the end of the 1620s, the Mahicans were defeated and the Dutch opened trade with the Mohawks. To the east, the Iroquois fought with the Abenakis and commenced trade with the English. With two sources of trade goods, the Five Nations now focused on the Hurons to the northwest. The lure of furs increased the Iroquois desire to control Huron territory, which bordered the fur-rich areas around the upper Great Lakes. The Iroquois gave the Hurons one last chance by inviting them to join the Five Nations Confederacy. The offer was refused.

Guns provided the Iroquois an additional advantage and made them an even more formidable enemy. By 1639, they obtained firearms from English traders in the Connecticut Valley and then directly from Dutch traders on the upper Hudson River. The longer and heavier Dutch guns were superior to those that the French sold to their Christian converts. Thus equipped, the Iroquois could raid the nations to the north much more easily than before. In 1648, the Iroquois had more than 500 guns, while the Hurons had no more than 120. These guns were crude, awkward to handle, and in many ways little better than the bow and arrow, but their thunderous noise and their ability to inflict mortal wounds made them a source of terror.

The successful Iroquois attacks of the early 1640s caused some Huron traditionalists to question whether peace with their enemies, the Iroquois, with whom they shared common customs and speech, was not preferable to cultural extinction through association with the Jesuits. As one Huron told the Jesuits: "You tell us that God is full of goodness, and then, when we give ourselves up to him he massacres us. The Iroquois, our mortal enemies, do not believe in God, they do not love the prayers, they are more wicked than the Demons—and yet they prosper; and since we have forsaken the usages of our ancestors, they kill us, they massacre us, they burn us—they exterminate us, root and branch. What profit can there come to us from lending ear to the Gospel, since death and the faith nearly always march in company?"[1] In the end, however, the majority of the traditionalists mistrusted the Iroquois more than they did the French, and remained with the Christian Hurons in alliance with the French. The defeat of the anti-Jesuit Hurons ended organized resistance to the missionaries.Champlain attempted to neutralize the Iroquois through an armistice, but failed. With no choice, he looked to bolster the defences of New France. Trois-Rivières was established in 1634 in part as a buffer for Quebec. The Iroquois responded by harassing French fur brigades. By 1642, the Mohawk and Seneca were blockading the St. Lawrence, Ottawa, and Richelieu Rivers; by 1649 the Iroquois were attacking settlements along the frontier. The final conflict was at hand.

The Fall of Huronia

In mid-March 1649, a large Iroquois force struck a Huron village, killing or capturing all but 10 of the 400 inhabitants. The village was then used as a base camp to destroy other neighbouring settlements. Hurons who had earlier been captured and adopted by the Iroquois played a leading role in the attacks. The adopted Hurons, together with the Iroquois, tortured the French priests they captured, regarding them as sorcerers responsible for Huronia's destruction. Familiar with the frequent baptizing of dying children, the attackers repeatedly baptized Father Jean de Brébeuf and Gabriel Lalemant (the nephew of Jérôme Lalemant, now the superior of all the Jesuits in Canada) with boiling water, then further tortured and finally executed them.

The attacks threw the surviving Huron settlements into chaos. Seeing their position as untenable, the Hurons burned their villages and deserted them for the security of Quebec. Hunger and contagious diseases claimed many Huron refugees, who spent the winter on Christian Island, in Georgian Bay. A small number of survivors eventually accompanied the Jesuits to Quebec, where the order established a fortified mission for them on Île d'Orléans, just east of the town. Others joined the Algonquians to the north. In the next few years, some Hurons voluntarily joined the Iroquois. Huronia, like the Iroquois of the St. Lawrence in Jacques Cartier's day, was destroyed as a direct result of contact with the Europeans.

WHERE HISTORIANS DISAGREE

The Hurons and Christianity

In the 1640s large numbers of Hurons in good health accepted Christianity. Before 1639, the Jesuits' attempts to Christianize the Hurons met with limited success, mostly with individuals who were on the point of death and had nothing to lose. Yet by 1648, the "Black Robes" had converted several thousand people. Had it not been for the Iroquois defeat of the Hurons in 1649–50 and their subsequent dispersal, the Jesuits' dream of establishing a Roman Catholic Huronia might have been realized. The significant conversion of Hurons to Christianity in the last years of Huronia has aroused interest among historians in an attempt to understand why.

The impact of disease offers one explanation for the Hurons' sudden receptiveness to Christianity. From 1635 to 1640, a series of epidemics carried away more than half the population. The Hurons lost many of their most skillful leaders and craftspeople, and this had the effect of increasing their dependence on trade with the French. In the 1960s and 1970s, anthropologist Bruce G. Trigger pointed to the economic motives, among other factors, that led many Hurons to convert. They sought, through conversion, "to receive preferential treatment in their dealings with traders and officials in New France," and in particular, to be able to secure guns, which were given only to converts. As Trigger points out, "in 1648, when only 15 percent of the Hurons were Christian, half of the men in the Huron [trading] fleet were either converts or were preparing for baptism."[1]

Trigger's secular explanation of the Jesuits' success in his later two-volume work[2] was strongly opposed by Jesuit historian Lucien Campeau in the 1980s. Referring to Trigger's work as "malheureusement biaisée et peu exacte sous l'aspect historique" [unfortunately biased and not very historically accurate], Campeau wrote an account of his order's work among the Hurons in order to prove that they understood the Christian message as it was preached to them and that this message was the primary reason for their conversion.[3] In reply, Trigger pointed out that Campeau failed to examine the most recent ethnohistorical research in preparing his study. Moreover, he was too ready to accept, uncritically and at face value, the Jesuits' account of their mission work. "What we have here is splendid hagiography but very old-fashioned historiography."[4]

The Eurocentric nature of the sources lies at the heart of the debate. While we have the perspectives of the Jesuits, complete with all their biases, we have little by way of Huron testimony. According to Trigger, "For the majority of Indians whose names have been preserved, only a few isolated events are recorded and even a skeletal life history of such individuals remains beyond our grasp."[5] Trigger did use the work, Jesuit Relations to provide an account of the Christian convert Joseph Chihoatenhwa.[6] Expanding upon Trigger's sketch, John Steckley, an anthropologist and student of the Huron language, completed a short biography.[7] In Chihoatenhwa's case, economic factors apparently played very little part in his decision to accept Christianity, as he traded with the neighbouring Petuns and not with the French. Steckley argues, as does Trigger, that Joseph Chihoatenhwa converted in 1637 for reasons deep within his Aboriginal culture. "As a Christian, Chihoatenhwa did have, or believed he had, a source of power on which he could draw, a spiritual source not unlike that upon which a pre-contact Huron shaman could rely. . . . The priest appeared to have an effective medicine when no other was forthcoming; a preventative or cure which Chihoatenhwa accepted much [as] he would have in earlier times accepted the curing vision or dream of a powerful shaman."[8]

1. Bruce G. Trigger, "The French Presence in Huronia," *Canadian Historical Review* 49 (1968): 134.

2. Bruce G. Trigger, *The Children of Aataentsic: A History of the Huron People to 1660*, 2 vols. (Montreal/Kingston: McGill-Queen's University Press, 1976).

3. Lucien Campeau, *La mission des Jésuites chez les Hurons, 1634–1650* (Montreal: Éditions Bellarmin, 1987), p. 18.

4. Bruce G. Trigger, "Review of *La mission des Jésuites chez les Hurons*, 1634–1650 by Lucien Campeau," *Canadian Historical Review* 69 (1988): 102.

5. Trigger, *The Children of Aataentsic*, vol. 1, p. 22.

6. Trigger, *The Children of Aataentsic*, vol. 2, pp. 550–51, 565–67, 594–95, 598–601.

7. One of the three biographies included in John Steckley's *Untold Tales: Three 17th Century Huron* (Ajax, ON: R.A. Kerton, 1981).

8. Steckley, *Untold Tales*, pp. 9–10.

The Consequences of Huronia's Destruction

The fall of Huronia led to Iroquois attacks on other First Nations in the region. The League of Peace looked increasingly like a League of War, and the Iroquois had many enemies. Historian Daniel Richter argues that the Iroquois were also devastated by epidemics after the mid-1630s and this led to the urgency behind the war. Economic motives played a part, but the demand for captives to replace the deceased relatives became increasingly important.[2]

The Five Nations' subsequent victories over the neighbours of the Hurons to the west (the Petuns) and to the south (the Neutrals) disrupted the fur trade for the French. The diversion of furs to the Dutch on the Hudson River and the consequent bypassing of the St. Lawrence threatened to ruin the fur-trading colony. Only in the short term, however, did the destruction of Huronia damage the colony's economy; ironically, in the long term, it helped it. Because the Hurons could no longer supply food to the northern Algonquians, the latter became a new market for the colony's farmers. In the 1650s the majority of the engagés began to stay in the colony after their contracts expired. Farming expanded, as did the French fur trade.

With the loss of the Hurons as middlemen, the French were forced to leave the fur trade posts and go in search of the more remote Aboriginal groups. By 1653, the French coureurs de bois travelled inland to live with the Algonquians of the upper Great Lakes, or the "Ottawa," as the French called them, and to take their furs to New France. In 1654, Médard Chouart des Groseilliers canoed into the interior, returning two years later with a rich cargo of furs. His brother-in-law, Pierre-Esprit Radisson, accompanied him on later journeys, including one in 1659 to the far end of Lake Superior, where they heard of a "Bay of the North Sea" hundreds of kilometres to the north.

Iroquois Attacks on New France

But the annihilation of the Hurons did not end the conflict between the French (and their allies) and the Iroquois. The ability of the French to adapt and continue the fur trade was indication enough that only their destruction would achieve the objectives of the Iroquois. The Five Nations had the French in a very vulnerable position. Their major ally had been taken out, and the colonists were confined to the walls of their settlements, where they were terrorized by Iroquois attacks. It was now a matter of delivering the death blow. Between 1650 and 1653, the Iroquois killed 32 French settlers and captured 22 others. A mere 50 settlers held Montreal, the advance guard of the colony. Even at Trois-Rivières and Quebec, few went out to work their fields because of the constant danger. When they did, they left with sickles in their hands and firearms slung across their backs. The Iroquois were a fearsome enemy. They were skilled warriors, but their use of geography and subterfuge, along with their reputations for torture and brutality, added a powerful psychological weapon to their arsenal. The three French settlements were utterly demoralized and terrorized. Marie de l'Incarnation, the founder of the Ursuline order in New France, recalled in a letter to her sister that the Iroquois "made such ravages in their regions that we believed for a time that we should have to go back to France."

A HISTORICAL PORTRAIT

Marie de l'Incarnation

In the mid-sixteenth century, France became the focal point for the Counter-Reformation. Hundreds of Roman Catholic missionaries left France in the seventeenth century in hopes of countering the effects of the Reformation and revitalizing Catholicism. The Counter-Reformation allowed female religious orders the opportunity to carry out their work alongside male orders. In the distant Canadian missions, Catholic French women, like Marie de l'Incarnation, could work alongside the Jesuits.

Marie Guyart, the founder of the Ursuline order in New France, was born in 1599 in Tours, a textile town of almost 20 000 people in the centre of France's rich Loire Valley. Her father was a baker. From early childhood, she believed she had a calling as a nun. She received religious visitations: when she was a small girl, she claimed that Jesus visited her and kissed her in a dream.

Pressed by her parents, Marie reluctantly married Claude Martin, a master silk-worker. A jealous mother-in-law and financial difficulties led to her husband's bankruptcy, and contributed to a troubled marriage. After two years of married life, Martin died, leaving his 19-year-old wife destitute and with a son only six months old.

The young widow went with her son to live with her sister's family. Marie was able to help her brother-in-law, a successful merchant wagoner who transported goods throughout France. She did everything from grooming horses to keeping the accounts. But Marie believed that she was on a path to serve God. She waited until her son was old enough so she could finally join a convent.

Marie secretly took a vow of chastity and began to prepare herself for what she called a "mystic union" with Christ. Away from work she committed herself to solitude and meditation. In order to share and understand the pain suffered by Christ on the cross, she practised mortification of the flesh: she wore harsh clothing, slept on a bed of boards, and sometimes rose at night to whip herself, first with thongs, then with nettles. Mortification was also undertaken as sacrifice and penance. It was an important practice of Ignatius Loyola and his Jesuits.

When her son Claude reached the age of 12, Marie arranged for her sister and brother-in-law to look after his education, and she entered the Ursuline convent. Madame Martin became an Ursuline nun under the name "Marie de l'Incarnation" and took her final vows two years later in 1633.

Marie de l'Incarnation learned about the Canadian missions from the *Jesuit Relations*. She wanted to bring the Gospel to the First Nations. When a wealthy female patron, Madeline de la Peltrie, came forward to fund a women's convent in Quebec, Marie de l'Incarnation and two other Ursulines arrived in 1639 at a tiny hamlet of only a few houses. They immediately started their school for First Nations girls, and also for an increasing number of settlers' children, who came to predominate (the school still exists today).

At the time of Marie's death in 1672, the Ursuline community numbered over 20, and Quebec had hundreds of houses and several substantial buildings. The Ursulines became a fixture in the education system of New France. Indeed, the female religious orders in the colony allowed girls to receive more education than in France and at times a superior education to that received by boys. To an extent, female religious orders defied the strict patriarchal society of New France. They lived and worked outside the traditional structures of family life.

It is estimated that Marie de l'Incarnation wrote about 13 000 letters in her lifetime. Unfortunately, only several hundred survive, many of them saved by her son, Claude Martin, who became a Benedictine monk. After his mother's death, he wrote her life story.

The Iroquois were also intent on breaking the ring of allies that had surrounded them during the height of Huron power. The outbreak of war between the Iroquois and the Eries (who had taken in large numbers of Huron refugees) to the west gave New France a temporary reprieve. A five-year truce was negotiated between the French and the Iroquois in the mid-1650s. Fortunately for New France, the population increased during this time, tripling from 1050 permanent French residents in 1651 to nearly 3300 by 1662. The colony was diversifying away from a strict reliance on the fur trade and toward farming settlements along the St. Lawrence. The French also developed more effective defences against Iroquois attacks. A small detachment of soldiers patrolled the St. Lawrence from Trois-Rivières to Montreal, the most exposed settlement. The French organized militia units and erected stockades. The war resumed in 1658.

Dollard des Ormeaux

The French took the offensive and made their first advance against the Iroquois in the spring of 1660. The military force consisted of Adam Dollard des Ormeaux, an ambitious young soldier recently arrived from France, and 16 other young Frenchmen, along with Annaotaha, an experienced Huron warrior, with several dozen warriors. They left Montreal intending to ambush a small Iroquois party on the Ottawa River.

But at Long Sault, northwest of Montreal, Dollard's party encountered an Iroquois invasion army of some 300 warriors on their way to rendezvous with 500 more who awaited them at the Richelieu River. The Iroquois besieged Dollard and his party in a former stockade, and then waited for the remainder of their warriors from the Richelieu to join them before making the final assault. In the interim, some of the adopted Hurons in the Iroquois camp persuaded some of the Hurons with Dollard to join them. Since the French had turned over several Huron refugees to the Iroquois not long before, most of the Hurons felt no obligation to fight to the death. Only five Frenchmen remained alive when the final Iroquois attack came at the end of the week-long Battle of Long Sault; all five died at the torture stake. But three Hurons escaped to recount the tragedy to the French.

According to historian André Vachon, Dollard and his companions repelled an attack on Montreal and "diverted the Iroquois army temporarily from its objective in 1660, thereby allowing the settlers to harvest their crop and escape famine and allowing Radisson to reach Montreal safe and sound with a load of furs."[3] The events remained relatively unknown until the late nineteenth and early twentieth centuries, when French-Canadian historians resurrected Dollard as a national French-Canadian hero, exemplifying martyrdom for his church and colony. In French-speaking Quebec, May 24 was popularly known as Dollard Day throughout most of the twentieth century.

But New France was saved, not by the colonists, but by France itself. After decades of struggling for its very survival, the French Crown came to the colony's rescue. In 1663, King Louis XIV elevated the small colony to a royal province of France. The previous year he sent 100 regular soldiers to New France, and in 1665 he dispatched the Carignan-Salières regiment, the pride of the French military establishment, numbering 1000 strong. Alexandre Prouville de Tracy, lieutenant-general of America from 1663 to 1667, was dispatched from the Caribbean to set things right in the colony. In 1666, the French went on the offensive and made two overland attacks on the Mohawks in present-day New York state, burning villages and food stores as they went. The Mohawks sued for peace in 1667. The Seneca were involved in a war with the Susquehannock (Iroquoian-speaking First Nation living in present-day Pennsylvania). They made peace several years later. New France was saved.

Upon the regiment's recall to France in 1668, some 400 officers and men of the Carignan-Salières took their discharge in New France. The officers received large tracts of land in the

The Battle of Long Sault on the Ottawa River. Le combat de Dollard des Ormeaux 1660 by M.-A. de Foy Suzor-Côté (1869–1937).

Abbé Lionel Groulx.

exposed region along the Richelieu River and near Montreal. Twenty years of peace and relative security followed, during which the colony became a permanent feature.

The Iroquois and the French, 1667–1701

New France would survive and peace was negotiated, but tension continued for decades. To obtain furs and sensing they were being outflanked to the west, the Iroquois sent raiding parties in the late 1660s to the Illinois country, but this interfered with French exploration of the Mississippi Valley. The Illinois First Nation rejected the Iroquois invitation to ally itself with the Iroquois League and turned to the French, who promised aid and protection. Relations between the Five Nations and the French deteriorated every year as the Iroquois increased their raids against the Illinois, now French allies.

At the same time that the Five Nations attacked the Illinois to the west, they attempted to improve their relations with the northern Algonquians in order to obtain furs. This move concerned the French, who aimed to keep their Algonquian allies at peace among themselves, but at war with the Iroquois. The establishment of Hudson's Bay Company posts on James Bay and Hudson Bay in the 1670s was already diverting northern furs to the English. If the Iroquois took more furs from north of the Great Lakes to the Atlantic seaboard, New France would lose its leading export.

The Iroquois moved into the territory along the north shore of Lake Ontario in the 1660s. They used this area as bases for trading with the northern Algonquians. These developing trade links led the French to establish the post of Cataraqui, or Frontenac (at present-day Kingston), in 1673 to control the trade at the eastern end of Lake Ontario. Around 1680, the French also briefly maintained a fort at Niagara to control the trade at the western end of Lake Ontario.

The truce between the French and Iroquois was terminated in the mid-1680s. The French wanted the Five Nations to cease their attacks on the Illinois and to stop trading the furs of the northern Algonquians to the English. An attempted invasion into the territory of the northern Seneca, led by Governor Lefebvre de la Barre, was a disaster for the French. When provisions ran out and fever ravaged the governor's troops, he signed a humiliating peace treaty with the Iroquois that led to his dismissal as governor.

In 1687, the French persuaded the Algonquians to join nearly 2000 French troops on a second expedition to the Iroquois country. The invaders burned a number of villages, destroyed cornfields, and looted graves. In 1689 the Iroquois, with the aid of the English, retaliated by attacking the French settlement at Lachine, about 15 kilometres west of Montreal. According to a French account, 1500 Iroquois laid waste the open country: "The ground was everywhere covered with corpses, and the Iroquois carried away six-score captives, most of whom were burned." Historian José António Brandão estimates that the Iroquois captured or killed close to 600 French colonists from 1687 to 1697.[4]

The early 1690s marked the high point of Iroquois success against the French. But then fortunes turned. The colonists of New France—now employing Aboriginal tactics such as the quick strike and withdrawal (*raid-éclair*)—together with 1500 regular troops sent from France, gained the upper hand. Led by Governor Frontenac, the French invaded the territory of the Mohawks and the Onondaga. By 1693, the Five Nations were suffering heavy losses as a result of both war and disease. In the face of the Algonquians' attacks, they could no longer maintain their forward position on the north shore of Lake Ontario. Their numbers fell from more than 10 000 in the 1640s to less than 9000 at the turn of the century, despite the adoptions of other Iroquoians.

Iroquois Christian Converts

Despite the war between the French and the Iroquois, the Jesuits worked among the Five Nations. The priests were successful in convincing some war captives who had previously encountered missionaries to move from the Iroquois villages in present-day New York state to their mission on the island of Montreal (later moved to

Iroquois allant a la Découverte

An eighteenth-century Iroquois warrior, by Jacques Grasset St. Sauveur.

Source: Library and Archives Canada/C-003165.

the Lake of Two Mountains, in Oka, in 1717), and at Sault St. Louis (Caughnawaga, now Kahna-wake) southwest of Montreal. Many of the Iroquois converts were recently adopted Hurons and other prisoners. In the mid-1660s, several Jesuit missionaries claimed that adoptees constituted two-thirds or more of the population of many Iroquois villages. The recently adopted Iroquois weakened the unity of the Five Nations' communities.

The most famous convert was Kateri Tekakwitha (pronounced *Teg-gah-kweet-ha*), daughter of a Mohawk father and an Algonquian mother. After her conversion she escaped to Sault St. Louis, where she organized with two other Iroquois women a special society of devotion. Until her death, in 1680, Kateri's band of devout women flourished. In 1980, three centuries after her death, Pope John Paul II beatified Kateri. Beatification is just one step from sainthood in the Roman Catholic Church.

The Southward Migration of the Algonquians

In 1671, the French claimed possession of the Great Lakes in the presence of a great convocation at Sault Ste. Marie. Fourteen nations witnessed the raising of a cross and of a post bearing France's coat of arms. But the Algonquians considered themselves the allies, not the subjects, of France. They had a different understanding of the proceedings, as evidenced by their oral history of the event, which William Warren, a nineteenth-century Aboriginal historian, later recorded. The Algonquians believed that the French had simply asked "for permission to trade in the country," and that the French king's representative had, in return, "promised the protection of the great French nation against all their enemies."[5]

With their alliance with the French confirmed, and the Iroquois Confederacy in such a weakened state, the Algonquians advanced south from Lake Superior and the north shore of Lake Huron to occupy the former Huron, Petun, and Neutral territories. By moving south, the Algonquians acquired rich new hunting and fishing grounds. Some even got a new name. The English colonists on the Atlantic coast termed all the newcomers in the area bounded by Lakes Ontario, Erie, and Huron as either "Chippewa" or "Ojibwa." But they reserved a new name, "Mississauga," for the Ojibwa on the north shore of Lake Ontario. In 1640, the Jesuit fathers first recorded the term *omisagai* (Mississauga) as the name of an Algonquian band near the Mississagi River on the northwestern shore of Lake Huron. The French, and later the English, applied this name to all the Algonquians settling on the north shore of Lake Ontario. Only a tiny fraction of these Aboriginal people could have been members of the Mississauga bands, but once recorded in the Europeans' documents, the name became the one most commonly used. The Ojibwa continued to call themselves by their own name: Anishinabeg.

Peace Established, 1701

The English made peace with the French in 1697. This truce led the Iroquois to reconsider their own conflict with the French. Their fear of being encircled was becoming a reality, particularly after the French established the colony of Louisiana to the south in 1699. In 1700 the Iroquois Confederacy made an offer to the French, who convened a council with them at Montreal. War and disease had weakened the Iroquois. The Five Nations had had approximately 2570 warriors in 1689; by 1700, there were only 1230.

The Iroquois south of Lake Ontario made peace with the French and the western nations in August 1701. Representatives travelled to Montreal for the ratification of the treaty. To ensure

A Canada Post stamp commemorating the Great Peace of Montreal in 1701.
Source: rook76/Shutterstock.

that the Iroquois continued to serve as a buffer between the English colonies and New France, the French allowed them to continue to trade some northern furs with the English. The Christian Iroquois at Kahnawake became the intermediaries in the lucrative Albany–Montreal trade route. In turn, the Five Nations promised their neutrality in any future colonial war between France and England.

SUMMARY

The Great Peace ended the Iroquois wars that had menaced New France for decades. The Iroquois Confederacy brought the French colony to the brink of annihilation and seriously hindered its development and expansion. The colony's very existence was in question after the dispersal of the Hurons and the Iroquois raids on the tiny French settlements in the St. Lawrence Valley in the early 1650s. Yet, in the long term, the destruction of Huronia contributed to New France's growth. Agriculture became more profitable as the colony inherited the Hurons' former role as the Algonquians' "provisioners." In addition, the French in the late 1650s and early 1660s entered the interior themselves to trade directly for the Algonquians' furs, and the coureurs de bois helped reinforce the existing Franco–Algonquian alliance. Together, the French and their Algonquian allies gained the upper hand over the Five Nations in the late 1680s and 1690s, which led to the Great Peace of 1701.

NOTES

1. As quoted in James P. Ronda, "We Are Well as We Are': An Indian Critique of Seventeenth-Century Christian Missions," *William and Mary Quarterly*, 3rd series, 34 (1977): 77–8.

2. Daniel K. Richter, *The Ordeal of the Longhouse: The Peoples of the Iroquois League in the Era of European Colonization* (Chapel Hill: University of North Carolina Press, 1992), p. 38.

3. André Vachon, "Dollard des Ormeaux," in *Dictionary of Canadian Biography*, vol. 1 (Toronto: University of Toronto Press, 1966), p. 274.

4. José António Brandão, *"Your Fyre Shall Burn No More": Iroquois Policy Toward New France and Its Native Allies to 1701* (Lincoln: University of Nebraska Press, 1997), p. 125.

5. William M. Warren, *History of the Ojibway Nation* (Minneapolis: Ross & Haines, 1957 [1885]), p. 131.

BIBLIOGRAPHY

A number of studies exist on the relationship between the Iroquois and the French. William N. Fenton provides an overview in "The Iroquois in History," in Eleanor Burke Leacock and Nancy Oestreich Lurie, eds., *North American Indians in Historical Perspective* (New York: Random House, 1971), pp. 129–68. This essay is reprinted in his encyclopedic work, *The Great Law and the Longhouse: A Political History of the Iroquois Confederacy* (Norman: University of Oklahoma Press, 1998). On First Nation–European relations in general during this period, see Bruce G. Trigger, ed., *Northeast*, vol. 15 of *Handbook of North American Indians* (Washington, DC: Smithsonian Institution, 1978); and Denys Delâge, *Bitter Feast: Amerindians and Europeans in Northeastern North America, 1600–64*, trans. Jane Brierley (Vancouver: University of British Columbia Press, 1993).

Bruce G. Trigger's summary in *Natives and Newcomers: Canada's "Heroic Age" Reconsidered* (Montreal/Kingston: McGill-Queen's University Press, 1985) covers the early period of contact to 1663. The best introduction to the Five (later Six) Nations, or Iroquois, remains Dean R. Snow, *The Iroquois* (Oxford: Blackwell, 1994). Francis Jennings reviews the period from the 1600s to 1744 in *The Ambiguous Iroquois Empire* (New York: W.W. Norton, 1984) and in his sequel, *Empire of Fortune: Crowns, Colonies and Tribes in the Seven Years War in America* (New York: W.W. Norton, 1988). Georges E. Sioui' *For an Amerindian Autohistory: An Essay on the Foundations of a Social Ethic* (Montreal/Kingston: McGill-Queen's University Press, 1995) redefines First-Nations history examining events from the perspective of Indigenous peoples.

Paul A.W. Wallace relates the story of the founding of the League of the Iroquois in *The White Roots of Peace* (Philadelphia: University of Pennsylvania, 1946; reprinted Ohsweken, ON: Iroqrafts, 1998). A shorter version by the same author titled "Dekanahwideh" appears in *Dictionary of Canadian Biography*, vol. 1, 1000–1700 (Toronto: University of Toronto Press, 1966), pp. 253–55, which is available online: www.bibliographi.ca. William Engelbrecht relies on archaeological as well as oral data to determine the league's origins in his article "New York Iroquois Political Development," in William W. Fitzhugh, ed., *Cultures in Contact* (Washington, DC: Smithsonian Institution Press, 1985), pp. 163–83. Anthony F.C. Wallace (son of Paul A.W. Wallace) has written a complete study of one of the Iroquois nations in *The Death and Rebirth of the Seneca* (New York: Alfred A. Knopf, 1969). On the status of women in Iroquois society, see the collection of essays edited by W.G. Spittal, *Iroquois Women: An Anthology* (Ohsweken, ON: Iroqrafts, 1990). A good summary of the culture of the Iroquois is Hazel W. Hertzberg's *The Great Tree and the Longhouse* (New York: Macmillan, 1966). For a look at Iroquois–European military relations, see Jon Parmenter, "After the Mourning Wars: The Iroquois as Allies in Colonial North American Campaigns, 1676–1760," *William and Mary Quarterly* 64(1) (2007): 39–82.

There are a number of studies on the Hurons (Wendat). Bruce G. Trigger, *The Huron Farmers of the North*, 2nd ed. (Fort Worth, TX: Holt, Rinehart and Winston, 1990); and Elisabeth Tooker, *An Ethnography of the Huron Indians, 1615–1649* (Syracuse, NY: Syracuse University Press, 1991), are the best starting points. See also Conrad Heidenreich, *Huronia: A History and Geography of the Huron Indians, 1600–1650* (Toronto: McClelland & Stewart, 1971). Bruce G. Trigger provides a review in *The Children of Aataentsic: A History of the Huron People to 1660*, 2 vols. (Montreal/Kingston: McGill-Queen's University Press, 1976).

Short summaries of the Jesuits' contact with the Hurons are contained in Henry Warner Bowden, *American Indians and Christian Missions* (Chicago: University of Chicago Press, 1981), pp. 59– 95; and in James Axtell, *The Invasion Within: The Contest of Cultures in Colonial North America* (New York: Oxford University Press, 1985), Rachel Major, "Les jésuites chez les Hurons en 1648–49," *La revue canadienne des études autochtones* 26(8)1 (2006): 53–70. These can be supplemented by John Webster Grant's *Moon of Wintertime: Missionaries and the Indians of Canada in Encounter Since 1534* (Toronto: University of Toronto Press, 1984). A review is provided by Father Lucien Campeau in *La mission des Jésuites chez les Hurons, 1634–1650* (Montreal: Éditions Bellarmin, 1987). S.R. Mealing has edited *The Jesuit Relations and Allied Documents* (Toronto: McClelland & Stewart, 1963), a one-volume anthology of selections from the *Jesuit Relations*.

Dean R. Snow, Charles T. Gehring, and William A. Starna provide a good selection of documents, including several translated from Dutch, in *Mohawk Country: Early Narratives About the Native People* (Syracuse, NY: Syracuse University Press, 1996). Cornelius Jaenen has edited a useful collection of French documents, *The French Regime in the Upper Country of Canada During the Seventeenth Century* (Toronto: Champlain Society, 1996). In her book *Chain Her by One Foot: The Subjugation of Women in Seventeenth-Century New France* (London: Routledge, 1991), Karen Anderson argues that the Jesuits introduced the subjugation of women by men in the Hurons' egalitarian society. For an extensive look at the *Jesuit Relations* on the subject of Aboriginal spirituality, see Claudio R. Salvucci, ed., *Native American Spirituality: Extracts from the Jesuit Relations* (Bristol: Evolution Publishing 2005); and for a look at Jesuit surveys of the Aboriginal people of the Canadian interior, see Claudio R. Salvucci, ed., *Lost Tribes of the Interior: Extracts from the Jesuit Relations and Primary Sources* (Bristol: Evolution Publishing, 2006).

Useful studies on the Iroquois and the Great Lakes Aboriginal peoples include Daniel K. Richter, *The Ordeal of the Longhouse: The Peoples of the Iroquois League in the Era of European Colonization* (Chapel Hill: University of North Carolina Press, 1992); Richard White, *The Middle Ground: Indians, Empires, and Republics in the Great Lakes Region, 1650–1815* (Cambridge: Cambridge University Press, 1991); Gilles Havard, *The Great Peace of Montreal of 1701: French–Native Diplomacy in the Seventeenth Century* (Montreal/Kingston: McGill-Queen's University Press, 2001); Alain Beaulieu and Roland Viau, *The Great Peace: Chronicle of Diplomatic Saga* (Montreal: Libre Expression, 2001); Brian J. Given, *A Most Pernicious Thing: Gun Trading and Native Warfare in the Early Contact Period* (Ottawa:

Carleton University Press, 1994); Matthew Dennis, *Cultivating a Landscape of Peace: Iroquois–European Encounters in Seventeenth-Century America* (Cooperstown, NY: Cornell University Press, 1993); and José António Brandão, *"Your Fyre Shall Burn No More": Iroquois Policy Toward New France and Its Native Allies to 1701* (Lincoln: University of Nebraska Press, 1997). For a comparative account of Iroquois and European women, see Natalie Zemon Davis, "Iroquois Women, European Women," in Peter C. Mancall and James H. Merrill, eds., *American Encounters: Natives and Newcomers from European Contact to Indian Removal, 1500–1850* (New York: Routledge, 2000).

For an extended look at both women and the treatment of women in New France, see Karen Anderson, *Chain Her By One Foot: The Subjugation of Native Women in Seventeenth Century New France*. (New York: Routledge, 1991) and Terrence A. Crowley, "Women, Religion, and Freedom in New France," in Larry D. Eldridge, ed., *Women and Freedom in Early America* (New York: New York University Press, 1997). See also Allan Greer, *Mohawk Saint: Catherine Tekakwitha and the Jesuits* (New York: Oxford University Press, 2005).

Information on the First Nations in the St. Lawrence Valley is contained in Marc Jetten, *Enclaves amérindiennes: Les "réductions" du Canada 1637–1701* (Sillery, QC: Septentrion, 1994). Allan Greer's *Mohawk Saint: Catherine Tekakwitha and the Jesuits* (Toronto: Oxford, 2005) is an important study. William N. Fenton and Elizabeth L. Moore have edited and translated the Jesuit Father Joseph-François Lafitau's perceptive study of the Iroquois at Sault St. Louis (Kahnawake) near Montreal in the early eighteenth century: see *Customs of the American Indians Compared with the Customs of Primitive Times*, 2 vols. (Toronto: Champlain Society, 1974). For an account of a New England captive at Kahnawake, see John Demos, *The Unredeemed Captive: A Family Story from Early America* (New York: Vintage Books, 1995). Gerald R. Alfred's *Heeding the Voices of Our Ancestors: Kahnawake Mohawk Politics and the Rise of Native Nationalism* (Toronto: Oxford University Press, 1995) contains one chapter on the history of Kahnawake in the late seventeenth and early eighteenth centuries. For a look at Algonquin–French relations in the St. Lawrence Valley, see Mario Marchand, "Le troc des cultures: Algonkiens et blancs dans la foret des Trois-Rivières," *Cap-aux-Diamants* 86 (2006): 10–13.

The best treatment of Dollard is by André Vachon in *Dictionary of Canadian Biography*, vol. 1 (Toronto: University of Toronto Press, 1966), pp. 266–75. Terry Crowley has collected a number of primary and secondary accounts of this famous son of New France in his edited work *Clio's Craft: A Primer of Historical Methods* (Toronto: Copp Clark Pitman, 1988), pp. 253–303.

For French views of the Iroquois, see Joyce Marshall, trans. and ed., *Word from New France: The Selected Letters of Marie de l'Incarnation* (Toronto: Oxford University Press, 1967). Studies on Marie de l'Incarnation and the First Nations include Natalie Zemon Davis, "Marie de l'Incarnation, New Worlds," in *Women on the Margins: Three Seventeenth-Century Lives* (Cambridge, MA: Harvard University Press, 1995), pp. 63–139, 259–95.

Useful maps showing France's inland expansion appear in R. Cole Harris, ed., *Historical Atlas of Canada*, vol. 1, *From the Beginning to 1800* (Toronto: University of Toronto Press, 1987).

Source: Library and Archives Canada/C-043730.

Chapter Five

PROVINCE DE FRANCE, 1663–1760

TIME LINE	
1643	King Louis XIV ascends throne of France at age four
1661	Cardinal Mazarin dies; Louis XIV begins to govern personally
1663	New France becomes royal province under Louis XIV First of *filles du roi* (daughters of the king) arrive in colony
1665	Colbert becomes minister of marine and begins to reorganize New France Jean Talon becomes first *Intendant* of New France
1669	Organization of Militia in New France
1672	The Comte de Frontenac, Governor of New France, begins first term of office Franco-Dutch War begins
1688	Bishop Laval, first bishop of New France, retires
1713	Treaty of Utrecht ends War of Spanish Succession
1715	Louis XIV, "The Sun King," dies
1737	The King's Highway, the first road between Quebec and Montreal, completed

By the 1660s, after decades of struggling to survive, the small French colony in the St. Lawrence Valley was finally in a position to expand and prosper. The threat of annihilation by the Iroquois had passed. The Hurons were scattered, but French traders took over their roles and moved farther into the interior, contacting more First Nations, gathering more furs, expanding the fur trade, and extending French territorial claims. As the colony stabilized and grew in size, agriculture became increasingly important. New France also became an important link in the triangular mercantile trade with the mother country and the Caribbean. But imperial rivalry between France and England posed a new threat. North America would become a minor theatre in a much larger struggle. New France would need to rely on its established alliances with the surrounding First Nations to pose a challenge to the more populous English colonies to the south.

As part of its effort to consolidate empire, between 1663 and 1672, the French Crown turned the struggling fur trade outpost into a royal province. The Crown strengthened the colony's economic infrastructure and introduced new political institutions that lasted nearly a century. The objective of King Louis XIV and his minister of the marine, Jean-Baptiste Colbert, was to transform the St. Lawrence Valley into La Nouvelle France—a new France overseas.

Royal Government

In 1643, at the age of four, Louis XIV became King of France. The "Sun King," as he became known, ruled France for the next 72 years, until his death in 1715. Louis did not begin to govern personally, however, until 1661 and the death of his prime minister, Cardinal Mazarin. During the reign of Louis XIV, France became the dominant power in Europe. The Crown brought stability to the kingdom by centralizing power, controlling the aristocracy, modernizing the army, rebuilding the economy, regulating the legal system, and stifling religious division. He ruled by "the divine right of kings" and created an absolute monarchy in which all authority descended from him ("L'état c'est moi" was his famous line).

Stability in France allowed for stability in its main North American colony. The French Crown sought to create a dynamic French presence in the new world by making New France a *province de France*, a colony directly under royal rule. The fur trade monopolies had clearly failed to provide the colony with the impetus and infrastructure for growth and expansion. New France now acquired the same administrative structures as other French provinces. In particular, the royal colony came under the supervision of Louis' new adviser, Jean-Baptiste Colbert, the minister of the marine, in 1665. Unlike previous ministers Cardinals Richelieu and Mazarin, Colbert was not an official of the Roman Catholic Church.

Under Colbert's efficient administration, France's economy became increasingly mercantilist. Colbert reduced the kingdom's debt through taxation and increased exports by building industry. The colonies were expected to profit the metropolis. Whatever manufactured goods the settlers needed, they purchased from France. The colonists, in turn, were expected to supply the mother country with natural products and to sell their exports in France. Only French ships could transport goods. In order to be profitable, however, the colony had to produce more wealth than it cost to administer.

New France was expected to produce furs, minerals, and timber (including ship masts), which France formerly had to import from Scandinavia and Russia. In addition, Colbert sought to develop a triangular trade network among France, New France, and the French possessions in the Caribbean. New France exported fish, wheat, peas, and barrel staves to France and the French West Indies. The islands exported rum, molasses, and sugar. France exported textiles and manufactured goods.

It was one thing to develop the plan; it was another to implement it successfully. New France had to become more stable and self-sufficient. Colbert was determined to turn New France into a self-reliant,

An artist's depiction of a member of the Carignan-Salières Regiment.

Source: Robert Rosewarne after Lucien Rousselot/Library and Archives Canada/C-010368. © Government of Canada. Reproduced with the permission of the Minister of Public Works and Government Services Canada (2011).

defensible colony, with a prosperous agricultural base and its own basic domestic industries. The minister wanted it to become a "compact colony," one centred in the St. Lawrence Valley, without unnecessary forts and outposts on the periphery. He opposed western expansion because it extended the territory France would then have to defend. In other words, Colbert was not content with a colony based around the fur trade. But before any reforms were implemented, the colony had to be saved from the Iroquois. Therefore, Colbert's first objective was to strengthen the colony militarily. In the mid-1660s, he dispatched regular troops to New France in the form of the Carignan-Salières regiment. When the Iroquois made peace in 1667, Colbert's program to transform New France into a profitable and well-populated colony took shape.

Reforming the Seigneurial System

Europeans viewed land as the basis of wealth and agricultural settlement as the foundation of "civilization." For Colbert, one of the least desirable aspects of the fur trade was that it did not encourage agricultural settlement. Without farms, there would be no settlers and the population of the colony would remain small. Without farms, there would be no families and the colony would consist mainly of male traders.

In fashioning the new royal province, Colbert reformed the system of land holdings to replicate that of France. Peasant settlers, or *censitaires*, depended on seigneurs, or lords (or, more appropriately, squires or gentry), in turn themselves vassals of the king. Title to all the land rested with the king, who granted fiefs, or estates, as he saw fit. The soil belonged to the seigneur, but the mineral or subsoil rights and all oak trees on the property belonged to the Crown. Landowners who acquired large domains and who did nothing to improve them lost their lands to more energetic seigneurs.

In 1627, the Crown granted the Company of One Hundred Associates legal and seigneurial rights over the territory of New France. The company in turn granted to favoured individuals—usually nobles or religious bodies such as the Jesuits, the Ursulines, or the Sulpicians—large tracts of land, called *seigneuries*, along the St. Lawrence between Quebec and Montreal. In return for their rectangular estates fronting on the river and usually extending into the foothills behind, the seigneurs undertook to bring out the censitaires (or *habitants*, to employ Canadian usage), who in turn paid them rent and dues. The Company brought out about 260 marriageable girls (*filles à marier*) by paying their travel expenses and lodging until they married. While the population of the colony gradually increased, the settlement policies of the fur trade monopolies failed.

Under royal government, Colbert created a new position—the *Intendant*. Among his other administrative duties, the Intendant granted seigneuries and supervised the seigneurial system. On his arrival in 1665, Jean Talon, the first Intendant of New France, implemented Colbert's plan. He made occupancy a condition of all future grants, to prevent land being distributed as patronage to aristocrats who remained in France. Talon and his immediate successors also kept the size of the seigneuries relatively small to prevent the rise of a class of large landowners who might challenge royal authority. Nearly 200 seigneuries were open for settlement by 1715, most of them along the St. Lawrence from Montreal to below Quebec.

Obligations of the Seigneurs and the Censitaires

Both the seigneurs and the censitaires had obligations to fulfill. The seigneurs were responsible for clearing their land, maintaining manor houses, and either residing there or having responsible persons living there throughout the year. They had to make land grants of up to 80 hectares to settlers. They also had to establish a flour mill on the seigneury for the use of their censitaires. Some seigneurs also maintained a court of law to settle minor disputes. Unlike in France, however, the seigneurial system in New France did not include military obligations, and the landholdings were much larger. By 1663, 69 seigneuries had been granted.

The censitaires, or habitants, also had responsibilities. They had to build their own houses, clear their tract of land, and pay their seigneur the

A reconstruction of the subdivisions of a typical seigneury in New France.

cens (a small cash payment) and rentes (another money payment). Together, these two charges amounted to approximately one-tenth of a censitaire's annual income. The habitants had to take their wheat to the seigneurial mill, paying the seigneur one sack of flour out of every fourteen for this privilege. In a few seigneuries, the lord had the droit de corvée (right to forced labour), usually three days per year, determined in the contract with the censitaire. As well, the censitaires were required by the Crown to work without pay for a day or two a year, doing general maintenance work on any seigneurial roads or bridges. In return for their grants of land, the habitants had to maintain the portion of road that passed through their farms. If they met these requirements, the habitants became owners of their land, which they could pass on to their children. If they sold their land outside their families, they had to pay the seigneur a portion of the money they obtained.

The seigneurial system, therefore, was more than a land-holding enterprise. It laid the economic, political, and legal foundations for the resulting society. For Colbert, the seigneurial system was the key to creating a society that mirrored France. From the outset, however, the North American environment altered the plan. The seigneurial system in the colony demanded a new stock of seigneurs. Many of these lords gained their positions and lands through social mobility. They often lived and worked much as their habitants did, thereby blunting the social distinctions that prevailed in France between lord and peasant. In the colony's early years, a handful of enterprising and ambitious settlers became seigneurs themselves. Pierre Boucher, a pioneer of modest means, managed to become a seigneur in early New France; in 1654, he was elevated to the governorship of Trois-Rivières. As historians Louise Dechêne and Fernand Ouellet argue, social distinctions remained important as the seigneuries became heavily settled and the opportunity for social mobility declined. But the fur trade provided lucrative opportunities for the habitants that did not exist in France. The lure of the wilderness beckoned the young men to become coureurs de bois and seek their adventure in the interior.

The French provinces of Normandy, Perche, and Aunis provided the bulk of the French emigrants. But New France was not a favoured emigration site. The West Indies colonies, including Guadeloupe and Martinique, attracted the bulk of French settlers.

The Growth of Settlement

To help populate the seigneuries, Colbert and his counterpart in New France, the Intendant Jean Talon, worked to correct a social imbalance in the colony: the abundance of eligible bachelors and shortage of French women. By its nature, the fur trade was an industry that drew young men seeking fortune and adventure. The French fur traders found female partnership in Aboriginal women. Samuel de Champlain initially encouraged such relationships because he believed that the resulting offspring produced an even superior breed of Frenchmen. "Our sons shall marry your daughters," he proclaimed, "and together we shall form one people." The arrival of the Catholic missionaries dampened the enthusiasm for such unions, because the Church viewed many of the Aboriginal customs and beliefs as immoral. But until there were more French women in the colony, there was little chance of ceasing the practice; and even then it would prove difficult. Unable to find a French wife, many returned to France when their work contracts ended. In Montreal in 1663, for example, there was only one marriageable woman for every eight eligible men. Before 1660 the average age of first-time French brides in the colony was 15. Most widows remarried within a year of their husband's death.

The Daughters of the King

In 1663 the Crown looked to export marriageable girls from France. Young women were sought who were strong enough for work in the fields, were healthy enough to have children, and had a good character. At first the Crown selected orphanage girls, but when they proved not to be rugged enough, it recruited young, healthy country girls. In 1668, Marie de l'Incarnation, mother superior of the Ursuline convent at Quebec City, requested that "from now on, we only want to ask for village girls who are as fit for work as men." A number of the *filles du roi* (daughters of the king) were not much older than 16. The king paid for travel expenses and provided dowries— "the king's gift"—usually consisting of clothing or household supplies. When the young women arrived in Quebec, the Ursulines and Hospital sisters looked after them. In all, the state sent out nearly 800 *filles du roi* between 1663 and 1673.

The young women were housed in dormitories under the control of the "directress," who taught them skills and chores. The directress also supervised the interviews between the girls and the eligible men, usually within two weeks after arrival. A young man in search of a wife had to declare his possessions and means of livelihood. The *filles* were able to refuse offers of marriage and it soon became apparent that the most important qualification for a suitor was to have his house built. To encourage marriage, the government fined bachelors and denied them trading rights. On average, the girls were married within four or five months. In addition, the new couple received an assortment of livestock and goods to start them off in married life: a pair of chickens and pigs, an ox, a cow, and two barrels of salted meat. As an incentive to raise large families, the couple was given a yearly pension if they had ten children with an increase if they had twelve.

Even if the young man had built a home, a difficult life awaited these women, whose marriage contract bound them for life. They faced relentless work in clearing and maintaining their new family farms. The severity of Canadian winters also came as a shock to the young French women. In northern France, snow covered the ground for a few days, at most. In New France, it remained for months—then there was the extreme cold, the freezing of lakes and rivers.

Fortunately, by the time the *filles* arrived, the French settlers had learned to adjust to winter conditions. They now slaughtered animals at the onset of winter and hung the meat in icy cellars. By eating fresh meat and the past season's vegetables through the winter, they escaped scurvy. They also learned to construct houses in ways that improved heat retention and heating efficiency, by digging cellars first and putting fireplaces in the centre of the houses. In addition, they built roofs with steep angles that readily shed the snow. In the late seventeenth century, settlers introduced another improvement: iron fireboxes that produced four times more heat than conventional fireplaces. They built larger barns to store fodder for the winter and to keep domestic animals inside during the coldest weather. Livestock was also dispatched to New France at the Crown's expense. The first horses arrived in 1665. The First Nations, who had never seen such animals, called them the "moose of France." By the 1720s, there was one horse for every five settlers.

In 1672 France and England went to war with the Dutch republic. With Talon advising that the colony could now populate itself, the French Crown terminated the program. The last *filles du roi* arrived in 1673.

WHERE HISTORIANS DISAGREE

The Seigneurial System in New France

Historians have debated the nature of the seigneurial system in New France for decades. Much of the debate has focused on comparing the system in the colony with the mother country. Early historians, such as François-Xavier Garneau, held that the system was much less harsh and oppressive. The institutions that France established in the St. Lawrence Valley, including the seigneurial system, were "purified" in the new setting, their negative aspects removed by the French Crown. In 1899, historian Benjamin Sulte suggested that the seigneur in New France was not an exploiter but a "colonization agent."[1] This interpretation of a "softer" feudal system led to the portrait of New France as a more open and egalitarian society than France. The view was supported by the Church, who had established a close relationship with the elite and was dominant in Quebec until the mid-twentieth century.

A more critical view of the seigneurial system emerged in the 1960s and 1970s with the rise of social history and a desire to examine history "from the bottom up." In 1974, Louise Dechêne published a detailed local study of the Montreal area that pointed to the oppressive nature of the seigneurial system in the late seven-

teenth century.[2] She sided with fellow historian Fernand Ouellet who, in his numerous writings from the 1960s to the 1980s, argued that, in the eighteenth century, New France was indeed a class-bound society. Both Dechêne and Ouellet maintained that seigneurial practices in the St. Lawrence Valley conformed more to French patterns than originally suspected. In some cases, the customs in Canada were more outdated, and therefore more authoritative, than those in France. As Ouellet wrote in 1981, "In brief, the *ancien régime* society that had developed in the St. Lawrence valley, far from being a modernized or purified version of that of the mother country, was in a sense more archaic."[3]

Anglophone historians were also divided on the seigneurial system. In the 1960s, W.J. Eccles sided with the traditionalists and presented a romanticized version of the habitants and their lives. He wrote that "The seigneurs were little more than land settlement agents and their financial rewards were not great."[4] The habitants enjoyed a relatively comfortable life. In the 1980s, R. Cole Harris questioned the interpretation that farmers in New France occupied a position comparable to that of peasants in rural France during the last two centuries of pre-revolutionary France: "Rural Canada provided relative opportunity (cheaper land and higher wages) for ordinary people, and relative disincentive (higher labour costs, land of little value, and weak markets) for a landed elite."[5] Harris argued that the rural population of New France was independent and self-reliant, and enjoyed opportunities for upward mobility.

Historian Allan Greer challenged this viewpoint.[6] In the mid-1980s, Greer claimed that "exploitation, domination, and the clash of interests were characteristics of rural Canada since the early years of the French regime."[7] More recently, he has argued that "By the end of the French regime, a substantial proportion of the surplus production, that is, of the grain not needed to keep family members alive, was being siphoned off by the colony's seigneurs. All in all, seigneurial extractions did tear a significant chunk out of the habitant household economy."[8]

1. Benjamin Sulte, "Le système seigneurial," *Mélanges historiques* 1 (Montréal, 1918): 80, cited in Serge Jaumain et Matteo Sanfilippo, "Le régime seigneurial en Nouvelle-France: Un débat historiographique," *The Register* 5(2) (Autumn 1984): 227.

2. Louise Dechêne, *Habitants et marchands de Montréal au XVIIe siècle* (Paris: Les Edition Plons, 1974).

3. Fernand Ouellet, "The Formation of a New Society in the St. Lawrence Valley: From Classless Society to Class Conflict," in Jacques A. Barbier, ed. and trans., *Economy, Class and Nation in Quebec: Interpretive Essays* (Toronto: Copp Clark Pitman, 1991), p. 33; originally published in French in *Canadian Historical Review* 62(4) (1981): 407–50.

4. W.J. Eccles, *The Canadian Frontier 1534–1760* (Toronto: Holt, Rinehart and Winston, 1969), p. 68.

5. R. Cole Harris, in the new preface to *The Seigneurial System in Early Canada: A Geographical Study*, 2nd ed. (Montreal/Kingston: McGill-Queen's University Press, 1984), p. xix.

6. Allan Greer, *Peasant, Lord, and Merchant: Rural Society in Three Quebec Parishes, 1740–1840* (Toronto: University of Toronto Press, 1985).

7. Greer, p. xiv.

8. Allan Greer, *The People of New France* (Toronto: University of Toronto Press, 1997), p. 38.

A modern photograph of the Richelieu River, showing the continued impact of the seigneurial system on land formation.

Source: Bernard Vallee, 1976/Archives nationales du Québec à Québec, E10,D76-533/P19A.

The Engagés

In the mid-to-late 1660s, the Crown sent several hundred *engagés*, or indentured workers, to the colony annually. These immigrants constituted the majority of the arrivals from France in the seventeenth century. Bound by a three-year contract, or *engagement*, to a settler, merchant, or religious community, they received a modest wage. They were nicknamed "Thirty-Six Months," since after that period they became free. Beginning in the 1650s, more than half stayed in the colony after their term of service ended. In the early days of Royal government, the engagés performed much of the colony's heavy labour, doing dockwork and construction and clearing more land for farming. The system proved advantageous to both

Immigrants by Gender and Decade, 1608–1759

Period	Men	Women	Total
Before 1630	15	6	21
1630–1639	88	51	139
1640–1649	141	86	227
1650–1659	403	239	642
1660–1669	1075	623	1698
1670–1679	429	369	798
1680–1689	486	56	542
1690–1699	490	32	522
1700–1709	283	24	307
1710–1719	293	18	311
1720–1729	420	14	434
1730–1739	483	16	499
1740–1749	576	16	592
1750–1759	1699	52	1751
Unknown	27	17	44
Total	6908	1619	8527

Source: R. Cole Harris, ed., *Historical Atlas of Canada, vol. 1, From the Beginning to 1800* (Toronto: University of Toronto Press, 1987), plate 45. Reprinted by permission of the University of Toronto Press Incorporated.

the seigneur, who used them to open up more land, and to the engagés, who gained valuable knowledge of local conditions before they began farming on their own.

In total, the Crown sent nearly 4000 men and women to Canada by 1672. Many died from disease, either on the voyage or in the colony itself. A number returned to France. Nonetheless, New France's population grew rapidly from roughly 3000 in 1663 to almost 10 000 a decade later. Most settled along the St. Lawrence River from below Quebec to Montreal, and they cleared more land east of Montreal along the Richelieu River.

A HISTORICAL PORTRAIT

Étienne Trudeau

Étienne Trudeau came to New France from the city of La Rochelle in western France. A master carpenter at 18, Trudeau signed a contract for five years of military service in New France. Upon arrival in Montreal in 1659, he began service with the Sulpician Fathers, who had hired him. Three years later, he and two others were ambushed by 50 Iroquois, but they survived the attack.

In 1667, the year of the Iroquois peace treaty, the 26-year-old Étienne married Adrienne Barbier, the daughter of a carpenter who was one of the original twelve colonists to arrive at Montreal in 1642. Étienne and Adrienne had four children; one child eventually settled in Louisiana, while three became voyageurs and went to the Great Lakes before their marriages. Étienne worked as a farmer, carpenter, and stonemason. He died in 1712 at Montreal; his wife died several years later. Étienne Trudeau was the ancestor of all the Trudeaus of New France, including a ninth-generation descendant—Pierre Elliott Trudeau, prime minister of Canada from 1968 to 1979 and from 1980 to 1984.

The Settlement of the St. Lawrence Valley

Throughout the French regime, the St. Lawrence River remained the colony's main thoroughfare, in summer by canoe or small boat, and in winter by sleigh over the ice. Frontage along the water highway was always desirable. In addition, the settlers wanted to be close to one another, ideally within hailing distance of their neighbours, particularly in the event of Iroquois attacks. Around Quebec, the shores of the St. Lawrence already looked like one sprawling, unending village street, with the habitants' whitewashed farmhouses huddled closely together. The narrow farms extending back from the river were often twenty times as long as they were wide.

The reorganization of New France by the Crown was successful. It achieved significant population growth between 1663 and 1672. The women sent out in Colbert's wave of immigrants married and produced large families. The sexes became evenly balanced in New France. By 1700, women were an average age of 22 when they were married, seven years higher than forty years earlier; men tended to be older, averaging 28 years of age. Despite disasters, such as the smallpox epidemic of 1701 that killed 1000 people, New France's population continued to increase rapidly. It doubled every 25 years, almost entirely as a result of the high birth rate rather than immigration.

Women gave birth to eight or nine children on average. After 1700, the figure dropped to seven. One out of every five children, however, died before the age of one. Hence the average "completed" family in the eighteenth century consisted of 5.65 children per couple. Midwives delivered babies at home. A new mother might have a woman friend stay for a week or so after the birth, and her own mother usually stayed with her for at least a month.

The example of the Tremblay family dramatically underlines the population increase that occurred in New France. Pierre Tremblay arrived in the colony in 1647, and married ten years later at Quebec. When he died, he left behind 12 children, four of them boys. His sons in turn had 15, 14, 14, and 6 children, respectively, and their descendants similarly had large families. By 1957, the 300th anniversary of Pierre Tremblay's marriage, there were 60 000 Tremblays in North America, all descended from this one marriage in New France.

Colbert's Administrative Reforms

Staving off the Iroquois threat, increasing the population, and diversifying the economy were only the beginning of reforms to the colony. In order to mark New France's new status as a royal colony, Colbert established administrative structures identical to those already existing in the other provinces. The structures also reflected the political hierarchy in absolutist France. At the top was the king, Louis XIV. His counterpart in the colonies was the governor. But the monarch delegated considerable powers to his ministers. In the past, these advisers were religious leaders, such as Cardinal Richelieu and Mazarin. By the 1660s, however, Louis XIV was served by Colbert, a bureaucrat, who represented the rise of the middle class. Colbert's influence was evident in the creation of the colonial position of Intendant, who in essence served as Colbert's equivalent. Both the governor and Intendant were appointed by the Crown. A third position of authority was the bishop, who represented the Catholic Church. This triumvirate formed the Sovereign Council.

The Governor

The governor general held supreme authority. Almost without exception, he was a noble and a soldier. Aside from being titular ruler of the colony and representing the Crown, the governor was in charge of the military. Military officers in the colony could not marry without first securing his permission.

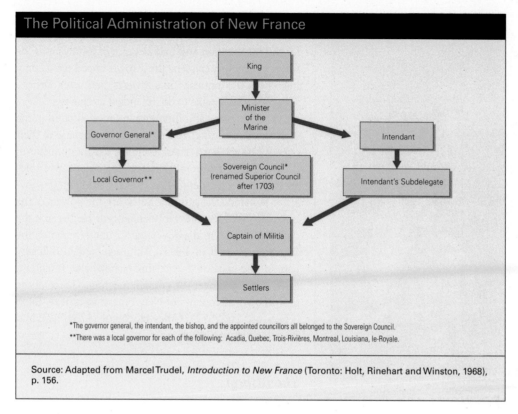

The Political Administration of New France

King

Minister of the Marine

Governor General*

Intendant

Local Governor**

Sovereign Council* (renamed Superior Council after 1703)

Intendant's Subdelegate

Captain of Militia

Settlers

*The governor general, the intendant, the bishop, and the appointed councillors all belonged to the Sovereign Council.

**There was a local governor for each of the following: Acadia, Quebec, Trois-Rivières, Montreal, Louisiana, le-Royale.

Source: Adapted from Marcel Trudel, *Introduction to New France* (Toronto: Holt, Rinehart and Winston, 1968), p. 156.

The governor also conducted diplomatic relations with the neighbouring First Nations and the English colonies. The administration of Daniel de Rémy de Courcelle, governor of New France from 1665 to 1672, was marked by important campaigns against the Iroquois. His successor, the Comte de Frontenac (1672–82 and 1689–98), spent much of his time dealing with the First Nations and with the English colonies.

The most celebrated governors of the eighteenth century included Philippe de Rigaud de Vaudreuil (1703–25) and his son, Pierre de Rigaud de Vaudreuil de Cavagnial (1755–60), the latter being the only Canadian-born governor of New France. The towns of Montreal and Trois-Rivières had local governors answerable to the governor general (who also served as the governor of the Quebec area). They functioned chiefly as military leaders. Claude de Ramezay, governor of Montreal in the early eighteenth century, remains one of the best-known local governors and his residence, the Château de Ramezay, built on Notre Dame Street in 1705, still stands.

The Intendant

The Intendant ranked second in the colonial hierarchy but in many ways, he was more influential in the administration. A skilled administrator with a good educational background and usually extensive legal training, he ran most of the daily affairs of New France, including responsibility for justice, public order, and finance. The Intendant managed the budgets of both the army and

Bishop François de Laval (1623–1708).

Source: Musée de la civilisation, collection du Séminaire de Québec. Portrait de Mgr François de Laval. Inconnu, d'après Claude Duflos. Vers 1788. Pierre Soulard, photographe. N° 1995.3480.

A portrait of Louis XIV (1643–1715) by Hyacinthe Rigaud, c. 1701.

Source: Louis XIV in Royal Costume, 1701 (oil on canvas), Hyacinthe Rigaud (1659–1743)/Louvre, Paris, France/ Giraudon/The Bridgeman Art Library International.

the colony. He headed the police and looked after road construction and maintenance. He was also responsible for the construction and maintenance of fortifications. As the population increased, the Crown appointed deputy intendants at Montreal, Trois-Rivières, and, later, Detroit. They were answerable to the Intendant at Quebec.

The governor and Intendant quarrelled often in the early years of royal government, largely because of their overlapping powers. These conflicts led the minister of the marine to define more clearly their respective roles and those of the other justice officers. Although the governor remained the supreme authority, the powers of the Intendant were considerably enhanced. He became the dominant figure in the Sovereign Council (renamed the Superior Council in 1703). Although ranked officially behind the governor and the bishop, the Intendant came to preside over the council meetings. Three of the best-known Intendants of New France were Jean Talon (1665–68, 1669–72), Gilles Hocquart (1731–48), and François Bigot (1748–60).

The Bishop

Under Louis XIV, there was a separation of church and state (an ideology and system called Gallicanism). The King and not the Pope was the head of the French Church. It was the King who nominated church officials and controlled religious orders.

The bishop was in charge of the spiritual affairs and well-being of New France. He played a role in the political life of the colony, even though the powers of the office were significantly reduced after 1663. When the Sovereign Council was first established, the bishop ranked behind the governor, reflecting the relationship of Louis XIV to the Pope in the Vatican. Thus, the first bishop, François de Laval, initially shared with the governor the responsibility of selecting the other council members from among the leading colonists. But after Laval clashed with the governor, he lost this right. Thereafter, the bishop's influence declined, and his attendance at the council became infrequent. The Crown respected the social and religious role of the Church, but opposed any political authority it might claim. Bishop Laval was responsible for creating the parish system after 1663 to serve the needs of the expanding colony.

Jean-Baptiste de La Croix de Chevrières de Saint-Vallier (1688–1727), who served for nearly forty years, followed Laval. He waged war on drunkenness, blasphemy, dancing, and immodest dress. The Church had long complained about the immorality of the colony. The lure of the fur trade—which the clergy argued drew the young men away from the colony where they could be observed and into the wilderness where they allegedly fell prey to the loose morals of the First Nations—was a constant source of frustration. But the priests and Jesuits also complained that the frontier environment in New France was creating a peasantry that lacked the discipline and respect of its counterpart in France. Complaints about the habitants fill the *Jesuit Relations*, covering such issues as men smoking and bringing their dogs to church to the parishioners not diligently paying the *tithe* (a tax to the church equalling one-tenth of the individual's earning). Laval had spoken against women appearing in church wearing fashionable gowns that revealed naked arms and bosoms, but Saint-Vallier went further and tried to stop women from wearing low-cut gowns even in their homes. The bishop also railed against the use of alcohol in the fur trade as a bartering item and a negotiation tool.

At the beginning of the period of royal government, Louis XIV and Colbert feared the excessive authority of the clergy in New France. The Jesuits had, in effect, run the colony for thirty years. Thus, the minister of the marine instructed the governor and the Intendant to subordinate the church to the authority of the state. After 1663, the King nominated the bishop and contributed 40 percent of the church's finances. When the parishioners complained about the tithe, and the Bishop recommended it being set at one-thirteenth of produce, it was raised to one-twenty-sixth. When Bishop Saint-Vallier replaced Laval, the parish system was in difficulty. There were only 21 priests residing in the parishes, and most had to live with parishioners because there was not enough money to construct rectories.

The Sovereign Council

The Sovereign Council, after 1703 known as the Superior Council, both made laws and heard criminal and civil cases. The members of the tribunal sat around a large table, with the governor, bishop, and Intendant at the head—the governor in the centre, the bishop on the governor's right, and the Intendant on the governor's left. As the population increased, the Council grew to seven members in 1675 and twelve in 1703. As the amount of litigation in the colony increased, the council restricted itself to legal functions, and the Intendant enacted legislation.

The Captain of Militia

Colbert also established the office of militia captain. In 1669, the Intendant organized the entire male population between the ages of 16 and 60 into militia units. He formed a company in each parish and appointed a captain from among the most respected habitants. The office carried with it no salary, but brought considerable status and prestige; the captains became the most influential men in their communities. In addition to drilling the militia, supervising their equipment, and leading them in battle, the captains acted locally as the Intendant's agents, communicating his regulations and ordinances to the habitants and ensuring they were carried out. They also

Historical reconstruction of the opening of the Sovereign Council, by Charles Huot.

Source: Commission de la Capitale Nationale.

directed the *corvées* for work on bridges and roads. During a corvée, even the local seigneur came under the militia captain's command. This new office thus prevented the seigneurs from becoming too powerful, in a sense parallelling the control Louis XIV maintained over his nobility at the palace in Versailles.

Public Meetings

The colony was to mirror the absolutist regime in France. Louis XIV ruled without calling parliament. Therefore, Colbert made no provision for local self-government. New France had no municipal governments, nor mayors or town councils. Furthermore, people could not call a meeting or arrange a public assembly. Government came from above, not from below. Even the magistrates of the Sovereign Council were appointed and paid stipends, and were, therefore, dependent on the governor and the Intendant. The only elected office in the late seventeenth century (and for the remainder of the French regime) was church warden.

Occasionally, the governor and the Intendant consulted the public on issues of general interest. They called together seventeen assemblies between 1672 and 1700. On at least one occasion, the Intendant subsequently acted on the assembly's requests. Thus, the people of New France had some say in the administration of their affairs, albeit very little. In 1709 in Quebec and in 1717 in Montreal, the governor and the Intendant also permitted the merchants to establish chambers of commerce. These bodies nominated a member to inform the governor and the Intendant of how best to promote commerce in their towns.

The Lower Courts

The lower courts in Quebec, Montreal, and Trois-Rivières stood below the Sovereign Council. The judges of these courts applied the municipal legislation drawn up by the Sovereign Council, such as regulations on street traffic, road maintenance, garbage disposal, and fire prevention. A few of the most populated seigneuries also had seigneurial courts, which heard minor civil disputes. In 1664 the law for the area around Paris, the so-called *coutume de Paris* (Custom of Paris), officially became the colony's legal code. The Civil Code in Quebec evolved from the *coutume*.

In reforming New France's justice system, Colbert constructed a system that would be provided with minimal expense to the state. First, he banned lawyers from practising in the colony; citizens argued their own civil cases in court. Notaries—not lawyers—drew up legal contracts. By 1700, the colony supported four notaries at Quebec, three at Montreal, and one at Trois-Rivières. Second, the Crown enforced a tariff of modest fees that legal officials, from judges down to bailiffs, could charge.

The courts operated as they did in France. When a crime was committed, the local magistrate or the attorney general of the Sovereign Council ordered the gathering of evidence. The judge, or a member of the Sovereign Council delegated by the attorney general, interrogated anyone thought to have knowledge of the crime. If the evidence revealed a suspect, that person was apprehended and put in jail. The judge or attorney general then interrogated the prisoner under oath (at this point, the suspect still had not been informed of the charge against him).

This form of interrogation was known as the *question ordinaire*. If, in important cases, the defendant proved reluctant to talk, torture could be used to extract a confession or the names of accomplices. This procedure was known as the *question extraordinaire* and was employed against at least 30 men and women during the century of royal government.[1] The *maître des hautes oeuvres*, or master of the means of torture, bound boards to the defendant's shins, inserted wedges, and then struck them with a hammer, painfully crushing the bones of the accused. After each hammer blow, the interrogators restated their questions until they believed the prisoner was telling the truth. According to legal historian Douglas Hay, "If the truth had to be sought in the bones, nerves and sinews of an unwilling witness, that was unfortunate," but the investigator "considered it much as a surgeon would his exploratory operation."[2]

If the Sovereign Council heard the trial, the attorney general received all the evidence and testimony, laid it before the court, and added a summation. The members of the council subsequently discussed the report and gave their opinions. The Intendant then delivered the verdict. The sentence was carried out either the same day or within a day or two.

Three categories of crimes existed in New France: crimes against God (heresy, blasphemy, sorcery); crimes against the Crown (treason, sedition, rebellion, desertion, duelling, counterfeiting); and crimes against person or property (murder, suicide, rape, slander, libel, theft, arson). Serious sentences were carried out in public to serve as a lesson. There were also three categories of punishment: capital (beheading, strangulation, burning at the stake, quartering, amputation of limbs, mutilation); infamous (jail, stocks, pillory, exile, loss of civil rights), and pecuniary (fines, confiscation of property). During the French regime, 85 people were executed.

Colbert's Economic Failures

With a new administrative structure established, Colbert sought capable men to fill the senior posts. For the restructuring of New France to be successful, the colony had to become more self-reliant. Colbert's objective was to create "a compact colony" in the St. Lawrence Valley. This colony would grow, develop, and prosper without further Crown expenditures. Intendant Jean Talon, a man who had been an Intendant in France as well, began investigating the colony's economic possibilities—discovering what the soil would grow, surveying the forests, and sponsoring expeditions to search for minerals. He also tried to develop a shipbuilding industry. The Crown sent skilled ship carpenters, tar makers, blacksmiths, and foundry workers, as well as the necessary supplies. Three ships were built, but the industry never became profitable. The imported skilled workers demanded high wages, iron had to be imported, and the industry required heavy capital outlays. In the end, ships cost much more to build in Canada than in France, and the Crown curtailed the program.

New France also failed to develop a significant overseas trade with the West Indies. The loss of two of Talon's ships at sea helped to cut short the experiment. Other difficulties arose as well. Ships out of New France could sail south only in the summer months—the hurricane season in southern waters. These ships had to run the gauntlet of English privateers in wartime and other nations' privateers at all times. As well, the Canadians had to compete with New England mariners, who could sell wheat and fish at lower prices year-round. For these reasons, New France failed to secure a foothold in the West Indies market.

Of the industries in New France, fishing offered the most promise. Colbert subsidized the necessary equipment. But Canadian fishers faced several disadvantages, the foremost being the failure to establish salt works in the colony. This meant a reliance on France for a supply of salt. In addition, merchants in France sent their ships directly to the Grand Banks, and they returned directly home without ever landing in New France and purchasing Canadian fish.

One of Talon's enterprises succeeded—the brewery at Quebec. Cheap beer brewed in the colony proved popular. Other industries he promoted included the production of hats and shoes. Unfortunately for Colbert's hopes, everything Canada produced, except for furs and beer, could be obtained more cheaply elsewhere. When Jean Talon left the colony in 1672, the industries he had promoted died. The Crown allocated no more funds because France had entered a costly war with the Dutch. New France had to depend solely on the fur trade, which remained its main economic activity.

Colonial administrators in New France also contributed to the failure of Colbert's "compact colony" ideal by using their positions to advance their own interests instead of those of the colony: "The idea that people with power should not use it to enrich themselves is a very modern notion.

The St. Maurice Forges as they stood in 1844.

Source: Library and Archives Canada/C-001241.

In the seventeenth and eighteenth centuries virtually all administrators of government—in Britain, France, and all their colonies—expected to gain personally from possession of their offices."[3]

Economic Development after 1713

In 1713, France and Britain signed the Treaty of Utrecht, which inaugurated a thirty-year truce. These years of peace enabled New France to consolidate itself economically and socially. Once again, the French government supported economic initiatives in New France. This time they proved more successful. The number of flour mills in the colony doubled between 1719 and 1734. The fishing industry also grew, with fish and seal oil becoming significant exports. Gilles Hocquart, the Intendant from 1731 to 1748, established tanneries at Quebec, Lévis, and Montreal.

The Crown also improved transportation. In 1737, the Intendant completed the "*Chemin du roi*" (King's Highway), which connected Montreal and Quebec. A return trip by water from Montreal to Quebec might take several weeks, while the trip by coach over the King's Highway could be completed in as little as nine days. The highway opened up new lands north of the St. Lawrence to settlement. It became the colony's lifeline in the summer of 1759, when the British fleet gained control of the St. Lawrence.

Private citizens also worked to develop the colony's industrial resources. Beginning in the 1720s, local contractors established small shipyards along the St. Lawrence. Intendant Gilles Hocquart helped with subsidies and assisted in establishing state-owned shipyards where workers were employed in sail making, rope manufacturing, tar works, foundries, sawmills, and tool and machinery making. He also encouraged the building of large ships, even though Canada's resources were better suited for small ones. In the 1740s, for example, the royal shipyard at Quebec constructed nine warships. On account of high labour costs, the shipyard cut back to only five naval vessels in the 1750s.

In 1729, François Poulin de Francheville established Canada's first heavy industry, the St. Maurice Forges, or ironworks, 15 kilometres north of Trois-Rivières. But by 1741, as a result of serious technical errors and lax administration, the company declared bankruptcy, at which point the Crown, which had given large subsidies, took control. Production under royal administration fluctuated greatly from year to year, but for a few years profits were reported. The ironworks employed about 100 workers, who produced sizable quantities of cooking pots, pans, and soup ladles, as well as cannons and cannonballs. They also made the first Canadian stoves.

By 1700, agriculture finally replaced the fur trade as the leading economic activity in New France. Three out of four Canadian families were involved in farming. The growth of agriculture transformed the colony's economic structure. Between 1706 and 1739, the population increased 250 percent and the amount of land under cultivation increased 430 percent. The colony became self-sufficient in wheat and flour. Wheat accounted for about three-quarters of the cultivated farmland and made up one-third of the colony's exports by the 1730s. The habitants also grew peas, oats, rye, barley, buckwheat, and maize. Surprisingly, the vegetable that in the early nineteenth century became the staple food of the habitants' diet was not grown in the colony: the English introduced the potato to the St. Lawrence Valley after 1760.

Market conditions limited production and the growth of livestock. The towns of New France were not large, and many town dwellers kept their own gardens and livestock. But, in the eighteenth century, an increase in the population and the opening of an export market improved the situation. Flour, biscuits, and peas were exported regularly to the new French fortress at Louisbourg on Île Royale (now Cape Breton Island) as well as to the French West Indies. The habitants needed to produce a surplus to pay church tithes and seigneurial dues and to purchase the things they could not make themselves.

The unlimited supply of land, and the high productivity of the soil, discouraged farmers from applying the intensive agricultural methods then commonly used in France, where land was scarce and expensive. When the good land became exhausted, the farmers cleared more with no concern for conservation. They avoided elaborate crop rotations, heavy manuring, and selective breeding of their cattle.

New France Society in the Eighteenth Century

About one-quarter of New France's inhabitants resided in towns during the eighteenth century. At the end of the French regime in 1760, nearly 8000 people lived in Quebec, with Montreal having only one-half of Quebec City's population. Quebec was the seaport and administrative capital; Montreal was a secondary town on the westernmost edge of French settlement. Trois-Rivières remained a small service centre with fewer than 1000 inhabitants.

Viewed from the St. Lawrence, the towns of New France looked impressive. The horizon was marked by Church spires and the roofs of church residences, as well as the homes of the governors and the Intendant, and the stone warehouses along the waterfront. Appearances, however, were deceiving. Well into the eighteenth century, pigs rooted among the refuse citizens

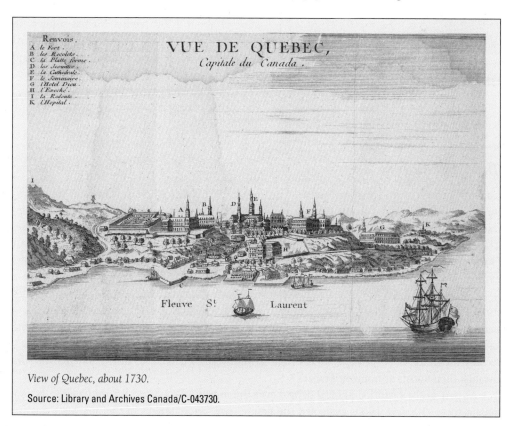

View of Quebec, about 1730.

Source: Library and Archives Canada/C-043730.

A French-Canadian couple in their Sunday clothes.

Source: Archives de la Ville de Montréal.

dumped in the narrow streets. On a few streets open sewers carried garbage down to the river during heavy rains and the uncobbled streets became quagmires. There was no street lighting.

Royal Administrators and Military Officers

Royal officials and military officers dominated life in Quebec, Montreal, and Trois-Rivières. The metropolitan French predominated in the Sovereign Council and held the top positions in the civil-service hierarchy. At the local level, a greater number of judges were born in the colony. The nobility kept alive the military and aristocratic values of Old France. In general, the sons of the nobles became military officers, obtaining commissions in the Troupes de la Marine, or colonial regular army.

The military formed a vital part of the community, especially considering that the St. Lawrence Valley had enjoyed only 50 years of complete freedom from war in the course of New France's 150-year existence. Every year, the Crown spent large sums for the maintenance of about 1500 regular French soldiers in New France, many of whom were stationed in the towns. Most of the soldiers were billeted in private homes. Within the army, tension arose between the French and the colonial-born officers. Colonial leaders enjoyed greater popularity with the troops than did the metropolitan French officers. Unlike the French soldiers, colonial troops had adapted to North American warfare based around Aboriginal tactics.

The Merchants

The merchants, or bourgeoisie, constituted an important social group in New France. The metropolitan French controlled the major commercial operations connected with the profitable wholesale trade. They had the necessary funds and contacts to obtain adequate supplies in France. These merchants provided most of the imported manufactured goods at Louisbourg and at Quebec. French merchants and their Quebec agents handled about two-thirds of the colony's external trade.[4] The colonial merchants dominated only the smaller-scale retail operations.

Colonial merchants dominated in smaller-scale trading, such as the fur trade. The companies usually consisted of three or four partners who obtained a three-year lease on the trade at a particular fur-trading post, and shared in the profits or losses according to the percentage of the capital they had invested. The partners obtained trade goods from the large Montreal merchants, usually on credit at 30 percent interest. These Montreal merchants in turn marketed the furs through their agents at home in France.

As part of the historiographical debate over the impact of the conquest on Quebec, historians in the 1950s and 1960s evaluated the nature, size, and strength of the merchant class in

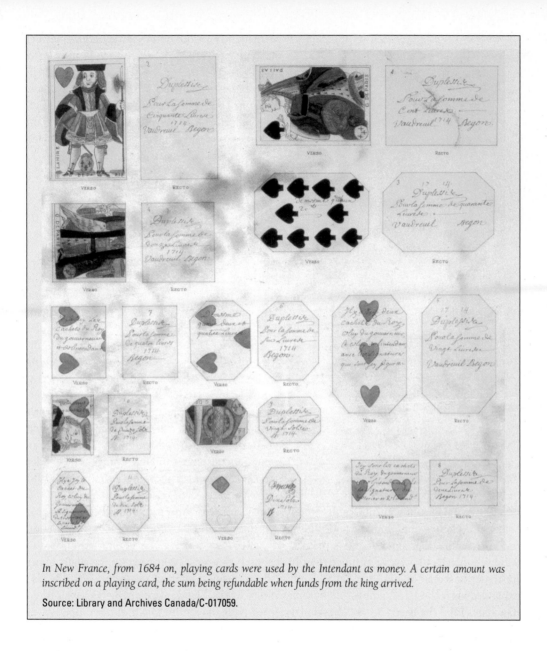

In New France, from 1684 on, playing cards were used by the Intendant as money. A certain amount was inscribed on a playing card, the sum being refundable when funds from the king arrived.

Source: Library and Archives Canada/C-017059.

New France. Historians questioned whether New France ever possessed a significant class of French entrepreneurs. If it did, as Maurice Séguin, Guy Frégault, and Michel Brunet claimed, the conquest "decapitated" the colony of its elites and allowed them to be replaced by English merchants. But Jean Hamelin and Fernand Ouellet contended that the existence of monopolies and state control over the economy stunted the development of a national bourgeoisie. There was no "decapitation."

Protestants in the Colony

In an attempt to avoid the religious division and wars that had long plagued France, Louis XIV attempted to turn New France into a strictly Catholic colony. As supreme protector of the Church, Protestants, Jews, and Jansenists (puritanical Catholics) were banned from settling

A portrait presumed to be that of Marie Charlotte Denys de la Ronde, a Canadian woman who ran several commercial enterprises in New France.

Source: Musée du Chateau Ramezay, Montreal C-009333. Copyright: Syndicat de la Propriété Artistique, 12, rue Henner, Paris IXe.

permanently in the colony. They could neither marry in New France nor bring a wife and family from France. The limited tolerance for French Protestants, recognized in the Edict of Nantes, ended in 1685 when the king revoked the edict. Although in the 1740s a few French Protestant import–export merchants were tacitly allowed to live at Quebec, they remained outsiders in the colony.

Women in the Colony

Historian Jan Noel argues that a number of women in New France enjoyed more liberties than their counterparts in France. The Catholic clergy certainly felt that women in the colony took more liberties in their dress and appearance. But even within the Church, the examples of Marie de l'Incarnation and Marguerite Bourgeoys of Montreal—the founder of the teaching order the Sisters of the Congregation of Notre-Dame—demonstrate that these *"femmes favorisées"*[5] enjoyed considerable influence. Girls educated by the female religious orders often received a superior education to both girls in France and also boys in New France. The gender imbalance provided the *filles du roi* more influence than peasant women in France.

Elite women in eighteenth-century New France did frequently run small businesses that sold cloth, clothes, furs, brandy, and utensils. During their husbands' absences in the interior, the fur traders' wives and daughters often looked after their stores and accounts. A number of widowed merchants' wives continued their husbands' businesses. Well versed in the affairs of her fur-trader husband, Marie-Anne Barbel continued his business after his death in 1745. She also expanded his real-estate holdings and began a pottery works. She was one of Quebec's well-to-do merchants until the Seven Years' War ruined her fur-trade operation. Much of her property was destroyed in the British bombardment of Quebec's Lower Town in 1759.

Other women also began successful commercial careers. Agathe de Saint-Père, Madame de Repentigny, headed a textile firm—New France's first—in the early eighteenth century. This energetic businesswoman ransomed nine English weavers held prisoner by the First Nations and hired them to teach Canadian apprentices the trade. Soon, she had twenty looms operating, turning out coarse cloth and canvas. Marie-Charlotte Denys de la Ronde, the widow of Claude de Ramezay, governor of Montreal, operated a sawmill, a brick factory, and a tile works. Her daughter, Louise de Ramezay, owned a flour mill, a tannery, and sawmills. After François Poulin de Francheville's death in 1733, his widow, Thérèse de Couagne, continued to operate the St. Maurice ironworks, at least until 1735.

Throughout New France, married women shared in the work of their husbands. At busy times of the year, they helped in the fields. In the urban areas, the wives of artisans and merchants assisted their spouses. Both rural and urban women often kept the family accounts and managed the servants (if there were any) or the apprentices, in the case of artisans.

But these few examples aside, by the eighteenth century the status of women in New France came to resemble more closely that in France. According to Allan Greer, "In a general sense, men ruled in New France, just as they did in old France."[6] Under the *coutume de Paris*, married women had a status far inferior to their husbands. Marriage was considered sacrosanct. Divorce did not exist in Catholic New France. In the case of abusive relationships, legal separations were difficult to obtain. According to Peter Moogk, "Since wife beating was tolerated in this society, occasional physical abuse was not sufficient proof of a murderous hatred…. Women bore the burden of preserving the union of husband and wife, and it could be a heavy yoke to bear."[7]

The Engagés in the Fur Trade

Small-scale fur traders and voyageurs, or *engagés*, ranked below the colonial retail merchants. They carried the products of the country to the town and vice versa; the voyageurs, under contract as engagés (as was increasingly the case after 1700), travelled thousands of kilometres, bearing trade goods for the First Nations and bringing furs to the St. Lawrence Valley from the distant interior.

Every year, 400 to 500 people received permission to enter the fur trade around the Great Lakes or in the upper Mississippi Valley. Many more went without permission. The trading firms recruited the majority around Montreal.[8] The engagés tended to be habitants from rural areas seeking to supplement their farm incomes.

Tradespeople

The colony had about 2000 trades workers by the 1740s. The most numerous in the construction industry were carpenters and masons; in transportation, navigators and carters; and in the food industry, bakers and butchers. As a rule, crafts workers owned all their own tools and worked in small workshops attached to their homes. The French authorities often accused habitant workers of being headstrong and insubordinate. Their self-confidence and independence were frowned upon by the administrators from Old France, where the average person had little, if any, personal freedom or opportunity for personal advancement.

The Habitant Culture

The habitants made up the largest group in the colony. By the 1740s, the oldest seigneuries had two (in some cases, three) rows of farms stretching back from the river. The habitants' lots, or *rotures*, were rectangular in shape and generally had a ratio of width to length of one to ten. The habitants paid no direct taxes, apart from the occasional tax for local improvements, whereas in France the peasants paid between one-third and one-half of their income in taxes. In addition, the habitants paid only half the rate for the church tithe that was required at the time in northern France.

The majority of the habitants ate well. They enjoyed almost daily pork and game, particularly venison and wild hare. Gradually, however, the habitants relied less and less on wild game as it became harder to obtain near the settled areas. The pig remained a mainstay of the diet because it was inexpensive to keep (it would eat anything from acorns to kitchen scraps) and because, as the old folk saying in both France and New France put it, "You can eat everything but the squeal." Fish formed part of the core diet of the French settlers, as did buckwheat, a hardy cereal used to make bread, pancakes, and porridges. Maple syrup was used for sweetening.

Vegetables from the garden, particularly peas and *fèves* (the large, tough-fibred beans from Normandy that were brought to the St. Lawrence Valley), were favourites. Dried peas and beans could be stored for years and then made into soups. And because legumes absorbed the flavour of either smoked or salted pork fat well, the habitants frequently used pork in their recipes for pea soup and baked beans. The habitants also enjoyed such fruits as apples, plums, and cherries. Apple trees, brought from the northwest of France, thrived in the cool, moist climate of New France. Wild fruits, especially raspberries, red and black currants, and cranberries, were there for the picking.

Wealthy habitants could obtain expensive tea and coffee from the traders. Milk, in contrast, was cheap and plentiful. Cider was drunk at most meals. The well-to-do could afford wine imported from France, while the habitants drank the cheaper beer brewed in the colony or, indeed, beer that they brewed themselves.

The lives of the habitants centred on their farms, which they cultivated with their families' help. The *curé* and the captain of militia served as the habitants' links with the outside world. As in France, the curés registered the births, deaths, and marriages in their parishes. Farmers in New France detested being called "peasants." As the Finnish traveller Pehr Kalm noted in 1749, "The gentlemen and ladies, as well as the poorest peasants and their wives, are called Monsieur and Madame." The habitants had more personal freedom than their counterparts in France. The royal officials in New France repeatedly complained that the independent-minded habitants always pleased themselves and paid little attention to the administrators' directives.

The Church in New France

During the years of royal government, and particularly during the years of the great migration from France in the late 1660s and early 1670s, the Church suffered from an acute shortage of priests. As late as 1683, the Intendant reported that three-quarters or more of the habitants heard mass only four times a year. This problem remained until well into the nineteenth century.

The parish priests played an important role in those communities they could regularly visit. As sociologist Jean-Charles Falardeau notes, "The Canadian curés were pastors of communities lacking resources, organization and, most of the time, local leaders. They soon became also the real leaders of these communities."[9]

Yet historians such as W.J. Eccles and Cornelius Jaenen, while not denying the Church's central role, take a different stance. They stress that the population of New France demonstrated a surprising independence from the Church. When, for instance, the Crown decided that the populace should pay tithes (or ecclesiastical taxes) for the support of a secular clergy, and the bishop stipulated that it be at the rate of one-thirteenth of the produce of the land, the people protested. The bishop reduced his demand to one-twentieth, and eventually had to accept only one twenty-sixth of the grain. To make up the difference, the Crown provided the clergy with annual subsidies. Only when more land came into production in the early eighteenth century did many parish priests become relatively well off.

The frequent *ordonnances* of the Intendant directed to the inhabitants of the parishes with priests provide further proof of the independence of many *Canadiens* from the clergy. The ordinances prohibited walking out of church as soon as the priest began his sermon, standing in the lobby arguing, brawling during the service, and even bringing dogs into church.

The clergy did, however, enjoy the respect of the community for their services. During the early history of New France, the clergy were actively involved in teaching, nursing, and other charitable work. In 1760, the nearly 100 diocesan or parish priests in the colony were assisted by 30 Sulpicians (a religious order that had begun work in the colony in 1657), 25 Jesuits, 24 Récollets (who had returned in 1670), and more than 200 nuns belonging to six religious communities. The clerically administered social institutions endured, in many cases, into the twentieth century.

Education and Charity

The Church controlled schooling in the colony and all the religious communities assumed some responsibility for education. Urban dwellers benefited most, as most schools were located in the major towns. In a study of three rural parishes in mid-eighteenth-century New France, Allan Greer discovered that only 10 percent of the men and women could sign their marriage act. In the urban centre of Trois-Rivières, in contrast, it was approximately 50 percent.[10] The Quebec Seminary ran the Petit séminaire, the most important elementary school in the colony. The Jesuit College at Quebec provided male students with a postsecondary education equivalent to that which could be obtained in a provincial town in France. The Congrégation de Notre-Dame and the Ursuline order established elementary schools for girls in the larger centres.

The Church also provided welfare services and maintained charitable institutions. Three female and two male religious communities became involved in this work. Each of the three principal towns in New France had a Bureau of the Poor, which served as a relief centre and employment agency. Those persons who were too elderly or too infirm to work, and who were not being cared for by their children at home, were placed in institutions at Montreal or Quebec, along with the chronically ill, the insane, and women of "loose morals" (the latter were put there to be reformed by the Hospital nuns). To help pay for these institutional services and for their hospitals, the Church held initially about one-tenth of the seigneurial lands in the St. Lawrence Valley, and by the 1750s about one-quarter of the land. In 1760, more than one-third of New France's population lived on Church seigneuries, providing the clergy with substantial revenue.

Marguerite Bourgeoys (1620–1700) by Pierre LeBer.
Source: © Collection Musée Marguerite-Bourgeoys.

Popular Religion

Popular religion remained strong in New France. Many habitants believed in magic and witchcraft. The colony, however, never knew the hysteria that swept through parts of New England in the 1690s, as exemplified by the infamous witch hunts of Salem. The clergy frequently performed exorcisms on individuals with the aid of prayers, candles, and holy water, and refused them burial in sanctified ground, but no executions occurred in New France as punishment for occult practices.

A Local Clergy

Gradually, the clergy of New France became localized. A native-born clergy had long been an objective of the Church. The seminary in Quebec trained priests at its theological college. During the eighteenth century, the native-born increasingly staffed the parishes in New France.

La Chasse-galerie (1906) by Henri Julien.

Source: Jean-Guy Kérouac/Musée nationale des beaux-arts du Québec/34.254.

By 1760, the colony had about 100 parishes, most of them run by diocesan clergy, about four-fifths of whom were born locally. Tensions, however, existed between the native-born clergy at the lower levels of the Church's administration and the French-born clergy who dominated at the top.

The First Nations Population

Despite the efforts of the Crown to create a monolithic culture, New France was a relatively diverse society with a considerable First Nations population and a small African community. The Aboriginal presence was greatest in the Montreal area, where, from the 1670s to the 1710s, the "mission" First Nations outnumbered the French settlers. Several thousand Aboriginal people lived in four major *réductions*, or missions, in the St. Lawrence Valley in the late seventeenth and early eighteenth centuries: the Hurons at Lorette, near Quebec; the Abenakis from present-day Maine at Saint-François, east of Montreal; and the Iroquois at Sault St. Louis (Kahnawake) and at the Lake of Two Mountains (Kanesatake or Oka), both west of Montreal. The Catholic missionaries did not insist on amalgamation with French civilization. As long as Aboriginal customs did not conflict with Christianity, they were tolerated.

These First Nations communities, however, served a practical purpose. They acted as a buffer against Iroquois and English invaders. But their existence had an unanticipated side effect. It expanded the contraband fur trade between New France and the American colonies, in which both the Catholic Iroquois and the Abenakis participated. The "mission" First Nations did not consider themselves subjects of French law.

The Christian First Nations of New France sometimes raised the children of colonists, as a consequence of the fact that unmarried pregnant women in the colony faced prosecution as criminals.[11] Some women concealed their pregnancies, then left their babies to perish. The death penalty could be imposed in such cases. Some unwed mothers gave their babies to the Aboriginals to raise instead. The midwives who assisted these women with their deliveries helped them escape detection. Aboriginals also adopted and raised American children who had been taken as captives during Franco-Indian raids. At Kahnawake, the captives received Christian and Mohawk names, and were assimilated into the community. Many assumed "leadership roles in both the political and military sphere."[12]

The French needed the resident Aboriginals for protection and assistance in their raids against the English, so they could not antagonize them by rigorously enforcing French laws. Although they regarded the Aboriginals in the colony as French subjects, they granted them special status. The French avoided the question of whether the First Nations were subject to French law "by tacitly granting [them] something akin to diplomatic immunity." The French did not usually prosecute them for breaches of the peace, "for one good reason; to have attempted to do so with any degree of vigour would have alienated the Indians, and this the French could not afford to do."[13]

Slavery

The legal status of slaves in New France was uncertain. In 1709, the Intendant proclaimed slavery legal. A slave class existed in the colony to help meet the acute labour shortage. Upon several occasions, merchants requested that the Crown dispatch African slaves to meet this labour situation.

From the late 1680s, Aboriginal slaves from the upper Mississippi Valley began arriving in the colony on a regular basis. These *panis*, or Pawnees (the name of a single nation was used despite the fact that the slaves were taken from many other groups as well), were sold to the French by other First Nations. Africans captured during raids on the English colonies or brought in from the French West Indies also increased the number of slaves in the colony. The African slaves were sold at an average price twice as high as that received for the more numerous Aboriginal captives because Africans had greater resistance to disease than did the First Nations. Aboriginal slaves were also

A Huron couple in the mid-eighteenth century.

Source: Archives de la Ville do Montreal. Philéas Gagnon Collection, BM7, 42500 (034-02-04-01).

more likely to run away. The average price of a black slave was 900 livres. In general, however, it was assumed that African slaves were poorly suited to the northern climate.

Montreal, the centre of New France's fur trade, had the largest number of slaves in the colony—several hundred by the mid-eighteenth century. Slaves were traded like cattle, at the marketplace and at auctions. Three-quarters lived in towns, where they worked mainly as domestic servants. The governors owned slaves: Rigaud de Vaudreuil, governor from 1703 to 1725, owned 11 slaves, while the Marquis de Beauharnois, in office from 1726 to 1746, owned 27. But the major slave owners were merchants, traders, and the clergy. Aboriginal and African slaves also worked at the convents and hospitals operated by nuns in Quebec and Montreal.

While no exact census of New France's slave population exists, local records reveal that approximately 3600 slaves lived in the colony from its origin to 1759. Of these, about two-thirds were Aboriginal and one-third were African. They lived brutally short lives: for Aboriginal slaves, the average age at death was about 18, and for Africans, 25 (compared to 50 for white colonists).

The Code Noir dictated the status of slaves throughout the French Empire. According to its provisions, slaves could be bought and sold as property, and could be inherited, but their owners had an obligation to provide the bare essentials, including food, clothes, and shelter. Slaves had to become Roman Catholics. Despite being property, slaves could be punished but not imprisoned or executed without recourse to the courts. Slaves were encouraged to marry with the permission of their masters, but their "produce" (their children) also became the owner's property. It was illegal to sexually exploit female slaves, and children could not be sold separately from their parents until they reached adulthood. This provision did not prevent owners from exercising the *droit de seigneur*, and mixed-blood children were common in families who owned slaves.

Marie-Joseph-Angélique

Marie-Joseph-Angélique, an African household slave of François Poulin de Francheville (a wealthy Montreal merchant and part owner of the St. Maurice ironworks), was about 21 years old when baptized on June 28, 1730. She gave birth to three children by César, the African slave of Ignace Gamelin, a business associate of Francheville. Twins followed a year later.

Like many slaves in New France, Angélique did domestic work. She washed dishes, cleaned house, and ran errands. Her meals were basic, and she slept in a corner of the kitchen, on the floor. Montreal, the centre of New France's fur trade, had the largest number of slaves in the colony—several hundred by the mid-eighteenth century.

Early in 1734, Angélique ran away with Claude Thibault, a French-Canadian servant in the Francheville household. Captured by the authorities, she was sent back to her owner, Madame Francheville, Thérèse de Couagne, now a widow because her husband had died in November 1733. Upon her return, Angélique's conflicts with Madame Francheville continued. Finally, Madame Francheville decided to sell the slave woman to a plantation in the West Indies as soon as the ice broke up and navigation resumed.

On the evening of April 10, 1734, fire broke out in the Francheville house, which stood near the Hôtel-Dieu Hospital. The fire spread quickly, and within minutes Montreal became a fiery inferno. The blaze, Montreal's worst disaster since the Iroquois attacks, destroyed 46 houses, as well as the hospital. Fearful of being sold, Angélique was accused of starting the fire

Marie-Joseph-Angélique. Painting by Alan Daniel.

Source: © Alan Daniel

to distract her owner, allowing her, in the confusion, to escape south with Claude to New England; however, she was caught not far from Montreal.

On June 4, the Montreal court read its judgment. Angélique would first be interrogated under torture to reveal her accomplice. She was then required to make a full apology for the fire, have her hand cut off, and be burnt alive. An appeal to the Superior Council in Quebec, the colony's court of appeal, moderated the sentence slightly. After torture to reveal her accomplice, she was to be taken to the parish church in a rubbish cart to confess her guilt. Immediately afterward, she would be hanged and her body burnt.

The authorities carried out the sentence in Montreal on June 21. But Angélique confessed her guilt only during the fourth round of torture. At no point did she reveal the name of an accomplice. She was hanged, her body burned, and her ashes were thrown into the wind. The authorities never found Claude Thibault.

The Rise of a *Canadien* Identity

By the early eighteenth century, the colonists called themselves *Canadiens*. Some families had already resided in the colony for two or three generations. A new people, self-confident and increasingly conscious of their separation from the French in France, emerged. As well, the regional dialects of France eventually died out in the St. Lawrence Valley, as the newcomers from various areas of France intermingled, settling together in one area and speaking a common dialect. They spoke *canadien–français*, a language with its own distinct expressions to describe Canadian realities—for example, *poudrerie* (drifting or powdering of snow), *cabane à sucre* (a cabin used at maple sugar time), and First Nations words, such as *canoë* and *toboggan*.

SUMMARY

By 1754, New France's population had reached 55 000. What had begun as a fragment of Old France became a new community in Canada. Little by little, the French had become *Canadiens*, with values, manners, and attitudes that differentiated them more and more from the metropolitan French. The *Canadiens* resented the assumption of superiority by the military and ecclesiastical leaders of Old France. The French officer Louis-Antoine de Bougainville, who came to Quebec in 1757, was struck by the increasing differences between the French and the *Canadiens*: "We seem to belong to another, even an enemy, nation."[14]

NOTES

1. André Lachance, "Tout sur la torture," *Le magazine Maclean*, December 1966, p. 38.

2. Douglas Hay, *The Meanings of the Criminal Law in Quebec, 1764–1774*, in Louis A. Knafla, ed., *Crime and Criminal Justice in Europe and Canada* (Waterloo, ON: Wilfrid Laurier University Press, 1981), p. 77.

3. Michael Bliss, *Northern Enterprise: Five Centuries of Canadian Business* (Toronto: McClelland & Stewart, 1987), p. 44.

4. Bliss, p. 70.

5. Jan Noel, "New France: Les femmes favorisées," in R. Douglas Francis and Donald B. Smith, eds., *Readings in Canadian History: Pre-Confederation*, 6th ed. (Toronto: Nelson Thomson Learning, 2002), pp. 91–110.

6. Allan Greer, *The People of New France* (Toronto: University of Toronto Press, 1997), p. 74.

7. Peter N. Moogk, *La Nouvelle France: The Making of French Canada—A Cultural History* (East Lansing: Michigan State University Press, 2000), pp. 229, 231.

8. Gratien Allaire, "Fur Trade Engagés, 1701–1745," in Thomas C. Buckley, ed., *Rendez-vous: Selected Papers of the North American Fur Trade Conference*, 1981 (St. Paul, MN: North American Fur Trade Conference, 1984), p. 22.

9. Jean-Charles Falardeau, "The Seventeenth-Century Parish in French Canada," in Marcel Rioux and Yves Martin, eds., *French-Canadian Society*, vol. 1 (Toronto: McClelland & Stewart, 1964), p. 27.

10. Allan Greer, "The Pattern of Literacy in Quebec, 1745–1899," *Histoire sociale/Social History* 11(22) (November 1978): 299.

11. Peter N. Moogk, "*Les Petits Sauvages*: The Children of Eighteenth-Century New France," in Joy Parr, ed., *Childhood and Family in Canadian History* (Toronto: McClelland & Stewart, 1982), p. 27.

12. Gerald R. Alfred, *Heeding the Voices of Our Ancestors: Kahnawake Mohawk Politics and the Rise of Native Nationalism* (Toronto: Oxford University Press, 1995), p. 200.

13. W. J. Eccles, *The Canadian Frontier, 1534–1760* (Toronto: Holt, Rinehart and Winston, 1969), p. 78.

14. Quoted by Guy Frégault, *Canada: The War of the Conquest*, Margaret M. Cameron, trans. (Toronto: Oxford University Press, 1969), p. 64. On this important point, see the comments of George F. G. Stanley in *New France: The Last Phase, 1744–1760* (Toronto: McClelland & Stewart, 1968), p. 272.

RELATED READINGS

Module 3, "Seigneurial Tenure in Early Quebec, Seventeenth to the Nineteenth Century," in *Visions: The Canadian History Modules Project: Pre-Confederation*, offers a useful general introduction to New France. See specifically "The Feudal Burden" by Allan Greer and Colin Coates' "Seigneurial Landscapes," pages 118–142.

BIBLIOGRAPHY

Allan Greer provides a good introduction to the social history of New France in *The People of New France* (Toronto: University of Toronto Press, 1997). For other overviews, consult Dale Miquelon, *The First Canada: To 1791* (Toronto: McGraw-Hill Ryerson, 1994); Jacques Mathieu, *La nouvelle-france: Les français en Amérique du Nord XVIe–XVIIIe siècle* (Quebec: Les Presses de l'Université Laval, 1991); and John A. Dickinson and Brian Young, *A Short History of Quebec*, 3rd ed. (Montreal/Kingston: McGill-Queen's University Press, 2003), pp. 3–104. More detailed treatments include W.J. Eccles, *Canada Under Louis XIV, 1663–1701* (Toronto: McClelland & Stewart, 1964); and Dale Miquelon, *New France, 1701–1744* (Toronto: McClelland & Stewart, 1987). Older works include W. J. Eccles, *The Canadian Frontier, 1534–1760* (Toronto: Holt, Rinehart and Winston, 1969), and his *France in America*, rev. ed. (Markham, ON: Fitzhenry & Whiteside, 1990).

Allan Greer's new work, especially "National, Transnational, and Hypernational Historiographies: New France Meets Early American History," in the *Canadian Historical Review*, December 2010: 695–724, explores transnational examinations of North American history. Another transnational consideration is Colin G. Calloway's *The Scratch of a Pen: 1763 and the Transformation of America* (New York: Oxford University Press, 2007). Jay Gitlin's *The Bourgeois Frontier: French Towns, French Traders, and American Expansion* (New Haven: Yale University Press, 2010) expands the geographical considerations of New France.

Two bibliographical works for all aspects of New France's history, particularly its social and economic past, are Thomas Wien, "Canada and the *Pays d'en haut*, 1600–1700," in M. Brook Taylor, ed., *Canadian History: A Reader's Guide*, vol. 1, *Beginnings to Confederation* (Toronto: University of Toronto Press, 1994), pp. 33–75; and Jacques Rouillard, ed., *Guide d'histoire du Québec du régime français à nos jours: Bibliographie commentée* (Montreal: Éditions du Méridien, 1991). See also Patricia Simpson's *Marguerite Bourgeoys and Montreal, 1640–1665* (Montreal/Kingston: McGill-Queen's University Press, 1997) and Patricia Simpson, *Marguerite Bourgeoys and the Congregation of Notre Dame, 1665–1670* (Montreal/Kingston: McGill-Queen's University Press 2005).

Michael Bliss reviews the economic life of New France in *Northern Enterprise: Five Centuries of Canadian Business* (Toronto: McClelland & Stewart, 1987). Kenneth J. Banks explores the importance of communications to the maintenance of French imperialism in *Chasing Empire Across the Sea: Communications and the State in the French Atlantic, 1713–1763* (Montreal/Kingston: McGill-Queen's University Press, 2006). Twenty-two essays by John F. Bosher, chiefly on the business history of the French colony, appear in his *Business and Religion in the Age of New France, 1600–1760* (Toronto: Canadian Scholars' Press, 1994). A business history is Dale Miquelon's *Dugard of Rouen: French Trade to Canada and the West Indies, 1729–1770* (Montreal/Kingston: McGill-Queen's University Press, 1978). Martin Fournier has written a biography of one of the best-known coureurs de bois of New France, *Pierre-Esprit Radisson: Merchant Adventurer, 1636–1701*, translated by Mary Ricard (Montreal/Kingston: McGill-Queen's University Press, 2001). A study of the fur trade's voyageur work force is Carolyn Podruchny's *Making the Voyageur World: Travellers and Traders in the North American Fur Trade* (Toronto: University of Toronto Press, 2006). Jan Noel has written "'Nagging Wife' Revisited: Women and the Fur Trade in New France," *French Colonial History* 7 (2006): 45–60. For a look at economics and social class, see Fernand Ouellet, *Economy, Class, and Nation in Quebec: Interpretive Essays*, translated and edited by Jacques A. Barbier (Toronto: Pearson Education, 1991).

Several important articles by W. J. Eccles have been reprinted in his *Essays on New France* (Toronto: Oxford University Press, 1987). Louise Dechêne describes Montreal in the seventeenth century in *Habitants and Merchants in Seventeenth Century Montreal*, translated by Liana Vardi (Montreal/Kingston: McGill-Queen's University Press, 1992). See also Sylvie Depatie et al., eds., *Habitants et Marchands, Twenty Years Later: Reading the History of Seventeenth- and Eighteenth-Century Canada* (Montreal/Kingston: McGill-Queen's University Press, 1998). John Hare, Marc Lafrance, and David Thiery Ruddel review urban life at Quebec in *Histoire de la ville de Québec, 1608–1871* (Montreal: Boréal Express, 1987). André Lachance has written a study of urban life in the French regime, *La vie urbaine en Nouvelle-France* (Montreal: Boréal Express, 1987). Later contributions by the same author include his two books *Juger et punir en Nouvelle-France* (Montreal: Libre Expression, 2000) and *Vivre, aimer et mourir en Nouvelle-France* (Montreal: Libre Expression, 2000). Peter N. Moogk's *La Nouvelle France: The Making of French-Canada: A Cultural History* (East Lansing: Michigan State University Press, 2000), a series of exploratory articles on various aspects of French-Canadian culture before 1760, is invaluable. See also his article "The Liturgy of Humiliation, Pain, and Death: The Execution of Criminals in New France," *Canadian Historical Review* 88(1) (March 2007): 89–112.

For further information on other aspects of the social history of New France, see the following pamphlets published by the Canadian Historical Association: Marcel Trudel, *The Seigneurial Regime* (Ottawa: 1956); W.J. Eccles, *The Government of New France* (Ottawa: 1965); and Cornelius J. Jaenen, *The Role of the Church in New France* (Ottawa: 1985). Jaenen's study of religious life in New France is also titled *The Role of the Church in New France* (Toronto: McGraw-Hill Ryerson, 1976). Several important essays on New France's society appear in Fernand Ouellet, *Economy, Class and Nation in Quebec: Interpretive Essays*, edited and translated by Jacques A. Barbier (Toronto: Copp Clark Pitman, 1991). For a look at social class, see Francois-Joseph Ruggiu, "La noblesse du Canada aux XVIIe et XVIIIe siècles," *Histoire, économie et société* 27(4) (2008): 67–85. R. Cole Harris, in *The Seigneurial System in Canada: A Geographical Study*, 2nd ed. (Montreal/Kingston: McGill-Queen's University Press, 1984), reviews the seigneurial system. Roger Magnuson examines schooling in *Education in New France* (Montreal/Kingston: McGill-Queen's University Press, 1992).

For a view of New France in 1749, see Pehr Kalm's *Travels into North America*, 2 vols. (New York: Dover, 1966). An account of early French-Canadian food and cooking customs is Jay A. Anderson's "The Early Development of French-Canadian Food Ways," in Edith Fowke, ed., *Folklore of Canada* (Toronto: McClelland & Stewart, 1976), pp. 91–99. For a look at the early pioneers of New France, see Hubert Charbonneau et al., *The First French Canadians: Pioneers in the St. Lawrence Valley* (Newark/London/Toronto: University of Delaware Press and Associated University Presses, 1993). For a look at culture in New France, see Leslie Choquette, *Frenchmen into Peasants: Modernity and Tradition in the Peopling of French Canada* (Cambridge, MA: Harvard University Press, 1997). For more information on the story of Angelique, see Afua Cooper, *The Hanging of Angelique: The Untold Story of Canadian Slavery and the Burning of Old Montréal* (Toronto: HarperCollins, 2006).

For the activities of women in New France, consult Micheline Dumont et al., *Quebec Women: A History* (Toronto: Women's Press, 1987); and Lilianne Plamondon, "A Businesswoman in New France: Marie-Anne Barbel, The Widow Fornel," in Veronica Strong-Boag and Anita Clair Fellman, eds., *Rethinking Canada: The Promise of Women's History* (Toronto: McClelland & Stewart, 1986), pp. 45–58. An overview is "Women in New France," Ch. 2 of Alison Prentice et al., *Canadian Women: A History* (Toronto: Harcourt Brace, 1996), pp. 33–57, but the fullest account appears in Allan Greer, *The People of New France*, pp. 86–88. The best study of the "King's Daughters" is Yves Landry, *Les filles du roi au XVIIe siècle* (Montreal: Leméac, 1992). See too Jan Noel, *Women in New France* (Ottawa: Canadian Historical Association, 1998). In the article "Caste and Clientage in an Eighteenth-Century Quebec Convent," *Canadian Historical Review* 82 (2001): 465–90, Noel examines the influence of convents in New France. Noel has also edited an interesting collection of articles, *Race and Gender in the Northern Colonies* (Toronto: Canadian Scholars Press, 2000), that contains essays on women in New France and New England. Karen Anderson examines the treatment of Aboriginal women in *Chain Her by One Foot: The Subjugation of Native Women in Seventeenth Century New France* (New York: Routledge, 1991). See also Saliha Belmessous, "Assimilation and Racialism in Seventeenth- and Eighteenth-Century French Colonial Policy." *American Historical Review* 110(2) (2005): 322–49. For a further look at the Jesuits, see Carole

Blackburn, *Harvest of Souls: The Jesuit Mission and Colonialism in North America 1632–1650* (Montreal/ Kingston: McGill-Queen's University Press, 2000), and Katherine E. Lawn and Claudio R. Salvucci, eds., *Women in New France: Extracts from the* Jesuit Relations (Bristol: Evolution Publishing 2004).

See also Rachel Major, "Les jésuites chez les Hurons en 1648–49," *La revue canadienne des etudes autochtones* 26(8)1 (2006): 53–70. For a look at religious conversion in New France, see Leslie Choquette, "Religious Conversion in New France: The Case of Amerindians and Immigrants Compared," *Quebec Studies* 40 (2005–6): 97–110. Josette Brun examines gender and the family in her article "Gender, Family and Mutual Assistance in New France: Widows, Widowers, and Orphans in Eighteenth Century Quebec," in *Mapping the Margins: The Family and Social Discipline in Canada, 1700–1975*, Nancy Christie and Michael Gauvreau, eds. (Montreal/Kingston: McGill-Queen's University Press, 2004). For a look at the relationship between women and the Church, see Elizabeth Rapley, *The Devotes: Women and Church in Seventeenth-Century France* (Montreal/Kingston: McGill-Queen's University Press, 1990), and Dominique Deslandres, "In the Shadow of the Cloister: Representations of Female Holiness in New France," in *Colonial Saints: Discovering the Holy in the Americas*, Allan Greer and Jodi Bilinkoff, eds. (New York: Routledge, 2003). For further reading, see Allan Greer's profile of Catherine Tekakwitha in *Mohawk Saint: Catherine Tekakwitha and the Jesuits* (New York: Oxford University Press, 2005).

Peter N. Moogk studies the children of eighteenth-century New France in "Les petits sauvages," in Joy Parr, ed., *Childhood and Family in Canadian History* (Toronto: McClelland & Stewart, 1982), pp. 17–43. One can find in the previously cited collection of articles by J.F. Bosher, *Business and Religion in the Age of New France, 1600–1760*, his essay "The Family in New France," pp. 93–106. The story of the Tremblay family is told in Jacqueline Darveau-Cardinal's "De l'origine et de l'histoire de quelques patronymes canadiens," *La revue française de généalogie* 11 (1981): 20–23. Another interesting family history is the review of the Trudeau family in Canada in Thomas J. Laforest, *Our French-Canadian Ancestors* (Palm Harbour, FL: USI Press, 1981).

Two studies of the population of New France are Hubert Charbonneau et al., *The First French Canadians: Pioneers in the St. Lawrence Valley*, Paola Colozzo, trans. (Newark: University of Delaware Press, 1993), and *Frenchmen into Peasants: Modernity and Tradition in the Peopling of French Canada* (Cambridge, MA: Harvard University Press, 1997).

For biographies of prominent individuals in New France, see *Dictionary of Canadian Biography*, vols. 1–4 (Toronto: University of Toronto Press, 1966, 1969, 1974, 1979). It is now also available online: www .biographi.ca. For valuable maps of the St. Lawrence colony, consult R. Cole Harris, ed., *Historical Atlas of Canada*, vol. 1, *From the Beginning to 1800* (Toronto: University of Toronto Press, 1987). Jacob Ernest Cooke, ed., *The Encyclopedia of the North American Colonies*, 3 vols. (New York: Charles Scribner's Sons, 1993), contains information about various aspects of the social and economic history of New France. For bibliographical references to the First Nations in the St. Lawrence Valley, see the bibliographies provided in Chapters 3, 4, and 7 of this book.

Source: Photo of Lewis Parker artwork of *Deportation of the Acadians from Ile St. Jean.* Copyright Lewis Parker. Courtesy of Parks of Canada N.S.

Chapter Six
THE ACADIANS

TIME LINE

1605	Port-Royal founded by the French
1632	France regains North American colonies from England in Treaty of Saint-Germain-en-Laye France begins first serious attempt to colonize Acadia
1654	England retakes Acadia
1667	France regains Acadia in Treaty of Breda
1674	The Dutch sack Acadia
1686	Number of French settlers reaches 800
1701	War of Spanish Succession begins
1710	British capture Port-Royal and rename it "Annapolis Royal"
1713	France cedes "Acadia" to Britain in Treaty of Utrecht
1720	France begins construction of fortress Louisbourg on Île Royale (Cape Breton Island)
1740	War of Austrian Succession begins
1748	New Englanders take Louisbourg
1749	French regain Louisbourg at Treaty of Aix-la-Chapelle British found Halifax
1754	Hostilities break out in North America two years before beginning of Seven Years' War
1755	Expulsion of the Acadians
1758	Louisbourg falls to British Acadians suffer second expulsion from Île Saint-Jean (Prince Edward Island)

While the focus of the Crown was on its royal province of New France, based along the St. Lawrence, a second French colony was quietly developing and prospering on the east coast. The French used the name *l'Acadie* or "Acadia" to distinguish the eastern or maritime part of New France from the valley of the St. Lawrence, which they called "Canada." Under French rule, Canada and Acadia remained separate colonies. Just where Acadia ended and Canada began was never clearly defined, but Acadia included present-day New Brunswick, Nova Scotia, and Prince Edward Island. It held strategic importance, because it contained the gateway to the St. Lawrence and Canada, and was located in the middle of a war zone between France and England.

The interests of France were focused on its St. Lawrence colony because it controlled the fur trade and access to the interior of the continent. As a result, the Crown neglected Acadia, and the colony was left to develop on its own. Little contact existed between the two colonies. This situation suited the Acadians, who did not suffer the same threats and problems (low population, Iroquois attacks, reliance on fur trade) as Canada. Over the decades, Acadia developed a unique cultural identity. This period became known as the "golden age" of the Acadians.

The "golden age" did not last, however. Acadia may have enjoyed its relative autonomy from the French Crown, but when war broke out between France and England, the strategic importance of Acadia did not escape notice. By the terms of the Treaty of Utrecht in 1713, Acadia was ceded to the British. By the mid-eighteenth century, the Acadians now under British rule had become a distinct people. Nonetheless, the British regarded them as French and Catholic, and therefore as a security threat, when war broke out again with France. In 1755 the British decided to deport the people from their homeland. The expulsion of the Acadians became one of the most traumatic events in Canadian history.

The Beginnings of Acadia

The origins of Acadia go back to 1604, when the French wintered on an island on the western side of the St. Croix River, on the present-day boundary between Maine and New Brunswick. The following two winters the French stayed at Port-Royal, in what is now Nova Scotia. But with Champlain's founding of Quebec in 1608, France focused its colonization efforts on the St. Lawrence.

A French aristocrat—Jean de Biencourt, Sieur de Poutrincourt—arrived with the first expedition led by Pierre Dugua de Monts in 1604. De Monts granted Poutrincourt the area that would become Port-Royal on the promise of establishing a colony. The Crown confirmed the grant in 1606, including fur trading and fishing rights. Poutrincourt sailed to France with furs and returned to Port-Royal as lieutenant governor of Acadia. He was expected to organize another settlement along the coast to the south; but this never came to fruition, and instead the colony teetered on the edge of failure over the next few years.

Poutrincourt's plan for the colony was based on agricultural settlement. He established good relations with the local Mi'kmaqs and conducted trade in furs, but his focus was always on farming. In 1607 word arrived in Port-Royal that the King had revoked the ten-year trading monopoly provided to de Monts. The settlers were forced to return to France. In 1610, Poutrincourt convinced the King to allow him to return to his colony. This time, however, more attention was to be given to converting the Aboriginals. Despite Poutrincourt's opposition, he was pressured to accept Jesuits into the colony. Acadia, however, faced trading competition from both French and English merchants who ignored commercial rights to the area. By 1613 Port-Royal was in financial ruin and the settlers were starving. The final blow came when Samuel Argall, the leader of the first English expedition to contest French colonization in Acadia, struck from his base at Jamestown, Virginia, and destroyed Port-Royal.

L'Acadie disappeared until the 1630s, when Cardinal Richelieu wished to re-establish the colony. France regained its North American colonies from England with the Treaty of

Acadians repairing a dike in early eighteenth century. By Azor Vienneau.

Source: History Collection, Nova Scotia Museum, Halifax, NSM 87.120.2.

Saint-Germain-en-Laye in 1632 and Isaac de Razilly was dispatched to serve as lieutenant general of New France. Razilly set out to create an agricultural colony. In letters to Richelieu, Razilly praised the land of Acadia: "The soil," he noted, "is rich both on the surface and below; the sea abounds in fish that we are exporting to southern France."

Many of the settlers came from the west coast of France, near the Atlantic port of La Rochelle. Labourers skilled in harvesting salt joined the contingent of several hundred colonists. Rather than clear the forested upland areas, the settlers built dikes to reclaim the fertile marshland that the Bay of Fundy's strong tides flooded twice daily. To ensure the effective drainage of the diked marshlands, the Acadians also constructed a system of drainage ditches, combined with an *aboîteau* (a hinged valve in the dike itself), which allowed fresh water to run off the marshes at low tide and at the same time prevented salt water from flowing onto the diked farmland when the tide rose. For several years, the Acadians let snow and rain wash away the salt from the tidal marshes. At the end of that period they planted crops on the fertile, stone-free plains.

Razilly's death in 1636 proved disastrous for the colony. Years of strife and confusion followed, as three men vied for control of Acadia: Charles de Menou d'Aulnay, Nicolas Denys, and Charles de Saint-Étienne de La Tour. Each governed his own territory and claimed exclusive trading rights. An internal struggle broke out among them, ending only in the mid-1640s. Then, in 1654, the English conquered Acadia and held it until 1670. The English treated it chiefly as a strategically located fishing and fur-trading area.

Acadian Society in the Late Seventeenth Century

Acadia was falling into a pattern of being handed back and forth between the French and English. The Acadians had little choice but to accommodate their English rulers during these periods of occupation. They also had to subdue their attachment to France. Not surprisingly in this volatile atmosphere, the Acadians developed their own distinct identity and culture. Kinship, common beliefs, and a system of mutual aid and solidarity united the community. Unique speech patterns appeared in an amalgam of various dialects—mostly French, a few English, and one or two Aboriginal. The generation of Acadian children born during the occupation had little knowledge of France.

The descendants of the immigrants of 1632 intermarried and developed a tightly knit community. At Port-Royal, the average Acadian couple usually married in their early twenties, and had ten or eleven children, most of whom survived to adulthood. The population doubled every twenty years, a faster rate than in New France. By 1670, the colony had a population of about 500. The absence of war, famine, or epidemics (such as typhoid, smallpox, and cholera) contributed to the rapid population increase.

Although Port-Royal became Acadia's largest settlement, there were other small outlying communities on the Bay of Fundy and along the eastern coastline of present-day Nova Scotia. Settlements were established in the 1670s and 1680s at Beaubassin (Amherst), Grand Pré (Wolfville), and Cobequid (Truro). The addition of about 40 families brought out after 1671 increased the population to more than 800 by 1686.

By the end of the seventeenth century, the Acadians had established themselves in the region's fertile marshlands. Wheat and peas became the principal field crops and every farm included a plot of vegetables. Most farms also had a small orchard of cherry, pear, and apple trees. Almost all farmers kept cattle and sheep. Their pigs roamed freely in the forest behind their houses. Judging by the names they gave their settlements along the Bay of Fundy and the Chignecto Isthmus, which connects present-day Nova Scotia and New Brunswick, people seemed content: Beaubassin ("beautiful pond"), Cocagne ("land of plenty"), and a settlement near Port-Royal called Paradis Terrestre ("earthly paradise" or "Garden of Eden"). According to historical geographers R. Cole Harris and John Warkentin, "like the Canadians, [the Acadians] achieved a far higher standard of living than all but the most privileged French peasants."[1]

A modern recreation of a raised haystack similar to what the Acadians would have used in their salt marshes.

Source: Virginia C. d'Eon/Nova Scotia Museum.

Acadian society was allowed to develop unfettered by the French Crown. As a result, the structure of the colony differed from that along the St. Lawrence. Because the Acadians enjoyed relatively peaceful relations with the neighbouring Mi'kmaq, Abenaki, and Maliseet First Nations, there was no need for a significant military presence. Because there was no need for the Crown to save the colony, there was no need to reorganize it. Because Acadia was not viewed as the heart of New France, it escaped the vestiges of being turned into a royal province. In Acadian society, the family and the church, rather than the seigneurial system, served as the most powerful institutions. The Crown granted seigneuries at Port-Royal, at Beaubassin (the first major village settled after Port-Royal), and along the Saint John River, but the seigneurs had little influence on the settlers' daily lives. In the St. Lawrence Valley, the Intendant enforced the system, but in Acadia no such official existed.

The Church was very influential in Acadia, but it was less hierarchical and structured than in New France. No single religious order dominated. The Jesuits, Capuchins, Récollets, and Sulpicians all took part in religious and educational work. The inhabitants often sought the advice of their priests, who acted as unofficial judges in the disputes that arose among them. But the clergy did not rule the settlements.

The economy in Acadia was allowed to develop naturally, and there was no need for the Crown to impose monopolies or work toward diversification. The Acadians produced small agricultural surpluses to trade for items they did not make or grow themselves. They traded mainly with New England. In many respects, the Bay of Fundy colony became a commercial dependency of New England. Acadian governors were unable to prevent the entry of merchants and fishers from Britain or New England. British merchants even built warehouses at Port-Royal. There they purchased furs and surplus Acadian wheat and oats in return for West Indian sugar, molasses, and rum. In turn, the Acadians bought manufactured goods, knives, needles, dishes, and cloth from the British and colonial merchants. The Acadians also travelled to Boston to sell their wheat and furs. They brought back cloth, tobacco, and pipes. In the late 1680s, even the governor of Acadia bought stockings and shoes in Boston for his garrison at Port-Royal.

Relations with the Mi'kmaq

At first the Acadians maintained good relations with the Mi'kmaq, in part because they used only small sections of the tidal flats, and avoided clearing forested land for cultivation. Unlike

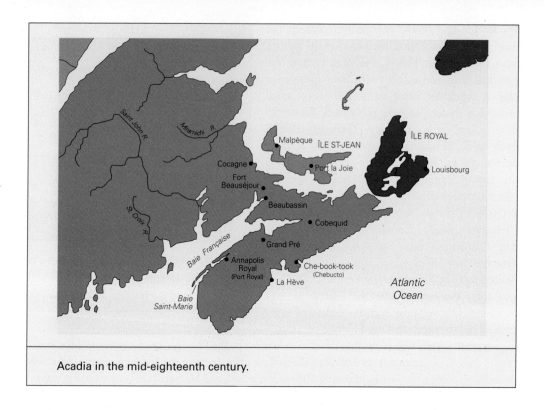

Acadia in the mid-eighteenth century.

the New England settlers, who antagonized the Aboriginal peoples by seizing their lands and clearing away the forests, the Acadians initially posed little threat. The community of La Hève (now LaHave, in Lunenburg County, Nova Scotia) became a mixed-blood settlement. But, as historian William C. Wicken has pointed out, the relationship became increasingly strained in the mid-eighteenth century. As the Acadian population increased, it began to compete with the Mi'kmaq for the same natural resources. The Acadian population multiplied by nearly thirty times between 1671 and 1755.[2]

Acadia Becomes Nova Scotia

Acadia was returned to France by the Treaty of Breda in 1667. Delays prevented the French governor from taking control of the colony until 1670. Although Acadia was now made a Crown colony, it received little aid from France and there was no significant reorganization. The Crown attempted prevent the Acadians from trading with New England, but the attempts failed. In 1674 Acadia was sacked by the Dutch.

The New Englanders also had their eyes on Acadia. When war broke out in Europe in 1689 (War of the League of Augsburg), the New Englanders, led by William Phips, attacked Port-Royal in 1690. They easily overpowered the garrison of 100 troops and sacked Acadia's capital. Even though many Acadians swore oaths of loyalty to Britain, the population suffered frequent attacks over the next years. The New Englanders held on to Acadia for seven years, until the signing of the Treaty of Ryswick in 1697, when France once again regained the colony.

With the outbreak of war in Europe in 1702 (War of Spanish Succession), Acadia again became easy prey for seafaring raiders from New England. Despite repeated attacks and looting, and with little help from France, Acadians held their ground against the British until 1710. That year, Britain supplied New England with money, arms, munitions, and naval aid to re-conquer Acadia.

The American colonies provided additional men and supplies. An expedition of 3400 men and 36 ships arrived at Port-Royal in September 1710. The French governor held only a ramshackle fort with fewer than 300 men. The French resisted for three weeks, then accepted the inevitable and surrendered in mid-October. While the area around Port-Royal was now in British hands, the rest of the colony remained French territory.

The Treaty of Utrecht

The Treaty of Utrecht in 1713 finally put to rest the question of the ownership of the peninsula. Acadia became Nova Scotia, and the British changed the name of Port-Royal to Annapolis Royal. But Louis XIV did obtain certain guarantees for the Acadians. One clause of the treaty stipulated that they had the right to leave Nova Scotia and settle elsewhere. Originally, they had one year in which to make up their minds, but this was later changed to allow more time. The Acadians were also promised religious freedom: "Those who are willing to remain here, and to be subjects to the kingdom of Great Britain, are to enjoy the free exercise of their religion according to the usage of the Church of Rome as far as the laws of Great Britain do allow the same."

A rivalry for the allegiance of the Acadians began. The war was over for now, but the imperial struggle between France and Britain ensured that the peace would not last. France retained Île Royale (Cape Breton Island), where it began in 1720 to build a fortified town to protect the Gulf of St. Lawrence and access to Quebec. The new fortress was named Louisbourg. Anxious to establish a strong colony there, the French tried to attract the Acadians. The community did send representatives to inspect the lands on Cape Breton, but the delegates reported negatively on the rocky soil and the lack of pasture land. Few Acadians embraced the idea of having to leave their rich farmlands and comfortable houses to pioneer once again. The British tried to prevent Acadians from leaving by forbidding them to construct boats or to sell their property and cattle. From the British vantage point, French immigration to Cape Breton would reinforce the French presence and weaken Nova Scotia, which would lose successful farmers and their livestock. The British also feared that the Acadians might destroy their homesteads and the restraining dikes as they left.

Acadians trading with New Englanders in the early 1700s, by Azor Vienneau.

Source: History Collection, Nova Scotia Museum, NSM 87.120.3.

The Neutral Acadians

The British administrators of Annapolis Royal faced a problem: How should a minority govern a majority? The government consisted of a council of soldiers that ruled by martial law. In 1720 a governing council of twelve was established, but it was not elected. The representative

Aerial photograph of the restored mid-eighteenth-century fortress of Louisbourg.

Source: © Parks Canada, Ron Garnett.

government practised in the Thirteen Colonies was not given to Acadia, because the majority consisted of French Catholics. The British rulers insisted that the Acadians become British subjects by swearing an oath of allegiance; this was customary, both after the succession of a new monarch to the throne and after a war. On five occasions, the governors of Nova Scotia tried to force the Acadians to swear such an oath, but the Acadians insisted on remaining neutral. As a border people between two rival empires, the Acadians proceeded cautiously. In particular, they feared reprisals from the Mi'kmaq, firm allies of the French. The authorities threatened the Acadians with expulsion, but they feared that the population would simply move to Île Royale.

Finally, in 1717, the Acadians worked out the terms on which they would remain under British government: they would have the right to practise their Catholic faith and the right to maintain neutrality in future wars against France, thereby avoiding retaliation from the Mi'kmaq. In 1730 the British agreed to their terms, and required in return that the Acadians take the following oath:

> I sincerely promise and swear on my faith as a Christian that I will be utterly loyal, and will truly obey His Majesty King George the second, whom I recognize as the sovereign lord of Acadia or Nova Scotia. May God so help me.

The Acadians took the oath, and thereafter were identified as "the neutral French." But as a result of maintaining their right to neutrality, they earned the wrath of both the French and the British. As historian Naomi Griffiths notes, "In 1748, the Acadians considered themselves Acadian, the French considered them unreliable allies, and the English, unsatisfactory citizens."[3]

The Golden Age, 1714–44

Despite being caught between the two rival empires and constantly under pressure to take the oath, the Acadians prospered. The Treaty of Utrecht at least halted the incessant raids of the New Englanders and English pirates. The high birth rate and longevity of the Acadians led to an impressive increase in population. In Port-Royal, 75 percent of the population reached the age of 21, at a time when only 50 percent reached that age in France. In 1711, there were approximately 2500 Acadians; in 1750, more than 10 000; and in 1755, more than 13 000 (Louisbourg excluded). The Acadian population spread into settlements along the present-day New Brunswick shoreline, as well as Île Saint-Jean (Prince Edward Island) and even into areas of present-day Nova Scotia that were surveyed and reserved for future English immigration.

The Acadians relied on their local priests or on the village patriarchs to solve problems of land boundaries, cattle theft, and other legal matters. The Treaty of Utrecht guaranteed the free exercise of Catholicism "insofar as the laws of Great Britain allowed." Although this guarantee was a contradiction in terms, because English laws made the practice of Catholicism in Britain difficult, the British authorities in Nova Scotia allowed a broad interpretation of the clause and granted the Acadians religious freedom.

The Catholic Church ministered to both the French and the Mi'kmaq population. The missionaries gained influence among the Mi'kmaq, who numbered about 1000 in the early 1740s in peninsular Nova Scotia and probably another 1000 on Île Saint-Jean, Cape Breton, and the mainland side of the Bay of Fundy. Abbé Pierre Maillard developed a Mi'kmaq alphabet, allowing them to learn selected prayers and chants and the catechisms. The Catholic priests probably "had something to do with the fact that the Mi'kmaq term for a Protestant person was *mu alasutmaq* ("he who does not pray")."[4]

Increasing Tensions between the Acadians and the British

The British paid little attention to the colony in the late 1730s. They left the melancholic Major Lawrence Armstrong in charge at Annapolis Royal from 1731 to 1739. Historian George Rawlyk describes him as "probably insane for much of the time."[5] Then, in 1740, war broke out between Britain and France once again (War of Austrian Succession). The French went on the offensive and, using Louisbourg as a base, made four attempts to capture Nova Scotia. The French tried repeatedly to convince the Acadians to rise up and fight for France. The population, however, realizing the implications of being on the losing side, refused. The decision proved wise when the French lost a large fleet crossing the Atlantic and the English, bolstered by a force of New Englanders led by Governor William Shirley, successfully captured Louisbourg in 1745. But the Treaty of Aix-la-Chapelle of 1748 restored the status quo. The English returned Louisbourg to France in exchange for Madras, an act that angered the New Englanders who, at great expense and loss of life, had captured it.

Britain consequently felt obliged to fortify Nova Scotia, to make it a counterbalance to Louisbourg. The English had earlier committed themselves to making Nova Scotia an effective part of their North American empire. Now they sought to make the Acadians into completely trustworthy subjects, to populate Nova Scotia with Protestant settlers, and to replace Annapolis Royal with a new military and administrative centre.

The new governor, Edward Cornwallis, then 36 years old (the uncle of the Lord Cornwallis who would surrender to the Americans at Yorktown in 1781), transported 2000 colonists to the port the Mi'kmaqs knew as "Che-book-took" (at the biggest harbour), a name the British rendered as "Chebucto." Cornwallis renamed it Halifax, after the Earl of Halifax, the president of the English Board of Trade and Plantations, the committee of Crown appointees in London who handled the administration of Britain's North American colonies until 1768.

In 1750–51, the British also brought in approximately 1500 "foreign Protestants," largely Germans, whom they settled at Lunenburg on the southeastern shore of the peninsula, within easy reach of Halifax. Lunenburg became the first British settlement in Nova Scotia outside Halifax. Authorities transferred the seat of government from Annapolis Royal to Halifax. Cornwallis introduced British institutions and laws to Nova Scotia, and fortified the new settlement to equal the strength of Louisbourg. These measures, together with the construction of roads to the Acadian settlements and the introduction of a large garrison, altered the balance of power in the colony.

Simultaneously, the French strengthened their position in what is now New Brunswick. While the British were constructing their naval and military base at Halifax and bringing Protestant immigrants into Nova Scotia, the French increased their garrison at the mouth of the Saint John River and occupied the Chignecto Isthmus. The French built Fort Beauséjour (near present-day Sackville, New Brunswick) in 1750. Beauséjour protected their overland communications from New France to Louisbourg.

The First Nations and the British

The French maintained their alliances with the Mi'kmaq and Maliseet (from present-day western New Brunswick). These alliances proved very important in providing critical support to the French, who were usually outnumbered by the New Englanders. The Mi'kmaq, however, needed little encouragement. The British were allies with the Iroquois and they were constantly encroaching on Mi'kmaq hunting grounds. The animosity went back almost to the arrival of the English in the area. More generally, the British policy of refusing to follow Aboriginal custom and provide annual gifts in return for the use of land increased hostility. The British took the view that France ceded its title to the land with the Treaty of Utrecht in 1713. It now belonged to Britain. From the Aboriginal perspective, the treaties signed in distant Europe meant little and were instead sources of frustration. They would result in their French allies ceasing to fight when the war was obviously not over. The First Nations were fighting a larger struggle against British attempts to take their land. According to anthropologist Harald Prins, the French might look upon the Mi'kmaq as proxy warriors, but in the Mi'kmaqs' eyes, they were "freedom fighters trying to liberate their homeland from the British intruders."[6]

The Acadians complained of regular raids by the New Englanders into their settlements, but the British had their own reasons to complain. Years of Mi'kmaq raids and harassment followed the Treaty of Utrecht. The Mi'kmaq even attacked at sea after they purchased European longboats from French fishers. They captured dozens of English trading and fishing boats in the course of these attacks. With the outbreak of war between Britain and France in 1744, the Mi'kmaq raids against the British in Nova Scotia reached a new level of intensity.

Governor Cornwallis responded with drastic measures. One plan was to recruit 50 rangers locally and bring in another 100 from Boston to kill Mi'kmaqs. On October 2, 1749, the British governor issued his proclamation commanding all "to Annoy, distress, take or destroy the Savages commonly called Mic-macks, wherever they are found." In wartime the French paid the First Nations for British scalps, just as the British paid for Aboriginal scalps. Cornwallis again promised payment and added that any person found helping the Mi'kmaqs would be treated as one. The plan, however, never went into effect. London advised a milder policy. The British had already learned from experience in other parts of North America that "gentler Methods and Offers of Peace have more frequently prevailed with Indians than the Sword, if at the same Time, that the Sword is held over their Heads."

Britain's Growing Anxiety about the Acadians

With frontier incidents and Mi'kmaq raids increasing, Cornwallis became more doubtful of the Acadians' loyalty to Britain in the event of another war. In 1749 the governor commanded them to swear an oath of unconditional allegiance to Britain or risk deportation. But when the Acadian delegates replied negatively to Cornwallis's ultimatum, he did not expel them, preferring to wait until British power became stronger in Nova Scotia.

By the 1750s, tension was increasing as France and Britain prepared for what would be the final stage in their war over North America. As the strategic importance of the maritime region increased, the issue of what to do with the Acadians neared a climax. Between 1500 and 2000 Acadians left peninsular Nova Scotia by choice or by coercion—many were forced by French raiding parties to move to French territory north of the isthmus. Yet the 80 percent who remained in the colony believed that the governor, by his refusal to remove them, had, like other British governors before him, accepted their "neutral" status.

When Charles Lawrence became lieutenant governor of Nova Scotia in 1753, the Acadians expected the situation to remain the same. This time, however, they were wrong. First and foremost, Colonel Lawrence was a soldier. He had no respect for "neutrals" who refused to take a stand. In Lawrence's view, the Acadians posed a serious

Indian Camp, New Brunswick *by William Robert Herries (1818–1845).*

Source: William Robert Herries. (Canadian) Indian Camp, New Brunswick (date unknown), watercolour on paper ht: 24.8 x wi: 37.2 cm. Purchased with a Minister of Communications Cultural Property Grant and funds from the Marguerite and Murray Vaughan Foundation and the Samuel Endowment. The Beaverbrook Art Gallery.

threat in the upcoming critical stage of the struggle between France and Britain. In the early months of 1754, Lawrence made one more attempt to coerce the Acadians to take the oath of unconditional loyalty.

The Expulsion of the Acadians

The Seven Years' War officially began in Europe in 1756, but hostilities broke out in North America two years earlier. In 1755, the commander-in-chief of British forces in North America, General Braddock, led a campaign against the French and First Nations in the Ohio Valley. As part of this campaign, Colonel Robert Monckton led a force composed largely of New England troops and captured Fort Beauséjour and the rest of the French garrisons on the Chignecto Isthmus in June.[7] Sufficiently impressed by the victories in his region, Lawrence made the decision to act on the Acadian question.

In July, Lawrence ordered representatives of the Acadians to appear before the Halifax Council, which advised the governor. With a significant British force near at head, he assumed the Acadians would capitulate quickly and agree to the oath. The council, dominated by military officers, insisted on an oath from the Acadians that they would support Britain in the event of war. The council was also aware that moving the Acadians would free up some of the richest land along the Bay of Fundy.

On July 23, two days before the first Acadian delegates from the villages arrived, the news of General Braddock's catastrophic defeat near Fort Duquesne in the Ohio country reached Halifax. Casualties approached 40 percent, and the British commander himself had been killed. Lawrence became further convinced of the need for the Acadians to make a declaration of unequivocal allegiance to Britain.

Upon arrival, the Acadian delegates pointed out that they had always been loyal to King George II and agreed to present all their firearms to the English as proof of their loyalty. They were prepared to abide by the oath they had sworn earlier, but not to take a new one. They asked to be considered neutral, pointing out that between 1713 and 1755 they had never fought for France. The Acadians underestimated the determination of Lawrence's council.

The final confrontation came on July 28. After hearing the delegates one last time, the council reached a decision. It endorsed the deportation of all Acadians under British jurisdiction who had refused to take the unqualified oath. In the general hysteria after Braddock's defeat, the British were prepared to remove them. The Acadians' fate passed into the hands of 2000 hostile, anti-Catholic New England militiamen working under the instructions of Lieutenant Governor Charles Lawrence.

The Deportation

Preparations for the deportation began immediately after the council's decision. Lawrence attempted initially to prepare carefully for the evacuation, providing adequate cabin space on transport ships and ample provisions for the duration of the journey. But, in the end, the evacuation was rushed and poorly planned. Mercantile ships were outfitted and sent up from Boston:

> Before leaving Boston the ships had been renovated by removing the balast stones and the bulk heads of the holds . . . creating a large area in the hold of the vessel measuring approximately 24 feet wide by 60 feet long. The removal of the floor timbers and the ballast stones increased the height to approximately 15 feet high. This enlarged hold space was then divided into three levels of just at or slightly over 4 feet high without windows for light or ventilation. The holds were locked creating a prison with no windows for light or ventilation, no sanitary conditions and no heat, except that of the huddled bodies.

The British troops camped among the Acadians during that last harvest and forced them to provide food. By September the transport ships began arriving. On September 5, a royal proclamation was announced to the gathered Acadians, announcing "That your Land & Tennements, Cattle of all Kinds and Livestocks of all Sorts are forfeited to the Crown with all other your effects Savings your money and Household Goods, and you yourselves to be removed from this Province." The British first herded the Acadians together at Annapolis Royal, Grand Pré, Beaubassin, and other settlements. Since sending them to Cape Breton or New France would only serve to build up the French militia in the two colonies, the British dispersed most of them among the Thirteen Colonies and sent some to Britain. Lawrence's troops, including those commanded by Colonel Robert Monckton, the victor at Fort Beauséjour, burned houses and barns to deprive those who escaped of shelter. Within several months, the work of more than a century of toil was turned to ashes.

The Destruction of Acadian Society

The expulsion destroyed Acadian society. It broke up communities and dispersed close-knit families. Some fought back—for the most part, ineffectively. Abbé François Le Guerne, who remained in what is now southern New Brunswick until August 1757, reported that women and children took to the woods to escape deportation and to flee the British soldiers who had burned their property. Some 86 Acadians escaped by digging a tunnel from barracks in their prison camp near Fort Beauséjour. On board a ship bound for the American colonies, an Acadian group seized their captors, sailed back to the Bay of Fundy, and then fled overland to the upper reaches of the Saint John River.

An estimated 2000 Acadians fled to Île Saint-Jean (Prince Edward Island), where the refugees outnumbered the original Acadian residents three to one. The exodus brought confusion to Île Saint-Jean. Many Acadian refugees came with only the clothes on their backs. Starvation was general, as the islanders had enjoyed only one good harvest over the previous five years. After the fall of Louisbourg in 1758, however, the British landed on the island and began to deport all the Acadians they could capture.

The Expulsion of the Acadians from Île Saint-Jean, 1758, *by Lewis Parker.*

Source: Photo of Lewis Parker artwork of *"Deportation of the Acadians from Ile St. Jean."* Copyright Lewis Parker. Courtesy of Parks of Canada N.S.

The conditions on the transport ships used to deport the Acadians were deplorable. Many died, victims of malnutrition and exposure. Storms at sea, a shortage of food and drinking water, and poor sanitary conditions meant that many ships lost more than one-third of their Acadian passengers. The *Cornwallis,* which left Chignecto with 417 Acadians on board, docked at Charleston, South Carolina, with only 210 still alive. The expulsions continued for seven years, until 1762.

The British military occasionally sent ships from the same village to different destination points. Inevitably, some family members were separated. Massachusetts, New York, Pennsylvania, Maryland, Virginia, the Carolinas, and

Georgia all received Acadians. For the most part, the Americans tried to settle the exiles in various small towns and villages, but these efforts proved to be largely unsuccessful. The Acadians, footsore and half-clad, wandered from town to town, looking for family and friends. They remained outsiders in the communities where they were settled. Their mortality rate in the American colonies was high. An estimated one-third of those deported died from diseases that had been practically unknown to them before 1755—smallpox, typhoid, and yellow fever.

WHERE HISTORIANS DISAGREE

The Expulsion of the Acadians

Canadian historians have long debated whether the expulsion of the Acadians in 1755 was strategically necessary and whether it was unnecessarily cruel. As historian Naomi Griffiths points out,

> Acadian history 1710—1755 provides endless questions of fact and interpretation, problems about what actually happened and whether it was brought about intentionally or not. . . . As the years lead on to 1755, the problems which divide historians multiply, and the events of the expulsion itself have been so diversely treated that one sometimes wonders whether the authors are writing about the same events.[1]

Some condemn the British; others believe the Acadians were to blame for their misfortunes by refusing to comply. A third group contends that interference from Quebec and Louisbourg resulted in the tragedy.

Early historians argued that the Acadians received surprisingly tolerant treatment by the British who conquered the area in 1713. The French Crown would not have been so tolerant. The Acadians had numerous opportunities to swear an oath and avoid persecution. Instead, they became complacent and took advantage of the "soft" British position. The expulsion should be seen solely as a military operation necessary for Nova Scotia's

defence. Archibald McKellar MacMechan, for instance, wrote in 1913:

> Before passing judgement on the men who conceived and executed this removal of an entire population, it should be remembered that they acted as did Louis XIV in expelling the Huguenots from France and the United States in expelling the tories. All were precautionary measures dictated by the need of national self-preservation; and they were regarded by those who took them as imperative in a dangerous crisis. Lawrence acted like the commander of a fort expecting a siege, who levels trees and houses outside the walls in order to afford the enemy no shelter and to give the garrison a clear field of fire.[2]

In 1956, popular historian Joseph Lister Rutledge reiterated this position:

> If ever a conquered people were treated with consideration by their captors, it was the Acadians. . . . The net result was generous and understanding treatment for people who represented a very stubborn breed indeed. This conquered people retained their land and freedom and the assurance of the exercise of their religion. The loyalty oath required of them was generous to a fault.[3]

Most French-Canadian historians are more sympathetic to the Acadians and condemn the expulsion. In the 1920s, Émile Lauvrière noted of Governor Lawrence's actions that "only a criminal soul could devise such a plot in all its details."[4] Henri Beaudé, a Catholic priest who wrote under the pseudonym of Henri d'Arles, considered the deportation order entirely undeserved and "conceived in hate, a prejudice of race and religion."[5]

While not overlooking the cruelty of the expulsion, two historians have tried to understand more fully the British decision to evict an entire people. In 1979, Naomi Griffiths wrote that the imposition in 1755 of a "declaration of unequivocal allegiance to British interests" was "reasonable enough" because war with France had begun.[6] Stephen E. Patterson also emphasizes the circumstances and the context in which the deportation occurred: "It took place in a time of war, a bitter war between inveterate enemies for whom possession of Nova Scotia had become symbolic of their power and prestige in the international world."[7]

Regardless of the historiographical debate, the expulsion of the Acadians remains a pivotal event in Nova Scotia's history. The traumatic event continues to stir up considerable emotion. It also remains an issue of historical contention between English and French in Canada, demonstrated by a resolution passed unanimously by the Quebec National Assembly in June 2002. The resolution supported the Acadians and demanded "that the British Crown officially recognize the historical wrongdoing in the deportation of their ancestors."[8] In mid-December 2003, the Canadian governor general officially acknowledged the Acadian expulsion in a royal proclamation. It acknowledged the wrongs done to the Acadians during the expulsion. It also stated that, beginning in 2005, and then annually thereafter, July 28 would become a commemorative day to mark the deportation.

1. Naomi Griffiths, ed., *The Acadian Deportation: Deliberate Perfidy or Cruel Necessity?* (Toronto: Copp Clark, 1969), p. 3.

2. Archibald McKellar MacMechan, in A. Shortt and A.G. Doughty, eds., *Canada and Its Provinces,* vol. 13 (Toronto: Glasgow Brook, 1914), p. 98.

3. Joseph Lister Rutledge, *Century of Conflict* (Toronto: Doubleday, 1956), p. 409. Published in the popular Canadian History Series, edited by Thomas B. Costain.

4. N.E.S. Griffiths, "The Acadians," in *Dictionary of Canadian Biography,* vol. 4, *1771–1800* (Toronto: University of Toronto Press, 1979), p. xxvi.

5. Henri d'Arles [Henri Beaudé] *La déportation des Acadiens* (Montreal: Bibliothèque de l'action française, 1918), pp. 21–26, translated and quoted in Griffiths, *The Acadian Deportation,* p. 156.

6. Griffiths, "The Acadians," p. xxvi.

7. Stephen E. Patterson, "1744–1763: Colonial Wars and Aboriginal Peoples," Ch. 7 of Phillip A. Buckner and John G. Reid, eds., *The Atlantic Region to Confederation: A History* (Toronto: University of Toronto Press, 1994), p. 145.

8. Rhéal Séguin, "Britain Made a Mistake with Acadians, Quebec says," *The Globe and Mail,* June 14, 2002.

It is difficult to determine the number of Acadians expelled between 1755 and 1763. Historians estimate that the British deported nearly three-quarters of the Acadian population of roughly 13 000. Approximately 7000 were deported in the first year alone. By the time the policy ended in 1762, the British had exiled perhaps another 3000 Acadians.

The Acadians from peninsular Nova Scotia were split into small groups. The British rounded up many who escaped to Île Royale (Cape Breton) and Île Saint-Jean (Prince Edward Island) after they took these two islands in 1758. Of the 2000 captives taken on Île Saint-Jean in 1758, 700 drowned when three transport vessels were lost at sea. Some Acadians sought refuge in the isolated Miramichi River valley, in what is now northeastern New Brunswick. About 1500 Acadians also fled to New France to establish homes near Quebec, Trois-Rivières, and Montreal. Others successfully made their way to St. Pierre and Miquelon, the two small islands off the coast of Newfoundland that France was able to retain under the peace treaty of 1763.

The Acadians in France and Louisiana

One thousand Acadians were sent to Virginia in 1756 and then immediately dispatched to England. The Virginians argued that the Acadians were British subjects, which therefore entitled them to Britain's support. About one-quarter of them died from an epidemic of smallpox during their first summer in England. The remainder spent seven years in internment camps in England, until France took them in 1763. Many of the Acadians who settled in France in 1763 had difficulty adjusting to French society. Although they spoke French and practised Catholicism, after a century and a half in North America, they were a people distinct from the French.

Not finding comfortable homes in France, seven shiploads of Acadians—nearly 1600 people—sailed for New Orleans, Louisiana, in 1785, where they joined other Acadians who had settled there earlier. Some 300 had arrived in 1764–65. Of those, some had initially sought refuge at Saint-Domingue (present-day Haiti), the French sugar island, but had eventually crossed over to New Orleans. In addition, about 700 Acadians from Maryland and Pennsylvania had arrived in Louisiana by ship between 1766 and 1770.

Although it was at that time a Spanish possession, Louisiana's main language was French, and the colony was officially Roman Catholic. Like the Bay of Fundy area, Louisiana had large marshes that needed draining—work at which the Acadians had prior experience. Today, Louisiana is home to more than one million descendants of the Acadians. As the Acadian settlements spread across the Louisiana bayous, their neighbours shortened the French name Acadien to "Cadien" and, eventually, to "Cajun."

The Return of Some Acadians

In 1764, the British permitted the Acadians to resettle in Nova Scotia. A steady stream of wanderers returned—in all, an estimated 3000. But since New Englanders now owned their farms, they could not regain their land.

By 1800, the Acadians in Nova Scotia numbered 4000 and in the new colonies of New Brunswick and Prince Edward Island, 3800 and 700 respectively—a result of high birth rates rather than the return of more exiles. They were concentrated around Baie Sainte-Marie (St. Mary's Bay) in southwestern Nova Scotia and Chéticamp on Cape Breton Island. They also settled around Malpèque on Prince Edward Island. Since present-day New Brunswick contained vacant land, especially along its east coast, the majority of returned Acadians went there. They joined a group who had previously sought refuge in this area during the expulsion. Finding themselves in many of these locations on infertile land, most of

The Martin house.
Source: Village Historique Acadien.

the Acadians became fishers rather than farmers. Subsequently they made a living from these lands, but it was at a much lower standard than what they had known on their well-developed farms before 1755.

The expulsion of 1755 became the unifying event in the history of the Acadian people. It became customary in Acadian villages for the older people to tell of their experiences in the deportation. The tradition remained an oral one until American poet Henry Wadsworth Longfellow, who first heard the story in the early 1840s, recorded it in his poem "Evangeline: A Tale of Acadie," which was subsequently published in several French translations. The romantic ballad centres on Evangeline Bellefontaine, a 17-year-old Acadienne who is separated in the deportation from her lover, Gabriel Lajeunesse. When, after a lifelong search, she finds him again, he is a broken old man. As she holds him in her arms, he dies. "Evangeline" confirmed for Acadians that they were a unique people with an identity and history of their own:

> *Still stands the forest primeval; but under the shade of its branches*
> *Dwells another race, with other customs and language.*
> *Only along the shore of the mournful and misty Atlantic*
> *Linger a few Acadian peasants, whose fathers from exile*
> *Wandered back to their native land to die in its bosom.*

In 1979, Antonine Maillet wrote a novel on the deportation, *Pélagie-la-Charrette*. It is the story of an unconquerable woman, Pélagie, who, after the expulsion, spent a decade travelling in a cart drawn by a cow. With others she met along the way, she journeyed from Georgia back to Acadia. "When they built their carts," Maillet wrote, "they were just families. By the time they returned to Acadia they were a people."

SUMMARY

Whether the expulsion of the Acadians can be justified or not, it was a tragedy. On the one hand, the Acadians were better off than the habitants of New France. Their colony did not suffer the attacks of the Iroquois and they were able to avoid the scrutiny of the French Crown. On the other hand, while the Acadians enjoyed a "golden era," they lived constantly in a war zone, an area contested by two European powers. They were often under threat of having their homes and valuables looted and burned by New Englanders and English pirates. In 1713 Acadia was conquered by the British. The Acadians tried to maintain a balance between the two competing powers by remaining neutral. They succeeded for more than a century, until wartime hysteria won out in 1755 and the British felt it necessary to expel the "neutral French." The habitants of New France were left wondering if the same fate awaited them, should they ever be conquered.

NOTES

1. R. Cole Harris and John Warkentin, eds., *Canada Before Confederation: A Study in Historical Geography* (Ottawa: Carleton University Press, 1991 [1974]), p. 30.

2. William C. Wicken, "Re-examining Mi'kmaq–Acadian Relations, 1635–1755," in Sylvie Dépatie et al., eds., *Vingt ans après: Habitants et marchands* (*Twenty Years Later*) (Montreal/Kingston: McGill-Queen's University Press, 1998), p. 96.

3. Naomi Griffiths, *The Acadians: Creation of a People* (Toronto: McGraw-Hill Ryerson, 1973), p. 37.

4. Harald E.L. Prins, *The Mi'kmaq Resistance, Accommodation, and Cultural Survival* (Fort Worth, TX: Harcourt Brace, 1996), p. 122.

5. George Rawlyk, "Cod, Louisbourg, and the Acadians," chap. 6 of Phillip A. Buckner and John G. Reid, eds., *The Atlantic Region to Confederation* (Toronto: University of Toronto Press, 1994), p. 113.

6. Prins, *The Mi'kmaq Resistance, Accommodation, and Cultural Survival*, p. 135.

7. Ironically, the largest Acadian community today is in Moncton, New Brunswick—named in honour of Robert Monckton, who became lieutenant governor of Nova Scotia in 1755.

RELATED READINGS

Module 4, "On the Edge of Empires: Acadians and Mi'kmaq in the Eighteenth Century," in *Visions: The Canadian History Modules Project: Pre-Confederation*, is a useful introduction to life in Acadia. The module offers five secondary-source articles covering many aspects of Acadian life and looks at both Acadian and Mi'kmaq culture. See pages 149–190.

BIBLIOGRAPHY

Naomi Griffiths has written three summaries of Acadian history: *The Acadians: Creation of a People* (Toronto: McGraw-Hill Ryerson, 1973); *The Contexts of Acadian History, 1686–1784* (Montreal/Kingston: McGill-Queen's University Press, 1992); and *From Migrant to Acadian: A North American Border People 1604–1755* (Montreal: McGill-Queen's University Press, 2005). Barry Moody provides bibliographical suggestions in M. Brook Taylor, ed., *Canadian History: A Reader's Guide*, vol. 1, *Beginnings to Confederation* (Toronto: University of Toronto Press, 1994), pp. 76–111. For a further general introduction to Acadian life, see Dean W. Jobb, *The Acadians: A People's Story of Exile and Triumph* (Etobicoke: Wiley, 2005).

For the early period, consult John G. Reid, *Acadia, Maine, and New Scotland: Marginal Colonies in the Seventeenth Century* (Toronto: University of Toronto Press, 1981); and John G. Reid et al., The *"Conquest" of Acadia, 1710: Imperial, Colonial, and Aboriginal Constructions* (Toronto: University of Toronto Press, 2003). Andrew H. Clark provides a historical geographer's view in *Acadia: The Geography of Early Nova Scotia to 1760* (Madison: University of Wisconsin Press, 1968). For additional works of historical geography, see R. Cole Harris, *The Reluctant Land: Society, Space, and Environment in Canada Before Confederation* (Vancouver: UBC Press, 2008), Andrew Hill Clarke, *Acadia: The Geography of Early Nova Scotia to 1760* (Madison: University of Wisconsin Press, 1968), and "The Acadians," by Naomi Griffiths, in *Dictionary of Canadian Biography*, vol. 4, *1771–1800* (Toronto: University of Toronto Press, 1979), pp. xvii–xxxi. See also A.J.B. Johnson, "De´fricheurs d'eau: An Introduction to Acadian Land Reclamation in a Comparative Context." *Material Culture Review* 66 (2007): 32–41. Jean Daigle's account, "Acadia, 1604–1763: An Historical Synthesis" in Jean Daigle, ed., The *Acadians of the Maritimes* (Moncton, NB: Centre d'études acadiennes, 1982), pp. 17–46, is useful. Valuable studies of the Acadians on Île Saint-Jean (Prince Edward Island) include D.C. Harvey, *The French Regime in Prince Edward Island* (New York: AMS, 1970 [1926]), and Georges Arsenault, *The Island Acadians, 1720–1980* (Charlottetown: Ragweed, 1989). Bibliographical references to Louisbourg appear in the bibliography of this text's Chapter 7. For a look at an early summary of Acadia, see J.B. Brebner, *New England's Outpost: Acadia Before the Conquest of Canada* (New York: Columbia University Press, 1927).

For an overview on the Atlantic region in the years preceding Canadian Confederation, see Philip A. Buckner and John G. Reid, eds., *The Atlantic Region to Confederation: A History* (Toronto: University of Toronto Press, 1994). See also W.J. Eccles, *The Canadian Frontier: 1534–1760* (Albuquerque: University of New Mexico Press, 1974). For a discussion of the challenges of Acadian history, see A.J.B. Johnston, "The Call of the Archetype and the Challenge of Acadian History," *French Colonial History* 5 (2004): 63–92.

Guy Frégault's "The Deportation of the Acadians, 1755–62," Ch. 6 in his book *Canada: The War of the Conquest*, translated by Margaret M. Cameron (Toronto: Oxford University Press, 1969), pp. 164–200, provides a French-Canadian historian's interpretation of events in Acadia in the 1750s. Various opinions on the issue of the expulsion appear in Naomi Griffiths, ed., *The Acadian Deportation: Deliberate Perfidy or Cruel Necessity?* (Toronto: Copp Clark, 1969). T.G. Barnes provides a good historiographical review in his "Historiography of the Acadians' *Grand Dérangement*, 1775," *Quebec Studies* 7 (1988): 74–86. An important study is Geoffrey Plank, *An Unsettled Conquest. The British Campaign Against the Peoples of Acadia* (Philadelphia: University of Pennsylvania Press, 2001). For a further look at the Conquest, see John G. Reid et al., *The "Conquest" of Acadia, 1710: Imperial, Colonial, and Aboriginal Constructions* (Toronto: University of Toronto Press, 2003).

The following articles on the Acadians appear in Phillip A. Buckner and David Frank, eds. and comps., *Atlantic Canada Before Confederation*, vol. 1, *The Acadiensis Reader* (Fredericton: Acadiensis Press, 1985): Gisa Hynes, "Some Aspects of the Demography of Port-Royal, 1650–1755," pp. 11–25; Naomi Griffiths, "Acadians in Exile: The Experiences of the Acadians in the British Seaports," pp. 26–43; and Graeme Wynn, "Late Eighteenth-Century Agriculture on the Bay of Fundy Marshlands," pp. 44–53. Robert G. Leblanc provides a short review of the expulsion in "The Acadian Migrations," *Canadian Geographical Journal* 81 (July 1970): 10–19. For the Acadians' arrival in Louisiana, see Carl A. Brasseaux, "A New Acadia: The Acadian Migrations to South Louisiana, 1764–1803," *Acadiensis* 15 (1985): 123–32. His more specialized studies on the topic include *The Founding of New Acadia: The Beginnings of Acadian Life in Louisiana, 1765–1803* (Baton Rouge: Louisiana State University, 1987), and *Acadian to Cajun: Transformation of a People, 1803–1877* (Jackson: University Press of Mississippi, 1992). Elsa Guery looks at French colonial administration in Acadia in "'Vous voyez par là Monseigneur, comme tout est icy dans l'indépendance!': La difficile adaptation de l'administration coloniale française en Acadie de Louis XIV," *Études canadiennes/Canadian Studies* 58 (2005): 79–96. For a look at missionary activity in Acadia, see Matteo Binasco, "Les activités des missionnaires catholiques romains en Acadie/Nouvelle-Écosse (1610–1755)," *Les cahiers de la Société´ historique acadienne* 37(1) (2006): 4–29.

The history of the Mi'kmaqs in Acadia under French and British rule is recounted in Olive P. Dickason, "Louisbourg and the Indians: A Study in Imperial Race Relations," *History and Archaeology* 6

(1976): 1–206; L.F.S. Upton, *Micmacs and Colonists: Indian–White Relations in the Maritimes, 1713—1867* (Vancouver: University of British Columbia Press, 1979); Harald E.L. Prins, *The Mi'kmaq: Resistance, Accommodation, and Cultural Survival* (Fort Worth, TX: Harcourt Brace, 1996); and Jennifer Reid, *Myth, Symbol, and Colonial Encounter: British and Mi'kmaq in Acadia, 1700–1867* (Ottawa: University of Ottawa Press, 1995). Daniel N. Paul takes a critical view of both French and English policies toward the Mi'kmaq in *We Were Not the Savages: First Nations History*, 3rd ed. (Halifax: Fernwood, 2000).

William C. Wicken challenges the presentation of Acadian–Mi'kmaq relations as harmonious in "Re-examining Mi'kmaq–Acadian Relations, 1635–1755," in Sylvie Depatie et al., eds., *Vingt ans après: Habitants et marchands (Twenty Years Later)* (Montreal/Kingston: McGill-Queen's University Press, 1998), pp. 93–114. In his study *Mi'kmaq Treaties on Trial: History, Land, and Donald Marshall, Junior* (Toronto: University of Toronto Press, 2002), Wicken examines a series of British–Mi'kmaq treaties (1726, 1749, 1752, and 1760–61). Stephen E. Patterson has written "Indian–White Relations in Nova Scotia, 1749–61: A Study in Political Interaction," *Acadiensis* 23(1) (Autumn 1993): 23–59. Wayne Kerr looks at Acadian-Mi'kmaq relations at Port Royal in *Port-Royal Habitation: The Story of the French and Mi'kmaq at Port-Royal (1604–1613)* (Halifax: Nimbus, 2005). See also Stephanie Inglis, "400 Years of Linguistic Contact Between the Mi-kmaq and the English and the Interchange of Two World Views," *Canadian Journal of Native Studies* 24(2) (2004): 389–402. For a further look at treaty negotiation, see Natasha Powers, "Beyond Cultural Differences: Interpreting a Treaty Between the Mi'kmaq and British at Belcher's Farm, 1761," *Atlantis* 29(2) (2005): 47–54. For a look at materials collected at the Canadian Museum of Civilization, see Stephen J. Augustine, *Mi'kmaq and Maliseet Cultural Ancestral Material: National Collections from the Canadian Museum of Civilization* (Ottawa: Canadian Museum of Civilization, 2005). Peter Sanger explores Mi'kmaq culture through textual study in *The Stone Canoe: Two Lost Mi'kmaq Texts* (Wolfville: Gaspereau Press 2007).

Léon Thériault provides an overview of Acadian history since the expulsion in "Acadia, 1763—1978: An Historical Synthesis," in Jean Daigle, ed, *The Acadians of the Maritimes* (Moncton: Centre d'études acadiennes, 1982), pp. 47–86. The story of the founding of Halifax is told in Judith Fingard, Janet Guildford, and David Sutherland, *Halifax: The First 250 Years* (Halifax: Formac Publishing, 1999). Biographical portraits of seventeenth- and eighteenth-century Acadians appear in *Dictionary of Canadian Biography*, vols. 1–4 (Toronto: University of Toronto Press, 1966, 1969, 1974, 1979), available online: www.bibliographi.ca.

Maps of Acadian marshland settlement and of the Acadian deportation and return appear in R. Cole Harris, ed., *Historical Atlas of Canada*, vol. 1, *From the Beginning to 1800* (Toronto: University of Toronto Press, 1987). For a complete overview of the area in the seventeenth and eighteenth centuries, consult the early chapters of Phillip A. Buckner and John G. Reid, eds., *The Atlantic Region to Confederation: A History* (Toronto: University of Toronto Press, 1994).

Source: Library and Archives Canada, C-073709.

Chapter Seven

THE STRUGGLE FOR A CONTINENT

TIME LINE

1670	Hudson's Bay Company established
1689	War of the League of Augsburg (called King William's War in the American colonies) begins
1697	Treaty of Ryswick
1701	The Treaty of Montreal ends conflict between French and Iroquois War of Spanish Succession (called Queen Anne's War in the American colonies) begins
1711	English expedition fails to take Quebec
1713	Treaty of Utrecht: France loses Hudson Bay, Newfoundland, and Acadia, to England
1744	War of Austrian Succession (called King George's War in the American colonies) begins
1748	Treaty of Aix-la-Chapelle
1755	General Braddock defeated
1756	The Seven Years' War begins
1759	British forces under General Wolfe win Battle of the Plains of Abraham and take Quebec
1760	British conquer New France and establish military government until the signing of peace
1763	Treaty of Paris

The English rivalled the French in North America from the beginning of settlement in the early seventeenth century. At approximately the same time that the French founded Quebec (1608), England established its first colonies in North America: Virginia in 1607, Newfoundland in 1610, and Massachusetts in 1620. Others followed on the Atlantic seaboard, and in 1664 the Dutch colony of New Netherlands passed into English hands and was renamed New York. The English also went north of the French holdings and sponsored expeditions into Hudson Bay. As early as 1610, the explorer Henry Hudson located an immense body of water, a "northern sea" the size of the Mediterranean, which provided access to the distant interior and possibly to the Northwest Passage. Half a century later, an English company established a string of fur-trading posts on the shores of the bay.

By the late seventeenth century and throughout the eighteenth century, Britain and France entered a series of imperial wars in Europe that spilled over into its colonies in North America and the Caribbean. In North America, the First Nations fought for their own objectives and played an essential role in these colonial wars (called the French Indian Wars in the Thirteen Colonies). This epic struggle continued, with several interludes of peace, until 1760, when the French forces capitulated at Montreal and the British took control of the continent.

English Interest in the North

In the early seventeenth century, the English joined the search for the Northwest Passage. The explorer, Henry Hudson, made several excursions in search of the Passage, including journeys for the Dutch East India Company around present-day New York in 1609 (the river was named after him). Hudson's expeditions laid the foundation for Dutch settlement in the area. In what turned out to be his last expedition in June 1610, Hudson went in search of the passage for the Virginia and British East India Company. His ship, *The Discovery*, entered an icebound strait previously noted (in the 1570s and 1580s) by English Arctic explorers, Martin Frobisher and John Davis. Hudson spent several months exploring the bay (which was later named for him), but the ship got caught in the ice in November. The crew went ashore and passed a difficult winter on the east coast of James Bay. Come spring, Hudson wanted to continue the search and exploration, but the crew mutinied. They seized Hudson, his son, and six others, and set them adrift. Henry Hudson was never seen again. Eight of the 12 mutineers returned alive to England, where they falsely reported that the expedition had found the Northwest Passage. The Welsh navigator Sir Thomas Button crossed Hudson Bay in 1612, but failed to find Hudson or a passage to the Indies.

Other English expeditions followed until 1631, when it became clear that, even if the Northwest Passage existed, it would not be a commercially viable trade route. Since both the Dutch and the English had already begun to make the longer but less hazardous journey around Africa to India and China, the lure of the passage diminished.

Even though it was the English who explored Hudson Bay, it seemed likely that it would be the French who would trade out of the area. The establishment of the French fur trade along the St. Lawrence, and the loss of the Huron as the middleman, sent the coureurs de bois further into the northwest (the area around the Great Lakes called the *pays d'en haut* or upper country) in search of fur reserves. In the late 1650s, Médard Chouart Des Groseilliers reached Lake Superior. The Ojibwa told him of a rich fur region even further to the north and west. In 1659, he joined with his brother-in-law, Pierre-Esprit Radisson, and traded heavily in the area. When the two returned to New France, however, they were arrested for trading without a licence. The authorities were seeking to reorganize the economic structure of the colony and diversify away from furs. They also did not want the free-spirited coureurs de bois expanding French territory on the continent and stretching its defences. In the years that followed, Des Groseilliers and Radisson tried to gain support for establishing a fur trade from Hudson Bay but they failed. The English, however, were interested.

The Last Voyage of Henry Hudson *by John Collier.*

Source: Tate Gallery, London / Art Resource, NY.

In 1668, a group of English merchants under the patronage of Prince Rupert, a cousin of King Charles II, sponsored an expedition, which was to winter on Hudson Bay and return with a cargo of furs. The enterprise, led by Des Groseilliers, proved so successful that in 1670 Charles II gave the Hudson's Bay Company exclusive trading rights and property ownership to "Rupert's Land," all the lands within the area drained by the rivers flowing into Hudson and James Bays (nearly half the area of Canada today). The English laid claim to the northwestern interior of the continent.

French Expansion

The English now threatened New France's fur trade from two sides: New York to the south and Hudson Bay to the northwest. The collapse of the French trading system with the Hurons in 1649 left a vacuum and forced the French to be more aggressive in gaining access to furs. In the early 1670s, the French sent overland expeditions to Hudson Bay (led by the Jesuit Charles Albanel), Lake Superior (led by fur trader Daumont de Saint-Lusson), and the Mississippi River (led by fur trader Louis Jolliet).

Frontenac, who became governor in 1672, defied Colbert's instructions to curtail expansion and openly promoted further westward expansion into the Mississippi Valley. A daring and ambitious fur trader by the name of René-Robert, Chevalier de La Salle, and Louis Jolliet, building on the earlier expeditions of Sulpician priests François Dollier de Casson and René de Bréhant de Galinée, reached the Mississippi delta and the Gulf of Mexico in 1682. La Salle raised the royal arms of France and claimed all the land drained by the Mississippi River and its tributaries for the King of France. He named the huge valley Louisiana, after Louis XIV. La Salle attempted to found a colony in Louisiana, but his efforts ended in failure—and his assassination in 1687.

In the mid-1670s, Montreal fur traders built Michilimackinac at the junction of Lakes Michigan and Huron, which became the starting point for the fur trade along the upper Mississippi River and beyond Lake Superior. The French then built a chain of trading posts from the Ohio River to Lake Superior and north to Hudson Bay. In 1682, a French military expedition led by the Chevalier de Troyes captured the English posts on Hudson Bay. The French were forced to return the posts, however, because France and England were not at war at the time.

La Salle's expedition down the Mississippi also raised the ire of the Iroquois, who were alarmed by his alliance with the Illinois nation. The Seneca attacked La Salle's fort at St. Louis in 1684, and the French retaliated with a military expedition, but were defeated. A much more impressive expedition was dispatched in 1687, consisting of 832 regulars, 900 militiamen, and 400 Aboriginal warriors, and it undertook a "scorched earth" campaign against the Seneca. French access to the Illinois country was secured by the construction of a garrison at the mouth of the Niagara. Or so it was thought. In August 1689, 1500 Iroquois attacked Lachine, a settlement just west of Montreal, causing mass terror among the population of New France.

A mixed Aboriginal and French population arose at the western posts, particularly at the larger centres, such as Michilimackinac, and later Green Bay and Detroit. This "people in between" over time developed their own unique culture and identity. They forged a niche in the fur trade and developed a new trade language, accommodating words and expressions from the French and Aboriginal tongues. Historian Richard White describes the vast territories of the fur trade as well as the contact zone between cultures as "the middle ground."[1]

Conflict with the English Colonies, 1689–1713

Frontenac's successors faced an increasingly difficult military situation by the 1680s. With the resumption of war between the Iroquois and the French, the Five Nations, with the encouragement of the English, resumed their raids on New France. Few in number and scattered over a vast area, the French realized the difficulties of defending the settlers along the frontier. They also realized the importance of their Algonquian allies. The coureurs de bois became even more important because they linked New France with its Aboriginal allies in the interior.

The Iroquois raid in 1689 on Lachine led to a new round of conflict between the French and the Iroquois, and their allies, the English colonies. Returning to New France as governor in 1689,

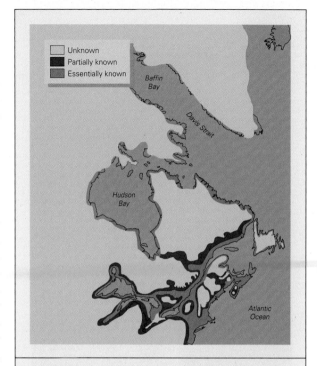

European knowledge of northeastern North America in 1670.

Source: Adapted from Richard I. Ruggles, *A Country So Interesting: The Hudson's Bay Company and Two Centuries of Mapping 1670–1870* (Montreal/Kingston: McGill-Queen's University Press, 1991), p. 27.

Frontenac launched attacks against the English settlements. At Schenectady, New York, and Salmon Falls, New Hampshire, the French and Aboriginal raiding parties terrorized the settlers. In what became known as *la petite guerre*, they scalped men, women, and children and took hundreds of prisoners.

War of the League of Augsburg

The clashes in North America formed a minor theatre in a major European conflict known as the War of the League of Augsburg. Louis XIV was threatening the Dutch on their borders with France. After the "Glorious Revolution" placed William of Orange and his wife Mary on the throne of England, the two Protestant nations formed a defensive alliance against Catholic France in 1689.

In the spring of 1690, a force of New Englanders led by Sir William Phips of Massachusetts attacked and looted Port Royal in Acadia. Phips returned to Boston to take command of a naval expedition of more than thirty vessels with 2300 men that would assault Quebec. But the ships took two months to reach Quebec and smallpox broke out en route. The New Englanders faced a determined French defence when they finally reached the walls of Quebec. When Phips demanded surrender, Governor Frontenac informed the invader that he would obtain his reply from "the mouths of my cannon and muskets." Phips also learned that New France had a formidable ally in the climate. It was an important lesson to be learned when attacking Quebec. The New Englanders arrived late in the season. Fearing entrapment in the ice during a lengthy siege, Phips had no choice but to withdraw. Frontenac's blistery response had its intended effect.

Twentieth-century promotional poster for Canadian Pacific's magnificent Chateau Frontenac.

After Phips's retreat, grateful residents of Quebec named the newly built parish church at Place Royale Notre-Dame-de-la-Victoire.

In 1694, the French naval commander, Pierre Le Moyne d'Iberville, devastated the coasts of Newfoundland. He also sailed into Hudson Bay, where he captured Fort York. D'Iberville continued his aggressive excursions in 1698 when he entered the mouth of the Mississippi and established the colony of Louisiana. Governor Frontenac used the war as a justification to build more forts in the interior, and by 1695, the fur traders had reached the western territories of the Sioux and the Assiniboine. One year later, the French sent an expedition that destroyed the villages of the Onondaga and the Oneida.

The War of the League of Augsburg continued for nine years, until 1697, when the Treaty of Ryswick ended hostilities with no territorial changes in North America. Peace came to the North American frontier only in September 1700, when a truce was negotiated at Montreal between four nations of the Iroquois Confederacy (all except the Mohawk) and the French (and their Aboriginal allies). In July the following year the "Great Peace" was signed at Montreal. But in the very year that New France's long conflict with the Iroquois ended, war broke out again with England.

The War of Spanish Succession

The War of Spanish Succession broke out in Europe in 1701. When Charles II of Spain died, his heir apparent was Philip, grandson of Louis XIV of France. Such a succession would have placed a member of the Bourbon dynasty as monarch of both Spain and France, dramatically altering the European balance of power. England, Portugal, the Holy Roman Empire, and the Dutch Republic moved to prevent the succession. In the English colonies, the conflict became known as Queen Anne's War.

By 1701 it became clear to authorities in New France that North America was a theatre of war in a much larger struggle. The policies and strategies of the remote colony were aimed at aiding France and Louis XIV in the struggle against European enemies. In North America, this enemy was England, its colonies to the south, and those First Nations that chose to fight alongside them. Increasingly, the fur trade became part of this struggle and the supply lines of the fur trade became the front lines. The French placed new importance on holding their forts along the Great Lakes and the Mississippi Valley in order to maintain their alliances with the First Nations and thus prevent English expansion. Colbert's idea of a "compact colony" on the banks of the St. Lawrence was shelved as the French built a chain of posts linking the Great Lakes to the Gulf of Mexico. Louis XIV also ordered the building of a new settlement, to be named *Détroit* (the straits), at the narrows between lakes Erie and Huron. Detroit replaced Michilimackinac as the western base. It was intended to prevent English access to the northwest and maintain French control of the upper Great Lakes. With their Aboriginal allies, the French planned to contain the English within the coastal strip between the Alleghenies and the Atlantic.

New France in Wartime

New France was now the centre of the French North American theatre of war. But the colony suffered three weaknesses. First, it had a small population in comparison with the English colonies, being outnumbered by nearly twenty to one. A second weakness was the precariousness of the fur trade. This one export industry was particularly vulnerable in wartime when the supply lines used to transport furs risked being severed. The colony's third weakness was the relatively small scale of its agriculture, also vulnerable to disruption in wartime. Even in good years, the habitants produced only a small surplus. In wartime, they had a deficit, because militia service took farmers off the land. War meant increased dependence on France for food and war materials at a time when the sea lanes to and from France became exposed to English attack.

Canadian on Snowshoes Going to War over the Snow.
Source: Library and Archives Canada/C-113193.

The French colony did, however, have a number of strengths. It had effective and centralized political leadership. Royal government in 1663 left New France with a unified command structure in times of war. Subject only to annual review, the governor had complete control over the marshalling of the colony's resources, its negotiations with the Aboriginal peoples, and the planning of its war strategy. Nature provided New France with a second strength: defences. The Adirondacks of New York, the Green Mountains of Vermont, and the White Mountains of New Hampshire and Maine all protected the French colony from a direct attack from the south. Two of the three gateways to the St. Lawrence—the river itself (closed half of the year by ice) and the Hudson River–Lake Champlain–Richelieu River waterway—could be sealed. Quebec commanded the St. Lawrence River, and a system of forts existed on the Richelieu River (later complemented by French fortifications at the southern end of Lake Champlain). Only the western approach from Lake Ontario remained open. Inadvertently, the Iroquois had built up the third strength of the French, by teaching the habitants the techniques of Aboriginal warfare. A cadre of tough and versatile French raiders had emerged from the wars with the Iroquois in the Illinois country—warriors who subsequently became Frontenac's most valued troops in his raids against English frontier settlements in New England and New York.

New France's Aboriginal Allies

New France's Aboriginal allies constituted her greatest asset. Through the fur trade and the wars against the Iroquois, the colony was allied with the Great Lakes Algonquians: the Ojibwa, Odawa, Potawatomi, Miami, and Illinois. These alliances were maintained out of necessity for the French, but also through a willingness to respect and honour Aboriginal diplomatic rituals. From the

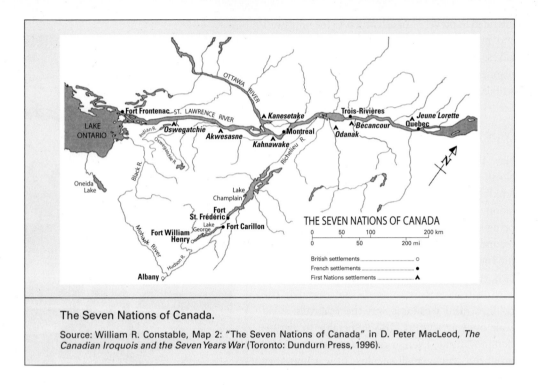

The Seven Nations of Canada.

Source: William R. Constable, Map 2: "The Seven Nations of Canada" in D. Peter MacLeod, *The Canadian Iroquois and the Seven Years War* (Toronto: Dundurn Press, 1996).

First Nations' perspective, an alliance with the French was logical because it aided them against their Iroquois and English enemies. While the English benefited from the Five Nations' support in the 1680s and 1690s, the majority of the Aboriginal groups in northeastern North America sided with the French.

Closer to home, New France had created an Aboriginal buffer to help protect itself. The colony had trading (and hence military) ties with the Abenakis from Maine, many of whom had sought refuge in Canada at Odanak (St. François) and Bécancour. These Catholic converts joined the other Aboriginal groups in the St. Lawrence Valley, living beside the French. The "mission" First Nations included the Iroquois near Montreal: at Kahnawake (Caughnawaga), Kanesatake (Oka), and Akwesasne (St. Regis); as well as the Algonquins at Kanesatake and Hurons at Lorette (Wendake) near Quebec. These close French allies, who numbered approximately 4000 in the mid-eighteenth century, helped to protect the St. Lawrence Valley. They formed an alliance network known as the Seven Nations of Canada. Anxious not to antagonize these allies, the French left them with a surprising degree of independence. They were, for example, largely excluded from the application of the French legal system.

Divisions Within the English Colonies

The French also benefited from divisions within the English colonies. While New France was restructured by the Crown in the mid-1600s, and became an authoritarian royal province under the Sovereign Council, the English colonies developed with relative autonomy and representative government. While Louis XIV's revoking of the Edict of Nantes ensured that New France would be a unified Catholic colony, the English colonies became a dumping ground for religious dissenters. The result was more freedom but also more friction in English America. These divisions prevented the English from taking advantage of its numerical superiority. Not all the English colonies were interested in fighting the French. The colonies of the Carolinas,

Virginia, Maryland, and Pennsylvania, for instance, believed themselves quite safe behind their mountain barriers. New York and Massachusetts shielded Rhode Island and Connecticut. In the north, only two highly populated colonies—Massachusetts and New York—supported the struggle.

Of the two English colonies that fought New France, New York might have proved Canada's match, had the colony's population not been divided in the 1690s between the descendants of the original Dutch colonists and the new English settlers. The Dutch in the north showed little enthusiasm for offensive operations in the name of the English king, and consequently New York posed little threat to New France. The same could not be said for the New Englanders from Massachusetts.

The church Notre-Dame-Des-Victoires, built in 1688 on the foundations of Champlain's trading post, as it appears today. During the summer there is music at Mass every Sunday. This picture appeared on the cover of La Revue d'histoire de l'Amérique française, *Spring 2003.*

Source: © Andre Jenny/Alamy.

Whereas the French colony of Acadia was exposed to constant English attacks, and changed hands numerous times, New France was much better protected. Two English attempts to seize Quebec by naval attack failed, including Phips's failed assault in 1690. Climate and fortune intervened for Quebec again 21 years later at the end of the War of Spanish Succession. In 1711, British commander Sir Hovenden Walker organized an army in Boston of some 7500 troops, while an additional 2300 troops worked their way up the Lake Champlain route by land. New France faced an invasion force equal to half the total French population of the St. Lawrence Valley. Once again, however, disaster struck the invaders. In gales, fog, and shoals along the St. Lawrence, the English lost eight ships and nearly 900 men. The Walker expedition turned back. Quebec's thankful citizens rejoiced by renaming the little church in the Lower Town Notre-Dame-des-Victoires, in honour of both victories.

The Treaty of Utrecht

The Treaty of Utrecht in 1713 ended the war. In Europe, Louis XIV lost his bid to have the empires of France and Spain united under his grandson. Philip V became king of Spain but he had to renounce his claim to the French throne. France did not suffer territorial losses in Europe but such was not the case in North America. The Treaty of Utrecht had serious ramifications for New France.

The losses in North America were ironic because, by the end of the struggle, the French had more than held their ground. They occupied York Factory, the most important Hudson's Bay Company. They retained Detroit and their forts on the Great Lakes. The establishment of Louisiana consolidated their position in the Mississippi Valley. Yet the peace treaty did not reflect these positions.

At the bargaining table at Utrecht, New France paid for Louis XIV's European losses. France had to make concessions, and the French monarch decided to make them in North America: France ceded all claims to Newfoundland, except for fishing rights on the north shore; Acadia was surrendered to England and became Nova Scotia; and France renounced its claims on Hudson Bay. In addition, the French recognized British suzerainty over the Iroquois Confederacy. As a result of these losses, New France was effectively hemmed in. With Nova Scotia and Newfoundland, the English now controlled access to the St. Lawrence from the east. From Hudson Bay to the north and the Ohio Valley to the south, the English forced the French fur trade into the northwest, through the Great Lakes.

Two years later, Louis XIV was dead. Louis XV, then a five-year old child, took the throne; but the real power lay with the regent, Philippe, Duc d'Orléans. The authorities in New France realized that while facing a serious setback, the epic struggle between the two colonial empires was not over. They prepared for the next stage in the conflict.

Military Preparations, 1713–44

The forfeiture of Acadia and Newfoundland was a serious setback for New France. But the French still held Île Royale (Cape Breton Island), whose cod fishery was worth more to France's economy than the entire fur trade. In an attempt to redress the strategic losses, France constructed the military fortress of Louisbourg on Île Royale in 1720. The formidable fortress also served as the administrative centre for Île Royale and Île St-Jean (Prince Edward Island). Although essentially a garrison town, Louisbourg also became an important fishing port and centre for the French triangular trade among the mother country, New France, and the West Indies. As one of the busiest seaports in colonial America—fourth after Boston, New York, and Charleston—it was visited in the 1740s, on average by 130 to 150 vessels every year. By the 1740s, its year-round population was 2500 to 3000. Soldiers made up about one-quarter of the population in the 1740s, and in the 1750s they constituted nearly one-half.

To protect the major towns in the St. Lawrence Valley, Governor Philippe de Rigaud de Vaudreuil built fortifications at Quebec and Montreal. The forts along the Mississippi were garrisoned. The French also moved to strengthen their military position on the Great Lakes and on Lake Champlain. They built Fort Saint-Frédéric on Lake Champlain, at the narrows of the lake near its southern end, to close off the main invasion route into Canada from New York.

The War Against the Fox

While strengthening their military position on the Great Lakes, the French became involved in an Aboriginal war west of Lake Michigan. As early as 1679, the French and the Fox nation had smoked the calumet (a ceremonial pipe) together, indicating their mutual friendship. In the face of the Iroquois threat, the two were natural allies. The problem, however, was that the Fox were enemies of the other French allies, including the Odawa, Ojibwa, Hurons, Miami, and Illinois. From the 1670s through the 1690s, the Fox were under constant attack from these groups. The Fox kept French traders and priests in their midst to discourage attacks from their enemies and the group was present at the Treaty of Montreal in 1701. As the French moved westward and established their settlement at Detroit, the Fox were in an ever better position to gain weapons as well as trade goods. Peace with the Iroquois removed the incentive of the other Aboriginal groups to remain at peace with the Fox.

The French attempted to maintain peace among their allies, but by 1708 the Ojibwa and Odawa were at war with the Fox around Detroit. By 1711, the Huron, Illinois, Potawatomi, and Miami were also fighting the Fox. Needing to maintain their Algonquian allies, the French were pressured into turning against the Fox. Relations deteriorated further because the French had accepted many Fox slaves into New France. Even Governor Vaudreuil had such slaves in his household. Peace between the Fox and French was restored in 1716, but two years later, animosities were increasing and the Fox were demanding the release of their kin from slavery. As Brett Rushforth points out, "to deepen the divide, allied Indians continued to attack Fox villages in violation of the 1716 peace agreement, trading or giving slaves to French officers as tokens of alliance."[2]

After requesting French intervention on four separate occasions in the 1720s to prevent their enemies from attacking their villages for captives, the Fox retaliated. By 1727, attempts at peace had failed completely. French colonial officials, many now with vested interests in the Indian slave trade, sided against the Fox. The French incited their allies to kill off the group. Charles de Beauharnois, Governor of New France, issued the order to "kill [the Fox] without thinking of making a single Prisoner, so as not to leave one of the race alive in the upper Country." This annihilation policy failed, but the Fox were reduced from a population of several thousand to one of several hundred.

La Vérendrye and Western Expansion

Pierre Gaultier de Varennes, Sieur de La Vérendrye, led French expansion further into the northwest. Born in Trois-Rivières, La Vérendrye was the son of a French soldier who had come to New France in the 1660s and the daughter of the Governor of Trois-Rivières. He joined the army and fought in the War of Austrian Succession in North America and the War of Spanish Succession in France. His brother fought against the Fox. As commander of a fur-trading post at the mouth of the Nipigon River, La Vérendrye heard tales about the west country. It is likely that other fur traders had travelled into the territory but did not leave records. From his Cree trading partners, he learned about a "muddy lake" (Lake Winnipeg) and a "great river" (Red River) to the west. Hoping these water routes led to the Pacific, and interested in competing with the English fur

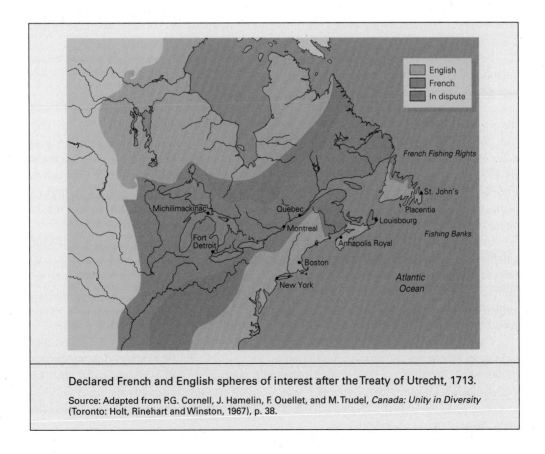

Declared French and English spheres of interest after the Treaty of Utrecht, 1713.

Source: Adapted from P.G. Cornell, J. Hamelin, F. Ouellet, and M. Trudel, *Canada: Unity in Diversity* (Toronto: Holt, Rinehart and Winston, 1967), p. 38.

trade based out of Hudson Bay, in 1732 La Vérendrye and his sons obtained permission from Louis XV to lead an expedition.

The result over the next decade was the construction of a chain of trading posts stretching from Lake Superior through the Prairies. These posts included sites at Lake of the Woods (Fort St. Charles), the Forks of the Red and Assiniboine Rivers (Fort Rouge), Lake Winnipeg (Fort Maurepas), Portage la Prairie (Fort la Reine), and further into the Saskatchewan (Fort Pascoyac). By 1735, La Vérendrye's trade was producing half the beaver pelts reaching Montreal. He travelled south to the land of the Mandan (present-day North Dakota). The excursions went as far westward as the foothills of the Rocky Mountains. In the process, La Vérendrye forged alliances with the Ojibwa, Cree, and Assiniboine. While he never reached the Pacific and his attempt to establish a monopoly on the fur trade failed, his enterprises did expand the French trade and Aboriginal alliances into an area supposedly controlled by the British and the Hudson's Bay Company. Most of the Aboriginal groups found it desirable to trade with the French, thereby forcing the English by the 1750s to push down from the Bay to facilitate their own trade links, and starting a fur-trade war.

War Returns, 1744–60

The War of Austrian Succession

Apart from the war with the Fox to the west and the Mi'kmaq raids against the British in Nova Scotia, peace prevailed in New France. It ended in 1744 with the outbreak of the War of Austrian Succession, known as King George's War in the English colonies. France and Prussia charged that Maria Theresa of Austria, as a woman, could not inherit the Hapsburg throne of her father, Charles VI. Britain and the Dutch Republic supported Austria. In North America, the New England business community welcomed the opportunity to attack Île Royale (Cape Breton) and Louisbourg. If it fell, they could secure a monopoly of the North Atlantic fisheries.

For 28 years, the French had been constructing the fortress of Louisbourg, located on the Atlantic coast of the island near its southeastern point. The site was chosen in order to protect against British naval excursions moving against Quebec, while a reef offered natural protection and a small island provided an ideal position for a battery. Over the decades, Louisbourg became the site of a substantial settlement. The population reached 1616 in 1734 and 4174 in 1752. The port became the third-busiest, behind only Boston and Philadelphia. Louisbourg took on economic importance for France due to the cod fishery. Indeed, the fishery rivalled the fur trade. By 1731, Louisbourg exported 167,000 quintals (about 49 kilograms) of cod and 1600 barrels of cod-liver oil. Almost 500 ships set out each day to fish. But Louisbourg was built for military purposes. The fortress cost thirty million livres, which prompted King Louis XIV to joke that he should be able to see the peaks of its buildings from his Palace at Versailles.

In 1745 Governor William Shirley of Massachusetts organized an expedition of over 4000 colonial militia to attack the French fortress of Louisbourg. In spite of the many years and considerable sums of money spent on construction, the fortress had a fatal weakness: Louisbourg was built to fend off a sea-based attack. The walls on the town's southern and northern flanks remained vulnerable to a land assault. The New Englanders bombarded the town for nearly seven weeks, reducing it to ruins. When no help came from France, the defenders surrendered on June 16.

The fall of Louisbourg caused great anxiety in New France. It revealed the precariousness of France's position in the interior. It also opened the gates of the St. Lawrence, clearing the way to Quebec. Fortunately for the colony, Britain could not mount an invasion of Quebec in 1745. Prince Charles Edward Stuart, "Bonnie Prince Charlie," had just rallied his Highland forces in Scotland. Until the British defeated Charles at Culloden Moor in April 1746, they could not afford to send troops elsewhere.

Realizing the importance of Louisbourg, the French attempted to retake the fortress in the summer of 1746. The attack, however, failed miserably. Scurvy and smallpox took their toll. Nearly 600 of the 7000 soldiers died and another 1500, stricken with disease, could not fight. Storms and British naval attacks ensured the mission's failure. The force returned to France without having attained any of its objectives.

British possession of Louisbourg seriously hampered the French because it prevented supplies of ammunition and trade goods, so badly needed for the fur trade and the maintenance of Aboriginal allies, from reaching the interior. This obstruction led to the defection of some French allies around the Great Lakes. When hostilities ceased in 1748, the French rushed trade goods to the interior.

France realized that without an Atlantic port, it would lose the interior of North America, and perhaps the St. Lawrence Valley as well. During the peace treaty negotiations at Aix-la-Chapelle in 1748, the French sacrificed their conquests in the Netherlands as well as the city of Madras in India in order to regain Louisbourg, much to the chagrin of the New Englanders.

The Seven Years' War

The Treaty of Aix-la-Chapelle in 1748 was no more than a glorified ceasefire. Empress Maria Theresa of Austria used the reprieve to consolidate her power in Europe, gain allies, and prepare for war with the rising power of Prussia under Frederick the Great. France and Russia joined Austria to oppose Prussia, who found an ally in Britain. But the imperial rivalry between Britain and France was coming to a head. The Seven Year's War (called the French and Indian War in the American colonies) would be the final stage in this long conflict. By its end, only one of the two would remain a power in North America.

The Seven Years' War in Europe began in 1756, but it had already been under way in North America since two years previously. The first clash occurred in the Ohio country. In 1753 the Marquis Duquesne, the new governor of New France, made French control of the Ohio River, the natural passage to the west, a top military priority. He sent a French military expedition to clear a route from Lake Erie to the forks of the Ohio River. The following year he commanded French soldiers to build Fort Duquesne at the forks of the river.

In early 1754, Virginia's Governor, Robert Dinwiddie, sent George Washington, a 22-year-old militia officer to dislodge the French from the Ohio. Washington's party ambushed a small French detachment in the Ohio country. Washington then withdrew to Fort Necessity, about 100 kilometres from Fort Duquesne. The French retaliated with a force of 500 French, Canadians, and Aboriginal warriors (Shawnee, Delaware, and Mingo). They attacked the Virginians and soon overpowered them. The French allowed Washington and the Virginians to return home, but their defeat brought wavering Aboriginal bands into the French alliance. When news of the defeat arrived in Britain, an expedition was organized to again attempt to dislodge the French. These skirmishes, in essence, began the Seven Years' War, two years before the first shots were fired in Europe.

New France at the Outset of the Seven Years' War

By the mid-1750s, New France had built up its military strength. The population tripled after 1713, to more than 55 000 in 1755, thus enlarging the militia. As well, settlers cleared new farmland along the Richelieu River, southeast of Montreal; along the Ottawa River, northwest of Montreal; and along the Chaudière River, south of Quebec, providing additional food for the army. Extensive road building allowed expansion back from the waterfront, thereby facilitating better communication and travel.

Historical reconstruction of French alliances with the First Nations by Frederic Remington.

Source: Library and Archives Canada/C-011198.

The French colony had weaknesses, however. First, New France's elongated frontier, which ran from the St. Lawrence to Louisiana, was a liability. It took a year to exchange letters between Quebec and New Orleans. To protect French interests, the Crown built a string of forts from Louisbourg to Fort Duquesne, but many of these outposts were mere trading posts. Canadian control of the interior depended on the support of the Great Lakes First Nations. Second, although the population of New France had increased to more than 55 000, the population of the American colonies now exceeded one million. American settlement extended nearly 200 kilometres from the coastline and now ran up against French territory. Third, although the 8000 militia of New France could be called up quickly and the majority of the First Nations were French allies, the Crown was unprepared to bolster these defences with French regular troops. The French strategy was to win victories in Europe and then use these victories at the peace table to regain colonial losses. As a result, theatres such as North America and the Caribbean received little military support. Fourth, the military command structure in New France was weakened by divisions and friction between the French and the Canadian-born. These frictions would take the form of a critical disagreement over strategy.

The British, on the other hand, were consolidating their position in North America. As a naval power with a superior geographical position to control the Atlantic trade routes, Britain's strategy was to win the overseas colonies. The alliance with Prussia worked well for Britain, because Prussia's formidable army complemented Britain's impressive navy. At the same time, the American colonies were increasingly unified. The coordination of strategy under a British commander-in-chief did much to draw the colonies together. In addition, the colonists viewed the conflict as more than an imperial war; they were fighting for their own territorial interests. They wanted to defeat New France in order to end the border raids and to gain access to the rich lands of the Ohio Valley. Nine colonies, each with populations larger than New France, gave the English colonists an advantage of roughly twenty to one. The foodstuffs available to them were enormous. In 1755, the governor of Pennsylvania claimed that his colony alone produced enough food to provide for an army of 100 000.

New France's Successes, 1754–57

In the early years, however, the war for North America went badly for the British. In 1755, General Edward Braddock planned a four-pronged offensive aimed at taking four French forts: Duquesne, Niagara, Saint-Frédéric, and Beauséjour (on the Isthmus of Chignecto, between present-day Nova Scotia and New Brunswick). But prior to departing England, plans of his expedition were leaked to the French and Louis XV dispatched additional troops. The British tried to obstruct French ships, leading to clashes on the seas. Braddock took command of the assault on Fort Duquesne, with a strike force of 1000 regulars and 1500 colonial troops. It took two months for the force to make its long march over the mountains. As they travelled, they constructed a road, a technique of war totally foreign to the French and their Aboriginal allies, who valued speed and the surprise attack. The advance column of 1450 men finally arrived within 15 kilometres of Fort Duquesne, but the British were ambushed at the Monongahela River. The French and their

Aboriginal allies unleashed a barrage of gunfire at the scarlet-coated regulars and blue-coated Virginians, inflicting 1000 casualties. General Braddock was killed. The defeat also resulted in the French obtaining the British war plans.

Upon receiving news of the defeat at Fort Duquesne, the British postponed their expedition against Fort Niagara under Massachusetts Governor William Shirley. Meanwhile, their attack on Fort Saint-Frédéric in the Lake Champlain area, under Sir William Johnson, resulted in the Battle of Lake George and both armies withdrawing. Johnson advanced no further than Fort William Henry. The newly appointed Canadian-born governor Pierre de Rigaud de Vaudreuil de Cavagnial (the Marquis de Vaudreuil) immediately built Fort Carillon (later Fort Ticonderoga) at the northern end of Lake George. Carillon, so named because it was located where the falling waters produced the sound of bells, became New France's first line of defence for the St. Lawrence Valley.

General Braddock's defeat by the French by Edwin Willard Deming.
Source: State Historical Society of Wisconsin, WHi-1900.

The Anglo-Americans scored their only clear success in Acadia, led by Colonel Monckton. Thanks to the assistance of Thomas Pichon, a traitorous French officer, the British took Fort Beauséjour as well as French Acadia. On the grounds of military necessity, the British captured and expelled nearly 10 000 Acadians, who numbered approximately one-sixth of the population of New France.

With the exception of their loss of Fort Beauséjour, the French and their Aboriginal allies humiliated the larger English colonies and the British army in 1755. The Anglo-American command was also divided. William Shirley took over as commander-in-chief after Braddock's death, but infighting resulted in his replacement early in 1756. The French command was much more impressive and experienced. Governor Vaudreuil wanted to keep up the momentum and maintain the offensive. In 1756, he sent out more than 2000 Aboriginal warriors and Canadians in raids from Fort Duquesne. The attacks caused so much terror along the frontier in Virginia and Maryland that these two colonies stayed out of the war until 1758, fearing that the raids might trigger slave uprisings. The French gained control of the Great Lakes by capturing Fort Oswego, at the eastern end of Lake Ontario, in 1756. The following year Vaudreuil attempted to take Fort William Henry, south of the French stronghold of Carillon (or Ticonderoga, as the English called it). This was a greater challenge, as Fort William Henry—unlike Oswego—lay at the end of a short and easy supply line and could be reinforced speedily from Albany. In addition, grain shortages proved to be severe and persistent in Canada, and the limited provisions would not permit a long siege of the English fort.

The Marquis de Montcalm

French regular forces arrived in 1756. But what should have been an advantage soon turned into a problem. A growing rift appeared between Governor Vaudreuil and the Marquis de Montcalm, the new military commander in New France. Montcalm led a successful attack on the Oswego forts, but this victory demonstrated that Montcalm, a veteran of the War of Austrian Succession, was uncomfortable with Aboriginal warfare. He was appalled at the Aboriginal custom of stripping prisoners of their valuables. French irregular forces harassed Fort William Henry and by

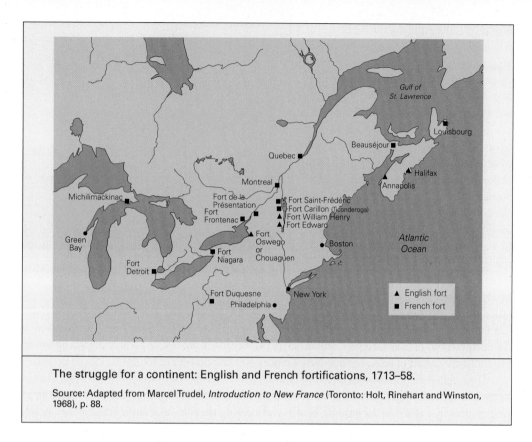

The struggle for a continent: English and French fortifications, 1713–58.

Source: Adapted from Marcel Trudel, *Introduction to New France* (Toronto: Holt, Rinehart and Winston, 1968), p. 88.

August of 1757 Montcalm besieged the fort. The British surrendered; but the Aboriginal allies, angered at the lost opportunity to gain loot, attacked the retreating force. When Fort William Henry fell, Vaudreuil wanted to harass the exposed British supply lines. He also wanted to march against Fort Edward, the English post on the Hudson River, 25 kilometres to the south, but Montcalm opposed such a plan.

Montcalm disagreed with the overall strategy being used in North America. He preferred shifting from the offensive to the defensive, and concentrating his forces in the St. Lawrence Valley in order to protect Montreal and Quebec. This tactic fit better with the larger French strategy of holding onto its colonial possessions while focusing on making gains in Europe. Vaudreuil disagreed because such a defensive plan largely neutralized the major French advantage: the Aboriginal allies. The French ministry resolved the dispute in late 1758 by putting Montcalm in command over Vaudreuil in military matters.

Montcalm's strategy and leadership has been maligned by historians, but by 1758, despite the French victories, it was justified, at least to an extent. The British were effectively blockading French sea lanes to North America, thereby limiting shipping and supplies. A poor harvest in New France in 1757 further strained resources. The alleged corruption of the Intendant, François Bigot, caused additional chaos, while the Aboriginal allies were beset by smallpox.

Britain Gains the Upper Hand

The direction of the war changed in 1757 with the accession of William Pitt the Elder—the self-styled saviour of the British empire—to the prime ministership of Britain. Pitt made the North American theatre and the conquest of Canada major objectives. The British offensive of 1758 aimed at the same four localities as that of 1755, but this time, the results proved different.

Several factors explain the improvement in Britain's fortunes. First, Pitt decided in 1758 to commit large numbers of regular soldiers to America. Second, by 1758 the Royal Navy had effectively blockaded France to prevent "escapes" of French support squadrons to Canada. Finally, Pitt greatly increased Britain's financial commitment to the war. More men, more ships, and more money made a significant difference in British fortunes in 1758 and 1759. North America was a priority for Britain.

French Losses in 1758

The first British objective in 1758 was to retake Louisbourg. On account of the effectiveness of the British blockade on France, Louisbourg on Île Royale lacked the protection of a full fleet. The combined British naval and army forces

The capture of the French ships Prudent *and* Bienfaisant *in Louisbourg harbour, July 26, 1758.*

Source: With permission of the Royal Ontario Museum © ROM, 956.94.

numbered approximately 27 000, outnumbering the defenders three to one. The British believed that Louisbourg had to be taken quickly if Quebec was to be captured in the same season. The defenders, however, held out for seven weeks—just long enough to rule out an expedition against Quebec before winter arrived and the St. Lawrence was frozen over.

The successful French defence at Carillon also served to prevent an attack on Quebec in 1758. Montcalm faced an English army of 15 000 with only 3500 men, yet won. But the French success had its price. Indirectly, it cost the French both Fort Frontenac on Lake Ontario and Fort Duquesne in present-day Pennsylvania. Since Fort Frontenac, with its small garrison and inadequate walls, could not be defended against an English attack, the French themselves destroyed the important post in August 1758. They also blew up Fort Duquesne and retreated. The English renamed the site "Pittsburgh," after their prime minister. While New France may have avoided an attack in 1758, the French lost control of the Upper Ohio Valley.

The largest single explanation for the English success in 1758 was the Royal Navy. It allowed the English colonies to obtain troop reinforcements and supplies, while also blockading New France. In 1759, New France faced odds of nearly three to one in ships, four to one in regular soldiers committed to North America, and ten to one in money.

The Fall of New France

In 1759, the British threw everything they had at New France. With the British resources in America, it could attack both Quebec and Carillon in equal strength. New France, by contrast, with its limited resources, had to concentrate its defence forces in the most vital area: Quebec. But the citadel at Quebec was, in many ways, the ideal defensive fortification. It commanded the heights overlooking the river and its natural defences made an assault precarious. Eighteenth-century warfare relied on artillery power. If properly equipped and outfitted, the citadel should have been nearly impossible to take. In Quebec, white-haired men and beardless boys turned out to defend their homeland. The Franco–Canadian army that gathered in the summer of 1759 numbered about 15 000, an impressive force for a colony of only about 60 000.

The French defenders at Quebec, however, faced several defensive problems. First, the walls on the western side facing the Plains of Abraham had no gun emplacements, seriously weakening the city's defence. Second, the French made a monumental error: they left undefended the south

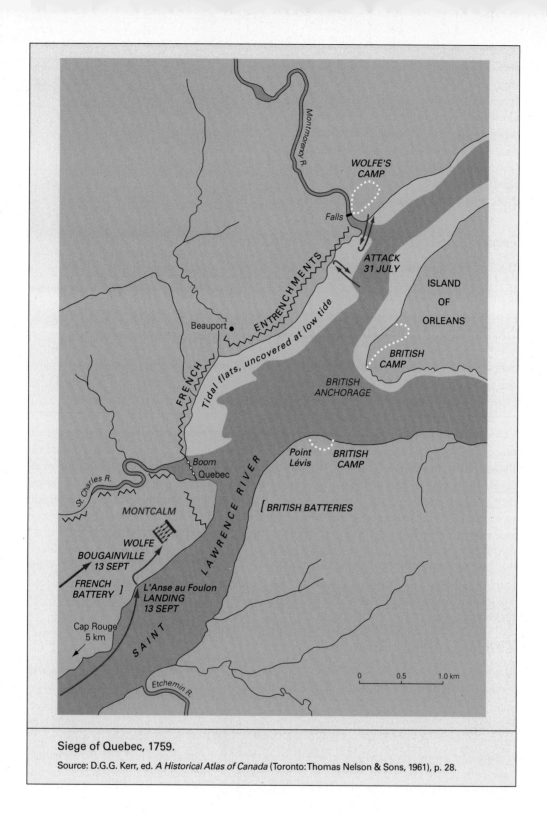

Siege of Quebec, 1759.

Source: D.G.G. Kerr, ed. *A Historical Atlas of Canada* (Toronto: Thomas Nelson & Sons, 1961), p. 28.

bank of the river opposite the city, assuming an attack could not come from this position. Worse still, the Royal Navy could transport its ships up the river beyond Quebec. In effect, the British army could land either above or below Quebec for an assault on the walled city.

Throughout the summer of 1759, the news went from bad to worse. A continuous stream of reports arrived in Quebec of inland French garrisons falling into enemy hands. By the end of June, the British reoccupied Fort Oswego. Fort Niagara succumbed to a British attack in late July. Rather than have the British take Fort Rouillé, France's small trading outpost in the area that the Aboriginals called Toronto, the French burned it to the ground. (An obelisk on the grounds of Toronto's Canadian National Exhibition marks the fort's location.) The French now lost control of lakes Ontario and Erie, and the Ohio country. In addition, they abandoned forts Carillon and Saint-Frédéric and retreated northward to the head of Lake Champlain. The French were falling back on Quebec.

The Notre-Dame-des-Victoires church after the naval bombardment of Quebec by the British in 1759. Note the extent of the war damage shown in this engraving by A. Bennoist, from a sketch by Richard Short, an English naval officer.

Source: Library and Archives Canada, Acc. No. 1970-188-17. W.H. Coverdale Collection of Canadiana/C-000357.

But time was on the side of the French. If Montcalm could hold out until the following year, it was expected that the war would end with Canada still in French hands. In the short term, the British also faced time constraints. They could lay siege to Quebec but if winter came before the citadel fell, the British army would be stranded outside the walls, surrounded by a hostile population, and with the river frozen, preventing reinforcements or supplies.

James Wolfe

Major-General James Wolfe, a 32-year-old professional soldier who was a veteran of the War of Austrian Succession as well as the Jacobite Rebellions, commanded the British invasion force of some 13 500 men against Quebec. An excellent battalion commander, he had never led an army before, although he had success in taking Louisbourg. At the time of the attack on Quebec, Wolfe looked ill and indeed was. Frequently in pain, he was often depressed to the state of despair.

Historian C.P. Stacey aptly called James Wolfe a "Hamlet-figure"—because of his difficulty making up his mind.[3] Only after several weeks of indecision did he decide to strike Montcalm and his forces at Montmorency, just east of Quebec. Wolfe's frontal attack on the French army's entrenchments failed, and the British retreated. The British commander spent the remainder of the summer systematically devastating the parishes around Quebec. On the south shore of the St. Lawrence, the British destroyed a thousand buildings as well as the crops. In the meantime, a second British force under General Jeffrey Amherst was marching on Montreal, but it was making slow progress and was not expected to be able to help Wolfe. Time was running out and Wolfe was becoming despondent.

The Battle of the Plains of Abraham

The British were forced into action. Wolfe knew he had to obtain a foothold on the north shore and then force Montcalm into an open, European-style battle. Fortunately, he found a small cove, L'Anse au Foulon, from which a narrow path led up the steep 65-metre cliffs. Believing an invasion force could not climb the heights on the tiny path, the French left it lightly guarded. Equally surprisingly, the French failed to establish a password for a French convoy expected to bring supplies on the night of September 12. Montcalm believed the British attack would come on the other side of the city or at its centre—but not at L'Anse au Foulon to the west. The daring British plan came as a complete surprise.

The French sentries on the shore believed that the boats gliding past them belonged to the French convoy expected that night. But the convoy had been cancelled. The British commander placed his few French-speaking officers in the forward vessels. In the darkness of night, they answered the sentries' challenges satisfactorily. A half-hour before dawn on September 13, the British landed near the cove. Three waves of landing ships reached the shore in total darkness. The advance party, two abreast, then walked up the steep pathway and, without detection, gained the summit of the cliffs. The risky plan paid dividends for Wolfe. The difficult naval landing succeeded and his advance guard of Scottish Highlanders overpowered the French post, securing a foothold on the cliffs. If the French sentries had identified the British in time, they could have sounded the alarm and easily eliminated the advance guard as they climbed the cliffs.

By daybreak, Wolfe deployed 4500 highly trained British troops and two small cannons on the Plains of Abraham, the grassy field close to the unarmed western walls of the citadel. At this point, Montcalm made a fatal mistake. Fearing that the British would carry more cannons up the cliffs and destroy the walls, the Marquis took action. Instead of waiting for Colonel Louis-Antoine de Bougainville to arrive with his 3000 regulars, stationed at Cap Rouge, about 15 kilometres upstream, he attacked. The decisive battle lasted less than half an hour. Wolfe was ready: to ensure accurate and concentrated firepower, he deployed three-quarters of his men in a single line confronting the French. The British held their fire until the French army was within 40 metres. Then the British officers gave the order to fire. Muskets roared, and a second volley followed, breaking the attack and causing the French army to retreat in disorder. Wolfe, leading a picked force of grenadiers, was shot three times and died on the battlefield. During the retreat, Montcalm was shot through the stomach. In the confusion after Wolfe's death, the French army retreated up the St. Lawrence by a circuitous route. Montcalm was carried from the battle and died the next morning. Both sides suffered about 650 casualties. On September 18, Quebec surrendered.

A HISTORICAL PORTRAIT

Joined in Death: Wolfe and Montcalm

Few military battles in Canadian history have been as celebrated, lamented, and romanticized as the Plains of Abraham. Regarded as the decisive engagement between France and Britain in the struggle for North America, the compelling personalities of the two rival commanders have come to embody the epic clash. The British Brigadier General James Wolfe and the French Major General, Louis-Joseph de Montcalm-Gozon, Marquis de Saint-Veran, were both experienced and competent military commanders. Although the British victory has traditionally been attributed to Wolfe's tactics and Montcalm's errors, both generals despaired of ever achieving their goals and shared a brooding fatalism that brought them to their demise at the Battle of the Plains of Abraham on September 13, 1759.

An aristocratic family, the Montcalms converted to Protestantism during the sixteenth century. When the persecution of French Protestants intensified in the mid-1680s, Montcalm's uncle took refuge in the Protestant stronghold of Geneva, Switzerland, while his father converted to Catholicism and thus was permitted to inherit the family's confiscated estates. Born in 1712 at the Château of Candiac in the south of France, near Montpellier, Montcalm began his military career at the age of 20. He was an impressive officer in the field. Wounded five times by sabre and musket ball during European conflicts such as the War of Austrian Succession, he was awarded the Order of St. Louis, the highest distinction a French officer could receive.

By all accounts, Montcalm was also a gentleman. His personal letters portray a devoted family man, writing often to his wife (Angélique Talon de Boulay, whose family had powerful connections at court, which helped her husband obtain his rapid promotions) and mother, and worrying about his children. Ever the cavalier, Montcalm's first duty was to his honour and his king. "I think that I would renounce every honour to join you again," Montcalm wrote to his wife at their home in Candiac, France, "but the king must be obeyed." According to the nineteenth century historian Francis Parkman, Montcalm was "a man of small [physical] stature, with a lively countenance, a keen eye, and, in moments of animation, rapid, vehement utterance, and nervous gesticulation."[1]

But as a commander trained in European tactics, Montcalm had nothing but disdain for the North American style of guerrilla warfare, and believed the depredations of his Native allies brought dishonour to the French colours. Montcalm favoured defensive strategies. At the Battle of Carillon (Fort Ticonderoga), Montcalm defeated a British army four times larger than his own, although many historians agree that this was owed more to the British commander's incompetence than Montcalm's ability. Sensing his lucky break at Carillon and the overwhelming odds against him, Montcalm asked to be recalled to France. The French authorities refused, and although Montcalm attempted to do all he could in the defence of Quebec, he believed that New France's only real hope was at a European treaty table.[2]

In contrast to the aristocratic Montcalm, James Wolfe was born into a modest, though well-regarded, military family in 1727. He became an officer while still a teenager and fought in the War of Austrian Succession and in the Jacobite Rebellion in Scotland at the Battle of Culloden. After distinguishing himself at the Battle of Rochefort in 1757, Wolfe was appointed Brigadier General and sent to North America, tasked with capturing Quebec.[3]

Wolfe often sat and chatted with his enlisted men and his Highland soldiers gave him the nickname "the red-haired corporal" for his simple uniform. Perpetually sick, however, Wolfe shared Montcalm's fatalism and was regarded as eccentric, if not mentally unbalanced, by his fellow officers. As the siege of Quebec wore on in 1759, he became despondent and feared he might succumb to his illnesses and die a failure. Frustrated with carrying out "Skirmishing, Cruelty & Devastation" in the countryside around Quebec, Wolfe finally decided to act.[4]

Unlike Montcalm, Wolfe was a flexible tactician. Ignoring the counsel of his fellow English generals, Wolfe secretly devised a plan based on the advice of a former prisoner of war held at Quebec. Rather than land his army on an open beach with room to manoeuver, his men would scale the cliffs at L'Anse au Foulon, up a little-known path southwest of Quebec City. Wolfe kept the landing site a secret even from his own officers until the evening before the attack and landed his men under cover of darkness. When the sun rose, the French defenders were shocked to see the redcoats arrayed on the Plains of Abraham. Montcalm had not considered such an audacious move possible.

Montcalm's decision to march out to meet the British rather than remain behind the walls of Quebec or await reinforcements has remained controversial to this day. But the Marquis knew that if he failed to stem the flow of redcoats up the cliff, his position would be hopeless. Wolfe, too, believed that if the British forces did not succeed, winter would end the campaign and he would return to England in defeat. Both generals staked everything in this gamble, and as honourable men, included their own lives in the wager.[5]

In the brief but decisive battle that followed, the French and Canadian lines

Montcalm's remains being carried to the Seven Years' War cemetery.

Source: Photo by Marc-André Grenier, Commission de la capitale nationale du Québec.

broke and both Montcalm and Wolfe were fatally wounded. Montcalm was carried from the field and died early the next morning. When his surgeon informed him that he had only a short time to live, the Marquis is reported to have replied "So much the better . . . I am happy that I shall not live to see the surrender of Quebec." Wolfe died on the field. After being told of the French rout, his final words were reputed to be: "Now, God be praised, I will die in peace."[6]

The British government erected a monument at Quebec to both generals in 1828 which still stands today. A Latin inscription reads: "Their courage gave them a common death, history a common fame, posterity a common memorial."

1. Francis Parkman, *Montcalm and Wolfe* (New York: Random House, 1999), pp. 346, 181, 184.

2. Lawrence Henry Gipson, *The British Empire Before the American Revolution,* vol. 7 (New York: Knopf, 1965), p. 232.

3. Fred Anderson, *Crucible of War: The Seven Years' War and the Fate of Empire in British North America, 1754–1766* (New York: Vintage Books, 2000), pp. 247–249.

4. Earl John Chapman and Ian Macpherson McCulloch, eds., *A Bard of Wolfe's Army: James Thompson, Gentleman Volunteer, 1733–1830* (Montreal: Robin Brass Studios, 2009), p. 12.

5. Anderson, p. 344.

6. Anderson, pp. 351–355.

The Death of General Wolfe *by Benjamin West.*

Source: Benjamin West, *The Death of General Wolfe, 1770.* Oil on canvas, 152.6 × 214.5 cm National Gallery of Canada, Ottawa. Transfer from the Canadian War Memorials, 1921. (Gift of the 2nd Duke of Westminster, England, 1918). Photo © NGC.

New France's Final Year, 1759–60

The Battle of the Plains of Abraham has become entrenched in the social memory as the pivotal event in the struggle for Quebec. The nature of the risky assault leading to the battle combined with the deaths of the two commanders provided irresistible fodder for the romanticized and heroic portraits to follow. But the fate of New France was not decided on the Plains of Abraham. The loss of Quebec was a serious blow to the French, but they still controlled the rest of the St. Lawrence Valley and their army remained intact. Ironically, the decisive battle for New France was a naval battle fought at Quiberon Bay, off the coast of France. The Royal Navy's destruction of the French fleet meant that France could not send a reserve force to save Canada. The success of the French army's offensive against Quebec in the spring of 1760 depended on the dispatch of a French armada, with fresh troops and supplies. But help would not arrive.

Before the ice left the rivers in April, the Chevalier de Lévis, Montcalm's successor as French commander, marched his 7000 troops to Quebec. James Murray, the British commander, had experienced a terrible winter, in which scurvy had reduced his garrison to only 4000. Lévis defeated him at Ste. Foy, immediately west of the city (near the site of Université Laval today). This battle proved bloodier than that of the Plains of Abraham, with about 850 casualties on the French side and nearly 1100 on the English side.

Though the details of The Death of General Wolfe *by Benjamin West might well be historically inaccurate, ethnologists regard this representation of a First Nations warrior as reasonably faithful. The artist had observed First Nations people while growing up in colonial Pennsylvania.*

Source: Benjamin West, *The Death of General Wolfe, 1770.* Oil on canvas, 152.6 × 214.5 cm, National Gallery of Canada, Ottawa. Transfer from the Canadian War Memorials, 1921. (Gift of the 2nd Duke of Westminster, England, 1918). Photo © NGC.

Lévis then besieged Quebec. Short of ammunition and supplies, Lévis—and all of New France—prayed for French ships to reach Quebec. But English, not French, ships arrived first at Quebec in mid-May. Lévis had to abandon his plans to retake the city. The rest of the year's operations were a foregone conclusion. General Jeffery Amherst, British commander-in-chief in America, advanced toward Montreal from the south, with a huge army. At Montreal that September, Lévis and 2000 troops confronted 17 000 British and American troops. The French capitulated on September 8, 1760, and the British took possession of Montreal. Canada passed into British hands.

And yet, the ultimate fate of New France was still unknown. As was so often the case during the colonial wars, what transpired in the North American theatre had little impact relative to what occurred on the battlefields of Europe. The Seven Years' War would not end in Europe until 1763. In the meantime, the British troops occupying New France had to wait anxiously until the peace was signed to determine who would control Canada. The *Canadiens* had reason to be even more anxious.

WHERE HISTORIANS DISAGREE

Montcalm: Asset or Liability for New France?

There is little doubt that the Marquis de Montcalm was an effective officer on European battlefields, but his ability in the New World has remained a point of debate among historians. Nineteenth-century Quebec historians such as François-Xavier Garneau and the Abbé J.B.A. Ferland regarded Montcalm as ineffective and defeatist, and credited the Canadian-born Vaudreuil for New France's early victories in the Seven Years' War. The American historian Francis Parkman saw the situation in reverse: Montcalm was the noble hero, a talented leader in a hopeless cause, undermined by the machinations of the conniving Bigot and Vaudreuil. According to Parkman, the conquest of New France and its "barren absolutism" was inevitable when faced with the "prolific vitality" of British liberties and institutions. Montcalm, for all his talents and virtues, was a tragic defender of a feudal system overwhelmed by the forces of modernism.[1]

In 1911, Quebec historian Thomas Chapais worked to rehabilitate Montcalm's image in French Canada. In *Le Marquis de Montcalm*, Chapais depicted Montcalm as an excellent commander and courageous defender of New France and her people. Far from being the haughty Old World General, dismissive of his colonial underlings, Chapais argued that Montcalm genuinely respected and liked the French Canadians.[2]

Chapais managed to salvage the reputation of the Marquis until the mid-twentieth century, when it was once again challenged. In his 1955 work, historian Guy Frégault depicted Vaudreuil as the hero of New France, who wisely used the strengths of his Native allies and Canadian militiamen.[3] W.J. Eccles agreed, painting Montcalm as a relentless self-promoter who, though achieving some success in spite of himself, was sorely out of touch with the necessities of North American warfare.[4]

Fred Anderson has provided the most recent interpretation of Montcalm in his book *Crucible of War*. Anderson argues that Montcalm's actions can be attributed to his devotion to the European attitudes of honourable warfare. Tactically, Montcalm adhered to the European orthodoxy of massing forces for the static defence of strong points. Montcalm thought that the thinly spread irregular forces favoured by Vaudreuil were doomed to fail against a large, conventional army, even in the wilderness. According to Anderson, Montcalm also believed that Vaudreuil's methods were little more than a "surrender to savagery" that stained the honour of France as well as the Marquis' personal reputation. According to Anderson, Montcalm "held as an article of faith what so few Canadians seemed able to grasp: that there were more important things in war than winning."[5]

Whether Montcalm was a liability or asset to New France is difficult to gauge, and may be irrelevant viewed with a wider lens. Engaged in a global struggle in Europe, India, and North America, France had few men and fewer materials to send to the defence of New France. While Britain's Prussian allies could keep France tied up on the European continent, Britain could employ its naval dominance and economic resources to deliver professional troops and supplies to North America. As Ian Steele argues, the fall of New France cannot be attributed to personalities, culture, religion, or supplies. Rather, "Canada fell to fortune's favourite—the biggest army."[6]

1.   Francis Parkman, *Montcalm and Wolfe* (Boston: Little, Brown, and Company, 1902 [1884]), p. 33.

2.   Thomas Chapais, *Le Marquis de Montcalm, 1712–1759* (Quebec: Garneau, 1911).

3.   Guy Frégault, *La guerre de la conquête* (Montreal: Fides, 1955); translated by Margaret M. Cameron as *Canada: The War of the Conquest* (Toronto: Oxford University Press, 1969).

4.   W.J. Eccles, "Louis-Joseph de Montcalm, Marquis de Montcalm," *Dictionary of Canadian Biography,* vol. 3, *1741–1770* (Toronto: University of Toronto Press, 1974), pp. 458–69.

5.   Fred Anderson, *Crucible of War: The Seven Years' War and the Fate of Empire in British North America, 1754–1766* (New York: Vintage Books, 2000), pp. 346–347.

6.   Ian Steele, *Guerillas and Grenadiers: The Struggle for Canada, 1689–1760* (Toronto: Ryerson Press, 1969), pp. 133–134.

SUMMARY

In 1763, Britain emerged as the dominant imperial power, triumphant after 60 years of colonial wars with France. The war for North America was over. But the empire now faced new challenges. The British had to determine policies to deal with the "conquered" French-Catholic population in Quebec and the hostile First Nations, most of which had long been enemies. To make matters worse, trouble was already brewing in the Thirteen Colonies to the south.

NOTES

1. See Richard White, *The Middle Ground: Indians, Empires, and Republics in the Great Lakes Region, 1650–1815* (Cambridge: Cambridge University Press, 1991).

2. Brett Rushforth, "Slavery, the Fox Wars, and the Limits of Alliance," *William and Mary Quarterly*, 3rd series, 63(1) (January 2006): 70.

3. C.P. Stacey, *Quebec, 1759: The Siege and the Battle* (Toronto: Macmillan, 1959), p. 171.

BIBLIOGRAPHY

Gilles Havard and Cécile Vidal's *Histoire de l'Amérique française* (Paris: Flammarion, 2006), although not yet translated, is an excellent recent overview of French expansion in North America. For an older treatment in English, see the following works by W.J. Eccles: *The Canadian Frontier, 1534–1760* (Toronto: Holt, Rinehart and Winston, 1969); *France in America*, rev. ed. (Markham, ON: Fitzhenry & Whiteside, 1990); and *Essays on New France* (Toronto: Oxford University Press, 1987). Bibliographical guides include Jacques Rouillard, ed., *Guide d'histoire du Québec du régime français à nos jours: Bibliographie commentée* (Montreal: Éditions du Méridien, 1991); and Thomas Wien, "Canada and the *Pays d'en haut*, 1600–1760," in M. Brook Taylor, ed., *Canadian History: A Reader's Guide,* vol. 1, *Beginnings to Confederation* (Toronto: University of Toronto Press, 1994), pp. 33–75.

Volumes on the military events of the late seventeenth and eighteenth centuries include Fred Anderson, *The Crucible of War: The Seven Years' War and the Fate of the Empire in British North America, 1754–1766* (New York: Vintage, 2000); and William M. Fowler, Jr., *Empires at War: The Seven Years' War and the Struggle for North America* (Vancouver: Douglas & McIntyre, 2005) and William Fowler's *Empires at War: The Seven Years' War and the Struggle for North America, 1754–1763* (Vancouver: Douglas & McIntyre, 2005). Francis Parkman's *Montcalm and Wolfe* is a classic that has recently been republished in multiple formats (see editions by Da Capo Press, 2001. Other treatments include I.K. Steele, *Guerillas and Grenadiers: The Struggle for Canada, 1689–1760* (Toronto: Ryerson Press, 1969), and his more recent book, *Warpaths: Invasions of North America* (New York: Oxford University Press, 1994); George F.G. Stanley, *New France: The Last Phase, 1744–1760* (Toronto: McClelland & Stewart, 1968); C.P. Stacey, *Quebec, 1759: The Siege and the Battle* (Toronto: Macmillan, 1959; new ed., Toronto: Robin Brass Studio, 2002); and Guy Frégault, *Canada: The War of the Conquest,* trans. Margaret M. Cameron (Toronto: Oxford University Press, 1969).

The first four volumes of *Dictionary of Canadian Biography* (Toronto: University of Toronto Press, 1966–1976) also contain important biographical sketches; of particular interest are C.P. Stacey, "James Wolfe," in vol. 3, pp. 666–74; W.J. Eccles, "Louis-Joseph de Montcalm," in vol. 3, pp. 458–69; and W.J. Eccles, "Pierre de Rigaud de Vaudreuil de Cavagnial," in vol. 4, pp. 662–74. These are available online: www.bibliographi.ca.

For a more recent biography of James Wolfe, see Stephen Brumwell, *Paths of Glory: The Life and Death of General James Wolfe* (Montreal/Kingston: McGill-Queen's University Press, 2007). Donald W. Olson et al. have provided a new look at the background to the Battle of the Plains of Abraham in "Perfect Tide, Ideal Moon: An Unappreciated Aspect of Wolfe's Generalship at Quebec, 1759," *William and Mary Quarterly* 59(4) (2002): 957–74. Summaries of the two respective armies in the 1750s appear in volume 3 of *Dictionary of Canadian Biography*. See the essays W.J. Eccles, "The French Forces in North America During the Seven Years' War," pp. xv–xxiii, and C.P. Stacey, "The British Forces in North America During the Seven Years' War," pp. xxiv–xxx. For an examination of the French defeat in the Seven Years' War, see Gregory H. McNiven, "Conquest! An Investigation into the Underlying Causes of the Military Defeat of New France During the French and Indian War," *Mirror* 28 (2008): 133–54. Martin L. Nicolai reviews the French forces in "A Different Kind of Courage: The French Military and the Canadian Irregular Soldier During the Seven Years' War," *Canadian Historical Review* 70 (1989): 53–75.

An illustrated volume on the Plains of Abraham has been prepared by Jacques Mathieu and Eugen Kedl, *Les Plaines d'Abraham: Le culte de l'idéal* (Sillery, QC: Septentrion, 1993). For a further look at the Plains of Abraham, see D. Peter Macleod, *Northern Armageddon: The Battle of the Plains of Abraham; Eight Minutes of Gunfire That Shaped a Continent* (Vancouver: Douglas & McIntyre, 2008). For a further look at Aboriginal and French military relations during this period, see Arnaud Balvay, "Les Relations Entre Soldats Français et Amérindiens: La question de la traite (1683–1763)," *Recherches amérindiennes au Québec* 35(2) (2005): 17–28.

For a look at the issue of both diplomacy and neturality during the colonial wars, see John Parmenter and Mark Power Robison, "The Perils and Possibilities of Wartime Neutrality on the Edges of Empire: Iroquois and Acadians Between the French and British in North America, 1744–1760," *Diplomatic History* 31(2) (2007): 167–206. See also Jon Parmenter, "After the Mourning Wars: The Iroquois as Allies in Colonial North American Campaigns, 1676–1760," *William and Mary Quarterly* 64(1) (2007): 39–82. For an examination of the taking of prisoners by the English, see Ian K. Steele, "When Worlds Collide: The Fate of Canadian and French Prisoners Taken at Fort Niagara, 1759," *Journal of Canadian Studies/Revue d'études canadiennes* 39(3) (2005): 9–39. For a look at the fortifications used during the Seven Years' War, see Matthew J. Wayman, "Fortifications at Quebec, 1759–1760: Their Conditions and Impact on the Sieges and Battles," *Journal of America's Military Past* 30(1) (2004): 5–25.

The history of Louisbourg is well documented. See *Louisbourg: An 18th Century Town* by A.J.B. Johnston et al. (Halifax: Nimbus, 1991), a lively popular account. A.J.B. Johnston has also written several important volumes on Louisbourg: *Life and Religion at Louisbourg, 1713–1758* (Montreal/Kingston: McGill-Queen's University Press, 1996), *Control and Order in French Colonial Louisbourg, 1713–1758* (East Lansing, MI: Michigan State University Press, 2001), and most recently *Endgame 1758: The Promise, the Glory, and the Despair of Louisbourg's Last Decade* (Sydney: Cape Breton University Press, 2007). Two overviews of the history of Louisbourg, one old and one new, are J.S. McLennan, *Louisbourg from Its Foundation to Its Fall, 1713–58* (Halifax: Book Room, 1990 [1918]); and the historical booklet by Terry Crowley, *Louisbourg: Atlantic Fortress and Seaport* (Ottawa: Canadian Historical Association, 1990). Students will enjoy the five well-crafted biographies of ordinary Louisbourg citizens in Christopher Moore's *Louisbourg Portraits* (Toronto: Macmillan, 1982). For a French-language study of Louisbourg, see Josette Brun's, *Vie et mort du couple en Nouvelle-France: Québec et Louisbourg au XVIIIe siècle* (Montreal/Kingston: McGill-Queen's University Press), 2006.

For background on Aboriginal involvement in the Seven Years' War, see Francis Jennings, *Empire of Fortune: Crowns, Colonies and Tribes in the Seven Years War in America* (New York: W.W. Norton, 1988); Peter MacLeod, *The Canadian Iroquois and the Seven Years' War* (Toronto: Dundurn Press, 1996); Jean-Pierre Sawaya, *La Fédération des Sept Feux de la vallée du Saint-Laurent* (Sillery, QC: Septentrion, 1998); and Richard White, *The Middle Ground: Indians, Empires and Republics in the Great Lakes Region, 1650–1815* (Cambridge: Cambridge University Press, 1991). Brett Rushforth's "'A Little Flesh We Offer You': The Origins of Indian Slavery in New France," *The William and Mary Quarterly* 60(4) (October 2003): 777–808, rethinks New France's approach to First Nations. See his article "Slavery, the Fox Wars, and the Limits of Alliance," also in *The William and Mary Quarterly*, 60(1) (January 2006): 53–80; Gauillaume Aubert's "'The Blood of France': Race and Purity of Blood in the French Atlantic World" from the same issue should also be consulted. The Michigan Historical Review devotes an entire issue to the question of borderlands; see *Michigan Historical Review* 34(1) (March 2008). The *William and Mary Quarterly* also devotes an issue to the middle ground; see 63(1) (January 2006). D. Peter MacLeod reviews the impact of smallpox on France's First Nations allies in "Microbes and Muskets," *Ethnohistory* 39(1) (Winter

1992): 42–64. Jan Grabowski underlines the independence of the "mission" First Nations in "French Criminal Justice and Indians in Montreal, 1670–1760," *Ethnohistory* 43(3) (Summer 1996): 405–29. An interesting look at the impact of the British invasion on the south shore of the St. Lawrence (east of Quebec, from Beaumont to Kamouraska) is Gaston Deschênes, *L'Année des Anglais: La Côté-du-sud à l'heure de la conquête* (Sillery, QC: Septentrion, 1988).

Maps depicting events of the Seven Years' War and the battles for Quebec, 1759–60, are contained in R. Cole Harris, ed., *Historical Atlas of Canada*, vol. 1, *From the Beginning to 1800* (Toronto: University of Toronto Press, 1987).

Part 2

COLONIAL SOCIETIES IN BRITISH NORTH AMERICA, 1760 TO 1815

INTRODUCTION

Britain now controlled most of North America. Policies were needed to deal with its new populations. But, first, Britain faced unprecedented Aboriginal resistance in Pontiac's Uprising in 1763. Most of the First Nations had fought against the British and its American colonies and did not negotiate peace.

New colonial societies emerged in British North America between 1763 and 1812. In Quebec, the Conquest represented a major upheaval for the French and Catholic inhabitants now under British rule. The British plan was to assimilate the French Canadians. It was expected that the colony would be British and Protestant within a generation or two. Certain events delayed the plan, however. As the eighteenth century closed, the Canadiens still retained many aspects of their culture, including their Catholic religion, the seigneurial system, and the French language.

The British government altered its policy to deal with Quebec three times between 1763 and 1791. In the Proclamation of 1763, Britain's objective was to assimilate the French. Then, in the Quebec Act of 1774, the authorities temporarily took a pragmatic approach and recognized French-Canadian institutions to gain the loyalty of the population when rebellion broke out in the Thirteen Colonies. The American Revolution brought further change, as large numbers of loyalists left their homes in the now-independent United States and immigrated to Britain's northern colonies. The Constitutional Act of 1791 created Upper Canada as a new loyalist homeland.

The first governor of Upper Canada, John Graves Simcoe, aimed to make Upper Canada a "model British colony." Large numbers of so-called "late loyalists" arrived, although more often in search of cheap land than from any attachment to Britain. On the eve of the War of 1812, this group represented the majority of the population. When the American invasion occurred, this population's "loyalties" were cause for concern.

Nova Scotia in these years was dominated by the aftermath of the Acadian deportation. New Englanders moved north in the post-Conquest era to settle the former Acadian lands. By the beginning of the American Revolution, over 60 percent of Nova Scotia's population consisted of New Englanders. Initially, it seemed that Nova Scotia might join the Revolution as a fourteenth colony.

Most loyalists who arrived just after the Revolution settled in the Saint John River valley. They appealed to London for their own government, free from the control of Halifax, as a reward for their loyalty. Britain complied, creating the colony of New Brunswick in 1784. Prince Edward Island continued to enjoy separate colonial status since 1769. Cape Breton, a separate colony since 1784, joined Nova Scotia in 1820, Newfoundland was constituted as a colony in 1824.

The distant northwest, meanwhile, remained the home of First Nations. They dominated the vast region outside the colonies of BNA, but a fur-trade war developed between the North West Company and the Hudson's Bay Company. A new colony developed amid this rivalry at the confluence of the Red and Assiniboine Rivers (present-day Winnipeg). The site was already home to a growing Métis population who worked the trade and hunted the buffalo. The arrival of Scottish settlers led by Lord Selkirk increased antagonism.

Source: Library and Archives Canada, Acc. No. 1970-188-1928. W.H. Coverdale Collection of Canadiana, C-041507.

Chapter Eight
THE CONQUEST OF QUEBEC, 1760–1774

TIME LINE	
1760	Britain proclaims military rule over Quebec
1763	Treaty of Paris cedes Canada to Britain General James Murray named governor of Quebec
	Royal Proclamation issued Pontiac's Uprising organizes Aboriginal resistance against the British
1764	Military rule ends in Quebec
1765	Fire ravages Montreal
1766	Jean-Olivier Briand named Roman Catholic bishop of Quebec
1768	Sir Guy Carleton (later Lord Dorchester) becomes governor of Quebec
1774	Quebec Act passed

With thousands of British troops massed at the gates of Montreal in early September 1760, the Marquis de Vaudreuil, Governor General of New France, saw no sense in continuing the struggle. Wishing to spare the colony further devastation and bloodshed, he resolved to surrender and set about drawing up the conditions to offer the attackers. Certain of victory, General Jeffery Amherst, the British commander-in-chief, was not, however, about to accept indiscriminately all the demands of the vanquished. He refused to accord the French the "honours of war"—the privilege, often conceded to a defeated army, of marching out under arms with colours flying and drums beating. Demonstrating his concern for the fate of the *Canadiens,* Vaudreuil capitulated regardless, thereby bringing upon himself the wrath of the French government, which was more concerned with the fate of the French army. On September 22, 1760, General Amherst proclaimed British military rule over Quebec. The British conquest became a reality, at least for the time being. Only the final peace treaty in Europe would determine the ultimate fate of the colony—whether it would be retained by Britain or restored to France.

British Military Rule, 1760–63

The roughly 70 000 *Canadiens* living in the St. Lawrence Valley faced harsh wartime conditions while they awaited their fate. Quebec City was in ruins. During the prolonged siege of the fortress in the summer of 1759, Wolfe's troops also laid waste the south shore of the St. Lawrence as far as Kamouraska, 150 kilometres downstream. The next year, General James Murray continued the ravages at Sorel and elsewhere. This devastation resulted in such severe food shortages that Murray, named military governor of the district of Quebec after the surrender, intervened to force merchants to sell hoarded grain stocks at uninflated prices.

The Articles of Capitulation

While the French Canadians faced harsh conditions and the terms of capitulation were severe, they feared worse. Henri-Marie de Pontbriand, bishop of Quebec, had warned them in 1755 that, if they lost, they risked suffering the fate of the Acadians—expulsion. And while the population may have feared deportation, particularly in the aftermath of the fall of Quebec and while awaiting the end of the war in Europe, Britain had no such intention. The expulsion of the Acadians was the exception and not the rule when it came to handling a conquered population. The Acadians were removed due to their strategic location at a tense time. The British viewed themselves and their empire as enlightened. The government was intent on distancing itself from the religious wars and the harshness of the past. There would be no expelling the French Canadians. Rather than encourage New France's inhabitants to depart, the British sought to make them loyal subjects of the Crown. As expected, the British refused to guarantee the survival of French laws, customs, and institutions, but His Majesty's new subjects were allowed to retain their "entire peaceable property and possession of their goods, noble and ignoble, moveable and immoveable." They could also continue to practise the Roman Catholic religion. Priests and female (but not male) religious orders were permitted to perform their functions.

Those wishing to return to France could do so. About three-quarters of the 2200 French troops that remained in Vaudreuil's desertion-plagued army sailed home with their officers. Perhaps another 2000 individuals, including the wealthiest members of colonial society, joined them. Some merchants returned to France, particularly those with commercial interests in Europe and the Caribbean. Others were forced into bankruptcy. François Havy and Jean Lefebvre, for example, began transferring their assets from Quebec to La Rochelle when the Seven Years' War officially broke out in 1756. Hostilities made it virtually impossible for them to ship their furs across the sea, and after the Battle of Ste. Foy in 1760, the French government's decision to

How the French and English forces might have appeared on the day of capitulation at Montreal, September 8, 1760. By Adam Sherriff Scott.

Source: LM: Lets get rid of Scott, Adam Sherriff and just leave the Library and Archives Canada/C011043

suspend payments on all colonial paper money consummated their ruin. Moreover, the shelling of Quebec's Lower Town destroyed much of the property of local merchants. For them the Conquest was a disaster. War and its aftermath seriously disrupted the colony's economy.

The Conquest also placed the Roman Catholic Church in a difficult position. The church suffered substantial property losses during the military campaign. Then, at the end of the war, numerous ecclesiastics returned to France. When Bishop Pontbriand died in June 1760, he left no successor. Without a bishop, no new clergy could be ordained. The Church of England became the established church, while the Catholic Church lost government support.

Some historians have argued that Quebec was "decapitated" by the Conquest. According to the decapitation theory, Quebec literally lost its head by having its military, political, commercial, and religious elites removed from the colony. This severing allowed a British elite to move in and replace the French hierarchy. The theory was used to explain the dominance of the British merchant community as well as the Anglo minority in the years to follow. But historians came to question this theory. Historians such as Dale Miquelon argued that the situation was more complicated. While sections of the French elite left Quebec after the Conquest, others stayed. While members of the British elite were sure to move in and take advantage of opportunities, they were positioned vertically, alongside the French elite. While there were certainly longer term effects of the Conquest on Quebec society, the social structure of the colony was not destroyed in the short term.

The French-Canadian population was given the opportunity to return to France, but few among the general population took up the offer. The colony was now home to most of the inhabitants. They had roots often going back to the mid-1600s if not earlier. Generations had grown up in New France; it was all they knew. Their ties had been cut to France decades ago and they would not go unless forced. Regardless, few could afford to make the journey.

The Royal Proclamation of 1763

The Treaty of Paris, signed in 1763, formally ended the Seven Years' War. Three long years after the fall of Quebec, it would finally be determined who would ultimately control Canada. As the victors, the British made considerable gains at the expense of the French. At the peace table, debate ensued in both the French and British delegations over whether it was preferable to have Canada or the West Indian sugar islands. In the end, it came down to who wanted Canada more (or in the case of France, perhaps less). British Prime Minister William Pitt allegedly pleaded with his cabinet: "Some are for keeping Canada, some (the West Indian sugar-producing island of) Guadeloupe. Who will tell me what I shall be hanged for not keeping?" In the end, the British government decided to retain Canada, thereby making Britain the dominant power outside Europe. The British also gained Florida from Spain and the eastern half of Louisiana from France (the rest of Louisiana was secretly ceded to Spain by France in the Treaty of Fontainebleu in 1760). Britain returned control of Guadeloupe, St. Lucia, and Dominique to France.

On October 7, 1763, King George III issued the Royal Proclamation. The objective was to organize Britain's North American possessions and stabilize relations with the First Nations. Canada was now a British possession, and the following year civil rule began. The three military districts of Montreal, Three Rivers (Trois-Rivières), and Quebec were united into the colony of Quebec, with James Murray as governor.

But the peace treaty confronted Britain with a difficult dilemma. It now administered a large French-Catholic population in North America whose loyalty would naturally be doubtful in the event of renewed war with France. The new colonial masters therefore hoped that the French population might be quickly assimilated, with the anticipated arrival of large numbers of English-Protestant immigrants from the American colonies. But rather than move north to Quebec, with its harsh climate and "foreign" population, New England migrants headed west to more fertile lands. Thus, by the outbreak of the American Revolution some fifteen years later, not only were the inhabitants of Quebec still Catholic and French, they were also more numerous (due to a high birth rate of 55 per 1000 annually).

Pontiac's War

With the return of peace, the "Indian" question posed a greater problem for Britain than the treatment of the *Canadiens*. The vast majority of the First Nations were French allies and British enemies. They would not willingly or peacefully submit to British sovereignty. A treaty signed in distant Europe meant little to the war being fought by the Aboriginals. The British colonies continued to encroach on Aboriginal land. This threat would only increase now that the French were removed from the continent. The First Nations had always been successful in playing off the European powers against each other. Now, with the fur trade declining and their role as military allies diminished, their position under the British Crown was precarious. For their part, the British recognized the dangers of the situation. They hoped that the Royal Proclamation of 1763 would reconcile the First Nations to British rule and prevent growing unrest in the vast territories acquired south of the Great Lakes and west of the Allegheny Mountains.

Pontiac, an Odawa chief in the Detroit region, organized a pan-Aboriginal confederacy and mounted the most formidable Aboriginal resistance that the British had ever faced. The First Nations resented settler encroachments on their lands and they realized that the British would now move into territories previously claimed by France. Dissatisfaction also arose from another source—a fundamental difference in French and English policy toward the Aboriginal peoples.

The French practised "gift diplomacy," the custom of making generous annual payments to Indigenous peoples. Due to the smaller French population in its colonies, there was little choice but to follow Aboriginal customs when it came to diplomacy. The English in the Thirteen Colonies, on the other hand, preferred treaties or one-time-only purchases for Aboriginal lands. Sir William Johnson, the British "superintendent of northern Indians," understood the need for the annual payments and urged a shift to the French policy. General Amherst refused. Amherst had contempt for the First Nations, and with 8000 troops in North America and the French out of the picture, he no longer feared them. He was under pressure to reduce expenses now that the colonial wars were over, so he drastically reduced money for "gift diplomacy." He also reduced the amount of guns and ammunition being traded.

In the summer of 1763, British garrisons and frontier settlements were attacked throughout the upper Mississippi and Ohio River basins. "Why do you suffer the white men to dwell among you?" Pontiac asked his fellow chiefs. "Why do you not clothe yourselves in skins, as your ancestors did, and use the bows and arrows, and the stone pointed lances, which they used? ... You have bought guns, knives, kettles, and blankets, from the white men, until you can no longer do without them; and what is worse, you have drunk the poison firewater, which turns you into fools. Fling all these things away . . . and as for these English . . . you must lift the hatchet against them." Pontiac and his confederacy captured every British post west of Niagara with the exception of Detroit, killing or taking captive an estimated 2000 settlers.

So relentless was Aboriginal resistance that Amherst contemplated waging biological warfare. In a letter he advised one commander: "You will do well to try to inoculate the Indians [against smallpox] by means of blankets, as well as to try every other method that can serve to extirpate this execrable race." It is not known whether Amherst put this policy into practice or whether it was effective. It did, however, indicate a low point in the relations between the First Nations and British. Amherst was recalled to London and replaced by Major General Thomas Gage. In 1764 the British undertook two expeditions to subdue the resistance in the Ohio country. Peace was made with Pontiac in 1765. The First Nations failed to remove the British from the territory but they did force the British to alter its policies.

The formidable resistance justified British plans, already drawn up by the Board of Trade and Plantations in London, to satisfy Aboriginal grievances. The Proclamation of 1763, issued by the British in October, at the height of the resistance, set aside a huge reserve west of the Allegheny Mountains for "the several nations or tribes of Indians with whom we are connected, and who live under our protection." Officials drew a boundary line (the "Proclamation Line") between the British colonies along the seaboard and First Nation lands west of the Appalachian Mountains, stretching from Florida to Quebec. By forbidding colonists from trespassing on Native lands, the British government hoped to avoid more conflicts like Pontiac's Uprising. The British agreed not to colonize First Nations territory without prior purchase by the Crown and the consent of the affected band. Colonial governors were forbidden to make any land grants to colonists or to survey within the area of the reserve. London alone was to manage trade relations with the First Nations.

This "ambitious programme of imperial control," as historian Pierre Tousignant describes the proclamation,[1] became the first legal recognition by the British Crown of Aboriginal rights. Events soon showed, however, that the policy was unenforceable without a substantial British military presence in the interior. In defiance of the British government, thousands of Americans began to push over the mountains into Aboriginal land, notably the fertile Ohio country.

Impact of the Proclamation of 1763

In creating the "Indian Territory," the Royal Proclamation reduced the colony of Quebec to a rough quadrilateral along both sides of the St. Lawrence River, extending from what is today eastern Ontario to Gaspé. But it was also intended to provide the colony with British governmental institutions, among them a council to assist the governor. Elected assemblies were promised, with a view to attracting immigrants from the New England colonies. While awaiting the expected wave of settlers that would permit the British to remake Quebec into a British colony, those few already living in Quebec could rely on "the enjoyment of the benefit of the laws of our realm of England." While Catholicism was tolerated, Catholics were excluded from all offices.

In the view of historian Philip Lawson, the Royal Proclamation of 1763 had "all the appearance of a hasty public compromise" that contained "many inadequacies and mistakes."[2] The government's priority was to satisfy British settler opinion. It therefore sought to establish British institutions and law in the colony. Certainly, it did not wish to be seen as overly concerned about the fate of the colony's overwhelmingly French-Catholic population. It was left to the colonial governors in Quebec to deal with the practical realities and to find appropriate compromises.

The Conquest

The debate over the effects of the British conquest on Quebec emerged when serious historical writing began in Quebec in the 1840s. The discussion over such an emotional historical event not surprisingly fuelled the antagonism between French and English in Canada. The impact of the Conquest, however, always held a more controversial and sensitive place in Quebec's social memory than in the rest of Canada.

How did the Conquest transform Quebec society? What was the fate of such groups as the seigneurs, the clergy, and the commercial elites? What repercussions did the Conquest have on economic and social development? How did life change for the habitants? Did the Conquest "decapitate" Quebec society and allow an Anglo minority to take control of the levers of society? Such questions dominated the historical debate, but the forces of nationalism made the event polemical, as the debate over the future of Quebec heated up in the 1960s.[1]

In the aftermath of the Rebellions of 1837–38, the nationalist François-Xavier Garneau, recognized as French Canada's first major historian, portrayed the Conquest as a tragedy, the beginning of his people's "sufferings and humiliations."[2] But Benjamin Sulte, who revered British liberties, emphasized the enlightened nature of British constitutional monarchy as compared to the absolutism of the *ancien regime*. He concluded in 1905 that, on the contrary, the Conquest signified the passage from "a reign of absolute subjection under the Bourbons to the free and untrammelled life of constitutional government."[3]

English-Canadian historians have also differed substantially on the impact of the Conquest. Francis Parkman claimed that "A happier calamity never befell a people than the conquest of Canada by the British arms."[4] A.L. Burt noted that "The years of this military régime are of supreme importance in the history of Canada, for they planted in Canadian hearts that trust in British justice which has preserved the country with its dual nationality from splitting asunder."[5] Arthur Lower disagreed. He wrote of the "bitter agony of Canada" in 1760: "If the French in Canada had had a choice of conquerors, they could not have selected more happily than fate did for them. But conquerors are conquerors: they may make themselves hated or they may get themselves tolerated; they cannot, unless they abandon their own way of life and quickly assimilate themselves, in which case they cease to be conquerors, make themselves loved. As long as French are French and English are English, the memory of the Conquest and its effects will remain."[6]

Many French-Canadian clerical historians, horrified by the excesses of the French Revolution in the 1790s, suggested that the British, by conquering the colony, saved Quebec from the atheism of republican France. Yet Abbé Lionel Groulx, who taught history at the Université de Montréal and whose historical writings spanned more than six decades of the twentieth century, viewed the Conquest as the "supreme catastrophe," from which French Canada would recover through the actions of the church, and also thanks to the qualities (and especially the fertility!) of rural families.[7]

In the 1950s and 1960s, historians Maurice Séguin, Guy Frégault, and Michel Brunet (known as the "Montreal School") argued that the Conquest had "decapitated" New France's bourgeoisie. The return to France of many of the colony's bourgeoisie inevitably condemned French Canada to economic inferiority. According to Frégault, Quebec was left "conquered, impoverished, socially decapitated, and politically in bonds."[8] To French-Canadian nationalists, the history of the Conquest helped explain Quebec's subordinate position vis-à-vis the rest of Canada in the era after World War II.

Other historians disagreed. Jean Hamelin disputed the claim that any decapitation occurred or that a "vigorous French-Canadian bourgeoisie" ever existed in the first place.[9] In his study of Canadian merchants involved in the fur trade, José Igartua concluded that the new British system of business competition was responsible for the economic decline of the French. "The Montreal merchants were not decapitated by the Conquest; rather, they were faced in very short succession with a series of transformations in the socioeconomic structure of the colony to which they might have been able to adapt had these transformations been spread over a longer period of time."[10] Fernand Ouellet questioned the existence of a significant Canadian bourgeoisie prior to the Conquest. He contended that the Conquest had the positive effect of opening up new markets for wheat for Quebec farmers. When French Canadians later fell behind economically, Ouellet blamed their traditional ideas and their inability to adapt to new circumstances.[11]

Historian Susan Mann captured in one trenchant phrase what might have been the sentiments of many *Canadiens* as they faced the realities of defeat and foreign takeover: "Conquest is like rape."[12] At the same time, however, Mann took pains to demonstrate that, for most people, the woes of political change surely took second place to the problems of everyday existence. Historians focused too much on what happened at the elite levels of society rather than on the common people.

In recent years, historians have preferred to focus on specific aspects of life at the time of the Conquest, such as the evolution of justice, a sphere in which the Conquest, by introducing English law, brought far-reaching change. Still, the controversy over the re-enactment of the Battle of the Plains of Abraham as part of the 250th anniversary in 2009 demonstrates that the Conquest remains one of the most controversial events in Quebec's history.

1. The historiographical debate is discussed in Dale Miquelon, ed., *Society and Conquest: The Debate on the Bourgeoisie and Social Change in French Canada, 1700–1850* (Toronto: Copp Clark Pitman, 1977); Serge Gagnon, *Quebec and Its Historians: The Twentieth Century* (Montreal: Harvest House, 1985), pp. 53–89; "The Conquest of 1760: Were Its Consequences Traumatic?," in Paul Bennett and Cornelius Jaenen, eds., *Emerging Identities: Selected Problems and Interpretations in Canadian History* (Scarborough, ON: Prentice-Hall, 1986), pp. 76–105.

2. François-Xavier Garneau, *Histoire du Canada*, 8th ed., vol. VI (Montreal: Éditions de l'Arbre, 1945), p. 82.

3. Benjamin Sulte, quoted in Ramsay Cook, *The Maple Leaf Forever: Essays on Nationalism and Politics in Canada* (Toronto: Macmillan, 1971), p. 102.

4. Francis Parkman, *The Old Regime in Canada*, vol. 2 (Toronto: n.p., 1899), p. 205.

5. A.L. Burt, *The Old Province of Quebec*, vol. I (Toronto: McClelland & Stewart, 1968 [1933]), p. 50.

6. Arthur Lower, *Colony to Nation: A History of Canada*, 3rd ed. (Toronto: Longmans, 1957), p. 64.

7. Lionel Groulx, *La naissance d'une race* (Montreal: Action française, 1919), p. 229.

8. Guy Frégault, "La colonization du Canada au XVIIe siècle," *Cahiers de L'Académie canadienne-française* 2 (1957): 53–81; Maurice Séguin, "La Conquête et la vie économique des Canadiens," *Action nationale* 28 (1947), cited in Miequelon, *Society and Conquest*, p. 78; Michel Brunet, *La présence anglaise et les Canadiens* (Montreal: Beauchemin, 1958).

9. Jean Hamelin, *Économie et société en Nouvelle-France* (Quebec: n.p., 1960), cited in Miquelon, *Society and Conquest*, pp. 105, 114.

10. José Igartua, "A Change in Climate: The Conquest and the *Marchands* of Montreal," Canadian Historical Association, *Historical Papers* (1974), reprinted in R. Douglas Francis and Donald B. Smith, eds., *Readings in Canadian History: Pre-Confederation*, 7th ed. (Toronto: Thomson Nelson, 2007), p. 221.

11. Fernand Ouellet, *Histoire économique et sociale du Québec, 1760–1850* (Montreal: Fides, 1966), p. 76.

12. Susan Mann, *The Dream of Nation: A Social and Intellectual History of Quebec* (Montreal/Kingston: McGill-Queen's University Press, 2002, [1982]), p. 31.

The Judicial System

The Royal Proclamation of 1763 also introduced British law to the conquered colony. In the three years of occupation after 1759, the British commanders set up military tribunals to judge important cases. These courts were most concerned with offences committed by soldiers, including desertion, insubordination, theft, and rape. Some cases involved civilians accused of criminal offences. One such example is the case of Louis Dodier. When Louis Dodier of St. Vallier, east of Quebec City, was found axed to death, suspicion first fell upon Joseph Corriveau, his father-in-law, who was tried and found guilty. Corriveau then accused his own daughter, Marie-Josephte, Dodier's wife, and a new trial took place. At this trial, a jury composed entirely of English army officers found Marie-Josephte guilty of having murdered her husband, and the judge condemned her to death. After her execution, her corpse was hanged in chains in a cage and exhibited for several weeks on a road in Lauzon, across the river from Quebec City. "La Corriveau" became a central figure in Quebec folklore for nearly two centuries.

Outside the large towns, the militia officers functioned as "the hands, the eyes, the ears, and the mouth of the government."[3] Among other responsibilities, they acted as magistrates, applying French law and, more generally, in accordance with Amherst's instructions, the principles of "due justice and equity." The Proclamation, however, introduced the law and legal system of England into the colony. Historian Evelyn Kolish sees the Proclamation as an "attempt to transform the colony, in its form of government, its laws and its customs, to make it conform to the model of other British colonies."[4] Historian Donald Fyson, emphasizes the fact that it was the governor's instructions, not the Proclamation itself, that set out the changes to be put into place.

With the coming of civil government in 1764, the militia captains were cast aside and replaced by Protestant justices of the peace, often merchants or half-pay officers, and by bailiffs, many of them French-speaking habitants. Under English law, these new officials could seize homes for minor debts and imprison debtors, although such punishments were rare in Quebec. As in the days of New France, in some prosecutions for assault, the alleged victims were bailiffs. At times, justices of the peace were accused by their detractors of deliberately stirring up feuds so that they might charge fees to settle them. Sir Guy Carleton, who was sent to Quebec as lieutenant governor in 1766, resented the opposition shown to his administration by the merchant community, which included several judges. In one famous comment, he vented his frustrations: "Not a Protestant butcher or publican became bankrupt who did not apply to be made a justice." Such accusations were probably groundless, and Carleton did admit that many judges were indeed worthy individuals. Early historians argued that the *Canadiens* boycotted the system of

A First Nations council with the British.

Source: By Benjamin West, from William Smith, *An Historical Account of the Expedition Against the Ohio Indians*, Philadelphia, 1766.

justice after the Conquest but more recent research suggests that they had frequent recourse to the courts. Still, they probably often relied on local priests, notables, or even former militia captains, who still retained their moral authority, to settle disputes informally.

Important criminal cases were heard by the court of King's Bench, but relatively few *Canadiens* went before it. A significant number of cases concerned alleged misconduct by soldiers. Trials in this court were held chiefly in English, but interpreters were used when the accused was French speaking. French Catholics were legally eligible to serve as jurors, but juries were often made up entirely of English Protestants. When Catherine Sauvage was brought before a court in 1766 and accused of attempted arson, twelve English jurors listened to the translated testimony of the French prosecutor and witnesses.

Despite the provisions of the Proclamation, in practice French civil law remained largely intact in the new colony. This situation at times provoked serious legal disorder. On questions related to marriage and inheritance, for example, decisions based on French law by lower courts were sometimes reversed by the court of King's Bench, which relied on English common law. Yet, because of their relatively minor importance and also because of the cost, most verdicts of the lower courts were not appealed. Juries in civil suits, as well as in some criminal cases, often included both English and French, particularly in lower courts. The demographic context also forced Murray to authorize Roman Catholic barristers to practise in the courts.

The Roman Catholic Church in Quebec

Governor James Murray found British policy pertaining to the Roman Catholic Church contradictory. Both the articles of capitulation and the Treaty of Paris granted freedom of worship, although only "as far as the laws of Great Britain permit." Although Catholics faced little overt persecution in England after 1689, anti-Catholic legislation remained in force until 1829. Moreover, London had instructed Murray to take measures to ensure that the *Canadiens* "may by degrees be induced to embrace the Protestant religion, and their children be brought up in the principles of it." Assimilation was at the heart of the policy.

During the war, Murray identified the clergy as "the source of all the mischiefs which have befallen the poor Canadians." In particular, he was suspicious of the French-born members of male religious orders such as the Jesuits and the Sulpicians. In time, however, Murray adopted a pragmatic attitude toward the Catholic Church. He realized that, even with all the support of the colonial administration, the handful of Protestants in the conquered colony had no chance of converting the *Canadiens* in the short term. He also realized that the Church enjoyed considerable influence with the habitants. By avoiding open oppression of Catholics and by rewarding loyal priests, the British administration, Murray reasoned, might even be able to rally the church's support. If he controlled the church, he believed he would control the people. The British viewed New France under the ancien regime as a colony of loyal peasants. The Canadiens were different from the American colonies in that they were not infused with a spirit of independence and democracy. Thus, he made no attempt to close the churches. Instead, he and his officials kept a watchful eye on their activities and administration.

The Precarious State of the Church

The period immediately after the Conquest was difficult for the Catholic Church. The male clergy, numbering close to 200 at the time of the Conquest, quickly declined to fewer than 140 by 1762, as a result of deaths and departures to France. Furthermore, male religious orders were forbidden to recruit. The British army was quartered at the Jesuit property at Quebec, and the fate of the wealthy Sulpician community in Montreal was in doubt.

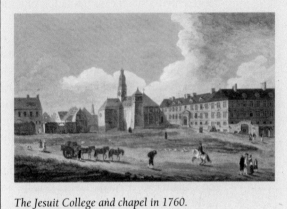

The Jesuit College and chapel in 1760.

Source: Library and Archives Canada, Acc. No. 1989-283-5/C-000354.

The female orders, also with about 200 members in 1760, enjoyed greater tolerance, because they were viewed as less threatening. The Jesuits were aggressive and they focused on conversions; they had direct links to France and the Vatican. Most of the nuns were born in Canada and their sphere of influence was associated with hospital work and other kinds of social assistance. The nuns were obliged to care for wounded soldiers, although they were explicitly warned not to minister to their patients' souls. Yet tolerance did not bring prosperity. The religious community of the Hôpital Général de Québec verged on bankruptcy; the Hôtel-Dieu de Montréal envisaged returning to France. Anxious to consolidate good relations with the British, the Ursulines at Quebec elected as their superior Esther Wheelright, an American captive who had been rebaptized Marie-Joseph and had become an Ursuline nun 45 years earlier.

The Selection of a New Bishop

The most delicate problem to be solved was the replacement of Bishop Pontbriand, who died in 1760. London instructed Murray not to re-establish the "Popish hierarchy," but when the New Englanders failed to come north, the governor needed someone with whom he could deal as the leader of French-Canadian society. Murray believed that such a leader should come from the church. He was thus ready, in spite of London's directives to the contrary, to accept a "superintendent of the Romish religion." But when the Quebec cathedral chapter chose Étienne Montgolfier, superior of the Sulpicians, as candidate for bishop, Murray balked and made known his preference for Jean-Olivier Briand, vicar general of the diocese of Quebec, who had shown respect for British authority. The cathedral chapter capitulated and nominated Briand for the position. With Murray's support, the nominee for bishop sailed for London to lobby the British government for its approval. After obtaining London's agreement, Briand went to France, where Rome named him bishop. In June 1766, six years after Pontbriand's death, the Canadian church had a new leader.

Cooperation with the British brought the Church benefits. Bishop Briand, for example, obtained an annuity from the governor for his "good behaviour." But the British exacted a high price for their concessions. After all, the governor had effectively chosen the bishop, and this represented a significant limitation of ecclesiastical authority. Furthermore, when Briand named priests to parishes, he sought the governor's approval. Murray consistently refused Briand's requests to recruit foreign priests. When, after eight years, Briand was finally permitted to name a coadjutor with the right to succeed him as bishop of Quebec, the new governor, Guy Carleton, forced him to choose a man five years his senior, who would attempt to run the diocese from the seclusion of his presbytery on the Île d'Orléans.

The governor used the church to communicate with the general population and, he hoped, to keep French Canadians loyal to the government. The church in turn issued pastoral messages in support of the state at the request of the governor. Priests made government announcements from the pulpits and on church steps. In 1762, Briand even prescribed special public prayers on the occasion of the coronation and wedding of King George III. To his critics, who thought him too obliging, he replied that the British "are our rulers and we owe to them what we used to owe to the French."

Canadien Society After Conquest

Although "conquered," the quality of life for the majority of French Canadians did not suffer. It certainly could have been worse. Land was still available in the old seigneurial region along the St. Lawrence. With the failure of the government to recruit immigrants from New England, the habitants did not feel threatened by an increase in the "foreign" English-Protestant population. The influence and control wielded by a small but vocal British merchant class was of concern, but excluding soldiers, the barely 500 British in the colony in 1765 hardly posed a threat to the 70 000 *Canadiens*.

The Seigneurs

The seigneurs, on the other hand, faced difficult times after the Conquest. With the end of the French regime, they lost their privileged, aristocratic links with the government, as well as their military commissions. Many were not wealthy, as their sparsely populated seigneuries produced little income. Some, however, seized the opportunity to buy lands abandoned by seigneurs who returned to France.

A few succeeded in managing the transition. Gaspard-Joseph Chaussegros de Léry, son of the famous engineer who built the fortifications of Quebec City, immigrated to France after the Conquest, hoping for a commission in the French army. Unsuccessful, he returned to Canada in 1764, going by way of London, where he was the first Canadian seigneur to be presented to King George III. Yet Governor James Murray received him coldly, because Chaussegros had left two sons in France, where they were preparing for careers in the French army.

Chaussegros considered selling his lands at a loss and returning to France, until he learned that the French authorities were questioning his loyalty and that he was now in danger of being arrested. His luck changed when Guy Carleton replaced James Murray as governor. Carleton befriended Chaussegros, gave him a pension and positions, and even named him to his Legislative Council in 1775. Chaussegros also became prosperous. He acquired several seigneuries with flour mills and sawmills. As for his sons left behind in France, one of them, François-Joseph Chaussegros de Léry, served with distinction in the French army for nearly half a century, fighting in 35 campaigns and 70 battles and sieges. Napoleon named him a baron in 1811. The name of this celebrated Quebec-born Marshal of France is inscribed on the Arc de Triomphe in Paris.

Another example is Michel Chartier de Lotbinière, a military officer, who married Louise-Madeleine, a sister of Gaspard-Joseph Chaussegros de Léry. He fared less well. Although he acquired several seigneuries after the Conquest, he lost two of them when the Royal Proclamation of 1763 situated them within the boundaries of the colony of New York. Incapable of paying his debts, he was compelled to cede most of the remaining lands to his son. He hoped for a restoration of the seigneurs' social status through the creation of a House of Assembly, grouping all large landowners, British as well as French. When the Quebec Act of 1774 failed to create such a body, he bitterly denounced Governor Carleton's "despotism" and left Quebec for France.

In general, both Murray and Carleton showed considerable favour toward the seigneurs. As aristocrats and military officers, the British governors had sympathy with their French counterparts. Recognizing that the "nobles" had been deprived of "their honours, their privileges, their revenues and their laws," Carleton recommended that the British government show them sympathy in return for their loyalty. London agreed, and by 1771 additional royal instructions had been issued to ensure the perpetuation of the seigneurial system. With the church and nobles on side, Carleton and Murray believed they could control the loyalty of the obedient French-Canadian "peasants."

Quebec's Hôpital Général in 1860, five years before it and more than 100 houses were destroyed by fire.

Source: Library and Archives Canada, Acc. No. 1970-188-320. W.H. Coverdale Collection of Canadiana.

The Canadiens

Barely 20 percent of the colony's citizens lived in towns. Quebec, the largest centre, had approximately 7000 inhabitants in 1765; Montreal had barely 5000. Beyond the new borders, the Detroit area contained perhaps another 2000 *Canadiens*. Although townspeople had access to goods and services, they suffered the hardships of their class. Labourers, for example, had to contend with the seasonal nature of much of the available employment. Disease caused untold misery. Epidemics due to contaminated water supplies and poor hygiene took many lives, especially among the old and the very young.

Fire was a serious threat. On May 18, 1765, Montreal suffered a great conflagration when a fire that began near the waterfront expanded to destroy more than 100 houses, as well as the Hôpital Général, run by the Grey Nuns, and many commercial establishments. Colonial authorities and charities distributed assistance to families who had lost all their possessions, but the loss of dwellings led to an acute housing crisis. Three years later, another fire destroyed 90 houses. The town was rebuilt, but the rising cost of land within the small city, with the ensuing increase in rents, pushed less affluent citizens, such as artisans and labourers, beyond the town walls. Although the bourgeois rebuilt their homes from stone, the poor continued to use wood, which was much cheaper. In spite of ordinances requiring regular sweeping of chimneys and forbidding the use of wooden shingles, fires occurred regularly.

The Commercial Elites

The area of greatest opportunity was in the commercial sector. Several hundred merchants involved in a wide variety of commercial pursuits, including the fur trade, vied for influence in Quebec. Many of these merchants were French. Some, however, were English, having arrived after the Conquest from Britain or the American colonies. This group quickly carved out an important place for itself in the local economy.

The respective roles of both groups have long been at the centre of historical controversy. Historian Hilda Neatby maintained that French merchants had little difficulty in adjusting to British rule. They could get the credit they needed and they enjoyed general prosperity after the Conquest. On the other hand, Michel Brunet argued that the Conquest established a new set of rules that placed the French at a decided disadvantage. Fernand Ouellet agreed that the French merchants suffered a relative decline. British investments in the fur trade as well as in other sectors surpassed French investments as quickly as the early 1770s. But according to Ouellet, the French merchants were much to blame for their own fate. They were too individualistic to build up the powerful associations that would have enabled them to remain competitive, and they were too conservative in their investments.

A major difficulty lay in the fact that many of the French merchants had to shift their mercantile interests away from France. Under these new conditions, a few tried to continue to import French merchandise to be sold in Quebec. Others, like François Baby, successfully made arrangements to shift their commercial relations from France to England. But most French merchants possessed meagre financial resources with which to undertake the post-Conquest struggle for control of the fur trade, the most dynamic sector of the economy. Moreover, the British army handed over its lucrative provisioning contracts in Quebec to leading English merchants. There may be historical debate as to how well or poorly the French merchants adapted, but there is little doubt that they faced considerable obstacles in the post-Conquest setting or that the British merchants were at an advantage.

A HISTORICAL PORTRAIT

Two Businesswomen: Louise de Ramezay and Marie-Anne Barbel

The effects of the British Conquest on the inhabitants of New France varied widely depending on such factors as social class, place of residence, occupation, and even gender. French law, for example, gave women, especially unmarried women and widows, considerable latitude in managing business activities. Indeed, prior to the Conquest, several women distinguished themselves in that sector of activity.

Louise de Ramezay, daughter of Claude de Ramezay, governor of Montreal, was born in 1705. She never married and spent most of her life in Montreal. Her earliest business interests were linked to a very profitable sawmill that her father built on the seigneury of Chambly, south of Montreal. This sawmill was well situated, taking delivery of logs from the upper Richelieu valley and Lake Champlain, and selling boards and planks to shipyards in Quebec City. In 1745, Louise de Ramezay entered into an association with Marie-Anne Legras, wife of Jean-Baptiste-François Hertel de Rouville, and built a sawmill and a flour mill on the seigneury of Rouville. She also owned a third sawmill at a site west of Lake Champlain. In addition, she became an important landowner, with an interest in five seigneuries. She had a tannery on the island of Montreal as well. Her commercial activities flourished, partly because of Louise de Ramezay's own administrative talents, and partly because of favours obtained thanks to her high position within the colonial aristocracy.

With the British conquest and the redrawing of the borders of Quebec, de Ramezay lost the seigneury that colonial authorities had granted her in upper New York state, as well as the sawmill situated on it. She continued, however, to manage her other activities for a time, but had sold these off by the time of her death in 1776. The Conquest appears to have had little to do with her departure from business.

Marie-Anne Barbel, daughter of a well-known royal notary, was born in 1703. In 1723, she married Jean-Louis Fornel, a well-to-do merchant. The colonial governor and the Intendant were among the guests at the wedding. These connections would later be highly useful to the couple.

Fornel had interests in the fur trade and, when absent from Quebec City, he gave his wife power of attorney to manage his affairs. When Fornel died in 1745, Marie-Anne Barbel took over the family business and continued to develop it. She retained the warehouse at Place Royale, in Quebec City's Lower Town, and, in addition, she obtained grants of two fur-trading posts on the St. Lawrence River. She joined with French merchants François Havy and Jean Lefebvre to promote exports of furs to France. She also owned several houses and considerable land in Quebec City and on the outskirts.

After 1756, when the Seven Years' War began, the presence of the British in the Gulf of St. Lawrence disrupted Barbel's fur-trading activities. The Conquest itself proved disastrous for Barbel: her properties in Quebec City were heavily damaged or destroyed. She withdrew from commerce and borrowed heavily to reconstruct her houses. She then rented these in order to pay off her debts. Barbel died in 1793. She was a capable businesswoman, but her links with the colonial administration in New France gave her significant advantages. With the Conquest, these advantages disappeared.

British merchants in Quebec enjoyed advantages. While they often lacked capital, credit, and lines of supply, they benefited from various types of favouritism. When shipping space was scarce, for example, they were able to get their shipments aboard government vessels. The English and Scottish merchants were accustomed to the greater competitiveness that accompanied British trade policy, while in New France trade had been well ordered and more state-regulated. Still, the French did enjoy one advantage: the Great Lakes First Nations preferred doing business with French families, such as the Cadots (Cadottes), St. Germains, and Grignons, who had intermarried with them and had mixed-blood families.

The arrival in Quebec of large numbers of British merchants, as well as officers and administrators, helps explain the rising numbers of mixed (French and English) marriages in the colony. New arrivals were willing, even eager, to marry *Canadiennes*. Merchant Justin Franck advertised in the *Quebec Gazette* for "a good woman for a wife." He wanted her to be healthy (he specified her ideal weight) and wealthy—"a genteel English, Scotch, Dutch or French girl, of middle size and age, fit for the care of a house and a shop, used to confinement and the keeping of her tongue." He promised that if she showed "good behaviour," she would be entitled to a housekeeper.

Conflict Between the Governor and the Merchants

The British merchants in Quebec quickly fell out of favour with the aristocratic colonial governors. Murray, for example, had contempt for the rising merchant class who did not come from the same "pedigree" as the aristocracy but were instead "self-made men." The governor preferred "gentlemen" such as the French-Canadian seigneurs (with whom he could converse in excellent French) to British tradesmen, whom he considered to be "in general the most immoral collection of men I ever knew and of course little calculated to make the new subjects enamoured with our laws, religion and customs."

In return, the British merchants viewed Murray as a despot. As an aristocrat and military officer, he did not seem to respect the traditions of the British parliamentary system or British representative government. They were not surprised that he seemed to admire the French peasantry, the Catholic Church, and the French seigneurial system. What he seemed to admire most was obedience. The merchants condemned Murray for the strict controls he imposed on the fur trade, conveniently ignoring the fact that British policy severely limited the governor's options. They denounced him for being too conciliatory to the colony's French-Catholic population, who constituted more than 95 percent of the total. They agitated for an elected assembly (in which no Catholic would be allowed to sit and therefore they would control). Finally, they petitioned the King for Murray's recall.

Murray's troubles were compounded by the fact that authority in the colony was divided between himself, as civilian governor, and Ralph Burton, as military commander. Friction between the two, who previously were warm friends, rapidly intensified. Murray sailed for England in June 1766, and, even though he successfully defended himself against the accusations of the local resident British merchants in Quebec and officially remained governor until 1768, he never returned to Quebec.

Murray's successor, Sir Guy Carleton, initially appeared sympathetic to the grievances of the British merchants. He endorsed Britain's decision to lift the constraints imposed on the fur traders and to leave control of trade relations with the First Nations to the colonial governments. The merchants were pleased but they soon began to complain of competition from wealthier traders from New York and Pennsylvania. As he came to know the colony, however, Carleton's sympathies shifted. Like Murray, he was impressed by what he viewed as the character of the *Canadiens*. He quickly grew tired of the constant griping of the merchants. In particular, he was concerned with maintaining the loyalty of the population who, he prophesied, would people this country "to the end of time," barring some unforeseen catastrophe. Before long Carleton found himself locked in the same struggle with the merchants, who accused him of being more sympathetic to the seigneurs and Catholic clergy.

The Quebec Act

The struggle between the governor and the merchants over commercial and legal issues could be contained as an internal power struggle within the colony. But the issues of representative government and the loyalty of the inhabitants were too serious to ignore and commanded the attention of the British government. From the late 1760s, pressures in North America began to force London to consider changes in its administration of Quebec. The small but vocal British minority, mostly merchants, urged the government to grant Quebec the liberties and representative institutions it had given the Thirteen Colonies, which were seen as inherent aspects of British rule. This group was convinced that the governors were incapable of recognizing that the local resident commercial class constituted the backbone of the colony and thus merited special consideration. French merchants supported some of their grievances, particularly in opposition to the seigneurs' own pretensions, but language and religion constituted a barrier to common action. While British merchants demanded that British commercial law apply to the colony, the *Canadiens* agitated in favour of a return to "our customs and usages." The British felt that, by right of conquest, only Protestants should occupy administrative positions in the colony. For the

Canadiens, more equitable arrangements between the king's old—that is, British—subjects and his new, French-Catholic, subjects were needed.

The Quest for Stability

For Britain, stability in North America was paramount. The Quebec Act of 1774 spelled out Britain's new policies in extending the colony's frontiers into the Ohio region and governing Quebec. The British hoped by extending the frontiers to put an end to the ferocious competition among traders that plagued the territory. Quebec's economy depended far more on furs than did New York's, and giving the West to Quebec would thus preserve the economic balance. London also viewed annexation of the Ohio region to Quebec as a wise decision, because the St. Lawrence traders and merchants had generally maintained good relations with the First Nations who lived there. Perhaps more importantly, they appeared to be the only traders capable of successfully competing with the French traders who worked along the Mississippi.

The Quebec Act revised the provisions of the Royal Proclamation when it came to governing the colony. It retained the application within Quebec of English criminal law, with its "certainty and lenity . . . and the benefits and advantages resulting from the use of it." It was presumed that the French Canadians were happy with English law. The French population probably did find the judicial system relatively lenient, due to high rates of acquittal and discharge. But punishments, such as whipping and fines, appear to have been of roughly equal severity with those meted out in the days of New France.

In civil matters, the act put into law the significant concessions that governors Murray and Carleton had already made to the seigneurs. In particular, it reintroduced French civil law with regard to property. This was an attempt to resolve the uneasy co-existence of two completely different legal systems. The return of French civil law enraged British merchants, but pleased the seigneurs. Britain now legally confirmed the existence of the seigneurial system and gave it a much-needed boost through the restoration of seigneurial dues.

The Act allowed public office holders to practice the Roman Catholic faith, by replacing the oath sworn by officials to Elizabeth I and her heirs with one to George III that had no reference to the Protestant religion. For the first time, French Canadians were able to participate legally in government affairs without formally renouncing their faith. The Act also re-established the collection of tithes, which had been halted, and allowed the Jesuit priests to return to the colony.

When it came to governance, this new constitution for Quebec substantially modified the political structures. It established an appointive Legislative Council that could make laws with the governor's consent. The governor could suspend or remove councillors. Significantly, these councillors could now be Roman Catholics. But the Quebec Act did not respond to the calls of the British minority to establish an elected assembly, thereby placing Quebec on par with the other colonies.

Reaction to the Quebec Act

The merchants, while satisfied with the colony's new boundaries, were furious that London had denied them the elective assembly for which they had so often petitioned. The British government justified the denial of representative government on the basis that Quebec was not ready for such an institution. The British Parliament refused to place the colonial government in the hands of a few hundred British-Protestant merchants, nor was it willing to countenance the establishment of a representative assembly that would be dominated by French Catholics whose ethnicity and religion made their loyalty suspect.

The Catholic clergy and seigneurs may well have looked upon the Quebec Act as a veritable charter of French-Canadian rights as well as a vindication of their dominant role in society. In addition, the seigneurs were likely pleased that no representative legislative body had been created. Carleton reported that the seigneurs, whom he described as "the better sort of Canadians," feared a popular assembly whose inevitable consequence would be to make the people "refractory and insolent." As for the habitants (whose response no one cared to petition), the legal recognition given to the tithe and seigneurial dues was surely disappointing, as was the refusal to allow an assembly.

Historians have also generally viewed the Quebec Act as beneficial to French Canadians and in particular, as the means by which they fended off the assimilationist designs of the Royal Proclamation. Some noted the humanity and "liberality" of the Quebec Act. Thomas Chapais wrote in 1919 that the act was a "victory" for the cause of French Canadians because it freed them from a "precarious toleration" and put them in possession of a "legal guarantee."[5] In the 1970s, Hilda Neatby argued that the act simply "confirmed . . . what had already been conceded in practice."[6] Pierre Tousignant cautioned that expediency also played a role in Parliament's adoption of the Quebec Act: any generosity shown toward Britain's new subjects had to "reinforce, not weaken, metropolitan authority."[7]

But perhaps the most important reaction to the Quebec Act came externally, from the Thirteen Colonies to the south. The extension of Quebec's boundaries embittered the Americans, still brimming over the prohibitive Proclamation Line. They viewed the Quebec Act as one more measure that continued the process of sealing off the west. The Americans had fought the colonial wars against France for decades, only to have their expansionist designs thwarted by their own government. They also bitterly resented the recognition that the Quebec Act bestowed on the colony's despised "papists" by conceding "the free exercise of the religion of the Church of Rome" and by firmly recognizing the right of the Catholic Church to collect tithes. The timing of the legislation was also critical. The Quebec Act became one of the "Intolerable Acts" leading shortly thereafter to the American Revolution. This "tyrannical act" figured prominently among the grievances of the Americans when they launched their rebellion in April 1775, three weeks before the Quebec Act was officially proclaimed.

Secret Instructions

The Quebec Act, however, cannot be fully appreciated without considering the secret instructions that accompanied it and, in many ways, contradicted it. These instructions required the governor to weigh the possibility of legal reform that would gradually introduce English civil law. They also explicitly detailed plans to subordinate the church to strict state control. Appeals to any "foreign ecclesiastical jurisdiction"—that is, to the Pope—were forbidden. Protestant ministers could at some future date collect tithes from Roman Catholics. Clergy were to be permitted to marry. The government was to oversee the bishop's performance of all his official functions and to regulate seminaries. The religious orders were to disappear, with the Jesuits being given an extra push through the outright suppression of the order and the confiscation by the state of all its holdings. Once all of these initiatives had been carried out, the Church itself would gradually wither away. That, at least, was the hope of the authors of the secret instructions. In other words, the Quebec Act appeared to guarantee the rights of the French Canadians but it was not intended to reverse the original intentions of the British Parliament at the time of Conquest. The objective was to keep them happy for now, and maintain their loyalty. The plan was still to assimilate the *Canadiens*. The plan would just take a bit longer to put into practice.

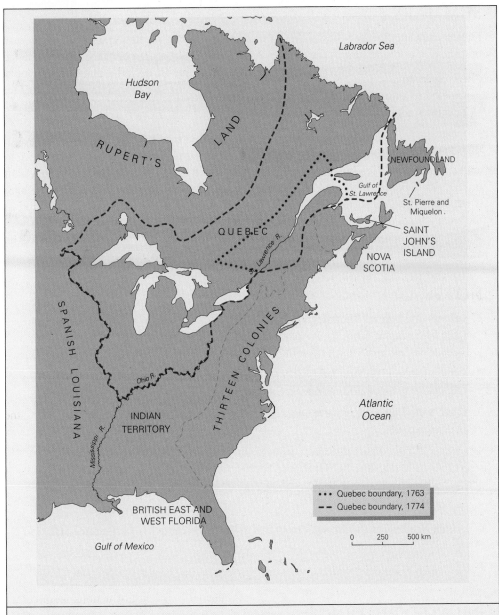

The Quebec boundary before and after the Quebec Act, 1774.

Source: Based on *The Integrated Atlas: History and Geography of Canada and the World* (Toronto: Harcourt Brace, 1996), p. 114.

Bishop Briand appears to have learned of these proposals, and they likely horrified him. Governor Carleton reassured Briand that he disapproved of the instructions and intended to ignore them. Carleton's major preoccupation was with the security of the colony he governed. His conservative and aristocratic bias led him to favour the clergy and the large landowners, who would support the government if the Americans invaded. Carleton's preferences, however, caused him to exaggerate the influence of these elites on the general population.

SUMMARY

Fifteen years after the Conquest, official British policy toward the new colony of Quebec was modified for a second time in the Quebec Act of 1774. Publicly, Britain gave the appearance of yielding to French and Roman Catholic desires. George III declared that the Act would have "the best effects in quieting the minds and promoting the happiness of my Canadian subjects." The French Canadians could now play at least a minority role in the administration of the province.

The Quebec Act also showed that the British believed the Catholic Church was powerful and held considerable sway over the *Canadiens*. There was no quick and easy way in which to anglicize and make Protestant a colony that had attracted but a few hundred British Protestant immigrants, largely merchants. The British did not reject assimilation as the ultimate aim; it was simply not a realistic policy in 1774. A year later, with the outbreak of revolution to the south, it was even less feasible. Eventually, with the arrival of thousands of loyalists who wished to cast their lot with Britain, the hopes of the assimilationists would revive. But for the moment, Quebec's population remained overwhelmingly French and Catholic.

NOTES

1. Pierre Tousignant, "The Integration of the Province of Quebec into the British Empire, 1763–91. Part 1: From the Royal Proclamation to the Quebec Act," *Dictionary of Canadian Biography*, vol. 4 (Toronto: University of Toronto Press, 1980), pp. xxxii–xlix.

2. Philip Lawson, *The Imperial Challenge: Quebec and Britain in the Age of the American Revolution* (Montreal/Kingston: McGill-Queen's University Press, 1989), pp. 36–37.

3. A.L. Burt, *The Old Province of Quebec*, vol. 1 (Toronto: McClelland & Stewart, 1968 [1933]), p. 28.

4. Evelyn Kolish, *Nationalismes et conflits de droits: Le débat du droit privé au Québec, 1760–1840* (LaSalle, QC: Hurtubise HMH, 1994), p. 30.

5. Thomas Chapais, *Cours d'histoire du Canada*, vol. 1 (Quebec: J.P. Garneau, 1919), p. 167.

6. Hilda Neatby, *The Quebec Act: Protest and Policy* (Scarborough, ON: Prentice-Hall, 1972), p. 137.

7. Tousignant, pp. xlvii–xlviii.

RELATED READINGS

For a discussion of Nova Scotia during the era of the American Revolution, see "The Fourteenth Colony: Nova Scotia and the American Revolution," which is Module 5 in *Visions: The Canadian History Modules Project: Pre-Confederation* textbook. This module offers a useful in-depth look at colonial life in British North America in the late eighteenth century. See pages 191–237.

BIBLIOGRAPHY

One of the earliest examinations of the post-Conquest period is A.L. Burt, *The Old Province of Quebec* (Toronto: McClelland & Stewart, 1968 [1933]); it remains useful, if dated. Hilda Neatby incorporated new research into her book *Quebec: The Revolutionary Age, 1760–1791* (Toronto: McClelland & Stewart, 1966). A study of British policy toward Quebec is Philip Lawson, *The Imperial Challenge: Quebec and Britain in the Age of the American Revolution* (Montreal/Kingston: McGill-Queen's University Press, 1989).

See also Pierre Tousignant's useful essay, "The Integration of the Province of Quebec into the British Empire, 1763–91. Part 1: From the Royal Proclamation to the Quebec Act," *Dictionary of Canadian Biography*, vol. 4, 1771–1800, pp. xxxii–xlix.

James H. Lambert provides bibliographical references for the period from 1760 to Confederation in his essay "Quebec/Lower Canada," in M. Brook Taylor, ed., *Canadian History: A Reader's Guide*, vol. 1, *Beginnings to Confederation* (Toronto: University of Toronto Press, 1994), pp. 112–83. For a look at the legacy of the French Empire in North America, see Philip Marchand, *Ghost Empire: The Legacy of the French in North America* (Toronto: McClelland and Stewart, 2005).

Fernand Ouellet reviews economic aspects of the period in *Economic and Social History of Quebec, 1760–1850* (Toronto: Macmillan, 1980). Several articles on the same topic are included in his *Economy, Class and Nation in Quebec: Interpretive Essays*, ed. and trans. by Jacques A. Barbier (Mississauga, ON: Copp Clark Pitman, 1991). Important surveys of life in Quebec at this time include Allan Greer, *Peasant, Lord, and Merchant: Rural Society in Three Quebec Parishes, 1740–1840* (Toronto: University of Toronto Press, 1985), and David Thiery Ruddel, *Quebec City, 1765–1832: The Evolution of a Colonial Town* (Ottawa: Canadian Museum of Civilization, 1987). The evolution of religious rites is studied in Ollivier Hubert, *Sur la terre comme au ciel: La gestion des rites par l'Église catholique du Québec (fin XVIIe-mi-XIXe siècle)* (Quebec: Presses de l'Université Laval, 2000). Law and justice are examined by Donald Fyson in *Magistrates, Police, and People: Everyday Criminal Justice in Quebec and Lower Canada, 1764–1837* (Toronto: University of Toronto Press and Osgoode Society for Canadian Legal History, 2006). See also Evelyn Kolish, *Nationalismes et conflits de droits: Le débat du droit privé au Québec, 1760–1840* (LaSalle, QC: Hurtubise HMH, 1994); and, in addition, two articles by Douglas Hay, "The Meanings of the Criminal Law in Quebec, 1764–1774," in Louis A. Knafla, ed., *Crime and Criminal Justice in Europe and Canada*, 2nd ed. (Waterloo, ON: Wilfrid Laurier University Press, 1985), pp. 77–110, and "Civilians Tried in Military Courts, 1759–64," in F. Murray Greenwood and Barry Wright, eds., *Canadian State Trials*, vol. I, *Law, Politics, and Security Measures, 1608–1837* (Toronto: University of Toronto Press, 1996), pp. 114–128. The fate of Canadien military elites is discussed in Roch Legault, *Une élite en déroute: Les militaires canadiens après la Conquête* (Outremont: Athéna Éditions, 2002).

Historiographical studies of the impact of the Conquest are available in Cameron Nish, ed., *The French Canadians, 1759–1766: Conquered? Half-Conquered? Liberated?* (Toronto: Copp Clark, 1966); Dale Miquelon, ed., *Society and Conquest: The Debate on the Bourgeoisie and Social Change in French Canada, 1700–1850* (Toronto: Copp Clark, 1977); Paul W. Bennett and Cornelius J. Jaenen, *Emerging Identities: Selected Problems and Interpretations in Canadian History* (Scarborough, ON: Prentice Hall, 1986), pp. 76–105; two volumes by Serge Gagnon, *Quebec and Its Historians, 1840–1920 and Quebec and Its Historians: The Twentieth Century* (Montreal: Harvest House, 1982, 1985); and Ronald Rudin, *Making History in Twentieth-Century Quebec* (Toronto: University of Toronto Press, 1997). See also Claude Couture, "La Conquête de 1760 et le problème de la transition au capitalisme," *Revue d'histoire de l'Amérique française* 39 (1985–86): 369–89.

Linda Kerr presents a view of the initial difficulties of the resident English-speaking merchants in Quebec in her Ph.D. thesis, "Quebec: The Making of an Imperial Mercantile Community, 1760–1768" (Edmonton: University of Alberta, 1992). The fate of French-speaking merchants is examined in José Igartua, "The Merchants of Montreal at the Conquest: A Socio-Economic Profile," *Histoire sociale/Social History* 8 (1973): 275–93, and in "A Change in Climate: The Conquest and the *Marchands* of Montreal," listed in this chapter's "Related Readings" section. Ronald Rudin provides a short review of Quebec's embryonic English-speaking community in *The Forgotten Quebecers: A History of English-Speaking Quebec, 1759–1980* (Quebec: Institut québécois de recherche sur la culture, 1985).

Lorraine Gadoury examines family relationships within the French-speaking colonial elite in *Échanges épistolaires au sein de l'élite canadienne du XVIIIe siècle* (Montreal: Hurtubise, 1998). Finally, there are biographies on all the major figures of these years in various volumes of *Dictionary of Canadian Biography*, an essential tool for this and other periods. One sketch is the biography of Marie-Josephte Corriveau, "La Corriveau," by folklorist Luc Lacourcière, in vol. 3: 1741–1770, pp. 142–43. For important maps of Quebec in this period, see R. Cole Harris, ed., *Historical Atlas of Canada*, vol. 1, *From the Beginning to 1800* (Toronto: University of Toronto Press, 1987).

The following provide a good introduction to the Aboriginal history of the period. Books: Francis Jennings, *Empire of Fortune: Crowns, Colonies and Tribes in the Seven Years War in America* (New York: W.W. Norton, 1988); Howard H. Peckham, *Pontiac and the Indian Uprising* (Chicago: University of Chicago Press, 1961 [1947]); Richard White, *The Middle Ground: Indians, Empires and Republics in the Great Lakes Region, 1650–1815* (Cambridge: Cambridge University Press, 1991). Articles: *The William and Mary Quarterly* devotes an entire issue to a forum on the middle ground in their January issue of 2006. See *The William and Mary Quarterly* 63(1) (Jan., 2006); W.J. Eccles, "Sovereignty-Association, 1500–1783," in his *Essays on New France* (Toronto: Oxford University Press, 1987), pp. 156–81; Jacqueline Peterson, "Many Roads to Red River: Métis Genesis in the Great Lakes Region, 1680–1815," in Jacqueline Peterson and Jennifer S.H. Brown, eds., *The New Peoples: Being and Becoming Métis in North America* (Winnipeg: University of Manitoba Press, 1985), pp. 37–71; and Harriet Gorham, "Families of Mixed Descent in the Western Great Lakes Region," in Bruce Alden Cox, ed., *Native People, Native Lands: Canadian Indians, Inuit and Métis* (Ottawa: Carleton University Press, 1988), pp. 37–55.

Specific developments in the province of Quebec are mentioned in Daniel Francis, *A History of the Native Peoples of Quebec, 1760–1867* (Ottawa: Indian and Northern Affairs Canada, 1983). On the Aboriginal history of the St. Lawrence Valley, see Jean-Pierre Sawaya, *La Fédération des Sept Feux de la vallée du Saint-Laurent, XVIIe–XIXe siècles* (Sillery: Septentrion, 1998); and Denys Delâge, "Les Iroquois chrétiens des 'réductions,' 1677–1770," *Recherches amérindiennes au Québec* 21(1–2) (1991): 59–70; 21(3) (1991): 39–50. For a look at the end of slavery in Montreal, see Frank Mackey, *Done with Slavery: The Black Fact in Montreal, 1760–1840* (Montreal/Kingston: McGill-Queen's University Press, 2010).

Source: With permission of the Royal Ontario Museum © ROM, 955.227.

Chapter Nine

QUEBEC SOCIETY IN THE LATE EIGHTEENTH CENTURY

TIME LINE

1775	American Revolutionary armies invade Quebec; Montreal capitulates
1776	Thirteen Colonies declare independence from Britain
	British reinforcements force Americans to retreat from Quebec
1782	Loyalists arrive in British North America
1783	Treaty of Paris ends war between Britain and United States
1784	Members of Six Nations Confederacy who supported Britain resettle in BNA
	Smallpox epidemic sweeps Quebec
1786	Guy Carleton returns to Quebec as governor
1788	Poor harvests cause famine throughout Quebec
1791	Constitutional Act is passed
	Quebec is divided into colonies of Upper and Lower Canada

Just over a decade after winning the North American continent, Britain lost the Thirteen Colonies. The American Revolution created the United States, and positioned an angry nation to the south of what was now called British North America (BNA). The creation of the United States would have massive long-term impact on the history of Canada. The short-term impact, however, was just as significant.

The rebelling Thirteen Colonies assumed that Quebec would join them in throwing off the "yoke of British tyranny." The British assumed the French Canadians would show their gratitude for the Quebec Act by remaining loyal. Both assumptions were wrong. The French Canadians took what can best be described as a neutral stance in the American Revolution. When the Revolutionary armies attacked Quebec, it would not be the last time Canada faced an American invasion. Fear of American annexation became a constant in the Canadian psyche for the next century.

In the aftermath of the Conquest, the British failed in their attempts to attract English-Protestant settlers to Quebec. But the American Revolution led to the arrival of Canada's first immigration boom. Many of those people in the Thirteen Colonies who wanted to live under the British flag or who had supported Britain during the Revolution left the United States. They were joined by nearly 2000 Iroquois members of the Six Nations who fought alongside Britain. Once again, the First Nations backed the losing side in their long war to prevent settler incursions into their lands. All told, approximately 15 000 loyalists came north to British territory. This "peaceful invasion" of English-Protestants drastically altered the ethnic, religious, cultural, and political landscape of BNA.

The American Invasion

By the early 1770s, it was apparent that trouble was brewing in the American colonies. Propaganda denouncing British tyranny, lauding democratic institutions, and proclaiming the people's rights and liberties circulated widely, even in Quebec. As revolutionary momentum increased, American colonial leaders looked north and expected to find a receptive welcome in the recently conquered colony of Quebec. American agents roamed the countryside, appealing to the French Canadians to choose between making the rest of North America their "unalterable friends" or their "inveterate enemies." France's support for the brewing rebellion was expected to help align Quebec with the American *patriots*. French-born expatriate, Fleury Mesplet, sent to Quebec by Benjamin Franklin, set about printing and distributing pamphlets on liberty. He took up residence in Montreal where, except for the three years he spent in prison for sedition, the founder of *The Gazette* defended democratic ideals, first American, and then, after 1789, French.

The Continental Congress in Philadelphia decided early in the Revolutionary War to invade Canada in order to prevent the British from concentrating their forces in the north and then sweeping down into the Thirteen Colonies. In May 1775, the Americans raided St. Jean, on the Richelieu River. The raid demonstrated British military weakness but also highlighted the lack of enthusiasm to fight among the Canadians. Then in September, the armies of General George Washington advanced into Quebec by way of Lake Champlain and Maine. The efforts of Governors Murray and Carleton to woo the French-Canadian elites paid dividends. Both the clergy and the seigneurs rejected the revolutionary ideals and upheld the traditional order. They urged the habitants to support the British cause and fight such radical and anarchistic notions as democracy. Few, however, came forward. Bishop Briand complained to one parish priest: "My authority is no more respected than yours. They tell both of us that we are Englishmen."

Governor Guy Carleton abandoned Montreal to the invading Americans in late 1775. After narrowly escaping the advancing enemy forces, he succeeded in reaching Quebec, although he doubted that the city could hold off the attack for long: "We have so many enemies within, and foolish people, dupes to those traitors . . . [that] I think our fate extremely doubtful, to say

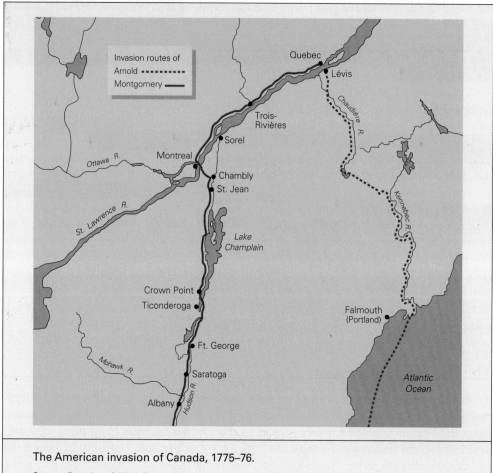

The American invasion of Canada, 1775–76.

Source: Based on C.W. Jefferys, *The Picture Gallery of Canadian History, vol. 2* (Toronto: The Ryerson Press, 1945), p. 5.

nothing worse." The Americans were confident of success. General Richard Montgomery boasted that he would eat Christmas dinner in Quebec City or in hell. The assault came in the early morning of December 31 and Montgomery was killed in a failed attempt to take the city. He did not eat Christmas dinner in Quebec City.

In London, the British government prepared for an expedition to relieve Quebec. An angry King George III declared that "when such acts of vigour are shown by the rebellious Americans, we must show that the English lion when aroused has not only his wonted resolution, but has added the swiftness of the racehorse." Five months later, in May 1776, a fleet of British ships sailed up the St. Lawrence, and the ill-equipped and demoralized Americans hastily departed.

Some British politicians demanded Carleton's recall for not preventing the American retreat up the Richelieu River and for not retaking the important fortress of Ticonderoga on Lake Champlain in preparation for the invasion of the Hudson River valley. Historian A.L. Burt argued that the governor's inaction "ruined the campaign of 1776 and possibly altered the outcome of the war."[1] Carleton did try to pursue the Americans, but his troops, after weeks spent on crowded transport ships, needed frequent rest and they were plagued by an outbreak of the "flux." The British also lacked supplies. According to historian R.A. Bowler, Carleton was over-prudent, but it was not errors in strategy that led to the failure to take advantage of the retreating American forces.[2]

In 1777, the British conceived a plan to crush the revolt by striking down from Quebec to New York City, thus dividing the rebellious colonies. These hopes were dashed when a larger American force surrounded and defeated the British at Saratoga, north of Albany. Thereafter, the British launched no more large-scale expeditions southward from the St. Lawrence.

The alliance of France with the American colonies in February 1778 changed the face of the war. A secret clause of the arrangement stipulated, however, that France would not invade Canada or Acadia. The Americans had no intention of allowing France back into the area. But for their part, the French did not wish to see the Americans take control of BNA either. King Louis XVI wanted to weaken British power by assisting the Thirteen Colonies in gaining their independence, but he did not favour an American conquest of Canada. Indeed, he hoped that a British Canada, by posing a continual check to the Americans, would ensure the latter's dependence on France. Neither France nor the United States wished the other to possess Canada.

The Response of the French Canadians

Governor Carleton was aware that there were elements within Quebec society that supported the American Revolution. During the American invasion, for example, some merchants welcomed the invading revolutionaries with enthusiasm. One French merchant who did so was Christophe Pélissier, director of the Forges du Saint-Maurice, who provided American troops with munitions for their march on Quebec City. Some habitants also supported the Revolution. In most cases, however, communities were divided. There was widespread anger and opposition to the policies of King George III. While the British had demonstrated tolerance in the Quebec Act of 1774, the legislation was designed more to win the elites than the common people.

In January 1776, Michel Blais, a landholder and militia captain, announced on the church steps of St. Pierre, a village near Montmagny east of Quebec City, that a certain Pierre Ayotte was in the area to recruit for the American cause. Later, speaking in his own defence, he insisted that he had spoken with such an ironical tone that no one came forward. Still, several inhabitants of the village and the surrounding area joined the rebel ranks. In March, British authorities ordered a former French army officer to assemble the royalist forces in the Montmagny region and to attack an American outpost at Pointe Lévy, across the river from Quebec City. Michel Blais's house at St. Pierre became the headquarters of the British. The Americans, warned by their *Canadien* followers, arrived on the scene with nearly 250 men, including 150 French Canadians, and a pitched battle was fought around the house. The Americans won the skirmish and took several prisoners, one of whom was Charles-François Bailly de Messein, future bishop of Quebec, then a young priest who had joined the British ranks as a chaplain in order to preach loyalty to England.

While some of the habitants agreed with the revolutionary ideals, in general the French-Canadian response was more conditioned by local issues. They listened sympathetically to the

Sir Guy Carleton, Lord Dorchester.

Source: © Library and Archives Canada/Mabel Messer Collection/C-002833. Reproduced with the permission of the Minister of Public Works and Government Services Canada (2007).

Americans' denunciations of tithes and seigneurial rents, both firmly established by the Quebec Act. But there was much uncertainty in the patriot cause. It seemed unlikely that the Thirteen Colonies would actually succeed and win their independence from the major European imperial power. And even if they did, what would it mean to a French-Catholic Quebec? The French Canadians had little love for the *Bastonnois*, or "people of Boston," as they called the Americans. In general, like many of the First Nations, the habitants felt little interest in this struggle and most preferred to keep their neutrality as long as possible. When American fortunes improved and American soldiers were willing to pay good prices in coin for supplies, the habitants sympathized with them. But when the invaders failed to take Quebec and the long winter siege dragged on, and—even worse—when they began to pay for their provisions with paper money or simply not at all, their popularity fell.

The reaction of the French Canadians embittered Carleton. He was certain he had read the tenor of Quebec accurately and the governor banked his political career on the colony's loyalty. He had gone to great pains to convince the British parliament to pass the Quebec Act. A few months before the invasion, he wrote that the French Canadians rejoiced over the Act and that the formation of a French-Canadian regiment "would complete their happiness." After the American withdrawal, a disappointed Carleton sent a commission into the rural parishes to inquire into the disloyalty of the habitants.

Throughout the war, the British reintroduced military *corvées* (forced labour for the government) that were previously levied under the French regime. The habitants were called on to furnish and transport materials for various construction works. They were not paid for their labour unless they were artisans. Moreover, army and militia officers were often arbitrary in their application of the ordinance on corvées. The correspondence of Frederick Haldimand, appointed governor of Quebec in 1777 to replace Carleton, who had resigned, demonstrates that desertions from the corvées were frequent and that the governor often imposed fines and prison sentences on recalcitrant workers.

The Catholic Church in Quebec feared and opposed the revolutionary ideals. Carleton's efforts did pay dividends with the clergy, who perceived a more advantageous position in a British than an American Quebec. In a pastoral letter that he ordered read in all churches in the colony, Bishop Briand condemned the rebellion as "contrary to religion as well as to good sense and to reason." Most priests, on Briand's orders, refused the sacraments to rebels, even at the hour of death. Pro-American priests such as the Jesuit Pierre-René Floquet were suspended from their functions. When the Americans departed, Briand demanded that parishioners who had sided with the Americans repent publicly. In one case, 12 rebel sympathizers, after being released from the Quebec City prison, went to the cathedral steps after high mass and pleaded for God and the King to pardon their scandalous behaviour.

Some habitant farmers who were able to avoid the armies benefited from a tripling of agricultural prices. In part, speculators caused this inflation by going out into the countryside and buying up crops.

Death of General Montgomery in the Attack on Quebec, 31 December 1775, *by John Trumbull*.

Source: Yale University Art Gallery/Art Resource, NY.

The rise in prices encouraged the habitants to clear and sow new land in order to increase their production of wheat and other crops. While certain parts of the countryside benefited, the towns suffered as prices for flour and other basic necessities soared. Harvests were generally abundant, but, in view of war needs, most of the crops were sold on the local market. Grain exports to both the West Indies and Britain fell considerably.

The American Revolution and the First Nations

Most of the First Nations in the affected areas were fighting their own war against the American colonists. While they were viewed as important military allies in the colonial wars, it is important to recognize that they had their own reasons for fighting. As Pontiac's Uprising demonstrated, the Aboriginals were not necessarily prepared to set their grievances aside just because peace was declared in Europe. Therefore, the American Revolution, for some, was a continuation of the war against American settlement moving westward. For the patriots, the Royal Proclamation of 1763 and the Quebec Act of 1774 were part of the "Intolerable Acts" because they demonstrated the British intention to prevent American incursions into Aboriginal territory.

Most of the First Nations were French allies against the British. When the Revolution broke out, most became British allies against the Americans. The Iroquois Confederacy, however, had long been British and therefore American allies. At the beginning of the American Revolution, the Six Nations Confederacy council declared its neutrality in what it perceived as a "family feud" between the British and their American offspring. Soon, however, it became clear that the Iroquois could not avoid being drawn into the struggle. The cost of their involvement in the conflict was heavy: the Iroquois League, which was several hundred years old, collapsed, and the Mohawks lost their lands along the Mohawk River in central New York state and elsewhere. Britain's defeat forced 2000 Iroquois to abandon their homelands and migrate to the western section of the colony of Quebec that would become Upper Canada.

After the defeat of Pontiac, the British cultivated good relations with the Aboriginal groups to ensure their military assistance. William Johnson, a large landowner in the Mohawk Valley who spoke Mohawk and served as the British government's northern superintendent of Indian affairs, was instrumental in carrying out this policy. Johnson, whose companion was Molly Brant, the sister of Six Nations war chief Joseph Brant (Thayendanegea), played an important role in the lengthy negotiations to define a boundary for the "Indian Territory" that took place after the Proclamation of 1763 and Pontiac's Resistance. After his death in 1774, his nephew and successor, Guy Johnson, argued that the annexation of First Nations territory to the Province of Quebec (by the Quebec Act) showed the British government's solicitude for its Aboriginal subjects and its desire to protect their territory from settlement.

In 1775, the British instructed Guy Johnson to pressure the Iroquois to "take up the hatchet against His Majesty's rebellious subjects." Johnson failed, however, to neutralize American efforts to enlist the aid of the Oneidas and Tuscaroras. The Iroquois were just as divided by the "family feud." Johnson then came to Montreal and attempted to build up support for the British cause among the several thousand Iroquois living at Kahnawake, southwest of Montreal, at Kanesatake (Oka), about 50 kilometres west of Montreal, and at St. Régis (Akwesasne), a settlement on the St. Lawrence River near present-day Cornwall, Ontario.

The efforts of Joseph Brant paid off. The Mohawks and some Senecas supported the British. The Onondagas and the Cayugas declared their neutrality, while many Oneidas and Tuscaroras, as well as some of the Iroquois in the Montreal area, showed a preference for the Americans. In 1779, however, American troops under General John Sullivan invaded the Six Nations territory, indiscriminately punishing the Iroquois by burning crops and destroying villages. These attacks on the hitherto neutral Onondagas and Cayugas brought them over to the British side. One thousand Iroquois warriors retaliated by burning and pillaging American farms throughout the vast territory between the Ohio and Mohawk rivers.

By 1782, with the British on the verge of final defeat, Frederick Haldimand, the governor of Quebec, instructed commanders to limit themselves to defensive actions. The First Nations, however, were not prepared to go on the defensive because it put them at a disadvantage, and meant their capitulation and surrendering of territory. Only with difficulty did Haldimand's orders prevail.

The Aboriginal Peoples and the Return of Peace

The American Revolution ended in 1782 and peace was declared with the Treaty of Paris in September 1783. The United States achieved their independence from Britain. As usual, however, the First Nations and their issues were ignored at the peace talks. They were not even mentioned in the treaty. The British recognized the area south of the Great Lakes, from the Appalachian Mountains to the Mississippi River, as American territory. But the Iroquois had never acknowledged direct British sovereignty over their land or the Crown's right to dispose of it. Outraged, Brant and the Iroquois were described as prepared to "defend their own just rights or perish in the attempt. . . . They would die like men, which they thought preferable to misery and distress if deprived of their hunting grounds." John Johnson, who had just replaced his cousin Guy as the British superintendent of northern Indian affairs, went with much trepidation to Niagara to negotiate with Brant. An embarrassed Governor Haldimand wanted to mollify the Iroquois and the Great Lakes First Nations in order to prevent them from taking revenge on the British, whom they now viewed as traitors. The governor urged the British to delay the surrender of the western posts of Oswego, Niagara, Detroit, and Michilimackinac, now in American territory.

COMMUNITY PORTRAIT

The Community of Odanak

Often overlooked in discussions of the Aboriginal history of the St. Lawrence Valley in the eighteenth century are the Algonquian-speaking communities, one of the most prominent being the Abenaki of Odanak. Located on the banks of the St. François River, near Sorel, just east of Montreal, "Odanak" means "at the village" in the Algonquian language of the Abenaki. The name "Abenaki" is itself an alteration of "Wabanaki," meaning "land of the dawn," or "country lying to the east." The community of Odanak was one of four major Roman Catholic mission stations in the St. Lawrence Valley, in the French regime, along with Lorette (Hurons) at Quebec, and Kahna-wake (Iroquois) and Kanesatake (Iroquois and Algonquian), both in the Montreal area.

The majority of the Abenaki at Odanak arrived in New France as refugees from Northern New England's Indian Wars. The Soroki nation originally constituted a majority in the refugee community, founded in the early eighteenth century. But Odanak was swept by smallpox in 1730, and the losses in the raids to the south proved destructive. Then another important nation, the Abenaki proper, arrived and gained predominance in the community. In total, the members of as many as twenty Algonquian-speaking

First Nations made their way as refugees from the encroaching American settlements to the south. At Odanak they all gradually lost their separate identities. As the majority, the Abenaki gave their name to the others in the community.

Abenaki war parties went forth from the St. François River against the *Bastoniak* (people from Boston), as the Abenaki called the New England settlers. These French allies fought until the end of the French regime. Odanak warriors joined other First Nations and the French in the ambush of British General Braddock in 1755, and fought beside the French at Quebec in 1759. In retaliation for their repeated raids on New England settlements, the British made an assault on the "St. Francis Indians" a priority in 1759. Only weeks after their victory on the Plains of Abraham, a company of American frontier rangers led by Major Robert Rogers made a surprise attack on Odanak, during which they burned the village church and all the houses to the ground, and killed many Abenakis.

In his report to General Amherst, the British commander, Major Rogers claimed his rangers killed 200 Abenaki, but French sources indicate that only 30 died. Anthropologist Gordon Day's investigation of Abenaki oral traditions helped demystify the event. In the late 1950s, Day spoke with several elders at Odanak who remembered traditions handed down to them as children by their grandparents, themselves born in the early nineteenth century. According to this oral history, an Aboriginal person serving with the American forces gave the village warning the night before the attack, which allowed the community to move their children, women, and old people into places of safe refuge. The Odanak Abenaki regrouped shortly thereafter, and the next year raided an American settlement in New

"Welcome to Odanak." The entry to the community on Highway 132 near Sorel, Quebec, 1984.

Source: © Paul-Émile Rioux.

Hampshire. Peace came late that year, and they re-established their village at the same location on the banks of the St. François.

Strangely, it was to this same village that Reverend Eleazar Wheelock sent recruiters in 1774 to obtain students for his Moor's Indian Charity School at Hanover, New Hampshire (later Dartmouth College). Normally, Odanak would have had nothing to do with the detested *Bastoniak*, who had occupied the Abenaki homeland. But at the time of the visit, an individual then in office as a principal chief proved sympathetic: Joseph-Louis Gill, "The White Chief of the Abenakis," the son of two New England captives. Gill was of European descent only in a biological sense. In the early eighteenth century the Abenaki had captured two English children, a boy and a girl, from the New England coast. Adopted into Abenaki families at Odanak, and raised as Abenakis and Catholics, these captives later married at Odanak, where they lived their entire lives. Joseph-Louis, the eldest of their seven children, became a chief in the community around 1750. His first wife, an Abenaki woman, died during Rogers's raid; his second wife was French Canadian. During the British regime, he met with the British authorities in 1764 to complain of encroachments by settlers in the Odanak area on the Abenakis' hunting territories. Toward the end of his life, Gill became prayer leader at Odanak, which meant he was the most important person in the Odanak church after the Catholic missionary.

Although a staunch Roman Catholic, Gill wanted his family to obtain an education, even if the welcoming school was Protestant and in Bastonki (New England). The chief sent four of his relatives to Dartmouth.

None of the Abenaki young men whom he sent to the school converted to Protestantism, but several Abenaki students from Odanak did, after Chief Gill's death in 1798. These Protestant Abenaki and their converts in the community added an additional layer of complexity to the already multi-ethnic Aboriginal community.

FURTHER READING

Thomas M. Charland, "Joseph-Louis Gill, Known Also as Magouaouidombaouit," *Dictionary of Canadian Biography,* vol. 4, 1771–1800 (Toronto: University of Toronto Press, 1979), pp. 293–94.

Gordon M. Day, "Oral Tradition as Complement," *Ethnohistory* 19(2) (Spring 1972): 99–107.

Gordon M. Day, "Western Abenaki," in Bruce G. Trigger, ed., *Handbook of North American Indians,* vol. 15, *Northeast* (Washington: Smithsonian Institution, 1978), pp. 148–59.

Joseph Brant, 1786. Painting by Gilbert Stuart.
Source: © Corbis.

The American victory in the Revolution ended any recognition of the Proclamation Line of 1763 (and as later extended in the Treaty of Fort Stanwix in 1768). As far as the Americans were concerned, in part they were fighting against such British policies as the Proclamation and the Quebec Act. The Americans intended to open the eastern part of the "Indian Territory" to settlement. In fact, hundreds of settlers had already crossed the former boundary line. The First Nations, now greatly outnumbered, had little choice but to cede extensive lands to the states of New York and Pennsylvania.

A disheartened Joseph Brant, backed by John Johnson, prevailed upon Haldimand to grant new lands to the Iroquois in the area north of lakes Ontario and Erie. In 1783–84, the Indian Department purchased vast tracts of land from the Mississaugas, as the British called the Ojibwa (Anishinabeg) on the north shore of Lake Ontario. While the Mississauga lost their lands through treaty, the "loyal" Six Nations gained a long, narrow strip of land along the Grand River, "to enjoy forever." The poverty of the reserve's new inhabitants, however, caused Brant to sell off large portions of the lands for European settlement. Brant personally received land in what is now Burlington, as well as a house and a military commission. His sister Molly was also given a house, and her daughters married English military men and officials.

WHERE HISTORIANS DISAGREE

The Anishinabeg–Iroquois War

Usually the lack of source material prevents Canadian historians from learning Aboriginal viewpoints. In the case of the Great Lakes Anishinabeg (Ojibwa, Mississauga, and Odawa), however, this is not the case. Several Anishinabeg authors, including Peter Jones, George Copway, William Warren, and Francis Assikinack, produced important historical accounts in the mid-nineteenth century. These works provide an alternative perspective on the Great Lakes First Nations in the late seventeenth century, and especially on the Anishinabeg–Iroquois wars that continued for half a century after the fall of Huronia in 1649.

William Warren (1825–53), the son of an American trader and a woman of mixed French and Ojibwa ancestry, wrote in the early 1850s that "their anxiety to open the road to the white traders, in order to procure fire-arms and their much coveted commodities, induced the Ojibways, Ottaways, Potawatomi, Osaukies, and Wyandots to enter into a firm alliance. They sent their united forces against the Iroquois, and fighting severe and bloody battles, they eventually forced them to retire from Canada."[1] An Odawa and Indian Department clerk from Manitoulin Island, Francis Assikinack (1824–63), also wrote about the Odawas' wars with the Iroquois in 1858. The Iroquois "used to go out into Lake Huron or Georgian Bay, by the Nahdowa Sahgi-River, until they got two or three severe defeats in the vicinity of the Blue Mountains, by Sahgimah, the most celebrated warrior of the Odahwahs at that time."[2] George Copway (1818–69), a Mississauga writer and lecturer of the late 1840s and 1850s, provided the most detailed description of the struggle. In his *History of the Ojibway Nation,* he gives references to the locations of the battles "which terminated in the subjugation of the eastern Iroquois."[3]

Peter Jones (1802–56), the Mississauga chief and Methodist minister, went one step further. He not only offered a summary of the battles but also provided evidence. In his *History of the Ojebway Indians,* published posthumously in 1861, he noted:

The last battle that was fought was at the outlet of Burlington Bay, which was at the south end of the beach, where the Government House formerly stood [present-day Hamilton, Ontario]. Near to this place a mound of human bones is to be seen to this day; and also another at the north end, close to the residence of the late Captain Brant. Besides these, there are traces of fortifications at short distances along the whole length of the beach, where holes had been dug into the sand and a breastwork thrown round them. They are about twenty or thirty feet in diameter, but were originally much larger. At this finishing battle the Ojebways spared a few of their enemies, whom they suffered to depart in peace, that they might go and tell their brethren on the south side of Lake Ontario—the fate of their nation—that all the country between the waters of the Ontario, Erie, St. Clair, and Huron, was now surrendered into the hands of the Ojebways.[4]

What primary evidence exists of an Anishinabeg victory in the late seventeenth century over the Iroquois? According to historian José António Brandão and anthropologist William A. Starna, none. In the 1990s, they argued that the Iroquois "had not been defeated" by the Anishinabeg.[5] The authors argued that claims of an Anishinabeg victory are "based on oral traditions published in the mid- to late nineteenth century that remain unconfirmed by the documentary record." In Brandão's study of "Iroquois Hostilities to 1701" (a list of nearly 500 Iroquois military encounters in the seventeenth century),[6] he found no evidence of an Anishinabeg victory over the Iroquois in southern Ontario.

Which interpretation is to be believed? How trustworthy and valuable is oral history? Gradually, historians are at least questioning their own biases toward written (and therefore Eurocentric) sources. If we are to open history to Aboriginal perspectives, we need to reorient our weighing of sources. When it comes to the Anishinabeg–Iroquois War, Historian D. Peter MacLeod argues for greater attention to these Anishinabeg oral sources in order to complement the documentary approach, which has produced "a distorted vision of post-contact North America in which Amerindians are fully visible only when they interact with Europeans."[7]

1. William W. Warren, "History of the Ojibways, Based upon Traditions and Oral Statements," reprinted in William W. Warren, *History of the Ojibway Nation* (Minneapolis, MN: Ross & Haines, 1957), p. 146.

2. Francis Assikinack, "Social and Warlike Customs of the Odahwah Indians," *The Canadian Journal,* new series, 3 (1858): 309.

3. George Copway, *The Traditional History and Characteristic Sketches of the Ojibway Nation* (London: Charles Gilpin, 1850), p. 85.

4. Peter Jones, *History of the Ojebway Indians* (London: A.W. Bennett, 1861), p. 113.

5. José António Brandão and William A. Starna, "The Treaties of 1701: A Triumph of Iroquois Diplomacy," *Ethnohistory* 43(2) (Spring 1996): 217.

6. José António Brandão, *"Your Fyre Shall Burn No More": Iroquois Policy toward New France and Its Native Allies to 1701* (Lincoln: University of Nebraska Press, 1997), pp. 177–278.

7. D. Peter MacLeod, "The Anishinabeg Point of View: The History of the Great Lakes Region to 1800 in Nineteenth-Century Mississauga, Odawa, and Ojibwa Historiography," *Canadian Historical Review* 73(2) (1992): 209.

The Loyalist Migration

During and after the Revolution, thousands of loyalists, bitterly denounced and often persecuted, fled north across the border into British North America. Governor Haldimand was overwhelmed at the numbers. In the case of the group who became known as the "late loyalists," it was suspected that they were coming more to receive free land than to live under the British flag. Many came to Quebec from upper New York and New England. They would immediately have settled in the area that was to become the Eastern Townships had not Haldimand, unsure of the location of the international border and perhaps fearing to settle an English population along it, forbid them to do so. The ban was lifted only in 1791.

Nor did the governor wish the loyalists to settle on the seigneurial lands along the St. Lawrence River, where he feared conflicts with French Canadians might erupt. He preferred that they move to Nova Scotia, or that they migrate to the western portion of the Province of Quebec that was to become Upper Canada in 1791. The Crown bore the costs of transporting the loyalists and, after forcing the Mississaugas off their land, assisted them in establishing their own farms.

The arrival of the loyalists immediately brought pressure to bear on the British administrators to make Quebec into an English-Protestant colony. The migration seemed to justify the complaints of the English merchants that the colony was being denied the traditions of British rule. For the first time since the Conquest, a significant contingent of English-Protestant immigrants settled in the province. Quebec's population of British origin increased to at least 10 percent of the total white population, estimated at about 160 000 in 1790.

Guy Carleton, now Lord Dorchester, returned to North America, where he was appointed Commander-in-Chief. He organized the evacuation of nearly 30 000 loyalists from New York City in 1782–83, including many slaves who had been promised their freedom for supporting Britain. Although officially Commander-in-Chief of all BNA, Carleton's rule effectively extended only over Quebec from 1786 to 1796. He took as his principal adviser William Smith, a prominent loyalist and former chief justice of New York (1780–83), whom he named chief justice of the Province of Quebec. Smith looked forward to the day when the French would be assimilated by waves of English settlers from the United States. Carleton himself no longer believed that Quebec was destined to remain predominantly French Canadian "to the end of time."

The Life of the Habitants

The life of the habitants continued as it had prior to the Revolution. Agriculture depended largely on the weather and yields were highly uncertain. A prosperous period in the mid-1770s was followed by several very lean years. Drought ruined the crop in 1779, and the harvests of the early 1780s were also poor, spoiled by late springs or early autumn frosts. Only in the mid-1780s did the situation improve, and then not for long. In 1788, rust or smut resulted in a serious drop in production, and the large surplus of 1787 had already been shipped away by the time the extent of the damage was realized. The results were catastrophic. In the wake of the shortage, prices more than doubled and both the urban and the rural poor suffered. Many died from famine, particularly in the Montreal area. Not until 1791 did harvests return to prewar levels.

After 1791, increased production necessitated larger markets, both at home and abroad. Fortunately for the colonial economy, the accelerating pace of industrialization, urbanization, and population growth in Britain meant that the mother country would buy virtually all surplus grain available in Canada. Whereas American farmers no longer had free access to the British markets, Canadian farmers received preferential treatment. In the aftermath of the American Revolution and the Napoleonic Wars in Europe, Canada's economy became ever more tightly integrated into the imperial economic system.

Even in relatively prosperous times, illness haunted the habitants. On several occasions, they fell victim to smallpox, typhoid fever, and other diseases transmitted through the water supply. In the disastrous epidemic of 1784, the death rate climbed to an extremely high 45 per 1000. Syphilis, one of the diseases for which no treatment existed, was prevalent in the port city of Quebec. Stricken individuals came from all social classes, from the recent immigrant to a top British administrator of the Province of Quebec—General Henry Hope, military commander-in-chief and lieutenant governor of Quebec, who died of the disease in April 1789. This reputedly handsome soldier died from "his improper Gallantries. . . . [He had become] the most shocking object that can be imagined—his Features & the greatest part of his Face entirely destroy'd."[3]

Château-Richer on the Côte de Beaupré, east of Quebec City, in 1787. By Thomas Davies.

Source: Thomas Davies, *A View of the Château Richer, Cape Torment, and Lower End of the Isle of Orleans near Quebec, 1787.* Watercolour on laid paper, 35.4 × 52.7 cm National Gallery of Canada, Ottawa Photo © NGC.

Medical practitioners in the colony (most of them without diplomas) numbered but a few dozen in the late eighteenth century. Most were British and lived in towns, at a time when 80 percent of the population remained rural. Moreover, the number of inhabitants per doctor was rising sharply and the colony had no school of medicine to train new doctors. The profession lacked prestige (except perhaps for medical officers in the army), and doctors had difficulty finding paying clients. They often ran notices in the newspapers requesting payment. In rural areas, folk medicines, many obtained from Aboriginal people during the French regime, remained in use.

Townspeople

After a period of stagnation due to war, agricultural crises, and epidemics, Quebec City and Montreal developed more rapidly, particularly after 1785, thanks to increased trade with Britain. Yet Quebec City's population reached only 7300 by 1795, and Montreal's was even more modest. Urban development proceeded according to the commercial interests of property owners. Poor areas of town were neglected. Roads into town were kept up by the habitants who used them. An ordinance in 1778 ordered farmers transporting wood, hay, fur, and other provisions into Quebec City to carry shovels, picks, and hoes in their carts to repair the road. Militia officers were often hired to supervise the work, but rules were difficult to enforce.

Colonial Elites

Governor Haldimand's relations with the British merchants in the early 1780s remained as hostile as under Murray and Carleton. All three governors were conservative, authoritarian, and generally unwilling to share power in the colony. For their part, the aggressive, arrogant, and uncompromising attitude of the merchants only added fuel to the fire. The scorn of government officials for the merchants was increased by their behaviour during the Revolution, when many supported the American invasion. The governors looked to check the power of the vocal and influential merchants by stacking the Legislative Council with their supporters, including some seigneurs.

Security became the major preoccupation of the governors in this troubled period. They continued to treat the French seigneurial and clerical elites with a certain deference. They assumed that these elites exercised great influence over the *Canadiens*.

Merchants

Although most of Quebec's inhabitants survived by cultivating the land, and agriculture was becoming a major industry, the fur trade still remained the colony's principal source of commercial wealth. In the late 1780s, furs represented more than half of total exports—even though the fur trade was being transformed at the time. Government regulations in wartime, such as the preference accorded military cargoes on transport ships, provoked numerous complaints from traders. Following the American Revolution, Albany ceased to be a centre for fur exports to Britain, a development that boosted the fortunes of the Montreal traders. But after 1794, when the British formally relinquished the Ohio country to the Americans in Jay's Treaty, the Montreal merchants lost their enormously productive fur-trading region and now had to look to the Northwest. The St. Lawrence–Great Lakes system became the new focus of the trade.

The industry became concentrated in the hands of fewer and fewer traders. The new barons of the North West Company (NWC), formed in the early 1780s, were almost all British. The French, who tended to work alone or in small associations, were pushed out. By 1789, they supplied only 15 percent of the trade goods sent inland. The surviving *Canadien* merchants could not pay the capital investment required for expeditions to the western posts. But *Canadiens* continued to provide most of the labour required in the trade. They were the *voyageurs*.

In the meantime, relations between the merchants and the colonial authorities went from bad to worse. The merchants' bitterness toward the Quebec Act intensified, and they petitioned London for its repeal. Buoyed by the arrival of the loyalists, they maintained that the province needed an elected assembly to defend their interests. As well, they demanded the granting of English commercial law, which would liberate them from French "custom and usage," as recognized in the Quebec Act. They sought recognition of legal rights, such as the right to trial by jury in civil cases, to protect themselves from the arbitrary authority exercised by the governor and appointed officials. The merchants also managed to arouse the ire of several public officials, whom they personally attacked. Although the government did make some effort to redress their grievances, Haldimand in particular felt that most British merchants were making their representations without considering the rest of society. The British officials could also point to the lessons of the American Revolution, as an example of what happens when colonies were given too much democracy.

Seigneurs

The Quebec Act helped confirm the social and economic status of the seigneurs. Some, such as the military engineer Gaspard-Joseph Chaussegros de Léry, the military officer René-Amable Boucher de Boucherville, and the businessman François Baby, were named to the Legislative Council. Several others received civil-service or judicial appointments. When Carleton re-established the militia in 1777, seigneurs such as Baby, who had been loyal to Britain during the American invasion, regained their traditional military role.

The growth of Quebec's population and the increases in wheat production should have brought the seigneurs important economic benefits. The development of new lands and investments in roads and mills, however, required capital that most seigneurs did not possess. Seigneuries, therefore, began to pass into the hands of the British, to individuals such as Gabriel Christie, whose properties in the upper Richelieu Valley assured his family material security with minimal risk. By 1784, more than one-quarter of the seigneuries, including the most lucrative, had British owners. The censitaires remained almost exclusively French, with British settlers preferring the freehold system of land tenure. Thus, despite the declining prestige of the seigneurs, the system itself appears to have served as a bulwark against assimilation.

The seigneurs belonging to Governor Carleton's councils resisted plans for immigration and worked for the conversion of seigneurial grants to freehold tenure. When talk of enacting a new constitution that would introduce a popularly elected assembly increased in the late 1780s, seigneurs such as Baby and Boucher de Boucherville pleaded against setting up a body that would surely boost the fortunes of the British merchants and thus endanger religion and property.

After the establishment of the Assembly, however, several seigneurs ran for office and, except for the merchants, they constituted the most numerous group in Lower Canada's first elected house. They also tended to view themselves as the representatives of the French-Canadians, although French merchants disputed this claim. Moreover, a slowly rising group of professionals, at first consisting of a few notaries and lawyers, increasingly challenged the seigneurs' attempts to assume leadership.

The Roman Catholic Church in Late-Eighteenth-Century Quebec

The Roman Catholic Church provided a more complex problem for the British authorities. Although it had remained loyal to the Crown during the American Revolution, the British tried to prevent it from becoming too powerful and independent. Many of the staunchly Anglican administrators of the colony scorned "Romanism" and looked to the day when the colony would be Protestant. While waiting for this change, they did not intend to support the institutions of the Catholic Church. Although the government did not officially persecute Catholics in the period from 1784 to 1791, it did intervene constantly in church affairs in an effort to weaken and control the institution.

Jean-François Hubert, c. 1790. He became Bishop in 1788.

Source: Bibliotheque et Archives nationales du Quebec. Fonds J. E. Livernois Ltee. P560,S2,D1,P534.

Ecclesiastical succession continued to pose a serious problem. Briand resigned in 1784 so that his elderly assistant, coadjutor Louis-Philippe Mariauchau d'Esgly, might become bishop and choose his own coadjutor before he died. D'Esgly picked the relatively youthful Jean-François Hubert, but Governor Haldimand, in England at the time, was furious at not being consulted. London's candidate was an elderly and reputedly senile Sulpician priest who declined the nomination. Hubert was finally accepted and became bishop upon d'Esgly's death in 1788. Governor Carleton then imposed as coadjutor the ambitious and worldly Charles François Bailly de Messein, a strongly pro-British cleric whose relations with Hubert were strained.

The Church confronted other serious problems, among them the perennial question of clerical recruitment. Immediately after the Conquest, Quebec had three priests per 1000 persons. By 1788, this ratio had declined to only one per 1000. Seventy-five parishes lacked priests, and the bishops worried about the quality of religious life. The government opposed any attempts to relieve the shortage by bringing in priests from France, or even priests from the Duchy of Savoy, who were not of French nationality. Only after 1791 were some priests, having fled the French Revolution for England, allowed to come to Canada. British interference ensured the Canadianization of the clergy. Of 64 new priests appointed between 1784 and 1792, 58 were born in Canada.

Male orders such as the Jesuits and the Récollets, although being allowed to return after the Quebec Act in 1774, were still prohibited from recruiting. Together, the two orders accounted for only 16 priests in 1790. Upon the death of the last Canadian Jesuit in 1800, the properties of that order were forfeited to the Crown. The Crown thus assumed title to the Jesuits' mission lands at Kahnawake. Since the Sulpician order remained intact, however, the British allowed it to keep its mission at the Lake of Two Mountains, or Kanesatake (Oka).

Although female communities could recruit, in practice they received few candidates because of their insistence on a dowry. The number of nuns in 1790—about 230—was scarcely higher than it had been in 1760. As in the past, Church officials lamented the lack of discipline in the communities—complaining of nuns who were discourteous to their superiors, who maintained small business operations for their private needs, and who played cards too much, or priests who drank or gambled too much, or read frivolous books.

In the late eighteenth century, the Church contributed to Quebec's cultural heritage through the work of artists and sculptors hired to create religious art for churches. The Baillairgés, father and son, founders of a dynasty that occupied a prominent place in Quebec's art and architecture for four generations, executed the interior decoration of the reconstructed Notre-Dame cathedral in Quebec City. Philippe Liébert, a painter and sculptor, devoted his considerable talents to church decoration in the Montreal region. Goldsmiths such as François Ranvoyzé showed imagination and versatility in the fabrication of hundreds of chalices and other religious objects.

A HISTORICAL PORTRAIT

The Baillairgés

The late eighteenth century witnessed a flourishing in Quebec art and architecture. Much of this cultural growth occurred as a result of the patronage of the Roman Catholic Church, which was recovering slowly from the effects of the Conquest. One family dynasty in particular, the Baillairgés, became noted for its contribution to the development of sculpture, painting, and architecture in Quebec City and the surrounding region. Four generations of this dynasty were active in these domains from the last days of New France until the beginning of the twentieth century.

Jean Baillairgé (1726–1805), a builder and carpenter from Poitou, France, settled in Quebec City in 1741. Lacking formal training, he gained his knowledge on site. After the Conquest, the parish authorities of Notre-Dame-de-Québec asked him to prepare plans for the reconstruction of the cathedral, which had been burned during the British bombardment of 1759. Bishop Briand objected to Baillairgé's plans for a simplified structure that he judged unbecoming for a cathedral. Disappointed, Baillairgé announced in 1769 that he was leaving Quebec. He changed his mind, however, when he obtained the contract to build the cathedral's spire. In a career that lasted sixty years, he built and decorated churches in Quebec City and its environs. His most notable work was the interior decoration of Quebec City's cathedral after 1787, a task in which he was assisted by his son, François. Art critics recognize that Baillairgé filled a void in the domains of architecture and sculpture created by the death or departure of artisans who had been active before the Conquest. Art historian Luc Noppen describes Baillairgé's work as "traditional," most of his models having been works done before the Conquest.

Jean's son, François (1759–1830), spent three years in Paris, studying at the Royal Academy. Primarily a sculptor, he devoted his talents to the interior decoration of churches, an activity in which he demonstrated considerable originality.

Between 1787 and 1793, he worked with his father in decorating the interior of Quebec City's cathedral. The fruit of his labour was destroyed when fire ravaged the cathedral in 1922. Fortunately, during extensive restoration work just prior to the fire, a great number of photographs of the interior of the church had been taken. These photographs made it possible to rebuild the cathedral's interior exactly as it had been before the fire.

Thomas (1791–1859), son of François, became Lower Canada's best-known church architect of his day. He was particularly noted for his harmonious facades with two towers, in which he synthesized French and English neoclassical styles. Thomas's close relations with the diocese of Quebec, and perhaps the colony's tiny number of practising architects, guaranteed him the contracts he needed.

Finally, Charles (1826–1906), in his role as municipal engineer, contributed to the beautification of Quebec City. The works of this architect and engineer still abound in the city and its environs, where he designed more than 200 buildings, including parts of the old Université Laval, the neo-Gothic church of Sainte-Marie, then the diocese's most sumptuous church, and the Quebec City prison. Charles's relations with the church were not always good, but he could turn to the Department of Public Works, the other major employer of architects. Charles also contributed through his writings to the diffusion of technical knowledge in his fields of expertise.

Proposals for Political Change

While the Church showed little interest in the colony's constitutional future, the British merchants discussed it with increasing urgency. They wanted a Legislative Assembly, preferably controlled by the colony's British minority. They saw themselves as responsible for economic growth and thus deserving of increased political power. Attorney General James Monk agreed that any Assembly would have to overrepresent the English to avoid French domination. But Chief Justice William Smith felt that the British element had to be strengthened through immigration before representative government could be established.

Many French-Canadian merchants and professionals also desired an Assembly, since the French, as the majority, hoped to control it. They tried to persuade the habitants that an Assembly would decide on the corvées and on militia laws—the implications being that a French-dominated legislative body would be unfavourable to both. But the seigneurs, who linked their interests and privileges to the maintenance of the status quo, warned that an Assembly could be dangerous for the colony, for it might tax land. Moreover, the seigneurs were outraged by the prospect of their tenants' becoming their political equals with the advent of elections.

The Woolsey Family *by William Berczy, Sr. (1809).*

Source: William Berczy, *The Woolsey Family, 1809.* Oil on canvas, 59.9 × 86.5 cm National Gallery of Canada, Ottawa. Gift of Major Edgar C. Woolsey, Ottawa, 1952. Photo © NGC.

Petitions and counterpetitions circulated. In reality, the great majority of the colony's 150 000 subjects had little understanding of representative government, since they had never enjoyed the privilege under the French *ancien regime*.

The Constitutional Act of 1791

The American Revolution and the arrival of the loyalists put new pressure on the British government to enact a new constitution. William Grenville, secretary of state for the colonies, drafted the Constitutional Act of 1791. The colony of Quebec was divided by executive order into two sections, the provinces of Upper and Lower Canada, with the upper part possessing a British-Protestant loyalist majority. The reasons for the partition of Quebec were not economic or geographic, for the colony functioned effectively as a single unit. Rather, Westminster's motivation was, as Grenville explained, to reduce "dissensions and animosities" among two "classes of men, differing in their prejudices, and perhaps in their interests."

The Constitutional Act of 1791 established an elective Legislative Assembly in each of the Canadas. Besides giving a voice to the population, this body could raise money through taxes for local expenditures, thus reducing the burden on the imperial treasury. At the same time, wary of what had happened in the American colonies, London moved to place the Assembly under strong executive control that would apply restraint if the people's representatives got out

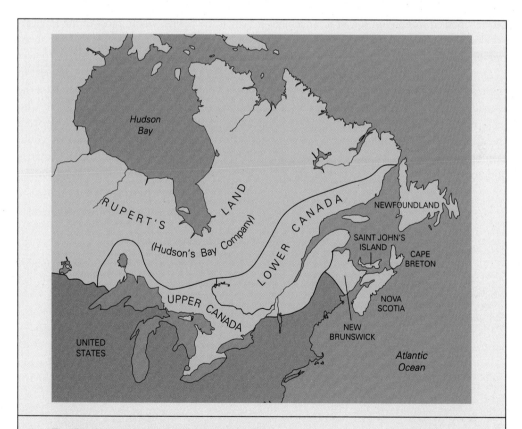

The British colonies in North America, 1791.

Source: Adapted from Ralph Krueger, Ray Corder, and John Koegler, *This Land of Ours: A New Geography of Canada* (Toronto: Harcourt Brace Jovanovich, 1991), p. 130. Used with permission.

of hand. A lieutenant governor was appointed in each province. He would name the members of the Legislative Council, the upper house. The Legislative Council's membership was intended eventually to be hereditary, like that of the British House of Lords. Thus, the "right men"—land-owners—would be assured of a place in power.

The governor enjoyed extensive veto powers and a measure of financial autonomy, thanks to the revenues from the Crown lands set aside by the Constitutional Act of 1791. Other lands were reserved for the maintenance of a "Protestant clergy," intended to mean the Church of England. Over the years, this system proved inefficient and increasingly unworkable. It also removed the Assembly's check on the Executive, by taking away the elected house's "power of the purse." Both the appointed executive branch and the elected Assembly possessed considerable powers and frequently used them to thwart each other's will.

On account of property qualifications in Britain, relatively few people (less than 3 percent of the population) could vote in elections. Essentially, the same qualifications applied in Lower Canada, but because of that province's distinct social structure, the majority of non-Aboriginal male farmers, or habitants, obtained the right to vote. Still, suffrage was far from universal. Most urban labourers and domestics were disqualified because they neither owned property nor paid sufficient rent. The property qualification eliminated most women from the rolls, although it was only in 1834 that the Assembly of Lower Canada specifically disenfranchised women.

The electoral arrangements disappointed Lower Canada's English Protestants. They had petitioned for an Assembly from which the French would be excluded, or at least in which there would be an English majority bolstered by further immigration. Montreal merchant Adam Lymburner lobbied in London for an arrangement in which the towns, where most of the English-speaking population lived, would get half the seats, even though they contained only about one-fifth of the total population. His avowed aim was to avoid putting the Assembly in the "power of ignorant and obstinate men" who held "the absurd idea that it is the landholders' interest to oppress commerce." In fact, although the towns obtained only 10 of the 50 seats, about 20 of the candidates elected in the first elections, held in 1792, were merchants, including a number who were French. There were also 14 seigneurs representing rural seats. Most members were from the upper bourgeoisie and, indeed, 21 were justices of the peace. Although the merchants would face opposition in the legislature, coming from the seigneurs and a handful of French notaries and lawyers, the Assembly as a whole was a "docile instrument in the hands of the governor."[4]

SUMMARY

After the Proclamation of 1763 and the Quebec Act of 1774, Quebec obtained, with the Constitutional Act of 1791, its third constitution in fewer than thirty years. The American Revolution and the arrival of thousands of loyalists had made change imperative. Reactions to the new legislation varied widely. In Britain there was satisfaction that the new colony of Upper Canada would be free to grow under British law and liberty, while the French majority in Lower Canada, confined to the House of Assembly, could do little damage. Some, like William Pitt, even hoped that the French, seeing the British system at work in Upper Canada, would gradually adopt English laws and customs. In the meantime, no force would be required.

Certain Lower Canadian groups, such as the seigneurs, the professionals, and the merchants, believed that they could use the new institutions profitably. The province's British minority, however, numbering some 10 000, were disappointed. The Constitutional Act of 1791 led to their separation from the growing British population in the new colony of Upper Canada. Moreover, the English inhabitants of what now became Lower Canada obtained few of the reforms for which they had agitated and did not even succeed in getting the Quebec Act repealed. The only real compensation received was the provision for the freehold system of land tenure in the area outside the seigneurial zone, in what became the Eastern Townships. Furthermore, the English were unsure of what to expect from the Assembly. The maintenance of a strong executive under British control was small consolation. After all, the government had been in British hands since 1760, and yet the merchants were more often than not at loggerheads with the colonial administrators. Nevertheless, regardless of political changes, the English merchants' economic power continued to increase. In the 1790s, they had reason to be optimistic about the future.

NOTES

1. A.L. Burt, *The Old Province of Quebec*, vol. 1 (Toronto: McClelland & Stewart, 1968 [1933]), p. 218.

2. R. Arthur Bowler, "Sir Guy Carleton and the Campaign of 1776 in Canada," *Canadian Historical Review* 55 (1974): 131–40.

3. A.J.H. Richardson, "Henry Hope," *Dictionary of Canadian Biography*, vol. 4, *1771–1800* (Toronto: University of Toronto Press, 1979), p. 367.

4. F. Murray Greenwood, *Legacies of Fear: Law and Politics in Quebec in the Era of the French Revolution* (Toronto: University of Toronto Press, 1993), p. 52.

BIBLIOGRAPHY

Hilda Neatby's synthesis, Quebec: *The Revolutionary Age, 1760–1791* (Toronto: McClelland & Stewart, 1966), provides a dated but solid review of political developments. Chs. 4 and 5 of Fernand Ouellet's *Economic and Social History of Quebec, 1760–1850* (Toronto: Macmillan, 1980) are also very useful.

On the American invasion, see Robert M. Hatch, *Thrust for Canada: The American Attempt on Quebec in 1775–1776* (Boston: Houghton Mifflin, 1979); George A. Rawlyk, *Revolution Rejected, 1775–1776* (Scarborough, ON: Prentice-Hall, 1968); and George F.G. Stanley, *Canada Invaded, 1775–1776* (Toronto: Hakkert, 1973). T.H. Breen's *The Marketplace of Revolution: How Consumer Politics Shaped Independence* (New York: Oxford University Press, 2004) provides a more recent examination of Revolutionary America and helps explain its national thinking. Nancy Rhoden's edited collection, *English Atlantics Revisited: Essays Honouring Ian K. Steele* (Montreal/Kingston: McGill-Queen's University Press, 2007) also considers the period's climate in the lead up to the American Revolution. A critical examination of Carleton's wartime conduct may be found in R. Arthur Bowler, "Sir Guy Carleton and the Campaign of 1776 in Canada," *Canadian Historical Review* 55 (1974): 131–40. L.F.S. Upton, ed., *The United Empire Loyalists: Men and Myths* (Toronto: Copp Clark, 1967), contains useful documents, while David V.J. Bell, "The Loyalist Tradition in Canada," *Journal of Canadian Studies* 5 (1970): 22–33, evaluates the impact of the arrival of the loyalists. A more thorough list of loyalist titles can be found in the bibliography of Chapter 10 of this book.

Françoise Noël has studied the management of an important group of seigneuries in *The Christie Seigneuries: Estate Management and Settlement in the Upper Richelieu Valley, 1760–1854* (Montreal/Kingston: McGill-Queen's University Press, 1992). Lorraine Gadoury examines family relationships within the French-speaking colonial elite in *Échanges épistolaires au sein de l'élite canadienne du XVIIIe siècle* (Montreal: Hurtubise, 1998).

For studies on the evolution of justice and the legal system, see Donald Fyson, *Magistrates, Police, and People: Everyday Criminal Justice in Quebec and Lower Canada, 1764–1837* (Toronto: University of Toronto Press and Osgoode Society for Canadian Legal History, 2006); and Evelyn Kolish, *Nationalismes et conflits de droits: Le débat du droit privé au Québec, 1760–1840* (LaSalle, QC: Hurtubise HMH, 1994). An article that examines how the legal system was used against pro-American rebels is Jean-Marie Fecteau and Douglas Hay, "'Government by Will and Pleasure Instead of Law': Military Justice and the Legal System in Quebec," in F. Murray Greenwood and Barry Wright, eds., *Canadian State Trials*, vol. I: *Law, Politics, and Security Measures 1608–1837* (Toronto: University of Toronto Press, 1996), pp. 129–71.

Church history is examined by Lucien Lemieux, *Histoire du catholicisme québécois: Les XVIIIe et XIXe siècles*, vol. 1: *Les années difficiles (1760–1839)* (Montreal: Boréal, 1989). See also Marcel Trudel, "La servitude de l'Église catholique du Canada français sous le régime anglais," *Canadian Historical Association Report*, 1963: 42–64; and Jean-Pierre Wallot, "Religion and French-Canadian Mores in the Early Nineteenth Century," *Canadian Historical Review* 52 (1971): 51–94. Attempts to bring French-speaking priests to Quebec from Savoy are described in Luca Codignola, "Le Québec et les prêtres savoyards, 1779–1784: Les dimensions internationales d'un échec," *Revue d'histoire de l'Amérique française* 43 (1989–90): 559–68.

Some information on women in late-eighteenth-century Quebec is available in Micheline Dumont et al., *Quebec Women: A History* (Toronto: Women's Press, 1987). The history of Quebec's English-speaking population is reviewed in Ronald Rudin, *The Forgotten Quebecers: A History of English-Speaking Quebec, 1759–1980* (Quebec: Institut québécois de recherche sur la culture, 1985). Important studies of life in rural and urban Quebec include Allan Greer, *Peasant, Lord, and Merchant: Rural Society in Three Quebec Parishes, 1740–1840* (Toronto: University of Toronto Press, 1985); and David T. Ruddel, *Quebec City, 1765–1832: The Evolution of a Colonial Town* (Ottawa: Canadian Museum of Civilization, 1987).

Pierre Tousignant studies the genesis of the Constitutional Act in "Problématique pour une nouvelle approche de la constitution de 1791," *Revue d'histoire de l'Amérique française* 27 (1973–74): 181–234. David Milobar shows how British needs and perceptions determined the nature of reform in Quebec in "Government and the Nature of Reform in Quebec, 1782–1791," *International History Review* 12 (1990): 45–64. Also very useful is Philip Lawson, *The Imperial Challenge: Quebec and Britain in the Age of the American Revolution* (Montreal/Kingston: McGill-Queen's University Press, 1989). For more on the American Revolution and its relationship to Canada, see also Gavin K. Watt, *I Am Heartily Ashamed: The Revolutionary War's Final Campaign as Waged from Canada in 1782* (Toronto: Dundurn, 2010.)

F. Murray Greenwood has written an account of political developments in the 1790s, *Legacies of Fear: Law and Politics in Quebec in the Era of the French Revolution* (Toronto: University of Toronto Press, 1993). For a discussion on the development of political liberty in the British North American colonies during the revolutionary era, see Michel Ducharme, *Le concept de liberté au Canada à l'époque des Révolutions atlantiques (1776–1838)* (Montreal/Kingston: McGill-Queen's University Press, 2009).

Useful maps of the St. Lawrence Valley in the late eighteenth and early nineteenth centuries appear in the first two volumes of *Historical Atlas of Canada*, vol. 1, *From the Beginning to 1800*, R. Cole Harris, ed. (Toronto: University of Toronto Press, 1987); and vol. 2, *The Land Transformed, 1800–1891*, R. Louis Gentilcore, ed. (Toronto: University of Toronto Press, 1993). For a look at the legacy of French colonialism on the Canada–U.S. border, see Paul A. Demers, "The French Colonial Legacy of the Canada–United States Border in Eastern North America, 1650–1783," *French Colonial History* 10 (2009): 35–54.

On the Six Nations, see Barbara Graymont, *The Iroquois in the American Revolution* (Syracuse: Syracuse University Press, 1972). Isabel Thompson Kelsay's book, *Joseph Brant, 1743–1807: Man of Two Worlds* (Syracuse: Syracuse University Press, 1984), is a biography of the important Mohawk war chief. For a more recent biography of Joseph Brant, see Joseph Paxton, *Joseph Brant and His World: 18th-Century Statesman and Warrior* (Toronto: James Lorimer, 2008). For other works on Aboriginal history of the period, see the bibliography of Chapter 8.

Finally, there are biographies on all the major figures of these years in various volumes of *Dictionary of Canadian Biography*, an essential tool for this and other periods.

Chapter Ten

MARITIME SOCIETY, 1760–1815

TIME LINE

1759	"Planters" from New England arrive in large numbers in Nova Scotia
1760–61	Mi'kmaq and Maliseet First Nations sign peace treaties with British
1764	Acadians allowed to return to Nova Scotia
1767	Saint John's Island, named Prince Edward Island in 1799, granted by lottery to British proprietors (absentee landlords)
1776	Jonathan Eddy's pro-American force unsuccessfully attacks Fort Cumberland Henry Alline begins career as preacher
1783	American Revolution ends
1784	New Brunswick and Cape Breton (to 1820) established as separate jurisdictions
1785	Parrtown incorporated as city of Saint John in New Brunswick
1792	Black loyalists leave Nova Scotia for Sierra Leone
1793	Britain and France go to war again
1806	Britain and France put up naval blockades to trade
1812–14	War of 1812

The Maritime region had long seen itself as distinct from Canada. Even in the days of the *ancien regime*, the colony of Acadia developed its own identity, distinct from New France. Acadia was conquered by the British in 1713, half a century before Quebec suffered a similar fate. But the Expulsion in 1755 transformed Acadia into Nova Scotia and replaced the majority French-Catholic population with one that was British and Protestant. Some Acadians would drift back to the colony, but they would never again dominate. They were forced onto poorer lands and became a minority in their homeland.

But the Maritime region was more than Nova Scotia. Distinct colonies developed on Newfoundland, Île St. Jean (established in 1769 and renamed Prince Edward Island in 1799), and Cape Breton. These islands seemed even more distant from the fur-trading world of the St. Lawrence–Great Lakes region. While the fur trade was pushing colonial interests further into the northwest, the world of the Maritime islands was transatlantic. Commercial interests looked to the seas, and eastward to Britain.

The end of the struggle between Britain and France in 1763 ushered in a temporary period of peace for the Maritime colonies. Nova Scotia enjoyed its traditional trade links with New England to the south. When the American Revolution broke out, there was considerable sympathy within the Nova Scotian population. There was enough sympathy that some questioned the colony's loyalty. Historian John Brebner dubbed them "the Neutral Yankees of Nova Scotia." If there was doubt as to the colony's loyalty before the Revolution, there was none in the years after. The loyalist migration transformed Nova Scotia and resulted in the creation of a new colony—New Brunswick.

Britain easily maintained control of the small, isolated colony of Saint John's Island, with its settler population of only 1000 recent British arrivals and Acadians. As for Newfoundland, its Anglo-Irish population looked eastward to Britain rather than southward to the Thirteen Colonies. In contrast, over half of Nova Scotia's approximately 20 000 inhabitants came from New England. They maintained strong economic and cultural ties with their former homeland. These loyalties would again be tested when the Americans invaded in 1812.

New England's Outpost

With the deportation of the Acadians in 1755 and the capture of Louisbourg in 1758, American colonists began moving north. The New Englanders had played a significant role in military actions against the French in Acadia. They were consistently frustrated when the area kept getting returned to France at the peace tables. Finally, in 1755, the Americans intended to take advantage of the fertile lands and commercial lands vacated by the deported French Catholics.

The British authorities wanted to attract loyal Protestant settlers in order to prevent the Acadians' return. In October 1758, Governor Lawrence issued a proclamation throughout British America that invited settlers to claim the unoccupied Acadian farmlands. The circular described Acadia's 80 000 hectares of "Plowlands producing Wheat, Rye, Barley, Oats, Hemp, Flax . . . cultivated for more than a Hundred Years past, and never fail of Crops, nor need manuring." The Nova Scotia government agreed to pay for the transportation costs of New Englanders and to provide 40-hectare grants of land to each family head and 20 hectares for each additional family member.

The opportunity held considerable appeal in the heavily settled areas of southeastern Massachusetts, eastern Connecticut, and Rhode Island, particularly among poorer farmers. Hundreds of fishers anxious to locate closer to the Grand Banks also came. These New England farmers and fishers became known as the "Planters." Between 1759 and 1767, some 8000 Planters from New England settled in Nova Scotia. Most of the immigrants went to the Annapolis Valley in peninsular Nova Scotia, to fertile lands previously cleared and diked by the Acadians, and to

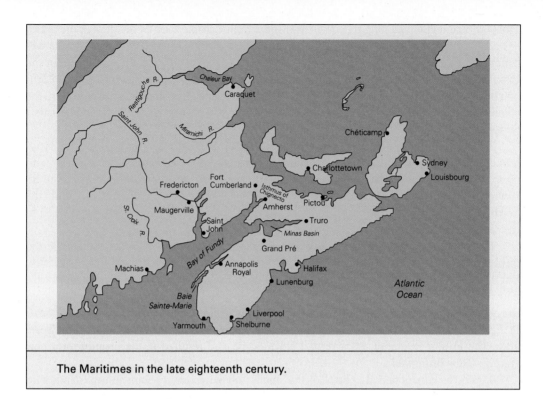

The Maritimes in the late eighteenth century.

the area around Cumberland, near present-day Sackville, New Brunswick. A smaller number entered the Saint John River valley, forming small frontier communities at the mouth of the river and at Maugerville (just south of present-day Fredericton), along the lower Saint John River. On account of the difficult conditions in what became known as "Nova Scarcity," a number of the recent arrivals returned to their homes in New England in the 1760s.

The Planters who remained worked to create a new English-Protestant Nova Scotia. They brought with them the political traditions formed in the Thirteen Colonies, including expectations of British parliamentary and representative government and expression. But the lack of roads linking the settlements prevented regular communication. As historian George Rawlyk noted, "on the eve of the American Revolution, Nova Scotia was little more than a political expression for a number of widely scattered and isolated communities."[1] Nevertheless, on the eve of the Rebellion, New Englanders constituted about half of Nova Scotia's total population of nearly 20 000. This population shaped the response of the colony when conflict broke out.

Americans were still migrating to the forested lands north of the Bay of Fundy when hundreds of Acadians began returning. In 1764, the British government permitted the Acadians to settle again in Nova Scotia, providing that they dispersed throughout the colony. This provision, along with the fact that their former farms were now occupied by New Englanders, led them to resettle in the Bay of Chaleur, on the present-day border between Quebec and New Brunswick. The settlement of Caraquet became a focal point for the region. Other Acadians lived on farms along the lower Saint John River.

British immigrants joined the migration into Nova Scotia in the 1760s and 1770s. These included some 2000 settlers from Ulster in Northern Ireland; more than 750 from Yorkshire, England, many of whom settled on the Isthmus of Chignecto; and, in 1773, nearly 200 Scots, who settled at Pictou. They joined the original British residents of Halifax, the approximately 1500 Acadians, and the approximately 1500 "foreign Protestants," largely Germans, who resided south of Halifax in the area around Lunenburg.

Halifax's Predominance in Nova Scotia

Halifax, as the only urban centre, became the colony's capital. It housed the military establishment and published the only newspaper. The elite of Halifax society, headed by the governor, included his senior officials and a group of merchants who had grown wealthy from army and navy contracts. A handful of merchants and professionals also lived in the colony's capital. The bulk of the city's population consisted of fishers, carpenters, mechanics, and labourers.

As expected in a British colony, Nova Scotia obtained an elected assembly in 1758, but few rural members could afford to take their seats. Even members of the "lower house" were expected to be men of means and the positions came with no salary. As a result, a small clique of Halifax merchants controlled both the Assembly and the governor's appointed Council. So influential were the merchants that they secured the recall of Governor Francis Legge to England. Sent to the colony in 1773, the reformist governor attempted to expose the spoils system operated by the Halifax merchants. They, in turn, protested to London, threatening that Nova Scotia would join the American Revolution if Legge's investigations continued. Already fearful of developments in the Thirteen Colonies, London overlooked the evidence of corruption that Legge had unearthed and ordered the governor home in early 1776. The incident demonstrated one of the results of the American Revolution in the colonies of British North America. The fear of democratic and republican ideas allowed the colonial elites to enhance their own bases of power, even to the point of weakening British parliamentary traditions.

Nova Scotia and the American Revolution

Not surprisingly, the rebellious rhetoric in the Thirteen Colonies in 1775–76 found an audience in rural Nova Scotia. Many New Englanders were critical of the "tyrannical" policies of George III. More locally, they resented Britain's unfulfilled promises of constitutional rights. At annual town meetings in New England, voters had become accustomed to electing their officers and deciding local issues. But in Nova Scotia in the 1760s, this form of local democracy did not exist. Instead, London implemented a tightly controlled, centralized government structure. The merchant-controlled Assembly in Halifax, which strongly supported the governor, worked to eliminate local township government. It appointed justices of the peace to administer the local areas and did not allow the election of township officials.

As tensions mounted in the Thirteen Colonies, settlements throughout Nova Scotia began holding town meetings similar to those held in the American colonies. When Governor Legge called out one-fifth of the provincial militia in November 1775 and levied new taxes to meet the cost, petitions from the settlements of Truro, Cumberland, and Onslow voiced opposition to military service. The Chignecto settlers objected to the new tax and to the idea that the governor might force them to "march into different parts in Arms against their friends and relations." In an ironic twist of fate, like the Acadians of twenty years earlier, most Nova Scotian settlers sought neutrality. On December 8, 1775, the inhabitants of Yarmouth, for example, sent a memorandum to the governor:

> We were almost all of us born in New England, we have Fathers, Brothers, & Sisters in
> that Country, divided betwixt natural affection to our nearest relations, and good Faith and
> Friendship to our King and Country, we want to know, if we may be permitted at this time
> to live in a peaceable State, as we look on that to be the only situation in which we with our
> Wives and Children, can be in any tolerable degree safe. . . .

Realizing the depth of the discontent, Legge backed down. He suspended compulsory military service, allowed the militia to stay at home unless an invasion occurred, and cancelled the new taxes, thus effectively neutralizing much of the anger.

Micmac Encampment *by Hibbert Newton Binney.*

Source: History Collection/Nova Scotia Museum, Halifax/NSM 79.146.1.

Responses to the American Revolution

The communities most distant from Halifax demonstrated the greatest enthusiasm for the American cause. The town of Machias, on the vaguely defined border between Nova Scotia and Maine, the Maugerville settlement on the lower Saint John River, and the Chignecto–Cumberland region at the head of the Bay of Fundy became active centres of support for the American Revolution. Jonathan Eddy, a New Englander who farmed in the Chignecto region, took the lead in organizing the revolutionary movement. His invasion force of about 180 men attacked British-held Fort Cumberland (the reconstructed French fort of Beauséjour) in 1776. But they lacked artillery to mount a siege. Few New Englanders on the isthmus openly supported Eddy's small, poorly trained, and undisciplined force. With the arrival of British reinforcements, Eddy's troops fled. The British burned the homes and barns of his supporters as punishment. The following summer, British naval vessels entered the Bay of Fundy and took control of the area.

The attempt to capture Fort Cumberland failed for a number of reasons. Historian John Brebner points out that General George Washington, whom Eddy approached for support, refused because he knew that the Americans had "little energy or material available for side shows, no matter how admirable the cause and its proponents."[2] As well, the presence of the Royal Navy in Halifax discouraged the Americans from making such an attempt. The Americans were able to win victories on the land, but the superiority of the seas still belonged to Britain.

The Maritime First Nations

The Maritime First Nations had long been enemies of the British and the New Englanders. The animosity was longstanding and bloody. The Abenaki were the first obstacle in a migration of New Englanders into the area. Their allies, the Mi'kmaq and Maliseet, fought on land and sea to protect their territories. When Acadia was ceded to Britain in 1713, there was no mention of the territorial rights of these Aboriginal groups. While the British attempted to pacify them and have them swear allegiance to Britain, the French encouraged them to continue fighting. The alliance between these First Nations and France went back 150 years and the effectiveness of the Roman Catholic missionaries was evident. When Governor Lawrence called for the "destruction" of the Mi'kmaq in May 1756, following the deportation, the animosity between the groups reached new heights.

In 1760 the British implemented a new Native policy. The British needed peace with the First Nations to protect their settlers and avoid costly wars. The Aboriginal peoples needed peace because they could no longer take advantage of the rivalry between the French and British to obtain advantageous prices for their furs and receive annual presents to confirm military alliances. The British imposed a centralized policy that prevented individual colonies from dealing with Aboriginal peoples. They also adopted the French techniques of gift diplomacy, providing their Aboriginal allies presents of food, medicine, and ammunition. Peace was negotiated with the Mi'kmaq and Maliseet in 1760 and 1761.

When the Revolution broke out, the Maritime First Nations sided with the British over their traditional New England enemies. Britain appeared to be the stronger of the two opponents during the Revolution after it extended its control over the Bay of Fundy and captured the coastline of northern Maine from the Americans. The Aboriginals ensured that the upper Saint John River valley remained in the British zone of influence throughout the war.

Growing Antagonism Toward the American Revolution

While the American insurgents consolidated their hold on the former Thirteen Colonies, Nova Scotia's sympathies lessened. American raids into the colony hardened attitudes toward the patriots. The military port of Halifax was the only Nova Scotian port to escape the privateers, who seized anything they could carry away. These attacks alienated wealthy citizens in Yarmouth, Lunenburg, and Liverpool, and prompted them to launch their own retaliatory attacks against American shipping. By 1781, settlements in the Minas Basin and the Bay of Fundy area, which in 1775–76 had opposed increased taxes for military defence, now willingly accepted militia service and taxes to meet the cost of defending the colony.

Henry Alline and the New Light Movement

The unwillingness of many New Englanders in Nova Scotia to support the American Revolution can also be explained by what some historians call the "missing decade."[3] Although these recent immigrants held many New England values and still possessed an attachment to their homeland, they had been absent during a crucial decade in New England's political development. It was during this decade that the revolutionary rhetoric of the early 1770s about the growing British oppression, and the need to defend New Englanders' liberties, reached its zenith. The "Nova Scotian Yankees" were absent from this politically charged atmosphere, and by necessity were more concerned about the need to clear land and develop the fisheries. In the late 1770s and early 1780s, a religious gospel rather than a political one monopolized the attention of Nova Scotians. They became part of a "great religious revival" that centred on a charismatic young man named Henry Alline.

Born and raised in Rhode Island, Alline belonged to the Congregational Church. It was this church to which most New England immigrants in Nova Scotia adhered. Henry received his early education at Newport, before his family moved to Nova Scotia in 1760. They settled in one of the richest farming areas in the colony—the Minas Basin, near present-day Windsor. With no school in his township, and no church, Alline was educated through family prayer, Bible reading, and religious discussions at home. But Alline came into contact with an evangelical group that emphasized the need for an intensely emotional conversion experience known as the "New Light."

In 1776, at the age of 28, Alline began his career as an itinerant preacher. From the reminiscences of one of his early listeners, Alline was an impressive orator and "mighty in prayer." He ignored the material world around him and focused on the spiritual. He taught the faith through music and song.

Initially, Alline confined his activities to the Minas Basin, but three years later several Annapolis Valley churches ordained him as their minister. Convinced that God had selected him to carry his message, he travelled constantly. The evangelist often rode as far as 80 kilometres a day, bringing religion to rural people. His willingness to preach under all conditions struck a responsive chord among the economically impoverished rural Nova Scotians on their frontier farms. They heard Alline and believed him when he told them that Nova Scotia had become the new centre of Christendom.

Alline's religious revival filled the spiritual vacuum in the new settlements far away from the revolutionary struggle. He preached the message that good Christians should work to secure their spiritual salvation rather than go to war. He convinced many Nova Scotians that they were performing a special role—bringing the world back to God—and that Christ merited their allegiance, not the British or the revolutionaries. Partly as a result, Nova Scotia's New Light communities chose political neutrality.

Alline died of tuberculosis in early February 1784, leaving behind scores of disciples and hundreds of followers. After his death, his manuscript journals were copied repeatedly by hand and circulated among his followers until they were published in 1806. Alline's disciples, popularly referred to as Allinites, later became members of the Baptist Church and carried on the teachings of the "Apostle of Nova Scotia."

The New England Loyalists

Approximately 20 percent of the white American population in 1776 (roughly half a million people) opposed the American Revolution and remained loyal to Britain.[4] Loyalist numbers were strongest in New York and weakest in Connecticut, Massachusetts, and Virginia. Generally, loyalists were politically conservative, and they found the revolutionary ideas and the notion of

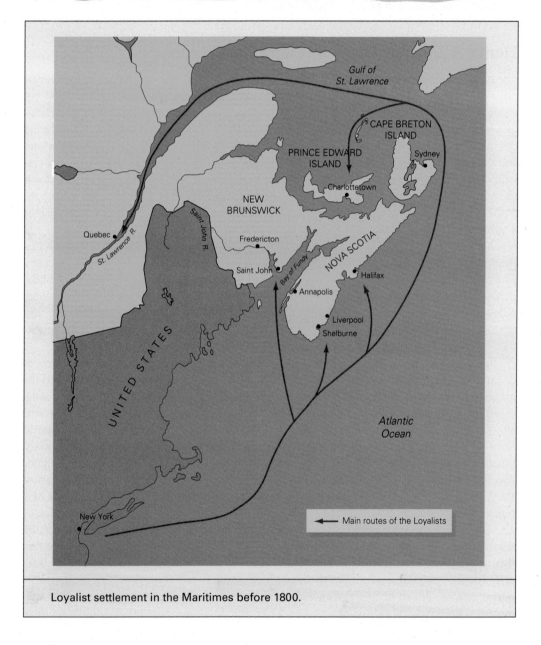

Loyalist settlement in the Maritimes before 1800.

rebelling against the Crown abhorrent. But the loyalists also came from every class, race, occupation, religion, and geographical region, and they supported Britain for a variety of diverse reasons.

Many loyalists (often called Tories, Royalists, or King's Men) were part of the ruling elite who had strong connections to the British government. These Tories served as colonial office holders and often had a vested interest in maintaining the status quo. Supporters of the Church of England (Anglican Church) were usually loyalists. Others resisted what appeared to be mob rule that was imposing pressure to conform to revolutionary ideas. Many believed that the Revolution would ultimately fail and they wished to be on the winning side. But the loyalist ranks were filled with more than members of the Tory and Anglican elite.

Many came from religious and cultural minorities. Not yet having joined mainstream American society, recent immigrants from Europe (Germany, the Netherlands, and the British Isles) and members of religious minorities (such as the French Huguenots, Maryland Roman Catholics, and Quaker pacifists) held on to the British connection for fear that an experiment in American republicanism could result in a loss of their religious freedoms.

Most First Nations had been French allies, but now looked upon Britain as the lesser of two evils. Britain at least demonstrated a desire to avoid wars with the Aboriginal groups and attempted to slow the advance of American settlers westward. Many African Americans saw an opportunity for freedom from slavery by joining the British and fleeing their owners.

Persecution of the Loyalists

Persecution of the loyalists began as early as 1774, when it became increasingly difficult to maintain neutrality in the face of the impending struggle. The term "lynch law," an informal system of law enforcement, originated to describe the treatment of loyalists in Virginia. One particularly nasty form of vigilante justice involved tarring and feathering outspoken loyalists. The victim was stripped naked, smeared with a coat of tar and feathers, then paraded through the streets.

With the passing of the Declaration of Independence, the local revolutionary committees stepped up their activities against loyalists. According to historians Wallace Brown and Hereward Senior, the means of persuasion "ranged from mild social pressure to murder."[5] Various states disenfranchised, put in prison, banished, and fined loyalists and confiscated their property as well. In loyalist-controlled areas, outrages were also committed against supporters of the Revolution.

WHERE HISTORIANS DISAGREE

Nova Scotia and the American Revolution

On the eve of the American Revolution in 1775–76, about half of Nova Scotia's 20 000 settlers were New Englanders. The colony appeared to be a northern outport of New England. Why, then, did it not join the revolution?

Historian Beamish Murdoch offered the first explanation. New England farmers, he argued, who had been given land previously owned by the Acadians when they arrived after the Conquest, were "full of intense loyalty and affection to the British government."[1] Some seventy years later, in the 1930s, Viola Barnes added an economic motive: Halifax merchants and Governor Francis

Legge kept Nova Scotia loyal to the Crown because it was in their best interest to do so. When the Americans boycotted West Indies commerce, Halifax merchants saw their opportunity to appropriate the trade themselves. "In short," she wrote, "Nova Scotia remained loyal because the merchant class in control believed the Province profited more than it lost by the connection with the mother country, and because the Governor, with their help, was able to prevent the radicals from stirring the people to revolt."[2]

W.B. Kerr challenged Barnes's interpretation. He questioned why Nova Scotia merchants would object to New Englanders carrying a monopoly of their trade, since they were New Englanders themselves. Furthermore, they were free to pursue their own trade if they so desired. For Kerr, Nova Scotia stayed out of the Revolution due to "the almost total want of sympathy among artisans, fishermen, and farmers for the American cause." The Nova Scotia legislature, made up of a majority of New Englanders, expressed their loyalty to the King on the eve of the Revolution. It acknowledged him to be the "supreme Legislature of the province" and claimed "it is our indispensable duty to pay a due proportion of the expense of this great Empire."[3] D.C. Harvey added yet another explanation. Nova Scotians "were inclined to submit to the will of the stronger."[4] With the British navy based out of Halifax, it only made sense to support the Crown.

In 1937, historian J.B. Brebner argued that geographical isolation, as well as close economic ties to Britain through mercantile trade, kept Nova Scotia insulated from activities elsewhere on the continent: "Nova Scotia had insulated and neutralized the New England migrants so thoroughly that as Nova Scotians they had henceforth to look eastward to London for direction and help rather than southward to Boston as they had done in the past."[5]

Beginning in the 1940s, historians became interested in religious revivalism as a factor in keeping Nova Scotians neutral. M.W. Armstrong saw the "Great Awakening" (as the revival was called) as "an expression of democratic ideals and spiritual independence" that raised the minds of Nova Scotians above worldly concerns. How could "King George" and the Revolution compete with "King Jesus" and redemption?[6] In 1959, sociologist S.D. Clark applied Frederick Jackson Turner's frontier thesis to an understanding of Nova Scotia's neutrality during the Revolution.[7] He saw the New Light religious revival in the outposts of Nova Scotia as a frontier movement of social protest that strengthened the spirit of local autonomy and resolved their determination to be politically independent of both Britain and its Halifax political agents, and New England.

Professors Gordon Stewart and George Rawlyk introduced their "missing decade" thesis in the 1970s. They argued that those New Englanders who migrated to Nova Scotia in the early 1760s missed the rebellious rhetoric and the intense anger against Britain that occurred between 1765 and 1775. They could not therefore identify with the fervour of the movement.[8] Rawlyk then went on to explore the role of Henry Alline, the charismatic leader of the religious revival in Nova Scotia, in keeping Nova Scotians neutral. Rawlyk argued that Alline's message to Nova Scotia "Yankees" that they had a divine mission "to lead the world back to God" gave them a purpose above and beyond that of worldly revolution.[9]

More recently, J.M. Bumsted has questioned both the size and the importance of the New England population in Nova Scotia during the American Revolution. He argues that as the war began, Nova Scotia "Yankees" who supported the rebel cause returned to New England and therefore played no part in Nova Scotia's decision. In addition, the strong British military presence in the colony, and resentment among Nova Scotians at the destructive behaviour of the American rebels within the colony, kept them neutral.[10]

1. Beamish Murdoch, *History of Nova Scotia or Acadie*, vol. 2. (Halifax: J. Barnes, 1865–67), p. 562.

2. V.F. Barnes, "Francis Legge, Governor of Loyalist Nova Scotia, 1773–1776," *New England Quarterly*, July 1931, quoted in George A. Rawlyk, ed., *Revolution Rejected, 1775–1776* (Scarborough, ON: Prentice-Hall, 1968), pp. 32–33.

3. W.B. Kerr, "The Merchants of Nova Scotia and the American Revolution," *Canadian Historical Review* 33 (1932): 22.

4. D.C. Harvey, "The Struggle for the New England Form of Township Government in Nova Scotia," *Canadian Historical Association Report* (1933): 22.

5. John Bartlet Brebner, *The Neutral Yankees of Nova Scotia* (Toronto: McClelland & Stewart, 1969), p. 310.

6. M.W. Armstrong, "Neutrality and Religion in Revolutionary Nova Scotia," *New England Quarterly* (March 1946): 57–58.

7. S.D. Clark, *Movements of Political Protest in Canada, 1640–1840* (Toronto: University of Toronto Press, 1959).

8. Gordon Stewart and George Rawlyk, *A People Highly Favoured of God* (Toronto: Macmillan, 1972).

9. G.A. Rawlyk, *Ravished by the Spirit: Religious Revivals, Baptists, and Henry Alline* (Montreal/Kingston: McGill-Queen's University Press, 1984).

10. J.M. Bumsted, "1763–1783: Resettlement and Rebellion," in P.A. Buckner and J.G. Reid, eds., *The Atlantic Region to Confederation: A History* (Toronto: University of Toronto Press, 1994), pp. 156–83.

The decisive battle of the American Revolution was fought on October 19, 1781, when Britain's Lord Cornwallis surrendered his army of 7000 troops at Yorktown, Virginia. This defeat was a shock to the British and effectively ended the war, although the general peace was not made until two years later. For many loyalists, the two years between the disaster at Yorktown and the final signing of peace was a difficult time. As the war ended, the British evacuated southern ports such as Wilmington, Charleston, and Savannah, to which the loyalists had fled for protection. Persecution reached new levels. Several of the newly independent states subjected the loyalists to double and triple taxation, and Congress encouraged the states to confiscate their property. Physical violence against loyalists continued. The British continued to hold New York City and Long Island, and many loyalists—at one point, 30 000—assembled there, awaiting evacuation.

At the peace negotiations, the American commissioners agreed that no further persecutions of loyalists would take place. But while Congress urged the states to grant restitution and amnesty, it had no power to enforce its requests. Except in one or two states, every clause in the Treaty of Paris relating to the loyalists was abrogated. When news of the preliminary peace reached the United States in the spring of 1783, the proscriptions, confiscations, and harassment of loyalists commenced anew.

The Loyalist Migration to Nova Scotia

The exodus of thousands of loyalists and their families began even before the peace treaty. According to historian Ann Gorman Condon, "the Loyalists were the first mass movement of political refugees in modern history."[6] The loyalists were estimated to constitute 20 percent of the

This imaginative sketch by American artist Howard Pyle shows the last boatload of British troops leaving the United States from New York on November 25, 1783. It appeared in Harper's New Monthly Magazine in November 1883.

Source: Library and Archives Canada, Acc. No. 1990-553-656, C-017509.

American population, and of this number approximately 20 percent are believed to have fled the United States. Wallace Brown and Hereward Senior estimate that British North America received more than 50 000 white, black, and First Nations loyalists. The British Isles received approximately 10 000, several thousand went to the British West Indies, and a small number (mainly Germans) returned to the Rhine Valley. The overwhelming majority of the loyalists were of European background, but about 6000 African-American loyalists migrated to the Maritimes, the West Indies, and Sierra Leone in West Africa. Some 2000 Iroquois also left New York. In all, 70 000 people—roughly the population of New France at the time of the Conquest—left the United States.[7]

As during the Conquest, the more influential loyalists—royal officials, wealthy merchants, landowners, professionals, and high military officers—sailed directly for England to press their claims for compensation. The lower and middling elements settled in the remaining British North American colonies. The loyalists favoured Nova Scotia over Quebec at a ratio of roughly two to one. Nova Scotia's fisheries, its large tracts of empty land, and the potential trade with the West Indies attracted them. Nova Scotia was also the shorter trip by sea. Small groups of loyalists had been finding their way to Halifax since 1775. The evacuation of New York in 1783, however, led to an unanticipated invasion. On April 26, 1783, the first or "spring" fleet set sail, carrying no fewer than 7000 men, women, and children. Half the vessels went to Port Roseway, about 150 kilometres south of Halifax, and the other half to the mouth of the Saint John River. They went ashore at Saint John on May 18, now commemorated in New Brunswick as "Loyalist Landing Day." Other fleets followed in the summer and autumn.

The First Loyalist Settlements

About 15 000 loyalists went to what became New Brunswick in 1784. About the same number went to peninsular Nova Scotia, and about a thousand each chose Prince Edward Island and Cape Breton, with a few families to Newfoundland. The great migration to the Atlantic colonies more than doubled their population with the arrival of more than 30 000 civilian refugees and disbanded soldiers.

Of those who came to Nova Scotia, approximately 40 percent came from New York state, 15 percent from the other middle colonies (particularly New Jersey), 20 percent from New England, and 25 percent (black and white) from the southern colonies. Even though New England sent a relatively small number of loyalists to Nova Scotia, "the New England states seem to have been represented more by quality than quantity, leadership than numbers."[8]

Arrival, however, proved a mixed blessing. In spite of British promises, the colonists found that almost no preparations had been made to receive them at Saint John. No shelter had been prepared, provisions were in short supply, and the land along the river was unsurveyed. Elizabeth Morgan later recalled her thoughts immediately after landing: "I climbed to the top of

Chipman's Hill and watched the sails disappearing in the distance, and such a feeling of loneliness came over me that, although I had not shed a single tear through all the war, I sat down on the damp moss with my baby in my lap and cried." (Her future great-grandson would be Samuel Leonard Tilley, one of New Brunswick's Fathers of Confederation.)

The loyalist migration infused the colonies of British North America with a powerful anti-American sentiment. Many loyalists brought with them vivid memories of American injustices. The Dribblee family of Long Island experienced particularly harsh treatment. As Polly Dribblee recorded in a letter to her brother in England, rebels had plundered their house and forced her and her five children out "naked into the streets." Two more times before they left Long Island, they were "plundered and stripped." Their misfortune continued in New Brunswick. During their first year at Saint John, Polly's husband, Filer Dribblee, who had spent six months in prison during the war, entered a deep depression and finally took his own life. As well, the Dribblees' log-cabin home burnt twice in one year.

The loyalist boom town of Shelburne, Nova Scotia, in 1789. Drawing by William Booth.

Source: Library and Archives Canada, Acc. No. 1990-289-1/C-010548.

Port Roseway, quickly renamed Shelburne after the current British prime minister, became the largest loyalist settlement. By 1784, the population had reached 10 000. The inexperienced loyalist settlers had initially picked Shelburne for its magnificent long, narrow harbour, but soon discovered that it had little else: the soil and timber were poor, the inland communications primitive, and the whaling and fisheries in the area disappointing.

The Black Loyalists

During the Revolution, in 1779, the British promised black slaves belonging to the rebels their freedom if they took up arms against the patriots. Military units such as the loyalist Ethiopian Regiment performed admirably. It is estimated that 12 000 black colonials fought for the British. About half of Nova Scotia's 3000 African-American loyalists settled in Shelburne's suburb of Birchtown. As many as 1200 still-enslaved peoples came to Nova Scotia along with the loyalists.

The establishment of Birchtown made it the largest free black community in North America. But the blacks suffered discrimination in their new homes. Their land grants were of the poorest quality, they received few tools and provisions, and they were harassed by neighbouring communities. They could not vote, sit in non-segregated sections of churches, or even fish in the Saint John harbour.

Thomas Peter, an African-American loyalist from North Carolina, went to England to protest. Here he met a group of British reformers promoting a "back to Africa" campaign for distressed blacks from all parts of the British empire. More than 1000 African Americans took advantage of the opportunity to go to Sierra Leone on the West African coast in 1792, where they established Freetown. In 1800, another 550 blacks arrived in Sierra Leone from Nova Scotia. These individuals were Maroons, descendants of slaves who had escaped from the Spanish two centuries earlier, and had lived free lives in the interior of Jamaica. Fearing the support they might give to a slave revolt in Jamaica, such as that which had broken out in neighbouring Haiti, the British expelled them to Nova Scotia in 1796. Now four years later, hoping to save the cost of keeping them in Halifax, Britain deported them to Sierra Leone in West Africa. Meanwhile, the population of Birchtown declined sharply, shrinking to 600 by 1815.

The Founding of New Brunswick

Shortly after their arrival, loyalists from the Saint John River petitioned London to have the section north of the Bay of Fundy separated from Nova Scotia and made into a loyalist colony. They argued that the distance of the Saint John settlements from Halifax made it difficult to transact business with the capital. They also realized that the creation of a new colony would provide themselves administrative offices and control.

In the summer of 1784, Britain created the new colony of New Brunswick. Colonel Thomas Carleton, the younger brother of Quebec governor Sir Guy Carleton, became the colony's first governor, a position he held for thirty years. In 1785, the major settlement at the mouth of the great river was named Saint John. The new capital, approximately 100 kilometres north of Saint John, was named Frederick's Town (Fredericton), in honour of Frederick Augustus, Duke of York, the second son of George III. Thomas Carleton selected Fredericton as the capital, to promote inland settlement. Moreover, the upriver location had a military advantage; Carleton could garrison his two regiments of British troops there, safe from a surprise coastal attack.

The possibility of an American attack was real, because the United States claimed one-third of the colony. The Treaty of Paris of 1783 established the St. Croix River as the boundary between Maine and New Brunswick. Unfortunately, identification of the St. Croix proved difficult, as three rivers flowed into Passamaquoddy Bay. The Americans pressed for the most easterly river as the boundary, while the British claimed the westerly river. Britain won its case by proving that Champlain and de Monts had wintered in 1604–05 on St. Croix Island, at the mouth of the most westerly river, thus claiming it to be the true St. Croix. They confirmed the site by conducting excavations on the island and revealing the ruins of the buildings as described by Champlain in his journal.

Chief Justice Ludlow's House *on the River St. John, New Brunswick by George Heriot.*

Source: With permission of the Royal Ontario Museum © ROM, 950.31.

Building a Loyalist Province

The loyalists turned to building a new society in the Saint John River valley. A severe labour shortage made the work particularly difficult. According to historian W.S. MacNutt, "Judges of the Supreme Court and other loyalist patricians took to the fields to raise the fruits and vegetables necessary to livelihood."[9] Gradually, a series of agricultural communities developed on favourable coastal locations and in the lowland river valleys. The town of Saint John became the major urban centre, with a population of 3500 in 1785. The Acadians' settlements, formed originally by those who had fled to the Miramichi to escape deportation between 1755 and 1758, were located along the eastern and northern shores of New Brunswick. Elsewhere, the forests prevailed.

Historical geographer Graeme Wynn notes that by 1800 the settlers had "done no more than trim part of the forest edge."[10]

Ironically, the First Nations, whose allegiance had been critical in retaining western Nova Scotia for the Crown, suffered the most. The loyalists encroached on their hunting and fishing territories. They helped themselves to Mi'kmaq and Maliseet land, fish, game, and timber. Clearly more intent on rewarding the whites than the First Nations for their loyalty, the British confiscated portions of their territories as Crown land without financial compensation. As historian Leslie Upton points out, the Mi'kmaqs and Maliseets in 1782 "were no longer of account as allies, enemies, or people." The correspondence connected with the arrival of 35 000 immigrants contained "not one word about the Indians who would be dispossessed by the new settlers."[11] In the Great Lakes area, the Royal Proclamation of 1763 protected First Nations land rights, but the British ruled that the Royal Proclamation did not apply in the Maritime colonies. Britain incorrectly assumed that the French had already dealt with the issue of Aboriginal title in the Maritime area.

The Loyalists on Prince Edward Island

About 800 loyalists travelled to Saint John's Island, soon to be renamed Prince Edward Island. They formed about one-fifth of the population. In Nova Scotia and New Brunswick, the authorities eventually supplied the loyalists with free land, government timber, and tools. On Prince

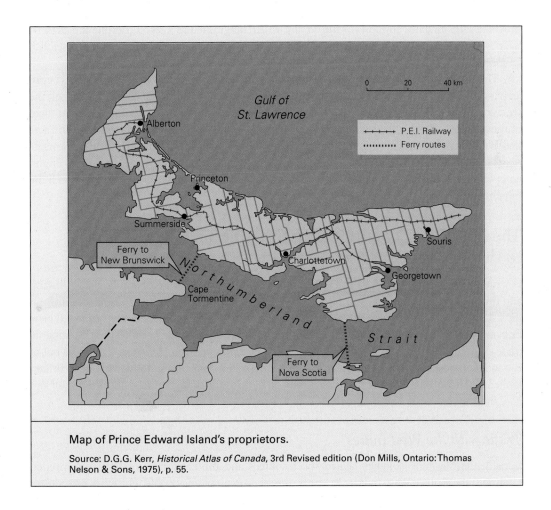

Map of Prince Edward Island's proprietors.

Source: D.G.G. Kerr, *Historical Atlas of Canada*, 3rd Revised edition (Don Mills, Ontario: Thomas Nelson & Sons, 1975), p. 55.

Edward Island, however, the hapless newcomers became tenant farmers on land granted to absentee proprietors.

In 1767, the British government divided the entire island into long belts of land, stretching from north to south. It then proceeded to grant all 67 townships of roughly 8000 hectares each to favourites of the Crown. The new landlords had to pay a small annual fee, or quitrent, for their land. They also had to promise to bring over settlers.

To attract loyalists, the landowners promised grants of land with secure titles. But once the settlers had cleared their lands, erected buildings, and planted orchards, the proprietors refused to grant land title to those who wanted to become landowners. Many settlers obtained no redress and left in anger. Those who remained fought for 75 years for justice. Only in 1860 would a land commission recommend that free grants be made to those who could prove that their ancestors had been attracted to the island by the original promises made to the loyalists. A final attempt to resolve the land question was made in 1873, in conjunction with Prince Edward Island's entry into Confederation.

Cape Breton Island

About a thousand loyalists came to Cape Breton Island. David Mathews, a former mayor of New York, and Abraham Cuyler, a former mayor of Albany, New York, convinced the British government to make the island a separate colony, essentially to obtain power and influence for themselves. Mathews became the new colony's attorney general, and Cuyler, its secretary and registrar. The new capital was named Sydney after the British colonial secretary. But the British government provided little financial support for the colony, which languished as a result, despite the fact that Sydney lay at the centre of the richest coal field in the Maritimes. London did not even establish an assembly for the island.

The society and economy of Cape Breton was developed after 1802, when immigrants began arriving from Scotland—Catholics and Protestants from the Hebrides, the coastal islands off the west coast, many of whom spoke only Gaelic. The magnificent hills and seacoast reminded them of their homeland. They became fishers and farmers. By the mid-nineteenth century the Scots had become the dominant community on Cape Breton Island, outnumbering the Mi'kmaqs, Acadians, and loyalist descendants combined. When the War of 1812 broke out, Cape Breton enjoyed a few years of prosperity. In 1820 the Colonial Office, without any consultation with the inhabitants, decided to merge Cape Breton with Nova Scotia.

The Maritime Economy from the American Revolution to the War of 1812

For more than a century before the American Revolution, trade linked New England, Britain, and the West Indies. New England sold fish, lumber, and foodstuffs to the West Indies, which in turn supplied molasses to New England and sugar to Britain. The mother country provided New England with manufactured goods. The Maritime region resided on the periphery of this imperial trade. While of strategic importance on the Gulf of St. Lawrence, the Maritime region was not of economic importance, apart from its fish. After the United States gained independence, Britain looked to the Maritime colonies to replace New England in the triangular trade between itself and its Caribbean colonies. Britain closed its West Indian ports to American ships.

Trade with the West Indies

Initially, the Maritime colonies lacked the resources and the economic infrastructure needed to supply the British West Indies. In truth, the Maritime colonies could not even provide for themselves. They could provide only a limited amount of their needs in fish and lumber, and they could not meet their demand for foodstuffs. Nova Scotia and New Brunswick had to import American farm products. Problems with labour shortages, an inadequate transportation system, and an inefficient land-granting system (which encouraged a general dispersal of the population) all contributed to the slow development of agriculture. Moreover, with cheap imported food from the United States available, little incentive existed to undertake full-time farming.

Direct trade between Nova Scotia and the British West Indies decreased further in the 1790s, when Britain met the Caribbean planters' demands for cheap foodstuffs by allowing American shipping access to the West Indies.

The Impact of the Napoleonic Wars

Real economic growth in the Maritimes began only after the outbreak of war between Britain and France in 1793. The British government spent lavishly on fortifications in Halifax, and constructed public and military buildings. Halifax became the strongest fortress outside Europe and the main supply base for the British West Indies.

After the beginning of the Napoleonic Wars, a flourishing timber industry developed in British North America. Britain required a safe supply of masts and spars for building war ships, and it needed timber for construction. Napoleon's blockade of continental Europe cut off Britain supplies of timber from Scandinavia. The imperial government gave tariff preferences for timber from BNA. This led to a lumber boom in New Brunswick, the Maritime colony with the greatest timber resources. The exports of fir and pine timber from New Brunswick increased twentyfold between 1805 and 1812. Wood products dominated New Brunswick's export economy for the next half-century. Every winter, armies of lumberjacks cut down the trees and then, every spring, tied them into huge rafts and floated them down the Saint John, St. Croix, and Miramichi Rivers. Heavily forested New Brunswick, being closer to Britain, was better situated than were the Canadas for this trade.

Inadvertently, the United States also promoted the prosperity of the Maritimes. After France and Britain imposed blockades on each other in 1806, President Thomas Jefferson, in retaliation against both countries' restrictions on neutral trade, prohibited all commerce out of American ports. The policy backfired, however. By closing American ports in 1807, the president ruined New England's trade—and enriched that of the Maritimes.

Since Britain depended on American foodstuffs as much as the United States needed British manufactured goods, Anglo–American trade continued, but now through illegal channels. An active smuggling trade developed, with cargoes being transferred at sea or carried overland across the British–American frontier. In defiance of their government, American ship captains sailed into British ports, turning the Maritimes in 1808 into a clearinghouse for international trade. The Maritime colonies purchased American produce and goods, and then exported these materials. Similarly, they sold British manufactured goods to the Americans. This thriving trade continued throughout the War of 1812.

The long-standing trade between the fish-exporting houses of Halifax and the British West Indies also expanded at the time of the American embargo acts. Britain encouraged this trade by paying bounties on fish exported from Nova Scotia and New Brunswick to the West Indies. Britain could also afford to provide convoy protection. After the British defeated the French navy at Trafalgar in 1805, the threat of a French invasion ended, and the admiralty could spare ships for convoy duty. The shipping of smuggled American flour, beef, and dry goods to the West Indies via the Maritime colonies began.

The War of 1812 brought more economic benefits. Throughout the war, New England was effectively neutral. The legislatures of the New England states openly condemned the war that

HMS *Shannon* and *Chesapeake* off Boston, 1813, *by Robert Dodd. In a short, fierce battle off Boston harbour in 1813, the* Shannon *captured the larger American frigate.*

Source: Universal Images Group/Art Resource, NY.

was ruining their commerce. New England trade with Britain and its Maritime colonies continued, so much so that the Halifax newspaper, the *Acadian Recorder*, announced on May 14, 1814: "Happy state of Nova Scotia! Amongst all this tumult we have lived in peace and security; invaded only by a numerous host of American doubloons and dollars, which have swept away the contents of our stores and shops like a torrent." Only naval activity on the high seas reminded Maritimers that they still lived in a war theatre. The occupation by the British in 1814 of part of the coast of present-day Maine allowed more opportunities for commercial profit.

The Emergence of a Maritime Identity

Within a generation, New England, the ancestral home of many of Nova Scotia's and New Brunswick's inhabitants, became a "foreign country." Gradually, the loyalists and the New Englanders in the Maritimes lost many of their Yankee customs. In the early 1780s, the bitterness on both sides remained strong. As time erased memories of their struggles, however, the loyalists accepted the newly independent United States. A number of loyalists returned to the U.S. in the late 1780s, particularly when Britain allowed half-pay officers to receive their pensions while living outside the empire. Cadwallader Colden, for example, the grandson of a royal lieutenant governor of New York, returned from self-imposed exile and was later elected mayor of New York City.

SUMMARY

The American Revolution had a profound influence on the Maritimes. It forced the area's inhabitants, many of whom were emigrants from New England, to choose sides: the insurgent Thirteen Colonies or the empire. Initially, like the Acadians before them, they attempted to remain neutral. Over time, circumstances shifted that neutrality toward a commitment to Britain.

At the end of the American Revolution, tens of thousands of loyalists came from the newly independent United States to live in the Maritimes. Their arrival transformed the region. It led to the creation of two new colonies: New Brunswick and Cape Breton Island (a separate colony until 1820). While life was not easy, the loyalists became the most influential group in the Maritimes. When war broke out in 1812, the population was again faced with the prospect of fighting their neighbours and former homeland.

NOTES

1. George A. Rawlyk, "The American Revolution and Nova Scotia Reconsidered," *Dalhousie Review* 43 (1963–64): 379.

2. John Bartlet Brebner, *The Neutral Yankees of Nova Scotia* (Toronto: McClelland & Stewart, 1969 [1937]), p. 285.

3. This thesis was first advanced by Gordon Stewart and George A. Rawlyk in *A People Highly Favoured of God* (Toronto: Macmillan, 1972); see especially pp. 3–4 and 43–44.

4. Paul H. Smith, "The American Loyalists: Notes on Their Organization and Numerical Strength," *William and Mary Quarterly*, 3rd series, 25 (1968): 269.

5. Wallace Brown and Hereward Senior, *Victorious in Defeat: The Loyalists in Canada* (Toronto: Methuen, 1984), p. 16.

6. Ann Gorman Condon, "1783–1800: Loyalist Arrival, Acadian Return, Imperial Reform," in Phillip A. Buckner and John G. Reid, eds., *The Atlantic Region to Confederation: A History* (Toronto: University of Toronto Press, 1994), p. 186.

7. The estimates of the loyalists' numbers are taken from Brown and Senior, *Victorious in Defeat*.

8. Neil MacKinnon, *This Unfriendly Soil: The Loyalist Experience in Nova Scotia, 1783–1791* (Montreal/Kingston: McGill-Queen's University Press, 1986), p. 59.

9. W.S. MacNutt, *New Brunswick: A History, 1784–1867* (Toronto: Macmillan, 1963), p. 70.

10. Graeme Wynn, *Timber Colony* (Toronto: University of Toronto Press, 1981), p. 18.

11. L.F.S. Upton, *Micmacs and Colonists: Indian–White Relations in the Maritimes, 1713–1867* (Vancouver: University of British Columbia Press, 1979), p. 78.

RELATED READINGS

Visions: The Canadian History Modules Project: Pre-Confederation, Module 5, "The Fourteenth Colony: Nova Scotia and the American Revolution," is a helpful introduction to the social, cultural, and political life of the colony during the late eighteenth century. The module has five secondary-source articles and seven primary-source documents included. See pages 191–237.

BIBLIOGRAPHY

Valuable overviews of the loyalists include Christopher Moore, *The Loyalists: Revolution, Exile, Settlement* (Toronto: Macmillan, 1984); and Wallace Brown and Hereward Senior, *Victorious in Defeat: The Loyalists in Canada* (Toronto: Methuen, 1984). The story of Polly Dribblee and her family is told in Wallace

Brown, *The Good Americans: The Loyalists in the American Revolution* (New York: William Morrow, 1969). For an estimate of the number of loyalists who came to Nova Scotia, see William H. Nelson, *The American Tory* (Oxford: Clarendon Press, 1961); and Paul H. Smith, "The American Loyalists: Notes on Their Organization and Numerical Strength," *William and Mary Quarterly*, 3rd series, 25 (1968): 259–77. For more recent overviews of immigration during this period, see Carl Bridge and Kent Fedorowich, eds. *The British World: Diaspora, Culture and Identity* (London: Frank Cass, 2003). Helen I. Cowan, *British Emigration to British North America: The First Hundred Years* (Toronto: University of Toronto Press, 1961), is also useful, if older. Elizabeth Jane Errington, "British Migration and British America, 1783 to the 1860s," in Philip Bruckner, ed., *Canada: The Oxford History of the British Empire* (Oxford: Oxford University Press, 2006), should be consulted as well. Tom Thorner and Thor Frohn-Nielsen have edited a pre-Confederation documentary reader that includes chapters on loyalists: *A Few Acres of Snow: Documents in Pre-Confederation Canadian History*, 3rd ed. (Toronto: University of Toronto Press, 2009). Norman Knowles examines loyalism in Ontario in *Inventing the Loyalists: The Ontario Loyalist Tradition and the Creation of Usable Pasts* (Toronto: University of Toronto Press, 1997).

For a general overview of Maritime history in this period, see Phillip A. Buckner and John G. Reid, eds., *The Atlantic Region to Confederation: A History* (Toronto: University of Toronto Press, 1994), pp. 156–260; Margaret R. Conrad and James K. Hiller, *Atlantic Canada. A Region in the Making* (Toronto: Oxford University Press, 2001); and W.S. MacNutt's *The Atlantic Provinces, 1712–1857* (Toronto: McClelland & Stewart, 1965), pp. 76–102. Margaret Conrad has edited several collections of articles on the Planters, the New England settlers who moved to Nova Scotia in the 1760s: *They Planted Well: New England Planters in Maritime Canada* (Fredericton: Acadiensis Press, 1988); *Making Adjustments: Change and Continuity in Planter Nova Scotia, 1759–1800* (Fredericton: Acadiensis Press, 1991); and (with Barry Moody) *Planter Links: Community and Culture in Colonial Nova Scotia* (Fredericton: Acadiensis Press, 2001). For more on agriculture and the domestic economy, see Rusty Bitterman's articles "Farm Households and Wage Labour in the Northeastern Maritimes in the Early 19th Century," *Labour/Le travail*, 31 (Spring 1993), and "Women and the Escheat Movement: The Politics of Everyday Life in Prince Edward Island," in Janet Guildford and Suzanne Morton, eds., *Separate Spheres: Women's World in the 19th-Century Maritimes* (Fredericton: Acadiensis Press, 1994). See also Béatrice Craig, *Backwoods Consumers and Homespun Capitalists: The Rise of a Market Culture in Eastern Canada* (Toronto: University of Toronto Press, 2008), and John G. Reid, *Essays on Northeastern North America, Seventeenth and Eighteenth Centuries* (Toronto: University of Toronto Press, 2008). Daniel C. Goodwin looks at evangelical religion in the Maritimes in *Into Deep Waters: Evangelical Spirituality and Maritime Calvinistic Baptist Ministers, 1790–1855* (Montreal/Kingston: McGill-Queen's University Press 2010).

In W. Brook Taylor, ed., *Canadian History: A Reader's Guide*, vol. 1, *Beginnings to Confederation* (Toronto: University of Toronto Press, 1994), consult the essays by Barry Moody, "Acadia and Old Nova Scotia to 1784," pp. 76–111, and Ian Ross Robertson, "The Maritime Colonies, 1784 to Confederation," pp. 237–79. For a look at Halifax as a colonial outpost, see Jeffrey L. McNairn, "'Everything was New, yet Familiar': British Travellers, Halifax, and the Ambiguities of Empire," *Acadiensis* 36(2) (2007): 28–54.

Nova Scotia's response to the American Revolution is reviewed by John Bartlet Brebner in *The Neutral Yankees of Nova Scotia* (Toronto: McClelland & Stewart, 1969 [1937]). See also George A. Rawlyk, ed., *Revolution Rejected, 1775–1776* (Scarborough, ON: Prentice-Hall, 1968). Ernest Clarke reviews a specific incident in these troubled years in *The Siege of Fort Cumberland 1776* (Montreal: McGill-Queen's University Press, 1995). For an overview of this period, see J.M. Bumsted, "1763–1783: Resettlement and Rebellion," in P.A. Buckner and J.G. Reid, eds., *The Atlantic Region to Confederation*, pp. 156–83.

For an introduction to Henry Alline and his New Light movement, see D.G. Bell's booklet, *Henry Alline and Maritime Religion* (Ottawa: Canadian Historical Association, 1993). For fuller treatments, consult: Gordon Stewart and George A. Rawlyk, *A People Highly Favoured of God: The Nova Scotia Yankees and the American Revolution* (Toronto: Macmillan, 1972); J.M. Bumsted, *Henry Alline* (Toronto: University of Toronto Press, 1971); and George A. Rawlyk, *Ravished by the Spirit: Religious Revivals, Baptists, and Henry Alline* (Montreal/Kingston: McGill-Queen's University Press, 1984).

Two guides to the loyalists and their influence on the development of the Maritimes are Robert S. Allen, *Loyalist Literature: An Annotated Bibliographic Guide* (Toronto: Dundurn Press, 1982); and J.M. Bumsted, *Understanding the Loyalists* (Sackville, NB: Centre for Canadian Studies, Mount Allison University, 1986). The impact of the loyalists in New Brunswick is reviewed by Ann Gorman Condon in *The Envy of the American States: The Loyalist Dream for New Brunswick* (Fredericton: New Ireland Press, 1983). W. Stewart MacNutt surveys the same subject in the opening pages of *New Brunswick: A History, 1784–1867* (Toronto: Macmillan, 1963). In *Benedict Arnold: A Traitor in Our Midst* (Montreal/Kingston: McGill-Queen's University Press, 2001), Barry K. Wilson recounts the New Brunswick sojourn of America's most reviled traitor, Benedict Arnold, the American general who changed sides in the American Revolution. Neil MacKinnon examines the loyalists' first decade in Nova Scotia in *This Unfriendly Soil: The Loyalist Experience in Nova Scotia, 1783–1791* (Montreal/Kingston: McGill-Queen's University Press, 1986). An older popular study, Thomas Raddall's *Halifax: Warden of the North*, rev. ed. (Toronto: McClelland & Stewart, 1971 [1948]), contains a lively review of the impact of the revolution and the loyalists on Halifax. A more recent review of the city by three professional historians is Judith Fingard, Janet Guildford, and David Sutherland, *Halifax: The First 250 Years* (Halifax: Formac Publishing, 1999). Graeme Wynn, a historical geographer, looks at early New Brunswick in *Timber Colony* (Toronto: University of Toronto Press, 1981). J.M. Bumsted's *Land, Settlement, and Politics on Eighteenth-Century Prince Edward Island* (Montreal/Kingston: McGill-Queen's University Press, 1987) covers the early British period in Prince Edward Island.

For information on the Aboriginal peoples of the Maritimes during the American Revolution, see L.F.S. Upton, *Micmacs and Colonists: Indian–White Relations in the Maritimes, 1713–1867* (Vancouver: University of British Columbia Press, 1979); and Harald E.L. Prins, *The Mi'kmaq Resistance: Accommodation and Cultural Survival* (Fort Worth, TX: Harcourt Brace, 1996). In *We Were Not the Savages: First Nations History*, 3rd ed. (Halifax: Fernwood, 2000), Daniel N. Paul provides a Mi'kmaq perspective on Aboriginal–newcomer relations. William C. Wicken reviews early British treaties with the Mi'kmaq in *Mi'kmaq Treaties on Trial: History, Land and Donald Marshall Jr.* (Toronto: University of Toronto Press, 2002).

James W. St. G. Walker's *The Black Loyalists: The Search for a Promised Land in Nova Scotia and Sierra Leone, 1783–1870* (Toronto: University of Toronto Press, 1992 [1976]) is the most important secondary source on the experience of black loyalists. See also Carole Watterson Troxler, "Re-enslavement of Black Loyalists: Mary Postell in South Carolina, East Florida, and Nova Scotia," *Acadiensis* 37(2) (2008): 70–85. For further reading, consult Harvey Armani Whitfield's two articles "African and New World African Immigration to Mainland Nova Scotia, 1749–1816," *Journal of the Royal Nova Scotia Historical Society* 7 (2004): 102–11, and "The Development of Black Refugee Identity in Nova Scotia, 1813–1850," *Left History* 10(2) (2005): 9–31. See also Van Gosse, "'As a Nation, the English Are Our Friends': The Emergence of African-American Politics in the British Atlantic World, 1772–1861," *American Historical Review* 113(4) (2008): 1003–28.

Important maps of the Maritimes in the late eighteenth and early nineteenth centuries appear in the first two volumes of *Historical Atlas of Canada*: vol. 1, *From the Beginning to 1800*, edited by R. Cole Harris (Toronto: University of Toronto Press, 1987); and vol. 2, *The Land Transformed, 1800–1891*, edited by R. Louis Gentilcore (Toronto: University of Toronto Press, 1993). See also William Welch, "Captain Thomas Durell's Charts of Nova Scotia," *Journal of the Royal Nova Scotia Historical Society* 11 (2008): 168–77.

Source: Library and Archives Canada, Acc. No. 1970-188-2092. W.H. Coverdale Collection of Canadiana/C-040137.

Chapter Eleven

UPPER CANADA, 1791–1815

TIME LINE

1781–1818	British negotiate treaties with Mississaugas
1784	Joseph Brant and the Six Nations (Iroquois) loyalists settle on Grand River
1791	Constitutional Act of 1791 divides Quebec into Upper and Lower Canada
1792	John Graves Simcoe first lieutenant governor of Upper Canada
1793	Simcoe founds York (Toronto)
1794	Jay's Treaty signed
1796	York becomes capital of Upper Canada
	Yonge Street opens from York (Toronto) to headwaters of Lake Simcoe
	Western posts finally surrendered to Americans
1812–14	American forces invade BNA in War of 1812
1812	General Isaac Brock killed at Battle of Queenston Heights
1813	Tecumseh, leader of First Nations confederacy, killed at Battle of Moraviantown

When the Quebec Act was signed in 1774, the colony was vast and included the territory north of the Great Lakes and immediately south of the Canadian Shield. But settlement was largely restricted to the St. Lawrence Valley. The only other settlement of significant size was located on the outskirts of present-day Windsor, where French-Canadian farmers, who supplied Fort Detroit just across the river, had established farms. The remainder of the western portion of the colony remained one continuous forest, and it was likely to remain so for some time. As economic historians Kenneth Norrie and Douglas Owram point out, "In the normal course of events, it would have been another generation before significant European settlement intruded upon the area."[1]

The American Revolution transformed the area and opened it for settlement. The loyalist migration led directly to the creation of Britain's first inland colony in 1791. John Graves Simcoe, commander of the Queen's Rangers (a loyalist corps), became the first lieutenant governor of Upper Canada (the terminology "Upper" and "Lower" derives from the flow of the St. Lawrence; Upper Canada lies to the south of Lower Canada). He spent four years constructing the framework for a colony intended to be the ideal home for loyalists. While loyalists came in significant numbers, so did other Americans in search of cheap land. This group formed the majority of the settlers, outnumbering the loyalists four to one at the beginning of the War of 1812. Upper Canada, therefore, had a notable American population when the United States invaded. The colonial authorities were left wondering how determined the population would be to resist American conquest.

The Anishinabeg

For most of the First Nations, it seemed they were constantly on the losing side of the colonial wars. After 1763, they jockeyed for position between the British and the Thirteen Colonies. The Royal Proclamation recognized the Great Lakes area as "Indian" country. As a result, settlement could not proceed until the First Nations had "surrendered" title to the land to the British Crown through treaty. In 1774, the Quebec Act brought the Ohio Valley and the Great Lakes under the jurisdiction of Quebec. The British promised to keep American settlers from further encroachments and most of the Aboriginal groups responded by fighting as British allies during the American Revolution. At the Treaty of Paris in 1783, the Americans refused to consider "Indian" concerns. Once more, the First Nations had to face the unpleasant fact that siding with the losing side in a European-style war meant loss of lands, even if they themselves were not defeated. Until the early 1780s, three nations lived in the area that would become Upper Canada: the Ojibwas (Chippewas), the Ottawas (Odawas), and the Algonquins. These three Algonquian-speaking nations called themselves the "Anishinabeg."

The Mississaugas

Sir Frederick Haldimand, governor of Quebec from 1778 to 1784, arranged for the "purchase" of land from the Mississaugas, as the British called

Sir Frederick Haldimand, Governor of Quebec from 1778 to 1784.

Source: © National Portrait Gallery, London.

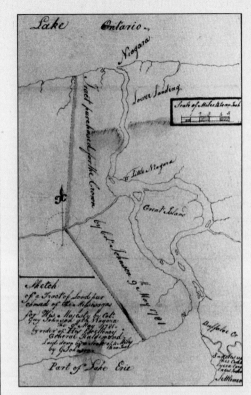

A map of the Niagara River, showing the first land surrendered by the Mississaugas, on May 9, 1781.

Source: Archives of Ontario/R.G. 1 A-I-1, vol. 1, p. 67.

the Ojibwa along the north shore of Lake Ontario. The first settlement of loyalist soldiers and refugees in the Niagara area began across the river from Fort Niagara, at what is now Niagara-on-the-Lake. In order to provide farms for settlers, the British made their first treaty with the Mississaugas in 1781. They paid them "three hundred suits of clothing" for a strip of land 6.5 kilometres wide on the west bank of the Niagara River.

The treaty process demonstrated the British inconsistency when it came to relations with the First Nations. Embittered after losing the Thirteen Colonies, the British embraced the French tradition of annual gift distributions to maintain Aboriginal alliances. Between 1784 and 1788, the British spent considerable amounts on this practice. But when it came to dealing with the Mississaugas, they resorted to their traditional approach of one-time payments. The British regarded the transactions as simple real-estate deals—complete title to the surrendered area in exchange for trade goods, paid on a once-and-for-all-time basis.

Other loyalists moved up the Hudson River valley to the St. Lawrence River, where Governor Haldimand housed them in temporary camps until he negotiated a treaty. In 1783, the Mississaugas surrendered all the land from present-day Gananoque to the eastern end of the Bay of Quinte, extending back from Lake Ontario "as far as a man can travel in a day," in exchange for guns, powder, ammunition for the winter's hunt, clothing for all of their families, and "as much coarse red cloth as will make about a dozen coats and as many laced hats."

In 1784, the British purchased the Niagara Peninsula and gave the Grand River valley to the Six Nation Iroquois, who had fought for Britain in the American Revolution. The British believed that they had obtained title to the entire Niagara Peninsula and the whole north shore of Lake Ontario, except for a large tract between the head of the lake (present-day Hamilton) and York (Toronto).

The Mississaugas did not believe they were giving up their lands forever. Their negotiating position was weak, however, because they relied on the trade with the British and on the gifts provided to them annually since the suppression of Pontiac's resistance. But regardless, they did not believe they were selling the land. The Aboriginal pattern of land ownership and use differed from that of the British. Among the Great Lakes Algonquians, an individual family could use a recognized hunting ground, fishing place, or maple sugar bush, but as soon as the family ceased to go there, it reverted to the collective ownership of the entire band. The Anishinabeg regarded the initial agreement as one with tenants for the use of the land as long as they practised good behaviour. There was little, however, the Mississaugas could do in the face of British pressure. The population was small, about 1000, and divided into a dozen or more separate groups along the 500 kilometres of lakefront. Thus, weakly organized, reliant on European trade goods, and believing that they would receive gifts in perpetuity for the use of their land, the Mississaugas reluctantly agreed to the proposals.

The Loyalists

The largest number of loyalist refugees arrived in 1784, the year after the peace treaty was finalized. The Crown bore the transportation costs and provided them with free land, as well as food, clothing, tools, seed, and shelter. Land was allotted according to status and rank. Each family head received 40 hectares, with an additional 20 hectares for each family member. Non-commissioned officers obtained 80 hectares, field officers 400, and captains 280. Subalterns, staff, and warrant officers were given 200 hectares.

Loyalist encampment at Johnstown, June 6, 1784. By James Peachy.

Source: Library and Archives Canada, Acc. No. 1989-218-1/ C-002001.

Loyalist settlements appeared throughout the area. In 1784, about 4000 loyalists settled in the townships along the St. Lawrence–Bay of Quinte area. They gradually transformed the forest into farms and settled communities. A large number were native-born Americans of German ancestry, while others were German regular soldiers who had fought as mercenaries for Britain.

Next in size was the Niagara settlement, a haven for the first refugees from the frontier districts of Pennsylvania and New York. A relatively small number of loyalists also settled on the northwestern shore of Lake Erie and in the towns of Sandwich (within the present-day boundaries of Windsor) and Amherstburg. In 1796, when Detroit passed into American hands, the population of these two towns increased. Many of Detroit's French-Canadian citizens crossed to the Canadian side. Some loyalists settled in the lower Thames River valley (below present-day Chatham) after the Crown purchased the land from the Anishinabeg in 1790. The Long Point Peninsula of Lake Erie became the last major centre of loyalist settlement, the majority of its inhabitants having originally settled elsewhere.

Iroquois Loyalists

Approximately 2000 Iroquois loyalists came to Upper Canada, leaving behind an equal number of their people. Of those that came, the majority were Mohawks, Cayugas, and Onondagas. Joseph Brant chose the location of their new settlement because of its proximity to their allies, the Senecas, most of whom decided to remain in western New York. A group of about 100 Mohawks antagonistic to Brant followed Chief John Deseronto and settled on a tract on the Bay of Quinte, at the community now known as Tyendinaga Mohawk Territory.

Anxious to retain Iroquois support in the event of another war with the Americans, the British provided the Six Nations on the Grand River with a church, a school, a sawmill, a grist mill, an allowance for a schoolmaster, and £1500 as general compensation for their war losses. The Mohawks on the Bay of Quinte also obtained a school, a schoolmaster, and a church. In keeping with Indian Department policy, all the First Nations received annual presents and, like the other loyalists, clothing, tools, and provisions.

Loyalist Settlements

In 1785, approximately 7500 loyalists (5500 non-Aboriginal and 2000 Aboriginal) lived in the region extending west from Montreal into present-day Ontario. By 1791, the number had risen to approximately 30 000. New settlements were established throughout the area, extending north from the St. Lawrence up the Ottawa River to the Rideau River. They were spread over

The oldest house of worship in Ontario.

Source: Eliza Field Jones

15 kilometres around the Bay of Quinte and formed a narrow strip along the Lake Ontario shore from the Bay of Quinte to York, where farms extended 25 kilometres up Yonge Street.

Settlers, mostly from rural New York and Pennsylvania, now occupied the narrow strip of fertile land below the escarpment around the Niagara Peninsula and part-way up the Lake Erie shoreline. From the concessions along the front of the Detroit River, settlement began to move along the south shore of Lake St. Clair, and into the lower Thames River valley.

The Life of the Loyalists

Most of the early Upper Canadian loyalists came from the lower classes. They lived in military tents until they built their first homes. They preferred sites by the lakes and rivers, the principal means of communication and travel before roads. Aboriginal trails, although narrow (seldom exceeding 50 centimetres in width), were important for travelling in the immediate area. Not until the wave of immigration from New Brunswick in the 1790s did Upper Canada receive what might be termed a loyalist elite, composed of families such as the Robinsons, the Jarvises, and the Ryersons.

A HISTORICAL PORTRAIT

David Ramsay

In the 1790s David Ramsay—fur trader, revolutionary war soldier, guide, and "Indian-killer"—was one of the best-known citizens of Upper Canada. He commanded considerable respect among the colonial administrators and the loyalist settlers. Joseph Brant, the Mohawk leader, however, regarded him as an "unworthy rascal." He was reported to have killed and scalped eight Anishinabeg, including a woman and two children. The Mississaugas apparently tolerated him because he provided a link with the dominant settler society.

What little is known about Ramsay's early life comes from a land petition that he submitted to Governor Simcoe and from notes made by a British traveller, Captain Patrick Campbell, whom Ramsay guided in 1792 from Niagara to New York. Taking great interest in Ramsay's adventures, Campbell stayed up with him one whole night to record his story, which he accepted completely because, as he wrote in his *Travels in North America*, "His honesty and fidelity is so well known, that he is entrusted with sums of money to any amount without requiring any token or receipt for the same." Ramsay claimed that he came from the town of Leven, Fifeshire, Scotland. As a young man he joined the crew of the British warship *Prince of Orange*, serving in the sieges of Louisbourg in 1758 and Quebec in 1759.

After the Seven Years' War, he entered the Great Lakes fur trade, operating out of Schenectady, New York.

Ramsay spent the winter of 1771–72 on the north shore of Lake Erie with his 17-year-old brother, who had just arrived from Scotland. Ramsay alleged that he had been forced, in self-defence, to kill several Mississaugas who, in a drunken state, attacked them. Sir William Johnson, the Indian superintendent for the northern colonies had a different account. Johnson argued that Ramsay deserved "Capital punishment." He dismissed Ramsay's argument of self-defence because "the Indians, whenever they meditate mischief, carefully avoid Liquor." But Johnson realized, however, that a jury would acquit him. As he wrote to an Indian Department assistant, "I don't think he will Suffer, had he killed a Hundred." Johnson was correct. In September 1773, a Montreal jury released Ramsay for "want of Evidence." Ramsay's brother, the only eyewitness of the killings present at the trial, supported his brother's story. No Mississaugas were present.

After his military service with the Royal Navy on the Atlantic coast during the American Revolution, Ramsay went back to live among the people whose relatives he had killed a decade earlier. He learned to dress like them, to live like them, and to speak their language. Yet Ramsay maintained his disdain for the Aboriginal peoples. He told Campbell, for example, in describing the killings of 1771–72: "After killing the first Indians, I cut lead, and chewed above thirty balls, and above three pound of Goose shot, for I thought it a pity to shoot an Indian with a smooth ball." Although he received death threats from some Mississaugas in the late 1780s and early 1790s, he remained among them.

The Mississaugas tolerated Ramsay because he proved an important and rare ally, however disdainful. He was astute enough to ensure he followed their customs. He "covered the graves" of the murdered, paying a certain number of gifts to the relatives of those that he had killed. This "eccentric white man," as the Mississauga Methodist minister Peter Jones later described him, forwarded their grievances to the government. In a petition sent in their name to Governor Simcoe in the winter of 1793, for instance, Ramsay outlined the settlers' encroachments on their hunting territories and fishing grounds.

David Ramsay claimed that the Mississaugas in 1789 gave him a large tract of land at the mouth of the Twelve Mile (Bronte) Creek, between present-day Hamilton and Toronto, as a gift. He stated that he and his heirs would allow the Mississaugas to use the land, to hunt and fish, and to plant orchards there, "forever as they now are or until they are half white. (But no black mixture allowed to inherit the above land.)" The government never recognized the gift, but it did give Ramsay two substantial land grants elsewhere in Upper Canada, together roughly 500 hectares in size. Ramsay died in New York City in 1810.

To support themselves in the first year or so, loyalist settlers relied heavily on the First Nations for food. On the open meadows, "Indian corn" (maize) became the most important first crop. Once the settlers cleared additional land, they planted wheat. The cutting of the forest became essential for the settlers and the shift to large-scale agriculture. According to Historical geographers R. Cole Harris and John Warkentin, "as a whole they were little interested in conservation or the long-term management of land and sought to maximize short-term profits."[2]

The typical loyalist home was a log cabin, with one or two rooms. These cabins had no cellar or foundation, an earthen floor, and roofs made of bark or small hollowed basswood logs that overlapped like tiles. They measured on average no more than 4 by 5 metres. Oil paper, not glass, usually covered the windows. Since bricks were not available, the chimneys were built of sticks and clay or rough, unmortared stones. At times the houses lacked chimneys, and the smoke found its way out through a hole in the bark roof. Clay and moss filled the chinks between the logs. Occasionally, furniture or family heirlooms survived the journey to Upper Canada, but most furniture was handmade. The settlers cooked on an open fireplace. In summer, flies and mosquitoes plagued the houses, and field mice and rats (introduced from Europe) infested the towns. Generally, the settlers preferred the winter cold to the summer heat and fevers. They found the Upper Canadian winters only slightly longer and colder than the winters most of them had known in New York and Pennsylvania.

In the process of settling the region and breaking the land, the loyalist settlers had one major complaint: Quebec's seigneurial system. As British subjects, they demanded that this archaic left-over of the French regime be abolished immediately. The loyalists had no intention of working land for a seigneur. They expected to own their own farmsteads. The authorities obliged and instituted a system of freehold tenure. The settlers could exchange land, by selling and purchasing it, well before the Constitutional Act of 1791 officially abolished the seigneurial system in Upper Canada.

The Constitutional Act of 1791

The Constitutional Act of 1791 created the colony of Upper Canada. It provided for freehold tenure and free land. Settlers paid only the fees for issuing and recording land titles. The legislation also set aside the equivalent of one-seventh of all lands granted in the future for "the Support and Maintenance of a Protestant Clergy." But the act failed to make explicit just what constituted the "Protestant Clergy" and whether the denominations other than the Church of England were included. This provision caused confusion and controversy. Initially the provincial government interpreted the phrase to refer only to the Anglican Church. In addition, the British government set aside another seventh of all lands as what were called Crown reserves. The revenues from the sale or rental of these lands were to be used to fund the colonial government.

On a Bush Farm near Chatham, Upper Canada, 1838, *by Philip John Bainbrigge.*

Source: Library and Archives Canada, Acc. No. 1983-47-21, C-011811.

A "Truly British" Colony

John Graves Simcoe, an energetic and enthusiastic military officer in the revolutionary war, then in his late thirties, became Upper Canada's first lieutenant governor. He wanted to make Upper Canada a centre of British power in North America. For Simcoe, the humiliation of the British empire in losing the Thirteen Colonies was a source of bitterness. "Democracy" and "republicanism" were bad words. As political principles they could only lead to anarchy. Believing that many in the new republic to the south remained actively loyal to Britain, Simcoe attempted to win Americans back to their old allegiance. He was convinced that a new colony with "a free, honourable British Government" would remind Americans of what they had lost in leaving the empire and the benefits of returning. Free grants of land, he reasoned, would be the first step in attracting them.

Simcoe's choice of place names highlights his vision of transforming Upper Canada into a "little England." In 1793, he travelled through the colony, choosing new designations. He went as far west as Detroit, confirming en route his choice of a site for the future capital at the place the Anishinabeg called "Ko-te-quo-gong" ("At the Forks"), at the headwaters of the Ashkahnesbe ("Horn" or "Antler") River. Kotequogong became London. The river that the Anishinabeg had named Ashkahnesbe, because its branches reminded them of a deer's antlers, became the Thames. The governor selected the title of York from the Duke of York (the same Frederick Augustus, second and favourite son of King George III, whom New Brunswick had honoured in naming their capital Fredericton) to replace the Iroquoian word "Toronto." He named the river east of York the Don and that to the west the Humber, after rivers in northeastern England, a region that also furnished the name for the bluffs east of the town site—Scarborough. To the north of York, he christened the large body of water the Anishinabeg called "Wah-weya-gahmah" ("Round Lake") Lake Simcoe, after his father. When asked what he thought of the governor's contribution to the colony, Joseph Brant replied, "General Simcoe has done a great deal for this province; he has changed the name of every place in it."

If Upper Canada was to take on a British character, for Simcoe it required a British hierarchy. The Anglican Church alone enjoyed the right of performing marriages. Reluctantly, Simcoe agreed that justices of the peace in remote areas might conduct marriage ceremonies, provided they followed the Anglican ritual. Only in 1798 was the right to solemnize marriages extended to Lutheran, Calvinist, and Presbyterian ministers. Methodists remained excluded until 1831. The Upper Canadian administration regarded the Methodists, who had strong links until 1828 with their American parent church, as a dangerous American denomination.

Establishing a Military Presence

Simcoe placed the new colony on a firm military footing. By the peace treaty of 1783, Britain and the United States agreed to an international boundary that ran through the upper St. Lawrence and the Great Lakes to the lands claimed by Spain in the Mississippi and Missouri river basins. But war with the Americans was a constant threat. In an attempt to appease their Aboriginal allies, the British delayed handing over their "western posts"—Oswego, Niagara, Detroit, and Michilimackinac—even though they were in American territory. By the same treaty, the Americans promised to allow the loyalists to return to their homes and collect their legitimate debts. The Americans failed to honour that promise. In the early 1780s, these issues caused considerable tension.

The British government allowed Simcoe to raise an infantry corps of 425 officers and men. The governor formed the Queen's Rangers (the name of his old loyalist regiment in the Revolution) to protect Upper Canada. The Upper Canada Legislative Assembly subsequently passed a militia bill in 1793 requiring all able-bodied men from 16 to 50 years of age to enlist and to drill for their local companies two to four times a year. By 1794, more than 5000 officers and men served in the militia. In the same year, Britain agreed to sign Jay's Treaty, which led to its withdrawal from the western posts by June 1, 1796.

Politics and Law in Upper Canada

Initially, Simcoe established his headquarters at Newark (now Niagara-on-the-Lake), only later changing it to York (Toronto). As a British colony, Upper Canada needed a Legislative Assembly. But as an aristocrat, Simcoe sought to avoid the unwieldy democratic element that he believed was one of the main causes of the American Revolution. He complained about the social background of the elected members, once describing them as "of a Lower Order, who kept but one Table, that is, who dined in Common with their Servants."

A British legal system was established by the legislature. William Osgoode, a well-regarded English lawyer, became chief justice, with responsibility for the Court of King's Bench, the new superior court of civil and criminal jurisdiction. Within each district, Simcoe created surrogate courts and a provincial court of probate. At a lower level, meetings for the courts of quarter sessions were organized. The justices of the peace presided over these and also performed a wide range of administrative and judicial duties. At the township level, the justices of the peace enjoyed considerable power, hearing court cases, supervising road and bridge construction contracts, and issuing various licences, including one for taverns. Township officials in Upper Canada were appointed, not elected as they were in New England.

York on Lake Ontario, Upper Canada, 1804, *by Elisabeth Francis Hale.*

Source: Library and Archives Canada, Acc. No. 1970-188-2092. W.H. Coverdale Collection of Canadiana/C-040137.

The Slavery Question

While the majority of African-American loyalists and slaves went to Nova Scotia after the Revolution, some slaves, perhaps as many as 500, were brought to Upper Canada. Joseph Brant, the Iroquois war chief, for example, had several, as did John Stuart, the first Anglican missionary at Kingston. But slavery did not prosper in Upper Canada. The more northerly clime meant a short growing season and prevented the cultivation of such crops as cotton, which required a cheap, plentiful labour force. Furthermore, owners had to feed, clothe, and house slaves throughout a long and unproductive winter. As a result, slavery was not as profitable or efficient as in the southern United States. In addition, attitudes toward slavery were gradually changing throughout the British empire. Many Upper Canadians, including Simcoe, found slavery abhorrent.

Under the governor's direction, the Assembly adopted a bill that gradually abolished slavery in Upper Canada. Slaves already in the colony had to remain slaves until death, but all children born after the act's passage would become free at the age of 25. Furthermore, no additional slaves could be brought to Upper Canada. After 1793, slavery steadily declined in the colony. The abolition of slavery in BNA indicated an enlightened attitude toward the issue, albeit one framed by economic motives. It did not, however, indicate an enlightened attitude toward race more generally. Blacks in the British colonies continued to be segregated and to face discrimination.

Land Grants

Simcoe hoped to cultivate an aristocratic class in Upper Canada. He assumed a population of loyalists—devoted to British Tory ideas, attached to the Church of England, and repulsed by American democracy—would be ideal for such a development. Through land policy, Simcoe believed that he could legislate such an elite into existence. Members of the Executive and Legislative Councils received large grants of 1200 to 2000 hectares, equivalent to those given the highest-ranked military officers. Their children could obtain 480 hectares. But the plan to create a landed gentry in Upper Canada failed. Few recipients had any intention of becoming country squires, preferring instead to sell their estates for profit. These grants locked up much valuable land and, to the resentment of many ordinary settlers, kept it out of their hands.

In reality, Upper Canada had two systems of land tenure. The first applied to the "official" settlers, who obtained land on account of their past service to the Crown or because of their social position. The second consisted of immigrants obtaining grants of 80 hectares on the promise to develop it. Once these individuals built their homes and fenced and cleared the road allowance, they gained title. This system involved mostly the "late loyalists."

Simcoe's land policies continued after his departure from the colony in 1796. Most of the "late loyalists," despite their name, came up from the United States not for political reasons, but rather for free land. Since the colony lay directly on the path of the advancing American settlement frontier, it received settlers en route from New York to the Ohio and Mississippi valleys. Most of these Americans did not necessarily intend to stay in Upper Canada and had no interest in Simcoe's plan for a "little England"; indeed, in future years, hostilities arose in the colony between the "official" and the "immigrant" settlers.

Communications

The colony could not develop a level of "civilization" if it did not have a decent system of transportation and communication. Simcoe worked to establish a road system in the remote and rural colony. In 1793, he began a military road from Burlington Bay to the Thames River, which he named Dundas Street after Henry Dundas, then secretary of state in the British cabinet. Simcoe built a second military road from York to Lake Simcoe, to ensure rapid communication with the upper lakes. The governor called this road, which he began in 1796, Yonge Street, after British secretary of war Sir George Yonge. Yonge and Dundas streets became the colony's principal pathways. Both roads allowed settlers to begin farms inland, away from the "front," at a time when most people clung to the navigable waterways.

Simcoe's Legacy

Simcoe left Upper Canada in mid-1796. Despite his achievements, while serving as governor he experienced many disappointments. The British government, not surprisingly, did not match Simcoe's enthusiasm and they did not share the extent of his vision for the future of the colony. The Colonial Office had requests coming in from across the empire. It turned down most of Simcoe's expensive schemes to build up Upper Canada economically and militarily. His proposal to create a provincial university, for example, received little support, as did his attempt to establish the Church of England in the colony under a bishop's tutelage. While Simcoe's vision of a "little England" echoed in the colony's place names, he failed to create a British system with its rigid class system. Simcoe did, however, succeed in establishing the basis for the colony. As historian Gerald Craig notes, "Simcoe had helped to nurse a new province into being, but its inhabitants, busy with their own projects and their own local affairs, showed only a tepid interest in the goals he had set for them."[3]

Loyalist Women

Loyalist families often had their homes and lives uprooted. The move to British North America was tumultuous and most of the burden of relocation fell on women. During the American Revolution, many faced harassment and persecution. The insurgents stole their property and seized their homes, and in some cases jailed them. Once the decision to uproot was made, the loyalist women travelled, in many cases with very young children through difficult terrain, to British

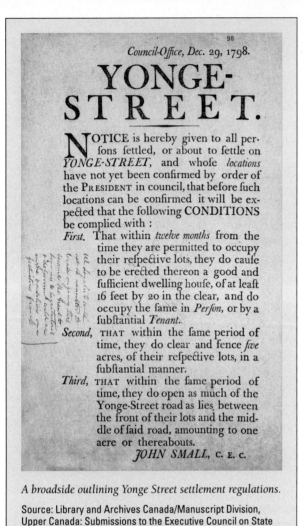

A broadside outlining Yonge Street settlement regulations.

Source: Library and Archives Canada/Manuscript Division, Upper Canada: Submissions to the Executive Council on State Matters, 1791–1841, R.G. 1, E 3, vol. 100, page 98.

refugee camps. Even here their struggles did not end. After demonstrating remarkable resilience and courage, as historian Janice Potter writes, once behind British lines, "They had to fit once again into a patriarchal power structure in which their inferiority and dependence were assumed."[4] A married woman had no legal identity separate from that of her husband. Some loyalist women did submit claims for compensation to Britain after the war. Without fail, however, the all-male adjudicators of loyalist claims awarded much more, proportionally, to men than to women.

The work of one loyalist woman helped maintain the British relationship with the Iroquois during the Revolution. Molly Brant (also known as Konwatsi'tsiaienni and Degonwadonti) was the older sister of Joseph Brant and partner to William Johnson, the British Superintendent of Indian Affairs. She was a Christian and anglicized Mohawk. After Johnson's death in 1774, she supported the British cause and used her affluent home to help other loyalists flee the country.

When British forces invaded New York in 1777, Brant sent Mohawk scouts to inform the British of an approaching patriot force. As a result, the Americans were ambushed and defeated at the Battle of Oriskany. In the aftermath, the Oneida (who were fighting with the patriots) and the Americans pillaged Brant's town of Canajoharie. Brant fled with her children to Onondaga. Here she used her influence to convince the Iroquois to fight alongside the British.

Iroquois society was matrilineal and Brant's influence was impressive. According to one British Indian agent, "One word from her goes farther with [the Iroquois] than a thousand from any white Man without Exception." Brant then moved to Fort Niagara to continue to use her sway as a diplomat with the Iroquois. The war forced her to move two more times with her family, first to Montreal and then to the British post at Carleton Island. With war's end in 1783, Brant moved her family to Cataraqui (Kingston), where the British government built her a house and provided her a pension. She remained there until her death in 1796.

The First Nations: A Displaced People

By the turn of the nineteenth century, the First Nations in the colony were becoming a displaced people. The fur trade was in decline, and with an end to the colonial wars and the drawing of international borders, they were losing their role as military allies. Many Aboriginal groups continued their struggle to resist the encroachment of white settlers, but it was a losing battle. While the British continued to fear "Indian uprisings," and sought to reward and appease various groups for their loyalty, the view of the First Nations was changing. They were now obstacles to "progress." The loyalist migration highlighted the need for Aboriginal land for white settlement.

The First Nations also recognized the change. Land treaties meant the loss of their traditional homelands in return for some material goods to help them survive in this new world. The elders, such as Kahkewaquonaby ("Sacred Feathers," known in English as Peter Jones), told the young people that when the British first came, they

> asked for a small piece of land on which they might pitch their tents; the request was cheerfully granted. By and by they begged for more, and more was given them. In this way they have continued to ask, or have obtained by force or fraud, the fairest portions of our territory.

Between 1805 and 1818, the Crown successfully pressured the Mississaugas to sell their last remaining tract, between Toronto and the head of the lake (present-day Hamilton). In two separate agreements, the British acquired the desired land.

Other tragedies followed. Between the 1790s and the 1820s, smallpox, tuberculosis, and measles killed almost two-thirds of the Mississaugas at the western end of the lake. The group's population in that area dropped to 200 in the 1820s, down from more than 500 a generation earlier. The Iroquois also experienced difficult times in the 1790s and 1800s, as land sales eliminated much of their reserve on the Grand River. Realizing that making the transition to a settled way of life was the only possible means of adapting, Chief Joseph Brant welcomed settlers to the Grand River to teach European agricultural techniques. Not all his followers agreed. Many objected to the presence of the outsiders who, by 1798, controlled two-thirds of the Six Nations' original grant.

A portrait of Kahkewaquonaby (Sacred Feathers, known in English as Peter Jones) by William Crubb.

Source: Peter Jones (Kahkewaquonaby), 1845 (calotype), by David Octavius Hill (1802–70) & Robert Adamson (1821–48) Edinburgh University Library, Scotland/With kind permission of the University of Edinburgh/The Bridgeman Art Library Nationality/copyright status: Scottish/out of copyright.

The Growth of Upper Canada

Upper Canada's population increased dramatically at the turn of the century. Many were "late loyalists" in search of cheap land. By 1812, settlers lived on all the vacant townships along the north shore of Lake Ontario and on several townships on Lake Erie as well. Although few roads existed, the waterways allowed for the dispersal of settlement along an 800-kilometre front in a period of less than twenty years.

The Plain Folk

Despite Simcoe's desire to create a model colony populated by English Anglican-Tories, the arrival of the late loyalists brought a relatively diverse range of people to Upper Canada. Among them were members of religious sects commonly called the "Plain Folk," because they believed in a pure religion

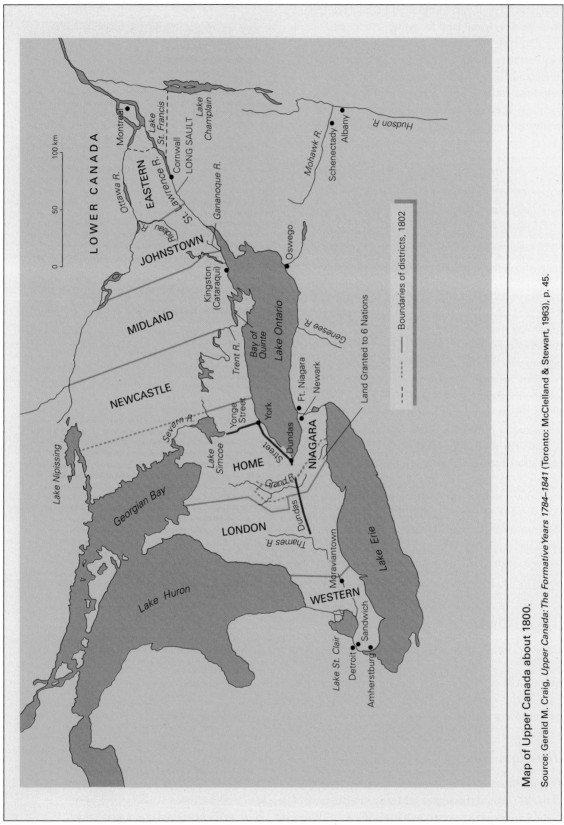

Map of Upper Canada about 1800.

Source: Gerald M. Craig, *Upper Canada: The Formative Years 1784–1841* (Toronto: McClelland & Stewart, 1963), p. 45.

and plain dress. They included Quakers, Mennonites, and Dunkards (a small group of Baptists who practised adult baptism by "dunking" the individual in water). Most of the Quakers originated in England, while the other sects came from Germany. But those that immigrated to Upper Canada came via the United States, mostly from Pennsylvania and New York. Many trekked north using heavy, broad-wheeled Conestoga wagons. They were pacifists who had remained neutral during the American Revolution. They also opposed taking oaths of allegiance to earthly rulers, believing that their allegiance was to God. The prospect of good land, the hope for stability, and the promise of religious tolerance attracted them to Upper Canada.

The largest number of Plain Folk settled in the Niagara Peninsula because of the easy access it afforded to the Quaker, Mennonite, and Dunkard settlements in Pennsylvania. The Bay of Quinte became another favourite area for religious minorities, as did Yonge Street, particularly in Markham and Vaughan townships. A sizable number of Mennonites from Pennsylvania came later and settled in Waterloo County. The additional migration of the Amish directly from Germany in 1824 strengthened the German character of the Waterloo

Mrs. Simcoe in Welsh dress.

Source: Library and Archives Canada, Acc. No. 1972-118-2/C-081931.

area, as did the later arrival from Europe of German Lutherans and Roman Catholics. The Plain Folk made ideal farmers. According to historian G. Elmore Reaman, they had three strengths that helped them succeed with breaking the land for agriculture: "They were physically equipped both in knowledge of what to do in the wilderness and the strength to do it; they came with money and equipment; and they aided one another, whether Quaker, Huguenot, Lutheran, or Mennonite."[5]

On the eve of the War of 1812, the population of Upper Canada reached 75 000. Scattered along the St. Lawrence River and lakes Ontario, Erie, and St. Clair, the settled areas rarely extended more than a few kilometres into the interior and away from the waterways. The work of establishing farms and clearing new land was hard work and took much of the settlers' time. The newcomers from the United States soon outnumbered the loyalists and the British immigrants four to one. The War would test the loyalty of the Upper Canadian population.

Upper Canada and the United States, 1791–1812

As long as Britain retained the western posts, war with the United States appeared likely. For the First Nations south of the Great Lakes, their war with the

Old Fort Erie with the Migrations of the Wild-Pigeon in Spring, April 12, 1804, *by Edward Walsh.*

Source: With permission of the Royal Ontario Museum © ROM, 952.218.

Tenskwatawa (1775–1836), the Shawnee religious leader and brother of Tecumseh. Painted in 1830 by George Catlin.

Source: Smithsonian American Art Museum, Washington, DC/ Art Resources.

Americans had never ended. Governor Simcoe held out hope that the Aboriginals would defeat the Americans. And for a short while, it appeared they might. In 1791, the First Nations of the Ohio Valley, led by the Miami and Shawnee, routed an American invasion army under General Arthur St. Clair, inflicting more than 900 casualties: "As an Amerindian victory, it ranked second to that over Braddock in 1755; it was the worst defeat ever for Americans by Amerindians."[6] The United States had to send another large military expedition to subdue them. In August 1794, General "Mad" Anthony Wayne defeated the Ohio First Nations at the Battle of Fallen Timbers, putting an end to Simcoe's dream of an Aboriginal buffer state.

International developments also contributed to Britain's decision to surrender the western posts. As a result of renewed war with France, Britain looked to ease tensions with the United States. In 1794 the two countries signed Jay's Treaty, named for John Jay, the American chief justice who negotiated the agreement. By its terms, Britain agreed to evacuate the forts on the south shores of the Great Lakes in 1796. With Britain's imminent withdrawal, the First Nations had little choice but to make peace with the Americans. In the Treaty of Greenville in 1795, they ceded their claims to most of the present-day state of Ohio. Aboriginal resistance to the Americans' westward march, however, continued.

Causes of the War of 1812

In the first decade of the nineteenth century, Tecumseh, a Shawnee chief, and his brother, Tenskwatawa, a religious leader, assembled the most formidable Aboriginal confederacy the continent had witnessed. Tecumseh ("Shooting Star," "Panther Across the Sky") was part Shawnee, part Creek. His early life was dominated by the struggle against the Americans. On numerous occasions, Tecumseh's family had to relocate after their village was attacked. As a young man, Tecumseh fought on the American frontier in the Ohio and Illinois country, and participated in the Battle of Fallen Timbers in 1794.

In 1808, tensions within the Shawnee caused a schism. Tecumseh and Tenskwatawa moved with their followers further into the interior to establish their own settlement, "Prophetstown," at the confluence of the Wabash and Tippecanoe rivers. Here, Tenskwatawa preached his vision that an apocalypse was coming that would destroy the American settlers. Meanwhile, he urged the Aboriginal peoples to return to their traditional ways and reject European culture, including their trade goods. Tecumseh came to prominence with his opposition to the Treaty of Fort Wayne, negotiated by Indiana Governor William Harrison, a questionable agreement that resulted in the First Nations ceding three million acres of land to the United States.

Tecumseh travelled widely, spreading his message of First Nations unity and the need to resist American encroachment. He gained the support of the Potawatomi, Ojibwa, Odawa,

Winnebagos, and Kickapoo; he had limited success with the Shawnee, Delaware, Wyandot, Menominee, Miami, Choctaw, and Piankeshaw, among others. Tecumseh's efforts held particular appeal with the younger warriors, while the older leaders often resisted, instead wishing to establish peace with the Americans and hold to treaties already made. The appeal was aided by the difficult situation facing the Aboriginal peoples of the area, including crop failure, drought, and the decline of the fur trade. While Tecumseh was away gathering support, Governor Harrison responded to the growing "Indian Confederacy" by attacking "Prophetstown" at the Battle of Tippecanoe in September 1811. The Americans won the battle and burned the town to the ground. Tecumseh rebuilt, and his confederacy entered open war with the Americans.

Many Americans from Ohio, Tennessee, and Kentucky suspected that despite Jay's Treaty, the British continued to encourage and finance the Aboriginal raids. Calls went out in these states for an attack against the British in their Canadian colonies. American "war hawks" argued that the United States could use the opportunity and justification to punish Britain by seizing Upper Canada.

Two direct provocations by Britain led many Americans to support war. In 1807, Napoleon's continental system closed all of western Europe, except Portugal, to British trade goods. Britain retaliated by imposing a naval blockade, preventing all ships, including American vessels, from trading with France. Officially neutral in the struggle, the United States called for freedom of the seas, especially since the size of its merchant marine had almost doubled in the past decade. The Americans were outraged and considered the blockade illegal.

The other provocation was that Britain ignored American sovereignty and regard for neutrality rights. Despite protests, British cruisers continued to stop and search U.S. ships on the North Atlantic. The British said they were looking for navy deserters who had gone over to American vessels to obtain higher wages, better food, and better working conditions. An estimated 11 000 had indeed deserted.

However, it was more than a legal matter. The Royal Navy during the Napoleonic Wars required over 140 000 sailors, and experienced men were difficult to find and even more difficult to keep. Even if a sailor produced his certificate of naturalization, the British ignored it, because they did not recognize the right of a British subject to transfer allegiance. Besides, there were many forgeries.

Because of these two issues, "Free Trade and Sailors' Rights" became the rallying cry of many Americans.

The *Chesapeake-Leopard* affair in 1807 highlighted the issue of impressment. When the American frigate *Chesapeake* refused demands by the British warship *Leopard* to halt and be searched off the coast of Virginia, the British fired, killing three men and wounding eighteen. The American ship surrendered and four men were impressed; one of them was later executed. The American public was outraged. President Thomas Jefferson said, "Never since the Battle of Lexington have I seen this country in such a state of exasperation." Jefferson opposed war and attempted to use diplomacy and trade restrictions to ease tensions. The new president, James Madison, was less conciliatory. Forced, as he put it, to choose between war and degradation, Madison sent a strong message to Congress that recounted American grievances. Both Congress and the Senate voted for war against Britain, and on June 18, 1812, President Madison signed the declaration into law. The United States declared war on a foreign nation for the first time.

The War of 1812

The Americans were seeking to expand westward into "Indian territory," but they were less anxious to expand northward into Canada. Most in the American government looked to attack Canada as a means of attacking Britain. It was believed that Canada, with its sparse population and meagre defences, would fall quickly and easily. The BNA colonies could then be used as bargaining chips with Britain. It would also punish Britain for allegedly supplying and supporting the First Nations southwest of the Great Lakes. Throughout the first year of the war, the Americans believed that Upper Canada's American population would welcome them as liberators. According to Thomas Jefferson, "The acquisition of Canada this year, as far as the neighborhood of Quebec, will be a mere matter of marching, and will give us the experience for the attack on Halifax, the next and final expulsion of England from the American continent." It proved more than "a mere matter of marching."

Despite the diplomatic tension and war of words, neither side was prepared for a major conflict in 1812. Britain was the less prepared, because it was completely engaged in the Napoleonic Wars with France: its army was involved in the Peninsular War in Spain and its navy was blockading continental Europe. The War of 1812 was a sideshow. But it might prove costly if the United States were able to take advantage.

As it happened, the British Prime Minister, Spencer Perceval, was assassinated on the eve of war, and his successor, Lord Liverpool, worked immediately to negotiate a solution. But his cables arrived in North America too late. It would not be the last time that the delay in communications across the Atlantic impacted the conflict.

The British could only afford to send 6000 regular troops to defend Canada. Lord Bathurst, the Secretary of State for War and the Colonies, ordered the commander-in-chief in North America, Lieutenant General Sir George Prevost, to maintain a defensive strategy. The United States was just as unprepared. For many in the U.S. government, the official declaration of war was enough to restore American honour. President Madison assumed that he could count on the state militias to carry out the fighting. The American regular standing army stood at only 12 000 troops. The militias were poorly trained and disciplined, and resisted leaving their home states to fight. But a major problem was that support for the war in the United States was divided by region. The New England states, for example, had no desire for war and instead vocally opposed it; the western states supported the conflict; and the southern states were indifferent. The president had difficulty funding the conflict.

The defence of Canada fell to Major General Isaac Brock. With limited military experience in Europe, Brock arrived in Canada in 1802. After dealing with desertions and mutinies in Montreal and Niagara, by 1805 he found himself in charge of British forces in North America. In the face of growing antagonism between Britain and the United States, Brock organized the defences of Canada. He strengthened the fortifications of Quebec and reorganized the maritime defences along the Great Lakes. The local militia was expanded and trained. Despite requests to be posted in Europe, Brock was given military and civilian command of Upper Canada in 1810. His request for a new posting was granted in 1812, but by this time he refused in order to defend the colony against the American invasion.

Canoe model made by an Odawa chief between 1814 and 1827.

Source: © Canadian Museum of Civilization, artist Jean-Baptiste Assiginack, catalogue no. III-M-10 a-n, image no. S89-1735.

Despite orders to take a defensive position, with only one British infantry regiment, a detachment of veterans, and a company of artillery to hold the vast colony, Brock went on the offensive. He used the armed vessels of the Provincial Marine that controlled the lakes to communicate with his posts quickly and effectively. Before news of the outbreak of war had even reached the American fort of Michilimackinac, Brock ordered his outpost at St. Joseph Island on Lake Huron to attack. The American fort was caught by surprise and surrendered. News of the victory spurred First Nations in the area to rally in support of the British. Meanwhile, Governor General George Prevost kept most of his troops for the defence of Lower Canada and opposed any offensive into American territory.

In July 1812, an American force under General William Hull launched a failed invasion with 1000 poorly trained militia at Sandwich (later Windsor). Brock used this failed attack as a justification to ignore Prevost's defensive order and counterattack. He commanded a small force of regulars and militia, and marched from York to reinforce the garrison at Amhertsburg on the western side of Lake Erie, across from Hull's position at Detroit. It was here that Isaac Brock met Tecumseh, and accounts indicate that the two leaders were equally impressed with each other.

Tecumseh and the First Nations, meanwhile, welcomed the outbreak of the second Anglo–American War. When word of hostilities reached Tecumseh, he rallied his confederacy and led hundreds of warriors to join the British in Upper Canada. They assisted the British in taking Michilimackinac, the leading fur-trading post in the Upper Great Lakes. Then, they helped to cut the Americans' communication and supply lines to Detroit. Brock's intelligence indicated that General Hull had lost the respect of his 2500 troops, was low on supplies, and feared a massacre if Detroit was lost to Aboriginal warriors. Outnumbered two to one, Brock and Tecumseh organized a daring attack. The militiamen donned the uniforms of regulars to create the appearance of a larger British force. Tecumseh's four hundred warriors paraded past the walls of Detroit and then doubled back to create the appearance of an even larger First Nations force. Finally, Brock sent Hull a letter demanding his surrender and playing on his rival's fears: "It is far from my inclination to join in a war of extermination, but you must be aware that the numerous body of Indians who have attached themselves to my troops will be beyond my control the moment the contest commences." The British artillery then began pounding the fort. The following day, on 16 August, Hull surrendered. The fall of Detroit led to the embarrassing loss of all American territory west of Lake Erie. It also substantially boosted the morale of both the British and the First Nations forces.

The unexpected victory at Detroit in August restored confidence among the population that Upper Canada could be successfully defended. Brock wished to continue the offensive, but Prevost opposed the move. Brock proved that the colony could indeed be defended again in October, when a large American invasion force crossed the Niagara River at the Battle of Queenston Heights. This time, the defence cost

Sir Isaac Brock wore this coat on October 13, 1812. In his charge up the strategic Queenston Heights, an American sniper's bullet pierced the major-general's coat just below the collar, killing him. Both the town of Brockville, Ontario, and Brock University in St. Catharines, Ontario, are named in his honour.

Source: © Canadian War Museum, CWM 19670070-009.

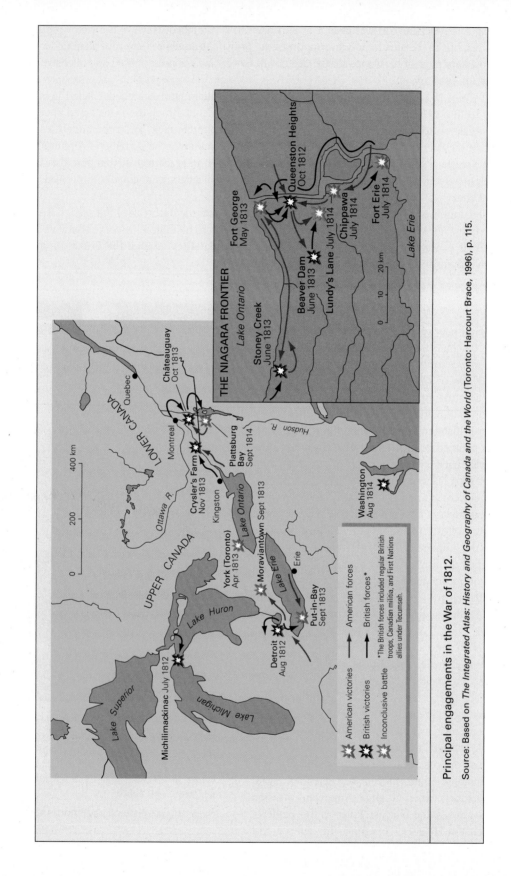

Principal engagements in the War of 1812.

Source: Based on *The Integrated Atlas: History and Geography of Canada and the World* (Toronto: Harcourt Brace, 1996), p. 115.

him his life. Isaac Brock was shot in the hand and the chest by American sharpshooters as he led a charge up the face of the heights to retake the British artillery position. He died where he fell. When 500 Iroquois joined 1000 British regulars and 600 Upper Canadian militia, the strategic heights were retaken. Among the militia units was "Captain Robert Runchey's Company of Blacks," a force of former American slaves. The British victors captured 900 American prisoners. Having lost one army at Detroit, the Americans lost another on the Niagara frontier.

After the war, it was claimed that the militia had won the contests at Detroit and Queenston Heights. In reality, regular soldiers constituted the first line of Britain's defence of Upper Canada, supplying the leadership and doing most of the fighting. Throughout the war, the Upper Canadian militia proved unreliable. Zeal for the fight always declined at harvest time or whenever news arrived of danger to the men's families from raiding parties. As historian George Sheppard has written: "Most Upper Canadian males, although obligated to fight, did not do so."[7]

The Campaigns of 1813 and 1814

The war had started off surprisingly well for the British. By the spring and summer of 1813, however, the tide was turning and the gains were reversed. The Americans twice briefly occupied York and launched a second invasion of the Niagara Peninsula, forcing the British to withdraw to Burlington Heights at the head of the lake (present-day Hamilton). Desertions from the militia grew, and two members of the Upper Canada Legislative Assembly joined the Americans. Only a surprise attack by British regular troops at Stoney Creek, immediately south of Burlington Heights, dislodged the Americans and saved Upper Canada. A second battle followed at Beaver Dams, where Iroquois from the Montreal area and from the Six Nations territory at the Grand River ambushed the Americans. The attackers benefited from vital information about the location of the American troops received from Laura Secord, a 37-year-old settler, who overheard American officers discussing their invasion plans. Slipping through the American cordon, she took a roundabout route to the British–First Nations camp with this information. Shortly after the Iroquois victory at Beaver Dams, the American invaders withdrew from the peninsula.

While their Niagara campaign in 1813 ended in failure, the Americans proved successful that same year in the Detroit sector of the conflict. American fortunes revived after Admiral Oliver Perry defeated the British at Put-in-Bay on Lake Erie. The lake, in effect, became an American possession, controlled by their naval forces for the remainder of the war. The victory also severed British supply lines and forced a withdrawal from Detroit. The Americans defeated the retreating British, the Upper Canadian militia, and Tecumseh's forces at Moraviantown on the Thames River. The Americans held onto southwestern Upper Canada until the end of the war. That autumn, their two-pronged attack on Montreal ended in defeat at Crysler's Farm in eastern Upper Canada and at Châteauguay in Lower Canada.

But the defeat at Moraviantown came at a heavy price. Tecumseh was killed on October 5, 1813, and with his death the confederacy collapsed. The link between the British and the First Nations peoples of the American Midwest was broken. Never again in the lower Great Lakes area

Perry's Victory on Lake Erie, September 10th, 1813, *drawn by J.J. Barralet.*

Source: Library and Archives Canada, Acc. No. 1992-698-5/C-007762.

First Nations chiefs at the commemoration of the Battle of Lundy's Lane.

Source: © City of Niagara Falls Museum, Lundy's Lane Historical Museum.

did the First Nations constitute a serious military threat; never again would they form such a united front.

The Americans were doing well on the lakes, and privateers caused British shipping serious damage as far away as the West Indies, but Britain maintained supremacy of the seas. The Royal Navy blockaded the American coastline except for New England. The British were able to raid at will, including an attack on Washington that resulted in the burning of the White House.

After Moraviantown, the battle lines consolidated for the remainder of the war. The Americans were more prepared and organized, but with Napoleon's abdication in 1814, the British were able to focus on North America. Four of the Duke of Wellington's ablest commanders, along with 15000 regular troops, arrived. On July 25, 1814, the British defeated the Americans' last attempt to capture Upper Canada, at Lundy's Lane on the Niagara Peninsula. Lundy's Lane was the site of the bloodiest battle of the War of 1812. The six-hour engagement lasted until darkness. Each side lost more than 800 men. Although each claimed victory, at the end of the battle the Americans had failed to dislodge the British. They withdrew, ending their final offensive in Upper Canada.

Outside Upper Canada, the British led by Prevost attempted but failed to take the offensive on Lake Champlain. In August 1814, a British expedition invaded Washington, and it was at this time that they burned the Capitol and

Battle of Moraviantown, October 5, 1813.

Source: Library and Archives Canada/C-007763.

the U.S. president's house, allegedly in retaliation for the American sacking of York in 1813. Madison was forced to flee to Virginia, and the British officers dined on the meal prepared for the president. The British advanced on Baltimore; the siege of Fort McHenry inspired the lyrics to "The Star-Spangled Banner." But the Americans took control of Lake Champlain and defeated the British at the Battle of Plattsburgh. The only other major battle of the war, at New Orleans in January 1815, ended in an American victory under General Andrew Jackson. This battle took place even though the Treaty of Ghent had been signed on December 24, 1814, as word had not yet reached North America that the war was over.

WHERE HISTORIANS DISAGREE

The War of 1812

The War of 1812 has been portrayed very differently in Canada and the United States. Nationalism continues to colour popular understandings of the conflict. Canadians often regard the war as a nation-building triumph and the pivotal moment when the future of Canada as a separate nation from the United States was ensured.[1] Americans sometimes regard it as a Second War of Independence, when the young, fragile republic successfully defended its rights against the might of the British empire. More often, however, the War of 1812 is America's "forgotten conflict."[2] Wedged between the War for Independence and the Civil War, it gets little attention in school curriculums or in the popular imagination.

Nationalism also influenced how the war was described by historians. One of the earliest Canadian histories of the War of 1812 was written by a participant in the events, Major John Richardson, a Canadian-born British officer captured by American forces at the Battle of the Thames in 1813. Richardson's goal was to share with "young men of the present generation" an account of the "brilliant

feat of arms, and sterling loyalty" of the Canadians who "rode triumphant over every obstacle, and came forth unconquered from the strife." He hoped, too, that his work would counter American histories of the war which had a "tendency to pervert facts . . . and weaken the energies of the national character."[3]

Nineteenth-century Canadian historians celebrated the War and embraced the myth that it was the loyalist militia who had won it for Upper Canada. "The U.E. [United Empire] Loyalists have been as a barrier of rock," wrote William Canniff in 1869, "against which the waves of Republicanism have dashed in vain."[4] In 1880, Egerton Ryerson, a loyalist descendent and one of the architects of the Ontario public school system, adopted the same interpretation when he wrote of how Upper Canada was saved by the "Spartan bands of Canadian Loyalist Volunteers . . . [who] repelled the Persian thousands of democratic American invaders."[5] Aside from uniting Canadians against a common enemy, late-nineteenth- and early-twentieth-century historians argued that the War of 1812 was the impetus for improving everything from roads and communications to economic institutions. For these men, it gave birth to Canada.[6]

By the mid-twentieth century, professional historians in Canada began to move away from the nationalist hype and question some of the "myths" of the war. Military historians such as C.P. Stacey, J. Mackay Hitsman, and G.F.G Stanley agreed that credit for defending Upper Canada properly belonged to the professionally trained British soldiers. Although the militia's role remained important, it played a supporting role at best and was mainly employed in constructing fortifications and conveying supplies.[7] More recently, George Sheppard has argued that most Upper Canadians could not even be relied upon for support service. Far from being an economic boon, the war caused shortages and destruction that nearly ruined the colony.[8] Furthermore, Robert Allen and others have highlighted the decisive role played by Britain's Aboriginal allies in the defence of Upper Canada.[9]

Historians have shown how the war, far from uniting the populations of Upper Canada or the United States, created deep divisions. As Jane Errington argues in *The Lion, the Eagle and Upper Canada,* there was a spirit of anti-Americanism among the elites of Upper Canada, but the attitude of the average settler was more complex. Most Upper Canadians had family ties in the United States, and trade flowed easily across the Great Lakes and the rivers. Culturally, the United States provided Upper Canada with print media and served as the British colony's "window on the world."[10] Some in Upper Canada who had only recently migrated northward from the United States welcomed an American invasion. In the United States,

New England and the Federalist Party were strongly opposed to the war, and some Boston merchants even continued to trade with Britain and her colonies in Canada. The War of 1812 nearly caused the disintegration of the United States, as some in New England seriously considered seceding from the Union. Some historians have seen the war as an earlier contributor to the sectional tension that later tore the United States apart in the American Civil War (1861–65).[11]

One of the most recent works on the war comes from the American historian Alan Taylor. In his work *The Civil War of 1812,* Taylor examines the events in light of the shared culture and internal divisions of the opposing sides, and the wider struggle between Britain and her former American colonies, which began decades earlier. It was, as Taylor writes, a "civil war between kindred peoples, recently and incompletely divided by the revolution." The idea of the War of 1812 as a civil war in the borderlands, as opposed to a clash of nations, more accurately reflects the experiences of many Upper Canadians torn between their loyalty to the empire and their loyalty to their friends and family across the border.[12]

Canadians have been particularly concerned with the issue of who won the War of 1812. This debate again focuses on questions of nationalism and national pride. Historians on both sides of the border generally agree that because it ended without any changes in territory, the war was a draw. But some historians disagree. Donald Hickey, for example, argues that the United States lost the war, because it was the aggressor who failed to achieve its objectives. Wesley Turner argues that both sides won, since Canada was preserved as a British colony and the

Americans crushed the Aboriginal resistance on the frontier.[13] The nature of the question, however, ignores the fact that even though there was no clear winner, the First Nations of the Great Lakes were unmistakably losers. Although allies to the British, they were ignored at the treaty table and left to fend for themselves against the Americans in the aftermath. The dream of the Indian Confederacy was destroyed.

1. Anne McIlroy, "Confederation Wins the Vote for Greatest Event in Our History," *The Globe and Mail*, September 18, 2000. The War of 1812 scored third overall, after Confederation and the Last Spike.

2. Donald Hickey, *The War of 1812: A Forgotten Conflict* (Urbana: University of Illinois Press, 1989).

3. John Richardson, *Richardson's War of 1812* (Toronto: Historical Publishing Co. 1902 [1842]).

4. William Canniff, *History of the Settlement of Upper Canada, with Special Reference to the Bay of Quinte* (Toronto: Dudely and Burns, 1869), p. 634.

5. Egerton Ryerson, *The Loyalists of America and Their Times, from 1620–1816,* vol. 2 (Montreal: Dawson Bros., 1880), p. 379.

6. Adam Shortt, "The Economic Effect of the War of 1812 on Upper Canada" (1913), reprinted in Morris Zaslow, *The Defended Border: Upper Canada and the War of 1812* (Toronto: MacMillan, 1964), pp. 296–302.

7. J. Mackay Hitsman, *The Incredible War of 1812: A Military History* (Toronto: University of Toronto Press, 1965). George F.G. Stanley, "The Contribution of the Canadian Militia During the War," in Philip Mason, *After Tippecanoe: Some Aspects of the War of 1812* (East Lansing: Michigan State University Press, 1963), pp. 28–48.

8. George Sheppard, *Plunder, Profit, and Paroles: A Social History of the War of 1812* (Montreal: McGill-Queen's University Press, 1994), p. 5.

9. Robert S. Allen, *His Majesty's Indian Allies: British Indian Policy in the Defence of Canada, 1774–1815* (Toronto: Dundurn, 1992).

10. Jane Errington, *Wives and Mothers, Schoolmistresses and Scullery Maids: Working Women in Upper Canada, 1790–1840* (Montreal: McGill-Queen's University Press, 1995), pp. 36–38.

11. James Banner, *To the Hartford Convention: The Federalists and the Origins of Party Politics in Massachusetts, 1789–1815* (New York: Knopf, 1970); Richard Buel Jr., *America on the Brink: How the Political Struggle over the War of 1812 Almost Destroyed the Young Republic* (New York: Palgrave MacMillan, 2005); Julius Pratt, *Expansionists of 1812* (Gloucester, MA: Peter Smith, 1957 [1925]).

12. Alan Taylor, *The Civil War of 1812: American Citizens, British Subjects, Irish Rebels, and Indian Allies* (New York: Knopf, 2010), p. 6.

13. Donald R. Hickey, *The War of 1812: A Forgotten Conflict* (Chicago: University of Illinois Press, 1989); Wesley Turner, *The War of 1812: The War That Both Sides Won* (Toronto: Dundurn Press, 1990).

SUMMARY

The War of 1812 ended in a stalemate, and the Treaty of Ghent essentially confirmed the status quo. But in the aftermath, both the Americans and the Canadians claimed victory. Ultimately, it was the First Nations who lost the most.

The war had a profound effect on Upper Canada in one respect, at least: the unsuccessful and destructive attacks of 1812–14 engendered anti-American sentiment among the settlers, and contributed to the work Simcoe had begun: the promotion of a nationalist spirit in Upper Canada.

NOTES

1. Kenneth Norrie and Douglas Owram, *A History of the Canadian Economy* (Toronto: Harcourt Brace, 1991), p. 161.

2. R. Cole Harris and John Warkentin, *Canada Before Confederation: A Study in Historical Geography* (Ottawa: Carleton University Press, 1991 [1974]), p. 112.

3. Gerald M. Craig, *Upper Canada: The Formative Years, 1784–1841* (Toronto: McClelland & Stewart, 1963), p. 41.

4. Janice Potter, "Patriarchy and Paternalism: The Case of the Eastern Ontario Loyalist Women," *Ontario History* 81 (1989): 20.

5. G. Elmore Reaman, *The Trail of the Black Walnut* (Toronto: McClelland & Stewart, 1957), p. 147.

6. Olive P. Dickason, *Canada's First Nations: A History of Founding Peoples from Earliest Times* (Toronto: McClelland & Stewart, 1992), p. 219.

7. George Sheppard, *Plunder, Profit, and Paroles: A Social History of the War of 1812 in Upper Canada* (Montreal/Kingston: McGill-Queen's University Press, 1994), p. 5.

BIBLIOGRAPHY

For an understanding of early Upper Canada, Gerald M. Craig's *Upper Canada: The Formative Years, 1784–1841* (Toronto: McClelland & Stewart, 1963) remains important. J.K. Johnson underlines its importance in "Gerald Craig's *Upper Canada: The Formative Years* and the Writing of Canadian History," *Ontario History* 90(2) (Autumn 1998): 117–33. Studies on the loyalists who settled in Upper Canada include Bruce Wilson, *As She Began: An Illustrated Introduction to Loyalist Ontario* (Toronto: Dundurn Press, 1981); James J. Talman, ed., *Loyalist Narratives from Upper Canada* (Toronto: Champlain Society, 1946); and Janice Potter-MacKinnon, *While the Women Only Wept: Loyalist Refugee Women in Eastern Ontario* (Montreal/Kingston: McGill-Queen's University Press, 1993). See too Norman Knowles' examination of loyalism in Ontario, *Inventing the Loyalists: The Ontario Loyalist Tradition and the Creation of Usable Pasts* (Toronto: University of Toronto Press, 1997). For a guide to the historical literature in general, see Bryan D. Palmer, "Upper Canada," in M. Brook Taylor, ed., *Canadian History: A Reader's Guide*, vol. 1, *Beginnings to Confederation* (Toronto: University of Toronto Press, 1994), pp. 184–236. Peter A. Baskerville has written a useful overview of all of Ontario's history: *Ontario: Image, Identity and Power* (Toronto: Oxford University Press, 2001).

Simcoe's years in Upper Canada are reviewed in Stanley R. Mealing, "John Graves Simcoe," in *Dictionary of Canadian Biography*, vol. 5, *1801–1820* (Toronto: University of Toronto Press, 1985), pp. 754–59. For an understanding of the mid-1790s in Upper Canada, Elizabeth Simcoe's diary is invaluable. John Ross Robertson's fully annotated version appeared as *The Diary of Mrs. John Graves Simcoe, Wife of the First Lieutenant-Governor of the Province of Upper Canada, 1792–6* (Toronto: Coles, 1973 [1911]).

Mary Quayle Innis has edited an abridged version, Mrs. Simcoe's Diary (Toronto: Macmillan, 1965). For information on Molly Brant, see Barbara Graymont's sketch in *Dictionary of Canadian Biography,* vol. 4, 1771–1800 (Toronto: University of Toronto Press, 1979), pp. 416–19; Earle Thomas, *The Three Faces of Molly Brant* (Kingston, ON: Quarry Press, 1996); and Gretchen Green, "Molly Brant, Catharine Brant, and Their Daughters: A Study in Colonial Acculturation," *Ontario History* 81(3) (1989): 235–50.

Studies on Upper Canadian women include: Elizabeth Jane Errington, *Wives and Mothers, School Mistresses and Scullery Maids: Working Women in Upper Canada, 1790–1840* (Montreal/Kingston: McGill-Queen's University Press, 1995); Katherine McKenna, *A Life of Propriety: Anne Murray Powell and Her Family, 1755–1849* (Montreal/Kingston: McGill-Queen's University Press, 1994); Janice Potter MacKinnon, *While the Women Only Wept: Loyalist Refugee Women in Eastern Ontario* (Montreal/Kingston: McGill-Queen's University Press, 1993); George Sheppard, "'Wants and Privations': Women and the War of 1812 in Upper Canada," *Histoire sociale/Social History* 28 (May 1995): 159–79; and Cecilia Morgan, *Public Men and Virtuous Women: The Gendered Languages of Religion and Politics in Upper Canada, 1791–1850* (Toronto: University of Toronto Press, 1997). Colin Coates and Cecilia Morgan have written *Heroines and History: Representations of Madeline de Verchères and Laura Secord* (Toronto: University of Toronto Press, 2002). See also Marjorie Cohen, *Women's Work, Markets, and Economic Development in Nineteenth-Century Ontario* (Toronto: University of Toronto Press, 1988).

For a look at the early economy of Upper Canada, see Catharine Anne Wilson, *Tenants in Time: Family Strategies, Land, and Liberalism in Upper Canada, 1799–1871* (Montreal/Kingston: McGill-Queen's University Press 2009); John Clarke, *The Ordinary People of Essex: Environment, Culture, and Economy on the Frontier of Upper Canada* (Montreal/Kingston: McGill-Queen's University Press 2010); and William N.Y. Wylie's article "The Blacksmith in Upper Canada, 1784–1850: A Study of Technology Culture and Power," in Donald H. Akenson, ed., *Canadian Papers in Rural History,* vol. 7 (Gananoque: Langdale Press, 1990).

For the early history of Upper Canada politics, consult Elizabeth Jane Errington, *The Lion, the Eagle and Upper Canada: A Developing Colonial Ideology* (Montreal/Kingston: McGill-Queen's University Press, 1987); David Mills, *The Idea of Loyalty in Upper Canada, 1784–1850* (Montreal/Kingston: McGill-Queen's University Press, 1988); Jeffrey L. McNairn, *The Capacity to Judge: Public Opinion and Deliberative Democracy in Upper Canada, 1791–1854* (Toronto: University of Toronto Press, 2000); Nancy Christie, ed., *Transatlantic Subjects: Ideas, Institutions, and Social Experience in Post-Revolutionary British North America* (Montreal/Kingston: McGill-Queen's University Press, 2008); and Julia Roberts, *In Mixed Company: Taverns and Public Life in Upper Canada* (Vancouver: UBC Press 2008).

Economic issues are examined in Ch. 6 ("Upper Canada") of Kenneth Norrie and Douglas Owram's *A History of the Canadian Economy,* 2nd ed. (Toronto: Harcourt Brace, 1996), pp. 115–45. Consult also Douglas McCalla's *Planting the Province: The Economic History of Upper Canada, 1784–1870* (Toronto: University of Toronto Press, 1993).

A variety of sources are available covering immigration to British North America. Carl Bridge and Kent Fedorowich present a multifaceted examination of the British colonial world in their edited volume *The British World: Diaspora, Culture and Identity* (London: Frank Cass, 2003). For a look at Scottish immigration to British North America, see J.M. Bumsted, *The People's Clearances: Highland Emigration to British North America, 1770–1815* (Edinburgh: University of Edinburgh Press; Winnipeg: University of Manitoba Press, 1982). See also Peter E. Rider and Heather McNabb, eds., *A Kingdom of the Mind: The Scots' Impact on the Development of Canada* (Montreal/Kingston: McGill-Queen's University Press, 2006), and Lucille H. Campey, *The Scottish Pioneers of Upper Canada, 1784–1855: Glengarry and Beyond* (Toronto: Natural Heritage Books, 2005). For a look at English immigration, see Helen I. Cowan, *British Immigration to British North America: The First Hundred Years* (Toronto: University of Toronto Press, 1961), and Elizabeth Jane Errington, "British Migration and British America, 1783–1860s," in Philip Bruckner, ed., *Canada: The Oxford History of the British Empire* (Oxford: Oxford University Press, 2006). See also Elizabeth Jane Errington's *Emigrant Worlds and Transatlantic Communities: Migration to Upper Canada in the First Half of the Nineteenth Century* (Montreal/Kingston: McGill-Queen's University Press, 2007). Irish immigration is covered in Bruce Elliott, *Irish Migrants in the Canadas: A New Approach*. 2nd ed. (Montreal/Kingston: McGill-Queen's

University Press, 2004). See also Michael Kenneally, "Irish Immigration to Nineteenth-Century Canada: Alternative Narratives," *Canadian Issues* 27 (2005): 38–40.

The experience of the Six Nations in early Upper Canada is reviewed in Isabel Thompson Kelsay, *Joseph Brant, 1743–1807: Man of Two Worlds* (Syracuse: Syracuse University Press, 1984); and Charles M. Johnston, ed., *The Valley of the Six Nations: A Collection of Documents on the Indian Lands of the Grand River* (Toronto: Champlain Society, 1964). For a discussion of the Ojibwas, see Peter S. Schmalz, *The Ojibwa of Southern Ontario* (Toronto: University of Toronto Press, 1990); Donald B. Smith, *Sacred Feathers: The Reverend Peter Jones (Kahkewaquonaby) and the Mississauga Indians* (Toronto: University of Toronto Press, 1987); and Janet Chute, *The Legacy of Shingwaukonse: A Century of Native Leadership* (Toronto: University of Toronto Press, 1998). Five useful studies of the First Nations in the War of 1812 include John Sugden, *Tecumseh: A Life* (New York: Henry Holt, 1997); Robert S. Allen, *His Majesty's Indian Allies: British Indian Policy in the Defence of Canada, 1774–1815* (Toronto: Dundurn Press, 1992); Gregory Evans Dowd, *A Spirited Resistance: The North American Indian Struggle for Unity, 1745–1815* (Baltimore: Johns Hopkins University Press, 1992); Colin Calloway, *Crown and Calumet: British–Indian Relations, 1783–1815* (Norman: University of Oklahoma Press, 1987); and Carl Benn, *The Iroquois in the War of 1812* (Toronto: University of Toronto Press, 1998). For land and justice issues, consult as well Sidney L. Harring, *White Man's Law: Native People in Nineteenth-Century Canadian Jurisprudence* (Toronto: University of Toronto Press, 1998). Michelle A. Hamilton examines how settlers collected and interpreted Aboriginal artefacts in *Collections and Objections: Aboriginal Material Culture in Southern Ontario* (Montreal: McGill-Queen's University Press, 2010).

Daniel G. Hill's *The Freedom-Seekers: Blacks in Early Canada* (Agincourt, ON: Book Society of Canada, 1981) is a popular summary of the history of blacks in British North America. Robin W. Winks, *The Blacks in Canada: A History*, 2nd ed. (Montreal/Kingston: McGill-Queen's University Press, 1997) is useful. In *The Trail of the Black Walnut* (Toronto: McClelland & Stewart, 1957), G. Elmore Reaman tells the story of the Plain Folk and their arrival in Upper Canada. Marianne McLean has written a well-researched monograph on Ontario's easternmost county, *The People of Glengarry: Highlanders in Transition, 1745–1820* (Montreal/Kingston: McGill-Queen's University Press, 1991). For a look at the Quaker Community in nineteenth century Toronto, see Robynne Rogers Healey, *From Quaker to Upper Canadian: Faith and Community Among Yonge Street Friends, 1801–1850* (Montreal/Kingston: McGill-Queen's University Press, 2006).

A short summary of the War of 1812 appears in Wesley B. Turner, *The War of 1812: The War That Both Sides Won*, 2nd ed. (Toronto: Dundurn Press, 2000). A fuller overview is Victor Suthren, *The War of 1812* (Toronto: McClelland & Stewart, 1999); and Mark Zuehlke, *For Honour's Sake: The War of 1812 and the Brokering of an Uneasy Peace* (Toronto: Knopf Canada, 2006). Pierre Berton has written two very readable accounts of the conflict: *The Invasion of Canada, 1812–1813* (Toronto: McClelland & Stewart, 1980), and *Flames Across the Border, 1813–1814* (Toronto: McClelland & Stewart, 1981). George F.G. Stanley provides the best scholarly account in *The War of 1812: Land Operations* (Toronto: Macmillan, 1983). George Sheppard has written a social history of the War of 1812 in Upper Canada, *Plunder, Profit, and Paroles* (Montreal/Kingston: McGill-Queen's University Press, 1994). See also Mark Zuehlke, *For Honour's Sake: The War of 1812 and the Brokering of an Uneasy Peace* (Toronto: Random House, 2006); Terry Mcdonald, "'It Is Impossible for His Majesty's Government to Withdraw from These Dominions': Britain and the Defence of Canada, 1813 to 1814," *Journal of Canadian Studies/Revue d'études canadiennes* 39(3) (2005): 40–59; and J.I. Little, *Loyalties in Conflict: A Canadian Borderland in War and Rebellion, 1812–1840* (Toronto: University of Toronto Press, 2008). French-Canadian participation is covered in Martin F. Auger, "French-Canadian Participation in the War of 1812: A Social Study of the Voltigeurs Canadiens," *Canadian Military History* 10(3) (2001): 23–41. For a look at the attack on York, see Robert Malcomson, *Capital in Flames: The American Attack on York, 1813* (Toronto: Robin Brass Studio, 2008). For a look at the Maritimes during the War of 1812, see John Boileau, *Half-Hearted Enemies: Nova Scotia, New England, and the War of 1812* (Halifax: Formac, 2005). For a look at the experiences of women during the war, see Dianne Graves, *In the Midst of Alarms: Women in the War of 1812* (Toronto: Robin Brass 2007). Cheryl Macdonald has written a biography of Laura Secord, *Laura Secord* (Canmore: Altitude, 2005). For a look at gun ownership and gun culture in nineteenth-century Ontario, see Douglas McCalla, "Upper Canadians and Their Guns: An Exploration via Country Store Accounts (1808–61)," *Ontario History* 97(2) (2005): 121–37. For a look at loyalism, see Maya Jasanoff, "The Other Side of Revolution: Loyalists in the British Empire," *William and Mary Quarterly* 65(2) (2008): 205–32. Wesley B. Turner examines military leadership during the war in *British Generals in the War of 1812: High Command in the Canadas* (Montreal/Kingston: McGill-Queen's University Press, 2011).

A selection of maps can be found in *History in Maps* (Toronto: University of Toronto Press, 1984); and consult R. Louis Gentilcore, ed., *Historical Atlas of Canada*, vol. 2, *The Land Transformed, 1800–1891* (Toronto: University of Toronto Press, 1993). See also J.P.D. Dunbabin, "Motives for Mapping the Great Lakes: Upper Canada, 1782–1827," *Michigan Historical Review* 31(1) (2005): 1–43.

Valuable portraits of early Upper Canadian figures appear in *Dictionary of Canadian Biography*, vol. 4, *1770–1800*; vol. 5, *1800–1820*; and vol. 6, *1821–1835* (Toronto: University of Toronto Press, 1979, 1985, 1987). The volumes of the *Dictionary* are available online: wwww.bibliographi.ca.

Chapter Twelve

THE FUR TRADE AND THE NORTHWEST, 1700–1821

TIME LINE	
1670	Hudson's Bay Company Charter granted
1690	Henry Kelsey journeys into interior of North America
1730s	Pierre La Vérendrye establishes French posts around lakes Winnipeg
1761	French traders withdraw from interior
1780s	North West Company formed
1812	Selkirk colony established at Red River
1816	Battle of Seven Oaks
1818	49th Parallel becomes boundary from Lake Superior to Rocky Mountains
1821	Merger of Hudson's Bay Company and North West Company

The colonies of British North America seemed a world away from the vast Northwest, a land still dominated by the First Nations. As historian Gerald Friesen observes, "It is fair to say that from the mid-seventeenth century to the first decade of the nineteenth century, the northwest was remote from the struggles of imperial armies, the missions of religious orders, and the quest for riches that marked the history of European overseas expansion."[1] Whereas the First Nations of the Canadas and Maritimes experienced the process and impact of contact in the sixteenth and seventeenth centuries, the First Nations of the Northwest underwent the process centuries later. While the Canadians viewed the region as largely empty and unsettled wilderness—a fur reserve and potential agricultural settlement frontier—the area was home to the Ojibway, Cree, Assiniboine, Sioux, Blackfoot, Chippewa, Dene, and Inuit.

White incursions into the Northwest were under way in the seventeenth century, led by explorers still seeking the elusive Northwest Passage, but more often by the fur traders. Posts were constructed along the major river routes, extending from the Great Lakes, through Red River, into the Saskatchewan, and beyond into the Athabasca all the way to the Pacific Coast. Even though the whites were greatly outnumbered by the Aboriginals, the region became mired in a fur trade war between the two competing companies—the North West Company (NWC) and the Hudson's Bay Company (HBC).

A significant colony emerged at the confluence of the Red and Assiniboine rivers (present-day Winnipeg). The Red River colony was strategically situated at the logical supply point for the fur trade coming from the east through the St. Lawrence–Great Lakes system. It was here that the largest *Métis* (mixed-bloods created by the union of European fur traders and Aboriginal women) population emerged. But the colony became the central battleground in the violent fur trade war between the two competing commercial empires. When the Selkirk settlers arrived from Scotland in the early nineteenth century to make their home in Red River, the animosity increased.

Red River's economy was primarily based around the fur trade. The Métis were able to adapt to their changing economic conditions and manoeuvre between their white and "Indian" identities. Over time, they developed their own identity as the "New Nation." They worked the fur trade, supplying *pemmican*—dried buffalo meat mixed with buffalo fat and berries, the crucial foodstuff and "fuel" of the trade—but they were also skilled buffalo hunters. Agriculture also developed in the colony as the predominantly French Métis farmed strips of land along the rivers, much as their forefathers had done in Quebec. The arrival of the Selkirk settlers introduced large-scale agriculture to the colony and the British system of landholding.

The Métis generally worked for the North West Company (NWC), the offspring of the old Montreal-based fur trade. The Selkirk settlers, however, were brought in as part of a Hudson Bay Company (HBC) endeavour. According to the Charter of 1670, all land draining into Hudson's Bay was under the control of the HBC, Red River included. But the area had long served as the critical supply point for the Nor'Westers. The Métis and the Scottish settlers became caught up in the fur trade war. By 1821, the rivalry ended and the NWC was amalgamated into the HBC.

The Aboriginal Fur Trade

The First Nations dominated the fur trade in the interior. They far outnumbered the white traders (estimates put the pre-contact population in the area from Lake Superior to the Rockies at 15 000 to 50 000 people), they determined prices for trade goods, and they used the trade and their relations with the Europeans as strategic factors in their rivalries and conflicts with their neighbours. When the white traders entered the interior, they were aware that they were intruding upon Aboriginal territory.

A Mutually Beneficial Trade

When the Europeans began entering the vast Northwest in the seventeenth century, the First Nations consisted of the Ojibwa in the forestlands and shield country north of the Great Lakes, the Cree between Hudson Bay and the Manitoba Lakes, the Assiniboine west of Lake Superior and onto the southeastern plains, the Blackfoot on the southwestern plains, and the Chippewas north along the Churchill watershed. These nations had well established trade patterns long before the Europeans arrived. When contact and trade did commence, the whites understood that they had little choice but to follow Aboriginal custom and ritual. The success of the trade depended upon this accommodation. The First Nations controlled the rhythms of the trade.

At first, relations were relatively harmonious and both native and newcomer benefited. As time passed, however, and the process of contact took its toll, the First Nations became dependent on European trade goods and an era of inequality set in. But throughout the process, the Aboriginals demonstrated more agency than historians have traditionally recognized. As Friesen points out, "The image of European culture as 'pattern-maker' and of native culture as 'clay' were never accurate descriptions of fur-trade relationships."[2]

The Importance of the "Middlemen" Role

By the mid-seventeenth century, the Ojibwa were trading at Sault Ste. Marie with the French coming along the St. Lawrence–Great Lakes system. They served as middlemen with the Cree and Assiniboine to the north and west. The arrival of the English on Hudson Bay in the 1670s and 1680s, however, allowed the wide-ranging Cree to step into the role of middlemen. The fur trade caused the Ojibwa to move northwest to take better advantage. Likewise, it led the Cree to migrate west and become allies with the Assiniboine. The Blackfoot Confederacy (Niitsítapi, comprising the Peigan, Kainai, and Siksika) hunted the buffalo herds of the plains. By the early eighteenth century, they traded for European goods with the Assiniboine and Cree. The Chippewas of the Lake Athabasca region began trading with the NWC and HBC in the 1780s and 1790s.

The Gun and the Horse

The major innovations brought by the Europeans were the gun and the horse. But even though these technological factors influenced the culture of the First Nations, the change was not immediate. The horse, brought to Mexico by the Spanish, entered the area from the southwest and reached the Blackfoot on the plains around 1730. The gun came to the Cree via the English trading on Hudson Bay, and reached the plains around the same time: "The image of mounted armed plains warriors has since become the epitome of 'Indians'—the origin of North America's 'cowboy–Indian' version of western history—but it represents merely a brief moment, a century of flamboyance, in a story that is at least ten thousand years old."[3]

Firearms were often unreliable and they needed to be regularly repaired. Difficulties in obtaining ammunition also diminished their reliability. For buffalo hunting, the Plains groups preferred sinew-backed bows with metal-tipped arrows, which did not make a noise that prematurely stampeded a herd. Their experienced hunters could easily reload a bow on horseback. In battle, however, the Plains peoples recognized the value of firearms. Guns had obvious advantages. Bullets travelled a longer distance than arrows and had greater killing power, particularly in the open spaces of the prairies. Rawhide shields and armour offered little protection against a musket ball. In addition, the gun's loud report provided a psychological advantage in battle.

In the early eighteenth century, the Chippewas, armed with guns, moved further into the forested areas immediately north of the Woodland Cree. Directly supplied by the English at Churchill, the Chippewas sold European goods to interior nations. A Chippewan woman, Thanadelthur, for example, became an invaluable interpreter and envoy for the Hudson's Bay Company in the 1710s. Like the Woodland Cree farther south, the Chippewas became the traders' middlemen. In addition, European guns gave them an advantage in their struggle with the Inuit to the north and with the Cree. In 1770–72, Samuel Hearne, a HBC explorer, made an epic journey with a group of Chippewas across the barren lands from Churchill to the Arctic Ocean. His account, *A Journey from Prince of Wales's Fort, in Hudson's Bay, to the Northern Ocean*, remains one of the classics of North American travel literature, although now it is recognized that his publisher embellished the original text, apparently inventing entire scenes.

Migration and the adoption of new ways characterized the experience of the Lakota, or Sioux, farther to the south. In the eighteenth century, they moved out onto the plains. No consensus exists about the reason for the move. According to historian Peter Iverson, the Sioux and their neighbours, the Anishinabeg, have their own explanations. "The Ojibwas, for example, say they forced the Sioux, their word for 'enemy,' out of Minnesota, but the Lakota people do not subscribe to this story. Instead, they speak of their imagination and initiative in following the bison and tell how they sought out opportunities for trade and expansion, which could be realized only in the West."[4]

The Cree already lived along the North Saskatchewan River in the late eighteenth century, but their repeated intrusions ended their initially friendly relations with the Blackfoot. Individual Cree bands travelled over the plains independently. No single chief coordinated the expansion. As historian Hugh Dempsey observes, the chiefs "did not order their people to move, they simply told them their own plans. A good chief had a faithful following, and they would go with him; but if for any reason his people disagreed with him, they were free to make their own decisions."[5]

The horse caused a cultural revolution on the Great Plains. It became a symbol of wealth. Some individuals owned up to 100 horses. By giving away or even lending horses, they enhanced their prestige. Horses were borrowed for hunting and for war parties, with the borrower returning in payment a portion of the game killed or of the goods seized.

The horse had the most impact on the Blackfoot, who used them for hunting buffalo. Horse-mounted warriors replaced those on foot in driving and luring the animals into buffalo pounds or over cliffs (buffalo jumps). Mounted hunters rushed straight into a herd, singled out an animal, rode beside it, and killed it at close range with two or three arrows from their bows. The Blackfoot sought five qualities in their buffalo horses: the ability to sustain a high speed over a distance of several kilometres; instant response to commands; quick movement alongside a buffalo while staying clear of it and its horns; the ability to run swiftly without stumbling over uneven ground; and finally, the ability to remain controlled in face of stampeding buffalo. A trained horse was worth several simple riding or pack animals.

The introduction of the horse had other consequences. It intensified warfare between First Nations. Combat on horseback with a bow and arrow, lance, war club, or knife—or a European rifle—led to increased casualties. The horse enabled the Woodland Assiniboine and many of the Woodland Cree to hunt buffalo on the prairies, lessening their dependence on European guns and trade goods but also increasing rivalry among First Nations. The Plains peoples, particularly the Blackfoot, became highly mobile.

The European Fur Trade

The first excursions into the Northwest came in search of the fabled passage to the Orient. Since Verrazzano's voyage in 1524, the French believed in the existence of a gulf that cut deeply into the continent from the Pacific, like Hudson Bay or the Gulf of Mexico. Jacques Cartier's journeys up the St. Lawrence in the 1530s and 1540s were driven by his determination to locate China. When René-Robert Cavelier de La Salle travelled inland in 1669 in search of China, his neighbours named his land grant on the south bank of Montreal Island "La Chine" (China), in recognition of his ambition

Indian Greeting White Man *by Frederic Remington.*

Source: Frederick S. Remington, *The Parley*, no date, Collection of Glenbow Museum, Calgary, Canada, 60.2.20.

to reach the Orient by way of "la Mer de l'ouest" (the Western Sea). Half a century later, the French still hoped that somewhere between the fortieth and fiftieth parallels of latitude a navigable strait joined the Western Sea to the Pacific Ocean.

The Search for the "Western Sea"

In 1717, the French Crown approved expeditions to discover the Western Sea, but would not pay for them. Instead profits from fur-trade posts west of Lake Superior were to cover the exploration costs. Then, in 1730, Pierre Gaultier de Varennes et de La Vérendrye, commander of the fur-trading post at Kaministiquia (present-day Thunder Bay), offered to establish a post on Lake Winnipeg. He agreed to conduct explorations for the Western Sea from this base, at no expense to the Crown.

From Kaministiquia, La Vérendrye travelled westward in the 1730s, building fur-trading posts in the Lake of the Woods district and around lakes Winnipeg and Winnipegosis. In 1753, the Chevalier de La Corne founded a fort farther west, near the forks of the north and south branches of the Saskatchewan River. The French never found "la Mer de l'ouest," but they did locate the route to the interior—the Saskatchewan River, whose twin branches flow through the central plains.

Inland Expeditions from Hudson Bay

With the French controlling the St. Lawrence and access to the interior through the Great Lakes, the English circumvented their influence by establishing a fur trade from the north in the late seventeenth century, on Hudson Bay. From these forts they traded with the Cree, who served as a buffer and came to live around the posts, known as "Homeguard Bands." The Cree and the Assiniboine to the south became the middlemen in the Hudson's Bay Company fur trade. By 1784, 300 canoes and 700 people visited York Factory, and 70 percent of the trade was conducted by these Aboriginal middlemen. European goods flowed through them and the established Aboriginal trade networks, and were dispersed throughout the southwest. It was through the Cree that trade goods reached the Assiniboine and the Blackfoot on the Great Plains.

The English sponsored only two inland expeditions southwest from York Factory, their major post on Hudson Bay. In 1690–91 they sent Henry Kelsey, a young employee, known to the HBC committee in London as "a very active lad, delighting much in Indians' company, being never more pleased than when he is travelling amongst them," to explore the interior. He left from York Factory with a Cree band and reached the prairies, around present-day east-central Saskatchewan. But upon his return the company decided not to establish costly forts in the interior. As long as the Cree and the Assiniboine brought good furs to them, the English would stay on Hudson Bay.

The French provided some opposition to the English trade from the Bay. In 1686, the Chevalier de Troyes captured several HBC forts. By the Treaty of Utrecht in 1713, however, France recognized England's possession of the coastline of Hudson and James Bays. But the French

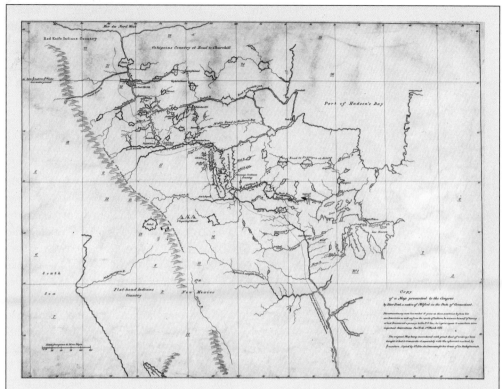

Peter Pond's map of the interior of North America c. 1785. This is one of the earliest maps that define the Prairies with the Great Lakes, the Canadian Shield, and the Rocky Mountains.

Source: Library and Archives Canada/NMC-44280.

continued to trade in the interior, building a chain of forts from the Lake of the Woods to the Saskatchewan, while for the next fifty years the English trade was restricted to the Bay, with only a handful of ships arriving annually. The French trade cut straight across the English trade. As competition intensified, the English had to change their tactics and become more aggressive.

In 1754, the HBC sent Anthony Henday inland to convince the Plains nations to give up their trade at the French posts and to come to the Bay. In his journal, which is far more precise than Kelsey's, Henday identified the specific groups in the interior (Assiniboines and Blackfoot) and provided notes on their way of life. The young trader became the first Englishman to describe the buffalo hunt. Henday returned to York Factory with an Aboriginal wife, who had helped him immeasurably as an interpreter, an assistant, and a reliable source of information. But he was less successful in convincing the Plains nations to make the long journey to the Bay to trade. His journeys did convince HBC traders to travel inland in pursuit of furs.

The Fur Trade After the Fall of New France

The Seven Years' War damaged the French fur trade out of Montreal. After the fall of New France in 1760, the Hudson's Bay Company expected to have a trade monopoly in the Northwest. The St. Lawrence trade, however, was quickly reorganized. The HBC failed to take advantage of the situation, and independent fur traders from Montreal, led by veteran voyageurs, maintained the trade. In

Hudson's Bay Company employees.
Source: Library and Archives Canada/C-82974.

York boats in front of Cross Lake, ca. 1910 *by Walter J. Phillips.*
Source: Hudson's Bay Company Archives, Archives of Manitoba

the early 1780s, Scottish and American fur traders formed the North West Company (whose agents came to be called "Nor'Westers"), a decentralized fur-trading operation that soon expanded beyond the French fur trade in the West to include the Peace, Mackenzie, and Columbia River districts.

The Emergence of the North West Company

The North West Company took over from the old French fur trade. Its major advantage was its transportation system, which ran from Montreal, up the St. Lawrence, and through the Great Lakes into the Northwest. It was serviced by a massive warehouse at Fort William, on the west shore of Lake Superior. Vast cargoes of trade goods and supplies traveled westward in the spring and great cargoes of furs made the journey eastward in high summer.

The North West Company relied on experienced French-Canadian, Métis, and Iroquois tripmen. These hardy voyageurs crossed half a continent. On the journey, they slept no more than six hours a day. They paddled 12 to 15, even 18, hours a day. With their light paddles and rapid strokes, they made 40 to 60 strokes a minute. They regularly "portaged" loads of 80 and sometimes 120 kilograms, on their backs over rocky trails.

The NWC had other advantages as well. It instituted a system of profit-sharing with its wintering partners while the HBC maintained a corporate structure with all decisions being made in distant London, England. As a result, the NWC reacted to the realities of the trade on the ground and its policies were more workable. In addition, the experience of the Nor'Westers led it to expand into the richest fur areas and to concentrate on the most valuable pelts (mink, marten, and beaver over wolf, bear, and moose).

The North West Company expanded in the 1780s and 1790s. In 1778, fur trader Peter Pond reached the Athabasca and Peace River country (in present-day northern Alberta), rich with fur-bearing animals. He was encouraged by the Chippewa to establish a post on Lake Athabasca. In 1789, Alexander Mackenzie journeyed down the Mackenzie River and, in 1793, reached the Pacific Ocean. The NWC then opened up posts in the Mackenzie Basin and, later, along the

Columbia River. Despite a chartered monopoly on all lands draining into Hudson Bay and an apparent geographic advantage, the NWC dominated the fur trade.

If the HBC ever took full advantage, however, the situation would change. The HBC had a shorter, hence less expensive, transportation route. The smaller company could take trade goods to the Athabasca country at about one-half the cost. The HBC York boats, although slower and much heavier than canoes, could carry greater amounts of trade goods in and more fur bundles out than the Nor'Westers' canoes could. The cost of sending goods over a supply line that stretched from Montreal to Fort Chipewyan on Lake Athabasca curbed NWC profits. Still the Nor'Wester organization grew and, in 1804, incorporated the XY Company (formed in the late 1790s by independent Montreal fur traders).

Rivalry between the North West Company and the Hudson's Bay Company

Competition from the NWC forced the HBC to go farther inland to obtain the best furs. In 1774 the HBC established a post at Cumberland House. The expansion of the two companies led to the elimination of the Cree and Assiniboine middlemen, as both the Nor'Westers and the HBC established direct contact with the interior hunting bands. The Woodland Assiniboine and the Woodland Cree moved out onto the prairies and became provisioners, supplying the two trading

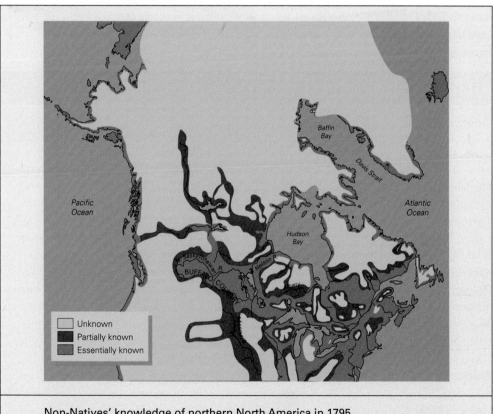

Non-Natives' knowledge of northern North America in 1795.

Source: Adapted from Richard I. Ruggles, *A Country So Interesting: The Hudson's Bay Company and Two Centuries of Mapping, 1670–1870* (Montreal/Kingston: McGill-Queen's University Press, 1991), p. 73.

companies with pemmican, which was easy to transport, kept well, and provided a nutritious, balanced diet. The demand for pemmican proved enormous: a voyageur consumed nearly a kilogram a day—the equivalent of about three kilograms of fresh meat.

Aboriginal Women in the Fur Trade

Aboriginal women played an indispensable role in the fur trade. Besides providing companionship and emotional support, they served as partners, guides, interpreters, diplomats, and scouts. The women knew how to survive in the harsh climate, and they could often carry almost as much of a load as their husbands. The daughter of a leading Aboriginal hunter or chief brought to her new husband the trade of his new father-in-law, as well as his immediate relations. Moreover, the women made pemmican, gathered berries, fished, dressed skins, and made moccasins and snowshoes. But the relationships were usually mutually beneficial. They were used by the First Nations to cement trade relations, gain credit, and guarantee weapons and supplies. Historians traditionally ignored this critical role, instead focusing on the economic functions of the trade and emphasizing the masculine character of the voyageurs.

By the early 1800s, interracial marriage between Europeans and the First Nations had become so common that about 1000 First Nations women and mixed-blood children lived at North West Company posts. The company encouraged its workers to marry the mixed-blood daughters of the older employees rather than First Nations women, in an effort to reduce the number of dependants at its posts and thereby the demands for assistance. Many young mixed-blood women had the ideal background for life as wives at a fur-trading post: they knew both the skills of their First Nations ancestors and the domestic duties required at the post—cleaning, planting, and harvesting.

A HISTORICAL PORTRAIT

George Nelson

Among the most celebrated fur traders of the late eighteenth and early nineteenth centuries were Samuel Hearne, David Thompson, Alexander Mackenzie, Simon Fraser, Peter Fidler, and Peter Pond. A less celebrated trader was the lowly, underpaid North West Company clerk George Nelson. He produced no great maps or surveys, made no great voyages of exploration, and never rose to administrative heights. In contrast to his younger brothers—Wolfred Nelson, a Patriote in the Lower Canada Rebellion of 1837 and later mayor of Montreal, and Robert Nelson, the Patriotes' leader in 1838 and later a successful surgeon in the United States—he achieved no fame in his lifetime.

But George Nelson was important. According to historians Jennifer Brown and Robert Brightman, his chief distinction comes from his sensitive recording, in a memoir written nearly two centuries ago, of western Cree and Ojibwa beliefs.[1] Nelson listened to the people and carefully recorded their stories. Historians Sylvia Van Kirk and Jennifer Brown describe his memoir as "one of the finest early ethnographic documents of its kind."[2]

George Nelson (1786–1859) was the son of loyalists from New York who fled to Quebec to escape the American Revolution. As the son of an English Protestant schoolmaster, Nelson received a good education. From the age of 16, when he entered the fur trade, he lived among First Nations people. From 1802 to 1823 he served as a clerk in present-day Wisconsin, northwestern Ontario, Manitoba, and Saskatchewan. He married Mary Ann, an Ojibwa woman, who was a valuable helpmate in his work. Upon his retirement from the fur trade, they settled with their four daughters at Sorel, just east of Montreal.

During his years in the Northwest, Nelson wrote constantly. Many of his fur-trade journals and his reminiscences (written ten to forty years after the events they describe) have survived and are valuable for an understanding of the Aboriginal peoples of the Northwest. His memoir of 1823, written in his last year in the fur trade, while Nelson was stationed at Lac la Ronge in northeastern Saskatchewan, however, is the most important because it offers insight into the religion and myths of the Cree and Ojibwa.

Nelson provided details of the religious lives of the Cree and Ojibwa, including an account of the shaking tent ceremony used by religious leaders to see into the future. He discussed the role, importance, and significance of dreams. Nelson also relayed the legend of the mythical being known as the Windigo: "Suffice it to say that they are of uncommon size—Goliath is an unborn infant to them: and to add to their dread, they are represented as possessing much of the Power of Magicians. Their head reaching to the tops of the highest Poplars (about 70, or 80, feet)."[3]

Nelson's life in Lower Canada after his retirement was unhappy. His wife died in 1831. Only one of their children survived into adulthood. Nelson became estranged from his brothers, Wolfred and Robert, on account of their participation in the Rebellions of 1837–38. He regarded their activities as treason. As a farmer he had little success. His greatest joy after his wife's death seems to have come from writing his reminiscences of his days in "Indian country," the 1823 portion of which has been edited by Brown and Brightman. He died in 1859 at the age of 73.

1. Jennifer S.H. Brown and Robert Brightman, *"The Orders of the Dreamed": George Nelson on Cree and Northern Ojibwa Religion and Myth, 1823* (Winnipeg: University of Manitoba Press, 1988).

2. Sylvia Van Kirk, in collaboration with Jennifer S.H. Brown, "George Nelson," *Dictionary of Canadian Biography,* vol. 8, *1851–1860* (Toronto: University of Toronto Press, 1985), p. 653.

3. Brown and Brightman, p. 86.

WHERE HISTORIANS DISAGREE

The Aboriginal Fur Trade

For years, historians took a Eurocentric approach to the fur trade. The Europeans, it was argued, were technologically advanced and brought "civilization" to the "savages" through their advanced trade goods. Whereas the Aboriginals obtained mere "trinkets," the Europeans gained valuable furs and pelts. Whereas the Europeans came from vast commercial empires with long economic histories, the Aboriginals possessed no concept of economics, land ownership, or material wealth. As a result, the First Nations were ignorant passive agents (often dupes) in a trade dominated by more advanced European traders.

Evidence of this one-sided relationship could be found in the dependent state in which most First Nations eventually found themselves. In *The Fur Trade and the Northwest to 1857*, for instance, E.E. Rich wrote

> within a decade of their becoming acquainted with European goods, tribe after tribe became utterly dependent on regular European supplies. The bow and arrow went out of use, and the Indian starved if he did not own a serviceable gun, powder, and shot; and in his tribal wars he was even more dependent on European arms.[1]

In the 1970s and early 1980s, historians such as Arthur J. Ray, Robin Fisher, Daniel Francis, Toby Morantz, and Paul C. Thistle challenged this interpretation by examining the trade from the perspective of the First Nations. What the Europeans considered mere trinkets were remarkable timesaving tools for the Aboriginals, such as steel-bladed knives, axe heads, and copper pots. In return, the Europeans were gaining mere animal skins, which were numerous and easy to obtain. Who was duping whom? These historians underlined the independence of the Aboriginal peoples and their power in the trade. The First Nations had well established trade patterns that went back centuries. While their notions of economics differed from the Europeans, they certainly existed. And they negotiated with marked skill in order to gain the best deals possible. Historian Olive Dickason summarized the new approach:

> Common to all of these works is the theme that Amerindians were as aware as Europeans in matters of self-interest, and during the early days of the fur trade at least, were able to manipulate matters to their own advantage. As long as they held the monopoly in fur production, they were also able to dictate the terms by which they were willing to trade. It was only when the exploitative nature of the fur trade began to affect the availability of resources, coupled with the widening technological gap that was a consequence of the Industrial Revolution, that Europeans were able to gain the upper hand.[2]

The move away from a Eurocentric approach led to a recognition of the roles played by the Aboriginals in the fur trade as partners and initiators, as well as consumers. They exercised agency and became involved on their own initiative. As historian Robin Fisher notes,

> The Indians of the Northwest coast exercised a great deal of control over the trading relationship and, as a consequence, remained in control of their culture during this early contact period.[3]

He added:

> Even in these early years, the Indians were not passive objects of exploitation. Rather, they vigorously grew accustomed to the presence of the Europeans; they also became shrewder in trading with them.[4]

The absence of Aboriginal voices in the form of written narratives helps explain the Eurocentric character of this early history but it remains a weakness for those doing research into the fur trade. Daniel Francis questions whether historians have actually overemphasized the importance of the fur trade in the life of the average Aboriginal. In his *Battle for the West: Fur Traders and the Birth of Western Canada,* he observes that

> the two groups met briefly at the posts to exchange goods, each receiving from the other things it could not produce for itself. Then they parted, the Indians returning to a world the trader never entered or understood, a world with its own patterns of trade, its own religion and social relations, its own wars and alliances. . . . [For] the most part traders were peripheral to the real concerns of the Indian people.[5]

Historians of Aboriginal descent are attempting to compensate for the absence of First Nations accounts. Within this field, there is also a debate on the accuracy and usefulness of oral history.[6]

1. E.E. Rich, *The Fur Trade and the Northwest to 1857* (Toronto: McClelland & Stewart, 1967), pp. 102–3.

2. Olive Dickason, "Review of *Indian–European Trade Relations in the Lower Saskatchewan River Region to 1840* by Paul C. Thistle," *Western Canadian Publications Project Newsletter* 21 (May 1987): 2.

3. Robin Fisher, *Contact and Conflict: Indian–European Relations in British Columbia, 1774–1890* (Vancouver: University of British Columbia Press, 1977), p. 1.

4. Fisher, p. 4.

5. Daniel Francis, *Battle for the West: Fur Traders and the Birth of Western Canada* (Edmonton: Hurtig, 1982), p. 62.

6. George Blondin, *When the World Was New: Stories of the Sahtú Dene* (Yellowknife: Outcrop Books, 1990); Edward Ahenakew, *Voices of the Plains Cree,* Ruth M. Buck, ed. (Regina: Canadian Plains Research Center, 1995 [1973]).

The Métis

As the fur traders intermarried with Aboriginal women, a group of "mixed-bloods," or *Métis,* appeared. The number of mixed marriages grew steadily. After a generation or two, Métis settlements extended from the upper Great Lakes west to the Red River and south through the Great Plains to the Arkansas River. Their culture blended Aboriginal and European customs. While some mixed-bloods lived with their mother's families and were accepted as "Indian" and others lived with their fathers and were viewed as white, many found themselves a people "in-between." Over time, they constructed a new identity and saw themselves as constituting a "new nation." In 1818, William McGillivray of the North West Company commented that the Métis "one and all look upon themselves as members of an independent tribe of natives, entitled to a property in the soil, to a flag of their own, and to protection from the British government."

The Métis (or "half-breeds" as they were then commonly known) emerged from relations with both NWC and HBC employees. In the period from 1770 to 1820 they exercised considerable influence in the fur trade. As historian Gerhard Ens has shown, they adapted remarkably well to their constantly changing economic milieu. They were buffalo hunters, farmers, trappers, traders, boatmen, intermediaries, and interpreters. While a British mixed-blood population emerged, the majority of the population was French and Catholic.

French and Métis voyageurs travelled throughout the area that is present-day western Canada and the United States. They introduced a number of French-based words to describe the new terrain: "coulee" (from *coulée*) for a deep gulch or ravine; "butte" for a flat-topped hill; and "prairie" (from *pré*) for meadow. The French also left a permanent record of their presence in the pronunciation of place names—for instance, in the silent terminal "s" of Arkansas and Illinois.

Susan, a Swampy Cree mixed-blood woman.

Source: Toronto Reference Library/T14359.

The blending of French and Aboriginal worlds through the Métis led to the development of a new language—French Cree, or, as the Métis call it, "Michif." According to linguist John C. Crawford, "The extraordinary characteristic of Michif is the manner in which French and Cree components combine; the noun phrase is a French domain; verb structure is clearly and thoroughly Cree, and syntax is Cree with French and probably English influence."[6] Bungee, a dialect of English with a strong Cree and Ojibwa component, evolved among the Aboriginal peoples who lived close to the Scottish settlement by the Red River.

The Métis at Red River

In the early nineteenth century, encampments of the French and their mixed-blood descendants developed at the junction ("The Forks") of the Red and the Assiniboine rivers (at present-day Winnipeg). The site on the borders of the shield and prairie, at a confluence of the rivers, had long served as an Aboriginal gathering point. It became the logical supply point of the fur trade.

The increasing number of intermarriages furthered the growth of the "new nation" of the Métis. Like the mixed-bloods on the upper Great Lakes, the Red River Métis built homes of squared logs covered with bark roofs. They made a special baking-powder biscuit called "bannock," a staple food in Métis communities. Although they undertook small-scale farming in the habitant tradition of riverfront lots or growing peas and potatoes in small gardens behind their cabins, they lived mainly off the buffalo hunt in the early nineteenth century.

The buffalo were the great wonder of the prairies. When Henry Kelsey and Anthony Henday first reached the vast open plains, they commented on the seemingly endless herds. Estimates indicate that 50 to 60 million roamed on the Great Plains in the early nineteenth century. John Tanner, a Virginia boy kidnapped and later adopted by the Odawa, recalled that near Pembina in the Red River area, he held his ear to the ground and heard the sound of a distant herd. Later he discovered that the herd at that point was still 30 kilometres away. Half a century later, in southern Alberta, John Palliser reported that he heard the approaching buffalo long before he saw them: "Their particular grunt sounded like the roar of distant rapids in a large river."

Yet by the mid-1860s, the buffalo had vanished due to overhunting by whites, Aboriginals, and Métis. According to historian Olive Dickason, "The bison, once 'countless' because they were so many, were rapidly becoming 'countless' because there were none left."[7] The slaughter of the buffalo had massive ramifications for the Plains nations.

As a mixed-blood people, the Métis introduced European technology to prairie life. For example, they introduced the small wagons used by the French Canadians in Quebec. These "Red River carts," built entirely of wood and tied together with leather, were easy to repair and efficient to use. To cross a river, one simply took off the wheels, some of which were 2 metres in diameter, strapped them underneath the cart, and used the vehicle as a raft. But the carts' constant rubbing of wood against wood made a terrible noise (one observer described it as the sound of a thousand fingernails being drawn across a thousand panes of glass at the same time). As well, the carts stirred up clouds of dust that could be seen several kilometres away. Still, the Red River carts aided the Métis during their communal buffalo hunts. An ox-drawn cart could carry a load of 400 kilograms more than 30 kilometres in a day. Several carts could be tied together in a caravan, enabling one driver to handle five oxen and carts. Soon, the Red River cart trails rivalled the rivers as transportation routes.

The Red River Colony

In 1811, Lord Douglas, the fifth earl of Selkirk, and a leading shareholder in the Hudson's Bay Company, persuaded the company to establish a

Red River carts by the North Saskatchewan River, 1871.

Source: Post Office Department / Library and Archives Canada/ PA-061689.

European agricultural colony at the forks of the Red and Assiniboine rivers. Legally, the area was under HBC control because the Red River flowed into Hudson Bay. But it was the NWC that dominated the Red River area. Selkirk hoped that a new colony in Red River would provide a home to retire in for HBC employees and their Aboriginal wives and families. It would become an agricultural centre to supply provisions for the company's workforce in the interior.

The following year, Selkirk recruited the majority of his settlers from Kildonan, Sutherlandshire, where the clearances of the tenant farmers to make sheep runs had been particularly brutal. Earlier, he had settled 800 displaced Highlanders on Prince Edward Island and had begun a less successful settlement at Baldoon on Lake St. Clair in Upper Canada. After his family acquired a controlling interest in the Hudson's Bay Company, Selkirk obtained from the company an enormous land grant of 300 000 square kilometres in the Red River valley—five times the size of Scotland—that he named Assiniboia. The location was contentious, because it lay across

A drawing of the Selkirk Settlement, established in 1812.

Source: Library and Archives Canada, Acc. No. 1993-208-1./C008714.

the North West Company's vital pemmican supply line in the heart of the Red River valley, thus threatening to curtail its supply of pemmican.

The Establishment of the Selkirk Colony

After arriving too late in the autumn and being forced to spend their first winter on the shores of Hudson Bay, and then having to undergo an incredibly arduous journey from the Bay to Red River, the advance party of 18 of Selkirk's settlers reached their destination in late August 1812. Another 120 joined them in late October. Miles Macdonell, Selkirk's choice as governor, established the settlers near the junction of the Red and the Assiniboine Rivers (now downtown Winnipeg).

Daily life for the Scottish settlers did not get any easier after arriving in Red River. The philanthropic but impractical Lord Selkirk sent them off without ploughs, with only hoes and spades to use for cultivation. To make matters worse, the colony's lifeline of communication stretched back more than 1000 kilometres to York Factory, a tiny fort on Hudson Bay, visited only once a year by ships from Britain. To survive the first winter, the newly arrived colonists had to travel 125 kilometres south to encamp near the HBC post at Pembina. The following year, only their potatoes yielded well, thus forcing the settlers to spend another rugged Red River winter at Pembina,

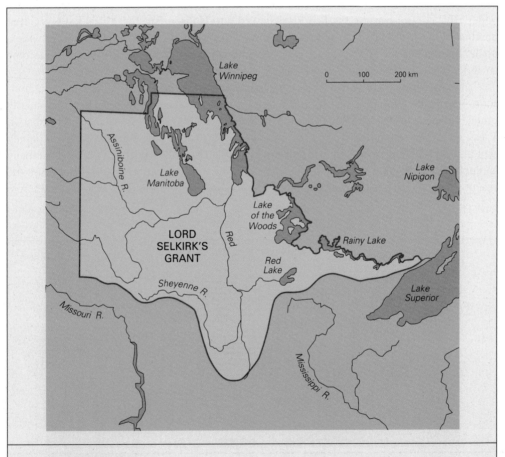

Lord Selkirk's Grant.

Source: Based on Gerald Friesen, *Canadian Prairies: A History* (Toronto: University of Toronto Press, 1984), pp. 90–91.

this time in log huts. Only the assistance of the local Métis and North West Company traders enabled the Selkirk settlers to survive those first two years.

Inevitably, the competition between the HBC and the NWC (which was reaching its peak) became a serious factor in the survival of the Selkirk colony. It did not take long for Governor Macdonell to take actions that went directly against the interests of the NWC, antagonizing the Métis. Facing food shortages for the colony, he issued a "pemmican proclamation" in January 1814 that placed an embargo on the export of that food from the Red River settlement. In July he issued another proclamation, forbidding the running of buffalo because the practice was driving the valuable food source further away from the colony. These actions posed a deliberate threat to the NWC. The proclamations confirmed the Nor'Westers' suspicions that the Hudson's Bay Company had planted the Red River colony to ruin them. They retaliated first by offering the Selkirk settlers free transport to new homes and better land in Upper Canada. In 1815, two-thirds of the 200 settlers accepted. Then, the Nor'Westers arrested Miles Macdonell, forced the remaining settlers to withdraw, and burned the settlement. Selkirk retaliated by sending more settlers to reoccupy the colony, along with a new governor, Robert Semple.

The following year, the fur trade rivalry intensified between the two companies. In the Athabasca region, in particular, the fur trade war took on a nasty character as the HBC tried to move in on NWC territory. It was, quite literally, a war. Rival traders, even though they were far in the interior and away from any official manifestation of the companies, still sought to obstruct each others' trade and kill each other, if the opportunity presented itself. The men would even allow their rivals to starve to death, rather than help them.

The NWC selected Cuthbert Grant, the well-educated son of a Scottish Nor' Wester and a Cree mother, and three French Métis to head a movement to drive out the Selkirk colonists. The Métis planned an attack on the settlement. They captured HBC pemmican boats and plundered posts.

The Battle of Seven Oaks

On June 19, 1816, near a shady grove called Seven Oaks, Grant and a party of some 60 or 70 Métis confronted Governor Robert Semple and about 25 settlers and Hudson's Bay Company employees. The Métis were attempting to move pemmican they had seized from the HBC posts on the Qu'Appelle River to NWC men on Lake Winnipeg. They tried to travel around the forks, controlled by the HBC. When fighting broke out, Semple and 20 of his men were killed. Only one of Grant's men was killed. Selkirk responded by bolstering the defences of the colony and hiring 90 mercenaries from the Swiss and German de Meuron regiment, fresh from service in the War of 1812.

The victory strengthened Métis unity by reinforcing their emerging identity in the Red River valley. Within hours,

The HBC and NWC forts at Pembina on the Red River, which had recently merged in 1822. Fort Gibraltar, belonging to the NWC, is on the left; the HBC post, Fort Douglas, on the right.

Source: Library and Archives Canada, Acc. No. 1988-250-33.

The Hudson's Bay Company flag, last flown in Winnipeg in 1925 for the 250th anniversary of the founding of the company. In the Canadian northwest, old hunters said the initials on the flag stood for "Here before Christ," because, as American writer Julian Ralph commented in 1892, "no matter how far away from the frontier a man might go, in regions he fancied no white man had been, that flag and those letters stared him in the face."

Source: AX 52, HBC Flag, North America, Cotton, Canvass, Brass, 91 cm × 45 cm, Collection of Glenbow Museum, Calgary, Canada

the conflict was retold in the "Chanson de la grenouillère," or "Song of Frog Plain," by Pierre Falcon, the prairie Métis bard. Their collective memory of the victory gave them a sense of unity and a common identity. To the Selkirk settlers, it was not a battle, but a massacre.

The Merger of the North West and Hudson's Bay Companies

By 1820, the tables had turned and the HBC was becoming the more profitable company. Internal divisions, the length of the supply lines, and the Athabasca War damaged the NWC. In addition, the violence at Red River prompted the British government to seek a forced solution to the "private war" and demonstrated a distinct lack of law and order in the territory. With Selkirk's death, the British pressured the two financially exhausted companies to unite. In 1821, the HBC and NWC companies merged. The consolidated company, the Hudson's Bay Company, ended the North West Company's trade route via Montreal. The company shipped its furs through Hudson Bay. After 1821, only 5 percent of the furs exported from British North America passed through Montreal.

George Simpson, nicknamed "the Little Emperor" by his employees, became the governor of the newly restructured Hudson's Bay Company for the next forty years, until his death in 1860. He had jurisdiction over an area that included Hudson Bay, the Arctic and Pacific oceans, and the Missouri River. Simpson introduced strict conservation measures in areas that had been overtrapped, laid off hundreds of redundant employees, kept salaries down, and closed unnecessary posts. The HBC became the undisputed colonial masters of the vast Northwest.

Red River Society

The fur trade war was over, but difficulties remained for the Red River settlers. Attempts to establish an agricultural colony were beset by plagues of grasshoppers in 1818–19 and a massive flood that levelled the settlement in 1826. Whenever the Red River overflowed its banks, the water spread quickly over huge areas because of the maturity and therefore the flatness of the valley. In 1826, in just one day, the flood waters rose nearly 3 metres, transforming the settlement into a lake. Houses were swept away that winter; the survivors dug cellars in the prairie, roofed them with sod, and lived underground. Floods would strike the Red River colony twice more during the century, in 1852 and 1882. Frosts destroyed the colony's crops totally or partially at least once every decade from 1810 to 1870.

Only by the 1840s, did the settlement of some 6000 inhabitants achieve a level of stability and prosperity. The land was fertile and well suited for agriculture, if the disasters could be avoided. The Métis, almost half the total population of the Red River colony, resided south and west of the forks of the two rivers. To the north, down the Red River toward Lake Winnipeg, lived the English mixed-bloods, the descendants of British fur traders and their Aboriginal wives; they comprised about a third of the settlement. Their neighbours, the original Selkirk settlers from

Scotland, represented about a tenth of the Red River population, and the local Ojibwa and Assiniboine made up another tenth.

The English Mixed-Bloods

The English mixed-bloods generally came from the northern HBC posts. Many of their ancestors actually came from the Orkney Islands, northwest of Scotland. Before 1800, the HBC recruited more than 80 percent of its personnel from the Orkneys. Most of them were under 21 years of age. They worked as contract labourers for three or four years before returning home, but some stayed and fathered families. Many used their savings to provide for their "country wives" and Aboriginal children before leaving to retire in the Orkneys or in Scotland.

Métis Encampment on a Buffalo Hunt, *a painting by Paul Kane.*

Source: With permission of the Royal Ontario Museum © ROM 912.1.25.

With the establishment of Selkirk's permanent settlement, many retired employees of the company now stayed in the Red River colony with their families and introduced their children to farming. Many also joined the Anglican Church, first established by the Reverend John West in 1820. A few obtained positions in the Hudson's Bay Company. Although racial bonds and the common use of the Cree or Ojibwa languages united the English and French Métis, ethnicity, religion, and their place of residence in the Red River colony divided them. According to historian John Foster, the "Country-born" (as he called the English mixed-bloods) "moved comfortably among the Métis. Others were more at home with the Indians. . . . Still others served a leadership role among the Kildonan Scots. Equal diversity could be found in terms of occupation and wealth."[8] Generally, however, the English mixed-bloods were viewed as more "white" than the Métis because they were more prone to be educated and to farm, considered markers of European "civilization."

The French Métis

The French Métis created a cohesive community, unified, in particular, by their Roman Catholic faith. The arrival of the first Catholic priests in the Red River settlement in 1818, followed by the first Oblate missionaries and the first sisters, the Grey Nuns, in the 1840s, strengthened the religious foundation of the Métis as well as their connection to the language and culture of their French-Canadian ancestors.

The Métis sense of community was also strengthened through communal participation in the buffalo hunt. Two annual hunts from the Red River took place—in June and in September or October. These expeditions included more than 1000 people and were highly organized. The Métis elected ten "captains" by vote at a general council, one of whom they named "chief of the hunt," or "governor." Each captain had ten "soldiers" under his command who helped the governor of the hunt maintain order. After the Métis elected the officers, they drew up regulations and the crier announced them. Such rules as "no person or party to run buffalo before the general order" demonstrated the discipline of the hunt. Rigid discipline prevented the premature stampede of the herds and was essential in the resistance to raids by the enemy Sioux.

SUMMARY

By 1821 the "fur trade wars" were over. The amalgamation of the Hudson's Bay Company and the Northwest Company signalled a period of transition for the diverse population of the vast territory. While the fur trade would continue, it commenced a long decline. Difficult times were ahead for the First Nations. While the Northwest remained a world away from events unfolding in the colonies of British North America, gradually the potential of a developing agricultural frontier focused the gaze of politicians and business interests onto the region.

NOTES

1. Gerald Friesen, *The Canadian Prairies: A History* (Toronto: University of Toronto Press, 1987), p. 45.

2. Friesen, p. 22.

3. Friesen, pp. 35–6.

4. Peter Iverson, "Native Peoples and Native Histories," in Clyde A. Milner II, Carol A. O'Connor, and Martha A. Sandwiess, *The Oxford History of the American West* (New York: Oxford University Press, 1994), p. 31.

5. Hugh A. Dempsey, *Big Bear* (Vancouver: Douglas & McIntyre, 1984), p. 48.

6. John C. Crawford, "What Is Michif?: Language in the Métis Tradition," in Jacqueline Peterson and Jennifer S.H. Brown, eds., *The New Peoples: Being and Becoming Métis in North America* (Winnipeg: University of Manitoba Press, 1985), p. 233.

7. Olive Patricia Dickason, *Canada's First Nations*, 2nd ed. (Toronto: Oxford University Press, 1997), p. 266.

8. John Foster, "The Country-Born in the Red River Settlement (c. 1820–1870)," Ph.D. thesis, University of Alberta, 1973, p. 264.

RELATED READINGS

See Module 9, "The Métis and Red River Society: Change, Adaptation, and Resistance—1830s to 1870s," in *Visions: The Canadian History Modules Project: Pre-Confederation*. The module includes articles by Sylvia Van Kirk, "The Impact of White Women on Fur Trade Society," Gerald Friesen, "The Métis and the Red River Settlement," and Gerhard Ens, "Dispossession or Adaptation? Migration and Persistence of the Red River Métis, 1835–1890." See pages 381–426.

BIBLIOGRAPHY

For a short overview, see Sarah Carter, *Aboriginal People and Colonizers of Western Canada to 1900* (Toronto: University of Toronto Press, 1999). Two illustrated books are William R. Morrison, *True North: The Yukon and Northwest Territories* (Toronto: Oxford University Press, 1998), and John Herd Thompson, *Forging the Prairie West* (Toronto: Oxford University Press, 1998), both in Oxford's Illustrated History of Canada series.

For the Mackenzie River basin, see Kerry Abel's *Drum Songs: Glimpses of Dene History* (Montreal/Kingston: McGill-Queen's University Press, 1993). R. Douglas Francis reviews changing perceptions of the Northwest in *Images of the West* (Saskatoon: Western Producer Prairie Books, 1989). Kerry Abel provides a complete bibliographic guide to the historical literature in "The Northwest and the North," in M. Brook Taylor, ed., *Canadian History: A Reader's Guide*, vol. 1, *Beginnings to Confederation* (Toronto: University of Toronto Press, 1994), pp. 325–55.

For an introduction to the history of the Northwest and its role in the foundation and formation of Canada's three Prairie provinces, see Gerald Friesen's *The Canadian Prairies: A History* (Toronto: University of Toronto Press, 1984). For an overview of the prehistory of the region, see Liz Bryan, *Stone by Stone: Exploring Ancient Sites on the Canadian Plains* (Victoria: Heritage House, 2005). For a look at the lure of the West for British travellers, see Terry Abraham, Mountains *So Sublime: Nineteenth-Century British Travelers and the Lure of the Rocky Mountain West* (Calgary: University of Calgary Press, 2005). For a look at law and society in the Northwest, see Louis Knafla and Jonathan Swainger, *Laws and Societies in the Canadian Prairie West, 1670–1940* (Vancouver: UBC Press, 2005). See also Walter Hildebrandt, *Views from Fort Battleford: Constructed Visions of an Anglo-Canadian West* (Edmonton: Athabasca University Press, 2009).

For information on the First Nations in the eighteenth and nineteenth centuries, consult Arthur Ray, *Indians in the Fur Trade* (Toronto: University of Toronto Press, 1974). On cultural change on the northern plains, an essential work is Theodore Binnema's *Common and Contested Ground. A Human and Environmental History of the Northwestern Plains* (Norman: University of Oklahoma Press, 2001). Deanna Christensen has written a valuable community study, *Ahtahkakoop: The Epic Account of a Plains Cree Head Chief, His People, and Their Struggle for Survival 1816–1896* (Shell Lake, SK: Ahtahkakoop Publishing, 2000). Hugh Dempsey's biographies of three Plains chiefs offer a vivid portrait of Blackfoot, Blood, and Cree life in the nineteenth century: *Crowfoot* (Edmonton: Hurtig, 1972); *Red Crow* (Saskatoon: Western Producer Prairie Books, 1980); and *Big Bear* (Vancouver: Douglas & McIntyre, 1984). John Milloy reviews the history of the Cree from 1790 to 1870 in *The Plains Cree* (Winnipeg: University of Manitoba Press, 1988). Laura Peers looks at the Ojibwa in *The Ojibwa of Western Canada: 1780 to 1870* (Winnipeg: University of Manitoba Press, 1994). In his provocative monograph *Eighteenth-Century Western Cree and Their Neighbours* (Ottawa: Canadian Museum of Civilization, 1991), Dale R. Russell questions the belief that the Cree and the Assiniboine came onto the plains only after their contact with the European fur traders. For background on the impact of disease, see the early section of Maureen K. Lux, *Medicine That Walks: Disease, Medicine, and Canadian Plains Native People, 1880–1940* (Toronto: University of Toronto Press, 2001). Hugh Dempsey's study *Firewater: The Impact of the Whiskey Trade on the Blackfoot Nation* (Calgary: Fifth House, 2002) reviews the topic of substance abuse. Kerry Abel examines Dene history in *Drum Songs: Glimpses of Dene History* (Montreal/Kingston: Queen's University Press, 1993).

A survey of the fur trade is that by Dan Francis, *Battle for the West: Fur Traders and the Birth of Western Canada* (Edmonton: Hurtig, 1982). A more in-depth treatment is Dan Francis's book, written with Toby Morantz, *Partners in Furs: A History of the Fur Trade in Eastern James Bay, 1600–1870* (Montreal/Kingston: McGill-Queen's University Press, 1983). A very useful collection of essays on the nineteenth century in Western Canada is Theodore Binnema, Gerhard J. Ens, and R.C. Macleod, eds., *From Rupert's Land to Canada* (Edmonton: University of Alberta Press, 2001). See also Jo-Anne Fiske, Susan Sleeper Smith, and William Wicken, eds., *New Faces of the Fur Trade: Selected Papers of the Seventh North American Fur Trade Conference, Halifax, Nova Scotia, 1995* (East Lansing: Michigan State University, 1998). For short sketches of the most important European fur traders, see the essays on Kelsey, La Vérendrye, Henday, Hearne, Thompson, Mackenzie, and others in the 15 volumes of *Dictionary of Canadian Biography* (Toronto: University of Toronto Press, 1968–2005). It is now available online: www.biographi. ca. Excerpts from the original narratives appear in Germaine Warkentin, ed., *Canadian Exploration Literature: An Anthology* (Toronto: Oxford University Press, 1993). Barbara Belyea presents the several phases of the fur trade's expansion westward in *Dark Storm Moving Westward* (Calgary: University of Calgary Press, 2007). For recent works on the fur trade, see Elle Andra-Warner's *Hudson's Bay Company Adventures: The Rollicking Saga of Canada's Fur Traders* (Surrey: Heritage House, 2009); James Raffan's biography of George Simpson, *Emperor of the North: Sir George Simpson and the Remarkable Story of the Hudson's Bay Company* (Scarborough: HarperCollins 2007); James Hargrave, *Letters from Rupert's Land, 1826–1840: James Hargrave of the Hudson's Bay Company*, Helen Ross, ed. (Montreal/Kingston: McGill-Queen's University Press, 2009).

The Métis are the subject of numerous studies. See, for example, Nicole St-Onge's *Saint-Laurent, Manitoba: Evolving Metis Identities, 1850–1914* (Regina: Canadian Plains Research Centre, 2004); also useful is her article "The Persistence of Travel and Trade: St. Lawrence River Valley French *Engagés* and the American Fur Company, 1818–1840," *Michigan Historical Review* 34(2) (2008). A popular work is D. Bruce Sealey and Antoine S. Lussier, *The Métis: Canada's Forgotten People* (Winnipeg: Manitoba Métis Federation Press, 1975). George Woodcock translated Marcel Giraud's classic *Le Métis Canadien* (Paris: Institut d'ethnologie, Université de Paris, 1945) into English, under the title *The Métis in the Canadian West*, 2 vols. (Edmonton: University of Alberta Press, 1986). Jacqueline Peterson and Jennifer S.H. Brown have edited *The New People: Being and Becoming Métis in North America* (Winnipeg: University of Manitoba Press, 1985). Guillaume Charette's *Vanishing Spaces: Memoirs of a Prairie Métis* (Winnipeg: Editions Bois Brûlés, 1980) contains the memoirs of Louis Goulet, who was born in the Red River Valley in 1859. Gerhard Ens reviews the movement of the Métis westward in *Homeland to Hinterland: The Changing Worlds of the Red River Métis in the Nineteenth Century* (Toronto: University of Toronto Press, 1996). Unlike Sprague, Ens sees the Métis people's movement west of the Red River as a response to "new economic opportunities," a pull westward rather than a push by outside forces. See Frank Tough's *As Their Natural Resources Fail: Native People and the Economic History of Northern Manitoba, 1870–1930* (Vancouver: UBC Press, 2006). A specific study of a country-born Red River community is Robert J. Coutts, *The Road to the Rapids: Nineteenth-Century Church and Society at St. Andrew's Parish, Red River* (Calgary: University of Calgary Press, 2000). See also Irene Gordon, *A People on the Move: The Métis of the Western Plains* (Surrey: Heritage House, 2009). Brenda MacDougall's *One of the Family: Metis Culture in Nineteenth-Century Northwestern Saskatchewan* (Vancouver: UBC Press, 2010) is another recent work, although focused only on the nineteenth century.

The story of Aboriginal women and the fur trade is told by Jennifer S.H. Brown in *Strangers in Blood: Fur Trade Company Families in Indian Country* (Vancouver: University of British Columbia Press, 1980) and by Sylvia Van Kirk in *"Many Tender Ties": Women in Fur Trade Society in Western Canada* (Winnipeg: Watson & Dwyer, 1980). See too Susan Sleeper-Smith, *Indian Women and French Men: Rethinking Cultural Encounter in the Western Great Lakes* (Boston: University of Massachusetts, 2001). Brian Gallagher questions the argument that increasing racism in the period before 1870 caused a decline in the marriage rate between European officers of the Hudson's Bay Company and Métis women: "A Re-examination of Race, Class and Society in Red River," *Native Studies Review* 4(1–2) (1988): 25–65. Edith I. Burley provides a detailed look at the labourers of the Hudson's Bay Company in *Servants of the Honourable Company: Work, Discipline, and Conflict in the Hudson's Bay Company, 1770–1879* (Toronto: Oxford University Press, 1997).

A book containing Aboriginal perspectives is Julie Cruikshank, *Reading Voices* (Vancouver: Douglas & McIntyre, 1991), on oral and written interpretations of the Yukon's past. George Blondin, *When the World Was New: Stories of the Sahtú Dene* (Yellowknife: Outcrop Books, 1990), provides a valuable Indigenous viewpoint on the history of the Great Bear Lake district of the Mackenzie River valley. Two volumes contain valuable information on the Inuit and First Nations: David Damas, ed., *Handbook of North American Indians*, vol. 5, *Arctic* (Washington, DC: Smithsonian Institution, 1984); and June Helm, ed., *Handbook of North American Indians*, vol. 6, *Subarctic* (Washington, DC: Smithsonian Institution, 1981).

Valuable maps of the Northwest appear in R. Cole Harris, ed., *Historical Atlas of Canada*, vol. 1, *From the Beginning to 1800* (Toronto: University of Toronto Press, 1987); R. Louis Gentilcore, ed., *The Historical Atlas of Canada*, vol. 2, *The Land Transformed, 1800–1891* (Toronto: University of Toronto Press, 1993); and Richard I. Ruggles, *A Country So Interesting: The Hudson's Bay Company and Two Centuries of Mapping, 1670–1870* (Montreal/Kingston: McGill-Queen's University Press, 1991). For an environmental history of the northern plains, see W.F. Rannie, "Summer Rainfall on the Prairies During the Palliser and Hind Expeditions, 1857–1859," *Prairie Forum* 31(1) (2006): 17–38. For a look at hunting culture in Rupert's Land, see Greg Gillespie, *Hunting for Empire: Narratives of Sport in Rupert's Land, 1840–1870* (Vancouver: UBC Press 2007).

INTRODUCTION

The colonies of British North America experienced a population boom between the end of the War of 1812 and Confederation in 1867. Growth was particularly evident in the two Canadas. In Upper Canada, the increase occurred as a result of large-scale immigration from Britain. In Lower Canada, growth—especially among the French Canadians—occurred as a result of a high birth rate. British immigration to Lower Canada, meanwhile, heightened tension between the two groups. The colony also experienced a large exodus of French Canadians in the 1850s and 1860s to the New England states. This loss of population stirred up fears that the French Canadians would gradually be overwhelmed by the English and lose their identity.

Population growth in the Canadas coincided with a period of economic prosperity. Until 1849, most trade occurred with the mother country through the mercantile system, by which the colonies supplied the raw materials in return for British manufactured goods. Once Britain adopted free trade, in the late 1840s, the BNA colonies looked increasingly to the United States for markets, especially between 1854 and 1866 when the Reciprocity Treaty was in effect.

The nineteenth century ushered in a period of industrial development in BNA. In order to develop and prosper in such a vast and geographically diverse area, transportation was crucial. The Canadas benefited from increased trade with Britain and the United States through a system of canals and then railroads that were in place by the mid-1850s and 1860s.

By the 1840s the beginnings of industrialization were indicated by the numbers of new factories in the growing towns and cities. But with industrialization came the class system. A new middle class emerged that largely benefited from industrialization, but the major benefits were enjoyed by the wealthy while the workers toiled in often miserable conditions.

The colonial elites took full advantage of their rewards as "loyalists". Anxious not to have a repeat of the American Revolution, the British government allowed these elites to exercise excessive influence and power, even at the expense of British political traditions. The result was the struggle for responsible government. In both the Canadas, the privileged group close to the governor opposed the elected members of the Assembly. The Rebellions in Upper and Lower Canada in 1837 demonstrated that all was not well in British North America.

The British government commissioned Lord Durham to look into the reasons for the rebellions and suggest solutions. Responsible government was achieved by 1849. One of Durham's more contentious recommendations, however, was a union of the Canadas, which took place in 1841, in order to assimilate the French Canadians. The two colonies were now reunited into one. But assimilation again failed. Instead, the union caused so much tension that effective government was impossible by the 1860s. One possible road out of the political mess was a federation of all the colonies of British North America.

Chapter Thirteen

REBELLION AND CHANGE ON THE ST. LAWRENCE

TIME LINE

1792	Legislative Assembly in Lower Canada meets for first time
1806	*Le Canadien* newspaper founded by four members of Parti canadien (later the Parti patriote)
1807–1811	Governor Sir James Craig's "reign of terror"
1813	French-Canadian militia defeats American invading force at Châteauguay
1817	The Bank of Montreal, Canada's first chartered bank, established
1832	First of a series of cholera epidemics sweeps Lower Canada
1834	Ninety-Two Resolutions adopted by Assembly Assembly ends all female suffrage
1836	Canada's first railway runs between Saint-Jean-sur-Richelieu and La Prairie
1837	Rebellion breaks out in Lower Canada
1839	Lord Durham's Report recommends union of Upper and Lower Canada

The half-century between the partition of Quebec in 1791 and the union of the two Canadas in 1841 was tumultuous and divisive. The Canadas went from having their British character reinforced with the coming of the loyalists to launching their own rebellions against British rule; from fighting off an American invasion to advocating the revolutionary ideals of democracy and republicanism in their own struggles. The people of Lower Canada ("obedient peasants," as they were characterized by Quebec's military governors) found their voices and stood up to the abuses of the colonial government and the elites. The *patriotes* (echoing the name given to the American rebels) shouted revolutionary rhetoric at mass meetings, laid plans to overthrow their British rulers, and took up arms. The British government was caught off guard by the insurrection in 1837. British troops intervened and brutally crushed the revolts, and in the aftermath the colonial authorities hanged, imprisoned, or exiled many patriotes; hundreds more fled. The uprisings in Lower Canada were also infused with an ethnic and religious character. As a result, they were much more widespread and violent than those that occurred at the same time in Upper Canada.

Economic Change in the Early Nineteenth Century

At the end of the eighteenth century, Quebec entered a period of intense, if uneven, economic growth, as Britain's industrialization and urbanization created new markets for the colony's food-stuffs and resources. The fur-trade era drew to a close and profits slumped because of declining demand for furs overseas and ruinous competition at home. Whereas furs constituted 76 percent of exports from Quebec in 1770, they made up only 10 percent by 1810. Yet some Montreal fur-trading firms survived by successfully diversifying their interests. Fur trader Simon McTavish, for example, became a seigneur and owner of several businesses. Other traders became timber exporters, shipowners, importers, bankers, and railway promoters.

The rise of the timber industry offset the decline of the fur trade in Lower Canada. By 1810, wood products accounted for three-quarters of Quebec's exports. Britain needed wood, especially to build ships. Napoleon's blockade of northern Europe from 1808 to 1810 cut off Britain's access to its traditional Baltic suppliers. As a result, imports of timber from Lower Canada and other North American colonies increased significantly. Shipowners, working through the English Board of Trade, pressured the British government into doubling import duties on foreign, but not colonial, timber. This effectively guaranteed a highly profitable monopoly to colonial suppliers, even if the Baltic ports reopened. William Price, who came to Lower Canada from England in 1810, was one of several entrepreneurs who made his fortune selling timber. The company he founded would, a century later, become a pioneer in the development of the pulp and paper industry.

Other sectors of the economy experienced significant, though less spectacular, growth. Ships were built at about 80 localities along the St. Lawrence River. Quebec City had the largest ship-yards, and much of their production went overseas to Britain. Sawmills, candle and soap manu-facturers, textile factories, flour mills, and an expanding construction industry contributed to this growth. Banks, beginning with the Bank of Montreal in 1817, were established to supply credit to new enterprises and commercial ventures.

English-speaking merchants took advantage of the economic opportunities. They were better situated to have commercial connections in Britain and they received patronage from the local colonial government. These English merchants were also able to displace the French as seigneurs. By 1812, two-thirds of the seigneuries were held by English-speaking merchants. The lack of commercial opportunities for the French Canadians led to the growth of the number of professionals. It also led to the rise of nationalist sentiments among the growing French-Canadian middle-class.

Urban Life in Lower Canada

Lower Canada's rapidly expanding population provided the labour needed for the increased resource exploitation and manufacturing. A high birth rate, that stayed slightly above 50 per 1000 throughout the period, as well as substantial immigration, caused the population to increase five-fold, rising to 890 000 in 1851 from about 160 000 in 1790. The population increased so rapidly that by the 1830s many young French Canadians emigrated to the northeastern United States in search of the land or work they could not find at home.

COMMUNITY PORTRAIT

The St. Maurice Forges—an Early Industrial Community

The Forges du Saint-Maurice National Historic Site is situated some 10 kilometres north of Trois-Rivières, Quebec. Set in rolling countryside along a small stream that dips through a gully to the St. Maurice River just below, it features the large reconstructed Grande Maison, the Master's House, built in 1738, and a modern blast-furnace interpretation centre describing the early development of the iron industry, from 1730 until 1883.

The Forges possesses a remarkable legacy, going back to the *ancien regime* era of New France. In this early period, it produced large quantities of muni-tions for the army. After the conquest, the British quickly realized the importance of the ironworks and made certain that masters and skilled employees continued working rather than returning to France. The British also used corvées to force the habitants to cut wood for charcoal.

But the Forges reached their pinnacle in the first decades of the nineteenth century. Wood charcoal was used in the process of ore reduction rather than the more modern and efficient coke-fuelled technology. The ore used was bog ore, found in the form of nodules close to the surface in swampy areas. The Forges employed

The iron forges on the St. Maurice River, 1832.

Source: Library and Archives Canada/C-004356.

400 people on site, but also provided work for the surrounding population. Men were hired to collect, prepare, and transport raw materials as well as products and goods. Work "campaigns," during which the blast furnace operated without interruption, lasted six to eight months. The pig iron that was produced supplied the Forges where blacksmiths fashioned tools and implements, pots and kettles, stoves, and munitions, including cannonballs. After the 1850s, the Forges found a new and ready market by selling huge quantities of iron to the burgeoning railway industry.

Recognizing the importance of the industry, for most of the company's history the Forges were under the control of the state. Until 1863, the state granted the Forges free access to vast timber and ore resources, a privilege that ensured profitability. When this privilege was withdrawn, and when the plant was forced to pay the real costs of raw materials, it soon collapsed under a crushing load of debt, in 1883.

Mathew Bell, a Scottish merchant, was master of the Forges from 1793 until 1846, when the government sold the enterprise. The government set favourable terms for the tenants, who could run the business for their profit. Bell used his influence as a member of the Assembly and then as a legislative councillor to ensure that the Forges disposed of adequate reserves of land for procuring raw materials, including 10 000 cords of wood annually. Bell's monopolistic control of huge tracts of land, however, provoked substantial criticism. The Assembly even accused him in one of the Ninety-Two Resolutions in 1834 of having been unduly and illegally favoured by the Executive.

Five generations of workers lived on the site, with fathers passing on the trade to their sons. Skilled workers and craftsmen lived in houses, while the families of unskilled labourers inhabited more modest tenements. Most workers had kitchen gardens, and kept livestock and poultry. The village boasted a chapel, while the Grande Maison contained a well-stocked store.

The St. Maurice Forges constituted the first industrial community in Canada's history, its character defined by its industrial vocation and its population of skilled workers. The village that grew up around the Forges was a precursor of the numerous mining and forestry communities that developed later, particularly in northern regions of Canada.

FURTHER READING

Michel Bédard, André Bérubé, and Jean Hamelin, "Mathew Bell," *Dictionary of Canadian Biography,* vol. 7 (1836–1850) (Toronto: University of Toronto Press, 1988), pp. 70–75.

Roch Samson, *The Forges du Saint-Maurice: Beginnings of the Iron and Steel Industry in Canada, 1730–1883* (Quebec: Les Presses de l'Université Laval and the Department of Canadian Heritage—Parks Canada, 1998), p. 10.

In British North America, urbanization proceeded industrialization. By the time the colonies underwent significant industrial development, cities were already rapidly growing. With the onset of industrialization, however, people flocked to the growing towns in search of work in the new manufacturing industries.

Lower Canada's two major cities developed rapidly, but this development was intended to serve the interests of the commercial elite rather than the workers. Towns and cities were not prepared for the population boom. In the early 1800s, the population of Quebec City grew at an annual rate of more than 5 percent. The Lower Town, around the seaport, was bustling, noisy, and dirty. One visitor commented on the "fearful scene of disorder, filth and intemperance," which

The Fire in the Saint-Jean Quarter, Seen Looking Westward, 1845, *a painting by Joseph Légaré (1795–1855).*

Source: Art Gallery of Ontario. Purchased with assistance of the Government of Canada through the Cultural Propert Exprot and Import Act, 1989. © 2011AGO.

he ascribed to the presence of a large number of sailors, lumbermen, and Irish immigrants. The narrow streets, crowded houses, and boarded roofs made the district "a most hazardous body of property," as one fire insurance agent put it to explain his refusal to insure buildings in the area. Fire was a constant danger in communities whose buildings were constructed largely of wood. In June 1845, a fire broke out in Quebec's Upper Town, destroying 1300 houses in the prosperous St. Jean quarter and leaving 10 000 people homeless. Only one month earlier, a fire in Quebec's working-class district of St. Roch in the Lower Town had demolished 1650 houses and left 12 000 people homeless.

Many impoverished French Canadians settled in the industrial district of St. Roch, located on a seigneury held until 1805 by William Grant, a wealthy merchant. Grant invested heavily in the purchase of properties disposed of by large landowners who returned to France after the Conquest. He also bought several large houses in Montreal, including the Château de Ramezay, and in Quebec, including Montcalm's former residence. In the 1790s, as St. Roch's population quickly increased, Grant ceded properties, developed industries and docks, and built mills, bakeries, and warehouses. In 1800, when Quebec City put forth a plan for road development, Grant, together with religious communities and other private-property owners jealous of their prerogatives, had it overturned by the courts. Not until 1833 was a new plan presented. Grant was thus able to build roads substantially narrower than those in town and to locate them where he wished.

While the poor lived in squalor, seigneurial rents and dues brought Grant and succeeding owners of St. Roch substantial profits. Class antagonism increased and, because the upper classes were often British, took on an ethnic character. In the fall of 1838, rumours circulated that the workers of St. Roch intended to sneak up to Quebec's Upper Town to strangle the bourgeois residents while they slept. Barrels of gunpowder and stocks of ammunition were discovered, and for some time thereafter the anxious burghers kept the city gates of Upper Town locked day and night.

Montreal also grew quickly. By 1825, it had 22 000 inhabitants. By the late 1830s it had overtaken Quebec, the administrative and ecclesiastical capital, and had become British North America's premier city, with a population of 37 000. French Canadians, however, constituted a minority of its residents. Well over half of the city's anglophones were Irish immigrants, most of them poor labourers who settled in industrial areas such as Ste. Anne and Griffintown, near the port. Increasingly, the upper classes settled in the suburbs. Wealthy British residents built grand residences with gardens on the verdant slopes of Mont Royal.

The old city of Montreal, along the river, contained the markets, shops, and administrative buildings. Many of its streets were narrow, muddy in wet weather, and dusty in dry periods. Small streams descended through the city from the hilly areas above. In spring, melting snow and rain caused floods, which impeded traffic and undermined the foundations of buildings. In summer, the water stank and posed a serious health hazard. By 1810, bylaws forbade people from dumping manure, refuse, privy waste, and dead animals into these watercourses. The laws were largely ignored. In response city authorities proposed "a new way of looking at the urban environment."[1] They instituted public works projects to drain away surface water through underground pipes.

Advances in communication and transportation stimulated Montreal's growth. In 1836, Canada's first railway, linking St. Jean on the Richelieu River (and hence Lake Champlain) to La Prairie on the south shore of the St. Lawrence opposite Montreal, was inaugurated. Goods destined to and coming from Upper Canada passed through the port of Montreal. The city's merchants, mostly British and often from Scotland, sold imported goods or set up shops to manufacture such products as leather goods, clothing, barrels, and beer, or to process agricultural products from the fertile farm belt around the city. To supply his Montreal brewery with locally grown barley, industrialist John Molson brought seed barley from England and distributed it among farmers. He also owned the first steamer on the St. Lawrence (which he acquired in 1809), sat in the House of Assembly and later on the Legislative Council, and was president of the Bank of Montreal. The same elite that built the colony's commercial ventures were also its politicians.

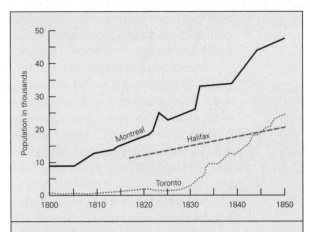

Population growth in Montreal, Halifax, and Toronto, 1800–50.

Source: R. Louis Gentilcore, ed., *Historical Atlas of Canada, vol. 2, The Land Transformed, 1800–1891* (Toronto: University of Toronto Press, 1993), plate 20. Reprinted by permission of the University of Toronto Press Incorporated.

The working classes were largely unskilled. Workers had no power and no voice. They were forced to accept the meagre wages, long hours, and dangerous and unhealthy working conditions. Prior to the 1830s, there were no unions, and legislation passed in 1802 authorized fines and prison sentences for striking employees. Labourers would usually spend more than half their earnings just to feed their families. They lived in crowded, poorly built, and unsanitary homes. Sickness and disease were common.

Women in Lower Canada

Over one-quarter of the women of Lower Canada were in the labour force in 1825, a figure higher than that at the end of the nineteenth century. In order to make ends meet and reach subsistence levels for the family, women toiled in a wide variety of occupations. At least 13 000 were weavers. Others made soap, candles, and dresses. A census taken in 1825 showed that Montreal had female innkeepers, mercers, blacksmiths, and coach makers. Many women were forced to earn money by taking in boarders, providing meals for them, and washing their laundry. Convents began to train some women as teachers.

Many female labourers worked as domestics. In the eighteenth century, parents often placed their very young daughters as servants in the homes of the affluent, where they would work until they married. They were paid no salary but received board, room, and clothing. By the early 1800s, however, domestic labour became salaried work, work that began at dawn and finished when the family went to bed. By 1820, about one family in five in Quebec City employed at least one servant.

The working world for girls and women was often dangerous and fraught with peril. Outside the home in the "public" realm, women were without the protection of the family patriarch. Instead, they were often vulnerable to other patriarchs. They received low wages. If they were subjected to sexual or physical abuse, they had nowhere to turn. The legal system was a male, gendered space that was unlikely to take the women's charges seriously.

Prostitution became an outlet for many lower-class women in Montreal and Quebec City. Many were destitute Irish immigrants. Before 1839, as historian Mary-Anne Poutanen points out, prostitution was a crime only if streetwalking and neighbourhood brothels annoyed passersby or neighbours. Laws were changed so that prostitutes could be apprehended and sentenced to hard labour for up to two months. Keeping a bawdy house was considered an indictable offence.[2]

Women increasingly played a leading role in the early nineteenth century in the founding of charitable institutions intended to alleviate some of the problems associated with urban poverty. After 1840, as gender roles became more entrenched, men took control of most new social-welfare institutions while women provided the labour.[3] Thérèse-Geneviève Coutlée was elected superior of the Sisters of Charity of Montreal's Hôpital Général in 1792. Particularly interested in assisting the poor and the sick, she was also, through government assistance, drawn into caring for the mentally ill, who were housed within the hospital in tiny rooms with grated windows. Only in 1845 was a government asylum built at Beauport, near Quebec City.

Another major function of the hospital was to take in abandoned newborns. Rather than face the harsh and repressive response of society (including their own families) to being unwed mothers, which could lead to being ostracized, women would often surrender their babies to charitable institutions. Nearly three-quarters of these died after being sent out to nurse. The nuns attributed the high mortality rate to the bad state of health of the children on arrival, "which proceeds from that shame which induces the mothers to resort to the utmost means of concealing the offspring of their crime from the eyes of the world." Male politicians often opposed these institutions, which they felt undermined marriage by encouraging unwed mothers to abandon their babies. Their existence, however, reduced the number of cases of infanticide.

Philanthropic organizations were established by middle- and upper-class women. Eleanor Gibb and other Protestant women, struck by the misery of poor Irish immigrants, founded the Female (later Ladies) Benevolent Society in 1815, while their Catholic counterparts established the Dames de Charité in 1827 to assist in providing housing, education, and employment to needy women and children.

Smallpox and Cholera Epidemics

In the early decades of the nineteenth century, disease posed a serious and constant threat to public health. This was particularly true in the towns, with their filthy living conditions and increasingly crowded populations. In 1815, Lower Canada's Assembly provided for public vaccination against smallpox. The method proved controversial, however, and public apathy and distrust kept many people away. In addition, politics intervened to undermine the credibility of the Vaccine Board. The government appointed as president of the board a doctor favoured by the British establishment rather than Dr. François Blanchet, a well-respected senior physician and prominent French-Canadian member of the Assembly. Disputes over regulations and payment of doctors helped seal the fate of the program, which was ended in 1823 with serious consequences. Smallpox continued to be a major source of death in the St. Lawrence Valley for many years. The last major outbreak, in 1885, killed 3000 people in Montreal.

In 1832, the first of a series of cholera epidemics provoked a wave of panic. The disease, transmitted mainly through contaminated water supplies, had spread from the delta of the Ganges River in India across Europe to Britain. Its attacks were sudden, extremely painful, and very often fatal. Death came within 48 hours, a result of complete dehydration of the victim's body. No known cure existed. In fact, most treatments hastened death. Patients were bled, even when they were in a state of collapse, and doctors administered laxatives, although the patients were suffering from uncontrollable diarrhea. Leeches and blisters were applied to the stomach. Fortunately for the victims of both the disease and the proposed remedies, physicians commonly prescribed opium as a painkiller.

The arrival in Lower Canada of large numbers of immigrants, very often indigents from Ireland, caused a vocal and critical reaction from the French-Canadian majority living in the

St. Lawrence Valley. The Irish had been migrating in large numbers to Lower Canada since 1815, although most went on to Upper Canada or to the United States. Some 50 000 arrived in 1831. They were destitute steerage passengers who had spent weeks on the ships, in filthy conditions, and often near starvation. Worried about the threat these immigrants posed to public health, the government of Lower Canada established a quarantine station on Grosse Île, a small island in the St. Lawrence River downstream from Quebec. The measure proved ineffective, because regulations could not be enforced and medical services were inadequate. Among those who perished in Lower Canada, likely on Grosse Île, was the wife of an Irish farmer named John Ford, who himself escaped illness. Ford went on to Detroit, where he began to farm. He was the grandfather of Henry Ford, the founder of the modern automobile industry.

Conditions in Lower Canadian towns contributed to the spread of infection. Houses were dirty and overcrowded, yards and streets were piled with refuse, and towns had open sewers. People emptied the remains of animal pens and latrines into the streets. Pigs and other animals ran loose. Slaughterhouses, often located in residential districts, dumped their waste into open water. In early spring 1832, the health board of Quebec City tried to force residents to clean up streets, houses, and yards. They were ordered to "scrape, wash and cleanse their premises and carry away all filth." Such regulations proved unenforceable.

Cholera struck Quebec City at the end of the first week in June 1832. Hospitals overflowed with victims, while hundreds more lay in tents on the Plains of Abraham. Many panic-stricken residents fled to rural areas, often carrying the disease with them. To prevent despair, church bells were no longer rung for the dead. Police had to be called to enforce the rapid burial of the deceased. By the end of October, 7500 residents of Quebec and Montreal—more than one-tenth of the population of each city—had died.

The disease had important political, as well as economic, social, and cultural consequences. The French Canadians, instinctively, blamed the spread of cholera on immigrants. The disease had come from somewhere else and the destitute Irish immigrants made convenient scapegoats. The fixing of blame increased ethnic tensions in the colony. French Canadian nationalists debated immigration policy and many, including the mayor of Quebec, blamed the British authorities for doing nothing to control the merchants and shipowners who profited by transporting immigrants who came with the disease. They denounced Governor Aylmer's administration for its inaction.

During a second, less severe, outbreak of cholera in Quebec City in 1834, Lord Aylmer fled to Sorel, and most of the Executive Council took up more healthy residence in the country. Even the rich, however, were not spared. Out of self-interest more than concern for the poor, they began to lobby for the public-health measures that, decades later, would dramatically reduce the incidence of deadly diseases.

The towns and cities of British North America were expanding and changing in the 1800s. Although daily life continued to revolve around the family unit, the city was becoming a strange and frightening place. Immigrants from foreign lands joined the tide of rural folk seeking work. Without the traditional networks of support offered by kin and community, many faced what historian David Sutherland calls "a sea of strangers." New networks, communities, and identities had to be formed, based around church organizations and local ethnic societies. Many identified with their "class" and formed a "class consciousness." Together, these factors produced complex identity patterns based around shared experience.

Rural Quebec

The towns and cities were drawing people from the country, but nineteen out of twenty French Canadians in the early nineteenth century lived in rural areas, where they practised subsistence farming. Rural Quebec, however, was also undergoing change. The bountiful harvests and high wheat prices of the 1790s and early 1800s allowed many habitants to accumulate small surpluses of wheat that they sold to grain merchants for export abroad. For a short time, farmers in Lower Canada saw their living conditions improve.

But yields varied enormously, and after 1815, crop failures became more frequent again. The productivity of even the best lands tended to drop after decades of cultivation without fertilization. New lands that had been opened up for colonization, especially those near the Canadian Shield, proved rocky and infertile. Crop diseases and insects posed a constant threat. The wheat midge, for example, almost destroyed the entire harvests from 1834 to 1836, forcing Lower Canada to buy wheat from Upper Canada, where yields were increasing.

Farmers also had to contend with international events. The War of 1812 severely disrupted the grain trade, and the depression in Britain following the Napoleonic Wars from 1815 to 1820 caused prices to fall dramatically. Tariff barriers, such as Britain's Corn Laws of 1815, blocked the entry of colonial grain when the British price fell below a certain level.

The 1830s witnessed a rapid deterioration of economic conditions. Famine was reported in 1837. Historian Fernand Ouellet blamed the farmers for failing to adopt more modern agricultural techniques, such as crop rotation, and for depleting soil nutrients while doing little to restore them. Historians Jean-Pierre Wallot and John McCallum contend that the habitants' alleged backwardness was the consequence, rather than the cause, of their economic plight. They argue that farmers in Upper Canada and in the northeastern United States were no better versed in innovative agricultural methods. Climatic factors and disease, as well as overpopulation, also played a role. Because they lacked the capital to invest in commercial substitutes for wheat, habitants turned more and more to peas, potatoes, and barley in order to avoid starvation. The economic plight of Lower Canadian farmers led many to support rebellion in 1837.

Alexis de Tocqueville, the French social philosopher, noted the existence of rural unrest during a visit to Lower Canada in the late summer of 1831. The superior of the Sulpicians in Montreal assured him that there were no "happier people in the world than the French Canadians" and that they paid trifling rents and acquitted their dues to the church "ungrudgingly and easily." But when de Tocqueville rode into the countryside around Beauport, near Quebec City, and spoke with the habitants, he found them worried about immigration, resentful of the seigneurs, and envious of the wealth that the tithe placed in the hands of some clergy. The habitants had annual seigneurial dues to discharge. Those who bought land had to pay a heavy mutation fine (transfer fee) to the seigneur. They were also obliged to grind their grain at the seigneur's mill—a lucrative privilege for the landed gentry. Historian Allan Greer asserts that this "feudal burden," while generally not crushing, made it difficult for the habitants to accumulate capital.[4] By the mid-1830s, as most seigneurs rallied to the colonial government and the habitants increasingly criticized seigneurial privilege, the conflict between seigneurs and habitants deepened. For Greer, this conflict played "a major part" in the outbreak of the rebellions.[5]

While the urban areas of British North America were seeing the first signs of industrialization, the rural areas were still based around a pre-industrial colonial economy. Within this economy, the basic and most important social and economic institution was the family household. While traditional historians have focused on the role of the export of staple products—fish, fur, lumber, and wheat—social historians have turned to the crucial role of the family unit. It was the family that provided order and stability; it was the sanctioned site of sexual activity; it was the hearth of child rearing. Economically, it was the family unit, with all members working together, that allowed the chance of financial security. Even as the pre-industrial gave way to the industrial, in rural areas the family household maintained its central role. While the division of labour was based around gender, the roles were complementary and flexible. During harvest time, for example, the entire household had to pitch in. But even household units often needed help from their communities. Kinship patterns, as in the urban areas, were important to the success of farms. Neighbours, friends, and kin helped each other when in need.

The Church

The habitants may have resisted the financial demands of the Roman Catholic Church, but this does not suggest a diminishing role for the Church in the lives of the people. The parish priest continued to play a pivotal role in the community, whether rural or urban. He baptized infants, confirmed the youth, married couples, accepted confession and offered contrition, and buried the dead. It was the parish priest who often brought news of the outside world and offered advice on how to deal with the rapidly changing world. The religious orders worked tirelessly to deal with social problems, particularly in urban areas. The Church maintained its place as the centre of leisure activities.

The role of the Catholic Church, however, was being challenged. While the Church was struggling to secure its independence from government dictates and to stand against the infusion of republican ideals, a new professional elite composed of notaries, lawyers, and doctors increasingly endorsed liberal ideas, particularly on political issues, and tended to be critical of the Church. Contemporary accounts detail the spread of religious indifference and even of anti-clericalism,

Manor house and mill of the Seigneurie des Aulnaies.
Source: © Michel Julien

particularly among the bourgeoisie. Liberals read the works of French secular philosophers such as Rousseau and Voltaire. The Assembly became the battleground for these conflicts.

The habitants did not generally challenge official dogma, although many were probably more superstitious and conformist than pious and fervent. They attempted to avoid paying tithes and other religious contributions and they argued over pews, the location of new churches, and other matters of a material nature. For its part, the clergy often complained of disorders and immorality, although that, admittedly, was their duty. Serious sexual misdemeanours were uncommon. Indeed, illegitimacy rates in Lower Canada were low by contemporary European and North American standards.

The habitants did enjoy their feast-days. Travellers reported frequently that the *Canadiens* danced, gorged themselves, got drunk to prepare themselves for Lent (which they scrupulously observed), then feasted again and got drunk to celebrate its passing. The Church was even obliged to abolish several feast-days because of excesses, pleasing the British merchants who did not approve of these kinds of pleasures or of the loss of time from work they entailed.

The habitants also commonly engaged in a popular custom known as the *charivari*, often a form of public rebuke for "mismatched" couples who appeared to marry for money or for mere sensual pleasure. Thus, for example, when an older man married a young woman, a crowd of young men would costume themselves and stage a noisy mock funeral on the couple's doorstep. They would return night after night, beating old pots and kettles to harass the newlyweds until the victims finally sued for peace by paying a substantial fine. Part of the money would go to the poor, and the rest would buy drinks for the revellers. The clergy disapproved of this ritual, which they viewed as a challenge to their authority over marriage.

One problem remained for the Catholic Church: the need to recruit more clergy. Indeed, by the early decades of the nineteenth century, the church faced a veritable crisis. The number of priests declined from 200 in 1760, to 150 in 1790, and then increased to 300 by the 1830s—but the population mushroomed from 70 000 to 500 000 in the same period. Bishop Ignace Bourget of Montreal complained that "there are not enough workers to help us cultivate the vine." During his tenure as bishop of Quebec from 1806 to 1825, Monseigneur Joseph-Octave Plessis encouraged the establishment of classical colleges and succeeded in increasing the number of vocations.

Education

Education remained in the realm of the church, but the rise of liberalism posed a new challenge. Some members of the Assembly supported universal and public education. In 1801 the colonial government founded the Royal Institution for the Advancement of Learning (RIAL), a system of voluntary public education. The Catholic Church entertained serious doubts about the value of universal primary schooling and viewed the initiative as a direct threat to its influence. Many curés did not want to spend parish money on schools and saw education as potentially dangerous, depending on what was taught and who was teaching it. Jean-Jacques Lartigue, named first bishop of the new diocese of Montreal in 1836, claimed that "It is better for them not to have a literary education than to risk a bad moral education." Since schools cost money and habitants generally did not want to pay for them, they tended to agree. The Catholic Church, led by Plessis, was suspicious of the RIAL schools, since a Protestant government that still hoped for the assimilation and conversion of the French Canadians had established them. The Church chose to ignore the schools, and few were established.

Education would become one of the major battlegrounds throughout the colonies of BNA throughout the first half of the century, as well as in the new Dominion of Canada after 1867. Because the issue dealt with the moulding of the youth, it encapsulated issues of religion, language, culture, and politics; it crossed over into issues of morality, assimilation, nationalism, and the role of the state. At the base of the issue was the traditional battle between church and state, which served as a central division between Catholicism and Protestantism. For the Catholics, the connection between church and state was strong; the church controlled education, as well as other "social" realms. For the Protestants, church and state were separate.

When, in 1818, the Lower Canadian Assembly set up a board of trustees to oversee education, Plessis refused to participate in this essentially English-Protestant body that clearly sought to establish education under state control. The board authorized separate religious worship, visits to schools by priests, and French textbooks. It appointed French-Catholic teachers in French areas of the province. Still, the local priests regarded the schools at best with indifference and usually with outright hostility. Many refused to become visitors, often on Plessis's orders.

In an effort to remodel educational legislation to make it more satisfactory to the Roman Catholic Church, the Assembly authorized the church to build its own schools, to be financed and directed by parish *fabriques*, or councils. In the Legislative Council, Plessis urged state financing, but the government replied that, because of the Assembly's obstruction, no money was available. It was becoming more apparent, however, that French liberals favourable to non-confessional schools constituted as much a threat to clerical ambitions as did Anglo-Protestant government officials. Indeed, in 1829, the liberals supported a bill that gave control of schools to the Assembly and to local officials called *syndics*. Within three years, many state-supported schools were built, leading to disputes between parish priests and town officials over their operation. Finally in 1836, in response to pressure from the Catholic Church, the Assembly abrogated the Elementary Schools Act.

Church–State Relations

At the time of Conquest, it was assumed that the British government (through its colonial administrators) would have an antagonistic relationship with the Catholic Church in Quebec. The Church, after all, was the bastion in the defence of the colony's French-Catholic character. Religion was culture, and to proceed with the assimilationist design as outlined in the Royal Proclamation of 1763, the hegemony of the Catholic Church had to be diminished. But the terms of such governors as James Murray and Guy Carleton indicated that the Church could be a valuable ally in controlling the population, particularly in the face of the threatening American Revolution. Plans to subvert the Roman Catholic Church were put on hold.

In the years following the American Revolution, anti-French and anti-Catholic sentiment often pervaded the colonial government. Herman Ryland, Governor Robert Prescott's secretary, hoped to undermine the Catholic influence through a reform of the educational system. Jacob Mountain, the Anglican Lord Bishop of Quebec, sought to raise the prestige of his church by increasing its status while decreasing that of the Catholic Church. He used his power as a legislative and executive councillor to block the creation of new Catholic parishes and to prevent the immigration of priests from France. His cathedral, inaugurated in 1804, boasted a steeple which topped that of the nearby Roman Catholic cathedral by fully one metre. Attorney General (later, Chief Justice) Jonathan Sewell, more moderate and more patient, wanted to diminish the powers of the Catholic bishops and, by giving Plessis and his coadjutor pensions and seats in the councils, make them obedient government servants. But by the time Sir George Prevost became governor in 1812, much of the momentum had gone out of these schemes. Plessis convinced the British government that an independent Catholic Church might be a powerful ally during renewed war with the Americans.

The Catholic Church managed to achieve considerable independence from government dictates. Until the 1830s, the government interfered with the nomination of bishops, although with decreasing success. When Bishop Bailly de Messein died in 1794, the governor gave the new bishop, Jean-François Hubert, a list of three names from which to choose a new coadjutor. But by 1825, the process was reversed. Bernard Claude Panet, the new bishop, submitted a list of three names to the governor, Lord Dalhousie. Furthermore, only one of the candidates was willing to accept the position. A somewhat humbled Dalhousie finally agreed to what was in fact the only choice. By 1840, ecclesiastical nominations became purely a church matter.

Church and state clashed on the issue of parish appointments. Here again the government sought to affirm its supremacy, examining lists of nominees and interfering occasionally, but aggressively, with the placement of priests. With the Constitutional Act of 1791, colonial administrators wanted amenable local clergy who could intervene to favour the election of candidates. Sir Robert Shore Milnes, sent to the colony in 1799 as the new lieutenant governor, prevented the entry into Lower Canada of French priests whose loyalty he doubted in the atmosphere of a renewed war with France. In time, the government eased up on this restriction also and allowed the Church to control its appointments.

The Catholic Church also prevailed on the question of dividing the large diocese of Quebec. In 1836, Lord Gosford finally agreed to the establishment of the diocese of Montreal. A grateful Bishop Lartigue later wrote to Gosford to request his portrait "as a monument to your good deeds in this country."

The local situation contributed to the Catholic Church's victory. Some governors were more willing to be flexible and even realistic. For their part, many church leaders were skillful diplomats who exploited opportunities to assert the Church's independence while at the same time providing the government cooperation and assuring British authorities of their loyalty. In addition, British hopes for converting the French Canadians were fading. Groups such as the Methodists, who used

Column to honour Horatio Nelson's victory over the French at Trafalgar in 1805, by John Murray, engraved by Adolphus Bourne, c. 1850.

Source: Print Collection, Rare Books and Special Collections Division, McGill University Library.

Swiss French-speaking agents, vainly attempted to proselytize. But the Protestants were often more preoccupied with their own denominational rivalries than with converting Catholics. Anglican Bishop Mountain, for example, tolerated Presbyterian and Lutheran ministers, but disdained the Methodist clergy. (The Methodists had left the Anglican Church and founded a separate church—as "a set of ignorant enthusiasts whose preaching is calculated only to perplex the understanding and corrupt the morals, to relax the nerves of industry and dissolve the bonds of society".)

International events afforded the Catholic Church additional opportunities to demonstrate its loyalty. The clergy vigourously opposed the liberal ideals of the "atheistic" French Revolution that broke out with the storming of the Bastille prison in Paris on July 14, 1789. Horrified by the Reign of Terror that soon took hold (among whose victims on the guillotine was King Louis XVI and his Queen, Marie Antoinette), Canadian prelates issued strong condemnations. Here was the prime example of liberal ideas run amuck. If Quebec felt any lingering ties to the former Mother Country, they were severed in the French Revolution when the populace overthrew the authority of both the church and state. Henceforth, the borders of Quebec would serve as the borders of the French-Canadian homeland.

Britain gained more support from the Catholic Church in Quebec when war broke out with France in 1793. Then, while Napoleon's military campaigns provoked new suspicions of all things French, the War of 1812 gave the church a welcome opportunity to preach loyalty through pastoral letters and sermons. Led by the clergy, loyal French Canadians praised the exploits of Charles-Michel de Salaberry and his militia, who forced a numerically superior American force to retreat at the battle of Châteauguay in 1813. French-Canadian troops won a glorious victory for the British—undeniable proof of loyalty. Governor Prevost could well declare that "The Catholic clergy are my firmest supports." The Catholic Church proved a good ally when it came to influencing its flock during the American Revolution and the War of 1812. It would prove an even more influential ally in the face of the Rebellions of 1837.

The rise of the Catholic Church in the early years of the nineteenth century took place partly at the expense of the colonial government and partly at the expense of the new professional elite. The professional class was the Church's only serious rival in the struggle for support and influence among the French-Canadian population. The Rebellion of 1837 brought this conflict to a head and decided its outcome in the Church's favour. By 1840 French Canada's clerical elite was poised to enter a golden age that would last for more than a century.

The Professional Elite

Many members of the new professional class were sons of small farmers and, as such, could scarcely base their social aspirations upon family wealth. Politics became an outlet for this group's ambitions. Espousing liberal, democratic, and republican ideals, the group sought government reform through enlarging the powers of the lower house and curtailing those of the executive.

These professionals were well aware of Lower Canada's colonial status and of the inferior position of French Canadians in the economy and in government circles. The situation was made worse by the aftermath of the American Revolution and the coming of the loyalists. Whenever such catchwords as democracy or liberalism were raised, they were quickly denounced as American. Such a pro-conservative environment worked to the benefit of the colonial cliques, who quashed the influence of the elected Assembly. The result was the further entrenching of the power of these cliques, to the point that they became effective oligarchies. The professionals in Lower Canada became champions of national and liberal values, and they easily associated the interests of French Canada with those of their own class. Not surprisingly, they framed their declarations of battle in the name of the French-Canadian nation.

This new middle class aspired to replace the seigneurs and, to a degree, compete with the clergy as leaders of French Canada. Many of its members viewed the seigneurs as exploiting the habitants when they raised seigneurial *rentes*, especially when the growing population in the seigneurial zone and better prices for timber enhanced the value of the seigneuries, more than half of which had passed to British owners. The French seigneurs also appeared as collaborators who bowed to the British to gain lucrative appointments and pensions. Many notaries and lawyers also condemned the Catholic Church for its support of Britain. Some were openly anti-clerical, espousing the ideals of the French Revolution and American democracy. Bishop Plessis denounced these radicals as early as 1809, accusing them of "tending to annihilate all principles of subordination and to set fire to the province."

The French professionals who formed the backbone of the *Parti canadien* (later called the *Parti patriote*) had increasingly hostile relations with the British merchants. Well represented in the governor's inner councils, the wealthy merchants numbered only a few hundred but, according to historian Donald Creighton, they were "the most self-conscious, purposeful and assertive of all the Canadian social classes."[6] The merchants wanted to control Lower Canada's political institutions in order to introduce new laws to promote economic growth, commerce, and transportation. Some demanded the abolition of the seigneurial system. They accused the Assembly's French-Catholic majority of systematically blocking necessary change. One solution they put forth was the union of the two Canadas, a measure intended to reduce the influence of the French. Twice, in 1822 and again in 1826, the British government examined such proposals, a harbinger of what was to come in 1840.

Liberalism and Reform

Liberals in Lower Canada vaunted such notions as liberty and democracy but there were limits to their extension. Despite their political radicalism, they were economically conservative. While critical of many aspects of the seigneurial system, they did view it as a rampart against English farmers (anxious to gain freehold title to their lands) replacing the habitants in the St. Lawrence Valley. The professionals defended traditional agriculture and denounced the threat of commercial capitalism because it was controlled by the English minority.

Liberals in Lower Canada were also reticent when it came to recognizing the political rights of minority groups. In 1807, Ezekiel Hart, of Trois-Rivières, became the first Jew in the history of the British empire to be elected to a legislative assembly. Yet the Assembly refused to let him take his seat, because he was a Jew and because he favoured the government party. A quarter of a century later, Hart and his sons were instrumental in having the Assembly adopt legislation according full political rights to Jews.

Reformers in Lower Canada, in tune with those across the British empire, denied women the right to vote (suffrage). In the early decades of the nineteenth century, women voted in numerous instances in Lower Canada. The restriction on the franchise was land (wealth), not gender.

In 1809, the mother of Louis-Joseph Papineau cast her vote for her son, whom she proudly described as "a good and faithful subject." But in 1820, after numerous complaints about voting by the wives of male property holders, the Assembly passed a resolution disenfranchising married women. Then, in 1834, it acted to end all female suffrage. Papineau and his party explained that electoral violence had reached such a point that "the public interest, decency, and the natural modesty of the sex" required that women not witness such scenes. The legislation of 1834 was found to be *ultra vires* for reasons that had nothing to do with women. The right to vote was finally taken from women in 1849.

The Rivalry between the Governor and Assembly

The Rebellion of 1837 indicated the serious British failures in governing its colonies in North America. To an extent, the experience paralleled the revolution of the Thirteen Colonies and indicated that the British had failed to learn their lesson. The colonists in Lower Canada found themselves governed by a repressive and even tyrannical regime. Ironically, the regime was created, or at least allowed to develop, due to the American Revolution. The coming of the loyalists infused the colonies of BNA with anti-American and staunchly conservative sentiment. In order to reward the loyalists, the British failed to check the growing influence of the elites. In a colonial system in which the executive branches of government (the governor and the Executive Council) already held considerable power, and perhaps more importantly, were able to raise money (the "power of the purse") outside the control of the elected Assembly, responsible government was a distant dream. Yet, responsible government was supposed to be the basis of the British parliamentary system. Instead, oligarchies were allowed to form and maintain power. These cliques were then supported by the established churches. Any opposition was branded radical, liberal, and pro-American.

The causes of the Rebellion of 1837 in Lower Canada were more complex than those in Upper Canada because of the colony's ethnic and religious divisions. The struggle pitted the English-Protestants against the French-Catholics, since Lower Canada's English minority dominated the Executive Council and the Assembly represented the French majority. The fight for responsible government, however, at times bridged the ethnic-religious divide and positioned a small group of English colonists in support of the patriotes. Some were Irish Catholics who opposed Britain's imperial policies in Ireland. Among these was the journalist Edmund Bailey O'Callaghan, a patriote close to Papineau, whose anti-British prose in the *Irish Vindicator and Canada Advertiser* was as bitter as anything found in the French-language press. Others, such as the brothers Wolfred and Robert Nelson, both supporters of reform, endorsed patriote demands for an executive that would be responsible to the Assembly.

The Financial Question

The "power of the purse" was at the crux of the British parliamentary system. In the seventeenth century, the British Parliament controlled the "purse strings" and the king had no choice but to go to Parliament for money. The English Civil War had been fought over this issue, resulting in the supremacy of parliament. The colonial governments were supposed to reflect this system. For three decades the Assembly in Lower Canada sought greater control of the colony's finances. Constitutionally, it alone could initiate money bills concerning taxes and expenditures. But in BNA the executive possessed revenues from Crown lands, from the military budget, and even from London, which enabled it to distribute patronage in the form of positions, salaries, and pensions to its supporters. Moreover, the Legislative Council could—and often did—refuse legislation from the Assembly. As a final nail in the coffin of responsible government, the governor possessed extensive veto powers.

Not surprisingly, the financial question dominated disagreements between the governor and the Assembly. As early as 1805, for example, a bill designed to raise money to build prisons provoked a debate that highlighted the intensity of the issue, as well as growing French-English conflict. French members favoured paying for the prisons through higher import duties, while British merchants wanted to tax the land. Because the British controlled trade and the French dominated farming, agriculture was arrayed against commerce, Catholic against Protestant. When the Assembly voted for import duties, the merchants appealed first to the Legislative Council, then to the governor, and finally to London. "If the [French] Canadians succeed in building so many churches, why couldn't they pay for the construction of prisons?" they argued. During this confrontation, a French-language newspaper, *Le Canadien*, was founded in November 1806. Edited by four members of the Parti canadien, it was intended to enable French Canadians to assert "the loyalty of their character and defy the designs of the opposition [British] party."

Relations between the Assembly and the governor deteriorated further during the mandate of Sir James Craig (1807–11). In the face of *Le Canadien's* vitriolic attacks on the beneficiaries of patronage and government land policies, and influenced by advisers such as the anti-Catholic Herman Ryland, Craig embarked upon a "reign of terror." When vocal Parti canadien members annoyed him, the governor used his power to dissolve the Assembly and call another election. When the dissolution stirred up popular agitation, resulting in the election of an almost identical body, Craig dissolved it again. After *Le Canadien* denounced the governor, he had the paper's presses seized and its editors thrown in jail on charges of treason. When the second election returned an even stronger slate of Parti canadien members, he used intimidation to force the Assembly into line. For Governor Craig, the problem in Lower Canada was not a struggle for responsible government; it was a struggle between the French-Catholics and English-Protestants. As a long-term solution to the problem, he recommended assimilation through a union of the provinces, large-scale British immigration, the subordination of the Catholic Church, and the abolition of "the representative part of government." Craig left the province, to the relief of the French-Canadian populace.

A HISTORICAL PORTRAIT

Hortense Globensky

Women took part in the Rebellions of 1837–38 by manufacturing bullets and cartridges, caring for wounded patriotes, and taking enormous risks by offering up their homes as sanctuary for rebels and their families. Hundreds of women suffered from the consequences. Their houses and property were destroyed by British troops and "volunteers." When the British destroyed crops, gardens, and supplies, they were often left without food to feed the elderly and children.

Some women participated directly in the rebellions as activists in the patriote cause. Emmélie Boileau Kimber came from a distinguished family with a long history in the Richelieu valley. She married a doctor who was a patriote leader. She held meetings at their *Tricolore*-flag-bedecked home in Chambly. Another patriote set fire to her own house to demonstrate to the British that she did not fear them and to prevent them from pillaging her house before they destroyed it.

Hortense Globensky, on the other hand, was a French-Canadian woman who sided with the British during the rebellions. Her father had immigrated to Lower Canada from Poland in 1776 as a surgeon in the Brunswick-Hesse regiment and her mother, a French Canadian, belonged to a wealthy family. Her brother Maximilien had fought with the British against the Americans at Châteauguay and Ormstown during the War of 1812. His loyal participation brought him rewards that included a lifelong pension and land. He sought election to the Assembly as a Tory. In 1837, the British military authorities asked him to form a unit of volunteers, whom he recruited from among society's "best known, most respectable, and most prosperous" members. His men participated in the ravages and reprisals around St. Eustache.

Like her brother, Hortense cast her lot openly with the British. In the election of 1834, she made no attempt to disguise her sympathies for the government party. In July 1837, friends warned her that patriotes intended to attack her home at Ste. Scholastique, north of Montreal. One of her children had just died, and Globensky decided not to abandon the body. Upon the arrival of some 50 patriotes one night, she took up position at a window, dressed in her husband's garb, with several pistols; seeing guns aimed directly at them, the attackers withdrew. As a souvenir of her exploit, friends styling themselves "loyal citizens of Montreal" gave her a silver teapot bearing the inscription: "in tribute for her heroism, greater than that expected of her sex, shown on the evening of July 6, 1837." Then, one Sunday in October 1837, after mass, as patriotes attempted to encourage the parishioners to rebel, Globensky urged them to remain faithful to the government. When rebels sought to silence her, she drew a pistol and threatened them. A similar incident occurred in November. After the rebellion, she responded to the pleas of neighbours and succeeded in obtaining the liberation of several rebel prisoners arrested. She was called "chevalière des Deux-Montagnes" and "héroïne du nord" by newspapers at the time.

Foremost among the leaders of the Parti canadien (called the Parti patriote after 1826), Louis-Joseph Papineau entered the Assembly in 1809 and became its speaker in 1815. Even though he was a seigneur, Papineau's education and political career acquainted him with liberal thought. As the political crisis deepened after 1830, Papineau's esteem for British institutions evolved into admiration for republicanism and American-style democracy. Liberal in his religious views, he refused to believe that he could not also be a good Catholic. He continued to view the Catholic Church as an important national institution and he attended mass to set an example for his tenants. Historian Fernand Ouellet portrayed him as a "divided soul."[7]

In 1828, believing that London would be more conciliatory once properly informed of the discontent in Lower Canada, the Assembly sent a petition bearing nearly 90 000 signatures and asking for curbs on the powers of the executive. But British politicians were convinced that a governor shorn of his powers would be unable to fulfill his constitutional obligations of responsibility to London. Britain's refusal to seriously consider reform of the colony's political structure led to the increased radicalization of the patriotes.

Radicalization

The British parliament adopted what it hoped would be perceived as a compromise solution. It gave the Assembly control of all expenditures on the condition that it agree to pay the civil list each year—that is, to pay for the civil administration of the colony, including the salaries of civil servants. But the patriotes were gaining strength. They won a sweeping election in 1834 with three-quarters of the popular vote. Papineau and a small committee drew up the Ninety-Two Resolutions, which called for the Executive Council to be elected and the Assembly to control revenues. The governor, Lord Aylmer, accused the Assembly of issuing what amounted to a declaration of independence. Rather than respond to the deepening crisis and seek to resolve the grievances, the British government bolstered the executive. To help resolve the executive's financial problems, London established the British American Land Company and granted it more than 400 000 hectares of land, in return for a commitment to build roads and make annual payments to the Crown. The company, however, showed little interest in colonization and much interest in speculation.

L'Assemblée des six comtés, in 1837 *by Charles Alexander Smith.*

Source: © Musée nationale des beaux-arts du Quebec, photograph by Jean-Guy Kérouac, 37.54. Transferred from the Hôtel du Parlement, 1937. Restored at the Centre de conservation du Québec with financial assistance from the Amis du Musée du Québec.

The Catholic Church, meanwhile, demonstrated its support for the status quo and its opposition to liberal ideas. The Church used its influence to encourage French Canadians to reject the reforms and the nationalism of the patriotes. Even Papineau was depicted as anti-clerical due to his support for secular schools, and he earned the animosity of Bishop Jean-Jacques Lartigue. The Church called on Catholics to reject the reform movement and support the authorities, forcing many to choose between their religion and their political convictions.

Britain was facing its own political problems, and as a result, the Parliament made the Lower Canadian question a low priority. The Whigs, then in power, opposed further concessions to Lower Canada's Assembly but they wanted to appear conciliatory. Procrastination in the form of establishing a commission to investigate the issue seemed the wisest policy. Unimpressed, the London *Times* in 1835 viewed this commission, headed by the Earl of Gosford, as "a frivolous and toad-eating embassy . . . a temporizing mission, a bribe to the Radicals in the British Parliament to tolerate the Whig ministry."

In March 1837, the British government responded with the Ten Resolutions prepared by Lord John Russell, government leader in the House of Commons. The Assembly's demands were categorically denied and the British government announced an end to conciliation. This series of resolutions constituted a refusal by the Colonial Office of all of the Assembly's Ninety-Two Resolutions. They went so far as to authorize the government of Lower Canada, if necessary, to pay its administrative costs from the tax revenues without the Assembly's approval. There would be no elective Legislative Council, thus preserving the English minority's political influence. The Executive Council, representing wealth and enterprise, would, as before, continue to be responsible to the governor alone, not to the Assembly.

Britain's strident response caused the political crisis to deepen and radicalization to increase. Papineau began to lose control of his party. Canadian considerations were temporarily forgotten by Britain. The events of November and December of that same year, however, abruptly brought them back to the floor of the British Parliament.

The Lower Canadian Rebellions

When they received news of Britain's response, the patriotes altered their tactics. It seemed obvious that only direct action through rebellion would force the hand of the imperial authorities. More moderate views prevailed, however, and the agreed-upon plan called for legal agitation to pressure the government to reconsider its positions. Rebellion would be the next recourse.

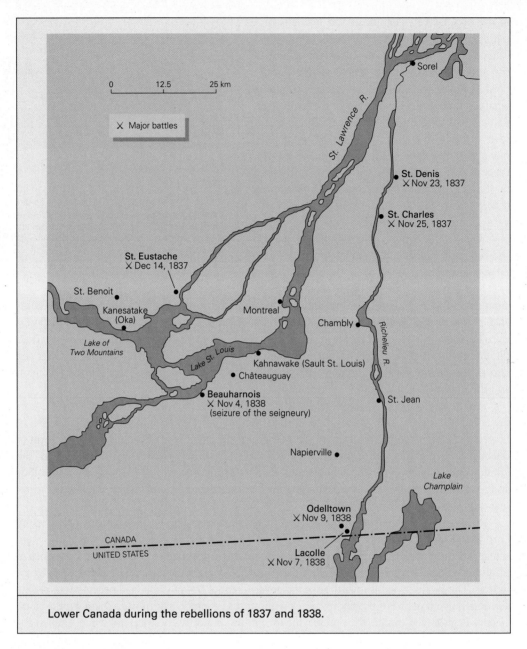

Lower Canada during the rebellions of 1837 and 1838.

Throughout the tense days of the summer and autumn of 1837, the patriote leaders organized. They staged assemblies and collected funds. Patriote women established an association whose objective was "to assist, insofar as the weakness of their sex made it possible, in the triumph of the Patriote cause."[8] They organized boycotts of imported goods in an attempt to strike at British merchants. In September an association with military sections, the Fils de la liberté, was founded. At a public assembly at St. Charles on the Richelieu River east of Montreal, attended by some 4000 people, patriote orators called for revolt. The meeting adopted resolutions that included a declaration of independence. They developed plans to take Montreal and then move on to Quebec City.

When the government issued warrants for their arrest, the principal patriote leaders, Papineau included, fled to the countryside south of Montreal. The prospective urban uprising was suppressed.

On November 23 a British force of 300 regulars marched through the night, in freezing rain, into the Richelieu valley. They expected little difficulty routing the rebels. But they met over 800 rebels led by Dr. Wolfred Nelson outside the village of St. Denis. Using barricades and then a stone wall, the rebels held the British troops at bay for several hours, until they were finally forced to withdraw to Sorel. Thirteen rebels and twelve British soldiers were killed. Two days later, the British were reinforced by 420 troops and they marched on the rebel camp at St. Charles. The British had little trouble smashing through the barricades and defeating the rebel force, numbering only 80 men. With victory in hand, the British advanced in the open, but some patriotes fired upon them, killing three soldiers. The British responded by massacring the remaining

British troops with Patriote prisoners, Rebellion of 1837, *by M.A. Hayes.*

Source: Library and Archives Canada, Acc. No. 1991-116-4/C-003653.

rebels. Prisoners were rounded up and sent to jail in Montreal. Throughout the St. Denis and St. Charles area, British troops torched twenty houses and barns.

Having pacified the Richelieu Valley, Sir John Colborne, the former governor of Upper Canada who had just been promoted to commander-in-chief of all British troops in the Canadas, turned his attention to the area north of Montreal. Here, Amury Girod, a Swiss immigrant, and Dr. Jean-Olivier Chénier, headed the resistance. News of the patriotes' defeat at St. Charles only hardened Chénier in his determination to "die fighting rather than surrender."

The British force under Colborne, consisting of 1280 regulars, 220 loyalist volunteers, and supported by artillery, approached St. Eustache on December 14, 1837. The patriotes hoped to assemble 800 defenders, but they only managed to muster 200, many of whom did not even have firearms. They were barricaded in the parish church, convent, and rectory. Girod fled before the skirmish, supposedly to get reinforcements from St. Benoit. He was later accused of treason and committed suicide. Some 70 patriotes, including Chénier, died by gunfire or were burned to death. The Rebellion in Lower Canada was crushed. In total, 250 men died in battle in Lower Canada, in the Richelieu Valley, and at St. Eustache, in late November and December 1837.

The British sought to make an example of the rebels. Hundreds were taken prisoner, including leaders, such as Wolfred Nelson. A policy of home-burning was initiated. St. Eustache was put to the torch, as was nearby St. Benoît, which had offered no resistance. One newspaper, usually favourable to the British, reported: "For a radius of 15 miles around St. Eustache, not a building escaped being ravaged and pillaged by these new vandals" who displayed "no feelings of humanity."

By the time news of the insurrection reached London, just before Christmas, many of the rebel leaders who had escaped found asylum in the United States, where they attempted to muster support and regroup. In February 1838, Robert Nelson led an incursion across the border. As provisional president of Lower Canada, he declared Canada's independence from Britain before fleeing back to safety on the American side.

In November 1838, revolt broke out anew, this time southwest of Montreal. Temporarily, the patriotes at Beauharnois took control of the seigneury. In one incident resulting from years of mistrust and tense relations, a patriote force raided the Mohawk community of Kahnawake (then also called Sault St. Louis). The raid failed, and the Mohawks captured some 60 patriotes, whom they sent off as prisoners to Montreal.

Defeat of the Insurgents by Sir John Colborne at St. Eustache, November 25, 1837, *by John Walker.*

Source: Library and Archives Canada/C-006032.

British troops intervened in response to the new troubles and soon crushed all resistance at Beauharnois. Patriote raids from across the American border were easily turned back. Colborne—nicknamed *le vieux brûlot* ("the Old Firebrand")—was to be long remembered for his ruthlessness in ravaging and pillaging the countryside. After the rebellion, a grateful British government raised Colborne to the peerage as Lord Seaton—but many French Canadians chose to pronounce his new title as "Lord Satan."

In the years that followed, clerical historians praised the role of clergymen such as Bishop Lartigue, for his attempts to avoid armed insurrection. Nationalist historians condemned the Catholic Church for siding against the French Canadians and instead collaborating with the enemy. Historian Fernand Ouellet described the patriotes as members of an ambitious professional elite, who sought political power and social prestige. Despite their revolutionary rhetoric, many patriote leaders were social conservatives. Papineau, for example, was a landowner—seigneur of Montebello—who nonetheless spoke fervently about American democracy. But his rhetoric became more ambivalent over time, and he denied ever advocating rebellion. Half an hour after the beginning of the Battle of St. Denis, he fled across the American border. Robert Nelson replaced Papineau as the patriote leader and introduced a more radical program, which advocated the abolition of the seigneurial system as well as an end to the payment of the tithe to the Catholic Church.

WHERE HISTORIANS DISAGREE

The Rebellions in Lower Canada

Early historians were concerned mainly with the politics of the Rebellions and as a result, their interpretations varied depending upon their ideological and nationalist positions. Abbé Lionel Groulx, a Catholic priest and the first professional Quebec historian, was conflicted when it came to the Lower Canadian Rebellion. As a nationalist, he perceived a just cause in the patriote movement that resisted British imperial domination, but he was critical of their anti-clerical and liberal message.[1] Maurice Séguin was less equivocal and portrayed the patriotes as

a vanguard struggling for the liberation of French Canadians.[2]

By the 1960s, historians began turning away from political explanations and instead emphasized economic causes. Mason Wade argued that the Rebellion pitted the popular agrarian majority against an oligarchy of "officials, placemen, and merchants" who were monopolizing power and frustrating the aspirations of the majority of Lower Canadians. Wade also observed that the rise of Jacksonian democracy in the United States reinforced the "long-established influence of the American Revolution upon Canadian political thinking," which made the colonial system intolerable to the popular leaders of the rebellion and their supporters.[3] Donald Creighton ignored Jacksonianism and emphasized the rebellions as a showdown between agriculture and commerce with Montreal merchants hostile to the interests of farmers.[4]

Fernand Ouellet argued that an agricultural depression led Lower Canadian farmers to grow impatient with the British colonial authority and to increasingly embrace nationalism. However, the patriotes not only consisted of farmers but included an aspiring professional elite frustrated by their failure to earn social and political power under British colonialism.[5] But not all historians accepted Ouellet's claim that an agricultural crisis existed. Allan Greer, in his study of the agricultural conditions of the lower Richelieu Valley, could not find evidence of a decline in wheat production and was unable to accept Ouellet's findings as the basis for rebellion.[6]

In a study of the predominantly English-speaking Eastern Townships, J.I. Little questioned the level of ideological polarization among the agricultural and mercantile interests, arguing that along the colony's frontier regions the Rebellions signalled the end of division between the Tory elite and agrarian radicals. By the 1840s, residents in the Eastern Townships were willing to support any political party capable of delivering economic growth. For Little, the Rebellions signalled "the transition towards increased political autonomy and capitalist expansion in North America."[7]

There has also been renewed debate about the role of ideology as a cause of the Rebellions. Political scientist Daniel Sallée has argued that the patriotes were members of a bourgeois that, like their European counterparts, adopted a liberalism that increasingly challenged aristocratic title.[8] Éric Bédard, however, downplays the role of individualism in the political thought of the patriotes. While they did hold many liberal views, they avoided the rhetoric of individualism and argued that French Canada must speak with one unified political voice. The patriotes were loyal to the Constitution of 1791, and their primary goal, Bédard writes, was always responsible government. What distinguished the patriotes was their emphasis not upon individual liberty but on the survival of the nation.[9]

Allan Greer claims that the increasing involvement of the masses in the Rebellions signalled that Lower Canada was experiencing a "classic revolutionary crisis."[10] In this spirit, F. Murray Greenwood has argued that the unwillingness of the Anglophone colonial elite to accede to the growing demands of the French Canadians precluded a peaceful negotiation of political differences.[11]

Gilles Laporte challenges the claim that the Rebellions were a truly "national" event by studying the events through the lens of region. He has found that the areas of greatest unrest existed where a large Anglo minority was present. Mobilization by both Tories and patriotes appears largely dependent upon the visible presence of an organized opposition, leading Laporte to argue that unrest often was regionally determined.[12]

1. Lionel Groulx, *Notre maître le passé,* vol. 2 (Quebec: Librairie Granger Frères, 1945), pp. 86–87.

2. Maurice Séguin, *L'idée d'indépendance au Québec: Genèse et historique* (Trois-Rivières: Boreal Express, 1968), p. 33.

3. Mason Wade, *The French Canadians 1760–1967,* vol. 1, *1760–1911* (Toronto: Macmillan, 1968), p. 152.

4. Donald Creighton, "The Economic Background of the Rebellions of Eighteen Thirty-Seven," *Canadian Journal of Economics and Political Science* 3 (1937): 322–34.

5. Fernand Ouellet, *Lower Canada, 1791–1840: Social Change and Nationalism* (Toronto: McClelland & Stewart, 1980), p. 135.

6. Allan Greer, *Peasant, Lord and Merchant: Rural Society in Three Quebec Parishes, 1740–1840* (Toronto: University of Toronto Press, 1985), p. 211.

7. J.I. Little, *Loyalties in Conflict: A Canadian Borderland in War and Rebellion 1812–1840* (Toronto: University of Toronto Press, 2008), pp. 104–106.

8. Daniel Sallée, "Revolutionary Political Thought, the Persistence of the Old Order, and the Problem of Power in an Ancien Régime Colonial Society: Ideological Perspectives of Lower Canada, 1827–1838," *British Journal of Canadian Studies* 3(1) (1988): 52.

9. Éric Bédard, *Les reformistes: Une generation canadienne-francaise au milieu du XIXe siecle* (Montreal: Boreal, 2009), pp. 321–322.

10. Allan Greer, *The Patriots and the People: The Rebellion of 1837 in Rural Lower Canada* (Toronto: University of Toronto Press, 1993), p. 5.

11. F. Murray Greenwood, *Legacies of Fear: Law and Politics in Quebec in the Era of the French Revolution* (Toronto: University of Toronto Press, 1993).

12. Gilles Laporte, *Patriotes et loyaux: Leadership régional et mobilisation politique en 1837 et 1838* (Quebec: Septentrion, 2004), pp. 10–11.

Drawing of a patriote by Henri Julien.

Source: Library and Archives Canada/C-017937.

There is little doubt that the various parties were seeking to protect their interests and ambitions. The patriote leaders had ambitions as a group and they saw the welfare of the masses as a function of their own interests. The church leaders were ideologically opposed to liberalism and reform, and they viewed the patriotes as anticlerical and out to diminish the Church's role. The seigneurs, such as Pierre de Boucherville, calculated that he would have lost an annual revenue of 500 *louis* (gold coin pieces) if the rebellions had succeeded. The English merchants certainly were protecting their interests and ambitions because they largely controlled the colony's economy. The increasing power of the French majority would only threaten their minority control. Responsible government threatened the oligarchic power of the British governor and his hand-picked councils.

Self-interest aside, however, the rebellions were ultimately caused by a situation that should never have been allowed to develop. In the aftermath of the American Revolution, colonial government had moved away from the British parliamentary of representative government. In the aftermath of the War of 1812 and the coming of the loyalists, oligarchic administrations and repressive regimes became entrenched. When legal protest proved futile, armed insurrection was the only option.

Consequences of the Rebellions

The British government declared martial law in Lower Canada, suspended the colony's constitution, and established a Special Council in 1838. It was composed of members of the English minority with a few "loyalist" French Canadians. During the rebellions, it suspended civil liberties and legal rights. It then set up a police force in Montreal, as well as a rural police force to pacify the people. The council also weakened French civil law by giving new guarantees to landed property and by undermining seigneurial tenure on the Island of Montreal.

The hanging of five patriotes on January 18, 1839.

Source: Library and Archives Canada/C-020295.

Lord Durham's Visit

Despite its draconian response, the British government realized that something had gone terribly wrong with its "loyal" colonies of British North America. Only sixty years after the humiliating loss of the American colonies, the British faced more rebellions. While they were crushed with relative ease, London needed to determine what was going wrong. The government formed a royal commission led by Lord Durham to visit both Lower and Upper Canada to study the causes. The future historian François-Xavier Garneau appealed to the commissioner on his arrival in Quebec: "Durham, close your ears to the counsels of vengeance; take upon yourself the defence of a helpless people." But Lord Durham was listening to other advice. Before he even left England, he had been lobbied by Canadian and British merchant groups who emphasized the ethnic and religious aspect of the conflict; they urged union of the Canadas to save themselves from "the designs of the French faction, madly bent upon [the] destruction" of the rights, the interests, and the property of Lower Canada's British population.

Durham's concerns for economic development made him sympathetic to the merchants' views. In his famous report, submitted in 1839, he drew attention to the "deadly animosity" between French and English. Ultimately the designs of assimilation, as laid out in the Royal Proclamation of 1763 at the time of Conquest, had never been implemented. The colonies, and the British imperial authorities by extension, were now paying for the consequences: "I found two nations warring in the bosom of a single state; I found a struggle, not of principles, but of races." A union of the two Canadas would yield a slight English majority, which immigration would further reinforce. Durham was convinced that "once placed, by the legitimate course of events and the working of natural causes, in a minority, [the French] would abandon their vain hopes of nationality." Union with Upper Canada would assure the assimilation of the French—the ultimate solution, Durham believed, to ethnic conflict in Lower Canada.

SUMMARY

The rebellions brought Lower Canada to its knees and made it easy to overlook the enormous changes that the colony had undergone since 1791. The colony lost its own government and was to be joined to Upper Canada in a union that the majority of the French Canadians did not want. Moreover, the avowed purpose of this union, as expressed by Durham, by British parliamentarians, and by English merchants, was to break the power of French Canada and eventually to assimilate it. But like the proponents of the Constitutional Act a half-century earlier, the advocates of union proved to be poor prophets.

NOTES

1. Dany Fougères, "Des eaux indésirables: Montréal et ses eaux de surface, 1796–1840," *Revue d'histoire de l'Amérique française* 60 (2006): 95–96.

2. Mary Anne Poutanen, "Reflections on Montreal Prostitution in the Records of the Lower Courts," in Donald Fyson et al., eds., *Class, Gender and the Law in Eighteenth- and Nineteenth-Century Quebec: Sources and Perspectives* (Montreal: Department of History, McGill University, 1993), pp. 99–125.

3. Jan Noel, "'*Femmes Fortes*' and the Montreal Poor in the Early Nineteenth Century," in Wendy Mitchinson et al., eds., *Canadian Women: A Reader* (Toronto: Harcourt Brace, 1996), p. 69.

4. Allan Greer, *Peasant, Lord, and Merchant: Rural Society in Three Quebec Parishes, 1740–1840* (Toronto: University of Toronto Press, 1985), pp. 122–39.

5. Allan Greer, *The Patriots and the People: The Rebellion of 1837 in Rural Lower Canada* (Toronto: University of Toronto Press, 1993), p. 293.

6. Donald Creighton, *The Commercial Empire of the St. Lawrence, 1760–1850* (Toronto: Ryerson Press, 1937), p. 23, quoted in Gilles Paquet and Jean-Pierre Wallot, "Groupes sociaux et pouvoir: Le cas canadien au tournant du XIXe siècle," *Revue d'histoire de l'Amérique française* 27 (1973–74): 539.

7. Fernand Ouellet, *Louis-Joseph Papineau: A Divided Soul* (Ottawa: Canadian Historical Association, 1960).

8. The original French text reads, "concourir, autant que la faiblesse de leur sexe peut le leur permettre, à faire réussir la cause patriotique." Quoted in Micheline Dumont et al., *L'histoire des femmes au Québec depuis quatre siècles* (Montreal: Le Jour, 1982), p. 145.

RELATED READING

Module 7, "The Rebellions of 1837–1838 in Lower and Upper Canada," in *Visions: The Canadian History Modules Project: Pre-Confederation*, offers an excellent introduction to the causes and events surrounding the rebellions. The module offers extensive primary source documentation and articles by Allan Greer, "Two Nations Warring" and Colin Coates and Ronald J. Stagg, "The Causes of the Rebellion." See pages 291–330.

BIBLIOGRAPHY

Fernand Ouellet's *Lower Canada, 1791–1840: Social Change and Nationalism* (Toronto: McClelland & Stewart, 1979) is useful for this period. His *Economic and Social History of Quebec, 1760–1850* (Toronto: Macmillan, 1980), and *Economy, Class, and Nation in Quebec: Interpretive Essays*, Jacques A. Barbier, ed.

and trans. (Toronto: Copp Clark Pitman, 1991), should also be consulted. Jean-Pierre Wallot and Gilles Paquet criticize Ouellet's interpretations and provide a contrary view on several issues. See, for example, "The Agricultural Crisis in Lower Canada, 1802–12; Mise au point: A Response to T.J.A. Le Goff," *Canadian Historical Review* 56 (1975): 133–61; "Stratégie foncière de l'habitant: Québec (1790–1835)," *Revue d'histoire de l'Amérique française* 39 (1985–1986): 551–81; and Gilles Paquet and Jean-Pierre Wallot, *Lower Canada at the Turn of the Nineteenth Century: Restructuring and Modernization* (Ottawa: Canadian Historical Association, 1988).

Allan Greer's *Peasant, Lord, and Merchant: Rural Society in Three Quebec Parishes, 1740–1840* (Toronto: University of Toronto Press, 1985) is an important study of a region in which patriote support was strong. John McCallum, *Unequal Beginnings: Agriculture and Economic Development in Quebec and Ontario until 1870* (Toronto: University of Toronto Press, 1980); Michael Bliss, *Northern Enterprise: Five Centuries of Canadian Business* (Toronto: McClelland & Stewart, 1987); and R. Cole Harris, "Quebec in the Century after the Conquest," in R. Cole Harris and John Warkentin, *Canada Before Confederation* (Ottawa: Carleton University Press, 1991 [1974]), pp. 65–109, are also helpful. Gérald Bernier and Daniel Salée argue in *The Shaping of Quebec Politics and Society: Colonialism, Power and the Transition to Capitalism in the 19th Century* (Washington, DC: Taylor and Francis, 1992) that social and class questions transcend ethnic issues in this period of Quebec's history.

Useful historiographical studies are Gérald Bernier and Daniel Salée, "Les insurrections de 1837–1838 au Québec: Remarques critiques et théoriques en marge de l'historiographie," *Canadian Review of Studies in Nationalism/Revue canadienne des études sur le nationalisme* 13 (1986): 13–30; Fernand Ouellet, "La tradition révolutionnaire au Canada: À propos de l'historiographie des insurrections de 1837–1838 dans le Bas-Canada," *Revue de l'Université d'Ottawa/University of Ottawa Quarterly* 60 (1985): 91–124; and Allan Greer, "1837–38: Rebellion Reconsidered," *Canadian Historical Review* 76 (1995): 1–18. Bibliographical suggestions appear in James Lambert's essay, "Quebec/Lower Canada" in M. Brook Taylor, ed., *Canadian History: A Reader's Guide*, vol. 1, *Beginnings to Confederation* (Toronto: University of Toronto Press, 1994), pp. 112–83.

On the history of the Roman Catholic Church, see Lucien Lemieux, *Histoire du catholicisme québécois: Les XVIIIe et XIXe siècles*, vol. 1, *Les années difficiles (1760–1839)* (Montreal: Boréal, 1989). James Lambert has made a notable contribution to social and religious history in his unpublished Ph.D. thesis, "Monseigneur, the Catholic Bishop. Joseph-Octave Plessis, Church, State, and Society in Lower Canada: Historiography and Analysis," 3 vols. (Université Laval, 1980). On conflict between the clergy and the laity, see Christian Dessureault and Christine Hudon, "Conflits sociaux et élites locales au Bas-Canada: Le clergé, les notables, la paysannerie et le contrôle de la fabrique," *Canadian Historical Review* 80 (1999): 413–39. For a look at evangelism, see Glen Scorgie, "The French Canadian Missionary Society: A Study in Evangelistic Zeal and Civic Ambition," *Fides et historia* 36(1) (2004): 67–81. The impact of the French Revolution is discussed in Pierre Boulle and Richard-A. Lebrun, *Le Canada et la Révolution française* (Montreal: Centre interuniversitaire d'études européennes, 1989); and in Michel Grenon, ed., *L'image de la Révolution française au Québec, 1789–1989* (Montreal: Hurtubise HMH, 1989). F. Murray Greenwood traces the development of a "garrison mentality" among Lower Canada's population in *Legacies of Fear: Law and Politics in Quebec in the Era of the French Revolution* (Toronto: University of Toronto Press, 1993).

Alexis de Tocqueville's Canadian journal offers a contemporary portrait of Lower Canada in the early 1830s; see Jacques Vallée, ed., *Tocqueville au Bas-Canada* (Montreal: Éditions du jour, 1973), as well as Stéphane Dion, "La pensée de Tocqueville—L'épreuve du Canada français," *Revue d'histoire de l'Amérique française* 41 (1987–88): 537–52. For a look at the 1830s in Lower Canada through the lens of the French-language press, see Steven Fontaine-Bernard, "Le Bas-Canada dans la presse française de 1830 à 1839," *Bulletin d'histoire politique* 13(2) (2005): 171–90. For an in-depth look at Lower Canadian politics in the decades leading up to the rebellions, see Louis-George Harvey, *Le Printemps de l'Amérique française: Américanité, anticolonialisme et républicanisme dans le discours politique québécois 1805–1837* (Montreal: Boréal 2005).

The cholera epidemics are discussed in Geoffrey Bilson, *A Darkened House: Cholera in Nineteenth-Century Canada* (Toronto: University of Toronto Press, 1980). Barbara Tunis examines the question of smallpox vaccination in "Public Vaccination in Lower Canada, 1815–1823: Controversy and a Dilemma," *Historical Reflections* 9 (1982): 267–76. Dany Fougères looks at an urban environmental issue in "Des eaux indésirables: Montréal et ses eaux de surface, 1796–1840," *Revue d'histoire de l'Amérique française* 60 (2006): 95–124.

Jean-Marie Fecteau analyzes social issues in *Un nouvel ordre des choses: La pauvreté, le crime, l'état au Québec, de la fin du XVIIIe à 1840* (Montreal: VLB Editeur, 1989). Serge Gagnon's research on social history is available in *Plaisir d'amour et crainte de Dieu: Sexualité et confession au Bas-Canada* (Ste. Foy, QC: Les presses de l'Université Laval, 1990), and *Mariage et famille au temps de Papineau* (Ste. Foy, QC: Les presses de l'Université Laval, 1993). Jean-Pierre Hardy examines body hygiene and other questions linked to daily life in *La vie quotidienne dans la vallée du Saint-Laurent (1790–1835)* (Quebec: Septentrion, 2002).

Françoise Noël proposes a case study of social organization in *The Christie Seigneuries: Estate Management and Settlement in the Upper Richelieu Valley, 1764–1854* (Montreal/Kingston: McGill-Queen's University Press, 1992). A brief examination of rural life may be found in Serge Courville and Normand Séguin, *Rural Life in Nineteenth-Century Quebec* (Ottawa: Canadian Historical Association, 1989) (Historical Booklet 47). Some personal accounts relating to this period may be found in Françoise Noël, *Family Life and Sociability in Upper and Lower Canada, 1780–1870: A View from Diaries and Family Correspondence* (Montreal/Kingston: McGill-Queen's University Press, 2003). Lucille H. Campey looks at Scottish immigration in Lower Canada in *Les Écossais: The Pioneer Scots of Lower Canada, 1770–1855* (Toronto: Natural Heritage Books, 2006). Sean Mills investigates the outbreak of the War of 1812 in Lower Canada in his examination of the Lachine Riot, "French Canadians and the Beginning of the War of 1812: Revisiting the Lachine Riot," *Histoire sociale/Social History* 38(75) (2005): 37–58.

Material on the history of the judicial system is available in Donald Fyson, *Magistrates, Police, and People: Everyday Criminal Justice in Quebec and Lower Canada, 1764–1837* (Toronto: University of Toronto Press and Osgoode Society for Canadian Legal History, 2006); and in Evelyn Kolish, *Nationalismes et conflits de droits: Le débat du droit privé au Québec, 1760–1840* (LaSalle, QC: Hurtubise HMH, 1994). Several articles on justice, martial law, and state repression during the rebellions may be found in F. Murray Greenwood and Barry Wright, eds., *Canadian State Trials*, vol. II, *Rebellion and Invasion in the Canadas, 1837–1839* (Toronto: University of Toronto Press, 2002). On the treatment of the mentally ill, see James E. Moran, *Committed to the State Asylum: Insanity and Society in Nineteenth-Century Quebec and Ontario* (Montreal/Kingston: McGill-Queen's University Press, 2000). The transformation of Lower Canada's landscape by settlers and the consequent emergence of community sentiment and its links with the rise of nationalism are studied in Colin M. Coates, *The Metamorphoses of Landscape and Community in Early Quebec* (Montreal/Kingston: McGill-Queen's University Press, 2000). See also his article on the interest in landscaping of some upper-class Britons in Lower Canada, "Like 'The Thames towards Putney': The Appropriation of Landscape in Lower Canada," *Canadian Historical Review* 74 (1993): 317–43.

A brief synthesis of the rebellions is available in English in Jean-Paul Bernard, *The Rebellions of 1837 and 1838 in Lower Canada*, Historical Booklet 55 (Ottawa: Canadian Historical Association, 1996). A fuller examination may be found in his book *Les rébellions de 1837–1838* (Montreal: Boréal Express, 1983). Allan Greer challenges earlier analyses of the events of 1837 and their origins in *The Patriots and the People: The Rebellion of 1837 in Rural Lower Canada* (Toronto: University of Toronto Press, 1993); and in "1837–38: Rebellion Reconsidered," *Canadian Historical Review* 76 (1995): 1–18. In "Historical Roots of Canadian Democracy," *Journal of Canadian Studies* 34(1) (1999): 7–26, Greer also contends that "ethnic nationalism" was much more characteristic of the anglophone Tories of Lower Canada than of the French-speaking patriotes. Joseph Schull's *Rebellion: The Rising in French Canada, 1837* (Toronto: Macmillan, 1971) is an older, popular treatment. Jacques Monet, *The Last Cannon Shot: A Study of French Canadian Nationalism, 1837–1850* (Toronto: University of Toronto Press, 1969), contains useful material on both the rebellion and its aftermath. Relations between Britain and Canada are analyzed in Peter Burroughs, *The Canadian Crisis and British Colonial Policy, 1828–1841* (Toronto: Macmillan, 1972); Ged Martin, *The Durham Report and British Policy: A Critical Essay* (Cambridge: Cambridge University Press, 1972); Phillip A. Buckner, "The Colonial Office and British North America, 1801–50," in *Dictionary of Canadian Biography*, vol. 8, *1851–1860* (Toronto: University of Toronto Press, 1985), pp. xxiii–xxxvii;

and James Sturgis, "Anglicisation as a Theme in Lower Canadian History, 1807–1843," *British Journal of Canadian Studies* 3 (1988): 210–29. See also Michael J. Turner, "Radical Agitation and the Canada Question in British Politics, 1837–1841," *Historical Research* 79(203) (2006): 90–114. Yvan Lamonde proposes an intellectual history of the period in *Histoire sociale des idées au Québec*, vol. I, *1760–1896* (Montreal: Fides, 2000). Janet Ajzenstat sees Durham as a mainstream liberal, but not as a cultural chauvinist, in *The Political Thought of Lord Durham* (Montreal/Kingston: McGill-Queen's University Press, 1988). See also the entire Spring 1990 issue of *Journal of Canadian Studies*, "Durham and His Ideas," and Michel Ducharme's study *Le concept de liberté au Canada a` l'époque des révolutions atlantiques (1776–1838)* (Montreal/Kingston: McGill-Queen's University Press 2009).

For material pertaining to women in Lower Canada in the early nineteenth century, see Micheline Dumont et al., *Quebec Women: A History* (Toronto: Women's Press, 1987). Women's work as domestics is examined in Claudette Lacelle, *Urban Domestic Servants in Nineteenth-Century Canada* (Ottawa: Parks Canada, 1987). Bettina Bradbury et al. look at changing marriage contracts in "Property and Marriage: The Law and the Practice in Early Nineteenth-Century Montreal," *Histoire sociale/Social History* 26 (1993): 9–39. Peter Gossage studies the work of the Grey Nuns with foundlings in "Les enfants abandonnés à Montréal au 19e siècle: la crèche d'Youville des Soeurs Grises, 1820–1871," *Revue d'histoire de l'Amérique française* 40 (1987): 31–59. Allan Greer analyzes the participation of women in the rebellions in *The Patriots and the People: The Rebellion of 1837 in Rural Lower Canada* (Toronto: University of Toronto Press, 1999), pp. 189–218. Urban violence involving women is examined in Mary Anne Poutanen, "Images du danger dans les archives judiciaires: Comprendre la violence et le vagabondage dans un centre urbain du début du XIXe siècle, Montréal (1810–1842)," *Revue d'histoire de l'Amérique française* 55 (2002): 381–405; in Sandy Ramos, "'A Most Detestable Crime': Gender Identities and Sexual Violence in the District of Montreal, 1803–1843," *Journal of the Canadian Historical Association/Revue de la Société historique du Canada* 12 (2001): 27–48; and in Donald Fyson, Colin Coates, and Kathryn Harvey, eds., *Class, Gender and the Law in Eighteenth- and Nineteenth-Century Quebec: Sources and Perspectives* (Montreal: Montreal History Group, 1993). For an extensive look at the history of slavery in Montreal, see Frank Mackey, *Done with Slavery: The Black Fact in Montreal, 1760–1840* (Montreal/Kingston: McGill-Queen's University Press, 2010).

Aboriginal issues are reviewed by Daniel Francis in *A History of the Native Peoples of Quebec, 1760–1867* (Ottawa: Department of Indian Affairs and Northern Development, 1983). Individuals mentioned in this chapter are also studied in various volumes of *Dictionary of Canadian Biography*; see, in particular, Fernand Ouellet's article on Papineau in vol. 10, *1871–1880* (Toronto: University of Toronto Press, 1972), pp. 564–78. Jack Verney has written a biography of E.B. O'Callaghan, one of the great English-speaking allies of the patriotes: *O'Callaghan, The Making and Unmaking of a Rebel* (Ottawa: Carleton University Press, 1994).

Useful maps relating to this chapter appear in R. Louis Gentilcore, ed., *Historical Atlas of Canada*, vol. 2, *The Land Transformed, 1800–1891* (Toronto: University of Toronto Press, 1993).

Chapter Fourteen

GROWTH AND REBELLION IN UPPER CANADA

TIME LINE	
1816	Upper Canada introduces Common School Act
1817	Society for the Relief of Strangers established
1819	Robert Gourlay banished from Upper Canada
1826	Canada Land Company established
1827	King's College, forerunner of the University of Toronto, founded by royal charter in York
1829	Welland Canal opens for navigation between Lake Ontario and Lake Erie
1830	Grand Lodge of British North America (Orange Order) established at Brockville, Upper Canada
1832	Completion of Rideau Canal Major outbreak of cholera in Upper Canada
1835	Kingston Penitentiary opens
1837	Rebellion in Upper Canada led by William Lyon Mackenzie
1838	Battle of the Windmill fought near Prescott, Upper Canada

From 1815 to 1840, Upper Canada experienced phenomenal growth and development. The population quadrupled, from less than 100 000 to more than 400 000. In contrast to Lower Canada, immigration, rather than the birth rate, accounted for much of this increase. Some of the new immigrants came from the United States, but most arrived from the British Isles, including northern Irish Protestants, southern Irish Roman Catholics, Lowland and Highland Scots, Welsh, and English. Many were fleeing desperate economic conditions in the aftermath of the Napoleonic Wars. This immigration wave recast the colony of Upper Canada. The newcomers settled the land, creating a new agricultural frontier. They also challenged the political, religious, and social order by bringing with them expectations of British parliamentary traditions that were being ignored in Upper Canada. The Scots and the Irish in particular challenged the oligarchic control of the English-Anglican elite. The result was rebellion in 1837.

Immigration and Settlement

After the War of 1812, anti-American sentiment was strong in British North America. The imperial government encouraged British over American immigration to the new frontier of Upper Canada. New laws pertaining to "aliens" prevented Americans from obtaining land grants until they had resided in the province for seven years. Nevertheless, some Americans did come: these included fugitive slaves from the South and freed slaves from the northern states. Most African Americans homesteaded along the border, with the exception of a small group of black veterans of the War of 1812, who settled in Oro Township on the western shore of Lake Simcoe.

Immigration from Britain

After 1815, the British settlers that Simcoe had sought in the early years of the colony finally arrived. The end of the Napoleonic Wars explains the migration. As was common, war was followed by economic recession. In this case, however, the peace brought severe economic dislocation and high unemployment to Great Britain. Postwar Britain encouraged emigration in the hopes that it would reduce the population pressure, alleviate unemployment, provide relief from social unrest, and strengthen its colonies.

In the late 1810s and early 1820s, the British government assisted the exodus with financial aid, similar to that given to the loyalists. The assistance included the cost of transportation, free grants of land to family heads, rations for eight months (or until families became established), agricultural supplies at cost, and a minister and school teacher on government salary for each settlement. Initially, the government intended this program mainly for demobilized soldiers and half-pay officers (those officers who received a reduced allowance when not in actual service or when retired).

Some 800 immigrants from four parishes in the Highlands of Scotland settled in Glengarry

Rare early depiction of an African-Canadian woman.

Source: Library and Archives Canada, Acc. No. 1950-29-64/C-093963.

County, Upper Canada, in 1815. Their early pioneering experiences would be made known through Ralph Connor's popular Glengarry novels after 1900. The government also helped several thousand Scots to settle in Upper Canada, chiefly in the Lanark area in the eastern part of the colony. Others received aid to settle in the Rideau district south of present-day Ottawa. In the 1820s, some 3000 Irish immigrants under government sponsorship arrived in the Peterborough area, administered by Peter Robinson, the commissioner of Crown lands for Upper Canada. A significant number from North Tipperary, Ireland, settled in the Bytown (Ottawa) area and, later, around London, attracted by next of kin who had gone before them and had succeeded in acquiring land for their children.

Under the auspices of the Petworth Emigration Committee, Reverend Thomas Sockett organized one of the largest of the assisted British emigration schemes in the years 1832–37. About 1800 men, women, and children, mostly from the Petworth parish in West Sussex, in the southeast of England, came under the sponsorship of the Third Earl of Egremont and under the guidance of the local rector, Reverend Sockett. Most were poor agricultural labourers who arrived in Upper Canada via Montreal and Toronto (as York was renamed in 1834), and were then dispersed to areas of south-central and western Upper Canada. The Petworth emigrants came too late to receive the generous government assistance.

In the mid-1820s, the British government stopped aiding emigrants. Some private charitable associations and landowners, anxious to rid their estates of impoverished tenants, provided minimal assistance. "Friendly societies" assisted single women wishing to emigrate by covering the cost of passage and also by providing a staff of matrons on board the ships. These societies included the London Female Emigration Society, formed in 1850; the British Ladies Emigration

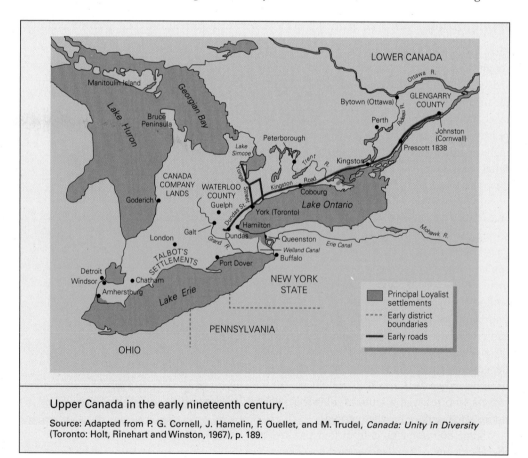

Upper Canada in the early nineteenth century.

Source: Adapted from P. G. Cornell, J. Hamelin, F. Ouellet, and M. Trudel, *Canada: Unity in Diversity* (Toronto: Holt, Rinehart and Winston, 1967), p. 189.

Society, formed in 1859; and the Female Middle Class Emigration Society, formed in 1861. Many immigrants were willing to come on their own, without government assistance, to escape a desperate situation in Britain and have a chance at a new life. This pattern holds especially true for the victims of the Irish potato famine.

Upper Canadian landowners, such as Colonel Thomas Talbot, also assisted immigrants in the hope of profiting from government incentives for settlement and land development. Talbot secured 2000 hectares on the remote northwestern shore of Lake Erie. He subsequently received 81 hectares of adjoining land for each colonist he settled on a 20-hectare lot of the original grant. Talbot eventually accumulated an estate of nearly 30 000 hectares, making him one of the largest landholders in Upper Canada. In return, he contributed to the transformation of more than 200 000 hectares of forest into 3000 farm lots in southwestern Upper Canada. His extensive road system made his lands more accessible and hence more valuable.

In 1826, the British government created the Canada Company, the first large-scale Canadian land company, headed by John Galt. The Canada Company purchased more than 400 000 hectares of land, consisting of Crown reserves and the huge Huron Tract (the latter in southwestern Upper Canada on the shores of Lake Huron), for the modest price of £350 000 sterling. The Company was allowed to withhold one-third of the price to develop public works and improvements in the Tract. The Canada Company initially suffered heavy losses due to incompetence, but it survived into the 1830s, when increased immigration enabled it to recover. The Company founded the town of Goderich, in the Huron Tract, and the town of Guelph in another of its parcels of land east of the Tract. Galt went on to launch another land company in Lower Canada, known as the British American Land Company, with large holdings in the Eastern Townships.

Land speculation was big business in the colonies. By purchasing land at a low price in undeveloped areas, speculators could become very wealthy when the prices increased dramatically, and transportation schemes opened the areas to settlement and development. In most cases, they paid next to nothing for the land, and then turned around and sold it to poor immigrants at inflated prices. Profits of 50 to 100 percent were not uncommon, although most received returns around 2 to 8 percent. Many successful speculators rose to positions of social prominence through this new wealth.

The Voyage Overseas

After the initial years of government assistance, most immigrants came at their own expense. Sea travel was becoming less dangerous, but it remained very expensive. Only the wealthy could afford the £30 for first-class accommodation, which included a cabin with one or two bunks, a sofa, a window, and full meals. The remainder had to share bunks in the steerage of crowded passenger ships or, worse, in the dank holds of timber ships. Timber merchants quickly realized that there was profit to be made, even from the poorest of would-be immigrants. Their ships were returning to Britain loaded with timber but they were making the journey to BNA empty. Even though these ships were of relatively poor quality and were not designed for passengers, they become the only possible mode of transportation for thousands of immigrants.

Makeshift 2-metre-square bunks stacked two or three tiers high lined the sides and ran down the middle of the vessels. The ship owners packed as many as 250 immigrants into a space 28.5 metres long by 7.5 metres wide and little more than 1.5 metres high. Often four people, even complete strangers, were crowded into a single berth. Food was often rancid and clean water and clean air sparse. Inevitably, communicable diseases spread rapidly. Few doctors and medical supplies were available.

The immigrants endured these squalid conditions for up to six weeks—and longer in times of poor sailing. Many had already spent a week or two waiting at dockside for their ships to sail.

In his first novel, *Redburn*, Herman Melville describes how the emigrants talked of soon seeing America:

> *The agent had told them that twenty days would be an unusually long voyage. Suddenly there was a cry of "Land," and emigrants crowded a deck expecting America, but it was only Ireland.*

Many never saw the New World and a chance at a new life. They died by the hundreds on these "death ships" and were dumped at sea. Cholera and typhoid spread through Britain and Europe in the 1830s and 1840s. The "death ships" were often disease-ridden. One of every 28 immigrants died on board. Quebec City was the destination of most. The wretched and bewildered immigrants faced the scrutiny of the French-Canadians, who saw them as a destitute, threatening, and disease-infected foreign population. Those who survived the trip were often quarantined upon arrival. They then confronted unscrupulous "runners," or profiteers at dockside, eager to take advantage of them. As if all this misery were not enough, the immigrants still faced the arduous overland journey to their new homes. And only at this point could they begin the arduous work of breaking the land and living an isolated existence on an often harsh and unforgiving frontier.

Still, the constant need for labour in Upper Canada gave even penniless immigrants an opportunity to earn a living and to save for farms of their own. In Upper Canada in the early 1830s, a landless labourer could still become a landed proprietor—something nearly impossible in Britain.

The Aboriginal Peoples

The land upon which the speculators made their fortunes and the immigrants settled was taken from the Aboriginal peoples, who, by 1815, were already outnumbered ten to one by whites. After the War of 1812, the First Nations in Upper Canada made seven major land surrenders, opening up much of present-day southern Ontario for settlement. In 1818, the government of Upper Canada changed the method of purchasing the land, offering to make annual payments or annuities in perpetuity instead of a one-time payment.

The First Nations were aware that they were losing their lands, but they had little choice but to strike the best possible deals. Their leaders recognized that the coming of the whites was inevitable. Their traditional lifestyles would not survive, and while they could retreat to more remote areas, the "march of progress" was inexorable. The Aboriginal people were not simply victims of government policy. They exercised considerable agency based on an assessment of their future possibilities in a time of change and uncertainty. The chiefs, therefore, looked to make the transition as smooth as possible. Most immediate, with the fur trade declining and their hunting grounds being taken away, the Aboriginal people required food, clothes, and supplies. Second, they needed medicine to help them stave off sickness and disease. Third, if they were to make the transition to farming, they needed tools and implements. Fourth, they required schools to educate their young to adapt and assimilate to the new realities.

Some Aboriginal groups from the United States migrated north to settle in Upper Canada. They came to escape the American government's removal policy, which dictated that Aboriginals east of

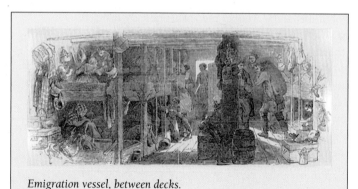

Emigration vessel, between decks.
Source: Toronto Reference Library.

the Mississippi must move west of the river. Several thousand Anishinabeg took up residence in Upper Canada in the 1830s and 1840s. Most of the Oneida, one of the Iroquois nations remaining in New York state after the American Revolution, also migrated around 1840 and purchased land on the Thames River west of London. In general, the government of Upper Canada allowed the First Nations to remain on their reserved lands (reserves). In 1836–37, Governor Francis Bond Head tried unsuccessfully to relocate the Anishinabeg of southern Ontario (the Ojibwas, Odawas, and Potawatomis) on Manitoulin Island. Instead, they were encouraged to farm in hopes that they would be acculturated and ultimately assimilated into the dominant society.

Colonial Oligarchy: The Family Compact

During the years 1815–40, a small, tightly knit elite popularly known as the "Family Compact" ruled Upper Canada. This elite was generally English, upper class, conservative, and Anglican. When novelist Charles Dickens visited Toronto in the early 1840s, he described the style of their tight rein on the province as "rabid Toryism." Through political domination of the Executive Council—the governor's "cabinet"—and the Legislative Council (the upper house of the government), this Toronto-centred group controlled government. Through political patronage, they appointed others from their clique in the outlying centres, thus creating or recognizing already-existing, smaller oligarchies throughout the colony. According to historian S.F. Wise, the Family Compact was "a quasi-official coalition of the central and local élites united for the purpose of distributing honours and rewards to the politically deserving."[1] Their aim was to create a government that regulated all aspects of society.

John Strachan

At the centre of the Family Compact stood Archdeacon John Strachan, cleric, educator, and leading adviser to the governors of Upper Canada. A story circulated in the colony about Strachan's son: One day someone asked him, "Who governs Upper Canada?" "I do," he replied. When asked to explain, he answered, "I govern my mother, my mother governs my father, my father governs Upper Canada."

Around Strachan gathered a group of men, many of whom were his former pupils. Foremost among them was John Beverley Robinson, who had become acting attorney general of Upper Canada in 1812, at the age of 21, and attorney general in 1818. About half of the Family Compact consisted of descendants of the original loyalist families. The other half included British immigrants who, like Strachan, had come in the early years of the colony. By maintaining control of the governorship and the executive, they directed government. In order to do this, they needed to prevent the elected Assembly from exercising its rightful role. Sir Peregrine Maitland, lieutenant governor from 1818 to 1828, for example, reinforced the Family Compact and allied himself with the members of the Executive Council. By maintaining a tight relationship with the Anglican Church, the oligarchy furthered its influence on the justification it was providing a "moral underpinning to society." Finally, the elite used

Sketch of Ojibwas by Titus Hibbert Ware.
Source: Toronto Reference Library/T14386.

A Methodist camp meeting.

Source: The United Church of Canada/Victoria University Archives, Toronto/Acc. no. 90.162 P/2019N.

its influence to build and expand the economy of the colony to its own benefit and profit. This economic progress included commerce, canal building, settlement schemes, and banks.

Crown and Clergy Reserves

In order to prevent the Assembly from exercising power, the Family Compact had to have its own sources of revenue through the Crown reserves. By the 1820s—due to increased settlement during the immigration boom—the wealth from the sale of the Crown lands was substantial. In 1826, the British government implemented a new policy for their sale. In each district, vacant Crown lands were evaluated and a minimum sale price established. The available land was advertised in the newspapers and sold to the highest bidder. The government appointed Peter Robinson as the commissioner of Crown lands. These payments went directly to the governor and his Executive Council, much to the resentment of an emerging reform group in the elected Assembly.

The clergy reserves became even more contentious. In 1791, the British government set aside one-seventh of the land in each township for the support of a "Protestant clergy." John Strachan argued that by the phrase "Protestant clergy," the Constitutional Act of 1791 meant the Anglican Church alone. The other Protestant denominations claimed entitlement to a portion of the reserves, but they were resisted by the influential Anglican clergy within the Family Compact.

Religious Disputes

The first denominational challenge to the Anglicans' ecclesiastical monopoly came from the Presbyterians. As the established Church of Scotland, this major Protestant denomination demanded a share of the clergy reserves. In 1829, the British government through the Colonial Office responded to the obvious injustice and authorized their inclusion. The Executive Council, however, denied the Methodists the same right. Since Methodism had come into Upper Canada from the United States, Family Compact members justified their opposition on the charge that it contained radical republican sympathies. The Methodists had to fight for a portion of the clergy reserves.

Regardless, Methodism gained popularity in Upper Canada, particularly among the poor, backwoods frontier community. Through hymns, campfire meetings, and fervent preaching, Methodist preachers used evangelicalism to reach out to a population far removed from the more aloof and elitist Anglican Church:

> Sometimes a wave of excitement would sweep over a gathering of this kind and as if moved by one impulse scores would rush to the altar, throwing themselves down, sobbing or groaning. This was the objective of the preaching and far into the night the ministers would move from group to group praying and exhorting the penitents.[2]

Using effective Mississauga preachers such as Peter Jones and John Sunday, the latter a veteran of the War of 1812, the Methodists converted 2000 First Nations people in Upper Canada to Christianity in the late 1820s. Aboriginal and white Methodists built missions for

Ojibwa-speaking converts at the Credit River, 20 kilometres west of York, and at Grape Island in the Bay of Quinte.

The growth of Methodism was of concern to such Anglican leaders as John Strachan and led to conflict. In 1825, Strachan used the occasion of a funeral eulogy for Jacob Mountain, the Anglican Lord Bishop of Quebec, to attack certain "uneducated itinerant preachers" of the Methodist Church. He described them as ignorant, incapable, idle, and above all, disloyal, because of their emotionally charged and "republican" views.

Egerton Ryerson

The Methodists counterattacked through Egerton Ryerson, a 23-year-old preacher of loyalist background, who wrote a thundering reply in 1826. Raised in a prominent Anglican family but a convert to Methodism, Ryerson upheld the educated quality of the itinerant preachers, denied that Methodists held republican views, and challenged the legality of Strachan's position that the Church of England was the established church in the colony. For a half-century Ryerson maintained a position of prominence in politics in Upper Canada, which he used to advance educational reform. Specifically, Ryerson advanced the Methodist belief that even the lower classes were deserving of an education. He championed the cause of universal and state-controlled education. He also moved Methodism away from American frontier–style camp

John Sunday.
Source: Library and Archives Canada/Bibliothèque et Archives Canada (R9266-2848).

meetings and itinerant preachers to urban churches and professionally trained and educated clergy, from public displays of emotion to rational principles. Methodists would also cease to look upon the state as a source of opposition and instead see it as an agency of stability and support.

As immigrants poured into Upper Canada, other Protestant denominations and religious sects emerged. Baptists, Quakers, Dunkards, Millerites, Campbellites, Christian Universalists, Mormons, and German-speaking Amish led to increased religious pluralism. Substantial numbers of Irish Catholics also arrived. These groups challenged the supremacy and tight grip of the Anglican Church.

Education

Religious disputes often focused on education. By doing so, they conjured up the old issue of church and state and took on political dimensions. Traditionally, education was controlled by the church and it was viewed as a privilege of the elite. There was little point, it was argued, in educating the masses. The lower classes spent their lives toiling on the land or, with the advent of industrialization, in workshops or factories. It was believed that education could also be dangerous. It could highlight the social injustices inherent in the class system and lead the masses to question their status, and possibly even revolt.

The Protestant sects placed increasing importance on education, particularly literacy, so that individuals could read the Bible and establish their own personal relationships with God. The Scots and the Irish placed considerable importance on education. They left established educational systems within their homelands before emigrating to Upper Canada and, upon arrival, they worked to establish schools. American immigrants also left communities that placed importance on education and they expected the same in their new homes.

Prior to 1815, schooling was informal and frequently occurred in the home. After the immigration boom, in most rural areas and local districts, schooling was considered important enough to be given priority in terms of building a schoolhouse or hiring a teacher. By the time of Ryerson's reform of the educational system in Upper Canada in the 1840s (he became superintendent of schools for Canada West in 1844), most townships had at least one and often as many as three or four public schools, not to mention private schools. In addition, Sunday schools began as a means of educating children who had to work the other six days of the week. A few grammar schools, or district schools, existed for the training of boys from affluent families who were destined for the professions. Girls fortunate enough to be educated were generally taught at home. In 1816, a committee of the Assembly introduced the Common School Act, which allotted £6000 annually to state-supported, common primary schools intended, at least in theory, for all children. Responsibility for building and maintaining the schools rested in the hands of local boards.

But the push for educational reform met powerful resistance in the form of the Family Compact. John Strachan wanted common schools under Anglican control to counteract the use of American textbooks and American-trained teachers. The battle played out within the government of Upper Canada. The Assembly opposed the idea and succeeded in establishing nonsectarian schools. It was a limited victory, however, since financial constraints reduced the annual appropriation for maintaining these schools to only £2500 in 1820.

Thwarted in his efforts for sectarian education in the common schools, John Strachan next directed his energy toward the grammar schools. These elite institutions, he believed, could offset the "Americanized" common schools. In 1819, he introduced legislation that required both an annual examination of all the grammar schools in the province and an annual report to the lieutenant governor. He also tried to introduce Andrew Bell's "monitorial" schools, an English system based on the teaching of Anglican doctrines. The Assembly defeated this suggestion.

Next, Strachan attempted to establish an Anglican university to connect higher education with the Church of England. He drew up a royal charter for the establishment of King's College in York in 1827. The university was mandated to hire only Anglican professors and to house a divinity school for training Anglican clergy. Strachan even offered the Mississauga Methodist leader Peter Jones a position in the proposed divinity school if he would convert to Anglicanism. Jones refused.

The Assembly opposed these "sectarian tendencies" and defeated the move to establish a provincial university at this time. Strachan had to be content with a preparatory school, modelled on the English classical schools and later known as Upper Canada College. King's College would not come into existence until 1843. By that time, the Methodists had already established their own university, Victoria College, in Cobourg, and the Presbyterians opened Queen's College in Kingston. Queen's began in 1841, when Thomas Liddell arrived from England with a charter from Queen Victoria to found a Presbyterian theological college.

Childhood in British North America

Historians have spent considerable time debating the schools question, but they have focused on religion and politics rather than the children themselves. Children were considered crucial for the future of the colonies of BNA. Having children and raising families was seen as the main role of women and as evidence of a successful marriage and home. Children were essential economically to allow a family to reach subsistence levels. But despite this emphasis, as historian Phillipe Aries notes, childhood was not a fixed category. The youth went to work so early that the transition from childhood to adulthood was blurred. There was no transitional "teenager" category in the nineteenth century.

Gender and class shaped the roles and identities of children. In working-class families, children as early as seven or eight years old were already working in the household or even outside the house as servants or in factories or mines. Childhood was a brief stage and there was little time for "play." Boys worked in the fields or workshops alongside their fathers and elder brothers; girls worked in homes alongside their mothers and elders sisters. The children received whatever education was possible in the household. Sometimes, this included being taught to read and write.

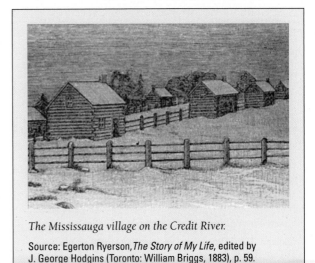

The Mississauga village on the Credit River.

Source: Egerton Ryerson, *The Story of My Life*, edited by J. George Hodgins (Toronto: William Briggs, 1883), p. 59.

Wealthy families placed great importance on formal education, but mainly for boys. They were often sent away to more "civilized" settings, such as Britain or the United States, to receive the best education possible. While girls were expected to be able to read and write, their education focused mainly on learning to be respectable and to carry themselves in society. By the latter nineteenth century, however, attitudes toward education were changing and society was beginning to view universal education as an essential mark of a "civilized" society. In an immigrant society such as BNA, it also became the crucial vehicle for assimilating future generations by instilling cultural, social, and national values.

Social, Criminal, and Humanitarian Concerns

One of the main arguments used against limiting schooling to the upper classes was that education could produce a more loyal and obedient citizenry. In addition to learning to read and write, the masses would be educated on morality and discipline. The need to use education as a means of social control became increasingly attractive with the rise of industrialization and urbanization.

Poverty threatened the maintenance of this respectable society. The large influx of immigrants, many of whom were destitute, raised the issue of poor relief. Traditionally, relief relied on Christian charity and was left to the churches and religious organizations. Publicly, it was granted to people in distress only on the recommendation of a magistrate. In 1817, the first major public-welfare agency, the Society for the Relief of Strangers, was established at York. Modelled on a similar society in London, England, this voluntary organization was created "to serve the wants and alleviate the misery" of destitute immigrants. In 1828, the society changed its name to "the Society for the Relief of the Sick and Destitute." The altered name reflected a change in attitude about social assistance: only individuals who were both sick and destitute would be eligible for relief. Able-bodied but unemployed individuals had to work in return for assistance. Those in authority assumed that work was available for everyone and that able-bodied people who did not work were lazy. They simply needed a moral lesson in frugality, hard work, and self-discipline. This myth laid the blame for poverty on the poor. The government established two "houses of industry" in 1837 to provide work for all "fit and able inmates," one in Toronto and one in Kingston.

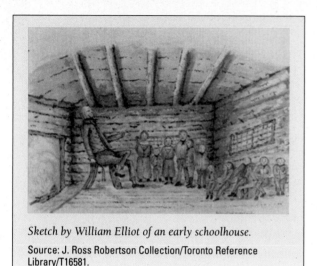

Sketch by William Elliot of an early schoolhouse.

Source: J. Ross Robertson Collection/Toronto Reference Library/T16581.

Crime and Punishment in Upper Canada

When charity failed to teach lessons to the poor, the legal system was prepared to step in. Gaols were established early on in Upper Canada to provide punishment and to deal with social outcasts, such as the mentally ill, the local vagrant, or the habitual drinker, as well as transients who had nowhere else to go. Ill equipped to retain people for extended periods of time, these cold, dark, and harsh places were designed to punish but not to rehabilitate individuals.

Beginning in the 1830s, penitentiaries replaced gaols as penal institutions. They were built to provide extended incarceration with the intention of using the time to rehabilitate the criminal. The Kingston Penitentiary opened in 1835 as the first of its kind in the country, reflected this new perspective. The usual sentence term lasted from one to six years for crimes such as grand and petty larceny, forgery, horse stealing, and assault. More than half of the convicted were under the age of 25 and believed to be young enough to be reformed. The building itself incorporated the most recent design features for penal institutions and had the distinction of being the largest and most expensive building in the country. It served, as well, as a showcase of the "civilizing" nature of Upper Canadian society. Criminal rehabilitation ranked with religion and economic growth as benchmarks of reform and progress in the nineteenth century.

Drunkenness was viewed as a major cause of crime in Upper Canada. Alcohol was believed to be the cause for most assault cases and was blamed for the breakup of families, poor work habits, and low productivity. Alcohol also contributed to social and political upheaval. Social reformers increasingly believed that temperance societies were the solution to the problem of "the drink." They aimed for abstinence through self-restraint rather than through government legislation, in the belief that drunkenness was a personal problem requiring a personal solution. The first temperance societies in Upper Canada appeared in the Niagara Peninsula, but by the 1830s, district societies existed throughout the colony. Most were affiliated with the Methodist, Presbyterian, and Baptist churches. In 1839, these temperance societies affiliated with the American Temperance Union in hopes of more effective action.

Sectarian, Ethnic, and Political Tensions

Violence and crime in Upper Canada often focused around sectarian, ethnic, and political tensions. An example was the antagonism between Irish Protestants and Irish Catholics, which originated in Ireland and carried over to the New World. The Orange Society was founded by Protestants in Ireland in 1795 and transplanted in British North America in 1830 when Ogle R. Gowan, an Irish Protestant from Dublin known for his anti-Catholic tracts, began the Grand Orange Lodge of British North America in Brockville, Upper Canada. Three years later, in 1833, some 90 lodges existed in the province with an estimated membership of more than 8000. Although these lodges served as social clubs, in some cases as insurance companies, and as hiring centres for Irish Protestants, they also held meetings designed to arouse sentiment against Irish Catholics, who organized their own associations and demonstrated the same antagonism towards the Protestants. Fighting between the "Orange and the Green" erupted in local bars, in communities where both groups lived in close proximity, and between work crews on the canals or in the lumber camps—especially on Irish festive holidays, such as March 17, St. Patrick's Day, and July 12, the anniversary of Protestant William of Orange's defeat of the Irish Catholics at the Battle of the Boyne.

Political violence often erupted at election time. Before the introduction of the secret ballot, voters had to show their support for candidates publicly. Some candidates hired thugs to intimidate and coerce voters to support them. During the election campaign of 1834 in Toronto, the streets were taken over by mobs brandishing sticks, representing the interests of opposing candidates. The authorities called in the infantry to restore the peace. Another example of corruption at election time involved using alcohol and the tavern to garner votes.

Ethnic clashes occurred frequently in the lumber camps in and around Bytown (Ottawa). Irish lumberers, known as "Shiners," fought with French Canadians for jobs. Owners of the lumber camps, especially Peter Aylen, deliberately incited these riots to take control of the lumber industry by undermining their competitors. The "Shiner Wars," as the disputes were called, were worse during springtime, when winter work was over and the lumberjacks had both money and idle time to drink and gamble in Bytown's many bars.

Class and ethnicity were important factors within the legal system of BNA, but gender also played a crucial role. The court system was a gendered institution. The court house, for example, was a distinctly gendered space. The judge, the lawyers, and the jury were male. It was often the reputation of the accused that was on trial and determined the verdict, more than the evidence:

> Authorities weighed the evidence in light of the complainant's and the defendant's class, race, age, and reputation. Judges and juries at rape trials interpreted a given situation based not only on the character of those involved but also on their understandings of cultural norms.[3]

Cholera Epidemics

Cholera, which entered the Canadas in the early 1830s as a result of British immigration, posed an immediate and pressing social problem. Near-panic prevailed in the summer of 1832, when the board of health recorded 273 deaths from the dread disease in York alone; in the province as a whole, at least 550 persons died: "Nothing is to be heard but the 'cholera.'" A poem that appeared in the *Kingston Chronicle* of April 7, 1832 recounted the mass fear of the disease:

> The months pass on, and the circle spreads,
> And the time is drawing nigh,
> When each street may have a darkened house,
> Or a coffin passing by.

When the cholera problem overwhelmed the local charities and because the colonial governments accepted no responsibility for health, each district was encouraged to establish its own board of health. Such boards became responsible for the caring of those with the disease and, in the case of port cities such as Kingston and York, for the inspecting of immigrant ships. The disease ran its course in 1832, only to return again in 1834 to cause 350 more deaths in Upper Canada. The first major medical breakthrough occurred only in the early 1850s, when cholera was linked to contaminated water or food.

Gender in Upper Canada

Gender roles in British North American society were regulated through social pressure. Men and women were seen as distinctly different and both were expected to "act" according to established codes of behaviour. While these codes were differentiated by class and ethnicity, the elites urged the masses to seek accepted levels of honour and respectability. If people acted outside these codes, they threatened the social fabric.

The behaviour of women in the early to mid-nineteenth century colonial society was strictly regulated. Their responsibilities consisted mainly of child bearing, child rearing, and social assistance to others, as well as "domestic employment," which included such tasks in the home as cooking, cleaning, sewing, knitting, spinning, and weaving, in addition to outdoor work, such as taking care of the poultry and the barnyard, the vegetable garden, and fruit growing. When her husband was away, a farm wife often assumed complete responsibility for outdoor work. Beyond the immediate family obligations, some women did sewing or laundry for others, took in boarders, served as seamstresses, kept inns or taverns in their homes, or taught school within their homes.

Women were regulated and restricted by rules, traditions, customs, and laws made by male social elites, church leaders, government officials, and legal authorities. The concept of domesticity was premised on the belief in a differentiation between women and men in work, with women restricted essentially to the "private" sphere of the home and family and men to the "public" sphere of the workplace. In the social sphere, however, such a division was more permeable. Studies of family life conclude that in Upper Canada before 1870, this seemingly stark division was often crossed and became more of a intermediate space. There existed a social space on the borders between the public and the private in which males and females, young and old, people of different religions and, even at times, of different races and cultures, interacted. As historian Julia Roberts has demonstrated, the tavern was one such space. There was social interaction on such occasions as births, marriages, illness, and death, and through such community activities as dances, picnics, and winter sleigh rides. As historian Nancy Christie concludes, "What new studies of masculinity make abundantly clear is that there can be no simple equation between domesticity and separate spheres or a gendered division between private and public."[4]

The legal system, however, was more clear on gender roles. British common law defined women as subordinate to their husbands, fathers, and even brothers. In the eyes of the law, husband and wife constituted one person—the husband. A wife did not have the legal right to sign a contract or to run a business without her husband's permission. A married woman *did* have the right of a dowry, a lifetime interest in one-third of her husband's property. But even when and where the law was operative, it applied only on the death of the husband and not in instances of separation or marriage breakdown. As well, it could be overridden, since the husband had the right to dispose of the family property to whomever he chose as heir; in most cases, the husband would choose a son, or even a grandson or son-in-law over a wife or a daughter. Divorce was possible but difficult, since in Upper Canada it required a special act of the legislature.

Colonial society sought desperately to regulate sexuality. Sexual conduct reflected standards of "proper" behaviour. Breaches to this code were seen as threatening the moral fabric of society. Sexual activity was supposed to be confined to a man and woman, and kept within the realm of marriage and the home. The role of white women in the empire was especially monitored because this group was expected to espouse the fundamental values of female respectability.

Christian law criminalized abortion and infanticide. The murder of a child was punishable by death, although the ruling was seldom applied. It was considered "criminal" to conceal the birth of a bastard, or a child born out of wedlock. The use of legal action in seduction cases reflected the attitude that a man had the "absolute right to his wife's body, and any man who dared have sex with a married woman could face a ruinous lawsuit from her husband." Clearly, a wife had few independent rights; she was "bound to submit to her husband, whatever the circumstances."[5]

Despite such restrictions, some women played active roles in education and religion. Some became schoolteachers in tax-supported schools. By 1851, women constituted almost one-fifth of "common" school teachers in Upper Canada. They were most often in rural schools, where few male teachers were available, or in districts where financial restraints necessitated hiring a female teacher, since she could be hired for half the price. Women were also active in the

Sunday school movement and in missionary societies, both of which played a social and educational role. Women were still refused entry into medical and law schools, and into the ministry. A few women did preach and prophesy, especially in the evangelical religious denominations, but even here they could not become ministers. Quaker women constituted the one possible exception. The Quakers believed that women should be separated from, but equal to, men.

Economic Developments

The economy of Upper Canada experienced rapid growth in the first half of the nineteenth century. Large-scale immigration in the years from 1815 to 1840 contributed to much of the development. Upper Canada became a thriving society based on an exchange economy, both export and domestic, and financed by both capital and credit. The expansion rested to a large extent on wheat farming: "Close to three-quarters of the cash income of Ontario farmers was derived from wheat, and wheat and flour made up well over half of all exports from Ontario until the early 1860s."[6] Much of this exported wheat, especially in the 1830s and 1840s, went to Lower Canada.

Timber rivalled wheat as the province's major export staple. In the Ottawa Valley, with its rich forests of pine and oak and the region's easy access to the St. Lawrence, lumbering not agriculture became the primary industry. Historian Douglas McCalla calculated that "forest products probably account for at least half of all the province's export earnings between 1815 and 1840."[7] To an extent, the timber trade was a by-product of farming, since settlers had to clear the forests before being able to farm the land.

Conservation

The early settlers transformed the landscape of Upper Canada ecologically. In doing so, they had little interest in conservation or the long-term impact on the environment. According to the mindset at the time, the struggle to settle the frontier pitted man against nature. Success came when man was able to "master" his environment. The land had to be "cleared" and "broken." The settlers' relentless drive to conquer and subdue the wilderness constituted a form of "ecological imperialism." According to historian Peter A. Baskerville, "As in other colonial frontiers, progress was measured in acres cleared, wetlands drained, and bushels harvested. In the process, Native people were displaced and Nature despoiled. In the typical parlance of the time, the white man's conquest of the wilderness was all but complete."[8] The major objective on the Upper Canadian frontier was to transform the wilderness into a civilized, agricultural settlement by clearing the forest, planting crops, raising livestock, and designing efficient routes for the exporting of agricultural goods.

In the name of "progress," settlers and woodsmen cut down trees at an astonishing rate. The axe, more than the railroad, radically changed the early Ontario landscape: "The domain of southern Ontario was transformed from woodland to farmland in less than a hundred years by an army of axe-wielding settlers and woodsmen."[9] Journalist William Smith noted the determination by which settlers cleared the Oak Ridges Moraine, north of Toronto: "The universal Canadian practice has been followed in clearing the land, that of sweeping away everything capable of bearing a green leaf. The new settlers look upon trees as enemies." Already by the 1850s, over one-third of the forested areas of southern Ontario had been destroyed. Within the next generation, three-quarters were gone, and by 1914 and the outbreak of World War I, over 90 percent had vanished.

Some areas cleared were at the headwaters of rivers, resulting in soil erosion that caused silt to pour into streams that flowed into Lake Ontario. The water ecology was adversely affected, along with the fish and aquatic animals. Atlantic salmon, for example, lost their spawning grounds and by the mid-nineteenth century no longer migrated in vast numbers up the St. Lawrence River. The last Atlantic salmon in Ontario were caught in the 1890s. Not until 1988, when the Ontario Ministry of Natural Resources reintroduced Atlantic salmon to Lake Ontario, did they appear again.

The building of canals also had a negative impact on the environment. Construction of the Erie Canal, for example, enabled the sea lamprey, a parasite fish that weakens or kills other fish by sucking their blood, to enter Lake Ontario. Its entry put pressure on the lake's native whitefish, trout, and salmon. With the completion of the Welland Canal, the lamprey migrated to the upper Great Lakes, resulting in a dramatic decline in native fish species there as well.

The farmers of Upper Canada did learn from some of their mistakes. Soil erosion and exhaustion led them to introduce new strains of plants that were well adapted to the climate and yielded better crops. One new strain was Red Fife wheat, introduced by David Fife of Peterborough, Ontario. Frustrated by the devastation of traditional strains of wheat by early frosts, wheat rust, and other diseases, Fife experimented with wheat seed from northern European varieties and developed his own strain. It matured earlier and produced high yields. By the 1870s, Red Fife came to be the major strain grown on the Canadian Prairies until the turn of the century, when superior strains replaced it. In introducing new plants, however, farmers inadvertently introduced foreign weeds to the region, such as wild mustard, burdock, and ragweed.

Transportation

Export of wheat and timber required transportation networks. Aboriginal trails became roads that were built in the Huron Tract beside Lake Huron, in the Talbot settlement north of Lake Erie, and by the military settlers in the Ottawa Valley and the Kingston area. Around York, a road system was developed to link the capital to outlying regions dependent on it for trade.

In the 1820s, a regular stagecoach line began between York and Kingston. At first, the service was erratic. Coaches required anywhere from two to four days to complete a one-way trip, depending on road conditions. By the 1830s, daily service became available year round. At the same time, coach lines along Yonge Street began to service the towns, villages, hamlets, and farming communities north of Toronto.

The Road between York and Kingston, Upper Canada, 1830, *by James Pattison Cockburn.*

Source: Library and Archives Canada, Acc. No. 1934-402/ C-012632.

Canal Building

The waterways, however, remained the most efficient means of transportation. The St. Lawrence remained the major trade artery, but access through the Great Lakes, thereby connecting Upper and Lower Canada, was obstructed by natural obstacles, notably Niagara Falls and the rapids at Lachine near Montreal. Canals offered a solution. They linked the lakes together for shipping and they also enabled small naval vessels to enter the heart of North America to defend Upper Canada against possible American attacks. In 1825, the first canal was completed around the Lachine rapids.

Canals, however, were very expensive and there was insubstantial private capital in British

North America to undertake such endeavours. The British government paid for Upper Canada's first major canal project: the Rideau Canal. The colonial authorities envisioned the Rideau Canal linking Bytown (Ottawa) with Kingston for defence purposes. The canal would bypass the rapids along the St. Lawrence and be a safe distance from American territory. In 1826, Lieutenant Colonel John By of the Royal Engineers arrived to oversee the project. Over a six-year period, By supervised a force of 4000 men who worked with shovel and wheelbarrow, sometimes sixteen hours a day, six days a week. Swarms of mosquitoes and blackflies plagued the workers all spring and summer. In the swamps and marshes, swamp fever and malaria became rampant. A heavy, noxious mist arose from the decaying vegetable matter that had been excavated after stagnant water had been drained

Colonel By Overseeing the Construction of the Rideau Canal *by C.W. Jeffreys.*

Source: Library and Archives Canada, Acc. No. 1972-26-795.

off. Trees were cut back in an effort to provide freer air circulation at the work sites, in keeping with the prevailing medical belief that malaria was caused by foul air (in Italian, *mal'aria*—"bad air"). More than 500 men lost their lives in the work camps. When completed in 1832, the Rideau Canal, threading through a series of lakes, was more than 210 kilometres in length and contained 47 locks. It had been an ambitious undertaking to meet an American attack that never materialized. Nonetheless, its construction boosted the economy of the eastern part of the colony.

The construction of the colony's second megaproject, a canal bypassing Niagara Falls and linking Lake Ontario to Lake Erie, began at roughly the same time. The incentive behind the Welland Canal was strictly commercial. But, once again, the impetus for action came from the United States. In 1825 the Americans completed the Erie Canal, which linked the Great Lakes by water with the Hudson River and the ice-free port of New York. The new canal attracted trade from the American West and siphoned trade from Upper Canada. Farmers in the Great Lakes area on both sides of the border found it cheaper and faster to ship via New York City to Britain. As a result, New York City rose to economic primacy in North America. The city had, by the early 1830s, a quarter-million people—roughly the size of Upper Canada's entire population.

William Hamilton Merritt, a young merchant and second-generation loyalist, dreamed of building a canal to bypass Niagara Falls and thus make the St. Lawrence–Great Lakes waterway system an effective rival to the American Erie Canal. The British government agreed to underwrite one-ninth of the cost of construction in return for the right of government ships to pass toll free through the canal. John B. Yates, an American investor from Oswego, New York, became the largest shareholder in Merritt's Welland Canal Company, while the government of Upper Canada offered a land grant and a loan of £25 000. In the end, Merritt's "private" project became the largest publicly financed project of its time, costing the government of Upper Canada an estimated £450 000 in 1833.

Banks in Upper Canada

Megaprojects required large amounts of capital, which, in turn, created a need for banks. Banks did not appear in Upper Canada until after the War of 1812. The earliest ones were branches of the Bank of Montreal. These soon proved inadequate for Upper Canadian merchants, who wanted their own banks. In 1819, the merchants of Kingston applied to the government of Upper Canada to charter a provincial bank. Much to their dismay and anger, their appeal was denied, although at the same time prominent York merchants were granted a charter.

This York bank, known as the Bank of Upper Canada, was controlled by the government. Nine of its fifteen directors belonged to Upper Canada's Executive or Legislative councils. The provincial government also supplied more than one-quarter of the bank's stock: "It is no exaggeration to say that the Bank of Upper Canada was a creature of the emerging Family Compact."[10]

The establishment of the first Upper Canadian bank at York rather than at Kingston reflected York's dominance as the provincial capital, a position it had held since 1797, when the seat of government was transferred to York from Niagara-on-the-Lake for security reasons. Through wholesale trade with towns and rural areas within its radius of influence, York became the most influential community in central Upper Canada. Its population increased from 1200 in 1820 to more than 9000 in 1834, the year of its incorporation as the city of Toronto. Economic growth in the 1840s and 1850s further strengthened Toronto's dominance in Upper Canada. The areas immediately adjacent to the city, such as the Home and Gore districts, came under its metropolitan control. In 1841, when the Canadas were united, one in five Upper Canadians lived within a 125-kilometre radius of Toronto.

The Rise of Reform

By the 1820s, opposition to the Family Compact was growing. The Reform members of the Assembly opposed the oligarchic control and increasingly called for political change. They favoured an elected Legislative Council, or upper house, and an Executive Council that was responsible to the Assembly rather than to the governor. Economically, the Reformers advocated policies that promoted agriculture. While supporting commercial enterprises, such as canals and banks, they opposed the patronage system that allowed the Family Compact to profit from contracts through legislation they themselves enacted.

Gourlay and Mackenzie

Robert Gourlay, a 39-year-old Scot who arrived in Upper Canada in 1817, initiated the first serious criticism of the Family Compact. The elite, however, was determined not to tolerate any dissent. Soon after his arrival, Gourlay complained about the oligarchic control of the appointed Legislative Council. He attacked John Strachan, that "monstrous little fool of a parson," and his "vile, loathsome and lazy" circle. Gourlay favoured township meetings similar to those in New England, where people could voice their grievances. He also advocated more power for the elected Assembly. These "radical" views led to his prosecution (under a wartime act dating from 1804 that regulated the conduct of immigrants) and his subsequent expulsion from Upper Canada in 1819.

This "banished Briton" left a legacy of political protest. Before his arrest, he circulated a lengthy questionnaire. The last of his 31 questions asked: "What, in your opinion, retards the improvement of your township in particular, or the province in general?" He received a litany of complaints: the bad roads, the clergy and Crown reserves, and restrictions on American immigration. These and other complaints continued to be heard throughout the 1820s. A Reform party began to take shape in the Assembly by 1824.

William Lyon Mackenzie, who arrived in Upper Canada from Scotland in 1820, furthered Gourlay's cause. In 1824, at Queenston, in the Niagara district, he published a newspaper, the *Colonial Advocate*, and relocated it to York the following year. Mackenzie brought "exceptional gifts" to his editorship: "The essence of radical journalism is to probe for feet of clay beneath the togas of the high and mighty, and no one probed more fearlessly or relentlessly than he."[11]

Mackenzie's attacks enraged certain members of the Family Compact in York. In 1826, Mackenzie's office was broken into and his typesetting equipment thrown into Lake Ontario. At first, the legal system did nothing to prosecute the crime. After a long trial, however, Mackenzie was successful at winning redress. But such attempts to thwart freedom of speech only helped make Mackenzie a hero to the radical Reformers and strengthened his determination to continue his campaign. He succeeded in winning a seat in the Assembly in the election of 1828.

That election returned the first Reform majority to the Assembly. Reformers such as John Rolph, Marshall Spring Bidwell (whose father, Barnabas Bidwell, had been expelled from the Assembly in 1821 under the Alien Act as an American), and William and Robert Baldwin (father and son) led the new group. But in the election of 1830, the Reformers lost their majority to the Tories, who were bolstered by immigration from Britain.

The defeat did not dampen the enthusiasm of the Reformers. They saw themselves as part of a vanguard of reform, accomplishing for Upper Canada what like-minded Reformers in Britain and in the United States were doing for their countries. In Britain, the Whig government of Lord Grey introduced the Great Reform Bill in 1832, which broadened the franchise. In the United States, President Andrew Jackson led a democratic movement to open up the political process to more people.

This photo of William Lyon Mackenzie was kept in a place of honour in the family photo album of Thomas and Elizabeth Jackson, English immigrants who settled in Ontario. Their second son, William Jackson, became Louis Riel's secretary in 1885 in the North West. See the biographical sketch of William Jackson in Destinies, *7th ed. (Toronto: Nelson Education Ltd., 2012), Ch. 4.*

Source: Photo courtesy of Cicely Plaxton.

The Path to Rebellion

The Family Compact's obstinate refusal to contemplate change pushed the reformers to embrace increasingly radical positions and alternatives. William Lyon Mackenzie was radicalized as a result of a visit to the United States. In 1829, he met the American President and observed "Jacksonian democracy" in practice. Suspicious of the upper classes and big business, Andrew Jackson favoured the state extending voting rights (for white men at least) and opened up the political process to the middle and lower classes. Back in Upper Canada, Mackenzie renewed his attacks on the political elite to the point that he was expelled from the Assembly, only to be re-elected and expelled three more times. In 1832 he visited England and met such British reformers as Jeremy Bentham, Joseph Hume, and Francis Place. In London, the fiery newspaper editor presented the complaints of the Upper Canadian Reformers, as he saw them, to a sympathetic British government.

The Split in the Reformers

Mackenzie's views, however, were too radical even for most Reformers. By the mid-1830s he was becoming disenchanted by the slow pace of reform and by the British government's refusal to take serious action. He increasingly praised the American system. A rift developed between a moderate wing led by Robert Baldwin and a radical wing under Mackenzie and John Rolph. The moderates wished to preserve Upper Canada's allegiance to the monarchy and its ties to the British empire, and did not want the American form of elective government that Mackenzie advocated. Instead, they favoured the British model of responsible government—a government responsible to the elected Assembly. To the moderate Reform politicians who had spent years trying to dissociate reform from republicanism, Mackenzie's platform opened them to charges of being pro-American.

After the Reformers regained control of the Assembly in 1834, the radicals took action on their own. Mackenzie, just elected as Toronto's first mayor as well as an Assembly member, was selected to chair an Assembly grievance committee that produced the famous "Seventh Report on Grievances" in 1835. It contained a wide-ranging attack on the existing system of colonial government and demanded an elected Legislative Council, an Executive Council responsible to the Assembly, and severe limitations on the lieutenant governor's control of patronage.

The new governor, Sir Francis Bond Head, appointed in 1836, initially made a positive gesture to the Reformers by appointing two of their members, Robert Baldwin and John Rolph, to the Executive Council. He then proceeded, however, to ignore the Council's advice, prompting Reformers on the Council to resign. They persuaded their fellow members to follow suit. The Assembly censured the governor and then blocked the granting of supplies, preventing the government from making expenditures. Head retaliated by refusing to approve any money bills; then he dissolved the legislature and called an election for the early summer. He actively campaigned in the election for the Tories, playing the loyalist card and warning that the battle was between American republicanism and the British connection.

The Tories won the election. Head's intervention in the campaign and his appeal to the loyalty of recent British immigrants contributed to their victory. A large number in the colony sided with the governor and the Family Compact, fearing that the Reformers were dangerously radical and "republican." The conservatives also used bribery, corruption, the careful selection of polling places, and the rapid enfranchisement of new British immigrants to win the election. These tactics convinced Mackenzie and his followers of the impossibility of fair elections and peaceful reform.

In his new paper, *The Constitution*, established symbolically on July 4, 1836, Mackenzie hailed the American Revolution as a justified act to overthrow a tyrannical government. A group of his followers issued the Toronto Declaration, closely modelled on the American Declaration of Independence:

> *Government is founded on the authority and is instituted for the benefit of a people; when, therefore, any Government long and systematically ceases to answer the great ends of its foundation, the people have a natural right given them by their Creator to seek after and establish such institutions as will yield the greatest quantity of happiness to the greatest number.*

Economic and social factors contributed to unrest in Upper Canada. In 1836, an economic downturn occurred throughout the Western world. In the colony, this recession led to tight bank credit and even a recall of loans, which hit farmers especially hard. Such action intensified Mackenzie's already deep distrust of banks. Along with difficult financial times came a series of crop failures in 1835–37.

In the western region of the province, around London, a separate group led by Dr. Charles Duncombe prepared to join the brewing rebellion. News of the patriote uprising in Lower Canada under Louis-Joseph Papineau (see Chapter 13) further encouraged the rebels. By early November 1837, no British soldiers remained in Upper Canada because they had been dispatched to quell trouble in Lower Canada. According to historian Allan Greer, "the Lower Canadian drift towards war provided an impulse, as well as an opportunity, to Upper Canadian radicals."[12]

The Upper Canadian Rebellion, 1837

During the evening of December 4, 1837, about 500 people gathered at Montgomery's Tavern on Yonge Street (just north of present-day Eglinton Avenue in Toronto). Realizing that the capital was largely undefended, the next day Mackenzie and his followers seized an armoury and marched down Yonge Street toward the city to obtain more arms and ammunition. At a point just beyond Gallows Hill, near the present site of St. Clair Avenue, they met a party of about 30 loyalist volunteers. The rebels were inexperienced and poorly equipped. Despite their numbers, they dispersed and fled in the confusion of battle.

That same night, Colonel Allan MacNab, a lawyer, land speculator, and loyalist leader, brought reinforcements for the government side from Hamilton. By Thursday, December 7, the loyalist forces were 1500 strong (including future prime minister, John A. Macdonald). They marched up Yonge Street to attack Mackenzie's force at Montgomery's Tavern. The rebels had reassembled, now under the command of Anthony Van Egmond, a veteran of the Napoleonic Wars. During the second battle, the rebels were routed within half an hour. The loyalist forces then burned the tavern and marched back to Toronto. The Rebellion in Upper Canada was over. With a price on his head, Mackenzie escaped to the United States, while some of his followers were captured. Among them were two leaders, Samuel Lount, a former member of Parliament for Simcoe, and Peter Matthews, who were later tried and hanged.

In the western region of the province, Duncombe gathered 500 rebels by December 13 in London. MacNab led an opposing group of 500 loyalists. Upon hearing of Mackenzie's defeat, Duncombe's men began to desert the camp. When MacNab attacked on the morning of December 14, he found only a few rebels. Most, including Duncombe, had escaped to the United States.

Counterattacks from the United States

From across the border in the United States, the rebel leaders planned further attacks on the government of Upper Canada. Mackenzie found support among those Americans who saw the rebellion as a Canadian version of the American Revolution—an attempt to end British tyranny. Other Americans saw the uprising as an opportunity for the United States to annex Upper Canada.

Mackenzie gathered a motley band of supporters who occupied Navy Island, just above Niagara Falls, on the Canadian side of the Niagara River, where they proclaimed a provisional government. The Upper Canadian militia retaliated by burning the *Caroline*, an American ship used to ferry men and supplies from the American side to Navy Island. Mackenzie's supporters and American sympathizers abandoned Navy Island, but did not end their raids. Small, unsuccessful attacks occurred along the Detroit River.

The most serious counterattack occurred at the Battle of the Windmill along the St. Lawrence River near Prescott, in November 1838, in which 200 invaders barricaded themselves in an old windmill until they were forced to surrender. Thirty men were killed, and the rest were taken prisoner. The government hanged eleven of the

Execution of Samuel Lount and Peter Matthews.
Source: Library and Archives Canada/C-001242.

rebels for instigating and taking part in the battle. By the end of the Rebellion of 1837, the authorities jailed more than 1000 people on suspicion of treason. Nearly 100 of them were sent to the convict settlements in Australia (more than seventy of these individuals were Americans) and twenty were hanged.

Lord Durham's Report

The Rebellion of 1837 in Upper Canada was a minor affair from a military standpoint. The British government demonstrated that it intended to crush the insurrection and treat the instigators harshly. But the Rebellions in the Canadas were important from a political standpoint. Even though British North America was assumed to be a bastion of loyal support to the empire, something had gone terribly wrong. While stamping out the rebellion with one hand, the British government had little choice but to acknowledge serious problems with the political structure of the colonies by investigating the causes of unrest with the other.

The British cabinet responded by replacing Sir Francis Bond Head in early 1838 and sending out one of its most gifted politicians, Lord Durham, or "Radical Jack" (he had earned the nickname due to his support of liberal causes such as parliamentary reform). Durham was expected to inquire into the affairs of the colony and report back to the British government. The prime minister gave Durham broader powers than any of his predecessors, making him governor general of all the British North American colonies. He arrived in May 1838 with a vast entourage, including a full orchestra.

Durham spent only five months in the Canadas and most of this time in Lower Canada. But he made one short visit to Upper Canada, where he consulted with Robert Baldwin, the moderate Reform leader. Despite the brevity of his stay, Durham used the time to produce one of the most significant documents in Canadian history—the *Report on the Affairs of British North America*.

WHERE HISTORIANS DISAGREE

The Rebellions in Upper Canada

Amateur historians were the first to write about the Rebellions of 1837 in Upper Canada. They were partisan and emotional in their approach because of their closeness to the incident in time and circumstance. Charles Lindsey, the son-in-law of William Lyon Mackenzie, blamed the Family Compact's refusal to compromise for driving the reformers to rebellion. In a two-volume work on the rebellion, journalist J.M. Dent challenged Lindsey's view and depicted Mackenzie as an extremist who led the colony to an unnecessary struggle.[1] These early commentators believed that the cause of the rebellion was political—a classic struggle between "democracy" and "privilege." This liberal interpretation held sway in the late nineteenth and the early twentieth centuries. During the 1920s, when Canada was gaining autonomy from Britain, the liberal-nationalist school saw the rebellion as an early stage in the process of forging a distinct national identity. The rebellions became an important event on the road from "colony to nation."

In the midst of the economic upheaval of the Great Depression of the 1930s, an economic interpretation of the rebellion emerged. Donald Creighton depicted the rebellion in Upper Canada as a struggle between agrarian interests, represented by Mackenzie and his followers, and commercial interests, which controlled the appointed Executive and Legislative Councils. "The rebellions were," Creighton wrote, "the final expression of that hatred of the rural community for the commercialism of the St. Lawrence."[2] Creighton bolstered his economic argument by pointing out that the rebellions broke out in Upper Canada after a succession of crop failures that had brought farmers to the point of starvation and bankruptcy. The economic arguments broadened the causes of the rebellions, but they were still pitched politically as the struggle for responsible government.

William Lyon Mackenzie has also been the cause of debate. Some historians depicted Mackenzie as a man of ideas, who drew his inspiration and his direction from reform movements in both Britain and the United States. They see the rebellion in Upper Canada as part of a general reform impulse that swept Western Europe and North America. R.A. MacKay notes:

> Few public men in Canadian history have so represented the spirit of their age as did William Lyon Mackenzie, and particularly during the pre-Rebellion stage of his career. This was the age of Catholic Emancipation and the Great Reform Bill. . . . On both sides of the Atlantic the new wine of liberty and democracy was bursting the old bottles of restriction and privilege. . . . In the 1820's and 1830's William Lyon Mackenzie was the principal purveyor of these wines of liberty to the backwoods colony of Upper Canada.[3]

Other conservative-nationalist historians criticized Mackenzie for his pro-American biases and labelled him a rabble-rousing troublemaker.

In the 1960s, social historians questioned whether the rebellion in Upper Canada was a class struggle. Marxist historian Stanley Ryerson interpreted the rebellion as a bourgeois-democratic revolution caused by oppression and led by men who were fighting for the cause of popular liberty. "Workers . . . made up nearly half, and farmers over 40 per cent of the victims of oppression: a significant indication of the social forces that were engaged in action."[4] Leo Johnson saw the roots of the rebellion in an inequitable system of land grants designed at the time of Governor Simcoe to create a landed gentry class at the expense of the ordinary farmer. The rebellion was a fight between two different views of land ownership held by two different classes of people.[5]

In the 1980s, Colin Read challenged the image of the Upper Canadian rebellion as a "people's revolution." Using the less-known Duncombe uprising in the London area, Read concludes that "There is no basis for arguing that the rebels comprised a clearly disadvantaged sector of society and hence were driven to arms by economic despair or the prospect of plunder." What did distinguish rebels from loyalists was the large number of rebels who were either American born or born to American parents and who "may well have retained or adopted the deep American dislike of Britain and have been more willing to rebel, hoping to sever the provincial ties to Great Britain."[6]

Read also questioned the extent to which economic distress was at the root of the rebellion: "The rebels were, for the most part, well-settled members of a reasonably prosperous agrarian society." He saw "no single cause or grand overriding explanation" for their participation. Short-term economic dislocation played a part, as did more individual motivations based on family loyalties or personal friendships and animosities. But at root, the struggle was against undue privilege and oligarchy: "So too did specific political grievances as well as the general reform perception that the world was ordered too much in the interests of the few, too little in the interests of the many."[7]

1. J.M. Dent, *The Story of the Upper Canadian Rebellion,* 2 vols. (Toronto: C. Blackett Robinson, 1885).

2. Donald Creighton, *The Empire of the St. Lawrence: A Study in Commerce and Politics,* rpt. with Introduction by Christopher Moore (Toronto: University of Toronto Press, 2002 [1937]), p. 316.

3. R.A. MacKay, "The Political Ideas of William Lyon Mackenzie," *Canadian Journal of Economics and Political Science* 3 (1937): 1.

4. Stanley Ryerson, *Unequal Union: Confederation and the Roots of Conflict in the Canadas, 1815–1873* (Toronto: Progress Books, 1968), p. 131.

5. Leo Johnson, "Land Policy, Population Growth and Social Structure in Home District, 1793–1851," *Ontario History* 63 (1971): 41–60.

6. Colin Read, *The Rising in Western Upper Canada, 1837–38: The Duncombe Revolt and After* (Toronto: University of Toronto Press, 1982), pp. 207, 208.

7. Colin Read, *The Rebellion of 1837 in Upper Canada* (Ottawa: Canadian Historical Association, 1988), p. 18.

Lord Durham's stay in Canada was briefer than intended. Within a month of arriving, he abused his power by banishing eight patriotes to Bermuda, without trial, and refusing sixteen others from returning to BNA upon punishment of death. When the British government faced opposition and responded by disallowing Durham's decrees, he resigned in protest and returned home on November 1, 1838. His report was written in Britain.

The Durham Report concluded that British North America needed greater self-government and, ultimately, responsible government. Durham argued that local affairs should be handled by the colonial government and that only larger issues, such as constitutional concerns, foreign relations, trade with Britain and other British colonies, and disposal of public lands, should be decided by the mother country. But ultimately, the colonies required the traditions of British government: "I know not how it is possible to secure harmony in any other way than by administering the Government on those principles which have been found perfectly efficacious in Great Britain." Durham recommended that the governor should choose his closest advisers, the members of the Executive Council, from the majority party in the Assembly and abide by the wishes of these elected representatives. Although Durham did not call this "responsible government," it nonetheless came to be known as such.

The Durham Report called for a union of the two Canadas. Durham realized that this would primarily benefit Upper Canada, since it would improve trade for the inland colony and force Lower Canadians to assume part of the debt incurred by Upper Canadians during the building of the canals. But he viewed such a union as the nucleus of an eventual amalgamation of all the British North American colonies, which he highly favoured, and as a necessary precursor to the assimilation of the French Canadians. Durham had spoken with merchants in Britain who argued that the French Canadians were obstacles to the commercial development of the colonies. His bias against the French-Catholic majority in Lower Canada became increasingly evident during his brief stay in the colony. He viewed this group as backward and a barrier to progress. In large part, he came to blame the ethnic-religious division for the trouble in Lower Canada, where he found "two nations warring within the bosom of a single state." The answer, he believed, was assimilation through union. The protections provided by the Royal Proclamation of 1763 and the Quebec Act of 1774 should be rescinded. In time, immigration would increase the dominance of the British-Protestants, who would overwhelm the French-Catholics.

The British government accepted union, but rejected responsible government. Lord Sydenham, Durham's successor, implemented the recommendation for a union of the Canadas in 1840–41. Before it came into effect, Sydenham resolved a long-standing disagreement in Upper Canada. He worked out an arrangement by which the two leading Protestant denominations—Anglicans and Presbyterians—would share half the proceeds of future sales of clergy reserves, while the other half would be divided among the other denominations, according to their numbers.

By the terms of the Act of Union of 1840, the two Canadas were united into one colony with its capital at the loyalist centre of Kingston. English was recognized as the only official language of the Assembly, which consisted of 84 members—42 from what was now called Canada East (Lower Canada) and 42 from Canada West (Upper Canada). The new Province of Canada assumed Upper Canada's debt. Assimilation was back on the agenda.

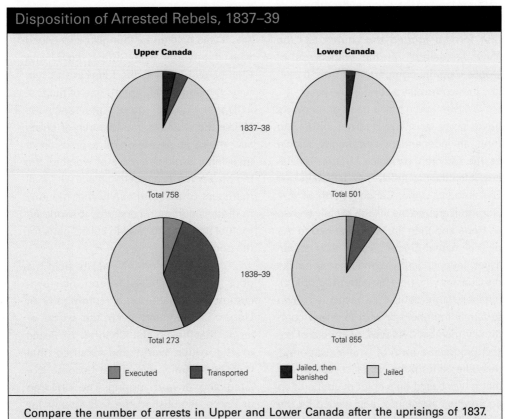

Disposition of Arrested Rebels, 1837–39

Upper Canada

Lower Canada

1837–38

Total 758

Total 501

1838–39

Total 273

Total 855

■ Executed   ■ Transported   ■ Jailed, then banished   ■ Jailed

Compare the number of arrests in Upper and Lower Canada after the uprisings of 1837. Although the crisis in Lower Canada was far more extensive, more arrests were made in Upper Canada.

Source: R. Louis Gentilcore, ed., *Historical Atlas of Canada, vol. 2, The Land Transformed, 1800–1891* (Toronto: University of Toronto Press, 1993), plate 23. Reprinted by permission of the University of Toronto Press Incorporated.

The Children of Peace

In 1801, David Willson left Pennsylvania with a group of fellow members of the Society of Friends, or Quakers, to establish a new community in Upper Canada based on Quaker values and beliefs. He claimed his vision for the new community came in the form of a dream. He dreamt of a poor man who could not find lodging in the city where he wanted to locate, and so moved on to the lake in front of the city, where he built a magnificent church in the shape of a house. The church, which was flooded with the light of God, served as a refuge for the poor and outcasts of society. He envisioned the community that formed around the church as "the New Jerusalem" in the wilderness of Upper Canada, comparable to the Israelites in the Promised Land.

Willson and a small band of followers broke away from the Quakers in 1812 to form an independent community known as the Children of Peace, or the "Davidites," after their founder. They settled in East Gwillimbury, Upper Canada, north of York (Toronto), around the village initially known as Hope and then, in 1841, changed to the biblical name Sharon. Here, they established independently owned farms (unlike the Quakers who held property in common), but these farms could only be handed down to family members or sold to fellow community members. As well, members of the sect practised a form of "moral economy" that differed from the capitalist economy in that it was based on a spirit of cooperation and mutual assistance, and guided by the Golden Rule: "Do unto others as you would have them do unto you."

The community was united through a close-knit ancestry, common religious beliefs, and a communal lifestyle. It was "less a physical community than a community of spirit." The Temple of Peace, a beautiful three-story, foursquare building, inspired by the biblical Solomon's temple and in the shape of a house as in Willson's dream, became the focal point of the community. There were four entrances to the temple, one door in the middle of each side so as to allow people to enter, as Willson noted, "from the east and the west, the north and the south on equal and the same footing." Men, women, and children were to enter as equals. In the centre of the temple was an altar in the shape of Noah's Ark. It was held up by four pillars inscribed with the words Faith, Hope, Love, and Charity, symbolizing the four cardinal virtues. A magnificent organ—one of the first in Upper Canada—graced the sanctuary. Unlike the Quakers, the Children of Peace saw music as an important expression of their faith. Besides a place of worship, the temple served as a meeting place where all members of the community met monthly to discuss common concerns, to work out mutual agreements, and to collect alms for the poor.

It was their commitment to help the poor, which extended beyond their own community to the larger community of Upper Canada and even the world at large, that linked the Children of Peace to the wider world and ensured that their community would not become isolated and inward turning. The Children of Peace established the first shelter for the homeless in the province and the first credit union, known as the Charity Fund, from which anyone in need could borrow money. As well, they created the first producer cooperative in Canada, known as the "Farmer's Storehouse Company." Situated in downtown Toronto next to the market square, it offered an alternative marketing centre to Toronto's competitive and individualistic merchant approach.

Some of the Children of Peace members were involved in political reform, hoping this would lead to social reform. They supported William Lyon Mackenzie's rebellion in 1837. Two members died in battle. After the rebellion, some members of the community organized "Durham meetings," to support reform based on Lord Durham's Report. The involvement by some members in the rebellion split the community, however, and it never regained its original cohesion. Still, the community continued to operate until 1889, when it disbanded. The community of the Children of Peace was one of the few success stories of alternative community life in nineteenth-century Upper Canada.

Temple of the Children of Peace, photo taken around 1860.

Source: Aurora Museum, Acc. No. X81.36.18.

FURTHER READING

Mark Fram and Albert Schrauwers, *4Square: An Introduction to the Sharon Temple National Historic Site* (Toronto: Coach House Books, 2005).

W. John McIntyre, *Children of Peace* (Montreal/Kingston: McGill-Queen's University Press, 1994).

Albert Schrauwers, *The Children of Peace and the Village of Hope, 1812–1889* (Toronto: University of Toronto Press, 1993).

SUMMARY

In the years 1815 to 1840, the society of Upper Canada underwent significant transformation as a result of large-scale immigration (some 300 000 people), economic development, and political reform. The arrival of thousands of Scots and Irish, in particular, placed pressure on established elites to implement social, educational, and political reform. The era of road and canal building opened up the isolated frontier to settlement. Agriculture and the timber industries boomed. Rule by the Family Compact was directly challenged, leading to a serious rebellion. Even though the rebellion was crushed, lessons were learned for the British government and the Colonial Office. Responsible government, while not immediately implemented, was a reality within a decade. By 1840, Lower Canada had become Canada West, a province of the united colony of Canada.

NOTES

1. S.F. Wise, "Upper Canada and the Conservative Tradition," in Edith G. Firth, ed., *Profiles of a Province: Essays in the History of Ontario* (Toronto: Ontario Historical Society, 1967), p. 27.

2. Fred Landon, *Western Ontario and the American Frontier* (Toronto: McClelland & Stewart, 1967 [1941]), p. 125.

3. Elizabeth Jane Errington and Cynthia R. Comacchio, *People, Places, and Times: Readings in Canadian Social History*, vol. 1, *Pre-Confederation* (Toronto: Thomson Nelson, 2007), p. 369.

4. Nancy Christie, ed., *Households of Faith: Family, Gender, and Community in Canada, 1760–1969* (Montreal/Kingston: McGill-Queen's University Press, 2002), p. 7.

5. Patrick Brode, *Courted and Abandoned: Seduction in Canadian Law* (Toronto: University of Toronto Press for Osgoode Society for Canadian Legal History, 2002), pp. ix–x.

6. John McCallum, *Unequal Beginnings: Agriculture and Economic Development in Quebec and Ontario Until 1870* (Toronto: University of Toronto Press, 1980), p. 4.

7. Douglas McCalla, *Planting the Province: The Economic History of Upper Canada* (Toronto: University of Toronto Press, 1993), p. 64.

8. Peter A. Baskerville, *Ontario: Image, Identity, and Power* (Toronto: Oxford University Press, 2002), p. 83.

9. J. David Wood, *Making Ontario: Agricultural Colonization and Landscape Re-creation Before the Railway* (Montreal/Kingston: McGill-Queen's University Press, 2000), p. xviii.

10. Gerald M. Craig, *Upper Canada: The Formative Years, 1784–1841* (Toronto: McClelland & Stewart, 1963), p. 162.

11. S.J.R. Noel, *Patrons, Clients, Brokers: Ontario Society and Politics, 1791–1896* (Toronto: University of Toronto Press, 1990), p. 88.

12. Allan Greer, "1837–38: Rebellion Reconsidered," *Canadian Historical Review* 76 (1995): 14.

RELATED READINGS

See Module 7, "The Rebellions of 1837–8 in Lower and Upper Canada: Why Did People Take Up Arms Against the Government?" in *Visions: The Canadian History Modules Project: Pre-Confederation*. Module 7 contains articles by Allan Greer (Lower Canada), "Two Nations Warring" and Colin Read and Ronald J. Stagg (Upper Canada), "The Causes of the Rebellion." The module also contains ten primary-source documents. See pages 287–330.

BIBLIOGRAPHY

Overviews of Upper Canadian society in 1815–40 are Gerald M. Craig, *Upper Canada: The Formative Years, 1784–1841* (Toronto: McClelland & Stewart, 1963); the relevant chapters in Peter A. Baskerville, *Ontario: Image, Identity, and Power* (Toronto: Oxford University Press, 2002); and R. Cole Harris's chapter "Ontario," in R. Cole Harris and John Warkentin, *Canada Before Confederation* (Ottawa: Carleton University Press, 1991 [1974]), pp. 110–68. Also of value are J.K. Johnson and Bruce G. Wilson, eds., *Historical Essays on Upper Canada: New Perspectives* (Ottawa: Carleton University Press, 1989); and David Keane and Colin Read, eds., *Old Ontario: Essays in Honour of J.M.S. Careless* (Toronto: Dundurn Press, 1990). Helen Cowan, *British Emigration in British North America: The First Hundred Years*, rev. and enlarged ed. (Toronto: University of Toronto Press, 1961), best describes the experience of immigrating to British North America from Britain. A shorter version is her pamphlet *British Immigration Before Confederation* (Ottawa: Canadian Historical Association, 1968). Also useful is H.J.M. Johnston, *British Immigration to British North America, 1815–1860*, Canada's Visual History Series, vol. 8 (Ottawa: Canadian Museum of Civilization, 1974). On the Petworth emigration scheme, see Wendy Cameron and Mary McDougall Maude, *Assisting Emigration to Upper Canada: The Petworth Project, 1832–1837* (Montreal/Kingston: McGill-Queen's University Press, 2000). Further studies on English immigration include Elizabeth Jane Errington, "British Migration and British America, 1783–1860s," in Philip Bruckner, ed., *Canada: The Oxford History of the British Empire* (Oxford: Oxford University Press, 2006), and Elizabeth Jane Errington's *Emigrant Worlds and Transatlantic Communities: Migration to Upper Canada in the First Half of the Nineteenth Century* (Montreal/Kingston: McGill-Queen's University Press, 2007).

Studies on Irish immigration and settlement in Upper Canada include D.H. Akenson, *The Irish in Ontario: A Study in Rural History* (Montreal/Kingston: McGill-Queen's University Press, 1984); and Bruce S. Elliott, *Irish Migrants in the Canadas: A New Approach* (Montreal/Kingston: McGill-Queen's University Press, 1988). See also Michael Kenneally, "Irish Immigration to Nineteenth-Century Canada: Alternative Narratives," *Canadian Issues* 27 (2005): 38–40. For a look at Scottish immigration, see Peter E. Rider and Heather McNabb, eds., *A Kingdom of the Mind: The Scots' Impact on the Development of Canada* (Montreal/Kingston: McGill-Queen's University Press, 2006), and Lucille H. Campey, *The Scottish Pioneers of Upper Canada, 1784–1855: Glengarry and Beyond* (Toronto: Natural Heritage Books, 2005).

Three books review the experience of blacks in Upper Canada: Robin Winks's *The Blacks in Canada*, 2nd ed. (Montreal/Kingston: McGill-Queen's University Press, 1997); Peggy Bristow et al., *"We're Rooted Here and They Can't Pull Us Up": Essays in African Canadian Women's History* (Toronto: University of Toronto Press, 1994); and the more popularly written *The Freedom-Seekers: Blacks in Early Canada* (Agincourt, ON: Book Society of Canada, 1981), by Daniel G. Hill. Roger Riendeau provides a good short summary of the Underground Railway in "Freedom Train," *Horizon Canada* 30 (1985): 704–9.

On crime and criminal justice in early Upper Canada, see Peter Oliver, *Terror to Evil-Doers: Prisons and Punishment in Nineteenth-Century Ontario* (Toronto: University of Toronto Press for The Osgoode Society for Canadian Legal History, 1998); David Murray, *Colonial Justice: Justice, Morality, and Crime in the Niagara District, 1791–1849* (Toronto: University of Toronto Press for The Osgoode Society for Canadian Legal History, 2002); and Patrick Brode, *Courted and Abandoned: Seduction in Canadian Law* (Toronto: University of Toronto Press for The Osgoode Society for Canadian Legal History, 2002). Margaret Atwood's novel *Alias Grace* (Toronto: McClelland & Stewart, 1996) recreates in fiction what life was like in an Upper Canadian penitentiary.

On the Family Compact, see Robert E. Saunders, "What Was the Family Compact?," *Ontario History* 49 (1957): 165–78, reprinted in J.K. Johnson, *Historical Essays on Upper Canada* (Toronto: McClelland & Stewart, 1975), pp. 122–40. The origins of an Upper Canadian elite and its transformation over time is the subject of S.J.R. Noel's *Patrons, Clients, Brokers: Ontario Society and Politics, 1791–1896* (Toronto: University of Toronto Press, 1990). On ideological differences in Upper Canada, see Jane Errington, *The Lion, the Eagle, and Upper Canada: A Developing Colonial Ideology* (Montreal/Kingston: McGill-Queen's University Press, 1987); David Mills, *The Idea of Loyalty in Upper Canada, 1784–1850* (Montreal/Kingston: McGill-Queen's University Press, 1988); and the essays by S.F. Wise in A.B. McKillop and Paul Romney, eds., *God's Peculiar Peoples: Essays on Political Culture in Nineteenth-Century Canada* (Ottawa:

Carleton University Press, 1993). See also J.I. Little, *Loyalties in Conflict: A Canadian Borderland in War and Rebellion, 1812–1840* (Toronto: University of Toronto Press, 2008).

For the treatment of religion in the context of American immigration and political reform, see Fred Landon, *Western Ontario and the American Frontier* (Toronto: McClelland & Stewart, 1967 [1941]). William Westfall's *Two Worlds: The Protestant Culture of Nineteenth Century Ontario* (Montreal/Kingston: McGill-Queen's University Press, 1989) examines the different world views that emerged out of the two dominant religious strains—Anglican and Methodist—in mid-nineteenth-century Upper Canada. An interesting survey is John Webster Grant's *A Profusion of Spires: Religion in Nineteenth-Century Ontario* (Toronto: University of Toronto Press, 1988).

On the role of image in religion and politics in Upper Canada, see Cecilia Morgan, *Public Men and Virtuous Women: The Gendered Languages of Religion and Politics in Upper Canada, 1791–1850* (Toronto: University of Toronto Press, 1996). Robynne Rogers Healey examines Quakerism in her book *From Quaker to Upper Canadian: Faith and Community among Yonge Street Friends, 1801–1850* (Montreal/ Kingston: McGill-Queen's University Press, 2006). On education, see S. Houston and A. Prentice, *Schooling and Scholars in Nineteenth-Century Ontario* (Toronto: University of Toronto Press, 1988). The best short account of Egerton Ryerson is Clara Thomas, *Ryerson of Upper Canada* (Toronto: Ryerson Press, 1969).

Douglas McCalla's *Planting the Province: The Economic History of Upper Canada, 1784–1870* (Toronto: University of Toronto Press, 1993) provides a good overview. See also Douglas McCalla, "Des pays d'en haut au Haut-Canada: La formation d'une économie de colonisation," *Histoire, économie et société* 27(4) (2008): 87–107. The importance of the wheat economy for Upper Canada is discussed in John McCallum, *Unequal Beginnings: Agriculture and Economic Development in Quebec and Ontario Until 1870* (Toronto: University of Toronto Press, 1980). For a short overview of the Upper Canadian economy, see Ch. 6 ("Upper Canada") in Kenneth Norrie and Douglas Owram, *A History of the Canadian Economy*, 2nd ed. (Toronto: Harcourt Brace, 1996), pp. 115–45. Transportation developments and canal building in particular are briefly described in Gerald Tulchinsky, *Transportation Changes in the St. Lawrence–Great Lakes Region, 1828–1860*, Canada's Visual History Series, vol. 11 (Ottawa: Canadian Museum of Civilization, 1974). Peter Baskerville reviews the history of banking in Upper Canada in the introduction to his edited work *The Bank of Upper Canada: A Collection of Documents* (Toronto: Champlain Society, 1987). On the impact of settlement and economic development on the environment, see J. David Wood, *Making Ontario: Agricultural Colonization and Landscape Re-creation Before the Railway* (Montreal/Kingston: McGill-Queen's University Press, 2000); Neil S. Forkey, *Shaping the Upper Canadian Frontier: Environment, Society, and Culture in the Trent Valley* (Calgary: University of Calgary Press, 2003); and W. Fraser Sandercombe, *Nothing Gold Can Stay: The Wildlife of Upper Canada* (Erin, ON: Boston Mills Press, 1985). Peter Russell looks at social mobility in Upper Canada in his book *Attitudes to Social Structure and Mobility in Upper Canada, 1815–1840* (Lewiston, NY: Edwin Mellen Press, 1990). Gordon Darroch has examined the formation of the middle-class in "Scanty Fortunes and Rural Middle-Class Formation in Nineteenth-Century Central Ontario," *Canadian Historical Review* 79(4) (December 1998). Douglas McCalla also looks at the gun culture in Upper Canada in his article "Upper Canadians and Their Guns: An Exploration via Country Store Accounts (1808–61)," *Ontario History* 97(2) (2005): 121–37.

On early social assistance in Upper Canada, see Rainer Boehre, "Paupers and Poor Relief in Upper Canada," in Johnson and Wilson, eds., *Historical Essays on Upper Canada*, pp. 305–40; and Stephen Speisman, "Munificent Parsons and Municipal Parsimony: Voluntary vs. Public Poor Relief in Nineteenth-Century Toronto," in M.J. Piva, ed., *A History of Ontario: Selected Readings* (Toronto: Copp Clark Pitman, 1988), pp. 55–70. On the Shiners' War, see Michael Cross, "The Shiners' War: Social Violence in the Ottawa Valley in the 1830s," *Canadian Historical Review* 54 (March 1973): 1–26.

Several studies exist on the development of the Reform movement. Besides Craig, *Upper Canada*, and Landon, *Western Ontario* (both cited earlier), see Aileen Dunham, *Political Unrest in Upper Canada, 1815–1836* (Toronto: McClelland & Stewart, 1963 [1927]). William Kilbourn's biography of William Lyon Mackenzie, *The Firebrand* (Toronto: Clarke Irwin, 1956), is a lively account. On the discontent in western Upper Canada, see Colin Read's *The Rising in Western Upper Canada, 1837–38: The Duncombe Revolt and After* (Toronto: University of Toronto Press, 1982); and, for the rebellion in general, Colin Read and Ron Stagg, eds., *The Rebellion of 1837 in Upper Canada* (Toronto: Champlain Society, 1985).

Colin Read contributes a brief but informative overview of the same topic in his pamphlet, also entitled *The Rebellion of 1837 in Upper Canada* (Ottawa: Canadian Historical Association, 1988). Allan Greer provides an interesting historiographical review of the two Canadian rebellions in "1837–38: Rebellion Reconsidered," *Canadian Historical Review* 76 (1995): 1–18.

The standard work on Lord Durham remains C. New, *Lord Durham's Mission to Canada*, with an introduction by H.W. McCready (Toronto: McClelland & Stewart, 1963). Gerald Craig has edited and introduced an abridged version of Durham's Report in *Lord Durham's Report* (Toronto: McClelland & Stewart, 1963). A more up-to-date account is Janet Ajzenstats, *The Political Thought of Lord Durham* (Montreal/Kingston: McGill-Queen's University Press, 1988). A valuable collection of articles, united under the title "Durham and His Ideas," appeared in *Journal of Canadian Studies* 25(1) (Spring 1990).

An overview of women in Upper Canada (and throughout North America) during this period is Alison Prentice et al., "Carders of Wool, Drawers of Water: Women's Work in British North America," Ch. 3 in *Canadian Women: A History*, 2nd ed. (Toronto: Harcourt Brace, 1996), pp. 58–83. Jane Errington has written on working women in *Upper Canada from 1790 to 1840: Wives and Mothers, School Mistresses and Scullery Maids* (Montreal/Kingston: McGill-Queen's University Press, 1995). See also Marjorie Cohen's *Women's Work, Markets, and Economic Development in Nineteenth Century Ontario* (Toronto: University of Toronto Press, 1988); and Cecilia Morgan's *Public Men and Virtuous Women: The Gendered Languages of Religion and Politics in Upper Canada, 1791–1840* (Toronto: University of Toronto Press, 1996).

On family life, see Françoise Nöel, *Family Life and Sociability in Upper and Lower Canada, 1780–1870: A View from Diaries and Family Correspondence* (Montreal/Kingston: McGill-Queen's University Press, 2003); and the relevant essays in Nancy Christie, ed., *Households of Faith: Family, Gender, and Community in Canada, 1760–1969* (Montreal/Kingston: McGill-Queen's University Press, 2002). See also Catherine Anne Wilson, *Tenants in Time: Family Strategies, Land, and Liberalism in Upper Canada, 1799–1871* (Montreal/Kingston: McGill-Queen's University Press 2009).

Edward S. Rogers and Donald B. Smith, eds., *Aboriginal Ontario* (Toronto: Dundurn Press, 1994), review the First Nations' history for this period in Ontario. For the Iroquois, see also Charles M. Johnston, ed., *The Valley of the Six Nations: A Collection of Documents on the Indian Lands of the Grand River* (Toronto: Champlain Society, 1964); and for the Mississaugas and other Algonquian groups, see Donald B. Smith, *Sacred Feathers: The Reverend Peter Jones (Kahkewaquonaby) and the Mississauga Indians* (Toronto: University of Toronto Press, 1987); Janet Chute, *The Legacy of Shingwaukonse: A Century of Native Leadership* (Toronto: University of Toronto Press, 1998); Peter S. Schmalz, *The Ojibwa of Southern Ontario* (Toronto: University of Toronto Press, 1990); and James A. Clifton, *A Place of Refuge for All Time: Migration of the American Potawatomi into Canada, 1830 to 1850* (Ottawa: National Museums of Canada, 1975). Tony Hall, "Native Limited Identities and Newcomer Metropolitanism in Upper Canada, 1814–1867," in David Keane and Colin Read, eds., *Old Ontario: Essays in Honour of J.M.S. Careless* (Toronto: Dundurn Press, 1990), pp. 148–73, reviews both the Iroquoian and Algonquian history of Upper Canada in the early nineteenth century. Hope Maclean discusses the Ojibwa experience with Methodist Residential Schools in "Ojibwa Participation in Methodist Residential Schools in Upper Canada, 1828–1860," *Canadian Journal of Native Studies* 25(1) (2005): 93–138. See also Michelle Hamilton's recent work, *Collections and Objections: Aboriginal Material Culture in Southern Ontario* (Montreal: McGill-Queen's University Press, 2010).

On the development of an Upper Canadian political culture, see John Clarke, *Land, Power, and Economics on the Frontier of Upper Canada* (Montreal/Kingston: McGill-Queen's University Press, 2001); Jeffrey L. McNairn, *The Capacity to Judge: Public Opinion and Deliberative Democracy in Upper Canada, 1791–1854* (Toronto: University of Toronto Press, 2000); and Carol Wilton, *Popular Politics and Political Culture in Upper Canada, 1800–1850* (Montreal/Kingston: McGill-Queen's University Press, 2000). See also Michel Ducharme, *Le concept de liberté au Canada à l'époque des Révolutions atlantiques (1776–1838)* (Montreal/Kingston: McGill-Queen's University Press 2009).

Maps appear in R. Louis Gentilcore, ed., *Historical Atlas of Canada*, vol. 2, *The Land Transformed, 1800–1891* (Toronto: University of Toronto Press, 1993). For an environmental history of the frontier in Upper Canada see John Clarke, *The Ordinary People of Essex: Environment, Culture, and Economy on the Frontier of Upper Canada* (Montreal/Kingston: McGill-Queen's University Press 2010).

Chapter Fifteen

THE UNION OF THE CANADAS: ECONOMIC AND SOCIAL DEVELOPMENTS, 1840–1864

TIME LINE

1843	Workers strike on Lachine Canal
1845	First volume of François-Xavier Garneau's *Histoire du Canada* published
1846	Britain introduces free trade, ending colonial timber and wheat preferences
	Lower Canadian School Act provides for both Catholic and Protestant state-aided schools
1849	Montreal merchants prepare annexation manifesto to join United States
	Anglican King's College becomes University of Toronto
1852	Université Laval founded
	Mary Ann Shadd Cary writes *A Plea for Emigration to Canada West* to appeal to African Americans
	Susanna Moodie's *Roughing It in the Bush published*
1854	BNA enters into reciprocity agreement with United States
1855	Great Western Railway completed
	School Act of 1855 establishes Catholic separate school system in Canada West
1859	The Grand Trunk Railway completed

The period from 1840 to the time of Confederation in the mid-1860s was tumultuous for the new united colony of Canada. Economically and socially, both sections of the colony (Canada East and Canada West) were shaped by the joint forces of industrialization and urbanization. Trade and transportation, in particular, dominated the economic agenda.

In the late 1840s, Britain reached the pinnacle of its power, symbolized by its adoption of free trade. The empire was unrivalled as the global power. Britain was confident enough in its economic prowess to drop its tariffs against foreign competition and encourage its trading partners to do the same. The move toward free trade, however, had an immediate and traumatic impact on its colonies in British North America. Gone was the colonies' preferential access to the lucrative British market; gone were the colonial timber and wheat preferences. BNA was forced to alter its reliance on markets in the mother country and instead look elsewhere, both internally among the colonies, and externally to the United States. The result was the signing of the Reciprocity Treaty with the United States in 1854 and a new north–south orientation in trade.

The most visible change to Canada came in the form of another transportation revolution. The era of canal building dominated the first half of the nineteenth century; the era of rail construction dominated the second half. The railroad became the symbol of progress, civilization, and modernity. During the 1850s, the new railway system transformed the agricultural, commercial, and urban character of Canada. With the emergence of rail transport, travel velocity increased tenfold, compared with that by horse or canal boat. Time and space were compressed. The railways also opened up new regions, not restricted to the waterways, for settlement, and linked BNA, facilitating inter-colonial trade.

Even though the immigration boom of the first half of the nineteenth century was over, migration patterns continued to reshape Canada. In the case of Canada West, immigrants continued to break land and build an agricultural frontier; in the case of Canada East, people continued to emigrate to the northeastern United States. The pace of industrialization increased during this period. As a result, so did urbanization, thereby bringing with it all the associated social problems. An influential social reform movement developed in an attempt to deal with the array of forces seemingly threatening the old order. Education increasingly was seen as a panacea and became a much-debated issue.

The Commercial Empire of the St. Lawrence

The Staples and Laurentian Theses

By the 1920s and 1930s, Canada's first generation of professional historians began producing large and sweeping interpretations of the nation's past. When they looked back at the nineteenth century, they searched for the main underlying forces that shaped Canada's history. In the 1920s, political economists, such as W.A. Mackintosh and Harold Innis, interpreted Canadian history as dominated by the *staples thesis*. The nation's natural resource "staple" commodities—fish, furs, timber, and wheat—determined its economic development, and in doing so, shaped its political, social, and cultural institutions. These commodities also determined the development of Canada's regions. The "heartland" exploited the "hinterlands."

In 1937, historian Donald Creighton built upon this idea and advanced the *Laurentian thesis* as an interpretation of Canadian history. For Creighton, the story of Canada was the story of the St. Lawrence. Whoever controlled this crucial waterway dominated the economic life of the continent.[1] From Cartier's first voyages up the St. Lawrence in 1534; to the expansion of the fur trade into the Great Lakes and beyond into the northwest; to the emergence of the timber trade, the development of the agricultural frontier in Upper Canada, and the building of the canals, Creighton argued that the economic life of BNA was based on staple trade, and the production and exporting of these resources. The American Revolution and the Treaty of 1783 created an artificial political boundary along the St. Lawrence and the Great Lakes, dividing the northern portion of the North American continent into two political units. However, the political boundary did not immediately become an economic one. Throughout the early nineteenth century, the British merchants of Montreal vied with those of New York for commercial dominance of the trade of the interior of North America.

Up to the mid-1840s, the commercial bourgeoisie of BNA competed successfully against their American counterparts, due to the highly favourable mercantile system of trade between the colonies and Britain. In particular, the British imported two staples readily available in the colony of Canada: timber and wheat.

British shipbuilders needed square-hewed timber, made from Canadian white and red pine, for the masts of sailing ships. In addition, lumber for construction found a lucrative market in Britain. Wood became BNA's most valuable export commodity, making up nearly two-thirds of the value of the colonies' exports to Britain by the 1840s. But the lumber industry remained vulnerable and volatile, subject to fluctuating demand in Britain, low tariffs after 1842, and overproduction—all of which caused many businesses to go bankrupt during the 1840s and 1850s. Without preferential treatment in British markets, it was difficult for Canadian lumber suppliers to compete with lumber exporters from the Baltic countries, with their lower transportation costs.

Wheat (in the form of either coarse grain or ground flour) came to rival timber. Canada West was the major producer of wheat in British North America. After 1840, a combination of good weather and increased hectarage, due to rapid settlement of the rich farmland of Canada West, greatly increased total production. The average farmer's export of wheat increased from 45 bushels (1 bushel = about 35 litres) in the 1840s to 80 bushels in the 1850s, and to as much as 135 bushels in the 1860s. Improved transportation on the St. Lawrence–Great Lakes with the completion of the canal system lowered transport costs and reduced insurance rates. This helped increase Canadian exports, making Canada West one of the chief suppliers of wheat to feed industrial Britain's growing urban population.

Transportation

Exporting bulky staples, such as wheat and timber, required a reliable and efficient transportation system. Roads were needed to move wheat to urban centres for local marketing or export. In the 1840s a series of roads, some of them little more than dirt paths or surfaced with gravel, crisscrossed the Canadas. By 1852, a comprehensive road system linked Windsor to Montreal, with branches northward to towns on Lake Huron and to Bytown (Ottawa).

More important for transportation, however, was the canal system linking Lake Erie with Montreal and the Atlantic Ocean. During the 1840s, the government of the Canadas widened and deepened existing canals, such as the Welland and the Lachine, to accommodate larger steamboats. It built new canals between Montreal and Prescott, where rapids and shallows impeded shipping, and at Beauharnois, Cornwall, and Williamsburg. By 1848, a chain of first-class canals enabled the St. Lawrence–Great Lakes route to rival the

Lumbering.
Source: Archives of Ontario/11778-4.

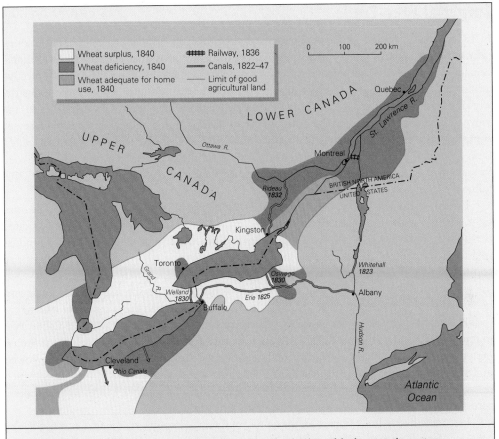

Map showing the wheat economy of the Canadas in the mid-nineteenth century.

Source: Thomas F. McIlwraith, "British North America, 1763–1867," in Robert D. Mitchell and Paul A. Groves, eds., *North America: The Historical Geography of a Changing Continent* (Lanham, MD: Rowman and Littlefield, 1990), pp. 244–45, figure 10.13.

Erie–Hudson River route, and Montreal to compete with New York as the major exporting and importing centre for the North American continent.

But New York had advantages. It was a larger city, with a heavily populated hinterland based on a diverse economy and, unlike Montreal, with a year-round ice-free port. Shipping rates from New York to Liverpool were also considerably lower than those from Montreal. In addition, in 1845–46 the American government passed the Drawbacks Acts, which allowed Canadian exports and imports to pass in bond through American waterways duty free, thus making it profitable for Canada West farmers and timber merchants to ship via the United States. Finally, New York had the advantage of being linked to the growing American Midwest by an extensive railway system.

Launch of the Royal William *by J.P Cockburn.*

Source: Library and Archives Canada, Acc. No. 1948-77-1/ C-012649.

Imperial Free Trade

In 1846, Britain adopted free trade. Pressure on the British government to end the old colonial mercantile system came chiefly from British factory owners, who wanted reduced tariffs to enable Britain to compete in a world market. They also sought the repeal of the Corn Laws (protective tariffs on grain), arguing that repeal of the laws would mean cheaper food for the industrial working class and hence an opportunity for employers to lower wages. On a global level, the move indicated a confidence in the British merchant marine and its protector, the Royal Navy, to compete and indeed dominate markets around the world. With global supremacy, Britain shifted from a "formal" to "informal" approach to empire. Its influence reached beyond areas that were formally part of the empire as colonies. Unrestricted trade was one of the means by which this influence spread.

Liberal economists such as Richard Cobden argued against traditional mercantile theories by pointing out the costs—economic and military—of maintaining colonies. Liberals argued persuasively in favour of laissez-faire economics and free trade as benefiting Britain, the industrial superpower of the day. Britain wanted to purchase raw materials at the lowest possible price and to sell manufactured goods wherever it desired. As historian J.M.S. Careless asks, "When the whole world was its domain for markets and supplies, what reason was there to guide and husband overseas possessions that cost much more to maintain than they could ever return?"[2]

These free-trade lobbyists convinced the government of British Prime Minister Robert Peel to repeal the Corn Laws in 1846. Other free-trade measures included the lowering of the timber preference in 1842, which cut the duty on foreign imports in half. Further reductions followed in 1845, 1846, 1848, and 1851. Then, in 1849, Britain repealed the Navigation Laws, which restricted trade with the colonies to British or colonial vessels. As well, the United States obtained access to the Canadian–British trade and to all the Great Lakes trade.

Free trade had a direct impact on the colony of Canada. Exports via the St. Lawrence fell by over one-third, from £2.7 million in 1845 to a low of £1.7 million in 1848. Many Canadian merchants regarded the abrupt end of the protected trading system as an unpatriotic act on Britain's part. They were resentful, especially the Montreal merchants, who prophesied the demise of their dream of expanding the commercial empire of the St. Lawrence. An international depression at the same time added to the city's problems as bankruptcies increased. If Britain was abandoning the colonies, perhaps it was argued by some, the colonies should abandon Britain. If the colonies lost their preferential access to imperial markets, perhaps they should look elsewhere. Annexation manifestoes circulated throughout the province, proposing union with the United States. Opponents of annexation formed the British–American League in 1849, which advocated tariff protection and a union of the British North American colonies. When free traders argued that high tariffs raised the price of consumer goods, Montreal journalist D'Arcy McGee rejoined that protection would "not be to make them dear, but to make them here."

From Transatlantic to Transcontinental Trade

The colony of Canada neither collapsed economically nor joined the United States. Commerce revived as British North America adjusted to new realities. Trade did increase with the United States, however. In addition, businessmen and politicians (often one and the same) placed increased emphasis on railways as the crucial vehicle of trade. These two goals were complementary. Just as the waterways facilitated east–west trade across the continent and ultimately with Britain, railways linked the Canadas and the United States for north–south trade. The transition from transatlantic to transcontinental trade was under way.

This transition came swiftly and dramatically. By the end of 1850, the international depression lifted and prosperity returned through increased trade. Whereas industrialism in Britain led indirectly to a temporary *decrease* in trade for the BNA colonies, industrialism in the United States led directly to an initial *increase* in markets for the Canadian staple products—timber and wheat. The rapidly growing cities of the eastern seaboard and of the American Midwest needed lumber, the universal building material at the time, to construct houses and commercial buildings, and wheat to feed the growing population. In the 1850s alone, 2.5 million Europeans immigrated to the United States. On the eve of the American Civil War, the United States had 31 million people, more than ten times the population of all the BNA colonies combined.

The 1850s inaugurated what historian A.R.M. Lower described as "the North American assault on the Canadian forest."[3] As demand for Canadian lumber increased, American lumber firms and sawmill owners established themselves in forest areas, especially the Ottawa Valley. Canadian timber found a growing market in Canada West, with its growing immigrant population. Saw and planing mills, sash and shingle factories, and cabinet-making firms arose to serve this local market. Britain also increased its demand for Canadian lumber in the prosperous years of the 1850s. Despite the move to free trade, Britain still remained, in relative terms, the most lucrative market for Canadian timber until into the 1860s, accounting for approximately 80 percent of wood exports.

Canadian wheat did equally well during the prosperous 1850s. As it turned out, the removal of the Corn Laws had little adverse effect on Canada's ability to compete in British markets. The demand for wheat during the Crimean War of 1854–56, when Britain prohibited the importation of Russian grain, helped the Canadas. Americans continued to purchased quantities of Canadian wheat to feed their growing urban population. Exports of Canadian wheat and flour via the St. Lawrence nearly tripled between 1845 and 1856, rising from 4.5 million bushels to 12 million bushels—a figure not surpassed until the next decade. Furthermore, prices tripled in the same period. As a result, agriculture surpassed timber as the major staple of the province of Canada—indeed, of all British North America—in the 1850s.

Farmers in Canada West benefited the most from this increased demand for wheat. High prices, along with high yields, provided farmers with capital to increase their hectarage and to diversify their produce. In addition to wheat, they exported wool, meat, eggs, butter, and cheese. Farmers in Canada East did not fare as well. Unlike Canada West, where new fertile land remained available until the mid-1850s, a shortage of good agricultural land, combined with problems of climate and fertility, led to problems. Farmers in Canada East produced little wheat for export, although they did export other grains such as oats and barley, along with dairy products in limited quantities.

Reciprocity with the United States

To expand its lucrative trade with the United States, merchants and politicians in Canada pushed for a reciprocal free trade agreement. Strong American protectionist sentiment, however, prevented acceptance of the idea. When the Americans finally became receptive in the early 1850s,

James Bruce, Earl of Elgin and Kincardine, 1848.
Source: McCord Museum, Montreal, Acc. No. 5338.

Canadian merchants were less enthusiastic due to the return of prosperity and increased trade with the United States. But, as J.M.S. Careless notes, "The emerging economic pattern of the early fifties indicated that if Canada could do without reciprocity, she could do much better with it."[4] The British government endorsed the idea, as a means of easing old tensions and reducing Canadian dependence on the mother country. The United States, however, still needed to be fully convinced of the benefits of reciprocity.

The first obstacle was the issue of slavery in the United States. The division between the pro-slavery states in the agricultural South and the anti-slavery states in the manufacturing North affected economic relations with the colonies of BNA. Many Northern senators favoured free trade because they believed it a prelude to annexing Canada, which would lead to a preponderance of anti-slavery states in the Union. Southern senators opposed it for the same reason, until Lord Elgin, who went to Washington in May 1854, convinced them that a prosperous Canada through free trade would be more likely to want independence from, rather than annexation to, the United States.

The other roadblock to reciprocity concerned Maritime fisheries. Britain and the United States had different interpretations of the territorial waters in BNA, from which American fishers were excluded under the Convention of 1818. New England fishers claimed a right to fish in Maritime waters 5 kilometres out from shore, following the shoreline. Nova Scotian and other Maritime fishers claimed a boundary 5 kilometres from headland to headland, thus leaving most of the bays and inlets as exclusive BNA territory. Britain was willing to use the fisheries issue as a negotiating tool for free trade of colonial natural products into the United States. In the end, Britain threatened to withdraw its patrol boats (which prevented American encroachment) unless Nova Scotia agreed to the treaty.

The Reciprocity Treaty

The Reciprocity Treaty of 1854, approved by the American Senate and ratified by the colonial legislatures, allowed for the free trade of major natural products, such as timber, grain, coal, livestock, and fish, between the BNA colonies and the United States; mutually free navigation on the American-controlled Lake Michigan and the Canadian-controlled St. Lawrence River; and joint access to all coastal fisheries north of the 36th Parallel. The agreement ran for a ten-year period commencing in 1855 and was subject to renewal or termination. For Canadians, the reciprocity agreement bolstered the prosperity that had already begun. In many ways, it became the symbol of the prosperity, and even though other factors (such as the Crimean War, demand created by the Civil War, and the building of railways) contributed, people looked back to the "Golden Age of Reciprocity."

The Railway Era

Closer economic ties with the United States coincided with the era of railway expansion in Canada. Increased Canadian–American trade provided the incentive for new rail lines and increased continental economic integration. The first British North American railway, the Champlain and St. Lawrence Railway, a 23-kilometre line made of wooden rails that linked Montreal and the Richelieu River, was completed in 1836. But the era of railway building occurred in the 1850s. At the beginning of the decade, only 105 kilometres of track existed in all British North America, as against 14 500 kilometres in the United States. By the end of the decade, the amount of track had increased to 2880 kilometres in the Province of Canada alone. By 1856, all the major urban centres in Canada West were linked by railways.

Such expansion came as a result of public and private financial support and promotion. As with canals, the railway projects blurred the lines between government and business. But unlike canals, in which the state often took control through public ownership, private companies built railways with extensive government financial assistance. The endeavours were often beyond the financial means of private investors and the lure of profits was not immediate or guaranteed. But the projects were attractive due to their nationalistic overtones. The railway became the new symbol of civilization, progress, and modernity. Governments became involved, for better or worse, and even though they were often taken to the brink of bankruptcy, railways seemed worth the price in order to build a nation.

The partnership between government and business made possible the construction of rail lines, but at a price. It led to waste, duplication of services, and an excessive drain on the public treasury (in the form of debt). It also contributed greatly to corruption through the granting of railway contracts for political purposes. In 1849, the Canadian government introduced the Railway Guarantee Act, which guaranteed interest at 6 percent on not more than half of the bonded debt of railways more than 120 kilometres long, over half of which had already been constructed. Of even more immediate value to railway promoters was the bill introduced in 1850 that permitted municipal governments to buy stock in railway companies and to make loans to them.

The colonies of BNA had insufficient credit ratings to borrow vast sums abroad. Since Canadians had arrived relatively late in the competition for railways, compared with Britain and the United States, and the country had hardly begun to industrialize, most of the capital came from these nations.

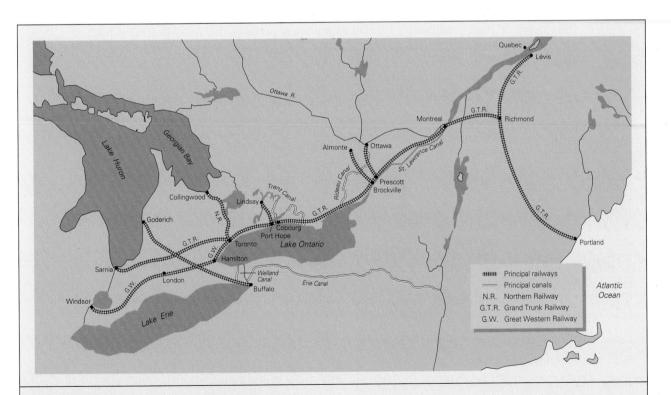

Canadian railways and canals before Confederation.

Source: Adapted from P.G. Cornell, J. Hamelin, F. Ouellet, and M. Trudel, *Canada: Unity in Diversity* (Toronto: Holt, Rinehart and Winston, 1967), p. 239.

Private companies built four key railway lines in the Province of Canada in the 1850s. The St. Lawrence and Atlantic line between Montreal and Portland, Maine, completed in 1853, gave Montreal access to a year-round ice-free port on the Atlantic, and made the city once more competitive with New York in continental trade. The second line, the Great Western Railway, completed in 1855, went from Niagara Falls via Hamilton and London to Windsor. In the east, the line joined the New York rail network, while in the west it connected with the Michigan Central. It sought to capture the trade of the American Midwest by offering a quick route from Chicago through to New York by way of the Canadas. Presided over by Sir Allan MacNab and backed by British and American capital, this 575 kilometres railway made a profit from the start. The third major line, the Northern Railway, went from Toronto, on Lake Ontario, to Collingwood, on Georgian Bay—a distance of roughly 160 kilometres. The Northern Railway serviced the rich farmland north of Toronto, opened up the forested area of the Georgian Bay and Muskoka regions, and provided access to Lake Huron. The fourth and most ambitious railway scheme of the decade was the Grand Trunk.

The Grand Trunk Railway

Chartered by the Canadian parliament in 1853, the Grand Trunk Railway was originally to run from Windsor, Canada West, to Halifax, Nova Scotia, linking the interior of British North America with an ice-free Atlantic port. The railway's name came from the intention to have several lines connect to one main line, much as the branches of a tree join its trunk. When plans to build the Maritime section failed, the company purchased the St. Lawrence and Atlantic line, which ran between Montreal and ice-free Portland, Maine. The scheme proved costly, however, because the St. Lawrence and Atlantic track needed major repairs. Equally expensive was the Grand Trunk directorate's decision (made after it failed in its attempt to purchase the Great Western) to build a competing line through the heart of Canada West from Toronto to Sarnia. As a result, the two railways often ran parallel and serviced the same area.

In 1859, the Grand Trunk completed the Victoria Bridge, one of the great engineering feats of the century. In 1858, the peak year of construction on the bridge, the enterprise employed more than 3000 workers. This 2700-metre bridge, opened by the Prince of Wales in 1860, spanned the St. Lawrence at Montreal and thus allowed for continuous rail connections between Sarnia and Portland.

Grand Trunk Railway locomotive with snow-clearing machine, Lévis, Quebec.

Source: Alexander Henderson/Library and Archives Canada/ PA-149764.

The Grand Trunk Railway, with 1760 kilometres of track, became the longest railway in the world. This distinction, however, came at great cost to the Canadian public. From the beginning, the company ran into financial trouble, leading its London bankers to approach the colonial government for help. The government consistently bailed out the company. If the symbolic and commercial power of the railroad was not enough to convince members to support the scheme, the fact that six out of twelve of the company's directors were also in the Canadian cabinet did.

By 1859, the Canadian government's debt from railway building exceeded $67 million. The Grand Trunk Railway accounted for a large part of that amount. "This sum alone," historians Kenneth Norrie and Douglas Owram note, "was greater than all the money spent on public works—canals, bridges, roads, buildings—by the Province of Canada between the Act of Union in 1841 and Confederation."[5] To make matters worse, this trunk line, designed to tap American trade for Canada, had a 1.65-metre track gauge—wider than that used in the United States. That meant American goods shipped via the Grand Trunk had to be reloaded at the border, causing the railway to lose most of the trade it was built to capture. In the 1850s and 1860s, the Grand Trunk Railway never made a profit.

Urban and Commercial Development

Railways may have been a nightmare for governments, but they were instrumental in promoting commercial development. They brought in millions of dollars of foreign investment. They required thousands of workers to lay track and then to maintain it. New related industries—engine foundries, car shops, rolling mills, and metalwork shops—sprang up across the Canadas and all needed skilled and unskilled workers. By 1860, Canadian railways had 6660 people on their combined payrolls.

Along with canal and shipbuilding, railways encouraged the development of secondary industries: flour mills, sawmills, tanneries, boot and shoe factories, textile shops, breweries, distilleries, and wagon and carriage manufacturers. Shipbuilders in Montreal and Quebec City built many of the steamboats that plied the St. Lawrence River and Great Lakes after 1809, using timber from the Ottawa Valley. Ironworks were established in Hamilton because of the city's easy access to the American coal fields in Pennsylvania. Significant developments in the manufacturing of agricultural implements occurred, especially in Newcastle, Canada West, where Daniel and Hart Massey produced a combined rake, reaper, and mowing machine in 1855, marking the beginning of a lucrative Canadian industry.

This industrial growth led to the creation of towns, mainly along the rail lines, to service the prosperous agricultural hinterland. In Canada West, the number of towns doubled to more than 80 between 1850 and 1870. Each provided a market centre for local produce and an import centre for manufactured goods. Fewer towns developed in the St. Lawrence Valley, where little fertile agricultural land remained.

On account of the lack of farmland and their inability to find work in Montreal and Quebec, many French Canadians emigrated to neighbouring New England or to the American Midwest, an area that was already attracting farmers from Canada West by the late 1850s. While Canada West was generally more fertile than the St. Lawrence Valley, it was "not nearly as rich as the long-grass prairie soils of parts of the American Middle West."[6] Moreover, by the late 1850s, the best farmland in Canada West was settled.

Within the hierarchy of towns and cities that developed in the 1840s and 1850s, London became the major centre in southwestern Canada West. This "hideous new raw place," as the artist Daniel Fowler described it in 1843, was "literally

Desjardins Canal disaster.

Source: Hamilton Central Library, Black Mountain Collection 3202218906000.

dug out of the woods—stumps up to the back doors." Nonetheless, between 1850 and 1856 its population tripled from 5000 to 15 000. The port of Hamilton dominated the hinterland to the west and south, extending its influence into the Niagara Peninsula. Both London and Hamilton became supply depots and manufacturing centres. Hamilton also became an early industrial city. A central location, however, could have some disadvantages. According to historian John Weaver, "A gang of pickpockets who worked the Great Western Railway and American trains settled in Hamilton on account of its proximity to major urban communities on both sides of the boundary."[7]

Railways in the 1850s and 1860s were also notoriously unsafe. During 1854, 19 serious accidents occurred, the most serious of which killed 52 people and injured 48. That same year, six times as many people were killed on the Great Western Railway as on all British railways, which carried 300 times as many passengers.

Rivalry between Toronto and Montreal

Toronto serviced a wealthy rural hinterland that extended roughly 20 kilometres to the east, 20 kilometres to the west, and 100 kilometres to the north, to Lake Simcoe. The city had the advantage of a central location and good harbour facilities on Lake Ontario, and became the railway hub of Canada West. Its leading commerce, the import trade, increased more than fivefold in value, from $1.2 million in 1849 to more than $6.6 million in 1856. Its export trade remained based on grain and wood to external markets, especially the United States and Britain.

An urban mercantile elite emerged in Canada West's leading city by the 1850s. Its members founded the Toronto Board of Trade. In 1852 the Toronto Stock Exchange opened, and in 1856 the Bank of Montreal inaugurated its Toronto office. By the end of the decade, the city had become the undisputed regional business centre of Canada West.

Toronto, however, could not supplant Montreal as the dominant metropolitan centre of the Province of Canada and the largest city in British North America. As one of the oldest centres, Montreal built upon its initial strengths. After a temporary setback caused by Britain's adoption of free trade in the late 1840s, the city rebounded as a prosperous centre in the 1850s. Its important location on the St. Lawrence gave it an advantage over inland Toronto, especially when the canal improvements of the 1840s made it cheaper and more efficient to ship goods by water than by rail.

Even in the competition for rail traffic, Montreal fared well with the completion of the Grand Trunk. The Portland branch provided the city with an ice-free port on the Atlantic and access to the agricultural hinterland of Canada West and, to an extent, the American Midwest. Montreal served as an import centre for the eastern portion of Canada West, rivalling Toronto for this lucrative market. The city also benefited from the Reciprocity Treaty of 1854, which helped it become a major export centre of Canadian timber and wheat for American markets.

Service industries in Montreal expanded, as footwear manufacturers, furriers, wood-products manufacturers, distilleries, breweries, tobacco factories, brickyards, and sugar refineries opened their doors. Metal-based industries, such as the Victoria Iron Works (the largest industry with 120 workers), also developed.

The Social Consequences

Immigration

Annually, 25 000 to 40 000 immigrants entered the Canadas, especially the western section. In 1851, the population of Canada West surpassed that of Canada East for the first time, to an extent fulfilling Durham's prediction. Overall, the population of the province went from 1.1 million in 1841 to almost 2 million in 1851. Almost half of the people were under the age of 18.

A large number of the new immigrants, estimated to be 90 000, came from Ireland, part of the famine migration resulting from the failure of the potato crop. Traditionally, historians have described these Irish as mainly impoverished Catholics from southern Ireland who lacked farming experience and money, and ended up in ghettos in the cities and towns. Research reveals, however, that by far the largest percentage (more than 75 percent) of Irish immigrants farmed on isolated homesteads in rural areas. Furthermore, more than two-thirds were Protestant. While many suffered from poverty, the extent of their "destitution" has been exaggerated.

COMMUNITY PORTRAIT

The Orange Community in Toronto's Cabbagetown

Formed by Irish Protestants in Ireland in 1795, the Orange Order spread rapidly throughout Ireland and England. It came to British North America in the 1820s. The Grand Lodge of British North America was organized in 1830. By 1870 Canada had more than a thousand Orange Lodges, with the largest number in Toronto. Although the Orange Order's membership was spread across all neighbourhoods in Victorian Toronto, Cabbagetown, or East Toronto, had the greatest number of lodges in the city.

East Toronto emerged in the mid-nineteenth century as an important destination for British immigrants to Ontario, particularly for Irish Protestants. The growth of railways and industries in Toronto created large numbers of jobs for urban workers north of the new rail and factory complex at the Don River end of the harbour. In the 1840s, after immigrants spread along both sides of King Street East, they settled on the vacant land to the north. There the newcomers built squatters' shacks and planted essential gardens, hence the district's name, "Cabbagetown." Small, low-priced houses followed, with some larger buildings.

The largely working-class neighbourhood, close to the adjacent factories and packing houses, soon was the home of a vibrant Orange community. Not all Protestant Irish males belonged, but a sub-

The Orange Order on parade on Toronto's King Street.

Source: Toronto Reference Library/T13222.

stantial number did. Although the initial strength of the order came from Irish immigrants, the spread of the organization owed much to the support of many non-Irish groups, in particular those of English and Scottish background. While the bulk of the membership came from the working class, the Toronto Orange community crossed class lines and had a significant middle-class component.

The Orange Lodge celebrated the British Crown and Protestantism. "No Surrender" was the order's rallying cry. The Orange Order opposed the influence of the Roman Catholic Church. In BNA, this antagonism entered the political realm over what became known as the Schools

Question. The Orange Order heralded the division between church and state and they opposed Catholic schools. The antagonism also highlighted the division between English and French in Canada. But in the British Protestant fortress of Victorian Toronto, Irish Catholics, not French Canadians, constituted the resident minority group. As John McAree, a prominent Toronto journalist, who was born of Northern Irish parents, wrote in his memoir *Cabbagetown Store* (1953), "Catholics were generally spoken of as Dogans, a term of contempt, I suppose. They were considered as foreign as if they had been Italians, and were viewed with suspicion." In mid-nineteenth-century Toronto, Protestants outnumbered Catholics by three to one. Religion, rather than race, was the focus of opposition, and the Orange Order in Canada allowed Protestant Aboriginal and black males to join.

The cohesion of Cabbagetown's Orange community came from a system of secret rituals, an internal hierarchy of five "degrees," and the public celebration of July 12, the date of William of Orange's ("King Billy's") victory at the Battle of the Boyne. The Catholics' defeat in 1690 led to the Protestant minority's maintenance of its domination of Ireland. In the nineteenth century and well into the twentieth, Cabbagetowners, on "the Glorious Twelfth," crammed with thousands of other Torontonians along downtown streets to catch a glimpse of "King Billy" on his white horse in the Orangemen's huge July 12 parade, their counterpart to the St. Patrick's Day celebrations. The celebrations were often used as means of inciting the Catholic community, just as the Catholics used St. Patrick's Day celebrations in the same manner.

Violence did occur between the Orange community of Cabbagetown and the residents of predominantly Catholic Corktown, located below Queen Street. In the late 1860s, the Young Britons arrived to strengthen the Orange community:

> A really militant organization was the Orange Young Britons, made up of husky, strutting young men, mechanics and labourers who were extremely provocative. They would parade frequently and always made it a point of invading a neighbourhood east of Parliament Street and south of Queen Street where there was quite a Roman Catholic settlement. These parades always wound up in fist fights and the throwing of stones.

Despite its bigoted overtones, the Orange community in Cabbagetown did much to benefit its members and their families. It served as a social club and as a mutual aid society, which the lower classes could afford to join. Lodge members assisted one another in times of sickness. A primitive insurance system existed to cover burial costs and even to provide lump-sum payments to widows. Orangemen also helped fellow members in the community to find work.

FURTHER READING

J.M.S. Careless, "The Emergence of Cabbagetown in Victorian Toronto," in Robert F. Harney, ed., *Gathering Place: Peoples and Neighbourhoods of Toronto, 1834–1945* (Toronto: Multicultural History Society of Ontario, 1985), pp. 25–45.

Cecil J. Houston and William J. Smyth, *The Sash Canada Wore: A Historical Geography of the Orange Order in Canada* (Toronto: University of Toronto Press, 1980).

Gregory S. Kealey, "The Orange Order in Toronto: Religious Riot and the Working Class," in Michael J. Piva, ed., *A History of Ontario: Selected Readings* (Toronto: Copp Clark Pitman Ltd., 1988), pp. 71–94.

J.V. McAree, *Cabbagetown Store* (Toronto: Ryerson Press, 1953).

The presence of Irish Protestants and Irish Catholics within the cities, or even adjacent rural settlements, resulted in the rise of "nativism," the practice of favouring native-born citizens over immigrants. In Montreal, Irish Catholics experienced less prejudice due to religious commonality with the French Canadians. But in Toronto, known at the time as "the Belfast of North America," nativist attitudes were very pronounced, especially after the Irish famine migration, when the city saw its Irish Catholic population increase from one-sixth in 1841 to one-quarter in 1851. Protestants feared that Irish Catholics would undermine loyalty to the British empire and Protestantism. In the presses and in pamphlets, the dominant Protestant population depicted the Irish Catholics as the "ignorant masses," "untameable barbarians," "priest-ridden," and "wretched." Such epithets lingered well after Irish Catholic immigrants had achieved economic success, thereby hindering their social advancement.

Harriet Tubman.

Source: Schomberg Center for Research in Black Culture, The New York Public Library, Astor Lennox and Tilden Foundations/ SC-CN-92-0675.

African Americans also came to the Province of Canada; an estimated 30 000 to 40 000 had arrived by 1861. Some came on the advice of Mary Ann Shadd Cary, the first woman publisher and editor of a Canadian newspaper in the 1850s. In 1852, she wrote *A Plea for Emigration to Canada West* to appeal in particular to African Americans by outlining the benefits of immigrating to Canada. The passage of the Fugitive Slave Act in the United States in 1850 meant that thousands of free African Americans living in the northern states were liable to be captured and sent back into bondage. Instead, many escaped to Canada by way of the Underground Railway—not literally a railway but rather a secret, complex network of free blacks, former slaves, and white American and Canadian abolitionists.

Those who led the slaves on foot or horseback, or transported them by wagons, barges, or steamers, became "agents" or "conductors" on the Underground Railway. The "passengers" were the runaways. The transfer points or hiding places were called "stations," and the final destination points were "terminals." The largest number of slave fugitives crossed at Amherstburg, situated at the narrowest point of the Detroit River. Other major "terminals" included Windsor, Sandwich, St. Catharines, Niagara-on-the-Lake, Hamilton, Toronto, and Kingston.

One of the most famous "conductors" was the former slave Harriet Tubman, who after escaping to freedom immediately returned to the South to help other slaves. In all she made nineteen trips, bringing out at least 300 slaves, and in 1857 she even succeeded in freeing her parents. Between 1851 and 1857, Tubman made St. Catharines her chief terminal. At one point, a group of slaveholders offered a $40 000 reward for her capture, dead or alive. But she evaded her would-be captors.

Many African Americans left Canada at the outbreak of the American Civil War to help the northern side. Others went home to join friends and relatives after the passage of the Emancipation Act of 1863, having found temporary refuge but no more tolerance than that experienced in the United States. It is estimated that around half stayed.

Migrant Mobility in the Canadas

Within Canada West, people moved frequently. In a case study of rural Peel County, just west of Toronto, historian David Gagan has shown that prior to 1840 the county had ample cheap land and a relatively self-sufficient population living off its own land and livestock.[8] Two decades later, it had become a major wheat exporting region. Young people moved away from the now overpopulated country areas, either to newer farming areas within the province, to the growing towns and cities of Canada West, or to other areas, such as the American Midwest. Those who stayed in Peel tended to be better off, with larger farms, a higher standard of living, and better-educated children than those who left. In general, people who did not move tended to be more prosperous than the transient in nineteenth-century North America. Canada West remained a society modelled on the agrarian values of hardy "yeoman farmers" and robust, self-reliant pioneers.

Transiency also characterized the urban centres of Canada West. Historian Michael Katz notes that the city's population increased in five years (1846–50) by 150 percent.[9] Individuals also moved frequently. More than one-third of those listed in the 1851 census could not be located for the 1861 census. This mobility characterized all social groups and ages in an attempt to improve living conditions.

In Canada East, people migrated as well. Many went to the United States, especially to New England. With a decline in agriculture and a sluggish timber trade, difficult times arrived in the 1840s and 1850s. Existing land was depleted, new agricultural land was scarce, seigneuries were subdivided to the point where the habitants could no longer support their families, and unemployment was high in the urban centres. This crisis, along with continued high birth rates, a declining death rate, and increased British immigration, forced many French Canadians to move. An estimated 30 000 emigrated during the 1840s alone.

The migration of French Canadians to the United States alarmed the clergy in Canada East, who feared, as Lord Durham had foretold, that the English population (roughly 25 percent of the total population in 1861) might one day become the majority in the province. After 1844, the Catholic Church became actively involved in the colonization movement designed to settle the northern areas of Canada East and, more important, to preserve the attributes of traditional family and religious life. This was best followed in the rural parishes, where the evil influencing vices of urban life could be avoided. The cities were also viewed as controlled by the English commercial interests. "Let us take possession of the soil, it is the best means of preserving our nationality" became the rallying cry of the agrarian nationalism of the 1840s and 1850s. The Catholic clergy may have rooted their nationalism and the survival of the French-Canadian race in an agrarian utopia, but the reality for most French Canadians was very different. Canada East was rapidly industrializing. Most French Canadians who did not leave for better economic conditions in *les États*, moved into the cities.

Urbanization in Canada West

Industrialization created a rigid class system in the urban centres of Canada West. Despite the rebellions, the Family Compact remained in place and commanded the upper classes. A growing commercial middle class, consisting of merchants, shopkeepers, and artisans, was gaining increasingly influence in society and was joined by a rising professional class of clergy, lawyers, doctors, and teachers. Gender divisions also remained in place. Middle-class women were expected to stay at home, in their "private sphere," where they performed domestic duties and reared children. Increasingly, women obtained positions as teachers (especially of girls at home), but they remained excluded from other professions. These middle-class women, however, did increasingly cross over into the "public sphere" through their charity work in voluntary associations and organizations. The seeming decay of industrial society opened the door to the reform movement.

The masses consisted of wage labourers, made up mostly of immigrants, both male and female. Few, however, had regular work. Wage-earning employment was usually temporary (as during a period of apprenticeship) or seasonal. This urban proletariat suffered the indignities of poverty: low wages, dangerous working conditions, long hours, seasonal unemployment, deplorable housing, and inadequate sanitation. The prevailing ethos of industrial capitalism held that success came to those who were diligent, frugal, and worked hard; failure came to those who were lazy, undisciplined, and immoral. The masses were kept in check by the belief that if they worked hard, their reward would come because anything was supposedly possible in this land of opportunity. Many working-class families hired out their children from about the age of seven or eight for additional family income. Other families expected children of that age to take responsibility at home while older children and the parents worked outside the home.

Urbanization in Canada East

In Canada East, urban concentration occurred in only a few centres. Even a long-established town such as Trois-Rivières had a population of only 3000 in the 1840s, while Sorel and Hull remained villages. The professional middle class of doctors, lawyers, and teachers constituted the elites in these communities. Sherbrooke was becoming the commercial centre for the predominantly English area of the Eastern Townships, but at mid-century it was still a village with a population of less than 1000.

·Only two urban centres claimed the title of "city" in Canada East in the 1850s: Montreal and Quebec City. The oldest, Quebec, was the centre of the timber trade. The majority of its commercial elite were English families associated with the trade in some respect. Many of the city's labourers, who inhabited the Lower Town (*basse-ville*) of the city, also worked in the timber industry. Here, in overcrowded and dirty conditions, French-Canadian and Irish workers intermingled. In contrast, the Upper Town, made up predominantly of the English, was considered "one of the cleanest cities in the world." In the northern section, around rue St. Jean, lived merchants, retail traders, artisans, and numerous tavern-keepers, while in the southern part resided officers and government officials.

Montreal was the largest and the most industrialized city in British North America. It also suffered from some the most negative industrial characteristics. As factories were built in the 1840s and 1850s, employment prospects attracted workers from the countryside who might otherwise have emigrated to the United States. In the 1860s, the French population once again outnumbered the English in Montreal. These French Canadians, along with the Irish immigrants, provided cheap labour for the new industries.

The eastern end of the city remained overwhelmingly working class and predominantly French Canadian, while the west end was decidedly bourgeois and British. The English-Canadian commercial entrepreneurs had begun to move "up the mountain" to build luxurious residences on Mount Royal. Historian Paul-André Linteau argues that "social divisions became so visible in Montreal's industrial sector that the city earned the fitting description 'City of wealth and death.'"[10]

Certainly Montreal's sanitation system contributed to the negative image of the city. Only in 1842 did an underground system replace open sewers on Craig Street. No regular garbage pickup existed. Drinking water was often contaminated. One in four babies did not live past the age of one year. Montreal's infant mortality rate was the worst in the industrial world.

The Working Classes

Working-class "consciousness" is an awareness that those within the class share a common lifestyle, situation, and interests. To an extent, it signifies an acceptance and even pride in the identity of being working class. It is, however, difficult to measure. In North America—"the land of opportunity" where "the streets are paved with gold"—the capitalist ethos emphasized social mobility and that "everyone can be rich." As a result, class-consciousness is even more

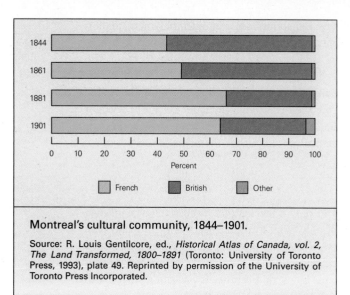

Montreal's cultural community, 1844–1901.

Source: R. Louis Gentilcore, ed., *Historical Atlas of Canada, vol. 2, The Land Transformed, 1800–1891* (Toronto: University of Toronto Press, 1993), plate 49. Reprinted by permission of the University of Toronto Press Incorporated.

difficult to gauge. A working-class consciousness was beginning to develop, however, in British North America by mid-century due to industrialization.

Skilled and semi-skilled workers joined together in the 1830s to form local trade unions and self-help organizations, such as the Ship Labourers' Benevolent Society. The objective was to protect and further the rights of workers while reacting to changing power dynamics. With skills to offer employers, they enjoyed more job security than did the labourers. Generally speaking, they preferred to strike over spontaneous rioting, which in the 1830s and 1840s was a popular form of protest among unskilled workers. Riots broke out when contractors on canal construction sites or on the developing railways could not pay their labourers. Occasionally, when conditions became desperate, skilled and unskilled workers united to stage riots and strikes.

Labourers organized two early strikes: one on the Lachine Canal in 1843, and the other on the Welland Canal in 1844–45. In both cases, they demanded improved working conditions and higher wages. In 1849, during the protests over free trade, shoemakers in Montreal ravaged a shoe factory and destroyed the sewing machines, in the tradition of the British Luddites, who opposed the mechanization of industry and the resulting loss of skilled labour. By the 1860s strikes had generally replaced riots as the main form of labour protest, although they, too, were illegal. In contrast to riots, strikes were usually more coordinated, longer-lasting, and likely to be less violent. As a result, they had a better chance of succeeding in gaining workers' redress. But the relationship between the state and capital was tight. In response to riots and strikes, employers often appealed for municipal or provincial government help (police or troops) to suppress them, often through violent means.

Children, as the most vulnerable members of society, suffered the most from the negative effects of industrialization. In Canada East the abandonment of children by poorer families to the Grey Nuns' Foundling Hospital was a serious problem. An estimated 12 000 children became wards of the church between 1840 and 1870. The majority died at a young age as a result of their weakened condition upon arrival and the lack of pasteurized milk. The Catholic Church also looked after the several thousand Irish orphans whose parents died on the Atlantic crossing, particularly in 1847, the worst year of the potato famine. Most of the Irish orphans were raised as French Canadians and intermarried. The alternative to abandoning children to orphanages or church societies in the Province of Canada was infanticide. Some destitute, unmarried, working-class women without family support resorted to such desperate measures, despite the fact that if caught they could be put to death.

The legal system, as the arm of the state, dealt harshly with crimes of poverty, even when they were the direct result of social inequality. Reform of the legal system did occur, however, in response. In 1849, William Hume Blake, solicitor general in the Baldwin–LaFontaine government, reformed the Court of Queen's Bench and the Court of Chancery and established a Court of Error and Appeals and a Court of Common Pleas. In 1857, George-Étienne Cartier centralized the legal system and made it more uniform. He also modernized the old Custom of Paris with a new Civil Code that revised contracts and labour law, and abolished dower rights unless they were formally registered.

The Prohibition Movement

Reformers increasingly focused on alcohol as a source of social problems. While all classes drank, the working classes were perceived as lacking the moral fortitude to handle alcohol. Drinking was thought of as a gendered problem, because "good" and "respectable" women did not partake, and working-class men were often accused of drinking their wages away in taverns and, returning home, beating their wives and children. The vices of gambling and prostitution, too, were associated with the urban working classes.

The rise of an urban working class spurred the "prohibition" movement (the use of the power of the state to control and, it was hoped, eliminate alcohol) throughout British North America. By the 1850s, there was a noticeable shift in emphasis from temperance (abstinence through self-discipline) to prohibition. Historian Graeme Decarie suggests that this shift in Canada West came about as a result of a perceived threat to traditional Protestant middle-class values from the growing working class, often made up of Irish Catholics. Prohibition became a means for some middle-class Protestants to reassert their position of power and prominence. The Sabbatarian movement, strong among the Protestant churches, advocated "all praying and no playing" on Sundays. It worked to ban alcohol altogether. Furthermore, many rural inhabitants saw alcoholism as a predominantly urban phenomenon, another example of urban moral decay. "To them," Decarie noted, "a vote for prohibition was a vote for rural virtue and against urban decadence."[11]

Quebec's "apostle of temperance" was Charles Chiniquy, a lively and eccentric Roman Catholic priest. He founded the Société de Tempérance in 1840, and by 1844 he had persuaded thousands to take the pledge of abstinence. "Everywhere his zeal goes, intemperance flies," the newspaper *Le Canadien* reported. His "zeal" took him to Kamouraska, Longueuil, and Montreal. His message, according to historian Jan Noel, could be summed up as follows: "The national survival of French Canada depends upon temperance. Giving up drinking might be unpleasant, but it was preferred to the decay and disappearance of a people."[12] Sexual escapades and charges of embezzlement later led to Chiniquy's excommunication from the Roman Catholic Church. In 1856 he became a Protestant and waged a war of slander against his former church until his death at the age of 89, in 1899.

Religion

Religion was central to the lives of most people in British North America. In Canada West in the 1840s, the Church of England was the declared church affiliation of 22 percent of the population. The Presbyterians followed at 20 percent, and the Methodists at 17 percent. The Baptists, Quakers, Lutherans, and Congregationalists together had 6 percent. The Roman Catholic population stood at 14 percent in 1841, most of it consisting of Irish Catholic immigrants.

Both the Methodists and the Baptists experienced internal dissension at mid-century. The union of Canadian and British Methodism in 1832 had led to the schism of the Episcopal Methodists and the growth of smaller British Methodist sects. The division appeared to be between the English brand of Wesleyan Methodism and Canadian Methodism. The same was true of the dissension in the Baptist Church. As a result, these two churches were more divided by 1850 than they had been in 1830, thus undermining their effectiveness.

The growth of new sectarian movements from within the Methodists and Baptists was accompanied by the rise of external religious sects and "heretical" religious groups that cut into Baptist and Methodist support. Among the largest and most influential of these sects were the Campbellites or Disciples of Christ, Mormons, and Millerites. These new sects received much of their support from the backwoods areas of Canada West as well as the working class in the towns and cities.

This religious shift from rural to urban was accompanied by a shift from evangelicalism and an emotional approach to religion to a rational approach to faith and the valuing of Baconian

The Reverend John Burwash.

Source: The United Church of Canada/Victoria University Archives, Toronto/Acc. no. 76.001 P/790N.

science. The latter entailed the study and classification of nature as a means to better understand God's design. After 1859, churches also faced the challenge of beliefs coming out of Darwinian science—that all living things had evolved from a primitive form of life through natural selection and the survival of the fittest. Such ideas brought into question Christian belief in humans as beings created in God's image. As well, urban-oriented society required churches to address issues of social reform with regard to such groups as the poor, the sick, and the mentally ill.

Ignace Bourget, appointed bishop of Montreal in 1840, encouraged religious orders from France to come to Canada East, in the case of some orders to return to Quebec, to help "Christianize" his diocesans. He also founded new male and female orders that took responsibility for elementary education, the classical colleges, hospitals, and charitable organizations. Bourget was an advocate of ultramontanism, the belief that the state should be subordinate to the church. By extension, the religious authority (the Vatican) held supreme power, even over state matters. To this end, he worked with Louis-Hippolyte LaFontaine to ensure that education remained under the control of the Roman Catholic Church instead of coming under state control.

Education and Culture

Education in Canada West

In the mid-nineteenth century, education often came to dominate public debate. Amid the social problems caused by industrialization, urbanization, and immigration, education was seen as the light in the darkness. It served a dual function of offering enlightenment for individuals to rise from their lowly situations while at the same time instilling social control through citizenship and propaganda. Gradually, even the elites recognized the value of education for the masses. Schools grew at a rapid rate to keep pace with the growing population. But whoever controlled education, controlled the youth and therefore the future of society. The nature and control of the schools, therefore, became highly contentious issues.

State-supported schools developed in the Union period. In 1841, the government of the Canadas passed an Education Act extending the common schools throughout the western half of the united province. The act created the office of superintendent of education to oversee educational matters, and established local boards of education with powers to tax inhabitants in each district to build and maintain schools. Opposition to the bill arose among those who argued that public funds should also be used to support separate schools for Roman Catholics, just as they were to support Protestant schools in Quebec. The votes of the French-Canadian members for Canada East gave the supporters of the separate-school clause in Canada West the majority they needed in the Assembly. After the clause was passed, Canada West's separate schools received funding in proportion to the number of children in attendance.

The central role of education in society lay at the heart of the separate-school controversy. Roman Catholic leaders believed that education should have a religious component and that religious instruction should be in keeping with the teachings and beliefs of the Catholic Church.

Catholic bishops argued that the common schools, while ostensibly "public" were in reality Protestant or, at best, non-religious in orientation. Only separate schools, they felt, could ensure a proper Catholic and moral education. Furthermore, church leaders such as Armand Charbonnel, bishop of Toronto, argued for the right of Catholic parents to direct the education of their own children.

Opponents of separate schools, such as Egerton Ryerson, the Methodist minister who served as superintendent of education for Canada West (Ontario) from 1844 to 1876, and George Brown, the influential political reformer and editor of the Toronto *Globe*, argued that education should be free, publicly funded, and nonsectarian. They believed that separate schools perpetuated sectarianism and undermined the common-school system. But beneath this "public" argument often resided anti-Catholic bigotry. Brown, for example, claimed that separate schools would allow the church to undermine the educational system and give the pope undue influence in national affairs. The debate between these two approaches to education continued throughout the mid-nineteenth century and often came to sit at the heart of Catholic–Protestant antagonism. As historian Peter A. Baskerville notes, "By the early 1860s, the school question would be the single most divisive issue in Canadian politics and a major cause of the political stalemate that characterized the last years of the Union period."[13]

Both separate and common schools proliferated in the 1850s and 1860s. By the School Act of 1853, a full-scale Catholic separate-school system came into being. The system had its own separate-school board, with tax support from parents, who were exempt from paying common-school taxes. A share of the provincial grant also paid expenses. The final pre-Confederation education bill, the Scott Act of 1863, allowed separate schools to receive a share of both the provincial and municipal grants. Separate schools were also extended into rural areas. In return for these concessions, separate schools, like their common-school counterparts, submitted to provincial inspection, centralized control of curriculum and textbooks, and government control of all teacher training.

Common or public schools also came under increased centralized control as a result of the efforts of Superintendent of Education Ryerson. His Common School Act of 1846 established a board of education (later the Council of Public Instruction) responsible for assisting the chief superintendent in establishing provincial standards, founded what were called "normal schools" to train teachers, and held locally elected school boards responsible for operating the schools in their sections. These schools were expected to teach children good moral values—that is, Christian values that included a sense of duty and attachment to Britain, and tolerance toward other ethnic groups and religions—as well as to prepare them for work in an expanding and changing commercial economy. Ryerson believed a centralized and highly regulated system could best achieve these goals.

In Canada West, a similar process of secularism occurred in higher education. In 1849, under the direction of Ryerson, the government changed the Anglican-affiliated King's College into the non-sectarian University of Toronto. Once King's College had been transformed into the "godless" University of Toronto, John Strachan, bishop of Toronto, founded the Anglican Trinity University in 1851. (At the turn of the century, Trinity, the Methodists' Victoria University, and St. Michael's, a Roman Catholic college founded in 1852, all became affiliates of the University of Toronto.)

Education in Canada East

In Canada East, the Lower Canadian School Act of 1846 provided for the two school systems: one Catholic and one Protestant. Within each Catholic school in Canada East, the *curé*, or priest, had the right to veto the selection of teachers and textbooks, leaving only the task of financing the schools to the provincial authorities.

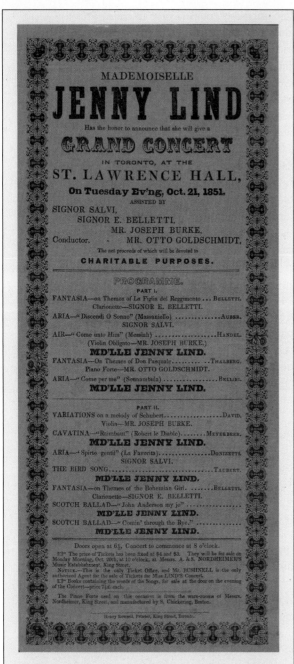

Jenny Lind's concert in Toronto's St. Lawrence Hall in April 1851 was a huge success. Due to over-subscription, it was repeated for three more evenings despite the high prices of $3 to $4 a ticket—several days' wages for a labourer. The money raised went to found the Protestant Orphans' Home.

Source: Toronto Reference Library, Baldwin Room Broadsides and Printed Ephemera Collection, 1851.

In 1851, the legislature passed an act to establish a normal school to educate teachers, but it took six years before it became operational. In 1859, it set up the Council of Public Instruction. Consisting of fourteen members (ten Catholic and four Protestant) and the superintendent of education, it assisted the superintendent in making regulations for the normal school, for the organization and administration of common schools, and for the grading of schools and teachers.

At the university level, McGill University, chartered in 1821, became an influential institution. Due to family litigation, however, it did not begin classes until the 1830s. It admitted both English- and French-speaking students (although instruction was in English only) for advanced education in law, medicine, and the arts. Under the guidance of its principal, William Dawson, appointed in 1855, McGill later acquired a distinguished reputation, especially in scientific research and medicine. In 1852, Université Laval was founded, having developed out of the Séminaire de Québec, founded by Bishop Laval in 1663. Steeped in the French-Catholic tradition, the first French-Canadian university soon held a position of respect in Canada East, with its courses in theology, civil law, medicine, and the arts.

Culture in the Canadas

"Culture" in the nineteenth century meant "high" culture and was assumed to be restricted to the elites who had the education and financial means to enjoy such pursuits. But the range, depth, and accessibility of cultural activities was increasing in the Canadas as a result of urban growth, educational opportunities, and the expansion of the middle class. Cultural pursuits, however, were notably divided between French and English Canada.

In Canada East, François-Xavier Garneau wrote his three-volume *Histoire du Canada*, a monumental history of French Canada, as a direct response to Durham's denunciation of French Canadians as a "backward people." Octave Crémazie was a French-Canadian poet, popular for his nostalgic references to the glories of New France and the miseries that followed after the Conquest. Newspapers, such as Montreal's *La Minerve* and Quebec City's *Le Canadien*, increased subscriptions. French-Canadian journalists and public figures gave popular lectures on important topics of the day: education, national traits, and *la position de la femme*. In 1843 Ludger Duvernay, the editor of *La Minerve*, organized the Société Saint-Jean-Baptiste de Montréal. Many prominent French Canadians joined this patriotic organization, established to promote the interests of French Canada.

Canadian literature in English had a slow start. Whereas Canada East was separated from France and developed its own tradition of writing, Canada West lauded its attachment to the British empire. There seemed less need to develop a "colonial" literature. In fact, the earliest novel to be written by a British-American-born author and published in the Canadas (Julia Catherine Beckwith's *St. Ursula's Convent*) appeared only in 1824, and the first anthology of poetry in English in 1864. Throughout the 1860s, poetry was popular

This sketch by James Duncan shows the dance at a French-Canadian wedding; the fiddler is on the right.

Source: With permission of the Royal Ontario Museum © ROM/ 951.158.14.

in Canada West. William Kirby described the migration of loyalists to Niagara in his poem *The U.E.L.*, while Charles Sangster captured the beauty of the Canadian landscape in *The St. Lawrence and the Saguenay*. Other writers included Susanna Moodie and her sister Catharine Parr Traill, both of whom obtained publishers, and a readership, in Britain. From 1847 to 1851, George Copway, an Ojibwa from Rice Lake in Canada West, published four books in English in the United States, including the first autobiography by a Canadian Aboriginal and the first history of the Ojibwa people. Peter Jones's History of the *Ojebway Indians* appeared in 1861, four years after the Ojibwa Methodist minister's death in 1856. Amateur historians, such as John Richardson (*The War of 1812*) and Robert Christie (*History of the Late Province of Lower Canada*), praised the early pioneers of the provinces. However, no significant publishing industry existed in the province until the late nineteenth century.

In 1855, journalist John McMullen produced the first history of English Canada, *The History of Canada from First Discovery to the Present Time*. While lacking François-Xavier Garneau's intensity and flair, McMullen did have a justification for his history: "To infuse a spirit of Canadian nationality into the people generally—to mould the native born citizen, the Scotch, the English

and the Irish emigrant into a compact whole." Newspapers, among them Toronto's *Globe* and *Leader*, helped cultivate a national feeling among English Canadians.

In the mid-nineteenth century, Canada attracted some impressive musicians. Famous artists such as Jenny Lind—"the Swedish Nightingale," the finest soprano of the day—and Henri Vieuxtemps, the Belgian violinist and composer, visited and inspired local artists and musicians. Due to the small population, however, few Canadian-born professional musicians could support themselves comfortably with only their performances and teaching.

Growing prosperity enlarged the market for portrait painters such as G.T. Berthon, landscape painters such as Robert Whale, and exploration

Ojibwa defeat of the Iroquois.

Source: Ontario Provincial Museum, *Archaeological Report for 1904* (Toronto: King's Printer, 1905).

Flier announcing the arrival in Quebec City of Levi J. North's circus.

Source: *Le Canadien,* 5 juin 1854, Montreal. Library and Archives Canada.

artists, including Paul Kane. By 1860, William Notman of Montreal had already established his reputation as a photographer.

Tourism and the Wilderness

Early Canadian writers focused on the climate and environment for their inspiration. For the Canadian elite, these areas of wilderness began to take on special significance as tourist spots by the mid-nineteenth century. As the wilderness began to be "conquered" and subdued, and thus lost its threatening nature in the Victorian mind, as Aboriginal people became more "civilized" and declined in numbers, and as landscape became imbued with a sense of the romantic and sublime, tourism emerged as a growth industry. Improved transportation facilities, including canals and railroads, made it easier for upper- and middle-class individuals to visit exotic or faraway places as tourist sites. As historian Patricia Jasen notes,

> The tourist industry was an ally of many forms of economic development in the nineteenth century, such as the growth of railways and steamer companies, and all of these industries were intimately associated with the gospel of expansionism, whereby the fate of the "unsettled" regions of Canada was identified with the interests of the metropolis.[14]

Tourism was, however, the preserve of the upper-and middle-classes. Only they could afford a holiday or even contemplate the "right" to leisure time. Many romantic tourist places—especially natural landscapes—took on a religious meaning. Tours to places of natural beauty were frequently compared to a secular pilgrimage.

Niagara Falls, above all other tourist attractions, became a special place, already attracting as many as 40 000 visitors a year by the later 1840s. To "do" Niagara, along with Boston and Quebec City, became the American equivalent of the European grand tour, a "must" for all affluent North Americans. With the opening of the Erie Canal in 1825 and the Welland Canal in 1832, and especially with the advent of railroads in the 1840s and 1850s, Niagara Falls became more accessible.

From the beginning, however, Niagara Falls also became associated with sexual pleasure, especially as "the Honeymoon Capital of the World." Historian Karen Dubinsky has shown how the "purity" of the natural falls, its gendered nature as a female icon, evident in such descriptions of the Falls as "the Queen of the Cataracts," "the Queen of Beauty," and "the Water Bride of Time," and the fact that the observer of such beauty was usually depicted as a male, "enhanced the spectatorial pleasure of 'doing' Niagara."[15] Already in the mid-nineteenth century, tourist agents realized the importance of identifying natural sites as places of pleasure—especially sexual pleasure, in a society that suppressed overt expressions of sex—thus enhancing the commercial value.

SUMMARY

Between 1840 and 1864, the Province of Canada underwent considerable economic and social change. Canadians adjusted to the end of the mercantile system of trade, to the advent of the railway age, and to rapidly changing social conditions in both rural and urban life. This was an age of transition from a British-oriented to an American-oriented economy and from a pioneer to a commercial society. The shift would take decades to complete, but it was underway. Culturally, a French-Canadian identity already existed, but beside it an Upper Canadian or English-Canadian collective identity continued to take shape. Its Protestant variant would be exported westward after Canada's acquisition of the North West in the late nineteenth century.

NOTES

1. See Donald Creighton, *The Commercial Empire of the St. Lawrence* (Toronto: Ryerson Press, 1937).

2. J.M.S. Careless, *The Union of the Canadas: The Growth of Canadian Institutions, 1841–1857* (Toronto: McClelland & Stewart, 1967), p. 111.

3. See A.R.M. Lower, *The North American Assault on the Canadian Forest* (Toronto: Ryerson Press, 1938).

4. Careless, *The Union of the Canadas*, p. 136.

5. Kenneth Norrie and Douglas Owram, *A History of the Canadian Economy*, 2nd ed. (Toronto: Harcourt Brace, 1996), p. 189.

6. R. Cole Harris, "Ontario," in R. Cole Harris and John Warkentin, *Canada Before Confederation* (Ottawa: Carleton University Press, 1991 [1974]), pp. 114–15.

7. John G. Weaver, Hamilton: *An Illustrated History* (Toronto: James Lorimer, 1982), p. 77.

8. David Gagan, *Hopeful Travellers: Families, Land and Social Change in Mid-Victorian Peel County, Canada West* (Toronto: University of Toronto Press, 1981), pp. 20ff.

9. Michael B. Katz, *The People of Hamilton, Canada West: Family and Class in a Mid-Nineteenth-Century City* (Cambridge, MA: Harvard University Press, 1975), p. 2.

10. Paul-André Linteau, "Montreal: City of Pride," *Horizon Canada* 4 (1984): 88.

11. Graeme Decarie, *Prohibition in Canada*, Canada's Visual History Series, vol. 29, Canadian Museum of Civilization, p. 3.

12. Jan Noel, "Dry Patriotism: The Chiniquy Crusade," *Canadian Historical Review* 71(2) (June 1990): 200.

13. Peter A. Baskerville, *Ontario: Image, Identity, and Power* (Toronto: Oxford University Press, 2002), p. 106.

14. Patricia Jasen, *Wild Things: Nature, Culture, and Tourism in Ontario, 1790–1914* (Toronto: University of Toronto Press, 1995), p. 152.

15. Karen Dubinsky, "'The Pleasure Is Exquisite but Violent': The Imaginary Geography of Niagara Falls in the Nineteenth Century," *Journal of Canadian Studies* 29(2) (Summer 1994): 75.

BIBLIOGRAPHY

J.M.S. Careless provides a survey in *The Union of the Canadas: The Growth of Canadian Institutions, 1841–1857* (Toronto: McClelland & Stewart, 1967). Eric Ross reviews life in the Canadas in 1841 in

Full of Hope and Promise: The Canadas in 1841 (Montreal/Kingston: McGill-Queen's University Press, 1991). For Canada East (Quebec), also consult the final chapters in Fernand Ouellet's *Economic and Social History of Quebec, 1760–1850* (Toronto: Macmillan, 1980). Donald G. Creighton develops the Laurentian thesis in *The Empire of the St. Lawrence: A Study in Commerce and Politics*, now reprinted with an introduction by Christopher Moore (Toronto: University of Toronto Press, 2002 [1937]).

Economic questions are addressed in Kenneth Norrie and Douglas Owram, *A History of the Canadian Economy*, 2nd ed. (Toronto: Harcourt Brace, 1996); and in Michael Bliss, *Northern Enterprise: Five Centuries of Canadian Business* (Toronto: McClelland & Stewart, 1987). For Canada West (Ontario), see the relevant chapters for this period in Douglas McCalla, *Planting the Province: The Economic History of Upper Canada, 1784–1870* (Toronto: University of Toronto Press, 1993). See as well G.N. Tucker, *The Canadian Commercial Revolution, 1845–1851* (Toronto: McClelland & Stewart, 1964); and D.C. Masters, *The Reciprocity Treaty of 1854* (Toronto: McClelland & Stewart, 1963). P.J. Cain, *Economic Foundation of British Overseas Expansion, 1815–1914* (London: Macmillan, 1980) explains British economic policies in terms of imperial developments.

On agricultural developments see McCalla's, *Planting the Province*, mentioned earlier and John McCallum's older, *Unequal Beginnings: Agriculture and Economic Development in Quebec and Ontario Until 1870* (Toronto: University of Toronto Press, 1980). See too R.M. McInnis' "A Reconsideration of the State of Agriculture in Lower Canada in the First half of the Nineteenth Century," in *The Canadian Papers in Rural History*, vol. III (Gananoque: Langdale Press, 1982). For Canada East, see R.L. Jones, "Agriculture in the St. Lawrence Valley, 1815–1850," in W.T. Easterbrook and M. Watkins, eds., *Approaches to Canadian Economic History* (Toronto: McClelland & Stewart, 1967), pp. 110–26; and Serge Courville and Normand Séguin, *Rural Life in Nineteenth-Century Quebec* (Ottawa: Canadian Historical Association, 1989). For Canada West, see R.L. Jones, *History of Agriculture in Ontario, 1613–1880* (Toronto: University of Toronto Press, 1977). A.R.M. Lower reviews the timber trade in *Great Britain's Woodyard: British America and the Timber Trade, 1763–1867* (Montreal/Kingston: McGill-Queen's University Press, 1973). On railway building in the 1850s, see G.P de T. Glazebrook, *A History of Transportation in Canada*, vol. 1 (Toronto: McClelland & Stewart, 1964). For an appreciation of the excitement of railway building, see T.C. Keefer's *The Philosophy of Railroads* (1849), reprinted with an introduction by H.V. Nelles (Toronto: University of Toronto Press, 1972).

Urban and commercial development in Canada West is discussed by Jacob Spelt, *Urban Development in South-Central Ontario* (Toronto: McClelland & Stewart, 1972 [1955]); and Douglas McCalla, *The Upper Canada Trade, 1834–1872: A Study of the Buchanans' Business* (Toronto: University of Toronto Press, 1979). See also Michael Katz, *The People of Hamilton, Canada West: Family and Class in a Mid-Nineteenth-Century City* (Cambridge: Harvard University Press, 1975). Also important is Robert Kristofferson's *Craft Capitalism: Craftworkers and Early Industrialization in Hamilton, Ontario, 1840–1872* (Toronto: University of Toronto Press, 2007). For Canada East, see G. Tulchinsky, *The River Barons: Montreal Businessmen and the Growth of Industry and Transportation, 1837–1853* (Toronto: University of Toronto Press, 1977). Henry C. Klassen recounts the life of an important Montreal entrepreneur in Luther H. Holton: *A Founding Canadian Entrepreneur* (Calgary: University of Calgary Press, 2000). Peter Baskerville reviews the history of the Bank of Upper Canada in the introduction to his edited work *The Bank of Upper Canada: A Collection of Documents* (Toronto: Champlain Society, 1987).

The chapters "Quebec in the Century After the Conquest," pp. 65–109, and "Ontario," pp. 110–68, in R. Cole Harris and John Warkentin, *Canada Before Confederation* (Ottawa: Carleton University Press, 1991 [1974]), provide an overview of social developments in the Province of Canada. For Canada East, see as well J.I. Little, *State and Society in Transition: The Politics of Institutional Reform in the Eastern Townships* (Montreal/Kingston: McGill-Queen's University Press, 1997). Donald H. Akenson's *The Irish in Ontario: A Study in Rural History* (Montreal/Kingston: McGill-Queen's University Press, 1984) is a valuable study. On nativist attitudes toward Irish Catholics, see Scott W. See, "'Unprecedented Influx': Nativism and Irish Famine Immigration to Canada," *American Review of Canadian Studies* 30(4) (Winter 2000): 429–53. For the story of blacks in the Canadas in the mid-nineteenth century, consult Robin W. Winks, *The Blacks in Canada*, 2nd ed. (Montreal/Kingston: McGill-Queen's University Press, 1997);

Daniel G. Hill, *The Freedom-Seekers: Blacks in Early Canada* (Agincourt, ON: Book Society of Canada, 1981); and Adrienne Shadd, "The Lord Seemed to Say 'Go': Women and the Underground Railroad Movement," in Peggy Bristow et al., eds., *"We've Rooted Here and They Can't Pull Us Up"* (Toronto: University of Toronto Press, 1994), pp. 41–68. Two good quantitative studies to consult are David Gagan, *Hopeful Travellers: Families, Land and Social Change in Mid-Victorian Peel County, Canada West* (Toronto: University of Toronto Press, 1981); and Michael Katz, *The People of Hamilton, Canada West: Family and Class in a Mid-Nineteenth-Century City* (Cambridge, MA: Harvard University Press, 1975). On French-Canadian migration, see Bruno Ramirez, *On the Move: French-Canadian and Italian Migrants in the North Atlantic Economy, 1860–1914* (Toronto: McClelland & Stewart, 1991.

Alison Prentice et al., *Canadian Women: A History*, 2nd ed. (Toronto: Harcourt Brace, 1996), examines changes in the lives of women in the mid-nineteenth century, while Micheline Dumont et al., *Quebec Women: A History* (Toronto: Women's Press, 1987), focuses on women in Canada East in the same period.

The First Nations' history in the Canadas in the mid-nineteenth century is reviewed in several sources, including Daniel Francis, *A History of the Native Peoples of Quebec, 1760–1867* (Ottawa: Department of Indian Affairs and Northern Development, 1983); and Edward S. Rogers and Donald B. Smith, eds., *Aboriginal Ontario: Historical Perspectives on the First Nations* (Toronto: Dundurn Press, 1994). For biographical treatments, see Donald B. Smith, *Sacred Feathers: The Reverend Peter Jones (Kahkewaquonaby) and the Mississauga Indians* (Toronto: University of Toronto Press, 1987); and Janet Chute, *The Legacy of Shingwaukonse: A Century of Native Leadership* (Toronto: University of Toronto Press, 1998). For an in-depth study of a First Nation community in Canada East, see Hélène Bédard, *Les Montagnais et la réserve de Betsiamites, 1850–1900* (Quebec: Institut québécoise de recherche sur la culture, 1988). A review of early Aboriginal residential schools is provided in J.R. Miller, *Shingwauk's Vision: A History of Native Residential Schools* (Toronto: University of Toronto Press, 1996). See also Michelle Hamilton's *Collections and Objections: Aboriginal Material Culture in Southern Ontario* (Montreal: McGill-Queen's University Press, 2010).

On the history of the Canadian working class, consult the relevant essays in Paul Craven, ed., *Labouring Lives: Work and Workers in Nineteenth-Century Ontario* (Toronto: University of Toronto Press, 1995); M.S. Cross, ed., *The Workingman in the Nineteenth Century* (Toronto: Oxford University Press, 1974); and S. Langdon's pamphlet *The Emergence of the Working-Class Movement, 1845–1875* (Toronto: New Hogtown Press, 1975). On strikes, see H.C. Pentland, "The Lachine Strike of 1843," *Canadian Historical Review* 29 (1984): 255–77; Ruth Bleasdale, "Class Conflict on the Canals of Upper Canada in the 1840s," *Labour/Le travailler* 7 (1981): 9–39; and Ruth Bloomsdale, "Class Conflict on the Canals of Upper Canada in the 1840s." *Labour/Le travail* 7 (1981). On labour protest in general, consult Bryan Palmer, "Labour Protest and Organization in Nineteenth-Century Canada, 1820–1890," *Labour/ Le travail* 20 (1987): 61–84; and Palmer, Bryan D. *Working Class Experience: Rethinking the History of Canadian Labour, 1800–1991*, 2nd ed. (Toronto: McClelland & Stewart, 1992). For a look at labour in 1840s Montreal, see Sherry Olson, "Ethnic Partition of the Work Force in 1840s Montreal," *Labour/Le travail* 53 (Spring 2004).

Educational questions are treated in J.D. Wilson, R.M. Stamp, and L.P. Audet, *Canadian Education: A History* (Scarborough, ON: Prentice-Hall, 1970), pp. 167–89, 214–40. For Canada West, see also S. Houston and A. Prentice, *Schooling and Scholars in Nineteenth-Century Ontario* (Toronto: University of Toronto Press, 1988); Franklin A. Walker, *Catholic Education and Politics in Upper* Canada, vol. 1 (Toronto: J.M. Dent and Sons, 1955); Gidney, R.D., and W.J. Millar, *Inventing Secondary Education: The Rise of the High School in Nineteenth Century Ontario* (Montreal/Kingston: McGill-Queen's University Press, 1992), and Bruce Curtis' books *Building the Education State: Canada West 1836–1871* (London: Falmer Press and Althouse Press, 1988) and *True Government by Choice Men? Inspection, Education, and State Formation in Canada West* (Toronto: University of Toronto Press, 1992). See also Clauidette Knight's article "Black Parents Speak: Education in Mid-Nineteenth Century Canada West," *Ontario History* 89(4) (December 1997).

William Westfall looks at the creation of Trinity University in Toronto in 1852 in *The Founding Moment: Church, Society and the Construction of Trinity College* (Montreal/Kingston: McGill-Queen's University

Press, 2002). See also William Westfall's *Two Worlds: The Protestant Culture of Nineteenth-Century Ontario* (Montreal/Kingston: McGill-Queen's University Press, 1989). For Canada East, see Andrée Dufour, *Tous à l'école: État communautés rurales et scolarisation au Québec de 1826 à 1859* (Ville La Salle: Éditions Hurtubise HMH, 1996); and Claude Galarneau, *Les collèges classiques au Canada français* (Montreal: Fides, 1978). A short but dated biography of Egerton Ryerson is Clara Thomas, *Ryerson of Upper Canada* (Toronto: Ryerson Press, 1969). On religion, see John S. Moir, *The Church in the British Era: From the British Conquest to Confederation* (Toronto: McGraw-Hill Ryerson, 1972); and John Webster Grant, *A Profusion of Spires: Religion in Nineteenth-Century Ontario* (Toronto: University of Toronto Press, 1988).

Cultural aspects of the era are reviewed in George Woodcock, *The Century That Made Us: Canada, 1814–1914* (Toronto: Oxford University Press, 1989). Jan Noel examines the temperance movement in *Canada Dry: Temperance Crusades Before Confederation* (Toronto: University of Toronto Press, 1995). Musical developments are reviewed in Helmut Kallmann, *A History of Music in Canada, 1534–1914* (Toronto: University of Toronto Press, 1960); and Timothy J. McGhee, *The Music of Canada* (New York: W.W. Norton, 1985). For information on art in the Canadas in the mid-nineteenth century, see Dennis Reid, *A Concise History of Canadian Painting*, 2nd ed. (Toronto: Oxford University Press, 1988). Douglas Fetherling reviews early Canadian journalism in *The Rise of the Canadian Newspaper* (Toronto: Oxford University Press, 1990). Denis Monière has written the biography of an important Montreal newspaper editor: *Ludger Duvernay et la révolution intellectuelle au Bas-Canada* (Montreal: Québec/Amérique, 1987). On tourism as an expression of popular culture, see Patricia Jasen, *Wild Things: Nature, Culture, and Tourism in Ontario, 1790–1914* (Toronto: University of Toronto Press, 1995); and Karen Dubinsky, "'The Pleasure Is Exquisite but Violent': The Imaginary Geography of Niagara Falls in the Nineteenth Century," *Journal of Canadian Studies* 29(2) (Summer 1994): 64–88.

Source: McCord Museum, Montreal, M11588.

Chapter Sixteen

THE UNION OF THE CANADAS: POLITICAL DEVELOPMENTS, 1840–1864

TIME LINE

1840	Union Act passed; Upper and Lower Canada become one colony
1841	Governor General Sydenham dies
1848	LaFontaine and Baldwin form government
1849	Governor General Elgin sanctions Rebellion Losses Bill Protesters burn Parliament building in Montreal Responsible Government becomes reality in BNA Annexation Association publishes manifesto
1854	John A. Macdonald and George-Étienne Cartier forge Tory alliance Seigneurial system abolished
1857	"Rep by Pop" becomes main plank of Reformers
1859	Queen Victoria selects Ottawa as Canada's capital.
1860	Britain (Crown) transfers authority over First Nations to Canadian government
1863	Political deadlock paralyzes Legislative Assembly

The Act of Union adopted by the British parliament in July 1840 followed Durham's advice and joined the two Canadas under a single colonial government. Although Lower Canada was officially renamed Canada East and Upper Canada renamed Canada West, people commonly used the pre-union names. The Act gave the old colony of Quebec its fourth constitution since the Conquest. The union, however, had a short and stormy existence. With the French-Catholic and English-Protestant colonies together, and each being given the same number of seats in the Assembly, political deadlock resulted. The situation became one of the main causes leading to a larger British North American confederation.

Although ultimately a failure, the union could boast some successes. The government adopted important laws providing for the education of children in both sections of the colony. As railway fever swept the business community in the 1850s, solicitous politicians oversaw a multitude of costly and often competing construction projects. While patronage and corruption was rife, and the expensive endeavours pushed governments beyond their fiscal means, the railways forged the economic structure of an emerging nation. The Reciprocity Treaty increased trade relations with the United States and led to an era of prosperity. Protective tariffs on manufactured goods stimulated industrial growth. While many governments came and fell during this period, and politics was divided into Tory and Reformer camps (and then subdivided into French and English groups), the foundations of Canada's political system were built. According to political scientist S.J.R. Noel, "The overall record of governmental accomplishment compares favourably with that of any other era, either before or since."[1]

Most importantly, the union years witnessed the coming of responsible government to British North America. It took a full decade after the rebellions of 1837–8, but London finally accepted the colonies' right to the British tradition of representative government. Power now lay in the hands of the elected Legislative Assembly rather than the governor and his clique. The power of the traditional elites was weakened. They were, however, largely replaced by new commercial and industrial elites, including many elected members of the Assembly.

The union of Upper and Lower Canada was primarily designed to assimilate the French Canadians. In this sense, the Act failed. While nationalist historians can congratulate the French and English groups in the Assembly for finding common ground in order to keep the colony functioning, and herald the era as a shining example of the type of ethnic cooperation needed in such a diverse nation, the era was dominated by political squabbling to the point of paralysis. Effective government came to a standstill. Certainly, French and English politicians often had to compromise, but there was little choice. The need to construct a *modus vivendi* may have helped restrain ethnic and religious bigotry, but it remained, brimming beneath the surface. In the end, French Canada again escaped assimilation. But for French-Canadian nationalist historians, the union had a traumatic impact, akin to a second conquest. It ended the separateness of Lower Canada and fused its destiny with that of Upper Canada. This process of subordinating Quebec's position would only continue with Confederation in 1867.

French–English Relations

The Colonial Office in London originally intended to use union of the Canadas to punish the French and assure their subjugation, if not their eventual demise, as a distinct ethnic-religious group. Certainly, the conditions of union constituted a severe blow for Lower Canada in general and for French Canadians in particular. English became the sole official language of parliamentary documents. The capital was to be the loyalist centre of Kingston. The elective Assembly had an equal number of representatives from both halves of the colony, even though in 1841 Canada East had 670 000 inhabitants and Canada West had 480 000.[2] The problem was compounded by the expectation that, as Canada West continued to develop and expand, its population would grow, and at this point, it would gain more representation.

The Act of Union also created "one consolidated revenue fund," making Upper Canada's heavy debt the responsibility of the Province of Canada as a whole. Upper Canada could no longer finance costly transportation facilities, such as roads and canals, by itself. It had already borrowed heavily in London, but union with the virtually debt-free Lower Canada would strengthen its position. Union would bring in higher revenues because the united colony could raise tariffs, a measure that Lower Canada, where most goods from Europe entered, could no longer block. The Act also recognized that the two Canadas formed a common economic bloc. Montreal's English merchants had been striving for such a union since the early 1820s.

Lord Sydenham

Charles Poulett Thomson, Lord Durham's successor as governor general of Canada, had spent eight years on the Board of Trade in London. He wanted to put Canada on a sound financial footing to attract development capital. Investment would assure progress and lessen the appeal of the United States, thus warding off the constant threat of annexation. He also hoped that substantial British immigration would further diminish the political and economic influence of the French Canadians.

When Thomson arrived in Canada in the autumn of 1839, he sought to convince the elites of Upper Canada to support political union. The English elites in Lower Canada needed no such convincing and the French elites were given no say in the matter. British Prime Minister Lord Melbourne wrote Colonial Secretary Lord John Russell to explain the policy: "We feel that we cannot impose this union upon Upper Canada without her consent, and therefore we give her a choice. We give Lower Canada no choice, but we impose it upon her during the suspension of her constitution." Upper Canada was on board for the most part. Union, it seemed, solved the colony's economic problem, offered future prosperity, and resulted in the subordination of the French. Thompson won over most of Canada West to his party, with the exception of a few Family Compact Tories such as Sir Allan MacNab (who judged the governor too sympathetic to the doctrine of responsible government), and some "Ultra Reformers" (who perceived him as too equivocal in his support of the same doctrine).

The union was officially inaugurated at the Château de Ramezay in Montreal on February 10, 1841. Thomson, now Baron Sydenham, announced: "Inhabitants of the Province of Canada: henceforth may you be united in sentiment as you are from this day in name!" Most French Canadians, however, were defiant and bitter. Pierre-Joseph-Olivier Chauveau, a future Quebec premier, condemned the British bankers whom he saw as the force behind union and prophesied: "Today a weeping people is beaten, tomorrow a people will be up in arms, today the forfeit, tomorrow the vengeance."

The French Canadians were aware that assimilation had simply taken on a new guise. In truth, however, it did not even make an attempt to be subversive. Augustin-Norbert Morin, a patriote of 1837 and Reform leader Louis-Hippolyte LaFontaine's lieutenant in Quebec City, commented frankly in a letter to Toronto politician Francis Hincks: "I am against the Union and against the main features, as I think every honest Lower Canadian should be." John Neilson, an urbane bilingual Scot who owned the *Quebec Gazette*, formed a committee in the fall of 1840 to work for the election of representatives opposed to union in order to express, by nonviolent means, "our reprobation of this injustice which is done to this Province."

Le poulet (the chicken), as the French disdainfully called Sydenham (his name was Charles *Poulett* Thompson) knew the French were hostile and would not support his candidates. Apart from areas with substantial English populations, he admitted, "We shall not have a man returned who does not hate British connection, British rule, British improvements, and everything which has a taint of British feeling." So the governor worked to elect as many English members as possible, so as to give the British-Protestants a majority in the Assembly. He gerrymandered riding boundaries to eliminate French votes from certain districts and staged polls in English localities situated far from French towns. He chose partisans as returning officers for the polls, and he used British troops as well as Irish construction labourers to intimidate French voters in the open voting (the secret ballot was established only in 1874). In LaFontaine's own district, the British candidate hired thugs who took possession of the polling station. Bitterly denouncing Sydenham's "law of the bludgeon," LaFontaine withdrew from the contest to avoid bloodshed and certain defeat that would risk compromising his own leadership. Not surprisingly, the governor won a comfortable working majority in the Province of Canada's first legislature.

Political Divisions

The French–English divide in Canada, however, was not so clear-cut; the political division between Reformer and Tory further complicated matters. It also allowed for collaboration across sectional and ethnic lines. Sydenham's heavy-handed tactics, for example, improved the chances for cooperation between Reformers in Canada East and Canada West. Since 1839 Francis Hincks, a pragmatic and ambitious Irish Protestant immigrant, assiduously cultivated good relations with Louis LaFontaine. Hincks assured the former patriote that, in return for cooperation in working toward responsible government, his followers would assist French-Canadian efforts to rid the union of objectionable features, such as official English unilingualism: "You want our help as much as we do yours," Hincks argued. At first suspicious, LaFontaine finally concluded that French Canada could obtain more by accepting union than by continuing to oppose it. In reality, there was little other choice.

The Baldwin–LaFontaine Alliance

Robert Baldwin, the prominent Toronto Reform leader, endorsed Hincks's overtures to LaFontaine. When LaFontaine could not get elected in Canada East, Baldwin arranged for him to run for the Assembly in a safe Reform riding north of York. Baldwin faced virulent opposition for the move from Tory opponents, such as William Henry Boulton, who became mayor of Toronto in 1845. As mayor, Boulton condemned the French as "tobacco-smoking, dram-drinking, garlick-eating . . . foreign in blood, foreign in race and as ignorant as the ground they stand upon." Despite the opposition, LaFontaine won.

Once elected, LaFontaine represented the farmers of Stouffville and Sharon in the Fourth Riding of York for one term. Later, the favour was reciprocated when Baldwin lost his seat in Canada West and LaFontaine found him a safe seat in Canada East. For one term Baldwin represented the voters of Rimouski, a French area on the south shore of the St. Lawrence River, 300 kilometres east of Quebec City. An influential French–English

The statue of Robert Baldwin and Louis-Hippolyte LaFontaine on Parliament Hill in Ottawa. Baldwin is on the left and LaFontaine on the right.

Source: Rolf Hicker Photography/Alamy.

coalition of Reformers was being formed. If successful, such a coalition would work against the main goal of union: assimilation.

The prejudices of ethnicity and religion, however, were not so easily cast aside. The pragmatics of politics brought Reformers together and the cause of responsible government was a powerful motivator, but old hatreds died hard. The myriad issues coming before the Assembly eventually touched on sensitive issues that sent members scurrying back to their traditional loyalties. The issue of the "prerogative" of the Roman Catholic Church in temporal matters was usually sure to raise the ire of the Protestant members. It spilled over into land, taxation, tariff, and education policy.

The Reform Coalition

In the early 1840s, Canada West's political spectrum was the most diverse, ranging from "Compact" Tories to "Ultra" Reformers. The Tories were conservatives, and vaunted their loyalty to the Crown and the Anglican Church. They supported privilege and the established elites. In their view, responsible government, while a British tradition, was premature to impose upon the colonies. It could lead to radicalism and anarchy (meaning republican democracy), as the disastrous American Revolution demonstrated. The Tories also represented the commercial interests and they worked to have the colonial government encourage and foster the development of trade and commerce. Toryism as a political ideology crossed class lines, however. Many of the working-class Irish Protestant immigrants supported the Tories. In return for Tory largesse, the Orange Order, notably in Toronto, provided the "votes and strong arms needed in the rough and tumble polling process of the day."[3]

The Reform cause was tainted by the failed Rebellions of 1837–8 and was vehemently denounced by both the Catholic and Anglican Churches as being liberal and therefore anti-clerical. The political cause was strong, however, and it was constantly bolstered by immigration from both Britain and the United States. Reformist ambitions were also given a powerful boost by Lord Durham's endorsement of responsible government in 1839. In order to prove their loyalty, the Reformists had to temper their radicalism and penchant for rebellion by demonstrating a willingness to work within the framework of the British constitution and traditions. Reformers reminded their opponents that they were attempting to do just that: party government and responsible government both existed in Britain.

The push for responsible government demanded a common front for the Reformers from the two Canadas, but such an accomplishment required time. If the Reformers consistently opposed the government of Lord Sydenham until responsible government was implemented, they jeopardized constructive policies, such as the public-works projects promised for their districts and desired by the voters.

The change needed to allow a Reformist breakthrough occurred suddenly and unexpectedly. The political landscape was transformed with Sydenham's death from lockjaw in September 1841, caused by an injury as a result of a fall from his horse. Sir Charles Bagot was appointed governor. Bagot had served as a British minister in the aftermath of the War of 1812,

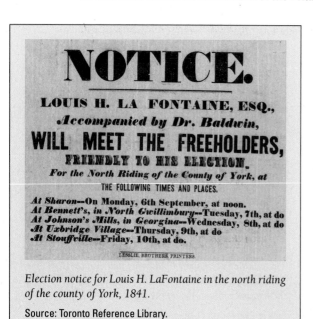

Election notice for Louis H. LaFontaine in the north riding of the county of York, 1841.

Source: Toronto Reference Library.

and had successfully negotiated the Rush–Bagot Agreement to limit naval forces on the Great Lakes and helped establish the border between the two countries. The new governor was ordered by the British government to resist the pressure for responsible government and to prevent the Reformers from forming a government under LaFontaine and Baldwin, despite their majority in the Assembly. But Bagot was not as anti-French as Durham and Sydenham, nor was he as focused on advancing the assimilationist objectives of the union. Bagot reported to Colonial Secretary Lord Stanley that it was all very well to wait for immigration to "hem in and overwhelm French Population and French Power"; in the meantime, he had to solve pressing political problems by giving positions to French members and making other "concessions." Bagot's term as governor was short-lived, however. He resigned in 1843 and died before reaching England.

The Great Blondin. *W.H.B. Bartlett, c. 1840.*

Source: With permission of the Royal Ontario Museum © ROM, 954.192.4.

Sir Charles Metcalfe, Bagot's successor, had a diplomatic career in India and Jamaica before being appointed governor of Canada. When appointed, he was also instructed to resist responsible government. Metcalfe agreed with Bagot that, while desirable, the anti-French assimilationist policies of the union were impractical. He recommended to the British government that the French language be provided official status. Lord Stanley disagreed, since the Act of Union was designed "to promote the amalgamation of the French and English races." Only in 1848, three years after Metcalfe's request, did the British Parliament amend the Act of Union to end the proscription of the French language.

The Achievement of Responsible Government

Responsible government was finally achieved by the end of the 1840s, a full decade after the rebellions. At the beginning of the decade, it seemed this achievement was impossible. The rebellions had been crushed and the leaders executed or exiled. The British government responded with the draconian Act of Union, intent on eliminating the French fact in Canada forever. The Act concentrated enormous power in the hands of the colonial governor, appointed by London. The governor, in turn, continued to create oligarchy by appointing for life the members of the Legislative Council. He continued the tradition of patronage by rewarding his clique through appointments. He chose his advisers, dismissing and replacing them at will. He also held broad veto powers over bills adopted by the legislature. Yet, over the course of the union's first decade, the forces of change were building momentum.

Responsible government would not come without a struggle. The Colonial Office consistently urged Canada's governors to avoid concessions lest things get out of hand and the colony agitate for independence. Gradually, however, even the resistant governors opened the door to increased representation. Governor Bagot appointed an Executive Council that had the support of a majority in the Assembly. He invited LaFontaine to join his council. When the latter demanded that Baldwin also have a place, Bagot again yielded. London was dismayed. The Duke of Wellington, Bagot's own uncle, called him "a fool." The governor responded that "Canada would have again become the theatre of a widespread rebellion, and perhaps the ungrateful separatist or the rejected outcast from British dominion."

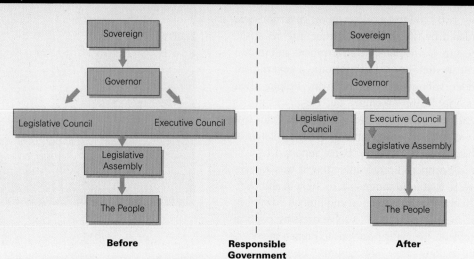

Governing in the Province of Canada Before and After Responsible Government

Before

Sovereign → Governor → Legislative Council / Executive Council → Legislative Assembly → The People

Responsible Government

After

Sovereign → Governor → Legislative Council / Executive Council → Legislative Assembly → The People

Before responsible government was introduced, the Legislative Assembly had no effective control over the Executive Council, on whose advice the governor relied. With the coming of responsible government, the Executive Council could remain in office only as long as it had the Legislative Assembly's support.

Source: Adapted from P.G. Cornell, M. Hamelin, F. Ouellet, and M. Trudel, *Canada: Unity in Diversity* (Toronto: Holt, Rinehart and Winston, 1967), p. 143.

WHERE HISTORIANS DISAGREE

The Union of the Canadas

On February 10, 1841 Upper and Lower Canada were united. The new province became Britain's largest North American colonial possession. The life of this union, however, was brief. Only 26 years would pass before Confederation joined Canada with the colonies of New Brunswick and Nova Scotia.

Historians have traditionally viewed union as a failed juncture that served as a mere preview to the inevitability of the national dream of Confederation. In the 1960s, W.L. Morton argued that union led to political deadlock in Canada between the English and French, and Confederation was the necessary remedy.[1] According to J.M.S. Careless, the union was imposed upon Lower Canada as part of Durham's assimilationist agenda. Not surprisingly, it met with strong disapproval: "French Canadians were bound to regard it not only as having been designed to undermine their national identity, but as magnifying that wrong by decisively under-representing their own section of the country." But the key for

Careless was how the colony responded. Canadians in both sections of the colony came together in an attempt to compromise and make the union work. The result was an innovative political system that included the practice of "dual ministerial leadership," the bicultural political party, and "self-government in partnership."[2]

French-Canadian historians failed to detect this "spirit of compromise." According to historian Maurice Séguin, union ensured that French Canadians remained in the political minority in perpetuity, as both Lord Durham and the British government intended. In addition, French Canadians remained under the domination of the English mercantile elite in Montréal, which further limited their economic prospects.[3] Mason Wade disagreed and claimed that despite intentions, the union did not fulfill its assimilationist goals. French-Canadian politicians pursued a reform agenda that linked their fate to likeminded reformers in Canada West.[4]

In the 1990s, Ged Martin took exception to both the "whiggish" and nationalist interpretations. Martin offered a more transnational perspective that placed the BNA colonies into a larger imperial context. He concluded that while political deadlock was persistent, Confederation was not the inevitable result. If the colony of Canada had reformed its electoral system to meet the demands of representation by population, the union was workable.[5]

More recently, Éric Bédard has accepted the view that union provided French Canadians with an important political opportunity. Despite Louis Hippolyte-LaFontaine's displeasure at both Lord Durham's Report and the Act of Union, he formed a fruitful partnership with Robert Baldwin and other Upper Canadian reformers, which led to the

achievement of responsible government in 1848. The philosophical and political basis of this bicultural partnership can be found in LaFontaine's famous "Speech to the Electors of Terrebonne" in 1840, in which he remarked upon the Canadian social experience that transcended linguistic, ethnic and religious divisions and that anyone, regardless of their origin, could become Canadian and share in its prosperity. Unlike Michel Brunet, who saw the speech as LaFontaine's abandonment of an exclusive French past for new forms of citizenship and loyalty, Bédard believes that LaFontaine was making the case for Canadian political autonomy and ending the domination of the colonial elite. LaFontaine was not abandoning his French origins, but instead arguing for a pluralist society where the French fact would be recognized.[6]

John Ralston Saul, in a recent biography of Robert Baldwin and Louis Hippolyte-LaFontaine, agrees and argues that the union was necessary for achieving responsible government because it provided an opportunity for Francophone and Anglophone reformers to join forces to create a bicultural reform movement. This was possible due to the remarkable friendship and political partnership of Baldwin and LaFontaine. These men led a party that not only achieved responsible government but also "created a new framework for power—a framework shaped by shared ideas rather than the European/English, even U.S., concept of a *natural* unity." Saul, like Bédard, cites the significance of LaFontaine's speech at Terrebonne, calling it "the key founding statement of what we understand Canada to be."[7]

According to the political scientist David E. Smith, union also set in place one of the defining political differences between Canada and the United States.

The introduction of responsible government, he argues, constituted the triumph of self-government by colonial statute: Canada would remain governed by the Crown and would not become a republic. Canadian politicians, including reformers like Robert Baldwin, believed that only parliament was capable of exercising political authority. Canada would continue the British tradition of parliamentary supremacy by limiting municipal jurisdiction, a practice that had been imposed upon the British North American colonies in response to the rise of republican radicalism in the town halls of New England before the American Revolution.[8]

1. W.L. Morton, *The Kingdom of Canada,* 2nd ed. (Toronto: McClelland & Stewart, 1969), p. 315.

2. J.M.S. Careless, *The Union of the Canadas: The Growth of Canadian Institutions, 1841–1857* (Toronto: McClelland & Stewart, 1967), pp. 5, xii.

3. Maurice Séguin, *L'Idée d'indépéndence au Québec: Genèse et historique* (Trois-Rivières: Boréal Express, 1968), p. 36.

4. Mason Wade, *The French Canadians, 1760–1967,* rev. ed., vol. 1 (1760–1911) (Toronto: Macmillan, 1968), p. 220.

5. Ged Martin, *Britain and the Origins of Canadian Confederation, 1837–67* (Vancouver: UBC Press, 1995), p. 5.

6. Éric Bédard, *Les Reformistes: Une generation canadienne-francaise au milieu du XIXe siecle* (Montreal: Boreal, 2009), pp. 72–73; Michel Brunet, *Canadians et Canadiens* (Montreal: Fides, 1954), pp. 21–23.

7. John Ralson Saul, *Louis-Hippolyte LaFontaine & Robert Baldwin* (Toronto: Penguin Canada, 2010), pp. 102, 108. This is a theme Saul also discusses in his book *Reflections of a Siamese Twin* (Toronto: Viking, 1997).

8. David E. Smith, *The Republican Option in Canada, Past and Present* (Toronto: University of Toronto Press, 1999), pp. 90–91.

Governor Metcalfe did not intend to submit to LaFontaine, and he would certainly not commit himself to taking his advice. Metcalfe assured Lord Stanley that he would strive to get a majority in Parliament, that if he failed he would dissolve the Assembly and try again, "and that if I fail then, still I cannot submit, for that would be to surrender the Queen's government into the hands of rebels, and to become myself their ignominious tool." In the rancorous election of 1844, Metcalfe obtained a slim majority by decisively defeating the Reformers from Canada West while losing badly in Canada East.

The regime that governed the colony from 1844 until 1847, led by the eloquent Conservative "Sweet William" Henry Draper as attorney general for Canada West, succeeded in adopting several important pieces of legislation, including school acts for both Canadas, legal reform, a revamped land-grant system that would lessen speculation, and a permanent civil list of salaried officials. Responsible government did not yet exist, however. Although the Executive Council now at least had the confidence of the Assembly, the governor's powers remained excessively broad.

Lord Elgin and Responsible Government

The pace of events quickened with the arrival of Lord Elgin, the new governor general, in 1847. It coincided, however, with a more significant shift in imperial policy from "formal" to "informal" empire. With the British move toward laissez-faire liberalism and the adoption of free trade, it became less imperative for London to wield such overt control of the colonies, particularly in regard to trade relations. The British empire would be governed by the principles of "trade, philanthropy, and good government." British politicians argued that as the greatest empire the world had witnessed, it was not necessary to use force or coercion to administer the colonies. Instead, it was seen as beneficial to allow them increased autonomy. Unlike previous governors, Elgin was instructed not to stand in the way of responsible government.

The elections of 1848 produced a strong majority for LaFontaine's group in Canada East and a significant majority for Baldwin's Reform movement in Canada West. Lord Elgin called on LaFontaine and Baldwin to form a government. Henceforth, the governor assented to legislation adopted by Parliament, unless he judged it as directly contrary to the interests of Great Britain. Responsible government came in 1849 when Elgin agreed to sign, despite personal reservations, the Rebellion Losses Bill, which compensated those who had lost property during the Rebellions of 1837–38 in Canada East (the question of losses in Canada West had been settled in 1845). The bill was bitterly opposed by the Tories because it also compensated "traitorous" rebels for their losses. When Elgin allowed it to pass on April 25, 1849, his carriage was pelted with stones, LaFontaine's house was sacked, and a riot broke out in Montreal that ended with the burning of the Parliament building. But despite the uproar, responsible government had arrived in Canada.

Responsible government moved Canada forward along the road to democracy and political autonomy. For that reason, most historians have viewed its coming as a great milestone in Canada's national history. The voters, through their elected representatives, would now exercise greater control over government—or rather the male property-holders would. Ironically, in 1849 the Reformers amended the election law to exclude women from the franchise. In spite of the common-law prohibition against female suffrage, a few women had voted. They had even helped a Tory win in 1844—an incident that the Reformers had not forgotten. It would not be the last time in Canadian history that a move toward democracy would come at the cost of disenfranchising others.

The achievement of responsible government was a progressive step on the road to democracy, but it did not lead to a reform of the political process. Patronage, in particular, was a widespread and accepted part of politics. There were limits to how far it could be pushed, but patronage was built into the system. Leaders of the governing party would now have access to patronage. Political scientist S.J.R. Noel asserts that the British resisted responsible government in part precisely because they "appreciated the central importance of patronage in the political process."[4] Responsible government also shifted power and influence toward the new commercial and industrial classes. Business and politics became intertwined. Most politicians were businessmen rather than landed gentry. They advanced their personal interests through their political positions. As a result, responsible government broke the oligarchies but did not shift power to the common people.

First Nations in the Canadas

The First Nations were increasingly marginalized and forgotten by both the British and colonial governments. As the percentage of Aboriginal peoples in the Canadas fell to less than 1 percent of the total population, they became increasingly invisible to the dominant society. Indeed, the Act of Union (1841) omitted to make provision for "Indians" or even to provide for the payment of annuities for earlier land surrenders. Officials only corrected this "oversight" in 1844.

With the coming of responsible government and Canadian autonomy in domestic affairs, colonial officials were forced to pay more attention to the First Nations. The British government transferred authority for "Indian affairs" to the Canadian legislature in 1860. The view of the "Indians" was changing. The idea of the "noble savage" was replaced by "the white man's burden." According to social Darwinism, a racial hierarchy existed and Indigenous peoples were near the bottom. But in such an advanced and enlightened empire, the whites were expected to alleviate the suffering of the "lesser" races. This was to be accomplished through assimilation: the poor, wretched "Indians" were to be aided in their transition from "savagery" to "civilization." Government reports indicated that the First Nations were a dying race. It was estimated that by the 1930s, there would be no more "Indians" in Canada. Politicians committed themselves to a system of First Nations education based on model farms and industrial or residential schools, in order to bring about the eventual assimilation of the Indigenous population. Christian missionaries would administer the schools. It was assumed that the First Nations should be, for their own well-being, absorbed into the settler society.

A HISTORICAL PORTRAIT

Nahnebahwequay

Nahnebahwequay is one of the few nineteenth-century Aboriginal women whose life can be described in some detail, using her own writings and those of others. She was one of the first Great Lakes women to acquire an English education and an understanding of the dominant society. Due to her attendance at a Methodist Indian mission school, a visit to England as a young girl, and her marriage to an English immigrant, she learned enough of the ways of the newcomers to be at ease in their society. Yet, she remained committed to her principles on matters of Aboriginal land claims and injustices to her people.

The year that Nahnebahwequay, or "Nahnee," as she later called herself, was born, her parents, Bunch and Polly Sunegoo, became Christians. They were among the first Mississaugas to help build the Methodist mission at the Credit River, 20 kilometres west of Toronto. The leading spirit of the mission was her uncle, Peter Jones, who became an ordained Methodist minister and a chief of the Mississaugas of the Credit.

Nahnee helped her parents with the chores in their log cabin home and on their farm. As a young child in the 1820s and early 1830s, she lost all her siblings through disease. On one occasion, she herself narrowly escaped death. Nahnee, in turn, also became a Christian. She

Nahnebahwequay ("Upright Woman").
Source: Grey Roots Museum & Archives.

was educated by her aunt, Eliza Field, the English wife of Peter Jones. At the Jones's home, Eliza taught Nahnee and other Mississauga girls sewing and other household skills. When Eliza returned to England for a visit in 1837, Nahnee accompanied her and her uncle.

Shortly after her return to the Credit at the age of 15, Nahnee married an English immigrant, William Sutton, who was 28. They seemed to have had a successful marriage. Both shared a profound religious faith. They left the Credit in the late 1840s for the Owen Sound area to the north, where William worked with the local Ojibwas as a farm instructor and local preacher. He cleared his own farm on a tract of land given them by the Ojibwas. In these years, Nahnee raised her growing family and helped run the farm.

When William agreed to be a farm instructor at Ojibwa Methodist missions around Sault Ste. Marie, the Sutton family moved north. Upon returning, they discovered that their land near Owen Sound was for sale. During their absence, the local Ojibwas had signed a treaty with the British, who did not recognize the validity of the Aboriginal grant of land to the Suttons. The Indian Department, at the same time, announced that it no longer considered Mrs. Sutton an Indian, "on the ground of her having married a white man."

In 1860, Nahnee, obtaining no redress, took her land claim and the grievances of the Ojibwas to Queen Victoria herself. Sympathetic Quakers in New York City provided her with passage to Britain.

In London, the Quakers assisted her in gaining an audience with the Queen on June 19, 1860. The Queen noted in her journal that her visitor spoke English quite well and had come to present a land petition on behalf of her people. Curiously, however, the Queen made no mention of Nahnee's pregnancy, which must, in her ninth month, have been quite obvious. Nahnee gave birth to a son, Albert, on July 11, 1860, at the home of Quaker friends in London.

Subsequently, the Suttons were allowed to buy back their farm near Owen Sound. This outcome did not appease Nahnee, who continued to fight for Aboriginal rights. She argued that the Europeans acted "as though their ideas of justice are that 'might is right.'" She criticized as "wholesale robbery" the government's attempt, in 1861, to purchase Manitoulin Island on the north shore of Lake Huron for non-Aboriginal settlers. A quarter of a century earlier, the Upper Canadian colonial administration had promised the large island, forever, to the Anishinabeg. For the last years of her short but eventful life, Nahnee suffered from poor health. She died at age 41 in 1865.

In another ironic twist, after gaining responsible government for themselves, Canadian politicians imposed even tighter control over the First Nations population. The government had established and surveyed reserves, but under the legislation adopted in the 1850s and 1860s, Aboriginal people were given little opportunity to administer their remaining lands. Subtle distinction also appeared in the manner in which the First Nations were referenced in treaties. In an 1819 treaty, the term "nation" was used; later, in the Robinson treaties (concerning the north shores of Lakes Huron and Superior) in 1850, the term "tribe" was used.

One group, the First Nations at Kanesatake (Oka), did not receive a reserve. During the Rebellions of 1837–38, the Sulpicians, who were the seigneurs at the Lac des Deux Montagnes, stood loyally by the British. The religious order encouraged Roman Catholics to enlist in British militia units and contributed money to support those units. Immediately after the uprisings, in 1840, the governor's Special Council issued an ordinance that gave title to the land to the Sulpicians.

The Annexation Movement

The achievement of responsible government led to a flurry of political activity in the years from 1848 to 1854. While Canada West did not explode with anger when the Rebellion Losses was passed in 1849, the area did experience considerable unrest. The Tories staged protest meetings to denounce the rewarding of "rebels" and "pardoned traitors," and thousands signed petitions demanding Elgin's recall. Robert Baldwin and William Lyon Mackenzie were burned in effigy, and Lord Elgin met a fiery condemnation from a Toronto mob. Another riot broke out in Bytown (Ottawa) in September that had to be dispersed by the military. The *Brockville Statesman* did not mince words: "Without peace there can be no prosperity, and that peace cannot be procured so long as his hated foot presses the free soil, or his lying lungs breathe the pure air of Canada."

If the Tories believed Britain was turning its back on them by allowing responsible government, they received another blow when Britain adopted free trade. The move signified an end to the imperial preferences that gave exporters in the British North American markets an advantage over traders in other nations to which higher tariffs had previously applied. Britain's new trade policies helped push large sectors of Canadian commerce into depression. It also redirected Canadian trade south to the United States. Shipping activity at Montreal declined by more than 40 percent between 1847 and 1849. Out of desperation, some Tories, who had hitherto proclaimed their loyalty to the Crown and condemned traitors and rebels, campaigned for annexation to the United States.

Montreal, as the centre of commercial activity and the home of the English merchants, became the hotbed of annexationist sentiment. In October 1849, the English press published the manifesto of the Annexation Association, signed by 325 citizens, many of them notable businesspeople, such as William Molson and John Redpath. Early in 1850 the formation of the Toronto Annexation Association, embracing "a large number of the most respectable merchants and inhabitants of this city, of all parties and creeds," was announced.

Three Indian Chiefs and Peter McLeod Presenting a Petition to Lord Elgin *by Théophile Hamel.*

Source: Private Collection/Photo courtesy of the owner.

French Canada and Annexation

Even French Canada displayed some interest in annexation, though for entirely different reasons. Louis-Joseph Papineau, who had returned to Canada from the United States after having been granted amnesty in 1844, was well known for his admiration of American democratic institutions and his hatred of the Act of Union. Radical young intellectuals belonging to the *Institut canadien*, a literary and debating society in Montreal, or who wrote for the newspaper *L'Avenir*, took up the annexationist cause. They declared that they preferred "Brother Jonathan" (a personification of the United States), with his egalitarian principles, to John Bull (signifying England), with his haughty and aristocratic airs. Louis-Antoine Dessaulles, Papineau's nephew, expressed his ardent desire that French Canada follow the path of Louisiana, with its large French population, in order to obtain the advantages both of a separate state and of American prosperity and democracy.

The annexationists, however, constituted but a small group. Their movement had no popular base, and other elites in French Canada vociferously condemned annexation. George-Étienne Cartier echoed conservative sentiment when he warned that American democracy signified that "the dominant power was the will of the crowd, of the masses." The Catholic clergy, for its part, feared that annexation would put an end to the liberty that it enjoyed under British rule.

In Canada West, annexationism, though noisy, made little headway and also remained a minority expression of frustration at British imperial policy. Newspapers frequently published citizens' statements lauding the benefits of the relationship with Britain. John Strachan, now Anglican bishop of Toronto, roundly denounced annexation as being opposed to "the plainest and most solemn declarations of the revealed will of God," because it signified union with republicans who sanctioned slavery. Opponents of annexation published their own manifestoes in the press.

In July 1849, a group of Tories, frustrated by the Reform government and by "French domination," gathered at Kingston to launch the British–American League. Future prime minister John A. Macdonald apparently played an active behind-the-scenes role in its organization, but the Toronto *Globe*, edited by George Brown, Macdonald's great political opponent, reported that Macdonald "said little in the convention and indeed he never says much anywhere except in barrooms." Patriotic delegates overwhelmingly rejected a resolution favourable to annexation. One delegate declared passionately, "It was never intended by Providence that the American, or Gallic, eagles should ever build their nests in the branches of the British oak, or soar over her prostrate lion." A later convention, held in Toronto in November, voiced support for a union of the British North American colonies, which many delegates viewed as a means of escaping from French domination. Macdonald judged this scheme "premature and impractical for the moment."

With the revival of prosperity in the early 1850s, annexationist sentiment receded rapidly. Although union with the United States had been much discussed, it had little popular support. The

The burning of the Canadian Parliament building in Montreal by Joseph Légaré.

Source: McCord Museum of Canadian History, Montreal, M11588.

Louis-Joseph Papineau, photograph by William Notman, 1865.

Source: Library and Archives Canada, Acc. No. 1986-36-1.

Americans' unresponsiveness to annexationist tendencies north of the border also hastened the movement's decline.

New Political Alliances

With responsible government achieved, the unity of the Reform movement began to splinter. By 1850, tensions arose between moderates and radicals on issues such as political reform, railway policy, financial affairs, and church–state relations. The more radical Reformers, with their stronghold in the area west of Toronto, denounced Montreal business interests, actively promoted agrarian democracy, and announced that they were seeking "only men who are Clear Grit" ("grit" being American slang for firmness of character).[5] Under journalist George Brown's leadership, the "Clear Grits" became vocal champions of "rep by pop," or representation according to population. The implication was that Canada West, with its now larger and rapidly increasing population, deserved a greater number of seats—and, therefore, a preponderant influence over government policy—than did francophone Canada East. The policy obviously alienated French-Canadian Reformers.

At the same time, with Louis-Joseph Papineau's political revival, the French-Canadian *Parti rouge* made a modest appearance in the Assembly in 1848. The *rouges* gained ground in the elections of 1851 and 1854, especially in the Montreal region. These radical reformers inherited the traditions of the *Parti patriote*. They tended to be more anti-clerical, republican, aggressively nationalistic, and critical of the close links between government and business, notably in matters pertaining to the railways.

The governing coalition faced mounting pressure from the *rouges* and the Clear Grits, particularly after the retirement of Baldwin and LaFontaine in 1851. With the Reform alliance breaking apart, a moderate conservative alliance emerged to replace it. After initial attempts to attract Clear Grit support, the government sought the endorsement of the Conservatives and of Hincks's moderate Reformers. In 1854, the so-called Liberal–Conservative alliance emerged, jointly led by Macdonald and Cartier.

A Canadian Capital

Choosing a seat of government and a capital proved difficult. Political, ethnic, and geographical rivalries transformed the issue into one of the most divisive confronting the union. It symbolized the deep divisions but also the potential for political deadlock over such controversial issues. In 1841, the British government chose the small loyalist town of Kingston as the first capital. Both Toronto and Montreal were difficult to defend in the event of American attack; moreover, Toronto was too far west. Quebec, with its majority French population, was not acceptable. According to Lord Sydenham, a capital somewhere in Canada West would be good for French members because it "would instil English ideas into their minds, [and] destroy the immediate influence upon their actions of the host of little lawyers, notaries and doctors." Kingston seemed a solid choice.

But many in the Assembly found Kingston too deeply permeated by Toryism and Orangeism. It proved to be an impractical location and the

Construction of the Parliament building on Barrack Hill, 1863.

Source: Library and Archives Canada/C-000773.

seat of government soon moved to Montreal. But in 1849, the burning of the Parliament building necessitated a move, and the seat of government migrated to Toronto. After a stormy debate, the legislators agreed that the capital would remain on the shores of Lake Ontario for two years, after which it would alternate every four years between Quebec City and Toronto. Canada now had a migrating capital. The established interests in both cities were reluctant to see the capital depart, but they preferred this "log-rolling compact" to losing the capital permanently. Between 1841 and 1859, the Legislative Assembly voted no fewer than 218 times on the location of the capital and seat of government.

On December 31, 1857, the Assembly appealed to Queen Victoria to choose a capital. After receiving memorials from various Canadian towns, the British government surprised Canadian politicians by selecting Bytown, which had recently been renamed Ottawa on being incorporated as a city in 1855. The Queen chose this rough and unruly logging town because it represented compromise. Ottawa was situated on the border between Canada East and Canada West. It was easier to defend from American attack than the other cities and the waterways gave it access to both sections of the colony. Ottawa was also well situated for railway development.

George-Étienne Cartier.

Source: Notman & Son/Library and Archives Canada/C-06166.

Despite the "compromise," groups in both sections of the colony were dismayed. The Toronto *Globe* was outraged by this choice of a city in which more than 60 percent of the population was Roman Catholic and half was French-Canadian. After more bickering, the Assembly finally deferred in 1859 to the Queen's decision and, six years later, Ottawa became the capital of the Canadas.

Politics and Business

While the divisions within the Assembly seemed to dominate politics, it was economic progress and, especially after 1845, railway development that most engaged the attention of the legislators. Railways required extensive government financial assistance through tax concessions, guarantees, bonds, the assumption of bad debts, and outright grants when private capital was insufficient (see Chapter 15). Despite the staggering financial burdens, the building of railways was seen as essential for the development of British North America.

Railway Promotion

The links between politics and business, personal and state interests, were nebulous at best. Sir Allan MacNab, co–prime minister in the MacNab–Morin and MacNab–Taché administrations (governments were named for the respective leaders from Canada West and East) from 1854 to 1856, affirmed candidly, after consuming "one or two bottles of good port," that "my politics

John A. Macdonald.

Source: Library and Archives Canada/C-010144.

are railroads." Reform leader Francis Hincks was an unabashed defender of railway schemes. While the links between business and politics were tight, there were limits, albeit broad. A parliamentary committee studied Hincks' conduct but found no evidence of corruption.

Alexander T. Galt, finance minister in the Cartier–Macdonald ministry in 1858, was also an influential business magnate. He was president of the St. Lawrence and Atlantic Railway that linked Montreal to Portland, Maine, by way of his home-town, Sherbrooke. The Grand Trunk Railway absorbed the line shortly after its completion in 1853. Galt also sat on the board of directors of the Grand Trunk and, in politics, sought to expand Montreal's influence westward.

George-Étienne Cartier actively concerned himself with Montreal business while serving as the director of a host of banking, insurance, transpor-tation, and mining companies. But railways were his main activity. Over many years, he held pos-itions as cabinet minister, chair of the Legislative Assembly's Railway Committee, and solicitor for the Grand Trunk Railway. Cartier guided the Grand Trunk's charter through the Assembly in 1854, claiming it was his proudest political moment.

Hugh Allan, a banker, shipping magnate, and railway promoter, made large contributions to Cartier's election campaigns. In return for the donations he received railway charters, favour-able legislation, and even the repeal of laws he disliked. Allan's lawyer, for example, later testified before the Railway Committee: "On every one of these subjects—steamships, railways, canals—the Government had a policy which was favourable to his [Allan's] views, and in my opinion three times the sum would have been well spent had it been necessary to keep a government in power which had . . . the improvement of the country so deeply at heart as this Government appears to." Cartier, who reportedly boasted that Irish voters could be bought for a "barrel of flour apiece and some salt fish thrown in for the leaders," was able to make good use of Hugh Allan's money.

Politicians waged fierce verbal battles in committee and on the floor of the Assembly over business-related decisions. Representatives from Quebec City, for example, such as Commis-sioner of Crown Lands Joseph Cauchon and Mayor Hector Langevin, protested vehemently that their pet project, the North Shore Railway to Quebec, was sabotaged by the Grand Trunk and its Montreal political allies Cartier and Galt, who had no intention of allowing trade to be diverted downstream.

"Rep by Pop"

The equal division of seats in the Legislative Assembly (42 for each section of colony) satisfied Canada West, as long as the population of Canada East was larger. As anticipated, however, the economy of Canada West developed more rapidly, as did its population. Once Canada West was more numerous, the call for representation based on population became louder.

Some representatives of both sections of Canada advocated the double majority vote. This notion implied that government ministers from each section of the colony needed the support of the majority of their section's members and, as a corollary, that controversial legislation could not be imposed upon one section of the colony by a majority composed largely of members from the other. Yet the government frequently had a difficult time building a simple majority, let alone finding majority support in both sections. In the 1840s, many measures were imposed on Canada East as a result of majorities in Canada West. After 1850, the shoe was often on the other foot, as large numbers of *bleus* (as the Conservatives were called in Lower Canada) helped adopt laws that were approved by only a minority of members from Canada West. One such law was the Scott Act of 1863, which gave added privileges to Canada West's Roman Catholic schools. The double majority principle proved unworkable.

In the early 1850s, Canada West's population surpassed that of Canada East. The Clear Grits now conveniently took up "rep by pop" as their campaign slogan. By 1857, it was the foremost plank in the Reform platform. And it was, after all,

George Brown.

Source: Hunter & Co./Library and Archives Canada/C-009553.

the intended result of the Union Act when passed by the British government in 1840. Not surprisingly, the French majority in Canada East bitterly opposed the policy. Union had instituted equality of representation in 1841, even though Canada East's population was then significantly greater than Canada West's. They would now resist the democratic logic, but obviously pragmatic timing, of "rep by pop" for what it was—assimilation.

Toward Confederation

By the end of the 1850s, it seemed that the union had run its course. Economic and demographic growth placed new strains on the political structure. At the Reform Party's convention in Toronto in November 1859, George Brown began to promote the idea, already advocated by the *rouges* of Canada East, of transforming the legislative union into a decentralized federative union of Canada West and Canada East. Many in Canada West were angry at having to pay for the expenditures voted by majorities built on eastern support. George Brown decried a situation in which, a century after the Conquest, the representatives of the British population still aspired to justice while having to wait while "the representatives of the French population [sit here] discussing in the French tongue whether we shall have it."

But the Conservatives formed the government at the time with support from the *bleus* in Canada East and they opposed such a scheme. Instead, they countered with suggestions for a wider British North American union. Alexander Galt entered the ministry only after extracting from the Conservatives a promise to work toward this "confederation," but initially the idea aroused only perfunctory interest. The Montreal *Gazette* believed that the proposal had possibilities and suggested forming a new English province that would join portions of eastern Canada

West with Montreal and the Eastern Townships. Then the French East could "stand still as long as it likes" and the West could "rush frantically forward," while the centre enjoyed "that gradual, sure, true progress which is the best indication of material prosperity." But most in Canada East opposed Brown's arguments on the basis that without Lower Canadian help to pay Upper Canadian debts, Upper Canada today would be "nothing more or less than a forest put up for auction by British capitalists to repay their investments."

Arguments for a new political structure became more pressing as politics in Canada ground to a standstill. Effective government proved increasingly difficult as governments were elected and then defeated with regularity. When the Macdonald–Cartier administration fell in 1858, for example, it was replaced by the Brown–Dorion Reform government. This government was defeated and fell within several hours. The governor general called upon Cartier and Macdonald to form another government. Newly appointed ministers, however, were obliged under parliamentary rules to resign their seats and face a by-election in their home constituencies. This rule did not apply to a minister who resigned one office and took another within a month. Cartier and Macdonald avoided their by-elections and the likely defeat of their government by taking new portfolios. The crafty move known as the "double shuffle" allowed the Macdonald-Cartier ministry to maintain power, but the "Short Administration" also made clear the desperate need for political change. Canada was sliding into political deadlock.

Political Deadlock

The deadlock that virtually paralyzed the union government provided the necessary push for change. In May 1862, the Macdonald–Cartier ministry resigned when, in the face of *bleu* defections over the issue of conscription, the legislature defeated its Militia Bill, much to the chagrin of the British government and "Little Englanders," who wished to shift more of the burden of Canadian defence away from British taxpayers. John A. Macdonald, the minister responsible for militia affairs, was inebriated and unavailable during most of the debate. A Liberal administration under John Sandfield Macdonald and Louis-Victor Sicotte (a moderate liberal, or *mauve*), took office. The following year it failed to survive a vote of confidence and fell. By 1863 both political parties were divided and the task of governing seemed hopeless. In 1864 Sandfield Macdonald gave up and the Conservative Étienne-Pascal Taché–John A. Macdonald regime tried to form a government. It too was defeated by June, after barely a few weeks in office. Canada in its present state was ungovernable.

At the same time, external pressures were pushing toward political change. They were also instilling a sense of urgency to break the political deadlock. Across the border in the United States, the Civil War raged and Britain's relations with the soon-to-be-victorious North were strained. Canadians, led by John A. Macdonald, feared that the Americans might decide to seek revenge on the British by again attacking Canada. Trade relations, which had been significantly stimulated by the Reciprocity Agreement of 1854, as well as by the North's needs during the Civil War, were now endangered. At the same time, British imperial policy was advancing the notion of informal empire. This included pressure for the colonies to take on increasing responsibility for their own affairs. Some form of larger BNA federation would possibly pose an escape from these external pressures.

SUMMARY

The Union period was formative for the development of Canadian politics. Despite the over-arching failures, the period resulted in the achievement of responsible government. It also resulted in the foundation of a party system. The design of assimilation failed again and despite the divisions, and the fact that ethnic and religious prejudice remained rampant, politicians realized the need for some form of compromise and even cooperation. By 1864, Canada was once again in the throes of constitutional change.

NOTES

1. S.J.R. Noel, *Patrons, Clients, Brokers: Ontario Society and Politics, 1791–1896* (Toronto: University of Toronto Press, 1990), p. 175.

2. Statistics vary. These are from J.M.S. Careless, *The Union of the Canadas: The Growth of Canadian Institutions, 1841–1857* (Toronto: McClelland & Stewart, 1967), p. 20.

3. Peter Way, "The Canadian Tory Rebellion of 1849 and the Demise of Street Politics in Toronto," *British Journal of Canadian Studies* 10 (1995): 10.

4. Noel, *Patrons, Clients, Brokers*, p. 151.

5. John Robert Colombo, "Grit," *The Canadian Encyclopedia*, 2nd ed., vol. 2 (Edmonton: Hurtig, 1988), p. 940. Grit is fine sand or gravel, often valued for its abrasive quality. The Clear Grits characterized themselves as "all sand and no dirt, clear grit all the way through."

BIBLIOGRAPHY

The union years are examined in J.M.S. Careless, *The Union of the Canadas: The Growth of Canadian Institutions, 1841–1857* (Toronto: McClelland & Stewart, 1967); and W.L. Morton, *The Critical Years: The Union of British North America, 1857–1873* (Toronto: University of Toronto Press, 1964). Also of use is Maurice Séguin's *L'idée d'indépendance au Québec: Genèse et historique* (Trois-Rivières: Boréal Express, 1968). Paul G. Cornell, *The Alignment of Political Groups in Canada, 1841–1867* (Toronto: University of Toronto Press, 1962), analyzes the rather complex development of party groupings. Carol Wilton's doctoral dissertation, "The Transformation of Upper Canadian Politics in the 1840s" (University of Toronto, 1985), represents a significant contribution to knowledge of the period. S.J.R. Noel studies the art of political brokerage in *Patrons, Clients, Brokers: Ontario Society and Politics, 1791–1896* (Toronto: University of Toronto Press, 1990). R.C. Brown, ed., *Upper Canadian Politics in the 1850s* (Toronto: University of Toronto Press, 1967), contains several informative articles, while J.M.S. Careless, ed., *The Pre-Confederation Premiers: Ontario Government Leaders, 1841–67* (Toronto: University of Toronto Press, 1980), constitutes a valuable addition to the political history of the period.

Much material on the development of the state in the Union period is available in Allan Greer and Ian Radforth, eds., *Colonial Leviathan: State Formation in Mid-Nineteenth-Century Canada* (Toronto: University of Toronto Press, 1992). In particular, this book contains an article on women and politics in the Canadas: Lykke de la Cour, Cecilia Morgan, and Mariana Valverde, "Gender Regulation and State Formation in Nineteenth-Century Canada," pp. 162–91. For biographies, albeit dated, of Canada West's two leading politicians, see Donald G. Creighton, *John A. Macdonald: The Young Politician* (Toronto: Macmillan, 1956); and J.M.S. Careless, *Brown of the Globe*, 2 vols. (Toronto: Macmillan, 1959 and 1963). Carol Wilton-Siegel has studied the role of Conservative politicians of the era in "Administrative Reform: A Conservative Alternative to Responsible Government," *Ontario History* 78 (1986): 105–25; see also Donald R. Beer, "Toryism in Transition: Upper Canadian Conservative Leaders, 1836–1854," *Ontario History* 80 (1988): 207–25. For a look at the relationship between population growth and politics, see Bruce Curtis, *The*

Politics of Population: State Formation, Statistics, and the Census of Canada, 1840–1875 (Toronto: University of Toronto Press, 2001). Janet Ajzenstat examines the political theory behind the genesis of confederation in *The Canadian Founding: John Locke and Parliament* (Montreal/Kingston: McGill-Queen's University Press, 2007).

Several other works also elaborate on the political developments of the period. On responsible government, see George Metcalf 's essay, "Draper Conservatism and Responsible Government in the Canadas, 1836–1847," *Canadian Historical Review* 42 (1961): 300–324. Another analysis may be found in Jeffery L. McNairn, *The Capacity to Judge: Public Opinion and Deliberative Democracy in Upper Canada, 1791–1854* (Toronto: University of Toronto Press, 2000). The annexation movement in Upper Canada is studied by Gerald H. Hallowell, "The Reaction of the Upper Canadian Tories to the Adversity of 1849: Annexation and the British American League," *Ontario History* 62 (1970): 41–56; and by S.F. Wise, "Canadians View the United States: The Annexation Movement and Its Effects on Canadian Opinion, 1837–1867," in A.B. McKillop and Paul Romney, eds., *God's Peculiar Peoples: Essays on Political Culture in Nineteenth-Century Canada* (Ottawa: Carleton University Press, 1993), pp. 115–48. For an examination of the American sympathies of some Canadian conservatives and for reflections on political culture, see Jeffrey L. McNairn, "Publius of the North: Tory Republicanism and the American Constitution in Upper Canada, 1848–54," *Canadian Historical Review* 77 (1996): 504–37. Jean-Paul Bernard describes annexationist sentiment in French Canada in *Les rouges: Libéralisme, nationalisme et anticléricalisme au milieu du XIXe siècle* (Montreal: Les presses de l'université du Québec, 1971), pp. 61–73.

Popular political culture in Upper Canada at the time of Durham is studied in Carol Wilton, "'A Firebrand Amongst the People': The Durham Meetings and Popular Politics in Upper Canada," *Canadian Historical Review* 75 (1994): 346–75. More general studies of this aspect of politics are David Mills, *The Idea of Loyalty in Upper Canada, 1784–1850* (Montreal/Kingston: McGill-Queen's University Press, 1988); and Jane Errington, *The Lion, The Eagle, and Upper Canada: A Developing Colonial Ideology* (Montreal/Kingston: McGill-Queen's University Press, 1987). The conflict over the choice of a capital is recounted in all its intricacies in David B. Knight, *Choosing Canada's Capital: Conflict Resolution in a Parliamentary System*, 2nd ed. (Ottawa: Carleton University Press, 1991). Carolyn Young reviews the history of Canada's Parliament buildings, with particular emphasis on the design competition of 1859, in *The Glory of Ottawa: Canada's First Parliament Buildings* (Montreal/Kingston: McGill-Queen's University Press, 1995). On corruption, see George A. Davison, "The Hincks–Brown Rivalry and the Politics of Scandal," *Ontario History* 81 (1989): 129–52. Michael J. Piva looks at finances in *The Borrowing Process: Public Finance in the Province of Canada, 1840–1867* (Ottawa: University of Ottawa Press, 1992). Peter Way, "The Canadian Tory Rebellion of 1849 and the Demise of Street Politics in Toronto," *British Journal of Canadian Studies* 10 (1995): 10–30, studies violence in politics in Upper Canada in the late 1840s.

British policy toward Canada is discussed in William Ormsby, *The Emergence of the Federal Concept in Canada, 1839–1845* (Toronto: University of Toronto Press, 1969); Peter Burroughs, *British Attitudes Towards Canada 1822–1845* (Scarborough, ON: Prentice-Hall, 1971); and Phillip Buckner, *The Transition to Responsible Government: British Policy in British North America, 1815–1850* (Westport, CT: Greenwood Press, 1985). See also Ged Martin, "Britain and the Future of British North America, 1841–1850," *British Journal of Canadian Studies* 2 (June 1987): 74–96; and the same author's provocative *Britain and the Origins of Canadian Confederation, 1837–67* (Vancouver: University of British Columbia Press, 1995). On French Canada in particular, see Jacques Monet's *The Last Cannon Shot: A Study of French Canadian Nationalism, 1837–1850* (Toronto: University of Toronto Press, 1969).

Biographies of the public figures of this age—including LaFontaine, Baldwin, Hincks, Cartier, and Morin—appear in various volumes of *Dictionary of Canadian Biography*, now available online. An inside look at the third generation of the Family Compact is provided by John Lownsbrough in *The Privileged Few: The Grange and Its People in Nineteenth Century Toronto* (Toronto: Art Gallery of Ontario, 1980).

For Aboriginal policy during the Union period, see John S. Milloy, "The Early Indian Acts: Developmental Strategy and Constitutional Change," in Ian A.L. Getty and Antoine S. Lussier, eds., *As Long as the Sun Shines and Water Flows: A Reader in Canadian Native Studies* (Vancouver: University of British Columbia Press, 1983), pp. 56–64; J.E. Hodgett's chapter, "Indian Affairs: The White Man's

Albatross," in his *Pioneer Public Service: An Administrative History of the United Canadas, 1841–1867* (Toronto: University of Toronto Press, 1955), pp. 205–25; and John F. Leslie, "Buried Hatchet: The Origins of Indian Reserves in 19th Century Ontario," *Horizon Canada* 40 (1985): 944–49. Tony Hall also reviews developments in Canada West in "Native Limited Identities and Newcomer Metropolitanism in Upper Canada, 1814–1867," in David Keane and Colin Read, eds., *Old Ontario: Essays in Honour of J.M.S. Careless* (Toronto: Dundurn Press, 1990), pp. 148–73. Legal issues are examined in Sidney L. Harring's *White Man's Law: Native People in Nineteenth-Century Canadian Jurisprudence* (Toronto: University of Toronto Press, 1998). For overviews of the Aboriginal peoples in the two Canadas at this time, see also Daniel Francis, *A History of the Native Peoples of Quebec, 1760–1867* (Ottawa: Department of Indian Affairs and Northern Development, 1983); and Edward S. Rogers and Donald B. Smith, eds., *Aboriginal Ontario: Historical Perspectives on the First Nations* (Toronto: Dundurn Press, 1994).

Biographical treatments include Donald B. Smith, *Sacred Feathers: The Reverend Peter Jones (Kahkewaquonaby) and the Mississauga Indians* (Toronto: University of Toronto Press, 1987); and Janet E. Chute, *The Legacy of Shingwaukonse: A Century of Native Leadership* (Toronto: University of Toronto Press, 1998). On Nahnee, the subject of this chapter's "Historical Portrait," see John Steckley, "Nahnebahwequay ('Standing Woman') or Catherine Sutton," in his *Beyond Their Years: Five Native Women's Stories* (Toronto: Canadian Scholars' Press, 1999), pp. 140–93; and Celia Haig-Brown, "Seeking Honest Justice in a Land of Strangers: Nahnebahwequay's Struggle for Land," *Journal of Canadian Studies* 36(4) (2001–2002): 143–70.

Useful bibliographical guides to the historical literature on the Canadas include the essays by James H. Lambert, "Quebec/Lower Canada"; Bryan D. Palmer, "Upper Canada"; and J.M. Bumsted, "British North America in Its Imperial and International Context," in M. Brook Taylor, ed., *Canadian History: A Reader's Guide*, vol. 1, *Beginnings to Confederation* (Toronto: University of Toronto Press, 1994), pp. 112–236, 394–447.

Part 4

COLONIES AND HINTERLANDS, 1815 TO 1867

INTRODUCTION

While events in the Canadas held the attention of the British Colonial Office, the Atlantic colonies to the east and the vast hinterlands to the west and north underwent significant transformations of their own. The colonies of New Brunswick, Nova Scotia, Prince Edward Island, and Newfoundland had already experienced distinct histories, but as a region they continued to share an economic link in their trade with Britain, the United States, and the West Indies. Politically, they joined the Canadas in the struggle against the oligarchies and the push for responsible government.

In New Brunswick, the economy was based on agriculture and lumbering. In Nova Scotia, seaport communities grew along the Bay of Fundy and the Atlantic seaboard. Fishing, shipbuilding, and agriculture were the main occupations. Independent communities also developed on Cape Breton Island (joined to Nova Scotia in 1820) and Prince Edward Island. Newfoundland, however, remained separate and distinct from the other Atlantic colonies. Its economy was heavily dependent on the cod fisheries of the Grand Banks and active trade with Britain and the West Indies.

In the seemingly distant and remote Northwest, the fur trade led to the construction of forts and took whites into remote First Nations communities. By the end of the eighteenth century, the ongoing search for the Northwest Passage took explorers across the continent to the Pacific Coast. Fur trading posts and communities developed in a world dominated by the First Nations. They seemed distant, even detached, from the events unfolding in BNA.

The economy of the Red River colony was still primarily based on the fur trade. But the amalgamation of the fur-trade companies in 1821 led to the development of a colonial society that began to mirror the rest of BNA. Industrial capitalism arrived, along with Victorian culture and sensibilities. As Hudson's Bay Company domination came to an end, Canada looked to expand westward by absorbing Rupert's Land before the Americans annexed it.

On the Pacific coast, Britain, the United States, and Russia competed for control of the area. Contact with the numerous First Nations, mainly centred on the trade in sea otter pelts, had been ongoing in the latter decades of the eighteenth century. In the nineteenth century, the British viewed the Pacific coast as an important naval base in its route to the Orient. But there was competition from the United States. In 1846, the two countries agreed to extend the boundary from the Rockies along the 49th Parallel to the coast, with Britain acquiring all of Vancouver Island. With the discovery of gold in the Fraser River valley in 1858, Britain created a separate colony on the mainland. In 1866, the mainland colony and Vancouver Island were united into the joint colony of British Columbia, with Victoria as the capital. To the north, the land remained under the control of the Inuit and the Dene, visited only by a small number of fur traders and, in the Arctic waters in the mid-1840s and 1850s, by explorers still searching for the elusive Northwest Passage.

Source: Library and Archives Canada/C-010103.

Chapter Seventeen

THE MARITIME COLONIES, 1815–1864

The loyalist migration reshaped British North America's Maritime colonies. After their arrival, the region consisted of four separate colonies: Nova Scotia, New Brunswick, Prince Edward Island, and Cape Breton. The population was widely scattered in isolated coastline communities and forested valleys, with only a few larger centres, such as Saint John, Halifax, and Fredericton. Economically, the Maritime colonies depended on fishing and farming, but the full development of the land-based resources began only in the early nineteenth century.

While Nova Scotia (to which Cape Breton was reattached in 1820) kept largely to fishing and trade, New Brunswick's economy benefited from the timber trade that began exploiting its extensive pine forests. On Prince Edward Island, agriculture became the mainstay of the colonial economy. By the mid-nineteenth century, coal mining near Pictou, Nova Scotia, and on Cape Breton Island had also grown in importance. On the eve of Confederation, Nova Scotia, New Brunswick, and Prince Edward Island had healthy economies based on fish, agriculture, and timber. Trade, however, remained focused southward and eastward with New England, the West Indies, and Britain.

The half-century following the Napoleonic Wars also witnessed major political developments. While the Maritime colonies avoided the ethnic conflict that plagued the Canadas, and the situation did not lead to rebellion, they faced their own struggles against the oligarchies. By the 1850s, Nova Scotia, New Brunswick, and Prince Edward Island achieved responsible government.

Economic Developments, 1815–1850

The Fisheries

The peace treaty of 1783 that ended the American Revolution and created the United States, granted Americans fishing privileges in the in-shore waters of the BNA colonies. But during the negotiations of the Treaty of Ghent, which ended the War of 1812, the British argued that the Americans had abrogated this privilege by declaring war. Under the Convention of 1818, the Americans lost the privilege of landing and drying their fish in the three Maritime colonies. They retained the right to do so only on unsettled shores in Newfoundland. American vessels continued to enter Maritime harbours to obtain water, purchase wood, or repair damages, but not until the signing of the Reciprocity Treaty in 1854 did the United States regain access to the in-shore fisheries.

Trade with the West Indies

After the War of 1812, the Maritimes increased trade ties with the West Indies. Commercial interests in Nova Scotia and New Brunswick argued that the privilege of trading with the British West Indies should belong only to loyal British colonies. Initially, the mother country agreed, and passed several measures favouring the shipping of goods between Saint John and Halifax and the West Indies, but Britain backed down in the face of subsequent American retaliatory measures. Officials in the British West Indies also complained about the higher cost of shipping American imports by the roundabout Maritime route. Finally, in 1830, Britain removed the restrictions on American trade to the West Indies but left duties on certain essential commodities. This arrangement allowed Nova Scotia and New Brunswick to import American produce duty free and then export it to the West Indies. As a result, colonial ships maintained much of their share of the trade.

Agriculture

Improved trade relations with the West Indies strengthened the Maritime economy, but agriculture remained weak. While farming flourished on Prince Edward Island, in Nova Scotia's Annapolis Valley, and in New Brunswick's Saint John River valley, it did not fare as well. Nova

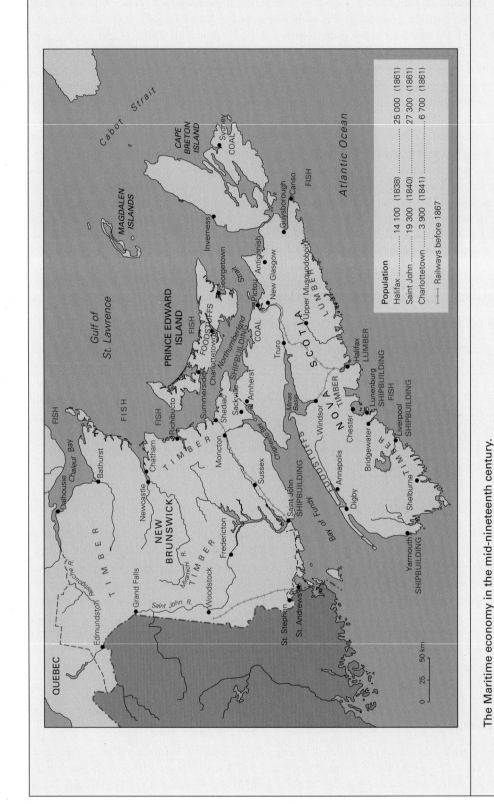

The Maritime economy in the mid-nineteenth century.

Source: Adapted from D.G.G. Kerr, *Historical Atlas of Canada*, 3rd Revised Edition. (Don Mills, ON: Thomas Nelson & Sons, 1975), p. 52.

Population
Halifax...........14 100 (1838)......25 000 (1861)
Saint John........19 300 (1840)......27 300 (1861)
Charlottetown......3 900 (1841)......6 700 (1861)
—— Railways before 1867

Scotia and New Brunswick as a whole continued to depend on American foodstuffs to feed their populations well into the nineteenth century. Commercial farming remained limited, with only Prince Edward Island, the "Garden of the Gulf," exporting large amounts of farm produce. In the cases of Nova Scotia and New Brunswick, the lack of good roads, a scattered population, and the absence of protection against American imports accounted for the limited agricultural exports. Nevertheless farming, more than either logging or fishing, remained the livelihood of a majority of Maritimers. A large number of those employed in logging and fishing also worked part-time in agriculture to support their families.

An increase in immigration after 1815 added to the size of the local market and encouraged agricultural production. New Brunswick had roughly 75 000 inhabitants in 1824 and almost 200 000 by 1851. During the same period, Nova Scotia's population increased from approximately 100 000 to 275 000. Prince Edward Island's population increased from 23 000 in 1827 to 72 000 in 1855, making it the most densely inhabited colony in British North America, due to its relatively small size.

The Axe Falls by Robert J. Wickenden.

Source: Musée nationale des beaux-arts du Québec/63 38. Don du ministère des Terres et Forêts du Québec. Photo by Jean-Guy Kérouac.

The Timber Industry

Timber became the leading growth industry in the Maritimes after the War of 1812. Local entrepreneurs, many of them farmers and small merchants, began operations in settled or semi-settled areas of the Maritimes. The timber industry also brought British traders and contractors, interested in quick profits, into the colonies. Timber companies cut trees on Crown land, even though the forests belonged to the government. By the 1820s, the New Brunswick government asserted itself against the timber barons by insisting on licences and taxing output.

Forest revenues became vital to New Brunswick's economy. As early as 1826, three-quarters of the colony's export revenues came from wood products—square timber, lumber, and ships. The industry was strong enough to survive the gradual reduction of the British preference on colonial timber. British and American demand remained high. By 1865, forest products made up two-thirds of New Brunswick's total exports by value, compared with about 10 percent of exports from Nova Scotia and Prince Edward Island.

Shipbuilding

Shipbuilding developed as a significant by-product of the timber industry. Square timber, a bulky commodity, had to be shipped in relatively large vessels, and because Britain could not meet the need for such ships in wartime, the Maritime shipbuilding industry expanded, making it the first major manufacturing industry in the region. The Maritimes soon supplied many of the new wooden ships used to ferry timber to Britain.

From the 1820s onward, the Nova Scotia and New Brunswick fleets grew steadily. Timber merchants found they could keep transportation costs low if they owned their own vessels. When prices for vessels increased, they made additional profits by selling the vessel as well as its timber cargo. Other entrepreneurs realized there was money to be made in owning ships involved in lucrative coastal trading, particularly in the West Indian trade. By the mid-nineteenth century, Maritime ships carried cotton from New Orleans, rice from India, and molasses from Cuba, as well as timber. From the 1850s to the 1870s, the Maritimes and Newfoundland accounted for over two-thirds of the tonnage registered in British North America, which claimed to have the fourth-largest merchant marine in the world, after Britain, the United States, and Norway.

WHERE HISTORIANS DISAGREE

The Timber Industry in New Brunswick

In 1989, historian Ramsay Cook lamented the lack of historical interest in the impact of settlement and industry on the natural environment: "Even the no longer so new social history has largely ignored the environment in the rush for class, gender and ethnicity."[1] Environmental history is a relatively new field in Canadian history, although its rapid rise and expansion now makes it one of the most vibrant.

Environmental concerns have long been raised about the exploitation of the forests of New Brunswick. As early as 1825, Peter Fisher raised the alarm in his *Sketches of New Brunswick,* the first historical study published in the province:

> The persons principally engaged in shipping the timber have been strangers who have taken no interest in the welfare of the country; but have merely occupied a spot to make what they could in the shortest possible time. . . . Instead of seeing towns built, farms improved and the country cleared and stocked with the reasonable returns of so great a trade, the forests are stripped and nothing left in prospect, but the gloomy apprehension when the timber is gone, of sinking into insignificance and poverty.[2]

A century later, historian Arthur R.M. Lower emphasized this same theme of senseless exploitation in three books on Canada's forest industries: *Settlement and the Forest Frontier in Eastern Canada* (1936), *The North American Assault on the Canadian Forest* (1938), and *Great Britain's Woodyard: British America and the Timber Trade* (1973). He concluded his last book by pointing out that "The Canadian forests contributed to the prosperity of the British timber importer and the enrichment of the American lumberman. . . . [But] it must be concluded that the new colonies got the minimum out of the wreck of their forests."[3]

Historian Michael Bliss took issue with Lower's interpretation in *Northern Enterprise,* a study of five centuries of Canadian business. While he did not disagree that the timber trade had negative long-term effects on the natural environment, he argued that the overall interpretation was a simplistic, knee-jerk reaction:

> The old idea that the rape of the forests was simply a using up of natural wealth with no compensating benefits is a romantic mockery of the realities and difficulties of colonial development. When A.R.M. Lower wove that theme into his writing about Canadian forest industries, with particular reference to New Brunswick, he was parroting some of the industry's least-informed critics.

Instead, Bliss focused on the economic benefits of the timber trade for colonial development. He cited a New Brunswick contemporary of Peter Fisher, who stated that the timber trade "has brought foreign produce and foreign capital into the Province, and has been the chief source of the money by means of which the country has been opened up and improved; by which its roads, bridges and public buildings have been completed; its rivers and harbours made accessible; its natural resources discovered and made available; its Provincial institutions kept up and its functionaries paid."[4]

Historical geographer Graeme Wynn agrees that the export staple of timber provided New Brunswick a critical economic boost. From 1805 to 1850 the exploitation of the forests transformed the colony from "an undeveloped backwater of 25 000 people to a bustling colony of 190 000." Profits were undoubtedly accrued by the timber barons the timber barons who received the greatest benefits and rarely concerned themselves with the environmental consequences. Conquest and exploitation of the wilderness was a dominant motif in nineteenth century nation-building and marked man's ascendancy into "civilization." At the same time, however, Wynn criticizes the indisputable waste and destruction: "Sawdust dumped into the rivers soon became sodden, sank to the bed of the stream, disturbed the river ecology, and obstructed navigation. In suspension it floated downstream, was deposited on banks and intervales, and drastically reduced fish populations." The debris of bark, slabs, edgings, mill rubbish, and sunken logs was carried over entire river systems.[5]

William Cronon's *Changes in the Land: Colonists and the Ecology of New England*[6] serves as a model for future histories of New Brunswick's timber industry by introducing interdisciplinary approaches. In particular, it offers ecological and biological knowledge. Such an approach is not completely new. In 1972 Gilbert Allardyce studied Alma Parish in Albert County in the nineteenth century.[7] At the beginning of the century, the parish's forests and fish life appeared inexhaustible; by 1850 sawmill dams blockaded the rivers and prevented the passage of salmon toward their headwater spawning grounds all along the Fundy coast. Still, lumbering increased, which meant more sawdust. The timber industry, he argues, killed fishing. When the lumber became exhausted in the early twentieth century, Alma Parish was left with nothing to support settlement. Alma Parish today forms Fundy National Park.

1. Ramsay Cook, "Review of *The Natural History of Canada*," *Canadian Historical Review* 60 (1989): 386.

2. Peter Fisher, *Sketches of New Brunswick* (Saint John: Chubb and Sears, 1825), p. 72; reprinted in Arthur R.M. Lower, *Great Britain's Woodyard: British America and the Timber Trade, 1763–1867* (Montreal/Kingston: McGill-Queen's University Press, 1973), p. 33.

3. Lower, *Great Britain's Woodyard*, p. 250.

4. Michael Bliss, *Northern Enterprise* (Toronto: McClelland & Stewart, 1987), p. 136.

5. Graeme Wynn, *Timber Colony: A Historical Geography of Early Nineteenth Century New Brunswick* (Toronto: University of Toronto Press, 1981), pp. 24, 33, 93, and 174.

6. William Cronon, *Changes in the Land: Indians, Colonists and the Ecology of New England* (New York: Hill and Wang, 1983).

7. Gilbert Allardyce, "'The Vexed Question of Sawdust': River Pollution in Nineteenth Century New Brunswick," *Dalhousie Review* 52(2) (Summer 1972): 177–90.

The Marco Polo, *New Brunswick's most famous sailing vessel, earned the title "the world's fastest ship" after making the round trip between England and Australia in less than six months in 1852.*

Source: New Brunswick Museum, Saint John, N.B./14462.

The Maritimes gained a reputation as one of the leading centres of the North American shipping industry. In 1851, the James Smith shipyard at Saint John, New Brunswick, launched the *Marco Polo*, which became the colony's most famous ship. It had a unique design, with the underwater body of a clipper and the midship of a cargo carrier. It was remarkably fast, able to cut a week off the previous record for the round trip between Liverpool, England, and Melbourne, Australia. It completed the trip in less than six months, earning the title of "the world's fastest ship."

Generally, however, Maritime shipbuilders built broad-beamed vessels designed to maximize carrying capacity, not speed. They increased sail capacity and improved the hulls of ships. They extended the average life of Nova Scotia and New Brunswick vessels from nine years in the 1820s to fifteen years by the end of the century. These shipbuilders also constructed their vessels relatively cheaply. An iron steamer in Britain cost four or five times as much in the 1860s as did a wooden vessel from the Maritimes. But the popularity of steamers grew rapidly due to their speed and reliability. The market for wooden ships diminished, leaving the Maritime economy vulnerable.

The major ship owners in New Brunswick included many timber exporters. In Nova Scotia, most were fish exporters, West Indies traders, and import–export merchants. Samuel Cunard, the most famous of the Nova Scotia ship owners, had interests in the West Indies trade, a tea business, a bank, and the sale of imported goods. In 1840, he initiated the first regular steamship service across the Atlantic. Cunard became one of the first Nova Scotians to build a business empire. He operated his interests, however, from London, England.

A number of the ship owners in the 1850s expanded their business interests and operations. By the time of his death in 1868, the operations of Thomas Killam of Yarmouth included a ship-outfitting business, a marine-insurance company, a telegraph company, a gas-lighting company, and a bank. Enos Collins of Halifax also diversified his shipping interests after the War of 1812. When he died in 1871 at the age of 97, he left behind an estate worth $6 million.

The timber and shipbuilding industries created jobs. Thousands of men and hundreds of women worked in the Maritime shipyards and in shops making materials for the ships. The sailors were most often in their twenties or early thirties. For most, seafaring was a short-term activity—a means of supplementing the family income, or a job when work was scarce on the mainland. It was demanding work with long hours, poor pay, and harsh masters. No unions existed on board ship, where the jobs were arduous and often unsafe. On any given

Dorchester, New Brunswick, shipbuilding village, 1875.

Source: Library and Archives Canada/C-010103.

voyage, a sailor faced odds of 1 in 100 of dying.[1] Desertion was one means of protection, and on average one-quarter of the crew deserted during a voyage. Until the sailing industry declined in the late 1870s, the numerous sailors in the ports of eastern Canada lived in what were called "sailortowns."

Banking

The financial needs of the merchants involved in the timber industry and shipbuilding led to the creation of banks. In Britain, commercial banks developed in the eighteenth century, and in the

Saint John, New Brunswick, around 1830.
Source: Toronto Reference Library/T14459.

1790s they began appearing in the United States. The Halifax Banking Company, the first bank in Nova Scotia, began trading in money in 1825. A group of merchants founded the Bank of Nova Scotia in 1832, and by 1840 it had branches in Windsor, Annapolis Royal, Pictou, Yarmouth, and Liverpool. New Brunswick's first bank, the Bank of New Brunswick, was chartered in Saint John in 1820; the second, the Commercial Bank, in 1834. Prince Edward Island's first bank opened in the mid-1850s. The banks dealt in foreign-exchange transactions, made loans, and circulated bank notes, on the understanding that the paper notes could always be redeemed, on demand, in real coinage. Depending on the risk the bankers were prepared to take, the banks could generally keep two or three times as many notes in circulation as they had gold or silver coins to redeem them. The issuing of notes in place of coins allowed the banks to double or triple the amount of interest they collected.

Saint John and Halifax

A rivalry developed between the two major urban centres in the Maritimes: Saint John and Halifax. Initially, Saint John held the advantage, because it was the largest city, controlled the timber trade of the Saint John River valley, had an important shipbuilding industry, and was the natural market for the farmers and fishers on both sides of the Bay of Fundy. Nearly half of the industrial output of New Brunswick was produced in and around Saint John. By the mid-nineteenth century, Saint John emerged as the region's major industrial centre, with foundry, clothing, and footwear industries. Together, these industries surpassed shipbuilding in value by the 1860s. But the merchants of Saint John delayed investing in manufacturing iron and steel. Such financial conservatism held back the development of a viable industrial base in New Brunswick by two decades.

Halifax, the military headquarters for the region, had a large, secure, ice-free harbour, with good proximity to major North Atlantic shipping lanes. It also benefited from the West Indies' trade and from its role as Nova Scotia's banking, judicial, and intellectual centre. In terms of industrial base, it developed a specialization in food-processing industries, such as sugar-refining, brewing, and distilling. But it lacked a readily accessible hinterland, and unlike Montreal and Saint John, it did not have a major waterway comparable to the St. Lawrence or the Saint John River. Halifax did succeed in bringing Prince Edward Island, Cape Breton Island, and the Miramichi country of eastern New Brunswick into its commercial orbit, but it lost the important Bay of Fundy region to Saint John.

Industrial problems plagued both cities. Urban poverty, particularly in the winter months, constituted a significant issue for both Saint John and Halifax. Charitable organizations, staffed by volunteer women and run by churches and ethnic organizations, assisted penniless immigrants as well as the urban poor. But they had limited resources. The seasonal nature of North Atlantic shipping meant that labourers, mill hands, sailors, carpenters, and other building-trades workers lost their jobs in the autumn. Only in the 1860s did the colonial governments make a modest entry into the charitable field by establishing orphanages.

The Maritimes and the United States

The relationship between the Maritimes and New England had been turbulent to say the least. From the days of the Mi'kmaq attacks to the constant incursions by the New Englanders during the colonial wars, the border region was the scene of frequent raiding and bloodshed. The expulsion of the Acadians in 1755 and the resettlement of their fertile farmlands by incoming immigrants from the Thirteen Colonies and Britain remained a bitter memory. The American Revolution and the War of 1812 increased antagonism. But despite the turbulent history, the trading relationship between the Maritimes and New England had always been strong.

Issues of borders and trade continued to dominate Maritime–American relations in the mid-nineteenth century. When Britain adopted free trade in the 1840s, many Maritimers looked to continental reciprocity—the free admission into British North America and the United States of each other's natural resources—as a viable alternative. New Brunswick saw free trade as the key to gaining entry for its timber into the American market of 23 million people.

The New Brunswick–Maine Border

There could be no chance of reciprocity until old feuds were laid to rest. In particular, a border dispute between New Brunswick and Maine had to be settled. The Treaty of Paris in 1783 set the boundary to run north from the St. Croix River to an undetermined height of land. In 1839, New

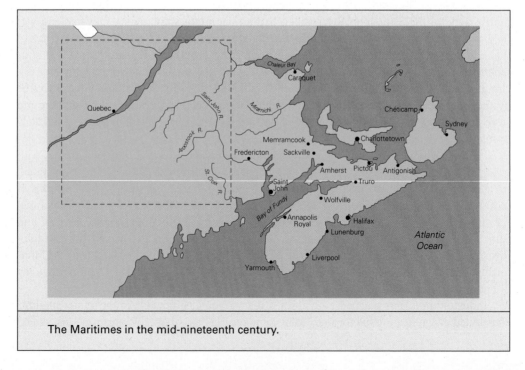

The Maritimes in the mid-nineteenth century.

Brunswick and Maine lumber workers almost caused a border war over which group had the right to cut at the headwaters of the Aroostook River, part of the disputed territory. Three years later Daniel Webster, the American secretary of state, and Lord Ashburton, the British envoy, resolved the controversy. The Webster–Ashburton Treaty of 1842 established the present-day New Brunswick–Maine boundary. The treaty left Maine a wedge of land projecting between New Brunswick and the Canadas, yet it kept intact the vital communication route between Quebec and Fredericton via Lake Témiscouata.

The Reciprocity Agreement, 1854–1866

The close trading relationship between the Maritimes and New England meant that reciprocity talks were likely to be well received in both regions. The Maritime colonies sought lucrative markets for their exports, such as fish and farm produce; the Americans, for their part, wanted access to the in-shore fisheries from which they had been excluded in 1818. Indeed, it was the inclusion of the fisheries that led the United States to sign the Reciprocity Agreement with the British North American colonies in 1854.

The Anglo–American boundary dispute.

The treaty led to the desired increased trade with the United States. The Maritime colonies now bought one-quarter to one-half of their total imports from the United States. In return, New Brunswick shipped increased amounts of lumber; Prince Edward Island shipped more foodstuffs; and Nova Scotia shipped slightly more fish. The twelve years that the reciprocity treaty lasted proved prosperous, but not solely on account of it. The high demand generated by the American Civil War (1861–65) led to high prices for fish, timber, and foodstuffs from the Maritimes. The carrying trade also benefited.

Railways

According to historian T.W. Acheson, "The railway was the new technological god that spelled progress and improvement to mid-nineteenth century minds."[2] It signalled a communication and transportation revolution that opened up remote areas to people and goods. More than anything else, the railway provided a link that connected people and places. It served as the essential link that could join the Maritimes to the Canadas. It could also link the Maritimes to New England. While it represented progress and intercolonial linkages, the railway was crucial for economic expansion.

The leading Maritime cities sought to build railways inland to expand their economic hinterlands. Between 1853 and 1866, New Brunswick built 350 kilometres of railways and Nova Scotia constructed 235 kilometres. Maritime promoters envisaged one day linking the ice-free Maritime ports with the St. Lawrence Valley and with the grain-producing American Midwest. Merchants in Halifax and Saint John had visions of their respective cities serving as the focal point from which European commerce could be channelled into the continent and from which American and Canadian exports could be sent abroad.

Yet these "symbols of modernity" proved expensive both to build and operate. The railway had to offer clear advantages over water transport. A single kilometre of track could cost as much as a sizable sailing vessel. Moreover, operating costs were much higher by rail than by sea.

To make money, the railway company owners needed both densely populated areas to provide local revenue and the shortest possible direct routes. Neither Halifax nor even Saint John had such hinterlands. Low population density and difficult terrain posed serious obstacles to railway development and, more importantly, to the bottom line—profits. The larger communities in the interior were too distant, in contrast with those neighbouring Boston, New York, or Montreal, and the land routes passed through long stretches of thinly populated territory. If profits were not to be accrued, private companies would not invest.

The People of the Maritimes

The immigration boom of the early nineteenth century transformed the character and identity of the Maritimes. Thousands of Scottish and Irish immigrants crossed the North Atlantic to British North America to escape overcrowding, famine, and poverty. They joined the already-established residents—English, Welsh, Acadians, Blacks, Mi'kmaqs, New Englanders, and loyalists.

The British

The British (English, Welsh, and loyalists) dominated the communities of the Saint John River valley and southeast New Brunswick. The descendants of loyalists and Planters were numerous in Nova Scotia. In the census of 1871, nearly 30 percent of Nova Scotians and New Brunswickers gave their national origin as English or Welsh.

The Acadians

Many Acadians, who had been deported in 1755, returned from exile. In New Brunswick in the mid-nineteenth century, they made up about 15 percent of the population, and in Nova Scotia and Prince Edward Island approximately 10 percent. The Acadians maintained their connection to the Roman Catholic Church as the one institution that maintained an interest in their well-being. The Church established elementary schools and, in 1864, the French-language Collège Saint-Joseph at Memramcook, New Brunswick. The college (which a century later became the nucleus of today's Université de Moncton) furnished the Acadian population with an educated professional elite from which the community drew many of its future political leaders.

By the mid-nineteenth century, the Acadians developed a distinct identity. Not surprisingly, the traumatic events of 1755 played a central role. Inspired by Henry Wadsworth Longfellow's poem *Evangeline*, an account of an Acadian woman and her lover separated during the deportation of 1755, that identity was based upon the diaspora of the Acadian people.

The Acadian community in northeastern New Brunswick incorporated, through intermarriage, many Irish, Scots, and English. Their modern-day descendants have British names like McGraw, Finn, McLaughlin, Ferguson, and Kerry, but their mother tongue is French and they consider themselves Acadian. French-Canadian immigrants from Quebec, who arrived in the late nineteenth century, also assimilated into these Acadian communities. In predominantly English-speaking areas, however—Prince Edward Island, for example—some Acadians were themselves assimilated into the English-speaking community. On Prince Edward Island, some Acadians anglicized their names: Aucoin became Wedge, Poirier became Perry, Bourque became Burke.

The Scots

The Highland Scots suffered "clearances" from their lands throughout the eighteenth and nineteenth centuries. Scottish Lords realized that their lands were more profitable when used for

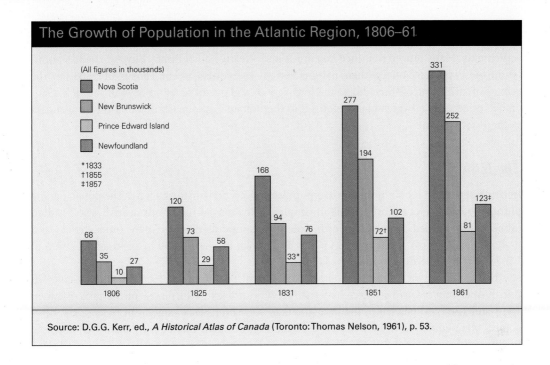

The Growth of Population in the Atlantic Region, 1806–61

(All figures in thousands)

- Nova Scotia
- New Brunswick
- Prince Edward Island
- Newfoundland

*1833
†1855
‡1857

1806: Nova Scotia 68, New Brunswick 35, Prince Edward Island 10, Newfoundland 27

1825: Nova Scotia 120, New Brunswick 73, Prince Edward Island 29, Newfoundland 58

1831: Nova Scotia 168, New Brunswick 94, Prince Edward Island 33*, Newfoundland 76

1851: Nova Scotia 277, New Brunswick 194, Prince Edward Island 72†, Newfoundland 102

1861: Nova Scotia 331, New Brunswick 252, Prince Edward Island 81, Newfoundland 123‡

Source: D.G.G. Kerr, ed., *A Historical Atlas of Canada* (Toronto: Thomas Nelson, 1961), p. 53.

sheep grazing than for peasant farming, and they often used unscrupulous means to drive out their tenants. Famines and cholera outbreaks added to the misery of a people already suffering government attacks on their identity and culture.

The promise of 40 hectares of free land led thousands of landless Scots to immigrate to Nova Scotia. Between 1815 and 1838, about 40 000 came to the colony, particularly to Cape Breton Island. The journey from Scotland was perilous. On one ship that left in 1827, 20 percent of those aboard died. Gaelic-speaking Highlanders came, usually in groups or clans. By the early nineteenth century, Gaelic was the third most common European language spoken in British North America. Although the magnificent hills and seacoast of Cape Breton reminded

National Origins: Nova Scotia (1871), New Brunswick (1871), and Prince Edward Island (1891)

	NORTH AMERICAN INDIAN		ENGLISH AND WELSH		SCOTS		IRISH		FRENCH	
	Number	%	Number	%	Number	%	Number	%	Number	%
Nova Scotia	1 666	0.4	113 520	29.2	130 741	33.7	62 851	16.4	32 833	8.5
New Brunswick	1 403	0.5	83 598	29.2	40 858	14.3	100 654	35.3	44 907	15.7
Prince Edward Island	281	0.3	21 568	19.8	48 933	44.8	25 415	23.3	10 751	9.9

	GERMAN		DUTCH		AFRICAN		SWISS		TOTAL
	Number	%	Number	%	Number	%	Number	%	Population
Nova Scotia	31 942	8.2	2 868	0.7	6 212	1.6	1 775	0.5	387 800
New Brunswick	4 478	1.6	6 004	2.1	1 701	0.6	64	—	285 594
Prince Edward Island	1 076	1.0	292	0.3					108 891

Source: R. Cole Harris and John Warkentin, *Canada before Confederation: A Study in Historical Geography* (Ottawa: Carleton University Press, 1991 [1974]), pp. 184–85. Data from Census of Canada.

them of home, the Scots were ill prepared for clearing virgin forest and faced many difficulties in establishing their farms. Some left, and some became fishers and boat builders in coastal settlements. Many moved to Prince Edward Island. Nearly half of Prince Edward Island's population (44.8 percent) stated their national origin as Scottish in the census of 1881. In the census of 1871, one of three did so in Nova Scotia, and one of seven in New Brunswick. Generally speaking, the Highlanders belonged to the Roman Catholic Church and the Lowlanders to the Presbyterian.

The Irish

Ireland's depressed economy and its overpopulation forced many to emigrate. The potato famine of the 1840s drove out nearly 2 million people. Of the tens of thousands of Irish who boarded timber ships headed for British North America, thousands died en route from cholera and typhoid. Nonetheless, 8000 arrived in New Brunswick in 1842, 9000 in 1846, and 17 000 in 1847. Only in 1848 did the numbers fall below 4000.

In New Brunswick, the Irish outnumbered even the numerous Scottish immigrants. No British American colony was more Irish than New Brunswick in the nineteenth century. Between 1815 and 1865, 60 percent of the immigrants to New Brunswick came from Ireland; the newcomers were equally divided between Protestant and Roman Catholic. By Confederation, the Irish constituted one-third of New Brunswick's population.

Although many Irish used New Brunswick as a stepping stone to the United States, a large number stayed. The poverty-stricken and destitute congregated in the ports and lumber camps of eastern New Brunswick. The main areas of Irish settlement in New Brunswick before 1850 were the upper Saint John River valley, the Bay of Fundy, and the south shore of Chaleur Bay. Although the loyalists and their descendants, together with a number of recent English immigrants, controlled the colony's political life, in many communities the Irish outnumbered them.

Black Maritimers

During the War of 1812, Britain offered sanctuary to runaway slaves as free citizens. Near the end of the war, some 3000 to 4000 blacks escaped from Chesapeake plantations during the British raids on Washington and Baltimore. Many sought freedom in British North America. They arrived at a time, however, when abundant, cheap white labour made it difficult to find work.

The British authorities may have offered freedom from slavery but they did not offer freedom from racial prejudice. The newcomers faced harsh discrimination, especially in Nova Scotia, which had the largest black population (1.6 percent of the total population, according to the Canadian census of 1871), and, to a lesser extent, in New Brunswick (where they formed 0.6 percent of the population). Historian W.A. Spray described how poorly the 400 refugees were treated in New Brunswick in comparison with the white settlers: "The policy in New Brunswick at this time was to give free grants of at least 100 acres to white settlers.... Yet the black refugees were to get only 50 acres, they were to pay for the surveys, and they were to receive licences of occupation for three years."[3] Furthermore, black Maritimers had no security of possession, since the government could simply refuse to reissue licences after the three-year term expired. The British empire prided itself on its enlightened and emancipated attitude toward slavery. Attitudes toward race, however, remained deplorable. In the decades to come, Canada would embrace a similar self-congratulatory attitude toward its role in offering "sanctuary" to freed slaves and in the "underground railroad". The treatment of the blacks of Nova Scotia, however, tells a very different story.

The First Nations

The First Nations of the Maritimes—the Mi'kmaqs and Maliseets—had long played a pivotal role in fighting alongside their white neighbours to defend the area. But now the people most indigenous to the region found it the most difficult to adjust to changing conditions. Unlike the Iroquois, the Mi'kmaqs and the Maliseets were not rewarded for their service as military allies. Unlike the First Nations in Upper Canada after the Proclamation of 1763, the British did not make land agreements or negotiate treaties with the Maritime First Nations. The Mi'kmaqs and the Maliseets demanded compensation for territory lost to settlement, and the situation only worsened as more immigrants arrived. But the British and the Maritime governments held that Aboriginal title to the land had already been extinguished—first, through French occupation and second, as a result of the Treaty of Utrecht in 1713, which the British claimed gave them sovereign title to Acadia.

The New Brunswick government set aside some reserves for the Mi'kmaqs and the Mali-

"Indian Basket Weaving, Prince Edward Island, Canada," late-nineteenth-century card issued by Keystone View Company.

Source: Library and Archives Canada/PA-024869.

seets, but the lack of adequate legal descriptions and surveys encouraged settlers to encroach into these areas. A similar situation developed in Nova Scotia. By the 1860s, the approximately 1000 Mi'kmaqs and 500 Maliseets in New Brunswick possessed an official land base of about 25 000 hectares. In Nova Scotia the Mi'kmaqs, who numbered between 1400 and 1800, had only 8000 hectares. The several hundred Mi'kmaqs on Prince Edward Island faced the most difficult situation. Until 1870, they held only a few campsites as reserve land. The division of the island into fiefdoms controlled by the absentee landlords left little room for reserves. In 1870, an English-based organization, the Aborigines' Protection Society, arranged to buy Lennox Island, a small island off Prince Edward Island for the Mi'kmaqs. By the time of Confederation, the First Nations constituted roughly 0.5 percent of the total population of Nova Scotia, New Brunswick, and Prince Edward Island.

But the Mi'kmaqs and the Maliseets did not disappear, and their cultures survived. Despite opposition and constant pressure to assimilate, they continued to speak their own languages, they passed on their traditions and folklore, and they practised their crafts. The women produced porcupine quillwork on birchbark, which they then sold in an international market. Mary Christianne Paul Morri, for example, was one of the best-known Mi'kmaq quillworkers. Mi'kmaq men were employed as furniture makers, ships' carpenters, and builders of small boats.

The Struggle for Responsible Government

After the American Revolution, the same rigid oligarchic political structures as formed in the Canadas were allowed to develop in the Maritime colonies. The governor, his appointed Executive and Legislative Councils, and the judiciary held the reins of power, and together they formed powerful cliques that were largely English, upper-class, and Anglican. The elected Assemblies had little authority or influence. The position of the small ruling cliques was bolstered by the

Joseph Howe in 1871.

Source: Library and Archives Canada/C-022002.

arrival of the anti-republican loyalists, while the Assemblies were aided by the New England and later Scottish and Irish migrations. Complaints about the lack of representative government increased.

With the dismantling of the mercantile system in the late 1840s, the Reformers increased their influence. Their push for responsible government gained momentum from the Rebellions in Upper and Lower Canada. As in the Canadas, the Reformers pushed to have the Executive Council (or Cabinet) held responsible to the majority party in the Assembly. If the Council lost a confidence vote in the Assembly or lost support in a general election, its members would have to resign. Second, the Reformers wanted the governor to accept the recommendations of the Executive Council, dependent as it was on majority support in the Assembly.

Nova Scotia

Joseph Howe emerged as leader of the Nova Scotia Reformers. Coming from loyalist stock, he was "a legendary political hero, a first-rate journalist, and perhaps the most renowned public speaker in the colonies during a century that greatly prized the art of oratory."[4] In 1827, at the age of 23, the self-educated Howe purchased the *Novascotian*, a Halifax newspaper, which he reorganized into the most influential newspaper in the colony. In 1835, Howe was charged with libel for publishing letters openly criticizing Halifax politicians and police for corruption. After he brilliantly defended himself by supporting his criticisms, the judge called for Howe's conviction but the jury acquitted him.

Elected to the Nova Scotia Assembly in 1836 on a platform of responsible government, Howe organized the Reform attack against the Council of Twelve, an interrelated Halifax-based merchant oligarchy, which controlled both the appointed Legislative Council and the Executive Council. The Reformers called for an elected upper house and for the Assembly's control over Crown revenues.

The Reformers dominated the Assemblies elected in 1836 and 1840. But Howe's critical editorials in the *Novascotian* so enraged John Haliburton (the son of the judge in Howe's libel trial), that he challenged Howe to a duel on March 14, 1840. Haliburton fired but missed. Howe played the role of the conciliatory gentleman and "deloped," deliberately firing his pistol in the air to abort the conflict.

Political division obstructed the Reform movement in 1843, but in the election of 1847, the Reformers fought on the issue of responsible government and won a majority. On February 2, 1848, the Colonial Office agreed that henceforth the Executive Council must collectively resign if it lost the Assembly's confidence. Nova Scotia thus became the first British North American colony to obtain responsible government, even though the winds of change were already blowing in the Canadas. Howe boasted that the Reformers had achieved their aims peacefully, without "a blow struck or a pane of glass broken." The Canadian Rebellions of 1837–38, however, had gone a long way in convincing Britain of the wisdom of conceding responsible government in British North America.

New Brunswick

In New Brunswick, Charles Fisher and Lemuel Allan Wilmot led the Reformers. They faced a situation similar to that in Nova Scotia but the small ruling clique in New Brunswick was even more entrenched because the colony was a loyalist creation. As a result, however, opposition took longer to emerge. Since Anglicans initially made up a majority of the population, the established position of the Church of England faced little opposition. The political battle for responsible government in New Brunswick happened relatively quickly and smoothly, compared to the other colonies.

By 1837 the oligarchy in New Brunswick allowed reform of the political system. The Assembly secured control of revenues from Crown lands, including timber land revenues, in return for the provision of a civil list guaranteeing the salaries of officers of government. As well, the Colonial Office made the Executive Council in New Brunswick responsible to the elected representatives in the Assembly. While these moves were steps forward, the colony had to wait until 1848 to obtain full responsible government along with the rest of British North America.

Responsible government opened up more than Executive Council seats to the Assembly. It provided the popularly elected body control over patronage—that is, the opportunity to make appointments to public office. Wilmot was one of the Reformers who took full advantage of the opportunity to benefit himself. C.M. Wallace, his biographer, has noted that "his pursuit of office, first on the Executive Council, then on the bench, and finally as lieutenant governor, might well be classed as rapacious."[5]

Prince Edward Island

The winning of responsible government became an important issue in Prince Edward Island only in the 1840s. The major political issue until this time involved the land question. In 1767 the island had been divided into 67 lots of approximately 20 000 acres (about 8000 hectares) each. They were distributed through patronage to favourites of the Crown. By the nineteenth century, these landholdings had been consolidated and were owned by 13 absentee landlords. The landlords refused

Mi'kmaq wigwam, probably near Dartmouth, Nova Scotia, in 1860.

Source: National Anthropological Archives/Smithsonian Institution/47728.

George Coles, local brewer in Prince Edward Island and the leader of the Reformers, in the early 1850s. Coles served as the first Premier of the province from 1851 to 1854.

Source: Public Archives and Records Office of Prince Edward Island. George Coles Portrait, ca. 1864, Acc. 2755/120.

to sell their lands, instead preferring to rent them out to tenants in what became a neo-feudal system. As late as 1841, only one-third of farmers owned their lands.

By the 1840s, the land question and the struggle for responsible government merged. Initially, the Colonial Office opposed granting self-government on the basis that PEI was a small and undeveloped colony, but in reality it opposed reforming the land system. In late 1847, a new governor, Sir Donald Campbell, was appointed. Campbell bitterly opposed responsible government. George Coles, a local brewer, was now the leader of the Reformers and his party won the elections of 1850 and took control of the Assembly. When the Assembly withheld supply (the governor and council in Prince Edward Island did not have access to revenues from Crown lands), Campbell appealed to the Colonial Office to curb the radicalism of the Reformers. The Colonial Secretary refused, and when Campbell died later that year, his replacement was ordered to implement responsible government.

Immediately, the population hoped that the constitutional change would lead to a settlement of Prince Edward Island's land question. The Colonial Office refused, however, to consider *escheat* ("take back")—the cancelling of the large grants to proprietors—and upheld the rights of private property. The island's Executive and Legislative Councils, both controlled by a small group of the leading families in Charlottetown, also protected the proprietors. To challenge this position, the Assembly set up an investigative commission to study the problem. It recommended in 1860 that tenants be allowed to purchase their land and that owners obtain a fair valuation of their property. Progress was slow. As late as 1873, the tenants still owned only one-third of the island.

Cultural Developments

As in economic and political matters, the Maritime colonies gained cultural maturity by the mid-nineteenth century. Throughout the colonies, local church choirs flourished. In the urban centres, the large Anglican and Catholic churches often had organs and skilled musicians. Music societies existed in the cities. Among the earliest in British North America were the New Union Singing Society of Halifax (1809) and the Philharmonic Society of Saint John (1824).

Throughout the nineteenth century, theatre was increasingly available to audiences in Maritime cities. At first, the Halifax garrison performed plays in makeshift theatres in taverns, but in 1789 it opened the New Grand Theatre. For the opening, the officers and men produced William Shakespeare's *Merchant of Venice*. Charlottetown built its first theatre in 1800, and by 1809 Saint John had its own Drury Lane Theatre. Professional companies and leading actors from both the United States and Britain visited in the mid-nineteenth century.

The Maritimes produced a major North American literary figure in the mid-nineteenth century: Thomas Chandler Haliburton. From 1823 to 1860, the Nova Scotia judge penned political pamphlets and many works on the history of the province, but he is best remembered for his fiction. Haliburton's classic, *The Clockmaker; or The Sayings and Doings of Samuel Slick of Slickville*, first appeared in 1836 and was followed by two more series of the same humorous stories about the shrewd Yankee peddler who crossed the province selling his poorly produced clocks to easily fooled Nova Scotians. As many as seventy editions of *The Clockmaker* have since appeared, and the book has remained in print for more than 150 years. Haliburton became the first British North American writer to gain an international reputation.

Religion and Education

By the mid-nineteenth century, the Christian churches were well established in the Maritime colonies. Considerable religious diversity existed. Among the Protestant denominations, the Anglicans remained numerous and influential, although the Baptists and Methodists made inroads and increased their membership. Charles Inglis, the former rector of Trinity Church in New York City, became Nova Scotia's first Anglican bishop in 1787, with jurisdiction over the colonies of Quebec, New Brunswick, Prince Edward Island, Newfoundland, and Nova Scotia. Inglis sought to make the Anglican Church predominant in the Maritimes. But the population, the majority of whom were not of English birth or tradition, resisted. "The Anglican church was strong in the cities and very strong among the cultivated and politically influential classes," historian T.W. Acheson observes, "but it never held the support of more than a minority of the freeholders and artisanal and labouring classes of the countryside and towns."[6]

Academy of Music, Saint John, New Brunswick.

Source: New Brunswick Museum, Saint John, N.B./W6725. Gift of the New Brunswick Historical Society.

Religious Denominations

By the mid-nineteenth century, the Anglicans had lost ground to the Baptists, the most active of the Protestant denominations, and to the Methodists. In New Brunswick, the Baptists were the largest denomination, making up nearly one-quarter of the colony's religious population in 1860. In Nova Scotia, the Baptists constituted one-fifth of the population. As a result of their close-knit organizations and high degree of church discipline, the Baptists filled the religious void left in the rural areas of the Maritimes after Henry Alline's death in 1784 (see Chapter 10).

Next in strength came the Wesleyan Methodists, who had succeeded by the 1820s in building up an influential following, including converts from the professional classes, taken largely from among the ranks of the evangelical Anglicans. Presbyterians came into their own with the large Scottish immigration to the Maritimes. Scottish Presbyterians settled throughout the Maritime colonies, but in large numbers on the north shore of Nova Scotia and in Prince Edward Island. Lutheranism was strong in the German community in Nova Scotia's Lunenburg County; small Quaker and Jewish communities existed as well.

The Roman Catholic Church had long been strong in the Maritimes. It held powerful sway among the Acadians and was then bolstered particularly by the immigration of the Scots and Irish. By the mid-nineteenth century, over 40 percent of the population of Prince Edward Island, a third of New Brunswickers, and a quarter of Nova Scotians belonged to the Catholic Church. Catholics gained full civil rights throughout the British empire in 1829. In the 1840s, the church hierarchy fought the integration of Catholics into the dominant Protestant community. They worked to build Catholic schools, to obtain equality for Catholics in all aspects of society, and to establish the paramount authority of the bishops for all Catholics.

Education

Education by the nineteenth century had become the main battleground for the churches. Maritime Catholics sought state financial support for their church-run schools, whereas the Anglicans, Baptists, Methodists, and Presbyterians favoured publicly funded, state-run primary schools that taught Protestant moral values. Fearful of the electoral consequences among Protestant voters, none of the colonial governments gave separate schools formal legislative approval. Without legal status, denominational schools would not be guaranteed financial aid in any of the three colonies in the 1860s, on the eve of Confederation.

Mount Allison Wesleyan College.

Source: Library and Archives Canada/C-58726.

Four generations of women, about 1880. Photographer unknown.

Source: Public Archives of Canada/Library and Archives Canada/C-088075.

Denominationalism prevailed in higher education. King's College at Windsor, founded by Bishop Inglis, excluded four-fifths of all possible candidates for degrees in the arts because they refused to swear an oath supporting the doctrines of the Church of England. The Anglicans also established the College of New Brunswick (to be reconstituted as the nonsectarian University of New Brunswick in 1859). Governor Dalhousie founded the college in Halifax that still bears his name, to provide an education to students of all religious denominations. However, when it finally began to offer classes in the 1860s, it had effectively become a Presbyterian institution.

In the early nineteenth century, Presbyterians built Pictou Academy, while in 1828 Baptists established Horton Academy at Wolfville, Nova Scotia (ten years later, it became Acadia College). Between 1838 and 1855, five new universities followed in the Maritimes: Prince of Wales and St. Dunstan's in Prince Edward Island; St. Mary's and St. Francis in Nova Scotia; and Mount Allison in New Brunswick. Each was associated with a religious denomination.

Gender Relations

The experience and plight of women in the Maritimes was similar to that in the rest of colonial British North America. Patriarchy prevailed when it came to gender relations. Men, for instance, owned almost all property and housing. At best, women had only limited rights under the law to protection and safety. In 1836 Prince Edward Island disenfranchised propertied women, as did New Brunswick in 1843 and Nova Scotia in 1851.

As with the Canadas, gendered "spaces" in the Maritimes were socially divided into the "public" and "private" realms, even though in reality considerable overlap occurred. One public space in which women played an increasing role was within the social reform movement. Women, particularly those representing the middle class, played prominent roles in their churches and charities. The caring and nurturing of society's ills seemed a logical and respectable place and role for women. In the early decades of the century, middle-class colonists organized Bible and missionary societies to help alleviate the suffering of immigrants. The evangelical reform movement had strong roots in the Maritimes. "Revivals" were intended to show individuals their sins and bring them to conversion. One of the main causes of this evangelicalism was the temperance and prohibition movements. Women became the main advocates of banning booze.

By the middle of the nineteenth century, women began to gain access to education. Progress in this regard, however, was slow. After 1849, New Brunswick finally allowed women to attend the provincial Normal School, and by the late 1850s, they numbered close to one-half of the colony's teachers. On the other hand, they were paid the same wage as domestic servants and were confined to teaching younger schoolchildren. And women were still denied entrance to colleges. It was assumed that higher education was the realm of men because the role of women was in the household, as wives, mothers, and homemakers. It was only respectable for women to have a profession (such as teaching) until she found a husband and was ready to raise a family. The idea of working women seemed to threaten the basic social unit—the family—and established gender relations based around patriarchy.

There was the occasional positive sign for women. While the legal system was heavily stacked in favour of men, Nova Scotia in 1857 became the only British North American colony to allow legal divorce on the grounds of cruelty, such as wife battering. New Brunswick and Prince Edward Island, however, took no steps to imitate this legislation. After surveying the status of Maritime women, historian Ian Ross Robertson concluded:

> It is doubtful whether the status of most women—dependency within a patriarchal world—was improving in the 1850s. . . . In most cases, the best a woman of the era could hope for was marriage to a man with the means to guarantee her a pedestal from which to supervise other, subordinate women of the household.[7]

SUMMARY

By the mid-nineteenth century, Nova Scotia, New Brunswick, and Prince Edward Island were developed colonies. Their economies were relatively diversified and industrialized, and the timber trade and the Reciprocity Agreement ushered in a period of prosperity. Railway development was well underway. The struggle for responsible government was successful and came without having to resort to rebellion.

Ethnically, the immigration boom rewove the social fabric of the region by introducing the Celtic element. But religious and ethnic divisions remained, and some groups, such as the Mi'kmaqs, the blacks, and even the Acadians were pushed to the margins of society. The colonies had become much more consolidated as a region than half a century earlier, but they felt little kinship with the Canadas to the east. Any proposal for a larger union of the BNA colonies was likely to encounter formidable opposition.

NOTES

1. Christopher Moore, "Writers of History, Who Killed the Golden Age of Sail?," *The Beaver* 71(5) (October 1991): 61.

2. T.W. Acheson, "The 1840s: Decade of Tribulation," in Phillip A. Buckner and John G. Reid, eds., *The Atlantic Region to Confederation* (Toronto: University of Toronto Press, 1994), p. 331.

3. W.A. Spray, "The Settlement of the Black Refugees in New Brunswick, 1815–1836," in Phillip A. Buckner and David Frank, eds., *The Acadiensis Reader, Atlantic Canada Before Confederation*, vol. 1 (Fredericton: Acadiensis Press, 1985), pp. 152–53.

4. Ian Ross Robertson, "The Maritime Colonies, 1784 to Confederation," in M. Brook Taylor, ed., *Canadian History: A Reader's Guide*, vol. 1, *Beginnings to Confederation* (Toronto: University of Toronto Press, 1994), p. 258.

5. C.M. Wallace, "Lemuel Allan Wilmot," *Dictionary of Canadian Biography*, vol. 10, *1871–1880* (Toronto: University of Toronto Press, 1972), p. 710.

6. T.W. Acheson, "The 1840s: Decade of Tribulation," in Buckner and Reid, eds., *The Atlantic Region to Confederation*, p. 317.

7. Ian Ross Robertson, "The 1850s: Maturity and Reform," in Buckner and Reid, eds., *The Atlantic Region to Confederation*, p. 353.

RELATED READINGS

Module 6, "Worlds of Work: Pre-Industrial Work, 1860–1880" in *Visions: The Canadian History Modules Project: Pre-Confederation*, while not explicitly focused upon the Maritimes, does contain two articles relevant to Maritime history. Rusty Bitterman's "Farm Households and Wage Labour in the Northeastern Maritimes in the Early 19th Century" and T.W. Acheson's article "Saint John: The Making of a Colonial Urban Community" are both included. See pages 273–284. Bitterman's article can also be found in *Labour/Le travail*, 31 (Spring 1993).

BIBLIOGRAPHY

An overview of the Maritimes' history to 1867 is Phillip A. Buckner and John G. Reid, eds., *The Atlantic Region to Confederation: A History* (Toronto: University of Toronto Press, 1994). Margaret R. Conrad and James K. Hiller, *Atlantic Canada: A Region in the Making* (Don Mills, ON: Oxford University Press,

2001), is very useful. An older survey is that by W.S. MacNutt, *The Atlantic Provinces: The Emergence of Colonial Society, 1712–1857* (Toronto: McClelland & Stewart, 1965). For New Brunswick, see also W.S. MacNutt's dated *New Brunswick: A History, 1784–1867* (Toronto: Macmillan, 1963) and Graeme Wynn's *Timber Colony: A Historical Geography of Early Nineteenth Century New Brunswick* (Toronto: University of Toronto Press, 1981). A.H. Clark reviews Prince Edward Island's story in *Three Centuries and the Island* (Toronto: University of Toronto Press, 1959). A lively popular history of the island is Douglas Baldwin's *Land of the Red Soil* (Charlottetown: Ragweed Press, 1990). Kenneth Donovan's two edited books *Cape Breton at 200: Historical Essays in Honour of the Island's Bicentennial, 1785–1985* (Sydney: University College of Cape Breton Press, 1985) and *The Island: New Perspectives on Cape Breton's History, 1713–1990* (Fredericton/Sydney: Acadiensis Press and University College of Cape Breton Press, 1990) review Cape Breton's past two centuries. See also Stephen J. Hornsby's *Nineteenth Century Cape Breton: A Historical Geography* (Montreal/Kingston: McGill-Queen's University Press, 1992). Ian Ross Robertson introduces the historical literature in his essay "The Maritime Colonies: 1784 to Confederation," in M. Brook Taylor, ed., *Canadian History: A Reader's Guide*, vol. 1, *Beginnings to Confederation* (Toronto: University of Toronto Press, 1994), pp. 237–79.

Economic questions receive attention in Ch. 4 of Kenneth Norrie and Douglas Owram, *A History of the Canadian Economy*, 2nd ed. (Toronto: Harcourt Brace, 1996), pp. 73–93; Michael Bliss, *Northern Enterprise: Five Centuries of Canadian Business* (Toronto: McClelland & Stewart, 1987); S.A. Saunders, "The Maritime Provinces and the Reciprocity Treaty," in George A. Rawlyk, ed., *Historical Essays on the Atlantic Provinces* (Toronto: McClelland & Stewart, 1967), pp. 161–78; Eric W. Sager and Lewis R. Fischer, *Shipping and Shipbuilding in Atlantic Canada, 1820–1914* (Ottawa: Canadian Historical Association, 1986); and Eric W. Sager with Gerald E. Panting, *Maritime Capital: The Shipping Industry in Maritime Canada, 1820–1914* (Montreal/Kingston: McGill-Queen's University Press, 1990). See also Daniel Samson, *The Spirit of Industry and Improvement: Liberal Government and Rural-Industrial Society, Nova Scotia, 1790–1862* (Montreal/Kingston: McGill-Queen's University Press, 2008). Beatrice Craig's *Backwoods Consumers and Homespun Capitalists: The Rise of a Market Culture in Eastern Canada* (Toronto: University of Toronto Press, 2009) should also be consulted.

The social history of the Maritimes in this time period is reviewed in the three editions of Phillip A. Buckner and David Frank, eds., *Atlantic Canada before Confederation*, vol. 1, *The Acadiensis Reader* (Fredericton: Acadiensis Press, 1985, 1988, 1998). The first edition contains Judith Fingard's essay "The Relief of the Unemployed Poor in Saint John, Halifax and St. John's, 1815–1860," pp. 190–211. Fingard's *Jack in Port: Sailortowns of Eastern Canada* (Toronto: University of Toronto Press, 1982) describes the life of merchant sailors in Saint John and Halifax, and her *Dark Side of Life in Victorian Halifax* (Porters Lake, NS: Pottersfield Press, 1989) focuses on the lives of about 100 habitual offenders in Halifax in the mid-nineteenth century.

See Harvey Amani Whitfield's *Blacks on the Border: The Black Refugees in British North America, 1815–1860* (Burlington: Vermont University Press and Hanover: University of New England, 2006) for a consideration of race. Bonnie Huskins examines issues of class in the role of the public feast in her article "From *Haute Cuisine* to Ox Roasts: Public Feasting and the Negotiation of Class in Mid-19th-Century Saint John and Halifax." *Labour/Le travail* 37 (Spring 1996). Jan Noel looks at the temperance movement in the early nineteenth century in British North America in *Canada Dry: Temperance Crusades Before Confederation* (Toronto: University of Toronto Press, 1995).

Several essays in Philip Girard and Jim Phillips, eds., *Essays in the History of Canadian Law: The Nova Scotia Experience* (Toronto: Osgoode Society, 1990), examine aspects of the province's legal history in the nineteenth century. For a look further at the law in Nova Scotia, see Blake R. Brown, "Storms, Roads, and Harvest Time: Criticisms of Jury Service in Pre-Confederation Nova Scotia." *Acadiensis* 36(1) (2006): 93–111. William B. Hamilton reviews the educational history of the three Maritime colonies in "Society and Schools in Nova Scotia" and "Society and Schools in New Brunswick and Prince Edward Island," in J. Donald Wilson, Robert M. Stamp, and Louis-Philippe Audet, eds., *Canadian Education: A History* (Scarborough, ON: Prentice-Hall, 1970), pp. 86–125.

A popular account of Halifax is Thomas H. Raddall's *Halifax: Warden of the North*, rev. ed. (Toronto: McClelland & Stewart, 1971 [1948]). For a more recent survey by three professional historians, see

Judith Fingard, Janet Guildford, and David Sutherland, *Halifax: The First 250 Years* (Halifax: Formac, 1999). T.W. Acheson's *Saint John: The Making of a Colonial Urban Community* (Toronto: University of Toronto Press, 1985) is an in-depth study of New Brunswick's largest city. Judith Fingard has also studied nineteenth century Halifax in her book *The Dark Side of Life in Victorian Halifax* (Porters Lake, NS: Pottersfield Press, 1989). T.W. Acheson examines evangelical religion in Southern New Brunswick in his article "Evangelicals and Public Life in Southern New Brunswick, 1830–1880," in Marguerite Van Die, ed., *Religion and Public Life in Canada: Historical and Comparative Perspectives* (Toronto: University of Toronto Press, 2001). See also Ross N. Hebb, "Samuel Cooke: Father of the Church of England in New Brunswick," *Journal of the Canadian Church Historical Society* 46(1) (2004): 27–47, and William Dawson Gerrior, "Father Hubert Girroir (1825–1884): One of the Two 'Human Milestones' in the Revival of Acadian Society in 19th Century Nova Scotia," *Journal of the Royal Nova Scotia Historical Society* 7 (2004): 160–79.

A collection of materials relating to Maritime women has been edited by Margaret Conrad, Toni Laidlaw, and Donna Smyth: *No Place Like Home: Diaries and Letters of Nova Scotia Women, 1771–1938* (Halifax: Formac, 1988). See also Janet Guildford and Suzanne Morton, eds., *Separate Spheres: Women's Worlds in the Nineteenth-Century Maritimes* (Fredericton: Acadiensis Press, 1994), and Rusty Bitterman and Margaret McCallum's book *Lady Landlords of Prince Edward Island: Imperial Dreams and the Defence of Property* (Montreal/Kingston: McGill-Queen's University Press, 2008). Interesting articles include Gail G. Campbell, "Disfranchised but Not Quiescent: Women Petitioners in New Brunswick in the Mid-19th Century," *Acadiensis* 18(2) (Spring 1989), reprinted in Phillip A. Buckner and David Frank, eds., *Atlantic Canada Before Confederation*, 3rd ed. (Fredericton: Acadiensis Press, 1998), pp. 282–314; Sylvia Hamilton, "Naming Names, Naming Ourselves: A Survey of Early Black Women in Nova Scotia," in Peggy Bristow et al., eds.,*"We're Rooted Here and They Can't Pull Us Up": Essays in African Canadian Women's History* (Toronto: University of Toronto Press, 1994), pp. 13–40; and W.G. Godfrey, "'Into the Hands of the Ladies': The Birth of the Moncton Hospital," *Acadiensis* 27(1) (Autumn 1997).

Maritime political developments are examined in Phillip A. Buckner, *The Transition to Responsible Government: British Policy in British North America, 1815–1850* (Westport, CT: Greenwood Press, 1985). The American border dispute, resolved in the Webster–Ashburton Treaty of 1842, is reviewed by Francis M. Carroll, *A Good and Wise Measure. The Struggle for the Canadian–American Border, 1783–1842* (Toronto: University of Toronto Press, 2001). A short sketch of Joseph Howe appears in *Dictionary of Canadian Biography*, vol. 10, *1871–1880* (Toronto: University of Toronto Press, 1972), pp. 362–70, in an entry by Murray Beck, who has also written the two-volume study *Joseph Howe* (Montreal/Kingston: McGill-Queen's University Press, 1982–83). John Ross Robertson examines Prince Edward Island's complicated land question in *The Prince Edward Island Commission of 1860* (Fredericton: Acadiensis Press, 1988).

Greg Marquis looks at the Maritime colonies during the American Civil War in *In Armageddon's Shadow: The Civil War and Canada's Maritime Provinces* (Montreal/Kingston: McGill-Queen's University Press, 1998). Important portraits of Maritime political, economic, and cultural leaders appear in the volumes of *Dictionary of Canadian Biography* devoted to the nineteenth century. It is now available online: www.bibliographi.ca. For a look at the Fenian threat in Prince Edward Island, see Edward Macdonald, "Who's Afraid of the Fenians? The Fenian Scare on Prince Edward Island, 1865–1867," *Acadiensis* 38(1) (2009): 33–51.

The peoples of the Maritimes in the late eighteenth and nineteenth centuries are the subject of several studies. On the history of the Aboriginal peoples of the Maritimes, see Harald E.L. Prins, *The Mi'kmaq: Resistance, Accommodation, and Cultural Survival* (Fort Worth, TX: Harcourt Brace, 1996); L.F.S. Upton, *Micmacs and Colonists: Indian–White Relations in the Maritimes, 1713–1867* (Vancouver: University of British Columbia Press, 1979); and Maura Hanrahan, "Resisting Colonialism in Nova Scotia: The Kesukwitk Mi'kmaq, Centralization, and Residential Schooling," *Native Studies Review* 17(1) (2008): 25–44. Daniel N. Paul provides an Aboriginal perspective in *We Were Not the Savages: First Nations History*, 3rd ed. (Halifax: Fernwood, 2000).

For a study of the Acadians on Prince Edward Island, see Georges Arsenault's *The Island Acadians, 1720–1980* (Charlottetown: Ragweed Press, 1989). Charles Dunn's classic *Highland Settler: A Portrait of the Scottish Gael in Nova Scotia* (Toronto: University of Toronto Press, 1953) and D. Campbell and R.A. MacLean, *Beyond the Atlantic Roar: A Study of the Nova Scotia Scots* (Toronto: McClelland & Stewart, 1974), deal with the Scots in Nova Scotia. A number of works have appeared on the history of the Irish in British North America. Scott W. See's *Riots in New Brunswick: Orange Nativism and Social Violence in the 1840s* (Toronto: University of Toronto Press, 1993) looks at social violence in the 1840s between Irish Catholics and Protestant Orangemen. Thomas P. Powell has edited *The Irish in Atlantic Canada, 1780–1900* (Fredericton: New Ireland Press, 1991). For a discussion of black Maritimers, consult Robin W. Winks, *The Blacks in Canada: A History*, 2nd ed. (Montreal/Kingston: McGill-Queen's University Press, 1997); and see W.A. Spray's "The Settlement of the Black Refugees in New Brunswick, 1815–1836," in Buckner and Frank, eds., *Atlantic Canada Before Confederation*, vol. 1, *The Acadiensis Reader*, 1st ed., pp. 148–64. An interesting study is James W. St. G. Walker, *The Black Loyalists: The Search for a Promised Land in Nova Scotia and Sierra Leone, 1783–1870* (Toronto: University of Toronto Press, 1992 [1976]). See also Jeffrey L. McNairn, "British Travellers, Nova Scotia's Black Communities and the Problem of Freedom to 1860," *Journal of the Canadian Historical Association* 19(1) (2008): 27–56.

For maps of the Maritimes in this period, consult R. Louis Gentilcore, ed., *The Historical Atlas of Canada*, vol. 2, *The Land Transformed, 1800–1891* (Toronto: University of Toronto Press, 1993).

Chapter Eighteen

NEWFOUNDLAND: THE LAND APART

TIME LINE

1583	Sir Humphrey Gilbert claims Newfoundland for England
1610	English establish first colony at Cupids
1620	French establish colony at former Basque haven of Plaisance
1696	Pierre Le Moyne d'Iberville ravages English settlements
1699	English government passes Newfoundland Act
1713	Britain gains control of Newfoundland in Treaty of Utrecht
1729	Admiral of fishing fleet made governor in summer months St. John's becomes capital
1763	Treaty of Paris gives France control of St. Pierre and Miquelon
1774	Labrador attached to Quebec
1784	British grant religious freedom
1800	Number of permanent residents reaches 20 000
1809	Labrador returned to Newfoundland's jurisdiction
1823	Newfoundland School Society founded
1824	Newfoundland gains colonial status
1829	Shawnadithit, last of the Beothuk, dies
1832	Newfoundland given representative government
1855	Britain grants responsible government to Newfoundland

The history of Newfoundland and Labrador goes back to Canada's earliest beginnings. It was this area that was first inhabited by the Dorset, the Innu, and then the Beothuk peoples. This was the zone of first contact between Europeans and First Nations when the Norse expedition of Leif Erikson arrived around A.D. 1000. It was this island and its coasts that European explorers first encountered in the "Age of Discovery." It was to Newfoundland that the fishing fleets of England, France, Spain, and Portugal sailed in the sixteenth century and began centuries of reaping the harvests of cod from the Grand Banks. Yet it was Newfoundland and Labrador that would remain distinctly separate from the rest of British North America.

Newfoundland offers a particularly sad story when it comes to the clash of European and First Nations civilizations. The Beothuks, the Aboriginal people of Newfoundland, were wiped out as a direct result of contact with the Europeans. Unlike the Mi'kmaqs in the Maritimes, the Beothuks did not establish a mutually beneficial trade relationship and military alliance with the newcomers. Instead they withdrew from the coastal areas where the Europeans set up shore stations and lost their access to the valuable coastal food supplies. They lost their traditional lifestyles and became weakened by starvation and European diseases. Within two centuries of the Europeans' arrival, the Beothuks were gone. The tragedy of the Beothuks provides a powerful lesson about contact. This Aboriginal group served no purpose to the Europeans; they were needed neither as fur trade partners nor as military allies. To make matters worse, they were on an island and had nowhere to flee. The results were tragic.

Like the Maritime colonies, Newfoundland was caught up in the colonial wars between France and England. After a half-century of conflict, France ceded Newfoundland to England by the Treaty of Utrecht in 1713. Powerful English merchants, mostly from Devon and Dorset in England's West Country, sought exclusive rights to the fishing grounds. They persuaded British monarchs and parliaments in the late seventeenth century to discourage additional permanent settlement on the island. In the eighteenth century, the British government finally sanctioned settlement. As a result, the island developed more slowly as a colony. It was only early in the nineteenth century that the island had a permanent population of more than 40 000 people. But the interests of this population were always eastward and southward to the sea. Their livelihood depended on exporting fish and on trade with Britain, the Mediterranean countries, and the West Indies. Newfoundland remained apart from the affairs of the other British North American colonies.

Early Settlement in Newfoundland

Five hundred years after the Norse settlements at L'Anse aux Meadows, fishermen from England, Ireland, France, Portugal, and Spain began accessing the rich cod pools off the Grand Banks. The English, under Sir Humphrey Gilbert, claimed Newfoundland in 1583. The remains of Basque whaling stations from this early period have been discovered at Red Bay.

By the early seventeenth century, England emerged as the dominant player in the Newfoundland fishery. Relative to England's colonies and France's possessions along the St. Lawrence, Newfoundland lacked Crown oversight and was instead left to privateers. On the high seas, many dangers awaited the English mariners, including fog, floating ice, and pirates. During the early seventeenth century, the "Barbary Rovers," North African Muslims who sailed along the coasts of Europe, allied with France and extended their operations as far as the English Channel. There they waited for the unarmed ships from Newfoundland to return to Britain. They sold the sailors into slavery except those needed to work on the pirate ships. The town of Poole in Dorset, which sent out twenty ships annually to Newfoundland, lost one-quarter of its fleet in a four-year period. Only after an Anglo–Dutch mission bombarded the pirates' North African headquarters in the late seventeenth century did the danger to English shipping diminish.

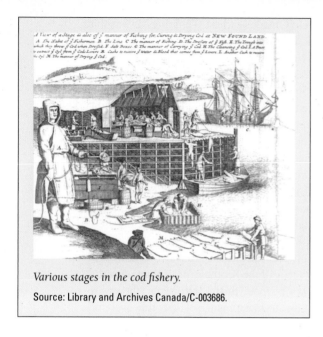

Various stages in the cod fishery.
Source: Library and Archives Canada/C-003686.

The London and Bristol Company

In 1610, a group of English merchants formed the London and Bristol Company. A "governor," John Guy, was dispatched to Newfoundland with 40 men to establish the island's first colony at Cupids on Conception Bay, 35 kilometres west of St. John's. The Company hoped that a settlement would offer an advantage over the rival fishers by being there at the beginning of the season. The settlement experiment, however, failed to produce the desired results. The Company did not produce a more fruitful harvest of cod and the costs of maintaining the settlement cut into profits. In addition, the rocky soil around Cupids had almost no agricultural potential, so settlers could not grow grain and their cattle died from lack of fodder. The Company also hoped that the island could produce mineral resources or establish a fur trade with the Beothuks, but both enterprises failed, leading to the colony's demise.

Ferryland

Another drawback to colonization was the weather. Lord Baltimore gained title to Ferryland, south of St. John's, in 1621. But after wintering on the island in 1628–29, his enthusiasm waned. Newfoundland in the seventeenth century was clearly not a place to raise a family: "I have sent them home after much sufferance in this wofull country, where with one intolerable wynter were we almost undone. It is not to be expressed with my pen what wee have endured." Lord Baltimore redirected his colonizing efforts southward to Virginia, where he received a charter to what became known as Maryland. Some of the Newfoundland settlers remained behind after the colony disintegrated, making Ferryland one of the oldest continuously inhabited settlements of English origin in the Americas. Despite the failures of the private companies, England attempted to secure a permanent foothold in Newfoundland, believing that whoever controlled settlement would control the fisheries.

Plaisance

The French also began a colony in Newfoundland. In the 1620s they founded Plaisance (present-day Placentia) on the southern coast, at the site of a former Basque whaling and drying station. The Basques used the abundant beach rocks to dry the fish rather than construct wooden stages. In 1655 the French, who now controlled half the island, made Plaisance their capital. It remained a small community, with only about 250 permanent residents by 1700.

Fishing Outpost

Without a concerted effort on behalf of either the English or French governments to establish permanent colonies, the population of the island grew slowly. By 1650, an estimated 500 English residents, including 350 women and children, lived in about forty settlements scattered along the eastern coast between Cape Bonavista and Trepassey. The population increased to an estimated

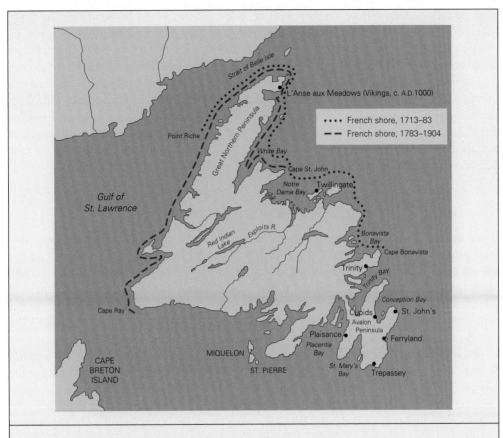

Early Newfoundland.

Source: Adapted from P.G. Cornell, J. Hamelin, F. Ouellet, and M. Trudel, *Canada: Unity in Diversity* (Toronto: Holt, Rinehart and Winston, 1967), p. 111.

2000 by 1680 and consisted of two groups: descendants of settlers brought out by colonizers such as John Guy and Lord Baltimore, and "bye-boatmen" from England's West Country, who came out as passengers on the fishing ships and returned in the autumn. They worked for the settlers or merchants who owned the bye-boats, the small fishing vessels left in Newfoundland harbours for use in the spring. As time went on, many of these skilled fishers remained in Newfoundland during the winter. Frequently, they stayed for several years, and some became permanent settlers.

But without an organized government on the island, the settlers and the bye-boatmen faced difficult times. They had to earn their living during the short season of cod fishing in the summer because there was no employment in the winter. When the fishing fleet departed in September or early October, it left the isolated communities on their own until the following spring. If food ran out, the communities starved. No births, marriages, or burials could be legally registered, since no clergy lived on the island between 1650 and 1702. The island had no law officers or courts because it had no official status as a colony. It was also vulnerable to constant attack by privateers.

Newfoundland posed a difficult problem for the English government in the late 1600s. On the one hand, England wanted a permanent colony because it would enforce England's claim to Newfoundland and make the island less vulnerable to being seized by France, which already controlled Acadia and New France. According to historian Frederick W. Rowe, three-quarters of the 10 000-kilometre coastline "was already, in effect, almost wholly under the control of the world's most powerful country. How long would it be before France would be occupying the entire Island of Newfoundland?"[1] On the other hand, England enjoyed the benefits of not supporting a colony. The Royal Navy relied on the annual fishing voyages to train its crews and maintain ships. In addition, the British feared that a Newfoundland resident fishery would end the English migratory fishery, as had been the case in New England. The English government resolved this dilemma in 1699. It formally recognized the permanent settlers on the island, but forbade them to encroach on the areas of the migratory fishers. It also announced that no government would be established on the island. The Act to Encourage Trade to Newfoundland, or the Newfoundland Act, the first English statute pertaining to the island, remained its only constitution for the next 125 years, until it became a British colony in 1824.

The Imperial Struggle for Newfoundland

While the English began settlements on the eastern Avalon Peninsula, the French claimed Newfoundland's south shore. In 1662, the French fortified Plaisance. The deep, ice-free harbour offered an excellent refuge for French ships and fish could be dried on its rocky beaches. But the rocky soil was not suited for agriculture. To build up settlement, the French government initially provided free passage and one year's financial support to settlers migrating to Plaisance. In the early 1670s, however, large-scale French assistance ceased, just as it did in New France. The colony's development ground to a halt.

Newfoundland became an inevitable theatre in the imperial conflict between England and France. With France controlling Quebec and Acadia, the island held strategic importance at the gateway to the St. Lawrence. War broke out in 1689. In 1694, Newfoundland's French Governor, de Brouillon, ordered a naval squadron under Chevalier Nesmond to lay siege to St. John's in retaliation for earlier English attacks. While the siege failed, two years later the French attacked again under the leadership of Pierre Le Moyne d'Iberville, sent from New France by Governor Frontenac. Attacking by both land and sea, New France's greatest soldier laid waste the English settlements in Newfoundland, killing 200 people and taking 700 prisoners. But an English expedition in 1697 recaptured all the settlements.

By the Treaty of Utrecht in 1713, England gained control of the entire island. The French ceded Plaisance and their evacuation of the port was complete by 1714, except for a small number of residents who accepted English rule and stayed behind. Many of the Plaisance evacuees were relocated to Île Royale (Cape Breton Island). The French also ceded Acadia to England. While France renounced its claim to Newfoundland, it retained the right to dry cod on what came to be known as the French Shore—between Cape Bonavista and Point Riche in the northeastern bays and around the Great Northern Peninsula, to a point located about a quarter of the way down the west coast, an area approximating one-third of Newfoundland's coastline.

By an Anglo–French agreement in 1783, Cape Ray, on the island's southwestern tip, was substituted for Point Riche and the eastern boundary moved from Cape Bonavista to Cape St. John. The French Shore now encompassed the entire west coast, the Great Northern Peninsula, and White Bay. British fishers were not allowed to interrupt the French fishery in that area, and the French disputed their right to settle there. The question of the French Shore troubled Anglo–French relations for nearly two centuries, until England purchased French landing rights in 1904.

Newfoundland now served as an essential British naval check on the French possessions of Louisbourg on Cape Breton Island. On account of French naval strength, Newfoundland remained in danger of French attack until the end of the colonial wars in 1763. In 1762, the French successfully captured St. John's, although the English recaptured the town the following year. When the Treaty of Paris ended hostilities in 1763, France's landing rights were reaffirmed, and to compensate for the loss of French fishing bases in Cape Breton, Britain ceded the islands of St. Pierre and Miquelon off Newfoundland to France, "to serve as a shelter to the French fisherman."

Law and Order in Eighteenth-Century Newfoundland

The lack of government in Newfoundland left law and order to the private companies and fishing fleets. As early as the seventeenth century, competition for favourable harbours reached such an intensity that the fishing fleets worked out the "fishing admiral system," a rough-and-ready means of keeping some kind of order in the harbours. This rough system of justice proved detrimental to the Beothuk, who competed with the settlers for food resources and endured poor relations with the fishers.

The Fishing Admiral System

To the first ship in a port, regardless of nationality, went the right to take the best fishing spot or strip of beach. The first ship's captain became the "fishing admiral," with the responsibility to maintain law and order in each harbour. The admiral's authority rested on his ability to maintain control. If he had a sizable and well-armed vessel and a large crew, he could enforce his will.

In 1634, the English government confirmed the admiral system in the First Western Charter, the first act regulating the Newfoundland fishery. The Newfoundland Act of 1699 again affirmed the rights and the authority of the fishing admirals. The system, however, had several serious defects. First, the admirals stayed for only three or four months in the spring and summer; for the rest of the year, no one was authorized to maintain law and order. Second, even when present, the admirals had no way of enforcing their rulings, and as settlement grew, the problems they had to resolve became more complex. Third, as the admirals received no payment for presiding over the courts and, since they had come primarily to fish, they had little interest in enforcing the law. Conditions on the island degenerated rapidly under the fishing admiral system. In the long period between the departure of the ships in the late summer and their return the next year, those guilty of murder, rape, and robbery had ample opportunity to escape.

Historian Keith Matthews offers two explanations for England's delay in establishing a proper legal system.[2] The establishment of law and other services on the island would have encouraged further permanent settlement, something the government opposed. In addition, the placement of law-enforcement officers in many parts of the island would have involved serious expenditures for the British government.

In 1729, Britain made a modest improvement in the system. The commander of the annual naval convoy to Newfoundland became the island's governor and commander-in-chief, but he lived on a ship and remained in Newfoundland only during the summer fishing season. Whenever the governor deemed a local regulation desirable, he could issue a proclamation, and his word became law. As governor, he also had the right to appoint magistrates from among the most respected local residents. The magistrates gained an increasing jurisdiction, both in terms of the nature of the cases they could hear and the time of year they would hear them.

A Fishing Station *by Gerard van Edema.*

Source: With permission of the Royal Ontario Museum © ROM, 957.91.

The Beothuks

The Beothuks suffered from the presence of the newcomers. *Beothuk* means "people," and was the term that the Aboriginals applied to themselves. While it was likely the ancestors of this group that contacted the Norse in the 11th century, the Beothuks first encountered European fishers in the sixteenth century. Population estimates at the time of contact vary from 500 to 700. The Beothuks lived in extended family groups numbering from 30 to 55 people. From their use of red ochre to decorate their bodies, clothing, and utensils during a spring celebration, the early Europeans called them "Red Indians."

Unlike the Mi'kmaqs in the Maritimes, who adjusted to living near the French, the Beothuks withdrew from the newcomers. Evidence indicates that they gathered and pillaged metal goods left by the fishing fleets to fashion into their own tools. This may help explain why the Beothuks never participated in a fur trade with the Europeans. The English under John Guy attempted to establish trade with the Beothuk in 1610, but the enterprise failed. The Mi'kmaqs also made life difficult for the Beothuk. In 1613 a conflict led to 37 French fishers being killed by Beothuk. The French invited the Mi'kmaqs onto the island for protection, but the presence of another Aboriginal group increased competition for food resources.

Beothuk foodstuffs included caribou, salmon, seals, and deer, and they followed their prey in migratory routes. With the increasing number of European fishers, however, it became difficult by the mid-seventeenth century for the Beothuks to gain access to their seaside summer campsites and, hence, to their food resources, particularly on the eastern and southern coasts. They increasingly retreated to the interior and food supplies became even more scarce. Starvation became common and made the Beothuks more vulnerable to European diseases.

The situation for the Beothuks worsened in the early 1700s as European settlement increased in the northeast and the interior. A salmon fishery was established near the river mouths of northeastern Newfoundland. Settlers began to trap fur-bearing animals in the interior; and the spring seal hunt, which was best operated from the northeastern coast, grew rapidly. The British settlers became seal hunters in the spring, salmon catchers in the summer, and trappers in the winter, thus depriving the Beothuks of their traditional sources of food and clothing.

Conflict between the Beothuks and the Europeans

When the Beothuks encountered the Europeans on the northeastern coast, violence often erupted. The settlers harassed them and raided their camps. George Cartwright, a prominent merchant in Labrador, provided a warning to the Colonial Office in 1784:

> Instead of a friendly intercourse with these Indians, our people dispossessed them from beaches and salmon rivers and it is now well known, that the poor Indians are put to the greatest difficulties to procure a scanty subsistence. If some effectual measures will not be taken, that unhappy race of mortals will soon be extirpated, to the disgrace of our Government, our country and our religion.

The Beothuks retaliated. According to contemporary reports and oral traditions, the Beothuks killed about a dozen settlers and wounded nearly as many more between 1750 and 1790. The settlers took their own revenge, killing and wounding Beothuks, and destroying their conical dwellings known as *mamateeks*. Lack of firearms put the Beothuks at a distinct disadvantage in these confrontations.

The violence continued unchecked but there was only a rudimentary legal system to punish transgressions. As a result, the culprits remained at large, unpunished. Even when murder trials were held at St. John's in the mid-eighteenth century, the court made few convictions.

Several naval officers and settlers in the late eighteenth and early nineteenth centuries worried about the Beothuks and their fate. A number of attempts to reach the Beothuks, who lived and hunted along the Exploits River from the interior down to Notre Dame Bay, failed, but one in 1811 succeeded. After trekking for twelve days up the Exploits River in heavy snow and subzero temperatures, Captain David Buchan and his party of 27 made contact with a band of about 40 Beothuks. The Beothuks remained suspicious and killed the two men left behind with them as hostages.

Attempts to locate the Beothuks the following summer failed. Apparently, many Beothuks had died, most likely from starvation, smallpox, and tuberculosis. From evidence accumulated by anthropologist Ingeborg Marshall, it appears that a few Beothuks joined the Mi'kmaqs in the southern part of the island, either voluntarily or because they were kidnapped.[3]

Demasduwit, a young Beothuk woman, was taken captive in 1819 by an expedition led by John Peyton Jr. During the capture, Demasduwit's husband and brother were killed, and her baby died after the mother was taken away. Peyton received a bounty for the capture of Demasduwit and it was hoped that the woman would learn English, teach the Beothuk language, and then serve as a liaison between the two peoples. But Demasduwit survived only a year and died of tuberculosis.

In 1823, three starving Beothuk women were captured. Both the mother and one of her two daughters died shortly after of tuberculosis. But the second daughter, Shawnadithit, a young woman between 16 and 20 and niece to Demasduwit, survived for six years. Shawnadithit lived at first as a servant in the household of John Peyton, but spent the last year of her life in St. John's, informing William Cormack about her people's culture, history, and language. Shawnadithit died on June 6, 1829 of tuberculosis. Apart from a few Beothuks who may have lived with the Mi'kmaqs, she was the last of her people.

A HISTORICAL PORTRAIT

Demasduwit

The story of Demasduwit, or Mary March as she was named in English, is one of the most authenticated of all Beothuk captivity stories. In March 1819, a group of ten armed settlers from Notre Dame Bay, out on a mission to recover stolen property, encountered a small party of Beothuks at Red Indian Lake in the interior. A fight ensued, in which the settlers killed Nonosbawsut, the chief, and captured his wife, Demasduwit. The settlers took the woman in the hope that she could be taught to speak English and might become an agent of contact with her people. In carrying her off, they separated her from her only child, a young baby, who died soon after. Taken to Twillingate on Notre Dame Bay, Demasduwit was placed in the care of the local Anglican missionary, the Rev. John Leigh. Demasduwit was named Mary March, her second name referring to the month of her capture. Twice she tried to escape, but after some weeks the young Beothuk woman appeared to accept her situation. When spring navigation opened on the coast, she was brought to St. John's, where she met the governor, Vice-Admiral Sir Charles Hamilton.

The governor seemed genuinely concerned about the fate of the Beothuks.

Appalled by the killings during her capture, he brought the perpetrators before the grand jury. But the jury accepted the settlers' story that they had not intended to kill the Beothuks, but had acted in self-defence. While Demasduwit stayed in St. John's, the governor's wife, Lady Henrietta Hamilton, a skilled artist, painted a watercolour portrait of her.

Sir Charles decided to return Demasduwit to her people. He hoped that she would become an intermediary between the settlers and the Beothuks. She was returned to Notre Dame Bay, but in a weakened state from tuberculosis. Although in poor physical condition, she joined several search parties looking for Beothuks at their summer stations near the mouth of the Exploits River. After these expeditions proved unsuccessful, the English decided that they would travel directly to Red Indian Lake.

Demasduwit did not live to see her home or people again. She died in early January. The military expedition returned her body, which they left in early February at the deserted Beothuk camp where she had been captured the previous year.

Shawnadithit, Demasduwit's niece, was taken captive three years later, in 1823. She learned a considerable amount of English during the six years that she remained among the settlers, until her death from tuberculosis in 1829. Her testimony provided additional insight into the story of Demasduwit. She had witnessed

Demasduwit.

Source: Library and Archives Canada/C-092599.

her aunt's capture and her uncle's killing. Shawnadithit also explained that the baby had died several days after being separated from its mother.

In 1976, a painting of a First Nations woman came up for sale in a New York auction house. The National Archives of Canada authenticated it as Lady Hamilton's miniature of Mary March, the only known portrait of a Beothuk. Lady Hamilton's portrait of a gentle and melancholy Demasduwit serves as a reminder of her personal tragedy, as well as that of her people.

Population Growth and Settlement

At the end of the eighteenth century, Newfoundland's population began to increase. The number of permanent residents increased from 2300 in 1730, to 20 000 in 1800, to 40 000 in 1830. As late as 1797, resident men outnumbered women five to one. As the settlers built dwellings and warehouses, and used increasing amounts of firewood, the forests rapidly disappeared. According to geographer Grant Head, the coastal forests were replaced by a "clutter of stages, flakes, boats, ships, warehouses, dwellings, vegetable patches, wandering cattle, and snaking trails."[4] Historical geographers R. Cole Harris and John Warkentin suggest that "the influence of

Europeans on the native flora and fauna of the northeastern rim of North America may have been almost as devastating as in the islands and perimeter of the Caribbean."[5]

Much of the population growth came from a large influx of immigrants, chiefly Irish. The first potato famines in the 1720s and 1730s led thousands of Irish to seek refuge across the Atlantic. Newfoundland became the first place in the New World to receive large numbers. Cheap transportation, the promise of work, and poor conditions at home brought them to the island. By the 1750s, Irish Catholics made up half the Avalon Peninsula's total population, and by the 1830s, they numbered half the entire island's population.

The Irish Catholic immigrants had little love for England, which had invaded Ireland repeatedly, seized Irish lands, and then proscribed the Roman Catholic religion. The English, likewise, had little love for the Irish and refused to allow Catholic priests on the island. Not until 1784 did the governor grant religious freedom. That same year, the first "legal" priest arrived in St. John's to minister openly to the Irish Catholics.

Mistrusting each other, the Irish and the English communities segregated themselves geographically. In the larger towns, such as St. John's, they lived in separate neighbourhoods. Intermarriages were rare. When the Irish Catholics moved away from the Avalon Peninsula, they settled in harbours not occupied by English Protestants.

As the population expanded, the economy diversified from the sole reliance on the shore cod fishery. The development of salmon fishing and sealing led to an expansion of settlement to the northern bays of the island. Settlers occupied hundreds of coves, harbours, and islands chosen for their proximity to the fishing grounds. They began to farm the Avalon Peninsula's scattered pockets of fertile land.

The Rise of St. John's

In the late eighteenth century, St. John's became the dominant urban centre on the island and the capital in 1729, when the British naval convoy commander was made governor. A number of St. John's settlers left the fishery to open taverns and stores, servicing the needs of the thousands of fishers who came to the island annually. An English garrison was also located in the town. As a result, the population of St. John's increased from about 1000 in 1790 to more than 5000 in 1810.

At first glance, St. John's, situated at the extreme eastern tip of the island, seems an odd choice as the island's major commercial centre. It was, however, located in Newfoundland's most densely populated area—the Avalon Peninsula, an area larger than Prince Edward Island. The peninsula itself was strategically located, being almost equidistant between the chief ports of England and New England. It was "the natural stepping stone between the old world and the new."[6] In addition, the peninsula lay immediately west of the North Atlantic's best fishing grounds—the Grand Banks.

The importance of St. John's increased in the late eighteenth and early nineteenth centuries. The governor made the town his headquarters. The establishment of the Newfoundland Supreme Court in 1792 and of customs and naval offices further raised the town's standing. After the American Revolution, merchants involved in the Canada and West Indies trade established themselves in St. John's. The town's merchants and ship owners financed the fishing trade, marketed dried cod, and distributed foodstuffs and manufactured goods to the outports. The merchants at St. John's, who were involved in exporting cod, directed the island's affairs by acting as suppliers to the smaller merchants and fishers in the outports. A small group of generally Protestant St. John's merchants controlled the fishery in the mid-nineteenth century.

As the town's wealth grew, newspapers, health services, and schools were established. Consequently, St. John's became the only community on the island with an educated and moderately wealthy middle class. The capital, however, could not escape its reliance on the fisheries. George Warburton, an Irish soldier and writer, visited St. John's in the mid-1840s on a tour of British

North America. In his book *Hochelaga; or, England in the New World* (1846), he described it as the "fishiest" capital in the world.

> *In trying to describe St. John's there is some difficulty in applying to it an adjective sufficiently distinctive and appropriate. We find other cities coupled with epithets which at once give their predominant characteristic: London the richest, Paris the gayest, St. Petersburg the coldest. In one respect the chief town of Newfoundland has, I believe, no rival: we may therefore call it the fishiest of modern capitals. Round a great part of the harbour are sheds, acres in extent, roofed with cod split in half, laid on like slates, drying in the sun, or rather the air, for there is not much of the former to depend upon. Those ships, bearing nearly every flag in the world, are laden with cod; those stout weatherly boats crowding up to the wharves have just now returned from fishing for cod; those few scant fields of cultivation, with lean crops coaxed out of the barren soil, are manured with cod; those grim, snug-looking wooden houses, their handsome furniture, the piano and the musical skill of the young lady who plays it, the satin gown of the mother, the gold chain of the father, are all paid for in cod; the breezes from the shore, soft and warm on this bright August day, are rich not with the odours of a thousand flowers but of a thousand cod. Earth, sea and air are alike pervaded with this wonderful fish.*

St. John's from Signal Hill, 1831.

Source: Library and Archives Canada, Acc. No. 1970-188-1508. W.H. Coverdale Collection of Canadiana/C-041605.

The Outports

Life was harsher in the outports. Jacob Mountain, a young Anglican priest, discovered as much during his seven years of missionary work on Newfoundland's south coast. There is no such thing, he wrote in his posthumously published *Some Accounts of a Sowing Time on the Rugged Shores of Newfoundland* (1857), as a typical Newfoundland fishing village:

Newfoundland coastal fishing village, about 1857.

Source: Paul-Émile Miot/Library and Archives Canada/ Photographie acquise avec le support financier du minstère du Patrimoine dans le cadre de la loi sur l'importation et l'exportation de biens culturels/PA-188225.

> *In one place you will find them clean, tidy, thriving; houses neatly and substantially built, and a certain air of sobriety and self-respect about the people, the children a picture of delight, with their beautiful eyes, well-formed faces, soft flaxen hair. In another close by, the very reverse of all this; houses, or rather hovels of studs, the crevices gaping wide or filled with moss, the roof covered with rinds of trees and sods, the entrance constructed by heaps of dirt, often nothing that deserved the name of door, the aperture so low that one must stoop to enter, the interior without any furniture but a low*

table and rough stool, scarcely raised three inches from the ground, the children wretchedly ragged and dirty, crouching round, or creeping into the smoky wood fire, an old sail and a few more studs forming the only partition between the kitchen and sleeping-room, if such terms can be applied to such miserable dens.

Scattered along 10 000 kilometres of coast, the population of almost all of Newfoundland's distant and remote coves and harbours lived without clergy or schoolteachers. A rich and varied language developed on account of this isolation. Numerous words and phrases survive in Newfoundland that are found only—if anywhere—in dialects of the British Isles. Residents of various Newfoundland outports can still be distinguished from one another by their accents, which hark back to western England or Ireland.

In the outports, women worked alongside men. While Newfoundland's population was heavily male-dominated and the fishing industry is characterized as inherently rough and masculine, women played an essential if largely undocumented role. At the beginning of the seventeenth century, the proportion of women was only 10 percent and children made up only 25 percent of the population. By the beginning of the eighteen century, the numbers were reaching "normal" proportions. While labour was divided according to gender, these lines were often blurred and women played a critical role in the functioning of the fisheries. "The colony depended on the export of saltfish, or salted dried cod fish, and it was often women who processed on shore the fish that men caught."[7] In effect, they ran the fisheries on shore but because their work was often not considered "productive" by economic standards, it has largely been ignored.

Religion and Education

Organized religion came to Newfoundland in the eighteenth century. The Anglicans arrived in 1703 with the appointment of John Jackson as the first missionary in Newfoundland for the Society for the Propagation of the Gospel in Foreign Parts (SPG). During the 1700s, two or three Anglican clergy were stationed on the island. Catholic priests arrived and worked secretly before freedom of worship was granted in 1784. After this date, other Protestant churches, such as the Methodists and the Congregationalists, also organized. On the Labrador coast, Moravian missionaries began their work among the Inuit in 1771.

With both church and state coming to Newfoundland so late, no schools existed until the eighteenth century. The Society for the Propagation of the Gospel organized the first schools for the poor and underprivileged. Later, the Wesleyan Methodists and other groups opened schools. Most children, however, had no schooling and remained illiterate. The availability of education improved with the foundation of the Newfoundland School Society in 1823. The society, which was closely identified with the Church of England, provided free grants of land on which to build schools, and free passage to the colony for teachers. It operated forty schools in the decades to follow. In the larger towns, particularly St. John's, the upper classes had private tutors and private schools and, in a few cases, sent their children off to be educated in England, since "respectable classes" did not want their children mixing with the "lower orders" in the SPG or Methodist schools.

From a Migratory to a Resident Fishery

In the first decades of the 1800s, Newfoundland increasingly became a "resident" rather than a "migratory" colony. For this to happen, the fishery—the economic mainstay of the island—had to become more permanently fixed. As long as the fishing fleets were based out of England and France, the population remained migratory. This essential characteristic changed when the American Revolution and the Napoleonic Wars influenced Newfoundland's fishing and trading patterns.

The sealing fleet leaving St. John's, Newfoundland.

Source: Drawn by Schell and Hogan from a sketch by J.W. Hayward, for *Harper's Weekly*, April 5, 1884

The end of the American Revolution in 1783 also ended New England's role in the British empire's carrying trade, and Newfoundland became the major supplier of fish to the British West Indies. Fishery production expanded, creating new jobs and, in turn, causing a sharp decline in emigration from Newfoundland to New England. Newfoundland ships and ports became an integral part of the triangular trade with Britain and the West Indies. It was illegal for British subjects to own American-built ships, leading the islanders to costruct their own vessels.

The Napoleonic Wars (1793–1814) also contributed to the new prosperity of Newfoundland. The Atlantic became a war zone between Britain and France. The price of dried fish increased substantially during the later years of the war because the French had to abandon their Newfoundland fishery. France could not protect its fishing fleet in wartime when the country needed to mobilize all of its naval resources to fight Britain. The presence of the Royal Navy led to a more controlled fishing industry, because many English vessels stayed at home. Fears of press-gangs in England forcefully seizing sailors for service in the Royal Navy also convinced many of the bye-boatmen to remain on Newfoundland instead of returning to Britain. As a result, the resident population, and the fisheries, expanded.

During these prosperous years, a resident Newfoundland fleet was created for the first time. Local merchants began sending ships to less crowded parts of the coast, to the northern part of the island, and on to Labrador. Each June, thousands of Newfoundland fishers sailed for Labrador to catch cod. Those who fished out of fixed locations with a "room" on shore became known as the "stationers" (or "squatters" or "roomers"); those who lived aboard their schooners and followed the fish were the "floaters" (or "green fish catchers"); those who chose to settle permanently on the Labrador coast became the "livyers" (a corruption of "live here"). As the Labrador fishery expanded, Britain reattached Labrador to Newfoundland, taking it out of Lower Canada's control in 1809. Before the Napoleonic Wars, the English migratory fishery produced more than half the total Newfoundland catch. By 1815, residents owned almost the complete fishing fleet and produced the entire yield of saltfish. The end of the Napoleonic Wars, however, led to an economic recession in Newfoundland, just as it did in Britain.

The hardy outlook and independent spirit of these rough and tumble Newfoundlanders on the Labrador coast echoes forth today in a favourite chantey, "Jack Was Every Inch a Sailor," a retelling of the Biblical story of Jonah in the whale with a Newfoundlander as the hero.

'Twas twenty-five or thirty years since Jack first saw the light.
He came into this world of woe one dark and stormy night.
He was born on board his father's ship as she was lying to.
'Bout twenty-five or thirty miles southeast of Baccalieu.

Chorus
Jack was every inch a sailor, five and twenty years a whaler,
Jack was every inch a sailor, he was born upon the bright blue sea.

When Jack grew up to be a man, he went to the Labrador.
He fished in Indian Harbour, where his father fished before.
On his returning in the fog, he met a heavy gale,
And Jack was swept into the sea and swallowed by a whale.

Repeat Chorus
The whale went straight for Baffin's Bay,
about ninety knots an hour,
And every time he'd blow a spray he'd send
it in a shower.
"O, now," says Jack unto himself, "I must
see what he's about."
He caught the whale all by the tail and
turned him inside out.

Repeat Chorus

The Seal Hunt

Sailors entered the waters off Newfoundland and Labrador's northern coasts to hunt the seal herds on the ice floes. Mammals and fish provided the bulk of the world's industrial oil in the early nineteenth century, and young seals produced ideal fat for fine-quality oil. Their skins could also be sold in Britain. The industry grew rapidly to take advantage of profitable markets. Between 1831 and 1833, the seal hunt produced between 30 and 40 percent of Newfoundland's total exports. More than 600 000 seals were harvested in 1831 alone. By the 1850s, 13 000 men were employed annually in the hunt. The industry supplemented the production of salt cod. But the lure of profits led to overhunting by the 1860s. The industry declined.

Dory and Crew Setting Cod Trawl-Lines on the Bank *by H.W. Elliott and Captain J.W. Collins.*

Source: G.B. Goode, *The Fisheries and Fishing of the United States* (Washington, 1887), plate 26. Reproduced in R. Louis Gentilcore, ed., *Historical Atlas of Canada, vol. 2, The Land Transformed,* 1800–1891 (Toronto: University of Toronto Press, 1993), plate 37. Reprinted by permission of the University of Toronto Press Incorporated.

Political Changes in the Nineteenth Century

As late as 1832, Newfoundland was unique among the British North American colonies in that it had no legislature and the naval governor still wielded vast powers. The resident population was rapidly increasing, however, and pressure mounted for normal colonial structures. By the early nineteenth century, the new mercantile and professional elite of St. John's led the push for social and political reform. The recession in Newfoundland's economy after the Napoleonic Wars began a debate as to the colony's future and created an atmosphere for reform. The objective was to shift power away from the naval governor and toward representative institutions; responsible government seemed far off in the distance. Cut off from regular communication with the capital, the outports remained isolated from the struggle.

The Rise of a Reform Movement

A Scottish physician, William Carson, who had come to St. John's in 1808, led the Reform movement. In his first tract, written three years after his arrival, he argued against the system of naval governors and called for constitutional reform. The first advance came in 1817 when Newfoundland was recognized as more than a summer fishery. The Colonial Office decided that the governor should

Sealers "copying" the floes (leaping from floe to floe), c. 1920.
Source: Provincial Archives of Newfoundland and Labrador.

William Carson, leader of Newfoundland's reform movement. Artist unknown.

Source: The Rooms Provincial Archives Division, A 23-91, Dr. William Carson [reproduced 193-?], Alfred Bishop Morine fonds.

remain on the island all year round and not just for two or three months in the summer. Then, in 1824, Britain recognized Newfoundland as a regular colony and abolished the naval government. Carson and other Reformers turned their attention to legal reform. Britain repealed the old fishing laws, an action that, among other things, allowed residents to hold clear title to land. In 1832 Britain instituted representative government. Parliament made provision for a Newfoundland legislature with elected and appointed chambers. Almost all of the male residents of the island gained the franchise.

The rapid pace of political reform heightened internal dissension between Protestants and Catholics (now almost evenly divided in number), between English and Irish, between reformers and conservatives, between merchants and fishers, and between St. John's and the outports. By the mid 1830s, this dissension plagued the new government and led to political deadlock. The Rebellions in the Canadas in 1837–8 spurred the push for responsible government in Newfoundland, but divisions among the Reformers now thwarted progress. In 1842, the Colonial Office experimented with an Amalgamated Legislature, consisting of eleven elected members and ten Crown appointees. This move reduced the Reformers to a small minority until Britain restored the two-chamber system in 1848.

With William Carson's death in 1843, the Reform movement lost momentum, but it revived in 1850 with a platform of obtaining responsible government. Carson's successors, such as John Kent, a fiery Reform politician, demanded that the island obtain responsible government. This goal was achieved in 1855.

SUMMARY

As the majority of British North America pondered federation, Newfoundland's gaze was fixed eastward, out to sea, and toward Britain. The island felt little kinship with the Maritime colonies and no connection to the mainland and the Canadas. Newfoundland's patterns of trade and settlement linked it to Britain, the West Indies, and the United States. The island's distinctive geography and distinctive history placed it very much apart: "In many ways it was an integral part of British North America, but in others it remained as remote as Bermuda had been from the thirteen colonies."[8]

NOTES

1. Frederick W. Rowe, *A History of Newfoundland and Labrador* (Toronto: McGraw-Hill Ryerson, 1980), p. 109.

2. See Keith Matthews's comments on the growth of law in Newfoundland in *Lectures on the History of Newfoundland, 1500–1830* (St. John's: Breakwater Books, 1988), pp. 131–50.

3. Ingeborg Marshall, *A History and Ethnography of the Beothuk* (Montreal/Kingston: McGill-Queen's University Press, 1996), pp. 157–58.

4. C. Grant Head, *Eighteenth Century Newfoundland: A Geographer's Perspective* (Toronto: McClelland & Stewart, 1976), p. 245.

5. R. Cole Harris and John Warkentin, *Canada before Confederation: A Study in Historical Geography* (Ottawa: Carleton University Press, 1991 [1974], p. 6.

6. William Menzies Whitelaw, *The Maritimes and Canada Before Confederation* (Toronto: Oxford University Press, 1966 [1934]), p. 29.

7. Ian Ross Robertson, "The 1850s: Maturity and Reform," in Phillip A. Buckner and John G. Reid, eds., *The Atlantic Region to Confederation* (Toronto: University of Toronto Press, 1994), p. 353.

8. Whitelaw, *The Maritimes and Canada*, p. 28.

BIBLIOGRAPHY

Frederick W. Rowe's *A History of Newfoundland and Labrador* (Toronto: McGraw-Hill Ryerson, 1980) remains a good study of Newfoundland's history. Peter Neary and Patrick O'Flaherty provide a short introduction to the island's history in their popular work *Part of the Main: An Illustrated History of Newfoundland and Labrador* (St. John's: Breakwater Books, 1983). Margaret R. Conrad and James K. Hiller, *Atlantic Canada: A Region in the Making* (Don Mills, ON: Oxford University Press, 2001), contains valuable references to Newfoundland and Labrador. Mark Kurlansky's popular "biography of the fish that changed the world" is good: *Cod* (New York: Penguin, 1998).

For a valuable biographical guide to the historical literature, consult Olaf Uwe Janzen's essay, "Newfoundland and the International Fishery," in M. Brook Taylor, ed., *Canadian History: A Reader's Guide*, vol. 1, *Beginnings to Confederation* (Toronto: University of Toronto Press, 1994), pp. 280–324. Important maps of Newfoundland and the fisheries before 1800 appear in R. Cole Harris, ed., *Historical Atlas of Canada*, vol. 1, *From the Beginning to 1800* (Toronto: University of Toronto Press, 1987). G.O. Rothney has written a short survey, *Newfoundland: A History* (Ottawa: Canadian Historical Association, 1964). For a pictorial history of Newfoundland, see Joan Sullivan's book *Newfoundland Portfolio: A History in Portraits*. (St John's: Jesperson, 2006).

Studies on the history of Newfoundland in the pre-nineteenth-century period include Gillian T. Cell, *English Enterprise in Newfoundland, 1577–1660* (Toronto: University of Toronto Press, 1969); Keith Matthews, *Lectures on the History of Newfoundland, 1500–1830* (St. John's: Breakwater Books, 1988); and Peter Pope, *Fish into Wine: The Newfoundland Plantation in the Seventeenth Century* (Chapel Hill: University of North Carolina Press, 2004). Specific information on Lord Baltimore's colony is contained in Luca Codignola's *The Coldest Harbour in the Land: Simon Stock and Lord Baltimore's Colony in Newfoundland, 1621–1649* (Montreal/Kingston: McGill-Queen's University Press, 1987). W. Gordon Handcock reviews English settlement in Newfoundland in *Soe Longe as There Comes No Women* (St. John's: Breakwater Books, 1989). Several essays on early Newfoundland appear in G.M. Story, ed., *Early European Settlement and Exploitation in Atlantic Canada: Selected Papers* (St. John's: Memorial University of Newfoundland, 1982). See also Sarah Glassford's article "Seaman, Sightseer, Storyteller, and Sage: Aaron Thomas's 1794 History of Newfoundland," *Newfoundland and Labrador Studies* 21(1) (2006): 149–76, and Robert C.H. Sweeney, "What Difference Does a Mode Make? A Comparison of Two Seventeenth-Century Colonies: Canada and Newfoundland," *William and Mary Quarterly* 63(2) (2006): 281–304.

For the eighteenth century, see C. Grant Head, *Eighteenth Century Newfoundland: A Geographer's Perspective* (Toronto: McClelland & Stewart, 1976). Several sections of Phillip A. Buckner and John G. Reid, eds., *The Atlantic Region to Confederation: A History* (Toronto: University of Toronto Press, 1994), and the older study, W.S. MacNutt's *The Atlantic Provinces: The Emergence of a Colonial Society, 1712–1857* (Toronto: McClelland & Stewart, 1965), contain extensive references to Newfoundland. Frederic F. Thompson's *The French Shore Problem in Newfoundland* (Toronto: University of Toronto Press, 1961) examines this complex question. Patrick O'Neill reviews the history of the economic and political capital of the island in *The Story of St. John's, Newfoundland* (Erin, ON: Boston Mills Press, 1975). Sean T. Cadigan looks at merchant–settler relations in Newfoundland from 1785 to 1855 in *Hope and Deception in Conception Bay* (Toronto: University of Toronto Press, 1995). John P. Greene has written *Between Damnation and Starvation: Priests and Merchants in Newfoundland Politics, 1745–1855* (Montreal/Kingston: McGill-Queen's University Press, 1999). For the history of St. John's, consult Patrick O'Neill, *The Story of St. John's, Newfoundland* (Erin, ON: Boston Mills Press, 1975).

The mid-nineteenth-century political history of the island is reviewed in Gertrude E. Gunn, *The Political History of Newfoundland, 1832–1864* (Toronto: University of Toronto Press, 1966), and in Patrick O'Flaherty's *Old Newfoundland. A History to 1843* (St. John's: Long Beach Press, 1999). P.B. Waite has written a sketch of John Kent, the Reform politician, in *Dictionary of Canadian Biography*, vol. 10, *1871–1880* (Toronto: University of Toronto Press, 1972), pp. 398–401. Other important biographies of prominent Newfoundlanders appear in this invaluable biographical series, now available online at www.biographi.ca. For a look at the growth of Methodism in Newfoundland during the nineteenth century, see Calvin Hollett, *Shouting, Embracing, and Dancing with Ecstasy: The Growth of Methodism in Newfoundland, 1774–1874* (Montreal/Kingston: McGill-Queen's University Press 2010).

A collection of references to Newfoundland in the nineteenth century is R.G. Moyles's *"Complaints Is Many and Various, But the Odd Divil Likes It"* (Toronto: Peter Martin Associates, 1975). James Hiller and Peter Neary have edited a collection of articles, *Newfoundland in the Nineteenth and the Twentieth Centuries: Essays in Interpretation* (Toronto: University of Toronto Press, 1980). Shannon Ryan reviews nineteenth-century economic developments in "Fishery to Colony: A Newfoundland Watershed, 1793–1815," in Phillip A. Buckner and David Frank, eds., *Atlantic Canada Before Confederation*, vol. 1, *The Acadiensis Reader* (Fredericton: Acadiensis Press, 1985, 1988, 1998), pp. 130–48. Shannon Ryan has also written *Fish out of Water: The Newfoundland Saltfish Trade, 1814–1914* (St. John's: Breakwater, 1986). For the history of the Newfoundland seal hunt, consult Shannon Ryan, *The Ice Hunters: A History of Newfoundland Sealing to 1914* (St. John's: Breakwater, 1984), and James E. Candow, *Of Men and Seals* (Ottawa: Canadian Parks Service, Environment Canada, 1989).

A substantial literature exists on Newfoundland's Aboriginal population. Book-length treatments include the essential study by Ingeborg Marshall, *A History and Ethnography of the Beothuk* (Montreal/Kingston: McGill-Queen's University Press, 1996); James P. Howley's *The Beothucks or Red Indians: The*

Aboriginal Inhabitants of Newfoundland (Toronto: Coles, 1974 [1915]); and Frederick W. Rowe's *Extinction: The Beothuks of Newfoundland* (Toronto: McGraw-Hill Ryerson, 1977). L.F.S. Upton has written a valuable article, "The Extermination of the Beothucks of Newfoundland," *Canadian Historical Review* 58 (1977): 133–53. On the Beothuk, see also Barbara Whitby, *The Last of the Beothuk* (Canmore, AB: Altitude Publishing, 2005). For the Mi'kmaqs' history, see also Dennis Bartels, "*Ktaqamkuk Ilnui Saqimawoutie*: Aboriginal Rights and the Myth of the Micmac Mercenaries in Newfoundland," in Bruce Alden Cox, ed., *Native People, Native Lands: Canadian Indians, Inuit and Métis* (Ottawa: Carleton University Press, 1988), pp. 32–36. Titles on both the Mi'kmaqs and the Beothuks are listed in Ralph Pastore's "Native History in the Atlantic Region During the Colonial Period," *Acadiensis* 20(1) (Autumn 1990): 200–225. Ralph Pastore and G.M. Story provide a valuable sketch of Shawnadithit, the last known survivor of the Beothuks, in *Dictionary of Canadian Biography*, vol. 6, *1821–1835* (Toronto: University of Toronto Press, 1987), pp. 706–9. In *Beyond Their Years: Five Native Women's Stories* (Toronto: Canadian Scholars Press, 1999), pp. 96–173, John Steckley includes an essay on Shawnadithit. G.M. Story completed the sketch of Demasduwit in *Dictionary of Canadian Biography*, vol. 5, *1801–1820* (Toronto: University of Toronto Press, 1983), pp. 243–44. See also Greg Mitchell's article "The Palliser Friendship Treaty: The Esquimeaux-British Treaty of Southern Labrador (August 21, 1765)," *Newfoundland Quarterly* 98(1) (2005): 48–51. For a look at exploration of Newfoundland, see William Gilbert, "Crout's Way: Retracing the Trail Cut by Settlers at Cupers Cove Between Conception Bay and Trinity Bay in September 1612," *Newfoundland Quarterly* 99(1) (2006): 44–51.

For a look at the history of whaling in Newfoundland, see Anthony B. Dickinson and Chesley W. Sanger, "Commercial Whaling in Newfoundland and Labrador: An Historical Overview," *Newfoundland Quarterly* 98(1) (2005): 28–31. Newfoundland's long relationship with the ocean is discussed in Farley Mowat's book *Sea of Slaughter* (Toronto: McClelland & Stewart, 1984). For a look at the economics of the Newfoundland fisheries, see Kenneth Norrie and Rick Szostak, "Allocating Property Rights over Shoreline: Institutional Change in the Newfoundland Inshore Fishery," *Newfoundland and Labrador Studies* 20(2) (2005): 233–64. Harold Innis has written a classic work on Newfoundland and the North Atlantic fishery in his book *The Cod Fisheries: The History of an International Economy* (Toronto: University of Toronto Press, 1940). Peter E. Pope offers an archaeological study of the French fishery in his article "The Archaeology of France's Migratory Fishery on Newfoundland's Petit Nord," *Archéologiques*, special issue 2 (2008): 38–54.

Interesting maps of Newfoundland appear in the first two volumes of *Historical Atlas of Canada*: vol. 1, R. Cole Harris, ed., *From the Beginning to 1800* (Toronto: University of Toronto Press, 1987); and vol. 2, R. Louis Gentilcore, ed., *The Land Transformed, 1800–1891* (Toronto: University of Toronto Press, 1993).

Source: Arthur Heming, *Mackenzie Crossing the Rockies, 1932* oil on canvas, Government of Ontario Art Collection, Archives of Ontario.

Chapter Nineteen

THE NORTHWEST

TIME LINE

1821	The Hudson's Bay Company and the North West Company unite
1832	Red River Academy established
1837–8	Great Plains First Nations ravaged by smallpox
1844	Franklin Expedition departs
1845	Oblate Mission established in Red River
1849	Sayer Trial results in declaration of free trade in furs
1850	Case of Sarah Ballenden heard in Red River
1851	The Battle of Grand Coteau is fought between the Sioux and the Métis
1857	Palliser and Hind Expeditions dispatched
1859	Establishment of regular steamboat connection between St. Paul and the Red River colony
1862	St. Albert Métis community founded
1864–5	Scarlet fever ravages Blackfoot

The Northwest was transformed in the era after the amalgamation of the fur trade companies in 1821. The fur trade declined and within decades, the seemingly endless herds of buffalo were gone. The lifestyles of the Métis and the First Nations underwent dramatic and often traumatic changes. The region fell under the gaze of Canada, and Britain helped prepare its absorption into British North America. White settlers began to move west and the colony of Red River was recast as a Victorian society. Historian Gerald Friesen argues that the 1840s serve as a "dividing line" in the history of the Northwest: "The institutions of European industrial capitalist society were taking root. New ideas such as race, respectability, and progress were becoming current."[1]

The Supremacy of the Hudson's Bay Company

The Hudson's Bay Company reigned supreme over the fur trade after 1821 when it merged with the Northwest Company. The HBC was also the unrivalled governing power in the vast Northwest, and its influence was remarkable. The Company's control, however, did not go unchallenged. Both the Métis and American traders from across the border looked to challenge the new monopoly in furs. The United States offered an alternative market for those prepared to defy the all-powerful Hudson's Bay Company.

In the years following the merger, the HBC reorganized its operations. The Company was coming under increasing scrutiny from the British government. Politicians realized that a unique situation existed in British North America, in which a commercial enterprise continued to exercise inordinate control over a massive area and a large population. The HBC licence over the area known as Rupert's Land was set to last for 21 years and came up for regular renewal. It was renewed for another 21 years in 1838. It would only be a matter of time, however, before some other arrangement would have to be made for the area and its residents.

As part of its restructuring, the Hudson's Bay Company established a hierarchy that followed the practice set by the Nor'Westers. Field officers were made Company partners. Chief factors supervised trade districts while chief partners supervised trade posts. Clerks worked below these officers, while engagés served as voyageurs and labourers. The Métis often filled these lower ranks.

George Simpson, "The Little Emperor," sat atop the hierarchy. Simpson had come to the Northwest in 1820, just prior to the amalgamation. He was made one of two field governors, but by 1826 (and until his death in 1860) he was the undisputed master of all HBC territories in North America:

> *He had a prodigious memory for business detail, an extraordinary ability to see beyond the ledger books and inventories to the vital broader patterns that affected policy and required decisions, a cold and even ruthless standard by which he measured his subordinates, a passionate devotion to the affairs of the company*

George Simpson, the "Little Emperor" of the HBC.

Source: Hudson's Bay Company Archives, Archives of Manitoba/ 1987/363-S-25/T78.

Pierre-Guillaume Sayer (left) and Louis Riel, Sr.

Source: Provincial Archives of Manitoba/N1445.

that can be seen as admirable but also as repellent, a prodigious enthusiasm for work and travel, and a smiling geniality that could charm a business acquaintance or an important politician in the wink of an eye."[2]

Simpson was an autocrat who focused on maintaining HBC profits during the decline of the fur trade. This was accomplished by ensuring tight control of operations and "trimming the fat." Unfortunately for the Aboriginal peoples, this often meant a reduction in prices and an elimination of the gift-giving tradition, which Simpson called a "ruinous practice."

The fur trade transformed the lifestyles and often the cultures of the First Nations. Increasingly, Aboriginal groups became dependent on the trade. But this dependency often worked to the disadvantage of the Hudson's Bay Company. While it could be profitable to have the Aboriginals dependent, it also taxed the resources of the Company. The HBC found itself having to deal with difficult issues of law and order. Of even greater concern, as the First Nations abandoned their traditional lifestyles, they became increasingly dependent on Company food and supplies. As the HBC looked to reduce expenses, Aboriginal groups faced starvation.

The Sayer Trial, 1849

The Métis, the largest group in the Red River colony, came to resent the control that the Hudson's Bay Company exerted over the settlement. As the fur trade declined, many Métis violated Company rule and did business across the border with American traders. The test case of Métis power came during the trial of Pierre-Guillaume Sayer, a Métis trader arrested in 1849 on a charge of illegally trafficking in furs.

The HBC argued that Sayer violated its monopoly. The Métis, who had not yet left on the spring hunt, organized an informal self-defence committee. Between 200 and 300 armed Métis, including committee member Louis Riel, Sr., gathered outside the courthouse during the trial. After hearing the evidence, and very aware of what waited outside the courthouse, the judge found Sayer guilty as charged but imposed no sentence and recommended mercy. It would have been difficult to impose a sentence, because the Métis hunters constituted the most powerful military force in the colony. The HBC dropped the charges. When Sayer emerged from the courthouse a free man, the Métis knew that they had broken the monopoly of the Hudson's Bay Company. "*Vive la liberté, le commerce est libre,*" they shouted. After the trial, the Company recognized French as an official language in the Red River colony.

The Slaughter of the Buffalo

The number of beaver and buffalo fell rapidly, to the point that the HBC had to introduce conservation measures. After the 1830s, the trade in buffalo robes across the border into the United States led to even greater pressure on the buffalo population. White hunters joined in on the massacre with their newest technology, the repeater rifle. A single American company traded in more than two-and-a-half million buffalo annually between 1870 and 1875. By the 1860s, buffalo hides for use in making industrial machinery belts took the animal to the point of extinction.

The decline of the buffalo increased competition and rivalry among the Plains nations. Cree and Assiniboine hunters travelled further westward, into the territory of their enemy, the Blackfoot, in pursuit of the herds. Meanwhile, the Métis journeyed further to the south and west from Red River, and came in conflict with their enemy, the Sioux.

For decades, the Métis carried out their annual buffalo hunts from their base in Red River. These highly organized, communal hunts involved men, women, and children travelling on the famous Red River carts in pursuit of the herds. But the Métis were slaughtering more buffalo than ever before, and as the Métis population increased, more buffalo were killed.

A Buffalo Rift *by Alfred Jacob Miller, 1837.*

Source: Library and Archives Canada, Acc. No. 1946-110-1 Gift of Mrs. J.B. Jardine.

The Battle of Grand Coteau, 1851

As the Métis moved farther to the southwest to hunt buffalo, they came into conflict with the Sioux. As the herds were slaughtered, competition among Métis, whites, and First Nations increased. The Métis–Sioux wars intensified in the 1840s and came to a head in 1851, at the Battle of Grand Coteau (big hillock), southeast of present-day Minot, North Dakota. During the clash, in which the Métis fought from behind a circular barricade made with their carts, packs, and saddles, at least twenty of the Sioux, but only one Métis, died. The Métis victory over a numerically larger party of Sioux demonstrated their growing military supremacy in the Red River and surrounding areas.

Missionaries in the Northwest

The Hudson's Bay Company and the British government disagreed about the future of the Northwest. The Company's motives were driven by profit. As long as Rupert's Land remained the preserve of the fur trade, those profits were relatively secure. The British government, however, looked to a time in the near future when HBC control would be replaced by colonial government. When British North America was ready, the Northwest and the Pacific Coast would be united with the eastern colonies. The population of the Northwest had to be prepared for absorption.

Bishop Joseph-Norbert Provencher.

Source: Société historique de Saint-Boniface MSB 0238.

The first Catholic missionaries arrived in Red River in 1818. Led by Bishop Joseph-Norbert Provencher, the Roman Catholic Oblates established their first mission in Red River in 1845. By 1847 the order established missions on the Columbia River, and by 1858 it reached Vancouver Island. Protestant missionaries were not far behind. The Scottish presence in Red River was strong in the form of the Selkirk settlers. Both Anglican and then Presbyterian ministers arrived in the colony.

The missionaries worked to convert the Aboriginals, but they also worked to ensure that Red River was a Christian, "civilized" colony. Fur trade society had to be stripped of its Aboriginal influences. The Métis were encouraged to give up hunting the buffalo and take up farming. The colonists were instructed not to marry Aboriginal women. By the 1830s, church marriage had replaced the fur trade custom of marriage *à la façon du pays*.

Red River Society

Red River increasingly became a "Europeanized" society in the decades after 1821. The colony's population was only 400, almost equally divided between Métis and Scots. When Cuthbert Grant moved his Métis followers from Pembina to St. Francois Xavier, about 32 kilometres west of the Forks, the population substantially increased.

Agriculture was viewed as the mark of "civilization" and both French and English mixed bloods took up farming. Their "river lots" along the banks of the Red and Assiniboine Rivers followed the French-Canadian pattern along the St. Lawrence. As the governing authority, the Hudson's Bay Company was responsible for settlement. Farmers were expected to obtain title to their property from the HBC. Many, however, failed to do so; and because the Company was more concerned with the fur trade and there was no shortage of available land, the HBC did not enforce the rules. This situation became a problem decades later when white settlement increased and the Métis were expected to prove that they held title to their farms.

Although both the French and English mixed bloods were united in their Aboriginal ancestry, they formed two distinct groups in Red River. The more numerous French-Catholic Métis population, such as that led by Cuthbert Grant, was perceived as more "Indian." They were less prone to devote themselves primarily to agriculture and instead followed the traditions of the buffalo hunt. As a result, they were viewed as more "savage" and less "civilized." The English-Protestant mixed bloods, led by the likes of Alexander Ross, took up farming. They placed more priority on education, often sending their sons out of the colony to Canada, Britain, or the United States for schooling. Because they adopted European culture, the English mixed bloods moved into positions of authority within Red River.

After 1821, former Company "servants" (as the HBC called its employees) retired to Red River. The white population was further augmented by the arrival of settlers from Upper Canada. This segment assumed they were bringing "civilization" to the remote colony. They expected to find European institutions and culture. Membership on the Council of Assiniboia (the governing authority), for example, was restricted to former company officials. They also expected to fill the upper levels of the social hierarchy. The English mixed bloods worked to assimilate into this group. By 1850, the population of Red River reached 5000.

While the English mixed bloods often sought to assimilate with the Anglo-Protestant minority, the French Métis continued to develop their own distinct identity and even nationality. They were distinctly French and Catholic, but they possessed their own vernacular as well as their own dress and culture.

But with "civilization" came new perceptions of race and class. Racial, ethnic, linguistic, class, and religious division marked the Red River colony. Aboriginal bloodlines became marks of inferiority. Whereas the Métis were once heralded for their ancestry, which gave them the benefits of both races and made them impressive hunters and warriors, they were now viewed as ignorant, lazy, and savage. Whereas mixed-blood women once held an advantageous position in Red River society, where they were coveted as wives, they were now replaced by white women arriving in the colony. HBC Governor George Simpson set the standard in 1830 by abandoning his "country wife" (mixed blood) and returning to Red River with his cousin as his bride. Company officers sent their daughters to boarding school to acquire "the accomplishments of ladies," including music, drawing, and dancing. Most importantly, their virtue was to be safeguarded. The Red River Academy was established in 1832 to supervise the education of fur traders' daughters. As the sensational case of "Mrs. Ballenden" demonstrated in 1850, social divisions were deepening.

The Case of "Mrs. Ballenden"

Sarah Ballenden was the Métis wife of John Ballenden, the chief factor in charge of the HBC's Red River district (and the man who had arrested Sayer in 1849). In order to retain social standing, a Victorian woman was expected to be free of any hint of impropriety. When Ballenden was charged with adultery, her reputation was ruined. When Captain Foss, her supposed lover, attempted to clear her reputation by suing her accusers for defamatory conspiracy, the trial in July of 1850 became a sensational event in Red River and did even more damage. As historian Sylvia Van Kirk has demonstrated, the case highlighted the issues of gender and race as Victorian notions of respectability were impressed on the colony.[3]

The Red River settlement changed rapidly in the 1860s. Louis Goulet, a Métis who grew up in the Red River valley during that decade, left a colourful account of the region and the Red River Métis immediately before union with Canada: "Everything had been improved, from transportation to food on the table. Craftsmanship was considerably improved, thanks to superior tools that could now be bought in almost any ordinary general store and at prices most people could afford." Most houses had floors, pane glass windows, and partitioned rooms. Spinning wheels and looms were also present in many Métis homes.

A HISTORICAL PORTRAIT

Sarah Ballenden

Born in 1818 in Rupert's Land to a mixed-blood mother and fur trader father, Sarah McLeod was one of eight children. Her father, Alexander, joined the Hudson's Bay Company after the merger with the North West Company in 1821. She was raised in various HBC trading posts along the Mackenzie River and in the Columbia district. As with many British mixed bloods, Sarah's identity was more white than Aboriginal and she was sent to the centre of "civilization" in the Northwest, Red River in the 1830s, to receive a formal education.

While in Red River, the "attractive and vivacious" young Sarah was under the guardianship of Chief Factor John Stuart. She met John Ballenden, a Scottish accountant working at Upper Fort Garry. According to historian Sylvia Van Kirk, "In a manner reminiscent of a Jane Austen novel, every eligible young clerk who set foot in Red River immediately found himself the object of marital speculation."[1] Marriages between HBC fur traders and mixed-blood women were falling out of fashion as British women, "exotic creatures" of "genteel breeding," came to Red River. When HBC Governor George Simpson resided in the colony in the early 1830s, unions with mixed-blood women were increasingly frowned upon. The Governor had turned his back on his own mixed-blood "mistress" and married his cousin. But Simpson had since left Red River, and attractive and acculturated young mixed-blood women could still aspire to social prominence through marriage to eligible young company officers. With Stuart's permission, the two were married in 1836. Sarah was 18 and John was 24 years old. Sarah's dowry was £350 and the marriage ceremony was one of the highlights on that year's social calendar. Sarah had a child a year later, naming her Ann Christie after the mixed-blood wife of Governor Alexander Christie.

The Ballendens left Red River in 1840 and moved to Sault Ste Marie. The couple had four more children over the next eight years, one of which died in infancy. They returned to Red River in 1848 when John was named chief factor. John suffered a stroke on the return trip and despite health problems, Sarah nursed him back to health. The couple became prominent in the active social life of Red River. Sarah became so socially prominent that her friends predicted she was "destined to raise her whole Cast above European ladies in their influence on society here." Sarah named her next child Frances Isobel Simpson after the Governor Simpson's white wife and cousin.

By the end of the 1840s, the strains on Red River society were evident.

Victorian concepts with regard to female propriety and virtue were taking hold. Aboriginal women, and by extension mixed bloods, were stigmatized as "loose and immoral." In 1849, Sarah's social prominence created scandal and she became the target of rumour and innuendo. Red River by this time was rife with gossip, as one chief factor complained: "I believe the World Canot produce Such a Set of ungrateful Wretches. Their whole Soul seems bent on Backbiting and Slander. I never heard a good word said of the Absent."

It seems Sarah flirted with Captain Christopher Foss, a handsome officer with the pensioners from the Royal Hospital, Chelsea (London), who frequented the HBC's mess table at Upper Fort Garry. Over the next few months, rumours circulated that the relationship between the two was such that John Ballenden had grounds for divorce. The gossip mill was fed by white women, such as Anne Rose Clouston and Margaret Anderson, recently arrived in Red River and who were resentful over the prominence of a "half breed" woman in respectable Victorian society. It is likely that they were also jealous over Sarah's beauty. According to one observer, "the poor woman seems to have had a watch set on her from the moment of her arrival, every act word or deed was marked and commented upon by certain parties." Anne Clouston in particular circulated gossip to discredit Sarah and demanded that the governor of Assiniboia, Major William Bletterman Caldwell, censure her immoral conduct.

When John Ballenden briefly left Red River on business in June 1850, the influential clique excluded Sarah from social engagements. Distressed, Sarah turned to the colony's Recorder, Adam Thom, for support and advice. Spurred on by their wives, HBC clerk Augustus Pelly (married to Anne Clouston) and Chief Trader John Black (married to Margaret Christie) accused Sarah publicly. It is notable that Sarah had spurned Pelly's own advances and that Foss had won a considerable sum of money when gambling with Pelly. Captain Foss appealed to the courts "to clear the reputation of a Lady." He brought a suit for defamatory conspiracy against the Pellys and HBC mess steward John Davidson and his English wife, who originated much of the gossip.

The three-day trial, which began on July 16, 1850, brought into the open the racial tensions that had been growing in the colony's social elite between incoming whites and the acculturated mixed-blood community, what one observer called "a strife of blood." Numerous witnesses were called, but the evidence was all based on gossip and insinuations. The jury decided in Captain Foss's favour and the defendants were assessed heavy damages (Pelly £300 and Davidson £100).

Despite this victory, the damage was done. As historian Frits Pannoekoek notes, "The social division accentuated by the scandal affected every aspect of life in Red River and either aggravated or created other conflicts."[2] According to Associate Governor of Rupert's Land, Eden Colvile, Sarah continued to be shunned by "the 'nobs' of the womankind." When her husband returned to Scotland to receive medical treatment in the fall of 1850, the knives in Red River came out again. A note, allegedly from Sarah to Captain Foss inviting him to visit her at the Lower Fort Garry, was intercepted and presented to Colvile. Now even her supporters, Colvile and Thom, turned against Sarah. For the anti-Ballenden camp, the new rumours proved their previous accusations. They never, however, attempted to gain redress in court. John reluctantly remained loyal to his wife, but she was now vilified and shunned by Red River society as a "fallen woman." Her health deteriorated so badly after the birth of her eighth child in 1851 that she was unable to accompany her husband to his new posting at Fort Vancouver.

Alexander Ross, whose friendship for Sarah had not been shaken, noted sadly that, "if there is such a thing as dying of a broken heart, she cannot live long." After a wretched winter at Red River she sought refuge in 1852 at Norway House with the family of Chief Factor George Barnston. The following summer John brought his family to Edinburgh. Their reunion was brief. Sarah Ballenden died of consumption on December 23, 1853, at the age of 35.

"The personal tragedy of this woman," Van Kirk concludes, "largely the result of rumour and innuendo, underscores the way in which the double standard punished women for any violation of the straight-laced moral code of the day. The controversy surrounding her fall from grace also reinforced the racial prejudice against native and mixed-blood women."[3]

---

1. Sylvia Van Kirk, "'The Reputation of a Lady': Sarah Ballenden and the Foss–Pelly Scandal," *Manitoba History* 11 (Spring 1986).

2. Frits Pannekoek, *A Snug Little Flock: The Social Origins of the Riel Resistance, 1869–70* (Winnipeg: Watson & Dyer Publishing, 1991), p. 130.

3. Sylvia Van Kirk, "Sarah McLeod (Ballenden)," *Dictionary of Canadian Biography,* vol. VIII, *1851–1860* (Toronto: University of Toronto Press, 1985), pp. 573–4.

Red River Society

Historians have disagreed over the tense and factious nature of Red River society. They also disagree as to how these divisions influenced the Red River Resistance of 1869–70. Some have argued that Red River was on the verge of collapse from the joint forces of internal racial, religious, linguistic, and class disputes, as well as pressures exerted by the annexationists that set the colonists at each others' throats. Others have portrayed Red River as a Métis community in transition and that the society, with its distinct groups, adapted well to changing conditions.

In the 1936 work *The Birth of Western Canada* George Stanley described a Red River in crisis. The colony was a backward, frontier society on the verge of being civilized by the expansionist white immigrants and settlers: "A primitive people, the half-breeds were bound to give way before the march of a more progressive people."[1] Stanley's portrayal of the Métis became known as the "civilization–savagery" (or "civ–sav") model. In a two-volume history of the Métis, Marcel Giraud, writing in the 1940s, argued that "in the Red River colony, civilization and barbarism met and mingled. . . . The result was a society quaint and unique, in which were reconciled the savagery of the Indian and the culture of Europe."[2]

In the 1950s and 1960s, Historian W.L. Morton rejected the frontierism of the earlier generation of historians in explaining Red River society: "The primary characteristic of the colony was the balance that existed ethnically between the buffalo hunt, river farm lots, and the canoe brigades." He argued that the central reason for the Red River Resistance was the French anxiety over English-Canadian rule in the colony and the increasing presence of the expansionists from Ontario. "What the Métis chiefly feared in 1869 was not the entrance of an agricultural frontier of Ontario into Red River—and they would have welcomed that of Quebec—but the sudden influx of immigrants of English speech and Protestant faith." Morton perceived Red River as a dual society. The roots of Canada's political bi-nationalism and cultural plurality could be found in Manitoba's early formation.[3]

Writing in the 1970s and 1980s, Frits Pannekoek presented a starkly divided community, but he offered a different explanation for the crisis. When Pannekoek examined Red River, he saw a colony torn asunder by religious division. Previous historians, he claimed, had failed to make use of Anglican Church source material and had fallen into the trend toward secularism that dominated the post–World War II period. The result was an underestimation of the separateness of the English mixed-bloods as well as the role of the Anglican Church in Red River: "The Halfbreeds and the Métis had been increasingly at odds at least twenty years before the Resistance, and the origins of their divergence lay in the nature of Red River and fur trade society."[4]

The arrival of European women and the Church Missionary Society altered cultural mores, particularly marriage patterns and racial stereotypes. "The case of Mrs. Ballenden" in 1850 revealed more than an atmosphere of muckracking and gossiping. It demonstrated a community fundamentally divided between European and Métis, Protestant and Catholic, English and French. As historian Sylvia Van Kirk noted, the scandal was "an event in Red River history which most historians would like to ignore. For those who would construct a rosy picture of racial harmony in the early days of Red River, it presents an embarrassing obstacle."[5] This division led the English mixed bloods to support the annexationists in future conflicts: "Red River, taken as a whole, was a society that was not the product of a delicate balance, but of brittleness, whose parts were mutually antagonistic and increasingly pitted one against the other."[6]

Historian Irene Spry took exception to Pannekoek's argument. "Very little evidence of conflict, let alone 'hatred,'" she argued, "has come to light except in the clerical sources on which Pannekoek's conclusion seems in large measure to be based." Instead, Spry agreed with Morton that the nature of relationships between French and English mixed-bloods was linked by "ties of blood and of long association on hunt and trip." Cleavages existed in Red River but they were not between the mixed-blood groups. They were rather class divisions emerging from education and positions in the Hudson's Bay Company and occupation divisions based around farmers and hunters.[7]

According to Gerald Friesen, both the interpretations of Stanley and Pannekoek depicted the settlement as divided and unstable: "Such a view exaggerates the weakness of the community and underestimates the abilities of its residents."[8] Instead, Friesen agreed with historian Gerhard Ens, who emphasized the ability of the Métis to adapt to changing conditions and circumstances, including new economic opportunities.

Ens argued that Pannekoek's portrait of "the colony in disarray" is unconvincing because it ignores examples of cooperation between the mixed-blood groups as well as "the more prosaic day-to-day existence that properly defined the Metis worlds."[9] Rather than being overwhelmed by the divisions created by European immigration, the Métis (both French and English) adapted and indeed became community leaders by the time crisis beset the settlement in the 1860s. But while Ens agreed with Spry's emphasis on the role of class as a source of division in Red River, the tendency of the Métis to remain fixed on the hunt was not a product of their "Indianness" but rather a pragmatic economic decision. Agriculture in Red River was not proving productive: "Thus the choice for the Red River Métis (at least before the 1870s) was not between a 'progressive agriculture' and the 'primitive hunt' but increasingly between a kin-based capitalist fur trade, wage labour, and peasant agriculture."[10]

Despite the criticism that Red River holds too much influence in the history and identity of the Métis, there is little doubt that the colony played a critical role. As John Weinstein argues, "Red River served as an incubator of the new nation and Métis nationalism. In eastern Canada, large-scale immigration and agricultural settlement had caused the absorption of people of mixed ancestry into the settler or Indian population, but in the Red River Settlement between 1820 and 1870 the Métis absorbed Europeans and Indians."[11]

1.   George F.G. Stanley, *The Birth of Western Canada* (Toronto: University of Toronto Press, 1960 [1936]), pp. 48–9.

2.   Marcel Giraud, *The Métis in the Canadian West,* vol. 1, trans. George Woodcock (Edmonton: University of Alberta Press, 1986), pp. ix–xvi.

3. W.L. Morton, *Manitoba: A History* (Toronto: University of Toronto Press, 1967), p. ix.

4. Frits Pannekoek, *A Snug Little Flock: The Social Origins of the Riel Resistance, 1869-70* (Winnipeg: Watson & Dyer Publishing, 1991), pp. 11–12; "The Anglican Church and the Disintegration of Red River Society, 1818–1870," in Carl Berger and Ramsay Cook, eds., *The West and the Nation: Essays in Honour of W.L. Morton* (Toronto: University of Toronto Press, 1976), pp. 72–90.

5. Sylvia Van Kirk, "The Reputation of a Lady": Sarah Ballenden and the Foss–Pelly Scandal," *Manitoba History* 11 (Spring 1986).

6. Pannekoek, *A Snug Little Flock*, pp. 11–12.

7. Irene Spry, "The Métis and Mixed-Bloods of Rupert's Land Before 1870," in Jaqueline Peterson and Jennifer S.H. Brown, eds., *The New Peoples: Being and Becoming Métis in North America* (Winnipeg: University of Manitoba Press, 1985), pp. 95–118.

8. Gerald Friesen, *The Canadian Prairies: A History* (Toronto: University of Toronto Press, 1987), p. 113.

9. Gerhard Ens, *Homeland to Hinterland: The Changing Worlds of the Red River Métis in the Nineteenth Century* (Toronto: University of Toronto Press, 1996), pp. 3–5.

10. Gerhard Ens, "Métis Agriculture in Red River During the Transition from Peasant Society to Industrial Capitalism: The Example of St. Francois Xavier, 1835–1870," in R.C. Macleod, ed., *Swords and Ploughshares: War and Agriculture in Western Canada* (Edmonton: University of Alberta Press, 1993), p. 240.

11. John Weinstein, *Quiet Revolution West: The Rebirth of Métis Nationalism* (Calgary: Fifth House, 2007), pp. 2–5.

Métis Migration

By the 1840s, the Red River Métis had developed a diverse economy based on the buffalo hunt, small-scale farming, and seasonal labour for the Hudson's Bay Company. In the 1850s the colony's horizons expanded, mainly as a result of more frequent contacts with St. Paul, Minnesota, to the south. St. Paul gradually replaced York Factory on Hudson Bay as the Red River's major *entrepôt* (duty-free trading post).

From 1851 to 1869, the number of Red River carts journeying to St. Paul to sell furs and purchase supplies increased from 100 to 2500. Mail service to the Red River colony came through St. Paul after 1853, rather than by the slower and more cumbersome route through York Factory. A railway reached St. Paul in 1855, and within a year the Hudson's Bay Company itself used it to bring in supplies. The establishment of a regular steamboat connection between St. Paul and the Red River colony in 1859 made the ties with Minnesota (with a population of nearly 200 000 by 1860) all the more binding. It is likely that the depression of 1857, the American Civil War in 1861–65, and the outbreak of war between the Americans and the Sioux in 1862 prevented Minnesota's annexation of the Red River country.

Many Métis moved farther west in the early 1860s, attracted by rising opportunities in the buffalo-hide trade and discouraged by the transformation of the Red River

Silhouettes of Pilgrims on Lac Sainte-Anne, 1862, *by William George Richardson Hind.*

Source: Library and Archives Canada, Acc. No. 1963-97-1.74R.

settlement. Those who spent the winter on the prairies to be nearer the herds became known as *hivernants* (winterers). They established settlements at the forks of the Saskatchewan River, in the North Saskatchewan River valley, in the Cypress Hills area of present-day southwestern Saskatchewan, and at Lac Ste. Anne, about 80 km northwest of Fort Edmonton. Lac Ste. Anne became the largest Métis settlement in the Northwest outside of the Red River colony until St. Albert (about 15 kilometres northwest of Edmonton) was founded in 1862. By the mid-1860s, the buffalo herds had migrated so far from present-day Manitoba that the Red River–based hunt had almost ended.

In 1871, an estimated 2000 to 4000 mixed-bloods lived along the North Saskatchewan River between the Red River and the Rockies, and about 11 000 at the junction of the Red and the Assiniboine rivers. The mixed-blood population of 13 000 to 15 000 was approximately one-half of the estimated number of Plains First Nations in British North America.

Métis traders, c. 1872, standing in front of a Red River cart.
Source: Library and Archives Canada/e000009381.

The First Nations in the Northwest

Red River deserves a central role in the history of the Northwest, but what some historians have called "Red River myopia" can obscure what was happening with the Aboriginal nations in the rest of Rupert's Land. While the mixed-blood population doubled in the Red River colony every fifteen to twenty years, the population of the Northwestern First Nations seriously declined in the mid-nineteenth century. The impact of contact—dependency on European trade goods, decline of the fur trade, decimation of the buffalo herds, loss of hunting grounds, disease, and starvation—decimated the Aboriginal populations. The increasing "efficiency" of the HBC made life more difficult. As Friesen points out, "The last half of the nineteenth century constituted a revolution for most of the native societies of the western interior, particularly those of plains and parkland. None of the changes in the native way of life in the preceding two centuries could be compared to the extraordinary upheaval in this period, and, what is even more striking, nothing could compare with the speed of the change."[4]

Adapting to Change

The streamlining of HBC operations meant difficult times for the First Nations. The restructured transportation routes requiring fewer posts led to a downsized workforce. As George Simpson explained in 1822, "Indians . . . must be ruled with a rod of Iron to bring and keep them in a proper state of subordination." As the buffalo moved south and west, and the moose and caribou disappeared, the Ojibwa living on the borders between woodlands and prairie had to adapt to their changing surroundings. Many found work in the fur trade and became dependent on the Hudson's Bay Company for food.

The condition of the Plains nations was dire due to sporadic warfare between the Blackfoot and the Cree and Assiniboine over the diminishing buffalo herds. The Sioux had long resisted Métis incursions into their territory. Now the Cree attempted to stop the Métis as well. As the Cree were pushed westward, conflict with the Blackfoot was inevitable. By 1865, the

A Blackfoot hay camp in Alberta, c. 1908.

Source: Glenbow Archives NC-43-49.

Cree moved into the "last refuge" on the western plains, the Cypress Hills (present-day southern Saskatchewan). White observers were alarmed by the gatherings of up to three thousand people. As the Plains nations became increasingly desperate, fears of "Indian Wars" increased—which became reality in 1870 when the Cree and Blackfoot went to war.

As historian John Thompson points out, while the Plains nations maintained some degree of autonomy, even as the buffalo were declining, "the woodland peoples, however, had become more dependent on trade with Europeans for guns, ammunition, and cloth."[5] The groups in the Athabasca country (Chippewa, Woodland Cree, and Ojibwa) were losing their traditional means of obtaining food and their dependency on the HBC, with its new rules, made life difficult. Restrictions were placed on trapping in areas where fur-bearing populations had been decimated. These restrictions, however, were not based on conservation principles. Governor Simpson ordered areas to the south, where the HBC competed with American traders, "trapped clean."

Sickness and Disease

In 1837–38, smallpox ravaged the Great Plains First Nations, just as it had a half-century earlier (in 1780–82). Such diseases tended to be carried along the trade routes—the drainage systems of the Missouri and Saskatchewan rivers. Crews of whites usually carried the smallpox viruses. The boat brigades' tight schedules often caused crews to be dispatched while the men were still infectious. They moved into the interior and infected the Aboriginals, who had gathered in their large summer camps. They, in turn, carried the disease farther inland.

The Aboriginal way of life inadvertently contributed to the spread of the new diseases. They lived in close-knit family groups in small living areas. In addition, the Aboriginal peoples had no idea that the disease was spread simply by contact. They insisted on visiting the sick, and in doing so, unknowingly spread the illness. As one Peigan told David Thompson, "We had no belief that one Man could give it to another, any more than a wounded Man could give his wound to another."

The efforts of the Hudson's Bay Company traders, however, saved some of the Cree around the company's posts. The discovery of a smallpox vaccine in Europe around 1800 checked the spread of the epidemic. The HBC began an extensive vaccination program. The vaccinated population constituted an effective barrier, and the highly contagious disease spread no farther than the posts on the northern fringes of the prairies. After the epidemic had run its course, the Cree could more readily move farther onto the prairies, because the strength of the Blackfoot nations had been so reduced. But, smallpox continued to take its toll. In 1870 alone, more than 3500 First Nations and Métis on the Canadian plains died because of the absence of vaccine.

Other infectious diseases also ravaged the population. In 1864–65, an outbreak of scarlet fever killed more than 1000 Blackfoot people. A measles epidemic hit the Cree. Influenza and whooping cough also spread through their communities. A new disease—tuberculosis—arrived in the 1860s, brought by refugee Sioux from the United States and by Red River people moving west (both groups had already been exposed to the deadly bacterium).

The Whiskey Traders

In the mid-1860s, the Blackfoot experienced another assault: American whiskey traders. In the 1850s and the early 1860s, the Blackfoot traded with both the Hudson's Bay Company and the American Fur Company. At Fort Edmonton and Rocky Mountain House, they exchanged pemmican and horses, as well as beaver furs, for British trade goods. At Fort Benton, in Montana, they traded bulky buffalo hides and robes (which were difficult for the HBC to transport profitably in their York boats) for American goods. The American Fur Company bought all that it could, shipping the furs down the Missouri by steamer to St. Louis.

The stability of the Missouri River fur trade suddenly ended, however, in 1864, with the collapse of the American Fur Company. Then, just after the end of the American Civil War in 1865, the discovery of gold brought a flood of prospectors and merchants to the mountains of Montana. With them came a flourishing whiskey trade. After U.S. marshals began to enforce laws against the trade, many of the traders moved north to present-day southern Alberta and Saskatchewan to make their fortunes. Their arrival led to social disruption among groups that had little acquaintance with alcohol and no social controls in place to deal with its consequences.

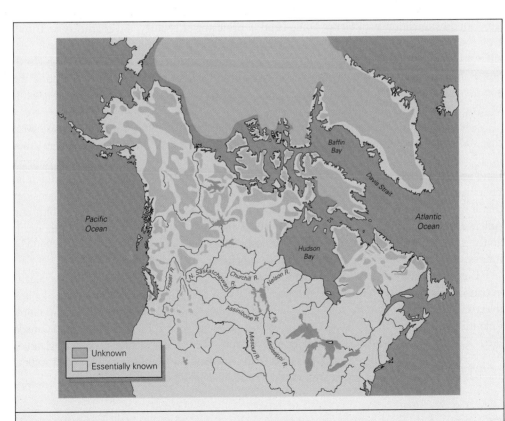

Non-Aboriginals' knowledge of Canadian territory in 1870.

Source: Adapted from Richard I. Ruggles, *A Country So Interesting: The Hudson's Bay Company and Two Centuries of Mapping, 1670–1870* (Montreal/Kingston: McGill-Queen's University Press, 1991), p. 119.

The Expansionists and Canadian Settlement

Until the late 1850s, the fur traders and the early visitors to the Northwest reported that the tree-less prairies, which stretched as far as the eye could see, were unsuitable for farming. According to Wreford Watson, a historical geographer, "There developed in the minds of Europeans an equation that went as follows: bareness equals barrenness equals infertility equals uselessness for agriculture."[6] This perception changed in the late 1850s.

Depictions in travel writings and fictions portrayed a rugged frontier full of adventure. Imperialists viewed the western interior as a region to be settled and linked to the Pacific. Canadian politicians viewed it as an agricultural settlement frontier and an eventual extension of Canada West. If Canada was to expand and become a great nation like the United States, it had to develop its own western frontier.

In 1857, the expansionists found a valuable ally in the British parliament. A select committee of the British House of Commons examined the possibilities of settlement in Rupert's Land and the question of renewing the HBC charter. The parliament was under increasing pressure from Aboriginal protection societies, who pointed out the failures of company rule and the sufferings of the First Nations.

Scientists also weighed in on the developing image of the Northwest. In the early 1860s, Canadian and the British expeditions to the area published their findings. Of the two, the British-sponsored expedition led by John Palliser is the best known. Dispatched in 1857, it was commissioned to report on the possibilities for agricultural settlement. In the same year, the Canadians sent out an expedition with Henry Youle Hind, a professor of geology and chemistry at Trinity University in Toronto, as scientific observer. Both expeditions reported on the magnificent possibilities for agriculture, particularly in the Red River area and in the "fertile belt" of the North Saskatchewan River valley. But they also reported on a triangular-shaped area constituting the southern prairies that was remarkably arid and extended northward from the United States. It became known as "Palliser's Triangle."

The expansionists in Canada focused on the positive findings. But it was really Canada West that was concerned with western expansion. Hoping to imitate the success of American cities in the east that had profited with the opening of their west, Toronto merchants viewed Rupert's Land as a logical extension of its hinterland. George Brown, editor of the *Globe* and influential politician, became the spokesman for the expansionists: "Let the merchants of Toronto consider that if their city is ever to be made really great—if it is ever to rise above the rank of a fifth rate American town—it must be by the development of the great British territory lying to the north and west." Farmland in the fertile area of the lower Great Lakes was becoming scarce. Railway interests saw the potential for great profits with expansion.

Even though the French Métis were the dominant "white" population in the area, French Canadians in Canada East were less excited by the prospects. They were only too aware that Canada West looked to expand its influence, thereby overcoming the deadlock that was developing in the Canadian colony. Colonies in the Northwest would be English-Protestant colonies when settlers moved in from Canada West. If settlers from Canada East looked for new horizons, they usually focused on New England or the regions to the north of their own borders. When the Hudson's Bay Company charter ended, settlers and business interests from Canada West would be ready to take advantage.

The North

The impact of contact came later to the Aboriginal peoples of the North. The First Nations and the Inuit enjoyed uncontested control of their homelands until the late nineteenth century and, in more isolated areas, into the twentieth. Arctic explorers, fur traders, and Christian missionaries were the first newcomers to come north. A small number of Christian missionaries, Roman Catholic and Anglican, arrived around 1850, approximately half a century after the fur traders. Until the late nineteenth century, the number of missionaries in the North remained low.

Northern Exploration

A decade or so after Alexander Mackenzie's 1789 voyage, down the river that now bears his name, the North West Company established its first posts in the Mackenzie River valley. Fort of the Forks (later renamed Fort Simpson) was built just after 1800. It was followed by Fort Good Hope, the first post on the lower Mackenzie, in 1805. After the merger of the fur trade companies in 1821, the revitalized Hudson's Bay Company extended its operations throughout the Mackenzie River valley as far as Fort McPherson, founded in 1840

"Encampment on the Red River," Henry Youle Hind Expedition, 1857–58. Photo taken by Humphrey Lloyd Hime.

Source: Humphrey Lloyd Hime/Library and Archives Canada/C-004572.

as Peel's River Post. By the 1840s, the company was expanding over the Mackenzie Mountains into the Yukon River valley.

European epidemics, brought north by the fur traders, devastated Aboriginal communities. The Gwitch'in (Kutchin) in the northern Yukon and adjacent area, for example, had a population of about 5400 in the early nineteenth century. By the 1860s, this number had been reduced to around 900. "In the 1860s, one Kutchin was alive where six had been originally."[7] That ratio can be applied to other First Nations groups in the Mackenzie River valley and the Yukon.

The Franklin Expedition

In the early nineteenth century, British naval parties resumed the search for the Northwest Passage—not for economic reasons, but for the international prestige of being the first to locate it. Sir John Franklin became one of the most famous explorers. Departing in 1844 with the latest technological assistance, including ships heated by pipes fired from steam boilers and with a three-year supply of canned food, the expedition seemed guaranteed of success. Yet Franklin, on this his third Arctic expedition, refused to use Aboriginal technology. He took no dogs, sleds, pemmican, or Inuit clothing. Within two years, the entire expedition of 129 men perished, as their ships became locked in pack ice near King William Island in the central Arctic.

More than thirty expeditions searched for Franklin and his missing party between 1847 and 1859, first for survivors and then, after evidence surfaced of their deaths, for explanations of the expedition's demise. The intensive search resulted

The Royal Navy ships HMS Assistance *and HMS* Pioneer, *shown in winter quarters, Devon Island, 1853.*

Source: New Brunswick Museum, Saint John, N.B./W5510.

in a large part of the Canadian Arctic Archipelago being charted and the northern limits of the North American continent established. Their sailing in and out of Arctic bays and inlets, and their wintering over on Arctic ice, led the British to claim sovereignty over the homeland of the Inuit.

In 1857, Captain Leopold McClintock was hired by Franklin's widow to solve the mystery. On the shores of King William Island, he found a stone cairn with a message dated April 1848. It indicated that 24 men, including Franklin, were dead and that the survivors were heading overland.

But McClintock's discovery did not end the mystery. In the early 1980s, anthropologists unearthed the remains of seven crew members. Their analyses indicated that the survivors had resorted to cannibalism to survive. Later in the decade, more bodies were discovered on Beechy Island. Almost perfectly preserved in the permafrost, autopsies revealed that while they died of pneumonia, they were also suffering from lead poisoning from their canned food. Inuit oral history indicates that the men were found with hard black mouths and emaciated limbs, also indicating that they suffered from scurvy.

SUMMARY

By the 1860s, the Northwest was on the eve of being "purchased" and incorporated into Canada. Change had come furious and fast: "The buffalo had disappeared, trains and fences now dominated the plains, the old ways had disappeared beyond recovery."[8] The days of First Nations and Métis dominance were replaced by the ideas of empire and industrial capitalism. Settlement expanded, first at the junction of the Red and Assiniboine rivers, and later in the 1860s, farther west, nearer the diminishing buffalo grounds. The intermarriage of fur traders and First Nations led to the creation of a new nation: the Métis. By the end of the 1860s, mixed-bloods numbered from 13 000 to 15 000 in the Northwest, roughly half of the Plains First Nations population, estimated to be 25 000. The Métis, with their sense of identity and feelings of being ignored in the designs of nation, confronted the Canadians when they tried to take control of the region in the late 1860s.

NOTES

1. Gerald Friesen, *The Canadian Prairies: A History* (Toronto: University of Toronto Press, 1987), p. 91.

2. Friesen, p. 85.

3. Sylvia Van Kirk, "'The Reputation of a Lady': Sarah Ballenden and the Foss-Pelly Scandal," *Manitoba History* 11 (Spring 1986).

4. Friesen, pp. 129–30.

5. John Herd Thompson, *Forging the Prairie West* (Toronto: Oxford University Press, 1998), p. 25.

6. Wreford Watson, "The Role of Illusion in North American Geography: A Note on the Geography of North American Settlement," *Canadian Geographer* 13 (Spring 1969): 16.

7. Shepard Krech III, "On the Aboriginal Population of the Kutchin," *Arctic Anthropology* 15(1) (1978), reprinted in Kenneth S. Coates and William R. Morrison, eds., *Interpreting Canada's North* (Toronto: Copp Clark Pitman, 1989), p. 66.

8. Friesen, p. 130.

RELATED READINGS

See Module 9, "The Métis and Red River Society: Change, Adaptation, and Resistance—1830s to 1870s," in *Visions: The Canadian History Modules Project: Pre-Confederation*. The module includes articles by: Sylvia Van Kirk, "The Impact of White Women on Fur Trade Society," Gerald Friesen, "The Métis and the Red River Settlement," and Gerhard Ens, "Dispossession or Adaptation? Migration and Persistence of the Red River Métis, 1835–1890." See pages 381–426.

BIBLIOGRAPHY

The best history of the Canadian West remains Gerald Friesen's book *The Canadian Prairies: A History* (Toronto: University of Toronto Press, 1984). Two traditional overviews are George F.G. Stanley, *The Birth of Western Canada* (Toronto: University of Toronto Press, 1960 [1936]) and W.L. Morton, *Manitoba: A History* (Toronto: University of Toronto Press, 1967 [1957]). For a more recent, short overview, see Sarah Carter, *Aboriginal People and Colonizers of Western Canada to 1900* (Toronto: University of Toronto Press, 1999). Two illustrated books are William R. Morrison, *True North: The Yukon and Northwest Territories* (Toronto: Oxford University Press, 1998); and John Herd Thompson, *Forging the Prairie West* (Toronto: Oxford University

Press, 1998), both in Oxford's Illustrated History of Canada series. For an overview of the prehistory of the region see Liz Bryan, *Stone by Stone: Exploring Ancient Sites on the Canadian Plains* (Victoria: Heritage House, 2005). For the Mackenzie River basin, see Kerry Abel's *Drum Songs: Glimpses of Dene History* (Montreal/Kingston: McGill-Queen's University Press, 1993). R. Douglas Francis reviews changing perceptions of the Northwest in *Images of the West* (Saskatoon: Western Producer Prairie Books, 1989).

Kerry Abel provides a bibliographic guide to the historical literature in "The Northwest and the North," in M. Brook Taylor, ed., *Canadian History: A Reader's Guide*, vol. 1, *Beginnings to Confederation* (Toronto: University of Toronto Press, 1994), pp. 325–55.

J.M. Bumsted examines the fur trade rivalry in *Fur Trade Wars: The Founding of Western Canada* (Winnipeg: Great Plains Publications, 1999). Frits Pannekoek examines the divisions in Red River Society in *A Snug Little Flock: The Social Origins of the Riel Resistance, 1869–70* (Winnipeg: Watson & Dyer Publishing, 1991). Sylvia Van Kirk offers valuable portraits of women in Red River and fur-trade society in *Many Tender Ties: Women in Fur-Trade Society, 1670–1870* (Winnipeg: Watson & Dyer Publishing, 1980). For a look at the lure of the West for British travellers, see Terry Abraham, *Mountains So Sublime: Nineteenth-Century British Travelers and the Lure of the Rocky Mountain West* (Calgary: University of Calgary Press, 2005). For a look at law and society in the Northwest see Louis Knafla and Jonathan Swainger, *Laws and Societies in the Canadian Prairie West, 1670–1940* (Vancouver: UBC Press, 2005). See also Walter Hildebrandt, *Views from Fort Battleford: Constructed Visions of an Anglo-Canadian West* (Edmonton: Athabaska University Press 2009).

For information on the First Nations in the eighteenth and nineteenth centuries, consult Arthur Ray, *Indians in the Fur Trade* (Toronto: University of Toronto Press, 1974). On cultural change on the northern plains, an essential work is Theodore Binnema's *Common and Contested Ground. A Human and Environmental History of the Northwestern Plains* (Norman: University of Oklahoma Press, 2001). Deanna Christensen has written a community study, *Ahtahkakoop. The Epic Account of a Plains Cree Head Chief, His People, and Their Struggle for Survival 1816–1896* (Shell Lake, SK: Ahtahkakoop Publishing, 2000). Hugh Dempsey's biographies of three Plains chiefs offer a vivid portrait of Blackfoot, Blood, and Cree life in the nineteenth century: *Crowfoot* (Edmonton: Hurtig, 1972); *Red Crow* (Saskatoon: Western Producer Prairie Books, 1980); and *Big Bear* (Vancouver: Douglas & McIntyre, 1984). John Milloy reviews the history of the Cree from 1790 to 1870 in *The Plains Cree* (Winnipeg: University of Manitoba Press, 1988). Laura Peers looks at the Ojibwa in *The Ojibwa of Western Canada: 1780 to 1870* (Winnipeg: University of Manitoba Press, 1994). In his monograph *Eighteenth-Century Western Cree and Their Neighbours* (Ottawa: Canadian Museum of Civilization, 1991), Dale R. Russell questions the belief that the Cree and the Assiniboine came onto the plains only after their contact with the European fur traders. For background on the impact of disease, see the early section of Maureen K. Lux, *Medicine That Walks: Disease, Medicine, and Canadian Plains Native People, 1880–1940* (Toronto: University of Toronto Press, 2001). Hugh Dempsey's study *Firewater: The Impact of the Whiskey Trade on the Blackfoot Nation* (Calgary: Fifth House, 2002) reviews the topic of substance abuse. Kerry Abel examines Dene history in *Drum Songs: Glimpses of Dene History* (Montreal/Kingston: Queen's University Press, 1993).

On the Métis, see Nicole St-Onge's *Saint-Laurent, Manitoba: Evolving Metis Identities, 1850–1914* (Regina: Canadian Plains Research Centre, 2004); also useful is her article "The Persistence of Travel and Trade: St. Lawrence River Valley French Engagés and the American Fur Company, 1818–1840," *Michigan Historical Review* 34(2) (2008). A popular work is D. Bruce Sealey and Antoine S. Lussier, *The Métis: Canada's Forgotten People* (Winnipeg: Manitoba Métis Federation Press, 1975). George Woodcock translated Marcel Giraud's classic *Le Métis canadien* (Paris: Institut d'ethnologie, Université de Paris, 1945) into English, under the title *The Métis in the Canadian West*, 2 vols. (Edmonton: University of Alberta Press, 1986). Jacqueline Peterson and Jennifer S.H. Brown have edited *The New People: Being and Becoming Métis in North America* (Winnipeg: University of Manitoba Press, 1985). Guillaume Charette's *Vanishing Spaces: Memoirs of a Prairie Métis* (Winnipeg: Editions Bois Brûlés, 1980) contains the memoirs of Louis Goulet, who was born in the Red River valley in 1859.

Gerhard Ens reviews the movement of the Métis westward in *Homeland to Hinterland: The Changing Worlds of the Red River Métis in the Nineteenth Century* (Toronto: University of Toronto Press, 1996).

See Frank Tough's *As Their Natural Resources Fail: Native People and the Economic History of Northern Manitoba, 1870–1930* (Vancouver: UBC Press, 2006). A specific study of an English mixed-blood Red River community is Robert J. Coutts, *The Road to the Rapids: Nineteenth-Century Church and Society at St. Andrew's Parish, Red River* (Calgary: University of Calgary Press, 2000). See also Irene Gordon, *A People on the Move: The Métis of the Western Plains* (Surrey: Heritage House, 2009). Brenda MacDougall's *One of the Family: Metis Culture in Nineteenth-Century Northwestern Saskatchewan* (Vancouver: UBC Press, 2010) is another recent work, although one focused only on the nineteenth-century.

Brian Gallagher questions the argument that increasing racism in the period before 1870 caused a decline in the marriage rate between European officers of the Hudson's Bay Company and Métis women: "A Re-examination of Race, Class and Society in Red River," *Native Studies Review* 4(1–2) (1988): 25–65. Edith I. Burley provides a detailed look at the labourers of the Hudson's Bay Company in *Servants of the Honourable Company: Work, Discipline, and Conflict in the Hudson's Bay Company, 1770–1879* (Toronto: Oxford University Press, 1997).

A book containing Aboriginal perspectives is Julie Cruikshank, *Reading Voices* (Vancouver: Douglas & McIntyre, 1991), on oral and written interpretations of the Yukon's past. George Blondin, *When the World Was New: Stories of the Sahtú Dene* (Yellowknife: Outcrop Books, 1990), provides a valuable Indigenous viewpoint on the history of the Great Bear Lake district of the Mackenzie River valley. Two volumes contain valuable information on the Inuit and First Nations: David Damas, ed., *Handbook of North American Indians*, vol. 5, *Arctic* (Washington, DC: Smithsonian Institution, 1984); and June Helm, ed., *Handbook of North American Indians*, vol. 6, *Subarctic* (Washington, DC: Smithsonian Institution, 1981).

Valuable maps of the Northwest appear in R. Cole Harris, ed., *Historical Atlas of Canada*, vol. 1, *From the Beginning to 1800* (Toronto: University of Toronto Press, 1987); R. Louis Gentilcore, ed., *The Historical Atlas of Canada*, vol. 2, *The Land Transformed, 1800–1891* (Toronto: University of Toronto Press, 1993); and Richard I. Ruggles, *A Country So Interesting: The Hudson's Bay Company and Two Centuries of Mapping, 1670–1870* (Montreal/Kingston: McGill-Queen's University Press, 1991).

For an environmental history of the northern plains see W.F. Rannie, "Summer Rainfall on the Prairies During the Palliser and Hind Expeditions, 1857–1859," *Prairie Forum* 31(1) (2006): 17–38. For a look at hunting culture in Rupert's Land, see Greg Gillespie, *Hunting for Empire: Narratives of Sport in Rupert's Land, 1840–1870* (Vancouver: UBC Press 2007).

Source: Library and Archives Canada, Acc. No. 1991-265-232/C-013415.

Chapter Twenty

THE PACIFIC COAST

TIME LINE

1774	Spanish expedition led by Juan Pérez encounters Haida off Queen Charlotte Islands
1778	British Captain Cook visits Nootka Sound
1793	Alexander Mackenzie reaches Pacific Coast
1821	Merger of Hudson's Bay Company and North West Company
1827	HBC builds Fort Langley near mouth of Fraser River
1843	HBC builds Fort Victoria on Vancouver Island
1846	Oregon Treaty creates 49th Parallel as border from Rocky Mountains to Pacific
1849	Colony of Vancouver Island established by HBC
1850–4	Douglas negotiates fourteen treaties with First Nations of Vancouver Island
1856	Legislative Assembly provided for colony of Vancouver
1858	Fraser River gold rush leads to establishment of British Columbia as mainland colony
1866	Colonies of British Columbia and Vancouver Island unite
1867	United States purchases Alaska from Russia

While explorers such as Sir Francis Drake may have explored the Pacific Coast for England as early as 1579, contact between the First Nations and Europeans occurred in the late eighteenth century. Relations were focused around the trade in sea-otter pelts. Explorers, such as Alexander Mackenzie, crossed the continent and reached the west coast in 1793. The fur trade war also reached the coast, crossing over from the Athabasca country, and both the Hudson's Bay Company and the Northwest Company built forts to facilitate trade. Throughout the nineteenth century, Roman Catholic and Protestant missionaries worked among the Aboriginal peoples.

Initially, Russia, Spain, Britain, and the United States competed for control of the Pacific Coast. Eventually only Britain and the United States contested the area between Russian Alaska and Spanish California. In 1818, the British and Americans agreed to joint occupancy and in 1846, the two countries consented to extend the international border along the 49th Parallel from the prairies to the Pacific, and to include Vancouver Island in Britain's jurisdiction. The Pacific Coast became an important imperial naval link in the "all red route to the Orient."

Significant colonization first came to the southern tip of Vancouver Island in the 1840s and then to the mouth of the Fraser River during the gold rush of 1858. The process occurred rapidly. By the 1860s, the newcomers claimed ownership of the entire coast and interior of British Columbia, even though the First Nations had not surrendered the land through treaty and they formed the majority of the population.

The First Nations of the Pacific Coast

The pristine wilderness of the Pacific Coast was home to a large number of First Nations. The region—which included the seas, the mountains, and the forests—was abundant in natural resources. Hemmed in by towering mountains, the narrow coastline was heavily populated. It is estimated that nearly half of the total Aboriginal population of Canada lived in present-day British Columbia at the time of European contact. The area became the most linguistically diverse in all of North America, with nineteen distinct languages represented. One of the oldest archaeological sites in the Fraser River canyon dates back at least 8500 years.

In general, the Pacific Coast First Nations were a more settled people. The abundance of resources meant they did not have to constantly move in order to follow their food supplies. As a result, they developed more permanent settlements, which explains the diversity in languages. It also explains similarities with Europeans when it came to notions of property and hierarchy. Because the groups were settled, they placed importance on the accumulation of material wealth and property. But as with all First Nations groups, generalizations can be misleading.

The Potlatch and Social Structure

Many of the First Nations had elaborate hierarchical social structures. The chiefdoms (Haida, Nuu'chah'nulth, Kwagiulth, and Tsimshian) were built upon clearly marked divisions among chiefs, nobles, and commoners, based on wealth and heredity. At the bottom were the slaves, acquired in war or by purchase. Anthropologist Philip Drucker notes that "each society consisted not of two or more social classes, but of a complex series of statuses graded relatively, one for each individual of the group."[1] The northern nations (Tlingit, Haida, and Tsimshian) were divided into exogamous moieties, which in turn were further subdivided into clans. Descent was recognized only through the female line. The southern nations (Kwagiulth, Bella Coola, and Nuu'chah'nulth) had no moieties and instead recognized descent "ambilaterally"—that is, rank and status were determined by membership in particular societies.

The dominant ritual on the Pacific Coast was the *potlatch*, which involved a distribution of gifts according to status. Originally the ritual had a subsistence function, facilitating food exchanges between groups with surpluses and those with shortages. In time, these elaborate "giveaway" feasts were used for more selfish purposes, such as allowing the ambitious to gain wealth and status, or providing the wealthy an opportunity to demonstrate their generosity. Anthropologist Wilson Duff describes the potlatch as

> *a large gathering to which important people were invited in order to witness some event,*
> *such as a young person assuming a new name or the completion of a new house and erection*
> *of a totem pole. On such an occasion the host would display his wealth and present gifts to*
> *his guests. The more he gave away, the more prestige he acquired.*[2]

Lineage played an important role. Each local kin group, for example, had identifiable privileges indicating common origins. One lineage of the Nimpkish, a village group among the Kwakwaka'wakw (Kwagiulth or Kwakiutl), on northeastern Vancouver Island, believed themselves descended from a giant halibut and a thunderbird that transformed themselves into human beings. People in this lineage proudly displayed the thunderbird and the halibut as crests on their houses, dance blankets, and painted screens.[3] The kin group also had the right to specific prerogatives in its intricate ceremonial system, such as the right to certain names, songs, and dances.

Warfare

Warfare also differed among the First Nations of the Pacific Coast. It was more widespread prior to contact, likely due to the later decimation of the populations as result of disease. Whereas war was carried out for honour, for territory, or to settle disputes, on the Pacific Coast it was also carried out to gain material wealth. In the south, in particular, the objective was often to gain booty (such as war canoes) and slaves. The Haida were feared slavers who often raided the Salish. The Tlingit were another nation renowned for their warlike nature.

Impressions of the Europeans

The Squamish tell about the first time their ancestors encountered the newcomers in the late eighteenth century. The Squamish paddled out to meet them. They hesitated going on board the floating wooden island with cobwebs hanging from the sticks growing on it until, with great misgivings, the bravest climbed the rope ladder onto the deck. The captain, who was pale as a corpse, advanced with outstretched hand. The chief assumed they were being challenged to a finger-wrestling match. He therefore waved away the man with whom the captain was trying to shake hands and called for the Squamish strongman to accept the challenge. Seeing that he was misunderstood, the captain shrugged and approached the chief with outstretched hand. The chief then said to the strongman, "He doesn't want you. He thinks you are not strong enough." With that, the chief refused to consider the captain's "challenge." The strangers' gifts also puzzled the Squamish. The newcomers offered warm snow in a sack (flour) and buttons (coins).

Seagoing canoes of the Northwest Coast.
Source: Library and Archives Canada/C-30193.

Kwakwaka'wakw village.

Source: Glenbow Archives, Calgary, Canada/NA-528-1.

European Exploration of the Northwest Coast

By the time the Europeans reached the Pacific Coast, they had considerable experience dealing with Indigenous peoples. Although Spain was the first European power to reach the Pacific Ocean, it took them two and a half centuries to advance northward from Mexico. Apostolos Valerianos, a Greek captain better known by his Spanish name of Juan de Fuca, spent forty years serving Spain in the Americas. He allegedly sailed north along the Pacific Coast and, in about 1590, entered a vast gulf or wide inlet between the 47th and 48th parallels that led into a broader sea with many islands. Fuca believed this to be the western outlet of the fabled Straits of Anian, a body of water that could provide a convenient sea passage between Europe and Asia. But the Spanish took so little interest in the expedition that they failed to preserve any authentic record of it, and only Fuca's later statement that he made the voyage survives. As Spanish power declined, rival empires seized its islands in the West Indies. These same rivals seldom ventured to the Pacific, however, until Russians arrived in the eighteenth century.

Vitus Bering, a Danish navigator in the Russian service, made the first documented voyage to present-day Alaska. In 1728, he sailed along the eastern coast of Siberia until he found the strait that now bears his name. In 1741, he explored an area in present-day southeastern Alaska. His return voyage proved disastrous, however, and the sixty-year-old mariner died of scurvy after being shipwrecked on an island off the Siberian coast. Nevertheless, his ill-fated expedition established Russia's claim to the Alaskan panhandle and led to economic expansion in the Pacific. The survivors from Bering's ship brought back a cargo of 900 sea-otter pelts. The Chinese prized the furs for their warmth and their glossy beauty, and they brought high prices. Within a half-century, the profitable sea-otter trade led to an international rivalry among Russia, Spain, and later Britain and the United States.

Rumours of Russian activity prompted Spain to advance northward to ensure the protection of Mexico. In 1767, the Spanish developed a major port at San Blas on Mexico's west coast and established settlements in California at San Diego, Monterey, and San Francisco. They also sponsored expeditions to investigate Russian advances along the Northwest Coast and to assert Spanish sovereignty. Juan Pérez sailed from San Blas in late January 1774 to Alaska, but bad weather forced him to turn back just north of the Queen Charlotte Islands. Pérez met 150 Haidas off the Queen Charlottes—the first recorded meeting between Europeans and Northwest Coast First Nations. The meeting was friendly, and the Spaniards traded small shipboard objects for

Cook's ships Resolution *and* Discovery *anchored at Resolution Cove in a 1778 painting by Gordon Miller.*

Source: Gordon Miller.

Aboriginal artifacts (now displayed in the Museo de América in Madrid). In 1775, Juan Franciso de la Bodega y Quadra claimed the North Pacific Coast for Spain.

Instead of the Russians, the British became Spain's major rival on the Pacific Coast. Captain James Cook was already renowned for his discoveries in Australasia and Antarctica. He had also been present at the French surrender of Louisbourg in 1758 and had helped to guide the English armada to Quebec. In the spring of 1778, he visited the Pacific Coast on his third expedition.

Cook's two vessels, HMS *Discovery* and HMS *Resolution*, arrived at Nootka Sound, which had been sighted by Pérez four years earlier. Here, Cook spent a month refitting his ships. Since no other European power knew of the Spaniard's previous visit, Cook (who was killed in January 1779 by Indigenous people in Hawaii) was credited with "discovering" Nootka, and the British claim to the Northwest Pacific Coast received international recognition. Captain Cook was welcomed by Maquinna, chief of the Mowachaht (a Nuu'chah'nulth group). Maquinna had already traded with the Spanish and he hoped to open trade with the British as well.

To strengthen their own claim, the Spanish in 1789 established a colony at Nootka Sound (with Maquinna's permission) and maintained a garrison of 200 to 250 men for six years, with only a brief absence during the winter of 1789–90. The dispute over territorial jurisdiction, known as the Nootka Sound Controversy, brought Spain and Britain to the brink of war. Spain argued that it had the exclusive right to trade and to control the coast, while Britain claimed that navigation was open to any nation. In 1795, Spain agreed to share the northern ports. It badly needed British assistance in its war against France. The agreement (which Maquinna helped negotiate) brought to an end Spain's attempts to exert a presence north of California.

In 1784, the publication of the official account of Cook's third voyage proved a turning point in Pacific Coast exploration. Captain James King, who had taken command shortly after the death of Cook, recounted in *A Voyage to the Pacific Ocean* (1784) how sea-otter pelts obtained in trade with the Nuu'chah'nulth had brought great profits in China. Other mariners saw their opportunity. The first was the sea captain James Hanna, who sailed in a British vessel appropriately named *Sea Otter*. Several other British and American ships followed. The trade in sea-otter pelts ushered in a brief but intense period of economic activity and contact between Europeans and First Nations.

Imperial Rivalry on the Northwest Coast

The withdrawal of Spain in the mid-1790s left the Northwest Coast open to three contenders: Russia, Britain, and the newly independent United States. In 1784, the Russians established a base at Three Saints Harbor on Kodiak Island in the Gulf of Alaska. The Russians now encountered intense British and American competition for sea-otter pelts. The Russian traders, however, laboured under several major handicaps. In contrast to both the Americans and the British, they possessed fewer and poorer trade goods, as well as inferior trading vessels. The Russian advance slowed in the Alaskan panhandle, where they faced strong competition from British and American traders, and from Tlingit middlemen, who traded European goods to the interior First Nations in what is now Yukon and northwestern British Columbia.

Britain strengthened its claim with the dispatch of a three-year expedition under George Vancouver, a naval officer who had served with Cook's expedition in 1778. From 1792 to 1794, Vancouver methodically charted the coastline from Oregon to Alaska. This thorough survey proved that Juan de Fuca Strait was not the entrance to the great inland sea that Fuca had reported. Vancouver later wrote in *Voyage of Discovery to the North Pacific Ocean*: "I trust the precision with which the survey . . . has been carried into effect, will remove every doubt, and set aside every opinion of a north-west passage, or any water communication navigable for shipping, existing between the north Pacific, and the interior of the American continent, within the limits of our researches." Before leaving the Northwest Coast, the British navigator named a huge island "Quadra's and Vancouver's Island" (sharing the honour with his friend Juan Francisco de la Bodega y Quadra, the Spanish commander at Nootka Sound). Later, it became known simply as Vancouver's Island, and finally as Vancouver Island.

The Napoleonic wars curtailed British voyages to the Northwest Coast. As Britain withdrew men from its merchant ships for service in the Royal Navy, American entrepreneurs captured Britain's trade in the North Pacific. After the mid-1790s, American traders dominated the coastal trade for the next quarter-century.

The First Nations and the Fur Trade

The First Nations welcomed the European fur traders and their iron trading goods. As with the Aboriginal groups to the east, the Pacific Coast groups quickly realized the advantages of metal tools and weapons. In fact, the Spanish discovered that the First Nations coveted iron so much that they even removed the metal strapping from the sides of their ships. Not even the rudder chains were safe. The Catholic missionaries were less impressed when some Aboriginals tore down

Man of Nootka Sound.

Source: Library and Archives Canada, Acc. No. 1991-265-232/ C-013415.

New tools and pigments became available to the Aboriginal peoples after contact with the fur traders. Carving became more elaborate and colourful. This photo, taken by C.F. Newcombe in 1901, shows the Kwakwaka'wakw village of Blunden Harbour.

Source: Image A-09132 courtesy of Royal British Columbia Museum, BC Archives.

a large cross to obtain the nails holding it together. In addition to purchasing iron goods, the people traded for muskets, cloth, clothing, blankets, rum, and molasses.

As with the fur trade elsewhere on the continent, the initial relationship was mutually advantageous. Both Europeans and First Nations gained benefits. In addition, it was the much more numerous Aboriginals in their home territory who initially controlled the trade. The first groups to commence trading took on the role of middlemen and worked aggressively to prevent the Europeans from coming into contact with the inland groups. Often, the Aboriginal middlemen imposed a 200 to 300 percent markup on the furs and goods they traded. Women also played a significant role in the trade. Anthropologist Loraine Littlefield notes "the many historical accounts that document the presence of women in trade transactions, their shrewdness and skill in bargaining, and their role as chief negotiators."[4]

Although the linguistic diversity of the Pacific Coast even exceeded that of Europe, a single trade language, called "Chinook jargon," came into use along the West Coast in the 1830s. Its 300 or so key words included borrowings from First Nations languages, as well as English and French: *skookum* meant powerful or fast; *chuck* water; *cheechako* newcomer; *Kinchotsh* ("King George Man") Englishman. Chinook jargon was spoken as far away as the inland districts. But the entry of European traders into the interior around 1810 took away much of the middlemen's trade. For nearly forty years, the maritime fur trade prospered along the coast. By 1825, however, the sea-otter population neared extinction.

The fur trade had an impact on the culture of the First Nations. The tools they made from their new supplies of iron allowed them to produce better and more refined headdresses, costumes, and masks for feasts and ceremonies. As well, new dyes and pigments became available. Although the First Nations carvers favoured the traditional colours, weavers supplemented the original pigments—red and yellow ochres, black and blue-green copper oxide—with the whole spectrum of European trade colours. Wood carving expanded. The totem poles, which displayed individual families' genealogies, underwent much elaboration and reached greater heights. More gradually, dress shifted from skins to cloth, and capes from cedarbark and mountain goat wool (or dog hair) to navy blue and red blanket cloth. Blankets became an important unit of trade.

But it did not take long for the negative results of contact to appear. To an extent, it repeated but condensed the 300 years of fur trade history on the eastern half of the continent. The Mowachaht people provide a good example. When incidents of theft occurred, it was common for the European traders to exact revenge against an entire Aboriginal group, which was then met by further vengeance. In 1803, the successor to Maquinna murdered the entire crew of the American ship *Boston*. Two men were left alive and taken into captivity. Upon being freed, they wrote a book describing their ordeal. A smallpox epidemic wiped out half the Nuu'chah'nulth population.

The absence of accurate statistics makes it difficult to provide even rough estimates of the casualties, but European infectious diseases such as smallpox, measles, influenza, and mumps took their toll, as they did elsewhere in the Americas. Smallpox ravaged coastal communities in 1835 and 1836. Measles and influenza wiped out villages in the Columbia Plateau in 1848 and 1849. Estimates indicate that the entire First Nations population declined from approximately 50 000 to 13 000. A smallpox epidemic that started in Victoria in 1862 killed about one-third of the First Nations population within two years. The Haida population fell from 6000 in 1835 to 800 in 1885.

The Inland Fur Trade

Not long after Europeans reached the Northwest Coast by sea, fur traders also arrived by land. Anxious to find a short supply line to the Pacific Ocean, the North West Company searched for a route westward from Lake Athabasca to the Pacific. The Nor'Wester Alexander Mackenzie, the first European to canoe the northern river that now bears his name and to reach the Arctic Ocean, completed the first crossing of North America (north of Mexico) in 1793 by travelling down what is now called the Fraser River, then over to the Bella Coola River, and down to the Pacific. On a seaside rock he simply wrote, "From Canada. By Land." The arduous route proved useless for transporting furs, but the journey made the 24-year-old Mackenzie's reputation as a fearless trader and explorer.

Two other Nor'Westers worked to find a commercial route to the Pacific. In 1808, Simon Fraser, who had first opened up fur-trading posts in the interior of what is now British Columbia, travelled with a small party down the treacherous river named after him. He succeeded, but pronounced the route unnavigable. Finally, in 1811, David Thompson, a partner of the North West Company, followed the Columbia River, and thereby connected the NWC route from east of the Rockies to the Pacific coast. A sea expedition sent by John Jacob Astor's Pacific Fur Company arrived in late March 1811, just months before Thompson. On the basis of having founded Fort Astoria, the Americans claimed the Oregon country.

Relations with the United States

As a temporary compromise, Britain and the United States agreed in 1818 to occupy the Columbia country jointly. The agreement left commerce open to both British and American traders between latitudes 42° and 54°40' (from the northern boundary of California to the southern limits of Alaska).

With the merger of the NWC and the HBC in 1821, the new Hudson's Bay Company under the management of Sir George Simpson began to exploit the rich fur resources of the Northwest Coast. Having obtained from the British Crown a 21-year lease to the exclusive trade of the "Indian Territory" (the lands between the Rocky Mountains and the Pacific), Simpson located a Pacific depot at Fort Vancouver, in an area of good farmland 150 kilometres up the Columbia River. Other forts followed. The three most important were Fort Langley, near the mouth of the Fraser River, built in 1827; Fort Simpson, on the boundary of the Russian territory to the north, in 1831; and Fort Victoria, strategically located on the southern tip of Vancouver Island, in 1843. The HBC's energetic commercial activities established a strong British presence on the Pacific Coast.

American interest in the Columbia country increased in the early 1840s. Americans began arriving in the 1830s, and by 1843 they numbered about 1000. In the next three years, another 5000 settlers arrived in the Columbia River valley. But due to the network of posts, inland trails, and shipping routes established by the HBC, Britain dominated the area north of the Columbia River. Nevertheless, the expansionist American president James Polk, who won the presidential election in December 1844 with the campaign slogan "54°40' or fight," demanded all of "Oregon," up to the Russian border.

In his inaugural address in March, President Polk reaffirmed his position that the United States held "clear and unquestionable" title to Oregon. His stand enjoyed popular support. In the summer of 1845, the newspaper, *The United States Magazine and Democratic Review*, introduced in an editorial the phrase "manifest destiny." The paper argued that foreign governments were attempting to check "the fulfillment of our manifest destiny to overspread the continent allotted by Providence for the free development of our yearly multiplying millions." Within months, the phrase became common usage throughout the United States.

The Americans began a war with Mexico in 1846 over Texas (and later New Mexico and California). Against Congressman Abraham Lincoln's objections that Congress and the public had been misled about the causes of the war (an alleged Mexican invasion), the President persisted in pushing for war. Polk did not, however, also want war with Britain. To avoid conflict, both signed the Anglo–American Treaty in June 1846, shortly after the United States had declared war on Mexico. The agreement extended the 49th Parallel (which had become the international border

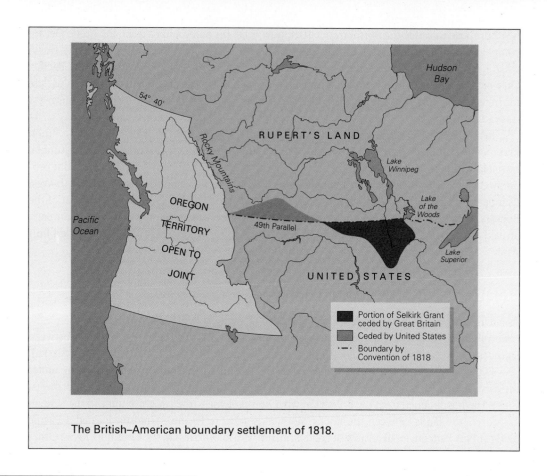

The British–American boundary settlement of 1818.

President James Polk, the expansionist eleventh president of the United States, 1845.

across the prairies in 1818) from the Rocky Mountains to the Pacific Ocean. Britain surrendered its demand for all the land north of the Columbia River, but gained recognition of its claim to all of Vancouver Island, a portion of which extended south of the 49th Parallel. Spared another war with Britain, Polk proceeded to defeat Mexico and to seize one-third of its territory for the United States.

The Establishment of Colonies

Anxious to counter the threat of American squatter settlement in its Pacific territory, the British government asked the Hudson's Bay Company to colonize, as well as to manage, Vancouver Island for ten years. A royal grant of 1849 stipulated that the company had to develop the island, make lands available to settlers at reasonable prices, and safeguard Aboriginal rights. By the end of 1849, Fort Victoria served as the company's western headquarters, its shipping depot, and its provisioning centre, as well as the capital of the colony of Vancouver Island. In 1852, the Colonial Office extended the jurisdiction of the governor of Vancouver Island to include the Queen Charlotte Islands.

At the time of the first census in 1855, fewer than 1000 white inhabitants lived in the Pacific colony of Vancouver Island. The discovery of coal at Nanaimo on the east coast of the island led to the founding of a small permanent European settlement. But until the Fraser River gold rush in 1858, the colony continued primarily as a fur-trading region, with its centre at Fort Victoria.

The fur traders consisted of immigrants from places as diverse as the Orkney Islands and Hawaii, along with French Canadians, Iroquois, and mixed-bloods. Many of the whites married First Nations or mixed-blood women. The existence of free land in Oregon and Washington

Nanaimo, around 1866.

Source: Toronto Reference Library/T14258.

attracted settlers; on Vancouver Island, land had to be purchased. At the time, perhaps as many as 200 whites lived in the various fur-trading posts on the mainland. On Vancouver Island and the mainland, the Aboriginal peoples outnumbered the whites by approximately fifty to one.

James Douglas

James Douglas became governor of the colony of Vancouver Island in 1851, replacing Richard Blanshard, the first governor, who resigned one year after arriving in Fort Victoria. In his brief term as governor, Blanshard used gunboats to launch attacks against the Newitty and Cowichan First Nations.

A "Scotch West Indian," Douglas was born in British Guiana (now Guyana), the son of "a free coloured woman" and a Scottish merchant. Sent to Scotland for his schooling at age 12, Douglas joined the North West Company at the age of 16 as an apprentice. After the union of the two rival companies, he entered northern "Oregon," or New Caledonia, as the HBC called it. There, in 1828, he married Amelia Connolly, the daughter of William Connolly, a fur trader from Lower Canada, and his Cree wife. In 1830, the HBC transferred Douglas to Fort Vancouver, and nine years later he became a chief factor. With his promotion to Fort Victoria in 1849, he became the senior company officer west of the Rocky Mountains.

Aboriginal Policy

Douglas found himself in charge of Aboriginal policy at a time of escalating violence. With white settlers arriving and the fur trade declining, the initial mutually beneficial relationship between native and newcomer had passed. The potential for violence was real. The First Nations, consisting of Songhees, Cowichan, Nanaimo, Nuu'chah'nulth, Haida, Kwakiutl, Sechelt, and Sto:lo drastically outnumbered the whites in the colony by 30 000 to less than 1000.

Douglas did not intervene in quarrels among the First Nations, but he did use his power, including Royal Navy gunboats, to settle disputes between them and whites. He claimed that he would not punish an entire group for the transgressions of one individual, as was often done by other administrators, and to have "invariably acted on the principle that it is inexpedient and unjust to hold tribes responsible for the acts of *individuals*." This approach, however, could also have negative effects. In 1828, Douglas is reported to have marched into a First Nations community to apprehend and then execute a man on the charge of murder. His aggressive tactics earned him considerable disdain among the local Aboriginals. But Douglas does seem to have at least made an attempt to understand First Nations society. Above all, he did not want the open

First elections to the Vancouver Island Assembly in 1856. Painting by Charles W. Simpson.

Source: Library and Archives Canada, Acc. No. 1991-35-14/ C-013947.

warfare that had broken out between the American settlers and the Aboriginal peoples (Cayuse and Yakima) in the Washington Territory to spill over the border.

The British Colonial Office realized that the fur trade was declining and that agricultural settlement was required to stake their claim against American competition. Vancouver Island, in particular, had to be protected. Under pressure from the British government, the HBC sent instructions to James Douglas to purchase Aboriginal land on Vancouver Island. Douglas took it upon himself to negotiate treaties. Following the dictates of the Royal Proclamation of 1763, he recognized "Indian Title" and believed that it was necessary to purchase the land before new settlement occurred. Between 1850 and 1854, he negotiated fourteen treaties. In all, he purchased roughly 1000 square kilometres of land, or about 3 percent of the total area of Vancouver Island. Douglas encouraged the Aboriginals to take up farming and he welcomed missionaries who would bring religion and education. He also encouraged them to work in the developing coal mines.

As the white population of the colony increased, Douglas' autocratic ways met increasing criticism. Settlers complained that he abused power and ignored obvious conflicts of interest. Most of all, they objected to his setting the price of land at £1 for one acre (0.4 hectares) when land in the neighbouring American Pacific Northwest went for one-quarter the price. The rising business class in Victoria objected to his "family-Company compact," composed of former Hudson's Bay Company officials and members of his own family, in particular his brother-in-law, David Cameron (appointed to the Supreme Court and the Legislative Council), and his son-in-law, Dr. John Sebastian Helmcken, the first speaker of the Assembly. In 1856, Douglas bowed to British pressure to establish a legislative assembly.

When settlement on Vancouver Island increased in the late 1850s, Douglas wished to purchase more Aboriginal land and to set aside reserves. Lack of funds, however, made the process difficult. The First Nations were realizing the value of the lands and were demanding better terms. The Assembly asked Britain to lend money to make land payments to the First Nations. The Colonial Office refused and replied that the funds should be raised locally. Settlement continued apace and the result was that while land was still taken, treaties were not signed and compensation was not provided the First Nations after 1859. White settlements were interspersed among small, autonomous Aboriginal villages. The government of Vancouver Island (and later British Columbia) set aside reserves without extinguishing title to the land. This situation placed the First Nations of British Columbia in a unique situation. Only a century and a half later, in the 1990s, would the treaty process resume on Vancouver Island and on the coastal mainland.

The Creation of British Columbia

When gold was discovered on the lower Fraser River and word reached California in the spring of 1858, the rush began. In 1849, 80 000 people had entered the California gold fields in one year alone. A decade later, the California gold rush had lost its momentum, and the gold seekers now

New Westminster, B.C., around 1863.

Source: Image A-03330 courtesy of Royal BC Museum, BC Archives.

headed north; some 27 000 men arrived from San Francisco. Seemingly overnight, a tent town arose at Victoria. Many new businesses or branches of American firms, financed by San Francisco capital, were established. One witness counted 225 new commercial buildings in Victoria in 1858.

Once in Victoria, the miners faced the challenge of reaching the gold fields in the interior. They needed boats to cross the Strait of Georgia to reach the mouth of the Fraser. In the "rush," many launched their own hastily made vessels and were drowned. Once the prospectors reached the mouth of the Fraser, they faced an additional 250 kilometres journey up the river to the first major strike, just south of Yale, an old trading post. In the last two weeks of May alone, 10 000 men travelled up the Fraser by canoe, sailboat, and raft. Another 15 000 arrived by the end of the year.

The main street of Barkerville, B.C., in the 1860s.

Source: Library and Archives Canada/PA-061940.

The arrival of thousands of Americans threatened British sovereignty on the mainland and raised the danger of a war between prospectors and the First Nations. In the fall of 1858, escalating tensions between the miners and the Nlaka'pamux First Nation led to the Fraser Canyon War. As the senior British official in the area, Douglas claimed the mainland and its minerals for the Crown. He drew up mining regulations, licensed miners, and hired constables. The Colonial Office praised Douglas, even though he was overstepping his bounds and lacked legal authority on the mainland. The British government quickly established a second colony on the mainland, British Columbia, separate from that of Vancouver Island.

James Douglas became British Columbia's first governor while still serving as governor of Vancouver Island (which in 1859 came under the direct control of the Colonial Office, after the royal grant to the Hudson's Bay Company ended). Colonel Richard Clement Moody, the first lieutenant governor of British Columbia, established the colony's new capital near the mouth of the Fraser River at New Westminster. Douglas, along with Matthew Baillie Begbie, British Columbia's first chief justice (and known as the "hanging judge"), established a uniform judicial system for the colony. Judge Begbie's circuit court tours established a frontier version of British law in the scattered mining camps.

Since no assembly was granted on the mainland (the British government did not want to give political influence to the increasing American population), Douglas retained his autocratic powers, including the power to legislate by proclamation. In May 1861, John Robson, the editor of New Westminster's *British Columbian*, commented on the lack of democracy: "We are in a state of veriest serfdom."

In 1860, about 4000 gold miners (the majority from California and Oregon; the rest from eastern Canada, Britain, Europe, and even China) proceeded eastward, pushing into the Thompson, Lillooet, and then the southern Cariboo regions. By 1861, with big strikes at Richfield, at Barkerville, and at Lightning on Williams Creek, the Cariboo region became the major mining field. But the gold resources could not be exploited without road links to the coast. Roads were also needed to guarantee British commercial and military control of the interior. Using public funds, the 650-kilometre Cariboo Road was completed in 1863, connecting the gold towns of Yale and Barkerville.

The First Nations obtained little economic benefit from the gold rush. The miners had no intention of sharing the area's rich lands and resources with the original inhabitants. Although Douglas allowed the First Nations to choose the locations of their reserves, he made no treaties

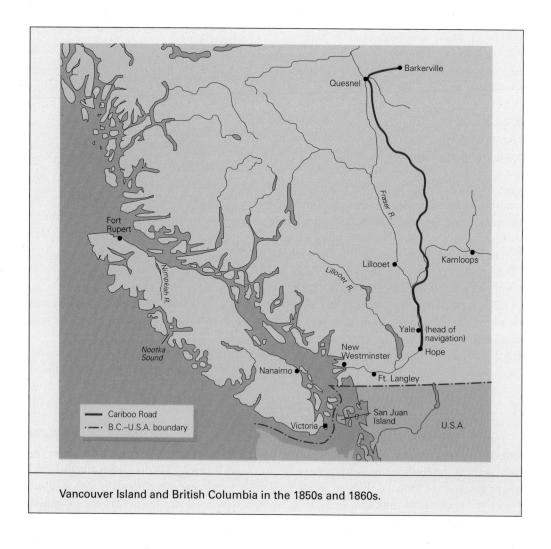

Vancouver Island and British Columbia in the 1850s and 1860s.

on the mainland. They received no compensation for the expropriation of their lands. Moreover, the miners intruded on their village sites, fishing stations, and cultivated areas. The increased number of whites also resulted in the outbreak of disease. Douglas remained governor of both British Columbia and Vancouver Island until 1864.

British Columbia in the Mid-1860s

British Columbia experienced a post–gold rush slump in the mid-1860s. Gold production fell, and people left the colony. Still, the region was rich in many natural resources. British Columbia's stands of Douglas fir produced ten times more wood per hectare than would New Brunswick's Miramichi or the Canadas' Ottawa Valley.[5] But in the 1860s, high transportation costs ruled out large-scale exploitation. Beginnings had been made in lumber and fishing as export industries, but coal mining, at centres such as Nanaimo, was still the most important industry, despite its decline. Some farming had begun, with specialization in wheat in the upper Fraser region, and with dairy and market gardening under way on the island. High American tariffs also reduced the trade that British Columbia and Vancouver Island had with the United States, although Vancouver Island did sell some coal to San Francisco.

James Douglas.
Source: Image A-01232 courtesy Royal BC Museum, BC Archives.

WHERE HISTORIANS DISAGREE

James Douglas

In the historiography of British Columbia, James Douglas is a figure comparable to Champlain in Quebec and Simcoe in Ontario. Few historians have been more laudatory of his contribution to British Columbia than historian Margaret Ormsby. In a biographical sketch of Douglas written in 1972, she states:

A man of iron nerve and physical prowess, great force of character, keen intelligence, and unusual

resourcefulness, Douglas had had a notable career in the fur trade. As colonial governor his career was even more distinguished. Against overwhelming odds, with indifferent backing from the British government, the aid of a few Royal Navy ships, and a small force of Royal Engineers, he was able to establish British rule on the Pacific Coast and lay the foundation for Canada's extension of the Pacific seaboard. Single-handed in the midst of a gold-rush he had forged policies for land, mining, and water rights which were just and endurable.[1]

Since that time, reassessments of Douglas have appeared, and his contribution, while still acknowledged as significant, is judged more critically. In her study *The West Beyond the West: A History of British Columbia*, Jean Barman criticizes Douglas for his "over-bearing style of governing." Moreover, "he alienated newcomers from Ontario and the Maritimes through his haughty demeanour and preference for Britons over Canadians."[2] His feverish road-building program, she added, left the mainland colony of British Columbia burdened by debt.

Douglas's Aboriginal policies have also been questioned. Earlier commentators such as Robert Cail,[3] Robin Fisher,[4] and Wilson Duff[5] regarded the governor's Aboriginal policies favourably. Anthropologist Wilson Duff, for instance, wrote in *The Indian History of British Columbia* that "As colonization progressed, his main concerns, in addition to maintaining law and order, were to purchase the Indian ownership rights to the land and to set aside adequate reserves for their use."[6]

Political scientist Paul Tennant, however, argues that the governor was far less generous to the First Nations than formerly believed.[7] Tennant admits that "at a time when aboriginal peoples elsewhere were routinely being forced from their lands and often actively exterminated, Douglas displayed a spirit of tolerance, compassion, and humane understanding."[8] The governor's decision to set aside reserves for First Nations communities at locations of their own choosing helped to protect these groups from cultural extinction: "The surviving members of traditional communities could thus remain resident on preferred sites within their ancestral homelands and so could retain a sense of communal unity and an active connection with historic places and communal memories. Confined to their small reserves, they could nurture a deepening sense of injustice as they witnessed the takeover of their surrounding traditional lands without regard to aboriginal title. Douglas's approach thus facilitated the retention of the communal and tribal group identities that he assumed would vanish."[9] Nonetheless, with the exception of fourteen small treaties signed between 1850 and 1854 on Vancouver Island, he made no further attempts to negotiate the transfer of land title with the First Nations peoples. Moreover, the man who had complete control of the mainland from 1858 to 1864 made no treaties there. Instead, he spent large sums of money, principally on roads, to take miners in and out of the interior.

After over a century of resistance, British Columbia is now discussing land claims with Aboriginal groups. This development has created much interest in James Douglas's early treaties on Vancouver Island, and, as well, in the reasons for his failure to complete further treaties on the island and on the mainland of British Columbia.

---

1. Margaret Ormsby, "Sir James Douglas," *Dictionary of Canadian Biography*, vol. 10, *1871–1880* (Toronto: University of Toronto Press, 1972), p. 248.

2. Jean Barman, *The West Beyond the West: A History of British Columbia* (Toronto: University of Toronto Press, 1991), pp. 80, 97.

3. Robert Cail, *Land, Man and the Law: The Disposal of Crown Lands in British Columbia, 1871–1913* (Vancouver: University of British Columbia Press, 1974).

4. Robin Fisher, *Contact and Conflict: Indian–European Relations in British Columbia, 1774–1890*, 2nd ed. (Vancouver: University of British Columbia Press, 1992 [1977]).

5. Wilson Duff, *The Indian History of British Columbia*, vol. 1, *The Impact of the White Man* (Victoria: Royal British Columbia Museum, 1992 [1965]), p. 61.

6. Duff, *The Indian History*, p. 61.

7. Tennant, *Aboriginal Peoples and Politics*, p. 29.

8. Tennant, *Aboriginal Peoples and Politics*, p. 38.

9. Paul Tennant, *Aboriginal Peoples and Politics: The Indian Land Question in British Columbia, 1849–1989* (Vancouver: University of British Columbia Press, 1990), p. 29.

In the late 1860s, about 12 000 non-Aboriginals lived in British Columbia and on Vancouver Island, more than half of them in the southwestern corner of the island. Between 1000 and 2000 resided in the lower Fraser Valley, with the remainder along the routes to the gold fields or at fur-trading posts. Since most Americans had left, at least three-quarters were British or Canadians and, of these, males predominated. A small community of African-American settlers from San Francisco, and a few settlers from the Caribbean, lived in Victoria and on the lower mainland. More than 1000 Chinese from California, mostly men, remained to work finds in the Cariboo. As late as 1871, there were only 53 Chinese women in the entire province. Most of the Chinese men came originally from poor rural backgrounds in southeastern China and could not bring over their families. Other reasons for the small number of females include prejudices in Chinese society against emigration and the hostile reception often given to Asians in British Columbia.

Christian Missionaries and the Pacific Coast Peoples

Missionaries worked to convert the First Nations to Christianity in the 1850s. William Duncan began his work at Fort Simpson in 1857 and continued at neighbouring Metlakatla, where he built a model mission. Other Anglican missionaries followed. Methodists from Canada West also came; Thomas Crosby worked on Vancouver Island and along the northern coastline. In the late 1850s, the Oblate fathers established Roman Catholic missions along the south coast, in the Okanagan, and in the Fraser Valley.

By the mid-nineteenth century, the ideas of Social Darwinism dominated throughout the British empire. The "lesser" races were caught up in the march of progress. As an "enlightened" empire, it was the "white man's burden" to alleviate the suffering of these races and ease their absorption into the dominant society. In British Columbia, on the "periphery of empire," a place where the First Nations were the majority population, missionaries were seen as essential agents of assimilation. This objective was revealed even in early church architecture. Historian Robin Fisher notes that "in the main, the churches expressed the missionaries' overall intent to replace that which was Indian with that which was European."[6]

First Nations' customs and rituals, including language, dress, and symbols, were viewed as obstacles to conversion and assimilation. In their zeal, the missionaries even banned totem poles. In 1900, the annual report of the federal Department of Indian Affairs noted that roughly 80 percent of British Columbia's First Nations were reported to be Christians. As historian Susan Neylan argues in the case of the Tsimshian, however, the process of conversion is not so straightforward. The First Nations demonstrated agency in how they "negotiated" Christian identities, often seeking links with their own forms of spirituality.[7]

It is also important not to exaggerate the extent to which European settlers disrupted First Nations culture or to assume that the process was a straightforward process of dependency. Anthropologist Rolf Knight points out that many Aboriginal people near the settlements adjusted well to the new economic conditions.[8] Independently of both mission and government direction, some First Nations tended potato gardens in the 1850s, and in the decades to follow, started mixed farming. As early as the mid-1850s, independent Aboriginal loggers delivered timber to sawmills. Many of the Hudson's Bay Company supply ships and several private trading schooners employed First Nations people as crew members throughout the nineteenth century. They worked as hunters and crew on European sealing ships and, on occasion, wintered in Japan. Schooners owned and sometimes constructed by First Nations people began to appear in the 1870s. From the 1870s on, the First Nations entered the commercial fishing and canning industry. Without diminishing the destructive impact of contact and colonization, it is important to recognize the complexities of these processes.

The Union of the Two Colonies

Major economic problems faced the two colonies of British Columbia and Vancouver Island in the mid-1860s. With the end of the gold rush, the economy was depressed and the two governments almost bankrupt. Anxious to save money, Britain promoted union of the two colonies, which would allow substantial reductions in administrative costs. In 1866, the colonies joined together and New Westminster became the capital; however, a vigorous lobby, led by John Sebastian Helmcken, James Douglas's son-in-law, convinced the governor to move the capital to Victoria in 1868. Despite the political consolidation of the two colonies, the depression continued.

In 1867, a new issue arose: the American purchase of Alaska. Since the gold rush, the threat of American annexation loomed large. Now, with the Americans also situated to the north, British Columbia was hemmed in. The other colonies of British North America seemed a world away. As Helmcken noted in his diary, the Americans "boasted they had sandwiched British Columbia and could eat her up at any time!"

COMMUNITY PORTRAIT

The Black Community of Victoria

Canadians have long congratulated themselves on their state of race relations, particularly in contrast with that in the United States. Although it is true that the British empire abolished slavery in 1833, approximately one-third of a century before the United States, African British North Americans did not achieve equality and full participation in their society. The existence of a vibrant, thriving community of people of African descent in Victoria, Vancouver Island, in the late 1850s and 1860s allows for comparisons to be made.

In the 1850s, African Americans faced increasing persecution and denial of civil rights in California. Several members of the African-American community in San Francisco sent a letter of enquiry to the government of the colony of British Columbia. A favourable reply was received, indicating that they would be welcome. James Douglas, the governor of

Vancouver Island, was of African ancestry from his mother's side of the family.

Approximately 400 people of African background emigrated from California to Victoria in 1858 and 1859. Since California was not a slave state, those moving to Vancouver Island were already free. A number came with business experience, and with the advantage of knowing a trade. A few, such as Mifflin Gibbs, brought capital with them. One of the central figures in the migration, Gibbs was a freeborn African American, originally from Philadelphia, and the son of a Wesleyan Methodist minister. As a young man in his mid-twenties he had moved to San Francisco and, within a year, had become a partner in a clothing business. But the discrimination against blacks rankled him. He became one of the first to emigrate northward. Once in the colony, he joined the Victoria Pioneer Rifle Corps, an all-black volunteer militia, known familiarly as the African Rifles, formed to protect the colony against possible American aggression.

In Victoria the newcomers pushed for integration. They sought what was denied to them in the United States: equal access to institutions, services, and the political process. Gibbs himself became a naturalized British subject, which allowed him to register as a voter. Elected to the Victoria city council in 1866, he served two terms—one as the chair of the important finance committee.

Unfortunately, full equality remained a distant dream. The immigrants suffered prejudice in their new home. Some churches established segregated sections. Some saloons and other public facilities refused service to them. Theatres made them sit for performances in the balcony seats. These divisions were backed up by physical intimidation. Even the loyal Pioneer Rifle Corps suffered humiliation, as they were barred from parades and public ceremonies. Legal equality prevailed, and some African Americans achieved acceptance, but the "colour line" remained.

By the late 1860s, a number of African Americans left the colony and returned to the United States. Gibbs departed in 1869 and settled in Little Rock, Arkansas. The American Civil War had ended, and opportunities surfaced for many in the country of their birth, but the persistence of the colour bar in British North America had also contributed to the exodus. In their new home on Vancouver Island, African Americans had contended with the same bigotry that they had tried to escape in pre–civil war California.

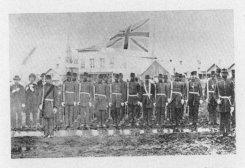

African-American volunteer militia regiment.

Source: Charles Gentile/Library and Archives Canada/ C-022626.

FURTHER READING

Sherry Edmunds-Flett, "Mifflin Wistar Gibbs," *Dictionary of Canadian Biography*, vol. 14, *1911–1920* (Toronto: University of Toronto Press, 1998), pp. 398–99.

Crawford Kilian, *Go Do Some Great Thing: The Black Pioneers of British Columbia* (Vancouver: Douglas and McIntyre, 1978).

James W. St. G. Walker, *Racial Discrimination in Canada: The Black Experience*, Canadian Historical Association Booklet No. 41 (Ottawa: The Canadian Historical Association, 1985).

Metlakatla, B.C., in the 1870s.

Source: Image G-04699 courtesy of Royal BC Museum, BC Archives.

As British North America completed the final arrangements for their union in 1867, British Columbia's settler population debated its own future. At no point did they consult the colony's 25 000 First Nations people. British Columbia had three options: remain a colony of Britain, join the United States, or accept union with Canada. Emotionally, most favoured the province's continuation as a British colony. Canada seemed so far away and logistics of being part of this far-flung enterprise made little sense. But Britain was seeking to make its colonies more self-reliant and the threat of American annexation was more real on the Pacific Coast. The path to becoming a colony had occurred relative quickly in British Columbia. There would not be much time to contemplate the colony's next step.

SUMMARY

The new united colony of British Columbia, only one year old, was the youngest of Britain's North American colonies in 1867. With the exception of a handful of fur traders, none of the approximately 8000 British Columbians of European descent in the colony had lived more than 25 years on Britain's Pacific coast. Thanks to the Hudson's Bay Company, Britain had retained this huge territory against Russian, and particularly against American, advances. The province's fate, however, still remained highly uncertain.

NOTES

1. Philip Drucker, "Rank, Wealth, and Kinship in Northwest Coast Society," in Tom McFeat, ed., *Indians of the North Pacific Coast* (Toronto: McClelland & Stewart, 1966), p. 137.

2. Wilson Duff, *The Indian History of British Columbia*, vol. 1, *The Impact of the White Man* (Victoria: Royal British Columbia Museum, 1992 [1965]), p. 21.

3. Peter L. Macnair, *The Legacy: Continuing Traditions of Canadian Northwest Coast Indian Art* (Victoria: British Columbia Provincial Museum, 1980), p. 21.

4. Loraine Littlefield, "Women Traders in the Maritime Fur Trade," in Bruce Alden Cox, ed., Native People, *Native Lands: Canadian Indians, Inuit and Métis* (Ottawa: Carleton University Press, 1988), p. 173.

5. Donald MacKay, *The Lumberjacks* (Toronto: McGraw-Hill Ryerson, 1978), p. 160.

6. Robin Fisher, "Missions to the Indians of British Columbia," in W. Peter Ward and Robert A.J. McDonald, eds., *British Columbia: Historical Readings* (Vancouver: Douglas & McIntyre, 1981), p. 123.

7. Susan Neylan, *The Heavens Are Changing: Nineteenth-Century Protestant Missions and Tsimshian Christianity* (Montreal: McGill-Queen's University Press, 2003).

8. Rolf Knight, *Indians at Work: An Informal History of Native Indian Labour in British Columbia, 1858–1930* (Vancouver: New Star Books, 1978), pp. 7–27.

RELATED READINGS

See Module 11, "Gender, Race, and Sexuality in Colonial British Columbia, 1849–1871," in *Visions: The Canadian History Modules Project: Pre-Confederation*. The module includes excerpts from Adele Perry's *On the Edge of Empire: Gender, Race, and the Making of British Columbia, 1849–1871* and five primary-source documents. See pages 477–521.

BIBLIOGRAPHY

Valuable histories of the two Pacific colonies are Jean Barman, *The West beyond the West: A History of British Columbia*, 3rd ed. (Toronto: University of Toronto Press, 2007), and Hugh J.M. Johnston, ed., *The Pacific Province: A History of British Columbia* (Vancouver: Douglas & McIntyre, 1996). Information on British Columbia can be found in Daniel Francis, ed., *Encyclopedia of British Columbia* (Madeira Park, BC: Harbour Publishing, 2000). Tina Loo provides a useful bibliographical guide in her essay "The Pacific Coast," in M. Brook Taylor, ed., *Canadian History: A Reader's Guide*, vol. 1, *Beginnings to Confederation* (Toronto: University of Toronto Press, 1994), pp. 356–93. See also N.E. Currie, *Constructing Colonial Discourse: Cook at Nootka Sound, 1778* (Montreal/Kingston: McGill-Queen's University Press 2005).

Keith Thor Carlson provides an innovative approach in *The Power of Place, the Problem of Time: Aboriginal Identity and Historical Consciousness in the Cauldron of Colonialism* (Toronto: University of

Toronto Press, 2010). Reviews of British Columbia's Aboriginal past appear in Wilson Duff, *The Indian History of British* Columbia, vol. 1, *The Impact of the White Man* (Victoria: Royal British Columbia Museum, 1997 [1965]); Robin Fisher, *Contact and Conflict: Indian–European Relations in British Columbia, 1774–1890*, 2nd ed. (Vancouver: University of British Columbia Press, 1992 [1977]); and two volumes by historical geographer R. Cole Harris: *The Resettlement of British Columbia: Essays on Colonialism and Geographical Change* (Vancouver: UBC Press, 1997) and *Making Native Space. Colonialism, Resistance, and Reserves in British Columbia* (Vancouver: UBC Press, 2002).

A source on the culture of the Aboriginal peoples is Wayne Suttles, ed., *Northwest Coast*, vol. 7 of *Handbook of North American Indians* (Washington, DC: Smithsonian Institution, 1990). Two studies of slavery are Robert H. Ruby and John A. Brown, *Indian Slavery in the Pacific Northwest* (Spokane, WA: Arthur H. Clark, 1993), and Leland Donald, *Aboriginal Slavery on the Northwest Coast of America* (Berkeley: University of California Press, 1997). Aldona Jonaitis has published the illustrated *From the Land of the Totem Poles* (Vancouver: Douglas & McIntyre, 1988) on Northwest Coast Aboriginal art. Paul Tennant's *Aboriginal Peoples and Politics: The Indian Land Question in British Columbia, 1849–1989* (Vancouver: UBC Press, 1990) is useful. See also Robert J. Muckle, *The First Nations of British Columbia: An Anthropological Survey*, 2nd ed. (Vancouver: UBC Press, 2006). For a study of the Aboriginal relationship with missionary Christianity see Susan Neylan, *"The Heavens Are Changing": Nineteenth-Century Protestant Missions and Tsimshian Christianity* (Montreal/Kingston: McGill-Queen's University Press, 2003). For a look at changing perceptions of the First Nations in British Columbia, see Dan Savard, "Changing Images: Photographic Collections of First Nations Peoples of the Pacific Northwest Coast Held in the Royal British Columbia Museum, 1860–1920." *BC Studies* 145 (2005): 55–96. See also Gerta Moray, *Unsettling Encounters: First Nations Imagery in the Art of Emily Carr* (Vancouver: UBC Press, 2006).

First Nations statements include *The Spirit in the Land* (Gabriola, BC: Reflections, 1987), which provides a summary of the land claim of the hereditary chiefs of the Gitskan and Wet'suwet'en people to nearly 60 000 square kilometres in northwestern British Columbia. First Nations traditions on the Northwest Coast are reviewed in Ruth Kirk, *Wisdom of the Elders* (Victoria: Royal British Columbia Museum, 1986). Several essays on early Indigenous–European contact on the North Pacific coast are included in John Sutton Lutz, ed., *Myth and Memory* (Vancouver: University of British Columbia Press, 2007). On the impact on the First Nations of European infectious disease, consult Robert Boyd, *The Coming of the Spirit of Pestilence: Introduced Infectious Diseases and Population Decline among Northwest Coast Indians, 1774–1874* (Vancouver: University of British Columbia Press, 1999). For a look at the Haida First Nation and environmental change in British Columbia, see Daryl W. Fedje and Rolph W. Mathewes, eds., *Haida Gwaii: Human History and Environment from the Time of Loon to the Time of the Iron People* (Vancouver: UBC Press, 2005).

Warren L. Cook's *Flood Tide of Empire: Spain and the Pacific Northwest, 1543–1819* (New Haven: Yale University Press, 1973), and three articles by Christen Archer—"The Transient Presence: A Re-appraisal of Spanish Attitudes Toward the Northwest Coast in the Eighteenth Century," *BC Studies* 18 (1973): 3–32; "Spanish Exploration and Settlement of the Northwest Coast in the 18th Century," *Sound Heritage* 7(1) (1978): 33–53; and "Cannibalism in the Early History of the Northwest Coast: Enduring Myths and Neglected Realities," *Canadian Historical Review* 61 (1980): 453–79—provide the background on Spanish activities. In *The Men with Wooden Feet: The Spanish Exploration of the Pacific Northwest* (Toronto: NC Press, 1985), John Kendrick also reviews the Spanish experience. Donald Cutter examines the Spanish expeditions of 1791 and 1792 in his *Malaspina and Galiano* (Vancouver: Douglas & McIntyre, 1991).

For a survey of Russian and American activities in the North Pacific, see James R. Gibson's *Otter Skins, Boston Ships and China Goods: The Maritime Fur Trade of the Northwest Coast, 1785–1841* (Montreal/Kingston: McGill-Queen's University Press, 1992). Barry Gough reviews early British contact in *The Northwest Coast: British Navigation, Trade, and Discoveries to 1812* (Vancouver: UBC Press, 1992), and he studies the later period in *Gunboat Frontier: British Maritime Authority and Northwest Coast Indians, 1846–90* (Vancouver: University of British Columbia Press, 1984). *Dictionary of Canadian Biography*, vol. 4, *1771–1800* (Toronto: University of Toronto Press, 1979), contains sketches of James Cook by Glyndwr Williams, pp. 162–67, and of George Vancouver by W. Kaye Lamb, pp. 743–48. They can also be accessed online: www.biographi.ca. Many aspects of Vancouver's voyage are reviewed in Robin Fisher and Hugh Johnson, eds., *From Maps* to Metaphors: The Pacific World of George Vancouver (Vancouver: UBC, 1993). Richard Somerset Mackie examines the coastal fur trade in Trading Beyond the Mountains: The British Fur Trade on the Pacific, 1793–1843 (Vancouver: UBC, 1997). For a survey of the inland fur trade, see Theodore J. Karamanski, Fur Trade and Exploration: Opening the Far Northwest, 1821–1852 (Vancouver: UBC Press, 1983). For a look at how the Pacific Northwest was an important crossroads for competing empires see Barry Gough, Fortune's a River: The Collision of Empires in the Pacific Northwest (Madeira Park: Harbour Publishing 2007).

Other items can be cited for the nineteenth century. Margaret Ormsby concisely reviews the life of James Douglas in Dictionary of Canadian Biography, vol. 10, 1871–1880 (Toronto: University of Toronto Press, 1972), pp. 239–49. Clarence G. Karr has written an interesting article on Douglas, "James Douglas: The Gold Governor in the Context of His Times," in E. Blanche Norcross, ed., The Company on the Coast (Nanaimo: Nanaimo Historical Society, 1983), pp. 56–78. Old Square Toes and His Family by John Adams (Victoria: Horsdal and Schubart Publishers Ltd., 2001) contains full biographical portraits of James and Amelia Douglas. Tina Loo's Making Law, Order, and Authority in British Columbia, 1821–1871 (Toronto: University of Toronto Press, 1994) is the first comprehensive legal history of British Columbia in the colonial period. For a look at the Vancouver colony's relationship with the British Empire, see Jeremy Mouat, "Situating Vancouver Island in the British World, 1846–49," BC Studies 145 (2005): 5–30, and J.F. Bosher, "Vancouver Island in the Empire.'" Journal of Imperial and Commonwealth History 33(3) (2005): 349–69.

An account of the British Columbia gold rushes is contained in Douglas Fetherling's The Gold Crusades: A Social History of Gold Rushes, 1849–1929 (Toronto: Macmillan, 1988). John Douglas Belshaw has written Colonization and Community: The Vancouver Island Coalfield and the Making of the British Columbia Working Class (Montreal/Kingston: McGill-Queen's University Press, 2002). Paul A. Phillips's essay, "Confederation and the Economy of British Columbia," in W. George Shelton, ed., British Columbia and Confederation (Victoria: University of Victoria, 1967), pp. 43–60, remains useful. For a study of the nineteenth century fur trade in British Columbia see Alan Twigg, Thompson's Highway: British Columbia's Fur Trade, 1800–1850 (Vancouver: Ronsdale, 2006). For a look at the impact of the gold rush on British Columbia, see Mark Forsythe and Greg Dickson, The Trail of 1858: British Columbia's Gold Rush Past (Madeira Park: Harbour Publishing 2007), and George Fetherling, Rivers of Gold: The Fraser and Cariboo Gold Rushes (Surrey: Heritage House, 2008).

In the field of gender and race history, Adele Perry has written On the Edge of Empire: Gender, Race, and the Making of British Columbia, 1849–1871 (Toronto: University of Toronto Press, 2001). Interesting accounts of non-Aboriginal and non-European groups in British Columbia in the nineteenth century include Crawford Killian, Go Do Some Great Thing: The Black Pioneers of British Columbia (Vancouver: Douglas & McIntyre, 1978); James Morton, In the Sea of Sterile Mountains: The Chinese in British Columbia (Vancouver: J.J. Douglas, 1974); and Tom Koppel, Kanaka: The Untold Story of Hawaiian Pioneers in British Columbia and the Pacific Northwest (Vancouver: Whitecap Books, 1995).

For important maps, consult the first two volumes of Historical Atlas of Canada: vol. 1, R. Cole Harris, ed., From the Beginning to 1800 (Toronto: University of Toronto Press, 1987); vol. 2, R. Louis Gentilcore, ed., The Land Transformed, 1800–1891 (Toronto: University of Toronto Press, 1993); and Derek Hayes, Historical Atlas of Vancouver and the Lower Fraser Valley (Vancouver: Douglas & McIntyre, 2005). Of additional interest is a recent edition of David Thompson's journals, edited with a new introduction by Barbara Belyea: David Thompson, Columbia Journals (Montreal/Kingston: McGill-Queen's University Press, 2007). For a further look at Thompson's writings, see David Thompson, The Writings of David Thompson, vol. 1, The Travels, 1850 Version, William E. Moreau, ed. (Montreal/Kingston: McGill-Queen's University Press, 2009).

Part 5

TOWARD CONFEDERATION

INTRODUCTION

The idea of a union of the British North American colonies was considered on a number of occasions since the 1790s. The British government encouraged the idea since the 1830s. Yet only in the early 1860s were the conditions favourable to attempt such a scheme. Pressure to form a federation came from both inside and outside BNA. Externally, the threat of American annexation loomed even larger than normal, due to a serious decline in Anglo–British relations during the American Civil War. The threat increased British pressure for a union of the colonies in the hopes of alleviating financial and military demands on the imperial government. Internally, Canada was paralyzed by political deadlock as a result of the Act of Union. The need to deal with the growing public debt as a result of overzealous railway building schemes and the possibility of acquiring the Northwest from the Hudson's Bay Company also pushed the Canadian politicians to take up the cause of confederation. The forces of nationalism, so strong throughout the Western world during this period, brought these conditions together.

But the dream of nation did not come easily. The forces opposing Confederation were formidable. In 1867, only three of the colonies—Canada, Nova Scotia, and New Brunswick—agreed to experiment with union, and even within these colonies, the debate proved acrimonious, the decision tenuous, and the process questionable. There was marked opposition in Canada East and the Maritimes. In Newfoundland and Prince Edward Island, Confederation was rejected outright.

Despite the opposition within BNA, the nation became a reality in 1867. The "Fathers of Confederation" hoped that this initial union would be the nucleus of a larger transcontinental entity. The motto for the new country, *A Mari Usque ad Mare* ("From Sea Even unto Sea") reflected their aspirations. But the difficulties facing the new dominion were only just beginning. The nation-building process occurred under pressure and with remarkable speed. Expansion proved just as hurried, and the resulting growing pains were debilitating.

Source: George P. Roberts/Library and Archives Canada/C-000733.

Chapter Twenty-One

THE ROAD TO CONFEDERATION

TIME LINE

1861	American Civil War begins
	Trent affair heightens tensions
1864	*Alabama* sunk by the Union
	Confederate soldiers launch St. Alban's Raid
	Britain sends 14 000 soldiers to BNA to defend against feared American attack
	"Great Coalition" formed in Canada to work toward BNA federation
	Colonial delegates meet in Charlottetown and Quebec City to discuss terms of union
1865	Canadian legislature approves Quebec Resolutions
	Joseph Howe fights against union in Nova Scotia
	Confederation is defeated in New Brunswick election
1866	United States terminates Reciprocity Agreement of 1854
	Leonard Tilley's pro-Confederation party wins election in New Brunswick
	Westminster Conference in London
1867	British North America Act passed, creating Dominion of Canada
	John A. Macdonald becomes Canada's first prime minister

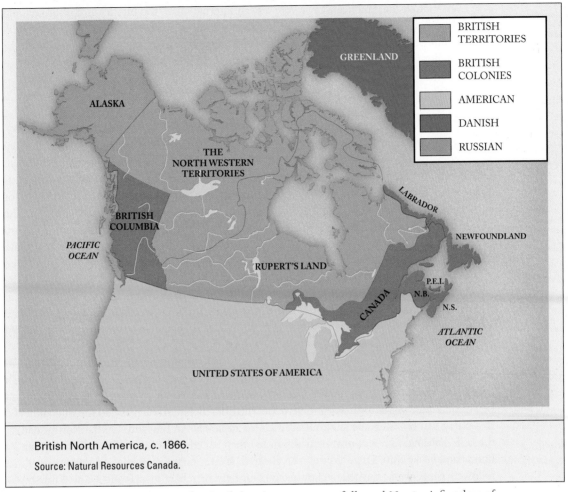

British North America, c. 1866.

Source: Natural Resources Canada.

According to historian P.B. Waite, "the Confederation movement followed Newton's first law of motion: all bodies continue in a state of rest or of uniform motion unless compelled by some force to change their state."[1] Proposals for British North American union were made well before the 1860s but did not come to fruition. By the 1860s, however, the stars were aligned: threats of an American invasion as a result of bitter relations during the American Civil War, pressure from Britain to reduce costs in administering the colonies, internal problems in the colonies, such as heavy public debt from railway building and, in the case of the Canadas, political deadlock, and the need to do something with the North West. While the desire to create a nation played a significant role, it was these immediate concerns, more than a spirit of nationalism, that prepared the way for the creation of Canada.

The Role of the American Civil War

By the 1860s, the fear of American annexation was an established reality in British North America. Since the American Revolution in the 1770s, the relations between the United States and the colonies of BNA were tenuous at best. On two separate occasions (during the Revolution and again during the War of 1812) the Americans invaded and attempted to annex the area. In 1837, American democracy and republicanism spurred rebellion in the Canadas. While relations improved in the following decades, culminating in the Reciprocity Agreement of 1854, paranoia lurked just below the surface for many politicians in BNA.

Even though the American Civil War was an internal affair, the interference of Britain and its North American colonies created hostility to the point of military conflict. Historian Frank H. Underhill once suggested that "somewhere on Parliament Hill in Ottawa . . . there should be erected a monument to this American ogre who has so often performed the function of saving us from drift and indecision."[2]

The Alabama *and* Trent *Affairs*

Although Britain (and its empire by extension) was officially neutral during the American Civil War, sympathy lay with the Southern states. The reasons were both pragmatic and emotional. Like Britain, the North was a manufacturing region and the two competed for the same markets. The South, on the other hand, was an agricultural region with substantial markets in Britain for such commodities as cotton. But on an emotional level, Britain had never recovered from the humiliating loss of its Thirteen Colonies. To have this experiment in American republicanism break apart on the shoals of civil war contained a certain degree of satisfaction for many in Britain and BNA. It was already apparent that the United States was a rising power. To have it divided into two nations would pose less of a threat to British hegemony. From the perspective of the colonies, a victory for the South would immediately lessen the threat of an American invasion. Even though slavery played a pivotal role in the Civil War, and the British empire which had already illegalized slavery supported Northern efforts toward emancipation, other factors shaped the British response.

Britain and its colonies in North America may have unofficially supported the South, but the international rules of neutrality dictated a policy of non-interference. Regardless, the British tested the boundaries of its neutral status by allowing the South to secretly build a swift and powerful cruiser in a shipyard near Liverpool. The Confederate strategists had the ship launched in a hurry, just one step ahead of outraged Union diplomats in England. On the North Atlantic, the CSS *Alabama*, as it was now named, hoisted the Confederate ensign of Stars and Bars, and a brass band broke into "Dixie" as the men cheered. In a 22-month rampage on three oceans that followed, the *Alabama* burned or captured 64 Northern merchant vessels and a Union warship—until the USS *Kearsarge* cornered and sank the Confederate raider off the coast of Normandy in June 1864. The North was furious and held Britain responsible for the destruction of ships and cargoes by the *Alabama* and other British-built Confederate vessels. Union leaders argued that since Britain knew the uses to which the South put these ships, it was effectively a contributor to the war and should pay for damages incurred. One Northern proposal included the takeover of all of British North America as compensation for what became known as the "*Alabama* claims."

Another incident during the Civil War that heightened Anglo–American antagonism was the *Trent* affair. In November 1861, in an ironic twist on the issue of impressment during the War of 1812, an American warship, the USS *San Jacinto* stopped the British steamer *Trent* and forcibly removed two Confederate envoys on their way to England and France to request diplomatic recognition for the South. Tempers flared on both sides, with Britain threatening retaliation if the North did not free these Confederate agents, seized in neutral waters, and the North denouncing Britain for aiding the Southern cause. In the end, President Abraham Lincoln released the prisoners on Christmas Day, 1861, to avoid war with Britain.

The St. Alban's Raid

In the early years of the war, the South held the advantage, and it looked as if Britain and BNA had backed a winner. As fortunes turned, however, and it became apparent that the United States would hold together, the colonies were faced with a victorious, armed, and angry North.

As the Union army continued its victorious march south in 1864, the Confederacy planned attacks on the North via Canada. At St. Alban's, Vermont, on October 19, 1864, 26 Confederate sympathizers terrorized the town, robbed three banks of $200 000, set several fires, wounded two men and killed another, and then fled across the border to Canada. The Confederate agents were arrested, but Charles Joseph Coursol, a Montreal magistrate, released them—and even returned the money to them—on a legal technicality.

More than the raid itself, this act of leniency infuriated the Union. The Canadian government quickly condemned Coursol's action. As well, in January 1865, the Canadian Assembly passed legislation that provided for the deportation of aliens involved in acts against a friendly foreign

The Trent *affair.*

Source: Library and Archives Canada/C-018711.

state. Nevertheless, BNA continued to be suspect in American eyes. General John A. Dix, commander of the American military district in the east, threatened Canada with retaliation if it refused to turn Southern border raiders over to American authorities immediately.

The Arrival of British Troops

Relations became so soured that, fearing an impending American attack, Britain sent 14 000 troops to defend its British North American colonies, the largest detachment of troops dispatched since the War of 1812. This policy decision was the exact opposite of what the British wished to achieve. The garrisons in North America were expensive and Britain was looking for an arrangement by which its colonies secured their own defence. A union of the BNA colonies, it was hoped, offered such an arrangement.

Dispatching the troops to BNA was one thing; transporting them within the colonies was another. A railway was needed that would extend from an ice-free port on the Atlantic into the interior of BNA territory for the purposes of defence and trade. Many of the 14 000 British reinforcements sent to the Canadas were forced to make an arduous journey by sled across New Brunswick because no rail link existed to the seaboard and poor relations prevented them from travelling through the United States. The Civil War demonstrated that BNA needed its own rail lines.

The Great Coalition

While the Civil War raged and politicians in BNA faced the spectre of American annexation, the Canadas looked for solutions to its political morass. With an equal number of seats distributed to both Canada West and Canada East in the Legislative Assembly, neither political party—the Tories or the Reformers—could form a stable government. Between 1861 and 1864, the Canadas experienced two elections and three changes of government. On June 14, 1864, the most recent administration, the Macdonald–Taché coalition, went down to defeat. Conservative leader, John A. Macdonald, requested dissolution of the Assembly, but rather than accept his request, Governor General Monck urged him to open negotiations with George Brown, leader of the Reform party, and attempt to form a coalition.

Brown and Macdonald, however, were old enemies. Their hostility resulted from a combination of political differences, conflicting personalities, and urban rivalry (Brown for Toronto and

Macdonald for Montreal). Nevertheless, faced with political paralysis in government, the two men agreed to negotiate. On June 30, a jubilant Assembly heard Brown announce that he would enter a coalition cabinet along with two others from his Reform party, Oliver Mowat and William McDougall, and work toward federation. The "Great Coalition of 1864" was born. Macdonald and Brown, however, made strange bedfellows. The window of opportunity to forge a union of BNA would only be open for a brief period of time.

Brown made three demands in return for compromising and supporting Macdonald's government. First, he insisted that the coalition government work toward a union of all the BNA colonies and, if this wider aim proved unattainable, toward a federation of the two Canadas alone. Second, Brown demanded representation by population, or "rep by pop," as it became popularly known. Now that the population of Canada West exceeded that of Canada East, the Clear Grits argued that representation in the Assembly should be based on population distribution, rather than on equality between the two sections. By 1861, Canada West had almost 1.4 million people, compared with the 1.1 million of Canada East. Third, Brown called for the incorporation of Rupert's Land into Confederation. He insisted that westward expansion accompany the entry of the Maritimes into a federal union. For nearly a decade, Brown's newspaper, the Toronto *Globe*, had kept Upper Canadians informed about developments in the Northwest. The *Globe* provided generous excerpts from the reports of the two scientific expeditions in the late 1850s—the British Palliser and the Canadian Hind expeditions. Brown's interest in the area lay in its potential for the development of Canada West. On January 22, 1863, the Toronto newspaper editor outlined his imperial vision:

> *If Canada acquires this territory it will rise in a few years from a position of a small and weak province to be the greatest colony any country has ever possessed, able to take its place among the empires of the earth. The wealth of 400 000 square miles of territory will flow through our waters and be gathered by our merchants, manufacturers and agriculturists. Our sons will occupy the chief places of this vast territory, we will form its institutions, supply its rulers, teach its schools, fill its stores, run its mills, navigate its streams.*

It was assumed that westward expansion would fit the designs of Canada West and that the vast territory would become an extension of the province. In doing so, it would serve the purpose of expanding the influence of Canada West over Canada East.

Maritime Union

The politicians in the Canadas may have taken a positive step forward in breaking their political deadlock and even in moving towards federation, but the "Great Coalition" meant little to the politicians in the Maritime colonies. These men had no time for the ethnic divisions plaguing the Canadas. They also saw only problems in Brown's demands for "rep by pop" and the purchase of the Northwest. The interests and future of the Maritimes remained tied to that of Britain. The problem, however, was that Britain wanted

The banquet and ball on the last night of the Charlottetown Conference at Province House. By Dusan Kadlec.

Source: *Province House Ball, 1864* © Dusan Kadlec and Parks Canada.

to loosen that tie. Economically, the major concern was the building of rail lines to link the colonies.

By the early 1860s, Nova Scotia, New Brunswick, and Prince Edward Island considered union amongst themselves. The Colonial Office endorsed the idea. While there were reservations in all three colonial governments, they agreed to meet. In July 1864, the government of the Canadas asked permission to attend the Maritime meeting and to present a proposal for a wider British North American federal union. The Maritimers agreed and arranged the meeting for September 1, 1864, in Charlottetown, Prince Edward Island.

The Charlottetown Conference

The Maritime delegates were lukewarm on the idea of Maritime union and most at this particular meeting were already envisioning a larger union of the BNA colonies. At the Charlottetown Conference, the Canadian delegation made their case. John A. Macdonald and George-Étienne Cartier set out the arguments in favour of Confederation and the general terms of the Canadian proposal, particularly those aspects dealing with the division of powers between the central and provincial governments. Alexander Galt, the minister of finance in the Canadas, dealt with economic issues and made the argument for the financial benefits for the Maritimes, while George Brown handled constitutional concerns. The main features of their proposals included: continued loyalty to the British Crown through membership in the British empire; a strong central government within a federal union in which the provinces retained control over their own local affairs; and representation in a lower house based on population and an upper house based on regional representation. Thomas D'Arcy McGee, the poet-politician, spoke eloquently and passionately for the need of a common British North American nationalism and vision.

The Maritime delegates were prepared to shelve their idea of Maritime union and endorse Confederation. Led by such premiers as Leonard Tilley and Charles Tupper, the Canadians were preaching to the converted. The problem, however, was that these politicians did not represent the dominant opinions in their respective colonies. Before the conference adjourned on September 7, the delegates agreed to meet again on October 10 at Quebec City to explore in greater detail the nature of a British North American federation.

The delegates to the Charlottetown Conference.

Source: George P. Roberts/Library and Archives Canada/C-000733.

The Charlottetown Conference as a Political Community

On September 1, 1864, 25 political leaders from the Atlantic colonies and the Canadas met in Charlottetown to discuss the possibility of a British North American union. The success of the conference depended on the ability to create a sense of political community—for the representatives to come to know and to trust one another, and to believe that they had something in common. In this respect, social events became as important as the political meetings.

The wives of the politicians, especially the wives of the island hosts who organized the social gatherings, made an important contribution. As historian Gail Cuthbert Brandt points out: "Mrs. Dundas, wife of the Lieutenant-Governor of Prince Edward Island, and the wives of Maritime politicians such as Mercy Haine Coles and Mrs. Haviland used their social skills to help transform the mutual ignorance and suspicion of Canadians and Maritimers into the personal bonds of esteem and friendship which facilitated political accommodation and new constitutional arrangements."[1] The presence of women reminded the politicians that their decisions affected all members of the community. As a result, some historians have now come to identity these women as the "Mothers of Confederation."

The politicians who met at Charlottetown came with different agendas and interests. Initially, the Conference was called to discuss Maritime union only. Then, the politicians from the Canadas asked to attend to put forward a proposal for a wider British North American union. The focus shifted. Mistrust, divisiveness, and differences had to be overcome in order to find points of common interests. Luncheons, dinners, banquets, and balls, dutifully organized and arranged by the wives of the Maritime representatives, were common occurrences during the seven days of deliberations.

In a letter to his wife and confidante Anne Nelson, daughter of publisher William Nelson, George Brown from Upper Canada noted the change that came over the delegates as they wined and dined: "Cartier and I made eloquent speeches, and whether as the result of our eloquence or of the goodness of our champagne, the ice became completely broken, the tongues of the delegates wagged merrily, [and] the banns of matrimony between all the provinces of British North America were formally proclaimed." Brown failed to note in his letter the important role that the women played in forging this sense of political community. But at the final banquet, the delegates made the last toast to Mrs. Dundas and the other women present as acknowledgment of their important role in making the Charlottetown Conference a success.

It is interesting to note that while the delegates may have been successful in creating their own sense of political community at the conference, the wider community in Charlottetown was much less interested. The delegates from New Brunswick and Nova Scotia originally planned on having the conference in Charlottetown because they realized that Prince Edward Island was the least interested in any form of union. The conference became even more of a "sideshow" because the circus was in Charlottetown at the same time. When the delegates arrived on the steamship SS *Victoria*, no one was working at the wharf. P.E.I. delegate William Pope had to handle receptions himself, including rowing out to greet the delegates. They even had to sleep aboard the ship because the circus had taken up most of the accommodations in town.

FURTHER READING

Moira Dann, *Mothers of Confederation*, CBC transcript (Toronto: Canadian Broadcasting Corporation, 1989).

Gail Cuthbert Brandt, "National Unity and the Politics of Political History," presidential address, *Journal of the Canadian Historical Association* 3 (1992): 3–11.

Christopher Moore, *1867: How the Fathers Made a Deal* (Toronto: McClelland & Stewart, 1997).

J.M.S. Careless, "George Brown and the Mother of Confederation, 1864," *Canadian Historical Association Annual Report*, 1960, pp. 57–73.

1. Gail Cuthbert Brandt, "National Unity and the Politics of Political History," Presidential Address, *Journal of the Canadian Historical Association* 3 (1992): 7.

The Quebec Conference

In the interim, the Canadian delegates reworked the general principles of Charlottetown into specific resolutions. They presented them at Quebec in the form of the Seventy-Two Resolutions. Over a two-week period, they established the political framework for a union of the British North American colonies. Their plan incorporated aspects of the British unitary and the American federal systems. The Maritime and Canadian delegates debated the resolutions, finally reaching agreement on the terms of what, with only a few minor alterations, would become the British North America Act.

John A. Macdonald clearly favoured a legislative union with a strong central government. He argued that the American Civil War was the direct result of overly powerful local governments. In the discussions, references to the American Civil War—with its death toll equal to the entire population of the Maritime colonies in the 1860s—constantly surfaced. The Colonial Office also favoured a strong central government to make all major decisions, as was done in Britain. The Maritime delegates, however, feared a loss of their identity and influence in a legislative union. They favoured a federal union with their own powerful local governments. The French Canadians, through their spokesman, George-Étienne Cartier, also insisted on a local government strong enough to protect their language, civil law, and customs.

The Quebec Conference was a success and the delegates reached a compromise. They granted some of the powers requested to the provincial governments, but gave the central government residuary powers (powers not specifically assigned to the provinces). They included the power "to make laws for the peace, order and good government of Canada." The federal government also gained the power of disallowance—the right to reject provincial laws.

The delegates confirmed their previous agreement at Charlottetown on a federal lower house based on representation by population and an upper house based on regional

Prince Edward Island Legislative Council.

Source: *Province House Confederation Chamber,* © Parks Canada.

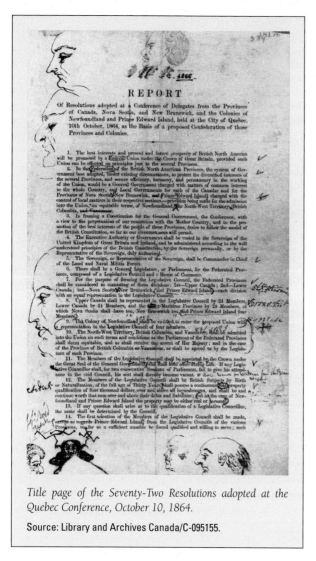

Title page of the Seventy-Two Resolutions adopted at the Quebec Conference, October 10, 1864.

Source: Library and Archives Canada/C-095155.

representation. But they disagreed on the number of representatives from each region in the upper house—the Senate. The issue became contentious because the smaller Maritime colonies saw the Senate as a means of strengthening their regional representation to offset their numerical weakness in the lower house. In the end, the delegates agreed that the Maritimes would have 24 seats, the same number given to each of Ontario (Canada West) and Quebec (Canada East). They also disagreed over the means of choosing senators. After discussing and eliminating a number of proposals, it was decided on appointment for life by the central government. In hindsight, the decision destroyed the possibility of the Senate becoming an effective voice for regional or provincial interests.

After acrimonious debate, the delegates accepted the financial arrangements proposed by A.T. Galt. He recommended that the new federal government assume the public debts—up to a specified maximum amount—of each province that joined. In addition, the federal government would finance the Intercolonial Railway, linking the Maritimes to the Canadas. The financial offer proved a powerful incentive in convincing the debt-ridden colonies to join.

Galt also argued successfully for the central government, with its heavy financial obligations, to control the main sources of revenue. It would have unlimited taxing powers, including the collection of both direct taxes and indirect taxes, such as customs and excise duties, one of the main sources of revenue at the time. In contrast, the provinces could levy only direct taxes. To compensate the provinces for the cost of education, roads, and other local obligations, Galt proposed that the federal government pay annual subsidies based on 80 cents per head of their population. The provinces could raise additional revenue by direct taxation or by selling their natural resources (public lands, minerals, and water power), which would remain in provincial hands.

Pushing Confederation

When the Quebec Conference ended, the delegates returned home to secure approval for the resolutions. The "Fathers of Confederation" considered submitting the draft constitution for popular approval, but later decided to follow the British procedure of ratification by the governments. They worried about public opposition to the scheme. There would be widespread opposition to the proposal, particularly in Canada East, Nova Scotia, Prince Edward Island, and New Brunswick. On the other hand, assembly ratification would provide a relatively quick path. Since the delegates represented the governments of the day, it seemed logical that the proposals would be passed.

Absent entirely from the constitutional process were the First Nations. To the "Fathers of Confederation," the Aboriginal peoples were wards of the state, upon whom sovereignty could be imposed.

They were not deemed people with rights of their own or even citizens. As political scientist Peter Russell notes, "Aboriginal peoples were treated as subjects, not citizens, of the new dominion."[3]

Canada West

Even though the Canadian assembly had formed the "Great Coalition" that originated the Confederation proposal, considerable debate ensued in the aftermath. In Canada West, the Reformers expressed concern about a wider union with the Maritimes. They also believed that the Intercolonial Railway would be another expensive publicly funded railway like the Grand Trunk. Nevertheless, George Brown agreed to overlook these reservations, since the proposed federation was to be based on representation by population. In general, Upper Canadian politicians favoured Confederation, realizing that they had the most to gain from the union.

Canada East

Members of the French-Canadian Reformers, the Parti rouge under the leadership of Antoine-Aimé Dorion, had serious reservations. It was not difficult to discern the intentions behind Brown's call for "rep by pop" or westward expansion. Brown was simply echoing the assimilationist designs of Lord Durham and the governors that followed. "It is not at all a confederation that is proposed to us, but quite simply a Legislative Union disguised under the name of a confederation," Dorion argued. "How could one accept as a federation a scheme . . . that provided for disallowance of local legislation?" He pointed out that in the proposed House of Commons, the English-Canadian representation from Canada West and the Maritimes would greatly outnumber the French-Canadian representation. The French Canadians had resisted assimilation for too long to voluntarily concede through a federation scheme. Dorion also noted that the union would heighten rather than diminish possible tension with the United States, as it would add the nearly 1000 kilometres long New Brunswick–American border to Canada's political boundary. Finally, he denounced the "Fathers of Confederation" for refusing to allow the people to make their views known on the proposed union, either through a plebiscite or by an election. In a prophetic statement, Dorion summarized his misgivings:

> I greatly fear that the day when this Confederation is adopted will be a dark day for Lower Canada. . . . I consider it one of the worst measures which could be submitted to us and if it happens that it is adopted, without the sanctions of the people of the province, the country will have more than one occasion to regret it.

The Conservative leader in Canada East, George-Étienne Cartier, countered Dorion's criticisms. He emphasized that Confederation, for the first time, offered French Canadians control of their own government. This was the means to cultural survival and an end, once and for all, to the designs of assimilation. In the new federal union, French Canadians would control their own legislature, have their own local administration, and retain the Civil Code. Furthermore, the French language would be official in the province of Quebec as well as in the federal administration, and the rights of religious minorities for separate schools would be recognized in all the provinces. On the question of English dominance, Cartier pointed out that the "new nationality" would be a "political nationality," not a "cultural nationality," and therefore did not require French Canadians to suppress their cultural differences for the sake of a pan-Canadian nationalism. He also reminded his French-Canadian compatriots of the importance of the British connection to offset the threat of American annexation and the loss of identity that would ensue.

Finally, Cartier presented Confederation to French Canadians as their best hope for cultural survival in a world of limited possibilities. The existing union, crippled by deadlock, could not go on.

For French Canadians, union with the United States would be the worst possible fate. The independence of Canada East was not feasible. Only a larger federation of British North American colonies, Cartier concluded, offered French Canadians possibilities beyond their own provincial boundaries at the same time as it protected their affairs within their own province. Cartier's close association with the Grand Trunk Railway (as one of the company's directors) and his desire to play a larger role as a statesman on a national stage no doubt contributed to his enthusiasm for Confederation.

Cartier faced a difficult struggle promoting Confederation in Canada East. He turned to the clergy for support, despite his personal concerns about mixing politics and religion. He could not, however, count on unreserved support. Ignace Bourget of Montreal, the most powerful French-Canadian bishop, feared for the future of the Roman Catholic Church in a new political union with other English colonies with large Protestant populations. He kept silent about his misgivings, however, since the other Quebec bishops were more favourably disposed, at least in principle. For the church to have opposed Confederation would have put them in the camp of their arch-enemies, the rouges, who were generally anti-clerical.

The Confederation debates in the Canadas lasted just over a month, from February 3 to March 11, 1865. In a final vote, 91 favoured and 33 opposed Confederation. In the breakdown of votes in the two sections, 54 of the 62 members from Canada West supported the proposal, as did 37 of the 62 members from Canada East. Of the 48 French-Canadian members present, 27 voted for and 21 against. Overall, Confederation won overwhelmingly, but among French Canadians the victory was narrow, indicating serious misgivings.

New Brunswick

The government of New Brunswick was led by Premier Samuel Leonard Tilley. He represented the colony at both the Charlottetown and Quebec conferences, and then led the campaign to have the deal passed by the Assembly. Tilley witnessed firsthand the economic impact of Britain's move to freer trade and informal empire (viewed as Britain's abandonment of its colonies). A supporter of temperance and responsible government, he also became an advocate of protectionism as well as railway development for New Brunswick. Tilley believed that only a union of all BNA could provide the political and economic structure required for the colonies "to bind together the Atlantic and Pacific by a continuous chain of settlements and line of communications for that [was] the destiny of this country, and the race which inhabited it." The Intercolonial railway was the critical stepping-stone in this process for New Brunswick. In the Confederation campaign, he argued that Saint John would be a year-round, ice-free port for the export of Canadian goods, and a lucrative market would exist in central Canada for Maritime coal and manufactured goods.

The opposition to Confederation in the Maritimes was as strong as it was among French Canadians in Canada East. A.J. Smith, the opposition leader, headed the anti-Confederation forces. He argued that Tilley had acted unconstitutionally at the Charlottetown Conference by endorsing Confederation (an idea conjured up in the "oily brains of Canadian politicians") when he was supposed to be discussing Maritime union. The terms of union with the Canadas, particularly in the Quebec Resolutions, offered few—if any—benefits to New Brunswick. It was meant to solve the Canadians' problems by exploiting the other colonies. No guarantee existed that the Intercolonial Railway would be constructed and, if it were built, where it would run and which area of the province (the north shore or the southern Saint John River valley) would benefit. One member of the Assembly asked derisively: "Mr. Tilley, will you stop your puffing and blowing and tell us which way the Railway is going?"

The opposition also pointed out that New Brunswick's economic trade pattern, especially since the Reciprocity Treaty of 1854, had been north–south rather than east–west. Commercial interests in the province had no economic ties with the Canadas. Furthermore, union with Canada could lead to a flooding of the New Brunswick market by Canadian imports and a high tariff structure. In addition, New Brunswickers would be forced to assume a portion of the heavy

Canadian debt from canal and railway building. Finally, Smith argued that Confederation would diminish New Brunswick's political power by giving the province representation of only 15 members of Parliament in a House of Commons with 194 members. The Roman Catholic clergy in the province also opposed Confederation based on the Quebec Resolutions, believing that a Canada dominated by Protestant "extremists" like George Brown could threaten Catholic schools and the Church itself throughout the proposed union.

Tilley mishandled the election of 1865 and the pro-Confederation forces were decimated. The Anti-Confederates swept into power with 26 of 41 seats. The people had spoken and Confederation was dead in New Brunswick, at least temporarily.

Nova Scotia

In Nova Scotia, Premier Charles Tupper faced a challenge at least equal to Tilley's in New Brunswick. Opposition to the Quebec Resolutions and to Confederation transcended party lines and was led by Joseph Howe, "Father of Responsible Government" and the most powerful political figure in Nova Scotia. The "voice of Nova Scotia" saw Confederation as restricting the colony's

Joseph Howe.

Source: Miscellaneous Collection/Library and Archives Canada/C-021463.

potential by reducing it to a backwater province in an insignificant North American nation. While Howe was an enthusiast of railways and an advocate of the Intercolonial, he favoured Nova Scotia's autonomy from the Canadas and preferred closer economic ties to Britain and the United States. Tupper, on the other hand, believed that Confederation would offer Nova Scotia more influence both in North America and within the empire: "British America, stretching from the Atlantic to the Pacific, would in a few years exhibit to the world a great and powerful organization, with British Institutions, British sympathies, and British feelings, bound indissolubly to the throne of England."

In early 1865, Howe presented his position in a series of letters written anonymously and entitled "The Botheration Letters." He argued that if Nova Scotia joined Confederation, it would lose its identity and cease to be an important colony in the empire. Furthermore, Howe pointed out that the colony looked eastward to the Atlantic Ocean and Britain, rather than westward to the continent and the Canadas: "Take a Nova Scotian to Ottawa, away above tide-water, freeze him up for five months, where he cannot view the Atlantic, smell salt water, or see the sail of a ship, and the man will pine and die." Howe also objected to Confederation being imposed without consulting the electorate. His arguments won particular support in those areas of the colony that looked to the sea and depended on ocean trade, shipbuilding, and fishing for their livelihood. In contrast, Charles Tupper drew his main support from the interior, where the coal, steel, and railway interests saw greater economic benefits from transcontinental, as opposed to oceanic, trade.

In the winter of 1866–67, Howe went to England to present his case to the colonial secretary and the British Parliament. Dissent in Nova Scotia against Tupper's School Act of 1864, which placed the cost of education on the localities rather than on the provincial government, aided Howe in his anti-Confederation campaign. Knowing full well that he could not win an election on the Confederation and schools issues, and with the example of Tilley's defeat in New Brunswick,

Tupper delayed and decided not to go to the people. Under pressure from the new lieutenant governor, Sir William Fenwick Williams, the premier introduced the issue of Confederation into the legislature in April 1866 but he promised changes to the Quebec resolutions. The motion passed in the Assembly but the electorate of Nova Scotia was given no say in the matter.

Prince Edward Island

Opposition to Confederation in Prince Edward Island was widespread. The first conference on union was held in Charlottetown because the delegates from Nova Scotia and New Brunswick realized that support there was the weakest. But Premier John Hamilton Gray, unlike the majority of the island's population, supported some kind of union of the BNA colonies. Still, at both Charlottetown and Quebec, Prince Edward Island's representatives had driven the hardest bargain, pressing for better political and economic terms.

Any enthusiasm declined after the delegates returned home. Disagreement broke out within the governing Conservative party between Premier Gray and another conference delegate, Edward Palmer. Gray promised that Confederation would provide a permanent solution to the vexatious absentee landlord issue by ensuring the sale of lands as well as funds to purchase them. Gray faced such widespread popular opposition to Confederation that he resigned in mid-December 1864. Palmer left government also and J.C. Pope became leader. Pope had not attended the Charlottetown and Quebec conferences, and his position on Confederation was ambiguous. He could not help, however, but sense the popular opposition.

Opposition centred on a number of issues. One was the old issue of absentee landlordism. In 1860, a British commission appointed to investigate the question issued a report favourable to the Islanders, only to have it rejected by the proprietors and the Colonial Office. Thus, when the Colonial Office pressured Prince Edward Islanders to adopt Confederation, they resisted. Many Islanders saw Confederation as simply replacing one set of distant landlords in Britain with another in Ottawa. In addition, Islanders believed that Confederation would give them very little economically. Union would mean higher taxes to support the Intercolonial railway project and higher tariffs to create interprovincial trade—neither of which would greatly benefit Prince Edward Island. They also disliked the proposed form of representation in the Senate and House of Commons, which would deny them a significant voice in distant Ottawa.

In the end, the majority of Islanders saw few if any benefits in Confederation. As the Charlottetown *Islander* wrote on December 30, 1864: "The majority of people appear to be wholly averse to Confederation. . . . We have done our duty. We have urged Confederation—the people have declared against it."

Newfoundland

Newfoundlanders felt even fewer ties to the rest of British North America. They failed to support Confederation as much out of apathy as anything else. Newfoundland had not participated in the Charlottetown Conference, but it had sent two observers to the Quebec Conference. The observers endorsed Confederation but returned to a colony that was initially mildly interested but soon largely indifferent.

The initial enthusiasm came as a result of Newfoundland's destitute economy. Fishing, the chief industry, was in decline throughout the 1860s. Agriculture and the timber trade, while distant seconds to fishing as commercial activities, also experienced hard times. Although Newfoundlanders first hoped that if they joined Confederation it might solve their economic ills, they soon thought otherwise. Most Newfoundlanders concluded that Canada was simply too far away to be of benefit to them. Essentially, the island continued to look eastward to Britain rather than westward to Canada.

As in the other colonies, the politicians were more supportive of Confederation than the general population. Premier Hugh Hoyles favoured Confederation, as did most members from both parties in the Legislative Council and the Assembly. But few people outside government circles endorsed the idea. In April 1865, Hoyles retired and was replaced by F.B.T. Carter. He allied with his political opponent, Ambrose Shea, to form a coalition government to persuade Newfoundland to join Confederation. They obtained the enthusiastic support of the pro-Confederation governor, Anthony Musgrave. But even this impressive political coalition could not stir up popular interest. R.J. Pinsent, a representative of the Legislative Council, spoke for many Newfoundlanders when he noted, "There is little community of interest between Newfoundland and the Canadas. This is not a Continental Colony."

External Pressures

By the end of 1865, Confederation was in deep trouble. Except for Canada West, the proposed union was unpopular. While the politicians, recognizing the gains to be made both personally and politically, were on board, the public was largely opposed. Had it not been for external pressure, Confederation would likely have died a quick death.

British Support

The British Colonial Office was frustrated by the opposition to Confederation. Britain's role was not so much one of "pressuring" as of "persuasively arguing" that the time was right for union of the British North American colonies. Since the 1830s the British had advocated some form of union that would allow the mother country to shed responsibility and expense for defending the colonies. Britain also hoped to ease tensions with the United States. Thus, when a pro-Confederation delegation from the Canadas arrived in London in the autumn of 1865, it was warmly welcomed, while a counter-delegation from Nova Scotia under Joseph Howe was not. The British government also replaced the governor of Nova Scotia with a new appointee, one more sympathetic to Confederation, and the Colonial Office ordered New Brunswick Governor Arthur Gordon to intervene in his province's politics to ensure the success of Confederation. Finally, Britain agreed to guarantee the loan interest for the proposed Intercolonial railway should Confederation come about, thus giving the Maritime colonies an additional incentive to unite with the Canadas.

The American Contribution

American pressure was less direct. When the Civil War ended in 1865, some Northerners called for the victorious Union army to be mobilized in order to annex British North America. Moreover, influential politicians in the American Midwest, such as senators Alexander Ramsey of Minnesota and Zachariah Chandler of Michigan, advocated annexation of Rupert's Land. Other American politicians, such as Congressman Nathaniel Banks, Senator Charles Sumner, and even Hamilton Fish, the secretary of state in Ulysses S. Grant's administration, wanted possession of all the British territory in North America. The New York *Herald* and the Chicago *Tribune* openly called for annexation.

Anglo–American relations were so strained by the end of the Civil War that the U.S. government terminated the Reciprocity Treaty of 1854. American protectionist interests had advocated abolition of the treaty as early as 1862. In December 1865, Congress passed a motion to end reciprocity as of March 1866. American annexationists argued that the treaty's abrogation would lead to such economic hardship among the British colonies as to force them to join the United States. Ironically, instead of forcing the British colonies into the arms of the United States, the announced abrogation of reciprocity encouraged the colonies to consider an alternative commercial union among themselves. If trade would not flow so easily north–south, it would have to flow east–west.

Fenian Raids

While the actual threat of an American military invasion was exaggerated, the Fenian Raids fanned the flames of paranoia. They also helped justify Confederation as means of defence for BNA. Extremist republican Irishmen, known as Fenians, had formed a brotherhood in 1859 in the United States to fight for the independence of Ireland. They looked to fight the hated British wherever they found them, and they did not have to look further than the border to the north. The Fenians devised a grandiose scheme by which they would capture the British North American colonies and use them as ransom to negotiate with the British government for the liberation of Ireland. Their marching song explicitly set out their goal:

The Fenians invade the Niagara Peninsula, 1866.

Source: Library and Archives Canada, Acc. No. 1946-35-1/ C-018737.

> *We are the Fenian Brotherhood,*
> *skilled in the art of war,*
> *And we're going to fight for Ireland,*
> *the land that we adore.*
> *Many battles we have won, along with*
> *the boys in blue,*
> *And we'll go and capture Canada for*
> *we've nothing else to do.*

The Fenians expected the sympathy and support of Irish Catholics in the British colonies to the north, but they were disappointed. Few supported them, and prominent individuals such as Thomas D'Arcy McGee came out strongly against them.

The Fenians posed little threat until the end of the American Civil War. In the summer of 1865, the Union army released thousands of Irish-American soldiers, who were trained, receptive to mobilizing in defence of their native country, and now idle. Furthermore, the Fenians met with little resistance and even had muted support from an American government that sympathized with their anti-British sentiments. Many American politicians also feared that if they failed to support the Fenians, they would alienate the large number of American Irish Catholic voters.

The Fenian threat was more psychological than real. Military activities were few and restricted to border skirmishes. The Fenians did, however, make two significant attacks that alarmed British North Americans. The first took place in New Brunswick. In April 1866, small bands of Fenians moved into the coastal towns of eastern Maine. New Brunswick mobilized its volunteer soldiers. The Fenians only succeeded in stealing the flag from a customs house before the militia and British regulars forced them back across the border. The raid helped the Confederation cause in the New Brunswick election that took place at that time. In April, the New Brunswick legislature passed the Confederation resolutions.

In late May, a much more serious incident occurred on the Niagara frontier, when 1500 Fenians crossed the Niagara River into Canada West. At Ridgeway on June 2, the Fenians defeated the Canadian militia, but they then withdrew. They never returned, although the Fenians continued to pose a threat until 1870.

The Turning of the Tides

In New Brunswick, A.J. Smith's anti-Confederation government, which took office in 1865, soon ran into considerable difficulties. It contained many conflicting interests and lacked internal unity. The first blow came in the autumn of 1865, when R.D. Wilmot and T.W. Anglin, two of Smith's ablest cabinet ministers, resigned. Wilmot was converted to the Confederation cause during a visit to the Canadas in September 1865. Anglin left for another reason: he opposed his government's decision to assist a private company to build an important railway. A second blow came in November, when the Smith government lost an important by-election in York County to Charles Fisher. The pro-Confederation forces interpreted the win in York as a victory, especially since the pro-Confederation government of the Canadas had contributed handsomely to Fisher's campaign fund. Finally, Smith failed in his bid to persuade the American government to renew the Reciprocity Treaty of 1854. In addition to these setbacks, Smith had to fight Governor Arthur Gordon who, at the British government's insistence, was pressuring New Brunswickers to support Confederation.

In exasperation, the Smith government resigned in April 1866. In the ensuing election campaign, Samuel Tilley resurrected his earlier arguments for Confederation and added new ones. He told the people of New Brunswick what they could expect from Confederation: lower taxes, the Intercolonial Railway, a fair share in the running of the nation, a market for their raw materials and manufactured goods—in other words, material progress and modernization. He argued that union would "open up and colonize immense tracts of fertile lands . . . lying unreclaimed and desolate. It will multiply the sources of industry and intensify the demand for labour. It will tend to keep our young men at home and allure those of other lands to our shores."

During the campaign, both parties benefited from external funds. The anti-Confederationists received money from Nova Scotia and possibly the United States, while the pro-Confederationists obtained financial support from the government of the Canadas. "Give us funds," a desperate Tilley cabled John A. Macdonald. "It will require some $40 000 or $50 000 to do the work in all our counties." Macdonald agreed. He did not want Confederation to go down to defeat in New Brunswick for lack of money. Direct British intervention and threatened Fenian raids assisted Tilley's cause. These circumstances resulted in a resounding victory for Tilley and his pro-Confederation forces. He immediately had the New Brunswick legislature endorse Confederation without referring it directly to the populace.

WHERE HISTORIANS DISAGREE

Nova Scotia and New Brunswick Join Confederation

The question of whether Confederation was forced upon Nova Scotia and New Brunswick has generated considerable debate among historians. In the 1920s, when regional and even separatist sentiments were strong, Maritime historians focused on the opposition to Confederation. They explained it in terms of the desire on the part of local communities to maintain the status quo and the absence among them of any feeling of identity with the distant Canadas. Historian George Wilson attributed the success of the pro-Confederationists in the election of 1866 to the Fenian raids (which led many New Brunswickers to fear for the security of their colony) and to the financial contribution of the Canadas to the election campaign.[1] Historian William Menzies Whitelaw, on the other hand, stressed the manipulative tactics of the Canadian politicians at the Quebec Conference of 1864 that won Maritime leaders over to Confederation.[2] Regardless, manipulation of the population, it was argued, played the major role.

In the 1960s, historians turned their attention to the external pressure coming from Britain and the United States. Donald Warner emphasized the perceived American military threat along with British imperial pressure as the decisive factors in overcoming Maritime opposition to union.[3] P.B. Waite argued that Confederation was "imposed on British North America by ingenuity, luck, courage, and sheer force."[4]

But whenever Confederation is discussed by historians, nationalism emerges as a major issue, both as a factor for the politicians at the time and for the historians writing about it later. Writing on the eve of the Canadian centennial in 1967, which saw an outburst of Canadian nationalism, Waite interpreted the Maritimers' support for Confederation as a desire to overcome parochialism by becoming part of a larger and greater transcontinental nation. A nascent Canadian nationalism was stirring. Kenneth Pryke, however, later challenged this assumption. "Support for union . . . did not always indicate a broadsighted vision," he wrote, "nor did opposition to it necessarily indicate a reactionary sectionalism."[5] Instead, Pryke argued, acceptance of Confederation in Nova Scotia was simply an acquiescence to colonial realities—an acceptance of the inevitable.

Historian Del Muise shifted the debate from politics (and the pressures exerted on Maritime politicians) to economics. He noted that the political divisions that arose in Nova Scotia over Confederation coincided with the economic divisions that existed in the province. Anti-Confederationists supported the old maritime economy, based on "wood, wind and sail"; they looked to Britain and the ocean for their livelihoods. Pro-Confederationists favoured a continental economy; from a younger generation, they saw a better future for the province in railways, coal, and industrialization. In the end, the latter outfought the former.[6] With regard to New Brunswick, Alfred G. Bailey associated the main opposition to Confederation with the "business fraternity who had been endeavouring for a decade to integrate the commerce of the province more closely with that of the United States."[7] By implication, the supporters of Confederation envisioned a brighter economic future for the province within a Canadian transcontinental economy.

Other historians viewed the division between the anti- and the pro-Confederationists as a cultural one, between native-born and British-born Maritimers. Ethnic historians found the greatest opposition to Confederation among Irish Catholics and Acadians, and the strongest support among the English elite. There are, however, sufficiently significant exceptions to these generalizations to put their validity in question.

Historian Ged Martin provides an interesting approach by examining Confederation from the British perspective. He argues that Britain did not put pressure on the recalcitrant colonies, such as Nova Scotia and New Brunswick, to accept the type of union proposed at Charlottetown and Quebec, but rather encouraged them to accept the idea of union as one that had been around for some time and whose time had now come, due to a variety of circumstances in the 1860s.[8] The process was inevitable and opposition largely futile.

Historian Phillip Buckner shifted the debate away from the opposition and toward union. He notes that "if one turns the traditional question on its head and asks not why were so many Maritimers opposed to Confederation but why so many of them agreed so easily to a scheme of union that was clearly designed by Canadians to meet Canadian needs and to ensure Canadian dominance . . . then the Maritime response to the Canadian initiative looks rather different." Buckner reveals the weaknesses and lack of effectiveness within the Maritime opposition to Confederation. He also argues that it would have taken more than external pressure to push the Maritimes into a union that they did not really want, and concludes that there was internal support for the cause. Buckner suggests that such popular support was evident in "those who equated consolidation with material progress and modernization."

Buckner also called for studies of the "intellectual milieu in which literary figures and the growing number of professionals functioned, of clerical thought, and indeed of changing views of the role and function of the state held by entrepreneurs and by other groups in society" to see to what extent support for Confederation came from those groups seeking "the emergence of larger and more powerful institutional units of government."[9]

1. George Wilson, "New Brunswick's Entrance into Confederation," *Canadian Historical Review* 9 (1928): 4–24.

2. William Menzies Whitelaw, *The Maritimes and Canada Before Confederation* (Toronto: Oxford University Press, 1966 [1934]).

3. Donald Warner, *The Idea of Continental Union* (Lexington: University of Kentucky Press, 1960).

4. P.B. Waite, *The Life and Times of Confederation, 1864–1867* (Toronto: University of Toronto Press, 1962), p. 323.

5. Kenneth Pryke, *Nova Scotia and Confederation, 1864–1871* (Toronto: University of Toronto Press, 1979), p. 6.

6. Del Muise, "The Federal Election of 1867 in Nova Scotia: An Economic Interpretation," *Nova Scotia Historical Society, Collection* (1968): 327–51.

7. Alfred G. Bailey, "The Basis and Persistence of Opposition to Confederation in New Brunswick," *Canadian Historical Review* 23 (1942): 382–83.

8. Ged Martin, *Britain and the Origins of Canadian Confederation, 1837–67* (Vancouver: University of British Columbia Press, 1995).

9. Phillip Buckner, "The Maritimes and Confederation: A Reassessment," *Canadian Historical Review* 71 (1990): 14–15, 22.

The Westminster Conference

In the autumn and winter of 1866, delegates from Nova Scotia, New Brunswick, and the Canadas met in London to prepare the passage of the British North America Act. The Quebec Resolutions served as the starting point for this final round of negotiations. Although the Maritime delegates pressed for modifications of those aspects of the resolutions that provided for a strong central government, in the end the resolutions were accepted as final except for a few significant changes. Rather than a "federation," the union would be known as a "confederation." Subsidies to the provinces would be increased beyond the agreed 80 cents a head by a fixed grant from the federal government. The contentious issue of separate schools, which had been heatedly debated in the legislature of the Canadas in the spring of 1865, was settled: the Quebec clause on education, which safeguarded the Protestant separate schools in Quebec, would be applied to all other provinces in the union, or to new provinces that had separate schools "by law" at the time they joined Confederation. Furthermore, religious minorities had the right of appeal to the federal government if the provincial government threatened their school systems, as they existed before Confederation.

Parliament Buildings, Ottawa, *by Frances Anne Hopkins* *(1867)*.

Source: Art Gallery of Ontario. Gift from The Canadian Club Classic Fund, purchased with assistance from the Government of Canada through the Cultural Property Export and Import Act, 1989. © 2011 AGO.

Right up to the time Confederation was ratified in the British parliament, opposition continued in Nova Scotia. While the delegates were meeting in London to finalize the terms of Confederation, Joseph Howe was meeting British officials to convince them to reject the union. He denounced British and Canadian politicians as attempting to force Confederation against the popular will. But the British government refused to retract its support. When the British North America Act was signed on March 29, 1867, Howe returned to Nova Scotia cured "of a good deal of loyal enthusiasm" and embittered against the Canadians. He was not alone. Many Nova Scotians saw Confederation as the beginning of the end for Nova Scotia. Elsewhere, Confederation was accepted, although not with enthusiasm, except in Ontario.

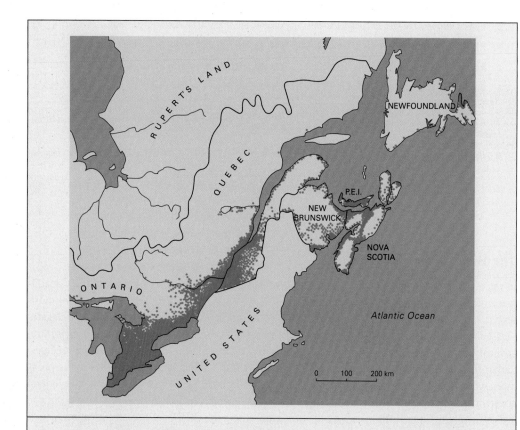

The extent of settlement in Canada, 1867.

Source: Adapted from John Warkentin, *Canada: A Geographical Interpretation* (Toronto: Methuen, 1968), p. 45.

Confederation

The study of Confederation has never produced a consensus on the political, economic, or cultural nature of Canada. Historians and political scientists have debated the motives, ideas, and conditions that informed the process of Canadian nation-building. Not surprisingly, Confederation has been perceived differently by historians of French and of English Canada.

For some French-Canadian historians, most notably Abbé Lionel Groulx, Confederation was not a shining compromise but a betrayal. According to Groulx, leading politicians such as George Étienne Cartier and the clergy of the Catholic Church would not have urged acceptance of Confederation among French Canadians had they known how Ottawa would subsequently prove unwilling to protect French linguistic, religious, and educational rights outside Quebec. French Canada did not enter Confederation to become a marginalized minority but to enjoy full partnership in the nation's expansion and evolution.[1]

Writing in the 1960s, Michel Brunet observed that the term "federalism" was an inaccurate description of Confederation. Canada is an executive state, not a compact or union of autonomous provinces. While Brunet agreed Confederation was a betrayal, he held that federalism did evolve.[2]

P.B. Waite, in *The Life and Times of Confederation* (1962), a study of newspaper coverage of the Confederation Debates, said Confederation was a compromise "between the federation of the United States and the legislative union of Great Britain." Rather than creating a new form of government, like the Americans, Canadians adapted the existing British colonial system by investing in Ottawa the powers of the old colonial legislatures "with a few more powers added." The new dominion would be centralized to accommodate the desire of colonial politicians for increased prestige and a larger platform to exercise their talents. The result was a regime in which the powers of the new provincial governments were "extraordinarily obscure."[3]

Historian Donald Creighton shared the view that Confederation was an extension of the old system.[4] It produced a central government in Ottawa charged with the responsibility of promoting trade and commerce to consolidate the new nation's vast geographic holdings. Following the work of economic historian Harold Innis, who viewed the Hudson's Bay Company as the forerunner to Confederation, Creighton argued that Canada had been formed by the relationship between geography and trans-Atlantic trade. A distinct commercial and agricultural society developed along the banks of the St. Lawrence, whose east–west orientation and connection to the British empire distinguished it from its neighbour to the south.

This interpretation, known as the "Laurentian thesis," influenced a generation of historians who saw Confederation as the culmination of a colonial system dependent upon centralized authority and monopoly-directed commercial enterprise. Creighton argued that for Confederation to work, executive and legislative authority had to be concentrated in Ottawa. Only Ottawa had the capability to promote, build, and protect a transcontinental union that would remain independent of the United States.

Historian W.L. Morton accepted the geographic and commercial basis of Creighton's "Laurentian thesis" but added an appreciation of the role of region and biculturalism in creating Canada. The "moral purpose of Confederation," Morton wrote, was "the union of the provinces in a partnership of English and French" joined "from sea to sea."[5] The genius of Confederation was that it formed a political union rather than a nationalist state like the United States. In a political union, linguistic groups and ethnicities could all live under the same government as long as they remained united under the Crown. Loyalty rather than consensus enabled the Fathers of Confederation to create a balanced federation. Political union also enabled the government to balance the interests of a widely diverse dispersed people. Morton posited that the federal cabinet enabled each region to enjoy representation within the national government, helping to ensure continuous balance between both national and regional self-interests.

The idea of Confederation as a political union has been taken up, more recently, by political scientist Janet Ajzenstat. Unlike Morton, Creighton, and Waite, Ajzenstat argues that Confederation was foremost an ideological exercise. In *The Canadian Founding: John Locke and Parliament*, she claims the founders arrived at the idea of a political union because of their adherence to John Locke's theory of liberal individualism. Instead of being "a Tory invention," Canada is a nation whose political life is defined by individual rights protected under common law and parliament.[6] According to this argument, it was Lockean liberalism, not cultural conservatism or allegiance, that provided the basis for Confederation.

Political scientist Peter J. Smith, in his article "The Ideological Origins of Canadian Confederation," argues that the founders were influenced by British, French, and American political thought and that Confederation was actually a debate between civic republicanism and commercialism, farmers and merchants. Unlike Ajzenstat, Smith does not consider Locke "the fountainhead of eighteenth-century Anglo-American political culture." Instead, he argues, the political economy of Adam Smith was more influential in creating a business class that sought a strong national government that could dispense patronage, underwrite large capital projects, and enhance the public credit. Farmers, on the other hand, were suspicious of a financially centralized and interventionist national government that supported large businesses and dispensed patronage to ambitious politicians, arguing that this bred corruption. While Smith argues that "the commercial ideology of Canadian Tories was to predominate politically in 1867," he contends that agrarian democracy was not extinguished in Canada, and that it made a dramatic return in Western Canada during the first decades of the twentieth century.[7]

In his book *Getting It Wrong: How Canadians Forgot Their Past and Imperiled Confederation*, Paul Romney attacks what he terms the centralist bias in Confederation historiography. Unlike Creighton, who saw Confederation as a continuation of the British colonial system, Romney argues it was a compact among the former colonies:

the Canadas supported union because they were looking to dissolve their legislative union; and Reformers, such as Oliver Mowat and George Brown, viewed Confederation as the culmination of the drive for responsible government in Upper Canada. Romney accuses Creighton and his disciples (whom he calls "centralists") of conflating John A. Macdonald's vision of a powerful central government with nationalism, marginalizing the Canadian reform tradition.[8] Confederation would not have been a failure, Romney argues, even if New Brunswick and Nova Scotia had failed to join, because the Canadas would still have achieved their compact and enjoyed responsible government. This argument not only contradicts Creighton's that Confederation almost did fail because of the ratification controversies in the Maritimes; it also challenges Morton's argument that a union of the British North American colonies was the moral purpose of union.

More recently, historian Andrew Smith has challenged both Ajzenstat's and Smith's interpretation of Confederation. According to Smith, Confederation's opponents were not civic republicans or Tories, but liberals who feared a national government with centralized and concentrated financial powers could not be trusted to manage public finances and would hinder free trade. The founding fathers, Smith argues, were the conservatives promoting a "'Tory-interventionist order.'" In his book *British Businessmen and Canadian Confederation*, he argues that British business investors in London played a vitally important role in urging the British colonial office to encourage the BNA colonies to form a political union. Confederation solidified a constitutional bond between Canada and Great Britain that was important to British investors and helped ensure that London remained the chief financier for Canada's capital investment projects.[9]

1. See "Les Canadiens français et l'établissement de la confederation," in Groulx, Lionel, *Notre maitre, le passé*, vol. 2 (Montreal: Librairie Granger frères limitée: 1936), pp. 233–54. Groulx also presented his case in a series of lectures early in his career, published in book form under the title *La Confédération canadienne* (Montreal: Imprimé au devoir, 1918).

2. Michel Brunet, "L'Acte de l'amérique du nord britannique," in *Québec Canada anglais: Deux itineraires un affrontement* (Montreal: Éditions HMH, Ltée, 1968), pp. 238–63.

3. P.B. Waite, *The Life and Times of Confederation 1864–1867* (Toronto: University of Toronto Press, 1962), pp. 326–7.

4. Donald Creighton, *The Empire of the St. Lawrence* (Toronto: Macmillan, 1956).

5. W.L. Morton, *The Critical Years: The Union of British North America 1857–1873* (Toronto: McClelland & Stewart Ltd., 1964), p. 277.

6. Janet Ajzenstat, *The Canadian Founding: John Locke and Parliament* (Montreal: McGill-Queen's University Press, 2007), p. xiii.

7. Peter J. Smith, "The Ideological Origins of Canadian Confederation," in Janet Ajzenstat and Peter J. Smith, eds., *Canada's Origins: Liberal, Tory, or Republican?* (Ottawa: Carlton University Press, 1995), pp. 48, 72.

8. Paul Romney, *Getting It Wrong: How Canadians Forgot Their Past and Imperiled Confederation* (Toronto: University of Toronto Press, 1999), p. 278.

9. Andrew Smith, "Toryism, Classical Liberalism, and Capitalism: The Politics of Taxation and the Struggle for Canadian Confederation," *Canadian Historical Review* 89 (March 2008): 2–3, 5; Andrew Smith, *British Businessmen and Canadian Confederation: Constitution-Making in an Era of Anglo-Globalization* (Montreal: McGill-Queen's University Press, 2008), p. 149.

Reading Proclamation announcing Confederation Market Square, Kingston, Monday, July 1st 1867.

The proclamation of Confederation, Market Square, Kingston, July 1, 1867.

Source: Queen's University Archives.

John A. Macdonald wanted to call the new nation the "Kingdom of Canada," but the British government objected because they feared the term would further offend the Americans, implying as it did a more autonomous country. Leonard Tilley had chanced upon an alternative title, as well as an appropriate motto, for the new country—*A Mari Usque ad Mare* ("From Sea Even unto Sea")—while reading Psalm 72:

> *He shall have dominion also from sea to sea, and from the river unto the ends of the earth.*

SUMMARY

The birth of the Canadian nation did not come easily. While Canada did not emerge out of violent revolution, the process occurred under considerable duress. In many ways, Confederation appeared to be a solution to the problems besetting British North America. The colony of Canada was paralyzed by political deadlock; all of BNA faced the threat, real or exaggerated, of American annexation; and the British government favoured a union of the colonies and applied its own pressure. But even with these factors, Confederation faced serious opposition within the colonies. On July 1, 1867, the Dominion of Canada was born. The difficult birth was over; the growing pains were just beginning.

NOTES

1. P.B. Waite, "Confederation," in *The Canadian Encyclopedia*, 2nd ed., vol. 1 (Edmonton: Hurtig, 1988), p. 488.

2. F.H. Underhill, *The Image of Confederation* (Toronto: Canadian Broadcasting Corporation, 1964), p. 4.

3. Peter H. Russell, *Constitutional Odyssey: Can Canadians Become a Sovereign People?*, 2nd ed. (Toronto: University of Toronto Press, 1993), p. 32.

RELATED READINGS

Module 12, "Confederation: What Kind of Country Are We To Have?," in *Visions: The Canadian History Modules Project: Pre-Confederation*, includes articles by Peter Russell, "Confederation," P.B. Waite, "Confederation and the Federal Principle," and Christopher Moore, "Nation and Crown." The module also includes documents from the Quebec Conference of 1864 and the Federal Union Debates, and a selection of maps of Canada from both 1849 and 1867. See pages 525–570.

BIBLIOGRAPHY

The three best general texts on Confederation, all written in the 1960s, are Donald Creighton, *The Road to Confederation: The Emergence of Canada, 1863–1867* (Toronto: Macmillan, 1964); W.L. Morton, *The Critical Years: The Union of British North America, 1857–1873* (Toronto: McClelland & Stewart, 1964); and P.B. Waite, *The Life and Times of Confederation, 1864–1867: Politics, Newspapers, and the Union of British North America* (Toronto: University of Toronto Press, 1962). The Canadian Historical Association has published a number of pamphlets on aspects of Confederation by leading scholars in their fields: J.M. Beck, *Joseph Howe: Anti-Confederate* (Ottawa: 1966); J.-C. Bonenfant, *The French Canadians and the Birth of Confederation* (Ottawa, 1966); P.G. Cornell, *The Great Coalition* (Ottawa: 1966); W.L. Morton, *The West and Confederation, 1857–1871* (Ottawa: 1962); P.B. Waite, *The Charlottetown Conference* (Ottawa: 1963); and W.M. Whitelaw, *The Quebec Conference* (Ottawa: 1966). Christopher Moore takes a more recent look at the topic in *1867: How the Fathers Made a Deal* (Toronto: McClelland & Stewart, 1997). Peter H. Russell looks at the history of the constitutional process from Confederation to the Charlottetown Accord in *Constitutional Odyssey: Can Canadians Become a Sovereign People?*, 2nd ed. (Toronto: University of Toronto Press, 1993).

Ramsay Cook has edited and written an introduction to *Confederation* (Toronto: University of Toronto Press, 1967), a collection of interpretive essays on the subject. Also useful are the articles included by Ged Martin in his edited work *The Causes of Canadian Confederation* (Fredericton: Acadiensis, 1990). A good primary source is P.B. Waite, ed., *The Confederation Debates in the Province of*

Canada, 1865 (Toronto: McClelland & Stewart, 1963). J.M. Bumsted provides a bibliographical guide to Britain's response to the Confederation idea, and to British North America's imperial ties in general, in "British North America in Its Imperial and International Context," in M. Brook Taylor, ed., *Canadian History: A Reader's Guide*, vol. 1, *Beginnings to Confederation* (Toronto: University of Toronto Press, 1994), pp. 394–447.

Confederation can also be studied through biographies of the protagonists; relevant biographies include D.G. Creighton, *John A. Macdonald*, vol. 1, *The Young Politician* (Toronto: Macmillan, 1952); Patricia Phenix, *Private Demons: The Tragic Personal Life of John A. Macdonald* (Toronto: McClelland & Stewart, 2006); Ged Martin, "John A. Macdonald: Provincial Premier," *British Journal of Canadian Studies* 20(1) (2007): 99–122; J. M.S. Careless, *Brown of the Globe*, vol. 2, *Statesman of Confederation, 1860–1880* (Toronto: Macmillan, 1963); Brian Young, *George-Étienne Cartier: Montreal Bourgeois* (Montreal/Kingston: McGill-Queen's University Press, 1981); O.D. Skelton, *Life and Times of Sir Alexander Tilloch Galt*, rev. ed. (Toronto: McClelland & Stewart, 1966 [1920]); and J.M. Beck, *Joseph Howe*, vol. 2, *The Briton Becomes Canadian, 1848–1873* (Montreal/Kingston: McGill-Queen's University Press, 1983). For a biography of Thomas D'Arcy McGee, see David A. Wilson, *Thomas D'Arcy McGee*, vol. 1, *Passion, Reason, and Politics, 1825–1857* (Montreal/Kingston: McGill-Queen's University Press, 2008). Important biographical sketches can be found in the volumes of *Dictionary of Canadian Biography* devoted to the late nineteenth century. It is now available online: www.biographi.ca. On women's role in the Confederation process, see Moira Dann, *Mothers of Confederation* (Montreal: CBC Transcripts, 1989). See also Irma Coucill, *Canada's Prime Ministers, Governors General, and Fathers of Confederation*, rev. ed. (Markham: Pembroke, 2005).

On the Maritime provinces and Confederation in 1867, see Phillip A. Buckner, "The 1860s: An End and a Beginning," in Phillip A. Buckner and John G. Reid, eds., *The Atlantic Region to Confederation: A History* (Toronto: University of Toronto Press, 1994), pp. 360–86; Martin, *The Causes of Canadian Confederation*, cited above; Kenneth Pryke, *Nova Scotia and Confederation, 1864–1874* (Toronto: University of Toronto Press, 1979); W.S. MacNutt, *New Brunswick: A History, 1784–1867* (Toronto: Macmillan, 1962); F.W.P. Bolger, *Prince Edward Island and Confederation, 1863–1873* (Charlottetown: St. Dunstan's University Press, 1964); and H.B. Mayo, "Newfoundland and Confederation in the Eighteen-Sixties," *Canadian Historical Review* 29 (1948): 125–42. On Quebec, see J.-C. Bonenfant, *La naissance de la Confédération* (Montreal: Leméac, 1969); and Marcel Bellavance, *Le clergé québécois et la Confédération canadienne de 1867* (Sillery, QC: Septentrion, 1992).

On the American and British influences on Confederation, consult Robin Winks, *Canada and the United States: The Civil War Years* (Montreal: Harvest House, 1971 [1960]); John A. Williams, "Canada and the Civil War," in H. Hyman, ed., *Heard Round the World: The Impact Abroad of the Civil War* (New York: Alfred A. Knopf, 1969), pp. 257–98; C.P. Stacey, *Canada and the British Army, 1841–1871*, rev. ed. (Toronto: University of Toronto Press, 1963 [1936]), and Andrew Smith, *British Businessmen and Canadian Confederation: Constitution-Making in an Era of Anglo-Globalization* (Montreal/Kingston: McGill-Queen's University Press, 2008). On the influence of the American Civil War on the Maritimes, see Greg Marquis, *In Armageddon's Shadow: The Civil War and Canada's Maritime Provinces* (Montreal/Kingston: McGill-Queen's University Press, 1998). A study of a specific incident that almost led to war between Britain and the North is Norman B. Ferris, *The Trent Affair: A Diplomatic Crisis* (Knoxville: University of Tennessee Press, 1977). Max Guérout has written a popular illustrated account of the most famous Confederate ship, "The Wreck of the C.S.S. *Alabama*, Avenging Angel of the Confederacy," *National Geographic* 186(6) (December 1994): 66–83. On the Fenian raids, consult Hereward Senior, *The Last Invasion of Canada: The Fenian Raids, 1866–1870* (Toronto: Dundurn Press, 1991). Studies of Britain's influence on the British North American federation include the new volume by Ged Martin titled *Britain and the Origins of Canadian Federation, 1837–67* (Vancouver: UBC Press, 1995); and John T. Saywell, "Backstage at London, 1864–1867: Constitutionalizing the Distinct Society?," *National History* 1(4) (Summer 2000): 331–46. Janet Ajzenstat examines the role of Lockean liberalism in the political philosophy of the fathers of Confederation in her book *The Canadian Founding: John Locke and Parliament* (Montreal/Kingston: McGill-Queen's University Press,

2007). Andrew Smith responds to Ajzenstat (and other scholars who see Confederation as a triumph of liberal individualism) in his article "Toryism, Classical Liberalism, and Capitalism: The Politics of Taxation and the Struggle for Canadian Confederation," *Canadian Historical Review*, 89(1) (March 2008): 1–25. For a collection of documents on pre-confederation history, see Tom Thorner and Thor Frohn-Nielson, *A Few Acres of Snow: Documents in Pre-Confederation Canadian History* 3rd ed. (Toronto: University of Toronto Press 2009).

Index